# Systemic Functional Grammar

Systemic Functional Linguistics (SFL) is a usage-based theory of language founded on the assumption that language is shaped entirely by its various functions in the contexts in which it used. The first of its kind, this book advances SFL by applying it comparatively to English, Spanish and Chinese. By analysing English alongside two other typologically very different major world languages, it shows how SFL can effectively address two central issues in linguistics – namely typology and universals. It concentrates in particular on argumentation, carefully explaining how descriptions of nominal group, verbal group and clause systems and structures are motivated, and draws on examples from key texts which display a full range of ideational, interpersonal and textual grammar resources. By working across three world languages from a text-based perspective, and demonstrating how grammar descriptions can be developed and improved, the book establishes the foundations for a groundbreaking functional approach to language typology.

**J. R. Martin** is Professor at the Department of Linguistics, University of Sydney and was Visiting Professor at the Department of Language Sciences, Pontificia Universidad Católica de Chile. He is best known for his work on discourse analysis, appraisal and genre. In April 2014 Shanghai Jiao Tong University opened its Martin Centre for Appliable Linguistics, appointing Professor Martin as Director.

**Beatriz Quiroz** is Associate Professor in Language Sciences at the Pontificia Universidad Católica de Chile. Her current research, informed by Systemic Functional Linguistics (SFL), focuses on developing a text-based and functionally oriented description of Spanish grammar.

**Pin Wang** is Associate Professor at the Martin Centre for Appliable Linguistics of the School of Foreign Languages, Shanghai Jiao Tong University, China. His chief research interests are Systemic Theory, Functional Grammar, and Functional Language Typology, with a particular focus on Mandarin Chinese and minority languages of China.

# Systemic Functional Grammar
*A Text-Based Description of English, Spanish and Chinese*

J. R. Martin
University of Sydney

Beatriz Quiroz
Pontificia Universidad Católica de Chile

Pin Wang
Shanghai Jiao Tong University

Shaftesbury Road, Cambridge CB2 8EA, United Kingdom

One Liberty Plaza, 20th Floor, New York, NY 10006, USA

477 Williamstown Road, Port Melbourne, VIC 3207, Australia

314–321, 3rd Floor, Plot 3, Splendor Forum, Jasola District Centre, New Delhi – 110025, India

103 Penang Road, #05–06/07, Visioncrest Commercial, Singapore 238467

Cambridge University Press is part of Cambridge University Press & Assessment, a department of the University of Cambridge.

We share the University's mission to contribute to society through the pursuit of education, learning and research at the highest international levels of excellence.

www.cambridge.org
Information on this title: www.cambridge.org/9781009284998

DOI: 10.1017/9781009284950

© J. R. Martin, Beatriz Quiroz and Pin Wang 2023

This publication is in copyright. Subject to statutory exception and to the provisions of relevant collective licensing agreements, no reproduction of any part may take place without the written permission of Cambridge University Press & Assessment.

First published 2023
First paperback edition 2025

*A catalogue record for this publication is available from the British Library*

ISBN 978-1-009-28500-1 Hardback
ISBN 978-1-009-28499-8 Paperback

Cambridge University Press & Assessment has no responsibility for the persistence or accuracy of URLs for external or third-party internet websites referred to in this publication and does not guarantee that any content on such websites is, or will remain, accurate or appropriate.

# Contents

| | |
|---|---|
| *List of Figures* | *page vii* |
| *List of Tables* | x |
| *Preface* | xv |

1 Systemic Functional Grammar ... 1
   1.1 An Introduction to Functional Grammar ... 1
   1.2 Introducing This Book ... 1
   1.3 Above Grammar: Context and Co-text ... 3
   1.4 Doing Functional Grammar ... 16
   1.5 Metafunction, Rank and Stratification ... 25
   1.6 Outline of This Book ... 32
   1.7 Notational Conventions ... 34

2 Nominal Group ... 35
   2.1 Approaching from Above ... 35
   2.2 English Nominal Group Resources ... 37
   2.3 Spanish Nominal Group Resources ... 52
   2.4 Chinese Nominal Group Resources ... 70
   2.5 Proper Name Challenge ... 90

3 Verbal Group ... 95
   3.1 Approaching from Above ... 95
   3.2 English Verbal Group Resources ... 97
   3.3 Spanish Verbal Group Resources ... 114
   3.4 Chinese Verbal Group Resources ... 143
   3.5 Verbal Group Corpus Challenge ... 166

4 Mood ... 169
   4.1 Approaching from Above ... 169
   4.2 English MOOD Resources ... 175
   4.3 Spanish MOOD Resources ... 192

|   |     |                                  |     |
|---|-----|----------------------------------|-----|
|   | 4.4 | Chinese MOOD Resources           | 211 |
|   | 4.5 | MOOD Challenge                   | 233 |
| 5 | Transitivity                         | 237 |
|   | 5.1 | Approaching from Above           | 237 |
|   | 5.2 | English TRANSITIVITY Resources   | 238 |
|   | 5.3 | Spanish TRANSITIVITY Resources   | 257 |
|   | 5.4 | Chinese TRANSITIVITY Resources   | 282 |
|   | 5.5 | TRANSITIVITY Challenge           | 302 |
| 6 | Theme                                | 304 |
|   | 6.1 | Approaching from Above           | 304 |
|   | 6.2 | English Information Flow         | 305 |
|   | 6.3 | Spanish Information Flow         | 322 |
|   | 6.4 | Chinese Information Flow         | 349 |
|   | 6.5 | Information Flow Challenge       | 365 |
| 7 | Envoi                                | 370 |
|   | 7.1 | Our Goal                         | 370 |
|   | 7.2 | Methodology                      | 370 |
|   | 7.3 | Functional Language Typology     | 374 |
|   | 7.4 | Off You Go                       | 380 |

Afterword: Describing Languages Systemic-Functionally
Christian M. I. M. Matthiessen                                382

*Appendices*     *402*
*References*     *439*
*Index*          *455*

# Figures

| | | |
|---|---|---|
| 1.1 | Language in context (field, mode and tenor) | 4 |
| 1.2 | Modelling context topologically | 5 |
| 1.3 | Field relations | 5 |
| 1.4 | Tenor relations | 6 |
| 1.5 | Mode relations | 7 |
| 1.6 | The stratified model of context assumed for this book | 9 |
| 1.7 | Extrinsic functionality (context) and intrinsic functionality (language) | 10 |
| 1.8 | Language strata | 11 |
| 1.9 | Discourse semantic systems | 16 |
| 1.10 | A simple TRANSITIVITY system | 20 |
| 1.11 | A simple MODALITY system in English | 22 |
| 1.12 | TRANSITIVITY and MODALITY systems in English | 25 |
| 1.13 | Dependency of MODALITY on MOOD in English | 26 |
| 1.14 | Verbal group systems realising 'periphrastic' MODULATION in English | 27 |
| 1.15 | Verbal group systems realising MODALITY through modal verbs in English | 27 |
| 1.16 | Word rank verb systems relevant to MODALITY in English | 28 |
| 1.17 | Basic ENGAGEMENT systems | 30 |
| 1.18 | Language strata realising register and genre systems | 32 |
| 2.1 | Field variables | 35 |
| 2.2 | Types of discourse semantic entity | 36 |
| 2.3 | Basic IDENTIFICATION system realised by English nominal group systems | 43 |
| 2.4 | General English nominal group systems | 47 |
| 2.5 | More delicate English nominal group systems | 48 |
| 2.6 | English nominal group systems | 50 |
| 2.7 | Basic IDENTIFICATION system realised by Spanish nominal group systems | 59 |
| 2.8 | General Spanish nominal group systems | 68 |
| 2.9 | More delicate Spanish nominal group systems | 69 |

viii    List of Figures

| | | |
|---|---|---|
| 2.10 | Basic IDENTIFICATION system realised by Chinese nominal group systems | 81 |
| 2.11 | General Chinese nominal group systems | 88 |
| 2.12 | More delicate Chinese nominal group systems | 89 |
| 2.13 | Chinese nominal group systems | 91 |
| 3.1 | Field variables | 95 |
| 3.2 | Basic ideational discourse semantic resources | 96 |
| 3.3 | Tenor variables | 96 |
| 3.4 | PRIMARY TENSE in English | 99 |
| 3.5 | Realisation of SECONDARY TENSE choices in English | 103 |
| 3.6 | English PRIMARY TENSE system in relation to one optional SECONDARY TENSE system | 105 |
| 3.7 | English PRIMARY TENSE and recursive SECONDARY TENSE systems | 108 |
| 3.8 | English verbal group systems – ideational resources | 109 |
| 3.9 | Spanish PRIMARY TENSE systems | 117 |
| 3.10 | Spanish SECONDARY TENSE system | 120 |
| 3.11 | Spanish PRIMARY TENSE and recursive SECONDARY TENSE systems | 122 |
| 3.12 | Tense choice and the temporal position of figures | 124 |
| 3.13 | Spanish verbal group NUCLEARITY, PRIMARY TENSE, SECONDARY TENSE and VOICE systems | 129 |
| 3.14 | Spanish verbal group MODALITY systems | 132 |
| 3.15 | Alternative realisations of SECONDARY TENSE in modalised verbal groups | 133 |
| 3.16 | Spanish POLARITY systems | 134 |
| 3.17 | Spanish verbal group systems | 136 |
| 3.18 | Basic Chinese verbal group ASPECT systems | 148 |
| 3.19 | Chinese verbal group ASPECT systems | 152 |
| 3.20 | Chinese verbal group PHASE systems | 155 |
| 3.21 | Chinese verbal group ASPECT and PHASE systems | 156 |
| 4.1 | Tenor variables | 169 |
| 4.2 | NEGOTIATION systems | 172 |
| 4.3 | Basic English MOOD systems | 177 |
| 4.4 | English indicative systems | 179 |
| 4.5 | Adjusted English indicative systems | 180 |
| 4.6 | Further adjusted English indicative systems | 182 |
| 4.7 | English MOOD including imperative systems | 184 |
| 4.8 | Basic ENGAGEMENT systems | 185 |
| 4.9 | English MOOD, MODALITY and POLARITY systems | 188 |
| 4.10 | English MOOD in relation to Comment Adjuncts | 190 |
| 4.11 | Spanish imperative INTERLOCUTION systems | 197 |

List of Figures     ix

| | | |
|---|---|---|
| 4.12 | Spanish indicative clause INTERLOCUTION and MOOD systems | 201 |
| 4.13 | Spanish indicative MOOD and MODALITY systems | 205 |
| 4.14 | Spanish MOOD and POLARITY | 206 |
| 4.15 | Basic Chinese MOOD system | 212 |
| 4.16 | Chinese imperative MOOD systems | 215 |
| 4.17 | Chinese interrogative MOOD systems | 229 |
| 4.18 | Chinese MOOD systems (oriented to NEGOTIATION) | 230 |
| 4.19 | Alternative Chinese MOOD systems (oriented to both NEGOTIATION and ENGAGEMENT) | 231 |
| 5.1 | Field variables | 238 |
| 5.2 | Basic English PROCESS TYPE system (types of clause) | 249 |
| 5.3 | English relational clause systems | 252 |
| 5.4 | Extended English PROCESS TYPE systems | 253 |
| 5.5 | Shared participant function in Spanish macro-phenomenal perception clauses | 275 |
| 5.6 | Spanish mental clause systems | 278 |
| 5.7 | Spanish mental clause systems extended | 281 |
| 5.8 | Basic Chinese PROCESS TYPE system (types of clause) | 295 |
| 5.9 | Extended Chinese RELATIONAL CLAUSE TYPE systems | 300 |
| 6.1 | Mode variables | 304 |
| 6.2 | Mode topology (with exemplary text types) | 305 |
| 6.3 | English THEME systems (for clauses) | 321 |
| 6.4 | English INFORMATION systems (for tone groups) | 322 |
| 6.5 | Spanish THEME systems (for clauses) | 336 |
| 6.6 | Spanish INFORMATION systems (for tone groups) | 340 |
| 6.7 | Spanish MARKED THEME systems | 347 |
| 6.8 | Spanish THEME and MARKED THEME systems (for clauses) | 348 |
| 6.9 | Chinese THEME systems (for clauses) | 354 |
| 6.10 | Chinese MARKED THEME systems (for clauses) | 359 |
| 6.11 | General Chinese THEME systems (for clauses) | 360 |
| 6.12 | Chinese information systems (for tone groups) | 360 |

# Tables

| | | |
|---|---|---|
| 1.1 | The main texts contextualising examples in this book | 7 |
| 1.2 | Key register variables for main texts | 9 |
| 1.3 | Discourse semantic systems (organised by metafunction) | 11 |
| 2.1 | Realisation statements for general English nominal group features | 47 |
| 2.2 | Realisations statements for more delicate English nominal group features | 49 |
| 2.3 | Epithet position in Spanish | 57 |
| 2.4 | Pronouns realising clause rank nominal groups in Chilean Spanish | 63 |
| 2.5 | Two instances of entity tracking in Spanish | 64 |
| 2.6 | Realisation statements for general Spanish nominal group features | 68 |
| 2.7 | Realisation statements for more delicate Spanish nominal group features | 70 |
| 2.8 | Realisation statements for general Chinese nominal group features | 88 |
| 2.9 | Realisations statements for more delicate Chinese nominal group features | 90 |
| 3.1 | Comparing primary and secondary future tense | 100 |
| 3.2 | Primary and secondary tense selections in relation to location in time | 101 |
| 3.3 | Tense selection in relation to a sequence of figures | 102 |
| 3.4 | Locating and sequencing figures in time through tense | 102 |
| 3.5 | English verb classes exemplified | 103 |
| 3.6 | Spanish verb classes exemplified | 117 |
| 3.7 | Spanish primary and secondary tense choice combinations | 121 |
| 3.8 | Pronominal clitics in Chilean Spanish | 126 |
| 3.9 | Participant roles and entity tracking as Gabriel's friends find him alive | 128 |
| 3.10 | Verb inflections used in congruent moves requesting goods & services | 134 |
| 3.11 | Spanish verbal groups in relation to Process and Participant structure | 137 |
| 3.12 | Contrasting structures involving modality vs attribution | 158 |

## List of Tables

| | | |
|---|---|---|
| 4.1 | Nub and terms exemplified in English dialogue | 173 |
| 4.2 | Nub and terms (further examples) | 173 |
| 4.3 | Nub and terms (additional examples) | 174 |
| 4.4 | Spanish INTERLOCUTION system and verbal group inflections realising indicative mood exemplified | 193 |
| 4.5 | Spanish nominal groups agreeing with verbal group inflection exemplified | 194 |
| 4.6 | Spanish INTERLOCUTION system and verbal group inflections realising imperative mood exemplified | 196 |
| 4.7 | Functional classifications of interrogatives in Chinese | 218 |
| 4.8 | Three types of interrogative in Chinese | 229 |
| 4.9 | Congruent realisations of SPEECH FUNCTION in English | 234 |
| 4.10 | Metaphorical realisations of SPEECH FUNCTION in English | 235 |
| 4.11 | Congruent and metaphorical modality in realising ENGAGEMENT | 235 |
| 5.1 | Transitive clause syntagms in English | 239 |
| 5.2 | More transitive clause syntagms in English | 239 |
| 5.3 | Sample syntagms for different types of clause | 240 |
| 5.4 | Reactances distinguishing action from sensing clauses | 245 |
| 5.5 | Structure and syntagm analysis of English material clauses | 246 |
| 5.6 | Structure and syntagm analysis of English 'emanating' mental clauses | 246 |
| 5.7 | Structure and syntagm analysis of English 'impinging' mental clauses | 246 |
| 5.8 | Reactances for English material, mental and relational clauses | 248 |
| 5.9 | Structure and syntagm analysis for English attributive relational clauses | 250 |
| 5.10 | Structure and syntagm analysis for English identifying relational clauses | 250 |
| 5.11 | Structure and syntagm analysis for English scoped intransitive material clauses | 254 |
| 5.12 | Structure and syntagm analysis for English existential clauses | 255 |
| 5.13 | Reactances for English behavioural, verbal and existential clauses | 257 |
| 5.14 | Reactances for Spanish material, mental and relational clauses | 261 |
| 5.15 | Reactances for Spanish behavioural, verbal and existential clauses | 269 |
| 5.16 | Extended reactances for Spanish material, mental and relational clauses | 270 |
| 5.17 | Summary of reactances for subtypes of Spanish mental clauses | 272 |
| 5.18 | Chinese clause syntagms | 284 |
| 5.19 | Reactances distinguishing material from existential clauses | 289 |
| 5.20 | Reactances for Chinese material, mental and existential clauses | 292 |
| 5.21 | Reactances for Chinese material, mental, relational and existential clauses | 295 |

| | | |
|---|---|---|
| 5.22 | Reactances for subtypes of Chinese relational clauses | 300 |
| 5.23 | Reactance for Chinese material, verbal and mentals clauses | 302 |
| 6.1 | Information flow in the 'waves attack' phase of the Bondi Beach text | 311 |
| 6.2 | Reworking information flow in the 'waves attack' phase of the Bondi Beach text | 312 |
| 6.3 | Theme and New in the 'waves attack' phase of the Bondi Beach text | 315 |
| 6.4 | Marked Theme, Theme and minimal New in the 'waves attack' phase of the Bondi Beach text | 317 |
| 6.5 | Two wave lengths of periodicity in the 'wave attack' phase of the Bondi Beach text | 318 |
| 6.6 | Information flow in the 'rescue' phase of the Bondi Beach text | 319 |
| 6.7 | Information flow in the 'medical response' phase of the Bondi Beach text | 320 |
| 6.8 | Information flow in the 'taking stock' phase of the Bondi Beach text | 320 |
| 6.9 | The macro-generic structure of the Ola Maldita text | 323 |
| 6.10 | Information flow in the 'Barrera escape' phase of the Ola Maldita text | 327 |
| 6.11 | Absence of co-referential nominal groups in non-finite clauses | 328 |
| 6.12 | Absence of co-referential nominal group in the continuing clause of a branching paratactic clause complex | 328 |
| 6.13 | Absence of co-referential nominal groups in clause complex initial clauses | 328 |
| 6.14 | Absence of co-referential nominal groups referring to Barrera | 329 |
| 6.15 | Absence of co-referential nominal groups referring to Blanca | 330 |
| 6.16 | Theme in the 'Valladares to the rescue' phase of the Ola Maldita text | 334 |
| 6.17 | Post-Predicator Themes in attributive relational clauses | 341 |
| 6.18 | Further examples of post-Predicator Theme | 342 |
| 6.19 | Marked Theme (Circumstances and P2/P3 Participants) | 347 |
| 6.20 | Information flow in the 'invasion of seaweed' phase of the Sea Lettuce text | 353 |
| 6.21 | Theme and minimal New in the 'invasion of seaweed' phase of the Sea Lettuce text | 356 |
| 6.22 | Marked Theme, Theme and minimal New in the 'invasion of seaweed' phase of the Sea Lettuce text | 358 |
| 6.23 | Participant Marked Themes | 359 |
| 6.24 | Information flow in the 'experts' advice' phase of the Sea Lettuce text | 361 |

6.25 Information flow in the 'members of the expert team' phase of the Sea Lettuce text ... 363
6.26 Information flow in the 'victory over sea lettuce' phase of the Sea Lettuce text ... 365
6.27 Information flow in the sopaipillas recipe ... 368

# Preface

This book was inspired by a series of meetings focusing on SFL language description, beginning at Shanghai Jiao Tong University (2015), and continuing at the Indonesia University of Education (2016), the University of Wollongong (July 2017), the Pontificia Universidad Católica de Chile (November 2017), Boston College (July 2018), the University of Sydney (November 2018) and the Pontificia Universidad Católica de Chile (July 2019).

As part of an international collaboration project (FRCAI1720, VRA-PUC) a first draft was composed by Martin and Quiroz in the second semester of 2017 at the Pontificia Universidad Católica de Chile, during Martin's sabbatical there. This draft was then circulated among colleagues who generously provided feedback. We are deeply indebted to Yaegan Doran, Giacomo Figueredo, Jing Hao, Basthian Medina, Estela Moyano, Teresa Oteíza, Fernanda Rojas, Margarita Vidal and Dongbing Zhang for their comments and suggestions. A revision was then prepared by Martin and Quiroz in the second semester of 2018 at the University of Sydney, taking advantage of Quiroz's time there as a visiting research fellow. During this same semester, Wang, also a visiting fellow at the University of Sydney, began work on translation of the chapters into Chinese and preparation of the sections on Chinese grammar. This work was completed (with the help of Zhu Yongsheng for the translation into Chinese) in September 2019, and shortly after Wang returned to Shanghai.

Once a decision was made in 2021 to publish the book in English (rather than as the bilingual English/Chinese version first envisaged), Wang began work on translating the sections on Chinese grammar in Chapters 2, 3, 4, 5 and 6 into English. Wang and Martin completed work on these sections over 2021 and 2022, alongside some minor editing and updating elsewhere in the book.

Our mentor, Michael Halliday, died in the middle of this project (in April 2018). He was aware of our endeavour and enthusiastically following reports of its development during the final year of his life. This book is our homage to his legacy, which has so inspired us all.

# 1 Systemic Functional Grammar

## 1.1 An Introduction to Functional Grammar

In 1985 Michael Halliday published the first edition of the consolidation of his work on English grammar, titled *An Introduction to Functional Grammar*. This work impressed many readers as a strikingly innovative contribution to the field; it and subsequent editions have generated well over 45,000 Google Scholar hits since that time. And few would quibble with assigning the title of genius to the author of a visionary work of this kind.

We need to remind ourselves however, as Halliday himself would have been the first to admit, that the genius of this description of English was entirely dependent upon the genius of the Systemic Functional Linguistic (SFL) theory which Halliday and his colleagues had concomitantly designed (rooted firmly as it was in the European functional/structuralist tradition). In this book we take up the challenge of showing how to do it – how to take SFL theory and use it to produce a grammatical description of this order. We do this by focusing on three world languages, English, Spanish and Chinese.[1] We don't do this primarily in order to compare and contrast these three languages. Our main purpose is, rather, to lead readers step by step through theoretical architecture and practical reasoning, which can be used to ground descriptions of the meaning-making potential of the grammatical systems and structure of languages (and related semiotic systems of any kind).

We can't all, of course, be Michael Hallidays and enact his unsurpassed 'feel' for the intricate ways in which English grammar means. But we can all learn how to take SFL theory and deploy it to formulate descriptions. This is the theoretical and practical knowledge we are attempting to share in this monograph.

## 1.2 Introducing This Book

This book builds in particular on two foundational introductions to SFL language description (Matthiessen and Halliday, 1997/2009; Martin, Wang

---

[1] For Spanish we focus on the Chilean variety; by Chinese we mean the modern standard variety, in common use and with official status in China, also known as Mandarin or Putonghua.

and Zhu, 2013) – with a view to modelling our perspective on the reasoning through which grammatical descriptions of languages can best be formulated.

The first of these, Matthiessen and Halliday (1997/2009), provides an overview of Systemic Functional Grammar (SFG), exploring its various dimensions and situating it as a model of one level of language within the linguistic theory known as Systemic Functional Linguistics. The second, Martin, Wang and Zhu (2013), takes one of these dimensions, axis, and introduces the basic principles of system network writing – including reasoning about the motivation of systems. That book reveals how the other fundamental dimensions of the theory (i.e. rank, metafunction and stratification) can all be derived from SFL's axial orientation to language analysis. These two books are critical resources as far as this publication is concerned.

This book pushes deeper, exploring in detail how SFG descriptions can be most effectively developed; it uses three major world languages, English, Spanish and Chinese, as exemplars. The book zeroes in on the grammar of clauses, groups and phrases – with chapters dedicated to central categories in the analysis of nominal groups, verbal groups, and MOOD, TRANSITIVITY and THEME clause systems respectively. Clause complex relations and word morphology will be brought into the picture only where needed to interpret clauses, groups and phrases. Each chapter begins with a discussion of English systems, followed by Spanish and then Chinese.

At the start of each chapter we review the context variables (i.e. register and genre choices) that are most relevant to the grammar systems considered. We next review the discourse semantic systems which bear critically on the grammar choices we will explore. We then move on to key grammatical systems and structures of English, Spanish and Chinese, building up a description step by step from first principles in order to make the reasoning involved as explicit as possible (including reasoning from above with respect to discourse semantics and, where relevant, from below with respect to prosodic phonology). This means, of course, that our descriptions cannot be as comprehensive as those found in grammars that are less explicit about their reasoning and which make more assumptions about SFL and about long-standing traditions of grammar analysis that are available for English, Spanish and Chinese. We have adopted this strategy because our goal is to model the way in which we feel SFL grammarians can best go about the work of developing rich functional descriptions. In doing so we hope to foster work on languages for which grammars informed by SFL have not yet been developed and to encourage critical appreciations and renovations of work that has already been done.

For many of our analyses we draw on published descriptions by SFL grammarians, work we acknowledge as we do so. For some of our analyses, we extend these extant descriptions and for others we propose alternatives. And in some of our analyses, we approach dimensions of English, Spanish and Chinese that haven't been described before.

In SFL the founding principle of our analysis is that of choice – of language as a system of systems enacting the registers and genres through which we live our lives. Inspired by Halliday (e.g. 1978, 1984a), SFL treats language as social semiotic behaviour and thus gives priority to modelling language paradigmatically as a meaning-making resource. We will develop grammar for English, Spanish and Chinese in precisely these terms.

The key to this modelling, as introduced in Martin, Wang and Zhu (2013), is axis – the dimension of SFL that privileges paradigmatic relations over syntagmatic ones, but at the same time motivates systemic choice in terms of its ultimate structuration. This book is about modelling how we believe this can most effectively be done.

In the next section we outline the model of language and context we will assume for purposes of this modelling. We assume a stratified model of context (as register and genre), as introduced in Martin (1992) and elaborated in Martin and Rose (2008). And we assume a stratified model of language (as discourse semantics, lexicogrammar and phonology/graphology), whose discourse semantic stratum is outlined in Martin (1992), popularised in Martin and Rose (2003/2007) and elaborated in Martin and White (2005). It is with respect to this framework that we reason about lexicogrammatical systems (as introduced in Section 1.4 below): (i) from above with respect to context and co-text, (ii) from around with respect to simultaneous systems and (iii) from below with respect to lower-ranking grammatical systems and phonology/graphology. For collections of grammatical descriptions assuming modelling and argumentation of this kind, see Martin (2018a); Martin, Doran and Figueredo (2020); Martin, Quiroz and Figueredo (2021); and Doran, Martin and Zhang (2021a, 2021b, 2022a, 2022b).

## 1.3   Above Grammar: Context and Co-text

In our approach to SFL, grammar systems realise higher-level systems that we refer to here as genre, register and discourse semantics. This allows us to bring patterns in context (i.e. the functions of language in use) and co-text (i.e. structure beyond grammar) to bear on grammar analysis. We introduce these higher-level systems here to emphasise the sense in which they offer an integrated holistic perspective on social semiotic behaviour. Grammar is a level of language, but it is one level among others. In a system where *tout se tient* 'everything interconnects' (Meillet, 1903), we have to take all meaning-making resources into account.

### 1.3.1 Context (Register and Genre)

First, context. In SFL, behaviour is brought into the picture by modelling context semiotically as systems of choice. There is general consensus in SFL that this model of social behaviour should include three key variables – referred to as field, tenor and mode. In SFL the relation of language to context is generally modelled using co-tangential circles, as in Figure 1.1, with the inner circle representing language and the outer circle context (factored as field, tenor and mode).

We begin by introducing some basic field, tenor and mode register variables – using topologies to exemplify the choices involved. Topologies are models of semiotic choice that treat systems of choice as clines. This kind of modelling allows us to treat registers as more or less the same, a useful modelling strategy in contextual analysis. The basic schema for topologies involving two variables is set out in Figure 1.2. Registers in this diagram are positioned at the prototypical centre of each quadrant; however, depending on their semiotic likeness to one another, they can, in principle, be positioned anywhere along either cline. For a more detailed set of proposals, alternatively organised as system networks, see Martin (1992); for discussion of topology in relation to typology, see Martin and Matthiessen (1991), Martin, Wang and Zhu (2013).

Field is a resource for construing phenomena as activities oriented to some global institutional purpose, or as items involved in these activities, along with associated properties (Martin, 1992; Doran and Martin, 2021). One key variable thus has to do with whether phenomena are construed dynamically as activity (unfolding through time) or statically as items (taxonomised by classification and composition). A second key variable has to do with whether phenomena are construed in everyday terms (through ostensive definition and by undertaking activities with others) or as technical discourse (through reading

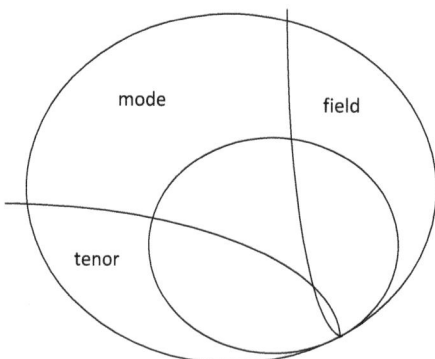

Figure 1.1 Language in context (field, tenor and mode)

## 1.3 Above Grammar: Context and Co-text

and writing activities in institutions that have been developed for regulating access to uncommon sense discourse). These two variables are presented as clines in Figure 1.3 and exemplified as recounting a holiday (an everyday activity perspective), explaining evolution (a technical activity perspective), classifying crocodiles (a technical taxonomy perspective) and describing a pet (an everyday taxonomy perspective).

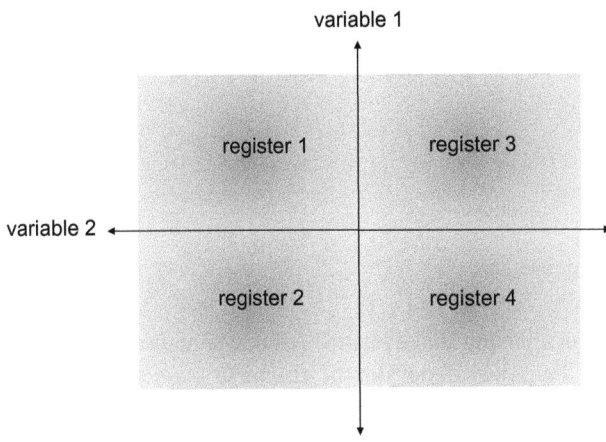

Figure 1.2 Modelling context topologically

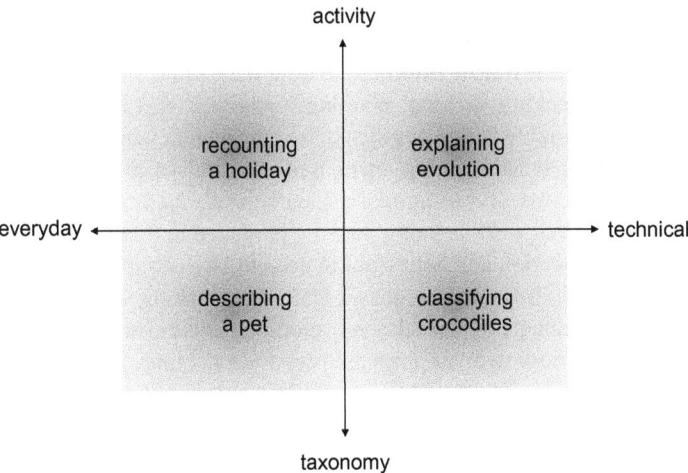

Figure 1.3 Field relations

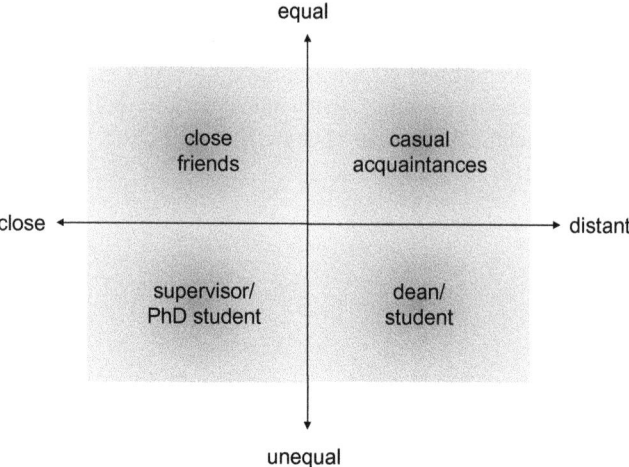

Figure 1.4 Tenor relations

Tenor is a resource for enacting social relations of power and solidarity. One key variable manages the power dimension of discourse – are the interlocutors of equal status or not, and if not, who will dominate and who must defer? A second key variable manages the solidarity dimension of discourse – how closely involved are the interlocutors with one another? These two variables are presented as clines in Figure 1.4 and exemplified as relationships involving close friends (close equal relations), casual acquaintances (distant equal relations), a faculty dean and students (distant unequal relations) and a supervisor and their PhD student (close unequal relations).

Mode is a resource for texturing information flow, depending on the medium of communication (speaking, writing, phoning, e-mailing, texting, blogging and so on). One key variable composes the context dependency of discourse – is the language part of what is going on or is it constitutive of the interaction taking place? In terms of multimodal discourse analysis, this variable is responsible for how much work is being done by language in relation to other modalities of communication and behaviour. A second key variable composes discourse as more or less interactive – does it feature turn-taking with immediate aural and visual feedback, or is it relatively monologic with various degrees of delayed response? These two variables are presented as clines in Figure 1.5 and exemplified as composing casual conversation (dialogic constitutive texture), news stories (monologic constitutive texture), sports commentary (monologic ancillary texture) and domestic exchanges (dialogic ancillary texture).

For some models of SFL, a stratified model of context has been developed, with genre as a higher level of abstraction, above register (Martin, 1992; Martin and Rose, 2008). In these models genre is treated as a recurrent configuration of field, tenor and mode variables, typically unfolding in stages as a text consummates its social purpose. In this book we deal with just a few genres which are instantiated as the key texts we use as sources of examples in our chapters. The texts we focus on are outlined in Table 1.1, aligned with the chapter sections they inform.

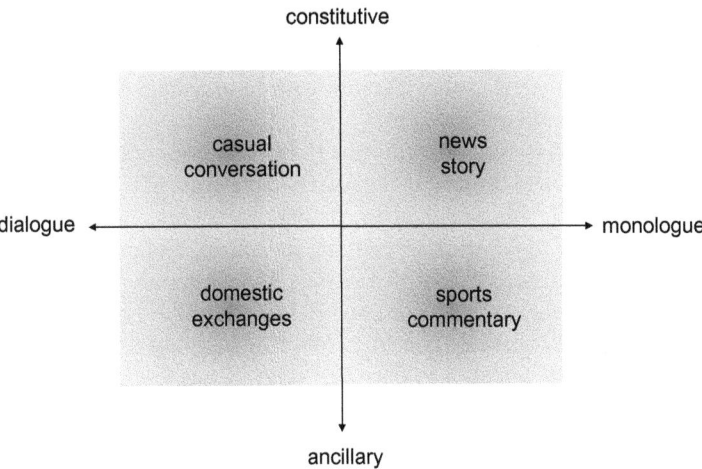

Figure 1.5 Mode relations

Our choice of data is opportunistic and designed for pedagogic purposes. Just a few texts play a central role in as many chapters as possible, supplemented only where necessary by additional material. We adopt this strategy so readers can see how texts with which they become increasingly familiar look from the perspective of different grammatical systems. For similar reasons we focus on just one dialect of English, Spanish and Chinese, so as not to have to spend time discussing dialectal variations. As we outline in Chapter 7, this is not the approach to data we recommend for research purposes.

Three main English texts are deployed. One is a feature article about a rescue operation by lifesavers at Bondi Beach, Sydney, when freak waves swept

Table 1.1 *The main texts contextualising examples in this book*

| Chapter | English texts | Spanish texts | Chinese texts |
|---|---|---|---|
| 2 Nominal group | Bondi Beach | La Ola Maldita | Sea Lettuce |
| 3 Verbal group | Random Chatty Vlog | La Ola Maldita | Interview with Curator |
| 4 MOOD | Youth Justice Conference | El Cambio de Plan; El Decodificador | Reckless Driving |
| 5 TRANSITIVITY | Random Chatty Vlog | La Ola Maldita | Interview with Curator |
| 6 THEME | Bondi Beach | La Ola Maldita; Sopaipillas | Sea Lettuce |

250 people out to sea; we refer to this as our Bondi Beach text. One is a vlog (i.e. a video blog) about the recent experiences of an American housewife and mother; we refer to this as our Random Chatty Vlog text. And one is a transcript of a New South Wales Youth Justice Conference, a legal process in which adolescent offenders meet with their victim and other community members to negotiate an apology and some form of community service by way of recompense for their offence (Zappavigna and Martin, 2018); we refer to this as our Youth Justice Conference text. These texts provide us with most of the range of spoken and written language features we need to ground our top-down approach to English grammar description.

Our main Spanish text is a feature article retelling the stories of the survivors of a massive earthquake and tsunami that devastated the coast of Chile in 2010; we refer to this as our La Ola Maldita ('the hellish wave') text. We also draw examples from two call centre texts, one asking for a change of cable TV plan and the other sorting out a problem with a set-top box; we refer to these as our El Cambio de Plan ('change of plan') text and El Decodificador ('set-top box') text respectively. We also include consideration of a pumpkin fritters recipe, which we refer to as our Sopaipillas ('fritters') text.[2] Once again these texts provide us with most of the range of spoken and written language features we need to ground our top-down approach to Spanish grammar description.

The description of Chinese is based on three main texts. One is a feature article published on the website of the Institute of Oceanology, Chinese Academy of Sciences – about controlling sea lettuce, a kind of green algae, that grows along the coast of East China's Qingdao city and which threatened sailing events during the 2018 Olympics; we refer to this as the Sea Lettuce text. Another is an interview with Mr Shan Jixiang, then retiring curator of Beijing's Palace Museum (also known as the Forbidden City) – reviewing his work experience in the Palace Museum and airing his wishes for the museum's future development; we refer to this as our Interview with Curator text. The third is a court trial dealing with a reckless driving case, in which two young drivers raced against each other, lost control of their vehicles and caused serious damage and injury; we refer to this as our Reckless Driving text. These texts provide us with most of the spoken and written language features we need to ground our top-down approach to Chinese grammar description.

The relevance of these texts is outlined, chapter by chapter, in Table 1.1. Except for the Youth Justice Conference text and Reckless Driving text (which are too long), they are presented in full in Appendices 2–4; relevant citations are provided there.

---

[2] The Spanish texts used in this book are part of the data of the research project supported by CONICYT-FONDECYT through grant 11170674. The grant also partially supported the analysis of Spanish nominal groups and experiential lexicogrammar shown in Chapters 2 and 4, respectively.

## 1.3 Above Grammar: Context and Co-text

The genres involved in these texts are outlined in Table 1.2, alongside the register variables through which they are realised. Our story genres are mainly monologic but do include some more interactive quotations. The El Cambio de Plan service encounter is constitutive; but the El Decodificador call includes phases of interaction in which the server gets the client to deal hands-on with the set-top box to get it working again.

The stratified model of language and context used to model these genres is imaged in Figure 1.6. In terms of realisation, the model treats choices among genres as realised through recurrent configurations of register choices, and register choices as realised through recurrent patterns of choices in language.

Table 1.2 *Key register variables for main texts*

| genre | | field | tenor | mode |
|---|---|---|---|---|
| stories | Random Chatty Vlog<br>Bondi Beach<br>La Ola Maldita<br>Sea Lettuce | domestic<br>natural disaster | close/equal<br>distant/unequal | ≈ monologic/<br>constitutive |
| procedure | Sopaipillas | cooking recipe | distant/unequal | monologic/<br>constitutive |
| service encounters | El Cambio de Plan<br>El Decodificador | pay TV contract<br>set-top box disorder | distant/unequal | dialogic/ ≈<br>constitutive |
| conference | Youth Justice Conference | restorative justice | distant/unequal | dialogic/<br>constitutive |
| interview | Interview with Curator | work experience | distant/unequal | dialogic/<br>constitutive |
| court trial | Reckless Driving | criminal offence | distant/unequal | dialogic/<br>constitutive |

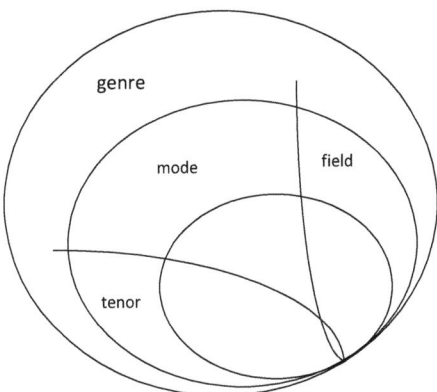

Figure 1.6 The stratified model of context assumed for this book

### 1.3.2 Co-text (Discourse Semantics)

In SFL the extrinsic functional organisation of language (field, tenor and mode) introduced above is correlated with the intrinsic functional organisation of language. Field is treated as by and large construed through ideational meaning, tenor as by and large enacted through interpersonal meaning and mode as by and large composed through textual meaning. In SFL these functional components of language are referred to as metafunctions. The correlations between extrinsic functionality (field, tenor and mode) and intrinsic functionality (ideational, interpersonal and textual meaning) are outlined in Figure 1.7. As the diagram implies, genre and register are modelled as strata of meaning – the social semiotic perspective on language as behaviour we outlined in Section 1.3.1.

Alongside being organised by metafunction, language is organised by stratum – as choices in discourse semantic systems realised by choices in lexicogrammatical systems realised in turn by choices in phonological systems (Figure 1.8). At the level of discourse semantics, we are concerned with meaning realised both inside and between clauses, whether these clauses have any grammatical relation to one another or not. The focus in other words is on co-text.

We will briefly introduce six discourse semantic systems here, organised by metafunction in Table 1.3. For a detailed presentation of these systems,

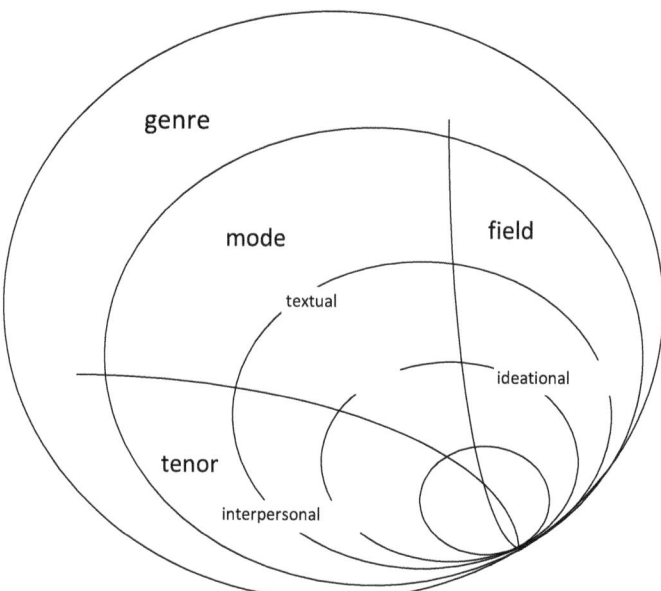

Figure 1.7 Extrinsic functionality (context) and intrinsic functionality (language)

see Martin (1992), Martin and White (2005), Martin and Rose (2007); useful handbook-style introductions include Martin (2015, 2018b) and Tann (2017). For each system we will note the diversification of grammatical systems realising discourse semantic ones, including what we will refer to as metaphorical realisations; and we will exemplify what we mean by co-textual relations between units of discourse that are not grammatically related to one another. By metaphorical realisations we mean grammatical choices that symbolise discourse semantic ones rather than realising them directly (as discussed in Halliday and Matthiessen, 2014, Chapter 10).

The key ideational systems are IDEATION and CONNEXION.[3] IDEATION comprises resources for construing experience as occurrences and entities in occurrence and state figures. In terms of diversification it allows us, for example, to position figures through a range of clause types (Halliday and Matthiessen, 1999; Hao, 2015, 2020a, 2020b).[4]

Table 1.3 *Discourse semantic systems (organised by metafunction)*

| metafunction | discourse semantic systems |
| --- | --- |
| **ideational** | IDEATION |
| | CONNEXION |
| **interpersonal** | NEGOTIATION |
| | APPRAISAL |
| **textual** | IDENTIFICATION |
| | PERIODICITY |

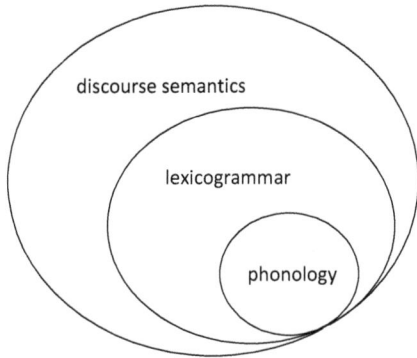

Figure 1.8 Language strata

---

[3] The system name CONNEXION is taken from Hao (2015, 2020a), replacing Martin's earlier term CONJUNCTION in order to differentiate discourse semantic and lexicogrammatical terminology.

[4] We are following Hao's (2020a) terminology here; in her model, discourse semantic figures can be positioned by projecting clauses.

"They've won", **she mused**. (behavioural clause realising the positioning of an occurrence figure)
**She knew** they'd won. (mental clause realising the positioning of an occurrence figure)
**She was aware** they'd won. (relational clause realising the positioning of an occurrence figure)

In terms of grammatical metaphor, IDEATION allows us to realise an occurrence figure congruently as a clause or metaphorically as a nominal group:

She knew **they'd win**. (congruent realisation of an occurrence figure)[5]
**Their win** delighted her. (metaphorical realisation of an occurrence figure)

In terms of meaning beyond the clause, IDEATION allows us, for example, to anticipate occurrence figures – using one clause to name what's to come (stock-taking below) and others to spell it out:

and it was time to **take stock**:
⇓
250 people had needed the lifesavers to pull them out, of whom 210 were OK once back on land. Thirty-five needed mouth to mouth to be restored to consciousness, while five people perished.

CONNEXION comprises resources for relating figures to one another. In terms of diversification, it allows us to connect various types of clause and clause complex to one another (via addition, comparison, time and cause):

**Thanks to** the lifesavers pulling them out, 210 were OK once back on land.
**Because** the lifesavers pulled them out, 210 were OK once back on land.
The lifesavers pulled them out **so that** 210 were OK once back on land.
The lifesavers pulled them out. **So** 210 were OK once back on land.

In terms of grammatical metaphor, CONNEXION allows us to realise relations between occurrences and states metaphorically as single clauses:

(congruent clause complex construing cause)
They were restored to consciousness
because the lifesavers gave them mouth-to-mouth.

(metaphorical cause in the clause)
Mouth-to-mouth resuscitation ensured their restoration to consciousness.

In terms of meaning beyond the clause, CONNEXION allows us to connect indefinitely long phases of discourse to one another (namely the long justification of the preceding sentence introduced by *for* below):

---

[5] The term congruent is used in SFL for direct non-metaphorical realisations.

## 1.3 Above Grammar: Context and Co-text

In their long and glorious history, this still stands as the finest hour of the Australian lifesaving movement.
⇑
**For**, ignoring their own possible peril, the Bondi boys now charged into the surf, some attached to one of the seven reels available, some relying only on their own strength. As one, they began pulling the people out. On the shore, many survivors were resuscitated, as the Bondi clubhouse was turned into a kind of emergency clearing house, and ambulances from all over Sydney town descended and carried the victims away. Finally, just half an hour after the waves hit, the water was cleared of bobbing heads and waving arms, and it was time to take stock: 250 people had needed the lifesavers to pull them out, of whom 210 were OK once back on land. Thirty-five needed mouth to mouth to be restored to consciousness, while five people perished.

The key interpersonal systems are NEGOTIATION and APPRAISAL. NEGOTIATION comprises resources for enacting social relations in dialogue. In terms of diversification it allows us, for example, to realise greeting moves through a range of more and less lexicalised structures.

Hey.
Good morning.
How's it going?
What a surprise!
Lovely to see you.
Didn't know you were back.

In terms of grammatical metaphor, NEGOTIATION allows us to realise moves directly or metaphorically through so-called 'indirect speech acts'.

What's your name? (congruent interrogative clause requesting information)
– Lionel.
Tell me your name. (metaphorical imperative requesting information)
– Lionel.
Your name is …? (metaphorical declarative requesting information)
– Lionel.

In terms of meaning beyond the clause, NEGOTIATION allows us to relate moves in conversation, including moves comprising several clauses (as in the following request and compliance sequence):

What I want you to do now is, I need you to tell us in a really loud voice, OK, what happened on that particular day, alright. So I want you to tell me everything that happened on that day that led to you being stopped by the police with the telephone, OK. Can you do that for us? Thanks. Off you go.
⇓⇑
– When I was walking to my mate's house, this guy just came up to me and he goes "Do you want to buy a phone?", and I go "Nah", and I go "Do you want to swap?" He wanted to swap, with my phone. And he looked at my phone and he goes, "Yeah, swap". And we swapped, and I went and stayed at my mate's house and then, when it came to

night time and I was going back home, I was walking and he was walking me up the road and the police just came and brought us.

APPRAISAL comprises resources for enacting social relations by sharing attitudes. In terms of diversification it allows us, for example, to realise affect across a range of grammatical structures:

**Sadly** they lost.
They **sadly** made their way home.
They were **sad** because they lost.
The **sad** fans drowned their sorrows.
The score **saddened** them.

In terms of grammatical metaphor, APPRAISAL allows us to realise feelings as if they were things, and deploy them accordingly.

They were so palpably sad that it darkened proceedings. (congruent adjectival feeling)
**Their palpable sadness** darkened proceedings. (metaphorical nominalised feeling)

In terms of meaning beyond the clause, APPRAISAL allows us, for example, to evaluate indefinitely long phases of discourse. The extended CONNEXION example we used above does more than justify a proposition; it also glorifies the lifesavers' rescue operations:

In their long and **glorious** history, this still stands as the **finest** hour of the Australian lifesaving movement.
⇓
For, ignoring their own possible peril, the Bondi boys now charged into the surf, some attached to one of the seven reels available, some relying only on their own strength. As one, they began pulling the people out. On the shore, many survivors were resuscitated, as the Bondi clubhouse was turned into a kind of emergency clearing house, and ambulances from all over Sydney town descended and carried the victims away. Finally, just half an hour after the waves hit, the water was cleared of bobbing heads and waving arms, and it was time to take stock: 250 people had needed the lifesavers to pull them out, of whom 210 were OK once back on land. Thirty-five needed mouth to mouth to be restored to consciousness, while five people perished.

The key textual systems are IDENTIFICATION and PERIODICITY. IDENTIFICATION comprises resources for composing discourse in terms of introducing entities and tracking them once there. In terms of diversification it allows us, for example, to track entities through a range of nominal resources:

**Pope Francis** arrived.
**He** was dressed in white.
**The Argentinian** thanked Chileans for their hospitality during **his** Jesuitical training there.
**This pope** publicly acknowledged the child abuse scandals.

## 1.3 Above Grammar: Context and Co-text

In terms of meaning beyond the clause, IDENTIFICATION allows us to identify and track indefinitely long phases of discourse; the pronoun *it* is used in this way below to reference the activity that subsequently unfolds.[6]

At three o'clock there was still not the slightest clue that this afternoon would forever be known as "Black Sunday" in the annals of Sydney. Then **it** happened.
⇓
With a roar like a Bondi tram running amok, an enormous wave suddenly rolled over the thousands in the surf, including those many standing on the large sandbank just out from the shore – knocking them all over as it went. And then another wave hit, and then another. The huge waves, just like that, piggy-backed their way further and further up the beach and grabbed everything they could along the way – from babies to toddlers to adolescents to beach umbrellas, to old blokes and young sheilas alike, and then made a mad dash for the open sea again, carrying all before it and sweeping everyone off the sandbank and into the deep channel next to it in the process.

PERIODICITY comprises resources for composing text as waves of information. The basic idea here is that there is a hierarchy of periodicity, extending from the small wave lengths of tone group and clause to an indefinite number of indefinitely long phases of discourse. In the example below we have a Kicker foreshadowing an entire feature article about a beachside tragedy, a topic sentence introducing what happened when the waves rolled up the beach further down and a retrospective summary of the effect of the inundations. A wide range of resources, including text reference and ideational grammatical metaphor (in bold below), co-operate with one another to scaffold information flow along these lines.

Big waves and Bondi Beach have always gone together, writes Peter FitzSimons, but no one had ever seen the ocean rise up with a **strength** such as **this**. ⇒

> At three o'clock there was still not the slightest clue that this afternoon would forever be known as "Black Sunday" in the annals of Sydney. Then **it** happened.⇒
>
>> With a roar like a Bondi tram running amok, an enormous wave suddenly rolled over the thousands in the surf, including those many standing on the large sandbank just out from the shore – knocking them all over as it went. And then another wave hit, and then another. The huge waves, just like that, piggy-backed their way further and further up the beach and grabbed everything they could along the way – from babies to toddlers to adolescents to beach umbrellas, to old blokes and young sheilas alike, and then made a mad dash for the open sea again, carrying all before it and sweeping everyone off the sandbank and into the deep channel next to it in the process.
>
> ⇐ In no more than 20 seconds, that peaceful scene had been tragically transformed into utter **chaos**. Now, the boiling surf, with yet more large waves continuing to roll over, was filled with distressed folk waving for help.

---

[6] Martin (1992) treats text reference of this kind as textual grammatical metaphor, since it involves a nominal group referring to a phase of discourse rather than an entity (a person, place or thing). It is, however, difficult to see how reference of this kind is symbolising a phase of discourse, and there is arguably no stratal tension (i.e. there are not two meanings in play, one of which could be interpreted literally). In retrospect the concept of grammatical metaphor was probably being pushed too far.

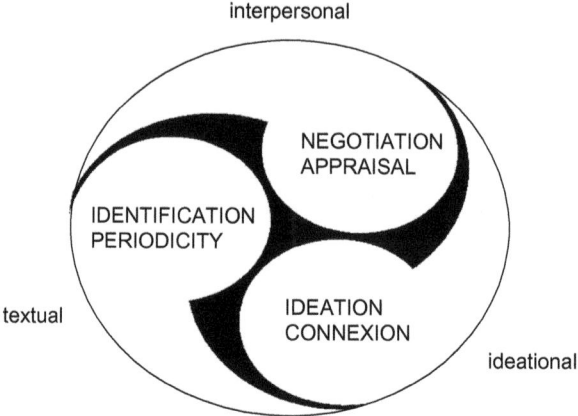

Figure 1.9 Discourse semantic systems

The discourse semantic resources briefly reviewed here are outlined by metafunction in Figure 1.9. They will be reintroduced, as relevant, in Chapters 2–6 of this book.

Since this is a book about grammar, albeit grammar analysis from a holistic linguistic perspective, we do not have room here to introduce discourse semantic systems in further detail. But we do need, perhaps, to emphasise that discourse semantic systems are organised differently from lexicogrammatical ones and that there is no one-to-one relation between discourse semantic and lexicogrammatical features. Rather, there is what Lamb has referred to as interlocking diversification – many-to-many relations between choices in systems on the two strata (see Lamb, 1964).

### 1.4  Doing Functional Grammar

There are, of course, many ways of approaching grammar analysis, falling roughly into the formal and functional traditions epitomised in the work of Chomsky and Halliday respectively in the second half of the twentieth century. Methodologically speaking, the complementarity of these traditions can be explored from many perspectives. We will highlight three that bear critically on this volume here.

First data. Rather than relying on a native speaker's intuitions about what can be said, SFG treats the texts that speakers produce as data. This is quite a challenge, since ultimately we want grammars that take responsibility for as wide a range of texts as possible. Ideally, SFG would draw on SFL register and genre theory to construct a representative corpus and design grammars based on what is found therein (e.g. Figueredo, 2021). In this book we will mimic this practice by using a key text as the main source of examples for each language in each chapter. Where practical, in terms of the range of linguistic resources in play, we have used the same text in more than one chapter so that we can show how SFG approaches a text from different dimensions of analysis. Where necessary, for pedagogic purposes, we have at times used constructed examples to simplify the presentation; at other times we have adjusted examples from the texts we used to make a point.

Second appliability. Ideally, rather than developing grammars dedicated to questions that only interest linguists, SFG also takes responsibility for questions about language that interest language users. This means that the grammars are expected to make a contribution to the regions of practice which we recognise as educational linguistics, forensic linguistics, clinical linguistics, translation studies and so on (e.g. Rose and Martin, 2012; Zappavigna and Martin, 2018; Rochester and Martin, 1979; Steiner and Yallop, 2001, respectively; for a more comprehensive survey see Caldwell, Knox and Martin, 2022). In this book we tackle this challenge by developing rich functional descriptions that show how grammar makes meaning. In doing so, we lay the foundation for the discourse semantic and contextual analysis needed to address communication issues of concern to speakers, wherever they arise.

Third argumentation. Ideally, SFG deploys what is often referred to as 'trinocular' vision – reasoning from above, from around and from below (Halliday, 1992/2003). This means that as grammarians we take (discourse) semantics and phonology into account, as linguistic resources that impinge directly on our analyses. And as far as grammar itself is concerned, it means that we take axial reasoning seriously, as promoted in Martin, Wang and Zhu (2013) and Quiroz (2013, 2018, 2020). What do we mean when we say "take axial reasoning seriously"?

As outlined in Martin, Wang and Zhu (2013), this means privileging paradigmatic relations over syntagmatic ones, but only on the understanding that any paradigmatic relations we establish must ultimately be motivated by syntagmatic ones. In Halliday's (1994, p. xx) terms, "Every distinction that is recognized in the grammar – every set of options, or 'system' in systemic terms – makes some contribution to the form of the wording. Often it will be a very indirect one, but it will be somewhere in the picture." What does he mean by "some contribution to the form of the wording"?

Minimally, some contribution to the form of the wording could be taken to mean focusing almost exclusively on syntagms – on sequences of classes of linguistic units. This would include focusing on word morphology (i.e. distinctive sequences of morphemes with words) and on syntax (understood as distinctive sequences of words in groups and phrases and distinctive sequences of groups and phrases in clauses).[7] A grammar conceived in just these terms is basically a catalogue of possible syntagms, including sometimes more and sometimes less information about how they are related to one another. All grammarians take syntagms, defined in these terms, into account when developing their descriptions.

In SFG grammarians push deeper, exploring the relations that syntagms enter into with one another. This paradigmatic perspective on deep grammar was developed by Halliday and his colleagues in the 1960s (e.g. Halliday 1964, 1966), including the formalisation of paradigmatic relations in system networks and specification of the structural basis of distinctions in realisation statements. Halliday (1967a, 1967b, 1968, 1970/2005) are the key papers introducing this perspective on deep grammar. Martin, Wang and Zhu (2013) is the basic introduction to the achievements of these functional grammarians; and Davidse (2018) synthesises their contributions. For foundational papers contextualising this work in SFL, see Martin and Doran (2015a, 2015b, 2015c).

To illustrate this grammatical perspective on meaning as choice, we begin with the following two sets of English clauses. As far as syntagms are concerned, the clauses look identical. The same kind of nominal group is followed by the same kind of verbal group followed in turn by the same kind of nominal group. We have the same pattern over and over again.

Lionel Messi has kicked the fullback.
Roger Federer has smashed the lob.
Adam Scott has putted the ball.
Sidney Crosby has deked the defenceman.

Lionel Messi has kicked the penalty.
Roger Federer has won the point.
Adam Scott has made the shot.
Sidney Crosby has scored the winner.

Now let's ask some questions about what went on, using the syntagm *What did (someone) do to (something)?* This works fine for the first set of clauses; we get a question and answer sequence that works out well.

---

[7] When it realises grammatical distinctions, prosodic phonology may also be brought into the picture; realisations of this kind are considered in relation to Spanish MOOD in Chapter 4.

## 1.4 Doing Functional Grammar

What did Lionel Messi do to the fullback? – Kicked him.
What did Roger Federer do to the lob? – Smashed it.
What did Adam Scott do to the ball? – Putted it.
What did Sidney Crosby do to the defenceman? – Deked him.

But for the second set our question doesn't seem to make sense. We would have to spend a very long time looking in an English corpus for examples of this kind.

*What did Lionel Messi do to the penalty?
*What did Roger Federer do to the point?
*What did Adam Scott do to the shot?
*What did Sidney Crosby do to the winner?

The difference between what we can do with the first set of clauses and what we can do with the second shows us that the same syntagm may in fact be realising different grammatical choices. In Halliday and Matthiessen's (2014, p. 229) terms, the first set of clauses is transitive and the second set intransitive.[8] This reflects the fact that in the first set what happens impacts on the entity realised by the following nominal group, while in the second what happens is realised through the verbal group and the following nominal group (the two together jointly construe what went on). For Halliday and Matthiessen, the clauses in the second set are more closely related to clauses without a second nominal group than they are to the clauses with a second nominal group in the first set. The intransitive clauses without a second nominal group they have in mind are exemplified in a third set of examples below.

Lionel Messi goaled.
Roger Federer lobbed.
Adam Scott putted.
Sidney Crosby scored.

We can't ask our *What did (someone) do to (something)?* question for either the second or the third set; instead, we have to ask *What happened?*

What happened? – Lionel Messi has kicked the penalty.
etc.

What happened? – Lionel Messi goaled.
etc.

We can express the relationships involved as proportions, using ':' to mean 'is related to' and '::' to mean 'as'.

---

[8] Note that Halliday and Matthiessen (2014) are therefore not using the terms intransitive and transitive to distinguish English clauses with one nominal group from clauses with two.

Messi goaled : Messi has kicked the penalty ::
Federer lobbed : Federer has won the point ::
Scott putted : Scott has made the shot ::
Crosby scored : Crosby has scored the winner

By grouping more closely related sets together in parentheses, we can bring all three sets into the picture.

(Messi goaled : Messi has kicked the penalty) : Messi has kicked the fullback ::
(Federer lobbed : Federer has won the point) : Federer has smashed the lob ::
(Scott putted : Scott has made the shot) : Scott has putted the ball ::
(Crosby scored : Crosby has scored the winner) : Crosby has deked the defenceman

As more relationships are introduced, this kind of notation gets rather cumbersome. In SFL, to overcome this problem, paradigmatic relations of this kind would be formalised as system networks like the one in Figure 1.10. The network classifies clauses as transitive or intransitive, and then subclassifies the intransitive clauses as optionally scoped.[9]

This kind of representation embodies a very important principle in SFL – namely its concern to model language and context as resources rather than rules (which resources comprise choices which constitute the meaning potential of a culture as whole).

The term [scoped] in the network is taken from the function term assigned by Halliday and Matthiessen (2014) to the nominal group following the verbal group in the second set of clauses; it contrasts with the function label they use for the second nominal group in the first set, termed Goal. The analysis they propose for the first two sets of clauses are tabled below. The function terms Actor, Process, Goal and Scope describe the role played by each group in the clause; the class terms nominal group and verbal group classify the linguistic units playing each role. By convention function terms are written with an initial uppercase letter and class terms are written in lower case. In our analyses, following Halliday (1981), the function terms constitute what we will refer to as structure (the first row of analysis in the tables) and the class labels

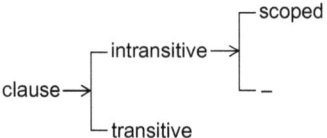

Figure 1.10 A simple TRANSITIVITY system

---

[9] For an introduction to system network notation, see Martin, Wang and Zhu (2013); for an introduction to systemic notation in Spanish, see Quiroz (2016). SFG notational conventions are summarised in Appendix 1 of this volume.

## 1.4 Doing Functional Grammar   21

(the second row of analysis in the tables) constitute what we will refer to as a syntagm.

|           | Lionel Messi  | has kicked   | the fullback  |
|-----------|---------------|--------------|---------------|
| **structure** | Actor     | Process      | Goal          |
| **syntagm**   | nominal group | verbal group | nominal group |

|           | Lionel Messi  | has kicked   | the penalty   |
|-----------|---------------|--------------|---------------|
| **structure** | Actor     | Process      | Scope         |
| **syntagm**   | nominal group | verbal group | nominal group |

In examples such as these, the function labels are used to distinguish the different choices realised by the same syntagm, a difference exposed by exploring the relationship between the verbal group and the following nominal group. The function structure as a whole thus reflects the distinctive relationships the syntagm enters into with other syntagms (e.g. the different possibilities for transitive and scoped intransitive clauses exemplified above).

By way of clarification of this paradigmatic perspective on grammatical relations, let's consider another set of English clauses.

Lionel Messi must goal every match.
Roger Federer must practise every day.
Adam Scott must birdie every round.
Sidney Crosby must score every game.

Each clause has an identical nominal group, verbal group, nominal group sequence, and the sequence of word classes in each group is also the same. But each clause is ambiguous. The modality realised in the verbal group may be giving someone's opinion of the probability of something having taken place; this meaning, termed modalisation in SFG, is foregrounded in the extended examples below.

Lionel Messi must goal every match to have scored that often.
Roger Federer must practise every day to have become so good.
Adam Scott must birdie every round to have ended up ranked number one.
Sidney Crosby must score every game to have won so many titles.

Alternatively, the modality realised in the verbal group may be encoding someone's advice about what must be done to achieve a certain goal; this meaning, termed modulation in SFG,[10] is foregrounded in the extended examples below.

---

[10] In formal semantics a distinction is drawn between epistemic and deontic modality, terminology which from an SFL perspective opposes ideational modality (epistemic) – the likelihood of a state of affairs, to interpersonal modality (deontic) – how the world should be. In SFL MODALISATION and MODULATION are both interpersonal systems, associated with propositions and proposals respectively (Halliday and Matthiessen, 2014, pp. 176ff., 689ff.).

Lionel Messi must goal every match for Barcelona to win the cup.
Roger Federer must practise everyday to win another grand slam.
Adam Scott must birdie every round to secure the championship.
Sidney Crosby must score every game for Pittsburgh to reach the finals.

Setting aside these extensions, we can observe that modalisation can be alternatively expressed as an adverb (*certainly*, *probably*, *possibly*, etc.), in which case there is no ambiguity. The following clauses are about degrees of certainty, not obligation.

Lionel Messi certainly goals every match.
Roger Federer probably practises every day.
Adam Scott possibly birdies every hole.
Sidney Crosby perhaps scores every game.

Modulation, on the other hand, is not alternatively realised in this way. Instead, a verbal group complex is deployed, with modulation encoded in the first verbal group. Once again there is no ambiguity. The following clauses are about degrees of obligation, not probability.

Lionel Messi is obliged to goal every match.
Roger Federer is required to practise every day.
Adam Scott is supposed to birdie every hole.
Sidney Crosby is expected to score every game.

We see again that the contrasting relations the syntagm enters into reveals that there is more going on in the first set of modalised clauses than the sequencing of classes reveals. In systemic terms we can express the relationships just reviewed as the set of choices formalised in Figure 1.11. The modalised clauses have verbal and adverbial realisations, while the modulated clauses have verbal group and verbal group complex ones.

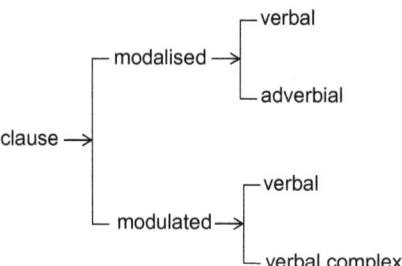

Figure 1.11 A simple MODALITY system in English

## 1.4 Doing Functional Grammar

If we want to reflect these distinctions in function structures,[11] then we need to extend our analyses to include the structure of verbal groups. A Modalisation and Event function structure is proposed for [modalised: verbal] groups below.

| Lionel Messi | must goal | | every match |
|---|---|---|---|
| Actor | Process | | Extent |
| nominal group | verbal group | | nominal group |
| | Modalisation | Event | |
| | modal verb | verb | |
| | *must* | *goal* | |

The structure for [modulated: verbal] groups could then involve a Modulation and Event structure.

| Lionel Messi | must goal | | every match |
|---|---|---|---|
| Actor | Process | | Extent |
| nominal group | verbal group | | nominal group |
| | Modulation | Event | |
| | modal verb | verb | |
| | *must* | *goal* | |

For [modalised: adverbial] clauses, a Modal Adjunct function could be inserted at clause rank.

| Lionel Messi | certainly | goals | every match |
|---|---|---|---|
| Actor | Modal Adjunct | Process | Extent |
| nominal group | adverbial group | verbal group | nominal group |

For [modulated: verbal complex] clauses, a verbal group complex with an $\alpha^{modulating}$ β structure could be proposed.

| Lionel Messi | is obliged to goal | | every match |
|---|---|---|---|
| Actor | Process | | Extent |
| nominal group | verbal group complex | | nominal group |
| | $\alpha^{modulating}$ | β | |
| | verbal group | verbal group | |
| | *is obliged* | *to goal* | |

As we can see, SFG pushes beyond syntagms when formulating its descriptions, adopting a paradigmatic perspective and asking how syntagms are

---

[11] Halliday and Matthiessen (2014) do not take the step of providing distinctive function structures for the two readings of the ambiguous clauses; they leave it to their system networks to distinguish the modality types involved.

related to one another. It formalises relations among syntagms as system networks – as sets of interconnected options accounting for the distinctions the grammar of a given language has evolved to make. And from a syntagmatic perspective, it reflects these systemic relations in function structures which tell us what the parts of a syntagm are doing (in addition to what they are). The extent to which function structures reflect distinctions in system networks is a variable. Reflecting every distinction in function labels would soon make an analysis of grammatical units difficult to view and time-consuming to draw. In practice, only very general grammatical distinctions are encoded in function structures; however, this can be adjusted as required for research projects that find a more delicate function structure specification revealing. In our treatment of modality options above, we have already pushed the function–structure description beyond that proposed in Halliday and Matthiessen's (2014) canonical English reference grammar.

The way in which SFG in effect treats syntagms as realising multiple structures has encouraged some linguists (e.g. Davidse, 1991/1999; Halliday and Matthiessen, 1999) to link the reasoning involved to Whorf (1945) and his interest in what he called 'covert' categories. Whorf's focus was on word classes, and he proposed that classification should not simply be based on overt morphological markers. For English adjectives, for example, he argued that although morphologically identical, there was a difference between the adjectives *pretty* and *French* in a phrase like *a **pretty** French girl*. The difference becomes apparent once we try to reverse the sequence of the two adjectives (i.e. \**a French pretty girl* is not grammatical); it is also reflected in the fact that *pretty* is gradable but *French* is not (so we find *a very pretty French girl* but not \**a pretty very French girl*, unless in the second case we are referring to her character and not her provenance). Whorf referred to the differentiating behaviour of words in these alternate syntagms as reactances and argued that reactances reveal covert categories ('hidden' categories he called cryptotypes). For discussion of the similarities and differences between Whorf's reasoning and axial reasoning in SFG, see Quiroz (2013, 2020). The SFG approach is, of course, concerned with the classification of grammatical units of all kinds, not just words. But the way in which SFG structures (reflecting paradigmatic relations) reveal what syntagms 'neutralise' does call to mind Whorf's proposals – a connection highlighted in the work of SFL grammarians who refer to their descriptions as cryptogrammars (e.g. Rose, 2001).[12]

In this section we have highlighted three critical dimensions of SFG methodology – data, appliability and argumentation. The three are in fact contingent upon one another. It is axial reasoning that enables the rich functional

---

[12] Fillmore (1968) acknowledges a comparable debt to Whorf in the introduction to his work on case relations.

descriptions that underpin discourse semantic, register and genre analysis in the model of SFL we are assuming here. This, in turn, informs the many applications of the theory across sectors. And it is these applications which more than anything else have pushed SFL grammarians to take responsibility for an ever-widening range of registers and genres. As we have illustrated, axial reasoning means giving prominence to relationships among syntagms – relationships which nonetheless have to be ultimately grounded syntagmatically. Modelling this approach to grammatical description is the main purpose of this book.

## 1.5 Metafunction, Rank and Stratification

The approach to axial reasoning introduced above and modelled in detail in Martin, Wang and Zhu (2013) and Quiroz (2013) underpins three further dimensions of SFL to which we turn our attention here – metafunction, rank and stratification. Metafunction deals with how axial reasoning organises multiple strands of meaning; rank is concerned with how axial reasoning shapes SFG's model of constituency; stratification focuses on how axial reasoning allocates resources to different levels of abstraction (referred to in the model of SFL assumed here as phonology, lexicogrammar and discourse semantics). We now deal briefly with each in turn.

First metafunction. In our discussion of axial reasoning above, we drew on examples from two English clause systems, TRANSITIVITY and MODALITY. We began by considering clauses with respect to the relationship between

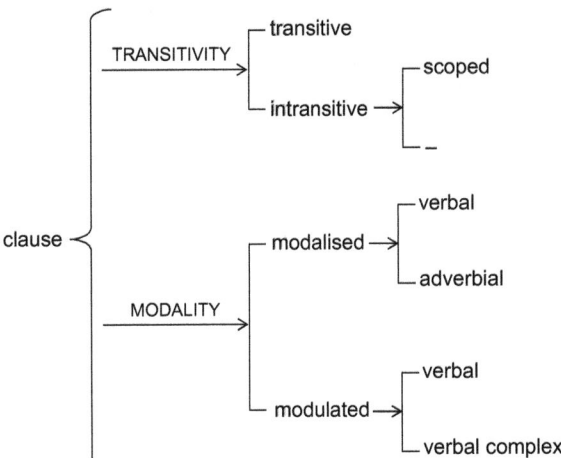

Figure 1.12 TRANSITIVITY and MODALITY systems in English

their verbal group and a following nominal group; and we then continued by exploring some ways in which assessments of probability and obligation can be brought onto the picture. The two system networks we proposed are brought together in the system network in Figure 1.12. In formalisations of paradigmatic relations of this kind, a brace (curly bracket) is used to show that a class is cross-classified (e.g. a clause cross-classified by the TRANSITIVITY systems and MODALITY systems below). As explained in more detail in Martin, Wang and Zhu (2013), several SFL grammarians working across languages have designed descriptions in which systems tend to cluster along the lines emerging in the network below – with some clusters of interdependent systems construing ideational meaning (e.g. TRANSITIVITY),[13] others enacting interpersonal meaning (e.g. MODALITY) and still others composing textual meaning (not illustrated in this chapter for clauses; see Chapter 6). In our experience clause grammars founded on axial reasoning will tend to reflect the metafunctional organisation of language by grouping systems in simultaneous clusters in this way.

Next rank. As we saw in our discussion of MODALITY above, systems can be realised in units of different kinds. In our examples MODALITY was realised as a modal adverb in clauses (e.g. *Lionel Messi **certainly** goals every match*), as a verbal group in verbal group complexes (*Lionel Messi **is obliged** to goal every match*) and as a modal verb in verbal groups (*Lionel Messi **must** goal every match*). This reflects the fact that alongside clustering as metafunctions, our models of systems of choice will also tend to cluster with respect to the basic units they classify. The MODALITY system in the network above is actually dependent on the MOOD feature indicative, since there is no modality in English imperative clauses. From the perspective of constituency, MOOD systems, including MODALITY, can be seen to cluster at clause rank, as outlined with a little more detail in Figure 1.13 (elaborated in Chapter 4).

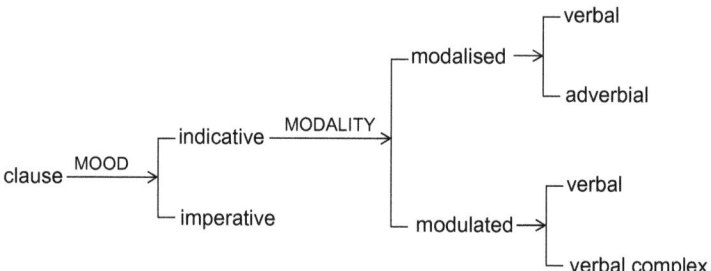

Figure 1.13 Dependency of MODALITY on MOOD in English

---

[13] We will introduce the distinction between the experiential and logical components of the ideational metafunction in later chapters.

## 1.5 Metafunction, Rank and Stratification

But as we have seen, only one of the MODALITY features included here is realised directly in clause structure – namely the feature adverbial, which triggers the insertion of a Modal Adjunct (e.g. ***perhaps*** *Messi will goal*). For the realisation of other MODALITY features, we need to move down a rank and bring groups into the picture, verbal groups in particular. As we have seen, verbal group complex modulations involve two verbal groups, one finite verbal group followed by one non-finite one (e.g. finite *is expected* and non-finite *to score* in *Messi **is expected to score***). The relevant systems are outlined in Figure 1.14. The loop in the network allows for complexing of groups (a recursive system). The left-facing brace establishes the verbal group complex environment in which modulation can be realised (read as if complex and verbal then optionally modulating).[14]

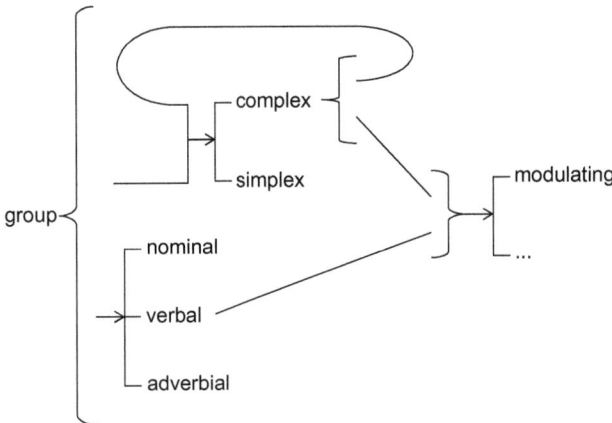

Figure 1.14 Verbal group systems realising 'periphrastic' MODULATION in English

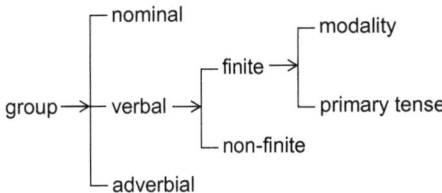

Figure 1.15 Verbal group systems realising MODALITY through modal verbs in English

---

[14] The alternatives to modulating verbal group complexes in English (e.g. *is expected to be able to score*) are not specified in the network; they include conative complexes such as *is trying to goal* and causative ones like *was forced to goal*.

Other MODALITY features are realised in English inside verbal groups, as modal verbs (e.g. M*essi* ***must*** *play there*). The relevant verbal group systems are outlined in Figure 1.15.

To take into account the realisation of these group rank systems, we have to move down a rank again and consider word classes (since the kind of verb we choose is crucial). A simplified word network is presented in Figure 1.16, including the relevant verb classes for verbal groups realising MODALITY in English.[15]

In short, exploring modality means bringing a consideration of clauses, verbal groups and modal verbs into the picture; clauses, groups and words are all involved. In SFG these units are organised along a scale of constituency known as rank.[16] The scale is organised the way it is because of the way the choices involved obtain for units of different kinds. Seen from a syntagmatic perspective, the key units are clause, group,[17] word and morpheme – with a clause understood as realised through one or more groups, a group as realised through one or more words, and a word as realised through one or more morphemes.[18] This is illustrated below for a clause with a verbal group realisation of modality. In order not to over-complicate the presentation, we have only broken down the verbal group realising the Process into its constituent structure.

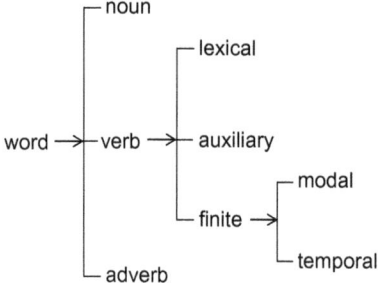

Figure 1.16 Word rank verb systems relevant to MODALITY in English

---

[15] Ideally the same term (the term [finite] is at issue here, used at group rank in Figure 1.15 and work rank in Figure 1.16) should not be used at different ranks; the Latin *finitus*, from which *finite* derives, is one possible alternative.
[16] Berry (2017) provides a useful introduction to rank in the theoretical and descriptive architecture of SFL; and Part III of Bartlett and O'Grady (2017) includes several group rank descriptions.
[17] We will introduce the distinction between groups and phrases in later chapters.
[18] For languages without morphology, a morpheme rank would be superfluous; since words have no structure, there is no need to recognise word and morpheme as distinct units.

## 1.5 Metafunction, Rank and Stratification

| clause rank | clause | | | | | |
|---|---|---|---|---|---|---|
| | Actor | Process | | | | Extent |
| group rank | nominal group | verbal group | | | | nominal group |
| | | Modality | Tense | Event | | |
| word rank | | verb | verb | verb | | |
| | | α | α | α | β | |
| morpheme rank | | stem | stem | stem | suffix | |
| | Lionel Messi | must | have | goal | -ed | every match |
| | *Lionel Messi must have goaled every match.* | | | | | |

The details of this kind of analysis will be spelled out in later chapters. Our main point here is to suggest that the grammatical systems introduced above are organised by rank (i.e. clause systems, group systems, word systems and morpheme systems) and that their realisation in function structures gives the shape it does to the constituency hierarchy illustrated above for English. As indicated in Figure 1.14 with reference to the recursive system for group complexes, units at each rank may enter into complexes, as illustrated below.

| clauses complex | **Serena Williams** won but **Venus Williams** lost. |
|---|---|
| group complex | **Serena Williams and Venus Williams** both won. |
| word complex | **Serena and Venus** Williams both won. |
| morpheme complex | Serena was gracious in both **pre- and post**-match interviews. |

The final dimension we need to consider in terms of clustering of systems is stratification. We will continue to explore clustering with reference to MODALITY. So far we have reviewed how MODALITY can be realised verbally and adverbially across ranks in English. But from a discourse semantic perspective, there are other ways of expanding the play of voices implicated in an exchange. Two are added below. The first uses a mental process, *I suppose*, to open up the exchange; it involves two clauses, one projecting the other. The fourth uses a relational process, with probability encoded as an attribute (*probable*) of an embedded clause (*he scored*).

**I suppose** he scored.
He **probably** scored.
He **would** have scored.
It's **probable** he scored.

In discourse semantics it is useful to bring these alternatives together, since they have comparable discourse functions. They all realise the APPRAISAL sub-system ENGAGEMENT, which in simple terms allows speakers to make a move in an exchange without reference to other opinions (monogloss), or to acknowledge other voices (heterogloss). Heteroglossic moves can then either

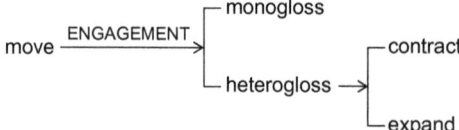

Figure 1.17 Basic ENGAGEMENT systems

shut down other voices (via negation and concession for example) or allow them room (the contract/expand system in Figure 1.17). MODALITY is a key resource for opening up discourse by implicating other opinions. Saying *Messi might have goaled*, for example, acknowledges that there might be someone believing he didn't, whereas *Messi goaled* does not.

From the perspective of grammar, the first and fourth examples are quite different from the others. In these cases we haven't modalised by simply adding a modal verb or modal adverb to an intransitive clause. Rather we've drawn on the English TRANSITIVITY system, as we will expand it in Chapter 5, and in each case added another type of clause (a mental clause and a relational clause respectively). In SFL the first and fourth examples are treated as grammatical metaphors – because, as we will argue, they don't directly realise discourse semantic choices; rather the grammar symbolises them.

**I suppose** he scored.
He probably scored.
He would have scored.
It's **probable** he scored.

In the case of probability, symbolising rather that directly realising means finding appropriate TRANSITIVITY resources to dress a statement or question up as probable. For our first example, a first person present tense mental clause of cognition is used to symbolise probability; in effect the grammar is saying, metaphorically speaking, that modalising is like thinking. A statement of this kind can be negotiated straightforwardly, using a modal adverb, as illustrated below; and because it is symbolising a modality, it will be tagged *I suppose he scored, didn't he?* rather than *I suppose he scored, don't I?*

I suppose he scored.
– Probably.

Alternatively, though this is less likely, it can be challenged – below by querying the thought process involved (so *Do you?* not *Did he?* below). In this case the mental process symbolising probability is taken literally, as if it was simply encoding what the speaker thought.

I suppose he scored.
– Do you?

1.5 Metafunction, Rank and Stratification

The general point we would like to reinforce here is that discourse semantic systems can be realised across a range of lexicogrammatical resources. One of the pay-offs of conceptualising the relationship this way is that grammar can be used either to directly encode meaning (termed congruent realisation) or to symbolise it (termed metaphorical realisation). For some SFL grammarians (e.g. Halliday and Matthiessen, 1999) recognition of this phenomenon is one of the key motivations for a model involving distinct systems of meaning on two levels of abstraction (their semantics and lexicogrammar).[19]

Turning from discourse semantics to phonology, we also have to take into account that fact that prosodic phonology (i.e. rhythm and intonation) can contribute significantly to the meaning being negotiated. In casual conversation, for example, the fact that the clause *I suppose* is symbolising probability means that it is likely to be phonologically reduced, reflecting the diminished status of its ideational meaning. In the first example below, its articulation is reduced to a single non-salient syllable (written below as *s'pose*).

//^ s'pose he /**scored**//[20]

The fast speech processes deployed here emphasise that the speaker is negotiating probability and is not, in fact, expecting his proposition to be challenged *Do you?* We can contrast this with a fully articulated version below and an alternative with two tone groups which follows. The first gives more informational prominence to the thinking clause; and the second offers it as negotiable in its own right, as an afterthought (undoing the grammatical metaphor of modality in the process).

//^ I su /ppose he /**scored**//
//^ he /**scored**//^ I su/**ppose**//

The ways in which the kind of language description we are promoting here draws on stratification to reason from above, around and below will be modelled in Chapters 2–6. In SFL the stratification hierarchy we are touching on here is usually modelled as co-tangential circles (Figure 1.18 below). The relationship between levels of abstraction is termed realisation. The increasing size of the circles reflects the fact that phonological systems realise lexicogrammatical systems, which in turn realise discourse semantic ones. So the choices in higher strata necessarily involve the choices in lower ones. The term metaredundancy is sometimes used to refer to this relationship among strata

---

[19] For further discussion of this point, see Martin, Wang and Zhu (2013), Taverniers (2018) and chapter 10 of Halliday and Matthiessen (2014) 'Beyond the clause: metaphorical modes of expression'. The ENGAGEMENT system underlying the direct and indirect realisations in English of MODALITY discussed here is introduced in Martin and White (2005).
[20] Our notation is based on Halliday (1967c, 1970) and Halliday and Greaves (2008). '//' stands for a tone group boundary, '/' for a foot boundary, '^' for a silent beat, and the tonic syllable carrying the major pitch movement in the tone group is in bold.

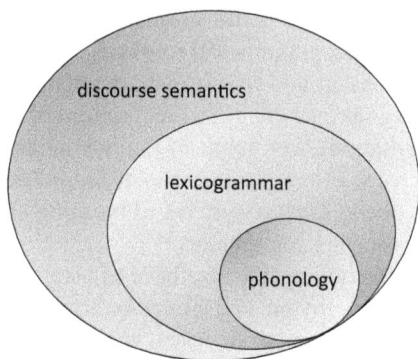

Figure 1.18 Language strata realising register and genre systems

(after Lemke, 1995; cf. Halliday, 1992/2002). This is a way of theorising the relationship between patterns on one level and patterns on another – a pattern of phonemes, for example, realising morphemes, or a pattern of clauses realising an exchange. Or, to put this the other way around, discourse semantics is a pattern of lexicogrammatical patterns, which are in turn a pattern of phonological ones. In SFL, lexis is treated as more delicate grammar, as explained in chapter 6 of Martin, Wang and Zhu (2013). For this reason the middle stratum is usually referred to as lexicogrammar.[21]

## 1.6   Outline of This Book

Following this introduction, this book comprises five main chapters followed by a brief culminative envoi. Each chapter is divided into three main sections, one each devoted to English, Spanish and Chinese; each chapter also dedicated to a specific dimension of grammatical description. A short outline of the pedagogic focus of each chapter is presented below.

Chapter 2 explores nominal group system and structure. In doing so, it concentrates on what in SFL is referred to as *multivariate structure*. Multivariate structures are structures involving a finite number of functions, each playing a distinct role. In this chapter we concentrate on developing multivariate structures for nominal groups in English, Spanish and Chinese.

Chapter 3 explores verbal group system and structure. In doing so for English and Spanish, it concentrates on what in SFL is referred to as *univariate*

---

[21] For writing, the least abstract stratum would be termed graphology (including alphabetic, syllabic and character-based systems, alongside the punctuation and layout resources they involve); a corresponding term for the sign languages of deaf communities would be signology.

## 1.6 Outline of This Book

*structure*. Univariate structures are structures involving a single variable, which is repeated over and over again; they thus function as the realisation of recursive systems. The unit complexes introduced above (clause complexes, group complexes, word complexes and morpheme complexes) are structures of this kind. And some languages develop more delicate clause and group systems organised along these lines.

The recursive tense systems in English and Spanish which we describe in this chapter are good examples. Chinese verbal groups, on the other hand, do not involve recursive systems realised by iterating structures and so have to be approached from a multivariate perspective.

Chapter 4 explores MOOD systems and structures. It concentrates on paradigmatic relations – and the ways in which these can be motivated in the grammars of English, Spanish and Chinese. This chapter foregrounds questions about the nature of functional language typology, when confronted with the diverse structural realisations of MOOD in three different languages. It highlights the need to focus on system rather than structure, on higher ranks rather than lower ones and ultimately on discourse semantics rather than grammar by way of establishing comparable ground whenever languages are being contrasted and compared.

Chapter 5 explores TRANSITIVITY systems and structures. It concentrates on the evidence used to motivate descriptions of paradigmatic relations. At stake here is the weight given to evidence of different kinds, including arguing from above, around and below. This chapter also foregrounds the cline of delicacy with respect to both system and structure, exploring what happens when general TRANSITIVITY classes are explored in greater detail and issues that arise with respect to how much subclassification should be reflected in function structure labelling.

Chapter 6 explores THEME and INFORMATION systems and structures. It concentrates on the need to argue from discourse semantics as far as the interpretation of information flow is concerned. This chapter brings some phonological analysis into the picture, since INFORMATION systems are realised through prosodic phonology (i.e. rhythm and intonation). This work draws on Halliday's analysis of English intonation, as presented in Halliday (1967c, 1970) and Halliday and Greaves (2008).

The final chapter rounds off the discussion, highlighting the distinctive nature of argumentation in the development of functional grammars informed by SFL and the importance of assembling data as a corpus of texts designed on the basis of a linguistic theory of register and genre.

In an ideal world, each one of these chapters would have had the strong discourse semantic orientation of Chapter 6. But this would have made the book very much longer than it is and might have backgrounded the pedagogic focus of the current chapters.

## 1.7 Notational Conventions

The notational conventions for this volume are basically those introduced in Matthiessen and Halliday (2009) and Martin, Wang and Zhu (2013). These are consolidated as Appendix 1. Any additional conventions will be introduced where required. The morpheme-by-morpheme glossing of the Spanish examples is based on the Leipzig glossing rules. Further glossing is based on the dedicated SFL glossing conventions available at https://systemiclanguagemodelling.wordpress.com/.

At various points this book adopts the convention of referring to participant roles in very general terms as Participant 1, Participant 2 and Participant 3 (P1, P2 and P3 for short). For languages with case relations, this can be understood in terms of nominative, accusative and dative oppositions. For languages in general it reflects the differentiation of participant roles in terms of nuclearity, with P1s more closely associated with a Process than P2s, and P2s more closely associated than P3s. In SFL this is generally reflected in the delicacy of transitivity networks, with P1s realising more general options than P2s, and P3s more delicate ones. Across languages P1s are strongly associated with both modal responsibility and unmarked Theme, associations which we explore in detail in Chapters 4 and 6 respectively.

# 2 Nominal Group

## 2.1 Approaching from Above

In this chapter we will approach nominal groups from an ideational and then a textual perspective. In terms of field (ideational context), nominal groups construe a static perspective on phenomena; they provide resources for classifying and composing items and associated properties. The outline of field in Figure 2.1 is based on Doran and Martin (2021).

In terms of IDEATION (ideational discourse semantics) nominal groups construe entities which play a variety of roles in relation to occurrences in figures. Most commonly these entities realise items – people, places and things (including objects and institutions). But they can also name activities, for example *process, trip, voyage, tour, journey, jaunt, junket, pilgrimage, outing, expedition, excursion* (activity entities). Less commonly, entities refer to discourse, for example *anecdote, joke, riddle, essay, paragraph, chapter, index, argument, factor, question* (semiotic entities). The entity system in Figure 2.2 is based on Hao (2015, 2020a).

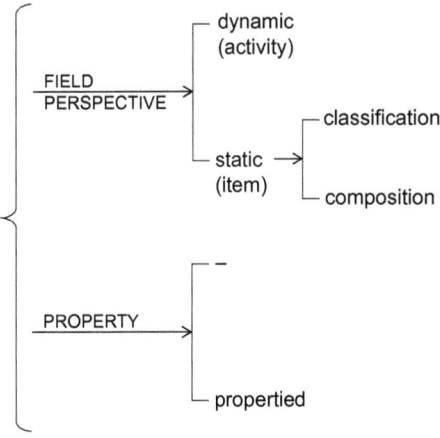

Figure 2.1 Field variables

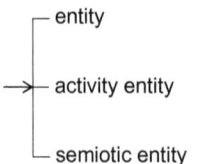

Figure 2.2 Types of discourse semantic entity

As far as grammar is concerned, all nominal groups include a nuclear function in their structure which we will refer to as Thing. This function may be all a nominal group needs to construe a discourse semantic entity, as happens when deploying a pronoun (*they*) or proper name (*Sydney*). But nominal groups can become much more complex, depending on the discourse semantic work they have to do.

In part this complexity is conditioned by mode (textual context). The more that language is just a part of what is going on (e.g. the sparse verbal interaction among players during a game of football), the less work nominal groups have to do. In contexts where the speaking or writing is basically what is going on (storytelling for example), the more work nominal groups have to do. In either mode, what matters from a textual discourse semantic perspective is IDENTIFICATION – introducing entities and keeping track of who's who, what's what, which is which and so on (Martin and Rose, 2007).

In Section 2.2 below we explore English nominal group resources, before turning to Spanish resources in Section 2.3 and Chinese resources in Section 2.4. In each section we first consider ideational resources, and then turn to textual resources. Our focus text for English is FitzSimons' (2005) story about a famous beach rescue at Bondi Beach, Sydney in 1938, which we refer to as the Bondi Beach text (Appendix 2.1). Our focus text for Spanish comprises stories about a famous earthquake and tidal wave in Maule and Biobío, Chile, in 2010 (Guzmán, 2010),[1] which we refer to as the La Ola Maldita ('the hellish wave') text (Appendix 3.1). Our focus text for Chinese is a news story about controlling the sea lettuce near Qingdao that once threatened the sailing events of the 29th Olympic Games in 2008, which we refer to as the Sea Lettuce text (Appendix 4.1). In Section 2.5 we present an analysis challenge concerning the grammar of proper name nominal groups. Our story genres provide us with rich range of nominal group resources as a variety of entities are introduced and tracked, and measured, described and classified.

---

[1] J. A. Guzmán (2010) La ola maldita. *Paula*. Retrieved on 5 August 2021 from www.latercera.com/paula/la-ola-maldita/.

## 2.2 English Nominal Group Resources

### 2.2.1 Ideational Nominal Group Resources

In this section we focus on Things realised by common nouns, setting aside Things realised by pronouns and proper names for Section 2.2.2 below.

From the perspective of field, the main taxonomies construed in the Bondi Beach text have to do with people and the beach. The Things realised by nouns dealing with these taxonomies are highlighted in the sentence below (people entities in bold, beach entities in italics; we set aside pronominal resources at this stage and the very general terms *everything* and *all*).

The huge *waves*, just like that, piggy-backed their way further and further up the *beach* and grabbed everything they could along the way – from **babies** to **toddlers** to **adolescents** to beach *umbrellas*, to old **blokes** and young **sheilas** alike, and then made a mad dash for the open *sea* again, carrying all before it and sweeping **everyone** off the *sandbank* and into the deep *channel* next to it in the process.[2]

The Thing only nominal groups (i.e. *babies, toddlers, adolescents*) would be analysed as follows for function and class.

(1)
| Example | *babies* |
|---|---|
| **group class** | nominal group |
| **group function** | Thing |
| **word class** | common noun |

For these, and the following nominal groups, the Thing function is sufficient to demarcate the entity being construed: *the huge **waves**, the **beach**, old **blokes**, young **sheilas**, all, everyone, the **sandbank**, the deep **channel***. For two nominal groups, however, the Thing function is not sufficient: *beach umbrellas* and *the open sea*. In these examples the Thing is subclassified by a Classifier function, realised by another common noun in the case of *beach umbrellas*.

(2)
| Example | beach | umbrellas |
|---|---|---|
| **group class** | nominal group | |
| **group function** | Classifier | Thing |
| **word class** | common noun | common noun |

This makes it clear that FitzSimons is referring to large umbrellas used for protection from the sun rather than rain and staked in the sand rather than held by hand, as the Thing alone (*umbrella*) would imply.

In the case of *open sea*, the Classifier is realised by an adjective, rather than a common noun.

---

[2] The word *process* realises an activity entity, which we set aside for purposes of this discussion.

(3)

| Example | *open* | *sea* |
|---|---|---|
| **group class** | nominal group | |
| **group function** | Classifier | Thing |
| **word class** | adjective | common noun |

At this point we need to ask two questions: (1) Why do we treat both the common noun and the adjective as realising the same Classifier function? (2) And why do we treat *umbrellas* as a common noun and *open* as an adjective?

Question (1) first. Reasoning from above we would argue that both nominal groups realise a single entity, which is not described – an entity which can be tracked as the text unfolds (e.g. *beach umbrellas* ← *they, the open sea* ← *it*). Reasoning from around in terms of their grammatical potential, we can note that neither Classifier can be graded by submodification: *\*very beach umbrella, \*very open sea*. And checking further nominal groups in the text, we can note that this is a general feature of Classifiers:

*summer sun, \*very summer sun*
*Bondi boys, \*very Bondi boys*
*Bondi clubhouse, \*very Bondi clubhouse*

Turning now to question (2), why do we say that *beach* is a common noun while *open* is an adjective? The distinction here has to do with the different potential of the common noun and adjective. Reasoning from above, *open* has the potential to describe an entity while *beach* does not; we can refer, for example, in another context to a *completely open door*. In this case *open* is gradable, because it is describing the door not classifying it (cf. *a stage door*, where grading is not possible). Conversely, *beach* has the potential to designate one beach or more (*beach/beaches*), while *open* does not. Reasoning from around this means that we can say *one beach* or *two beaches* (but not \**one open* or \**two opens*); and reasoning from below this is reflected in the fact that *beach* has singular vs plural number morphology (*beach/beaches*), while *open* does not.

As we can see, reasoning about function (e.g. Thing, Classifier) has to do with the role played by a unit in a given structure, whereas reasoning about class (e.g. noun, adjective) has to do with the potential of a unit to play different roles in different structures. Function labels are thus about what something is doing; class labels are about what something could be. And the relationship between function and class is not one to one; we can have a function realised by more than one class (e.g. Classifier by noun or adjective) and a given class can realise more than one function (e.g. noun as Classifier or Thing).

This brings us to the third ideational nominal group function we will consider – the Epithet. From the perspective of field, this function has to do with properties we assign to items; for discourse semantic ideation this means attributing qualities to entities. There are several examples in the sentence we quoted above, highlighted in bold below.

The **huge** waves, just like that, piggy-backed their way further and further up the beach and grabbed everything they could along the way – from babies to toddlers to adolescents to beach umbrellas, to **old** blokes and **young** sheilas alike, and then made a mad dash[3] for the open sea again, carrying all before it and sweeping everyone off the sandbank and into the **deep** channel next to it in the process.

In these examples the adjectives are realising Epithets not Classifiers, and so they can be graded: ***absolutely*** huge, ***very*** old blokes, ***quite*** young sheilas, ***rather*** deep channel. The structure would be analysed as in (4):

(4)

| Example | old | blokes |
|---|---|---|
| **group class** | nominal group | |
| **group function** | Epithet | Thing |
| **word class** | adjective | common noun |

Two sentences later we observe that Epithets can be realised by verbs as well as adjectives (highlighted in bold below):

Now, the **boiling** surf, with yet more large waves continuing to roll over, was filled with **distressed** folk waving for help.

These Epithets can also be graded, this time round using adverbs of manner (***intensely*** boiling, ***badly*** distressed), since the Epithets are realising occurrences[4] rather than qualities.

(5)

| Example | boiling | surf |
|---|---|---|
| **group class** | nominal group | |
| **group function** | Epithet | Thing |
| **word class** | verb | common noun |

Once again we see a function realised by more than one class (Epithet as adjective or verb), and a class capable of performing more than one function (verb as Epithet as in ***boiling*** *surf*, or as part of the Process of a clause as in *the surf was **boiling***).

In English, as we have seen, Epithets and Classifiers are sequenced before the Thing, with Epithets preceding Classifier if both are present:

The day was, in the vernacular of the time, a "stinker", and some thought it was in fact a record turnout on the beach, with the numbers perhaps swelled by the fact that those bronzed boys of the Bondi Surf Bathers' Life Saving Club had turned up in force to have one of their **popular surf competitions**.

---

[3] The word *dash* is a nominalisation realising an occurrence not an entity (cf. *the waves dashed to the sea again*), which we set aside for purposes of this discussion.

[4] The word *distressed* can also be graded like adjectives (e.g. *very distressed, more distressed*), and by this criteria is arguably an adjective, not a verb; in treating it as a verb we are privileging its morphology (its *-ed* suffix) and its potential to function as the Process of a mental clause as in *their fear of drowning **distressed** them*.

(6)

| Example | *popular* | *surf* | | *competitions* |
|---|---|---|---|---|
| **group class** | nominal group | | | |
| **group function** | Epithet | Classifier | | Thing |
| **word class** | adjective | common noun | | common noun |

There can be more than one Classifier, as many as are needed in fact to pinpoint the entity being construed and its place in the relevant field taxonomy. Two Classifiers, for example, are deployed to narrow down the movement FitzSimons is extolling: ***Australian lifesaving** movement*.

(7)

| Example | *Australian* | *lifesaving* | *movement* |
|---|---|---|---|
| **group class** | nominal group | | |
| **group function** | Classifier | Classifier | Thing |
| **word class** | adjective | adjective[5] | common noun |

There can also be more than one Epithet, adding as many descriptive and attitudinal qualities as needed to an entity. Instead of using the adjective complex *long **and** glorious* to appreciate the history of the Australian lifesaving movement, for example, FitzSimons might have used a sequence of Epithets: *their **long glorious** history*.

In their **long and glorious** history, this still stands as the finest hour of the **Australian lifesaving** movement.

The alternative modification strategies are presented below. For *long and glorious history*, we need to expand the table to allow for an adjective complex realising a single Epithet. The structure of this complex is 1 +2 (paratactic extension).[6]

(8)

| Example | *long* | *and* | *glorious* | *history* |
|---|---|---|---|---|
| **group class** | nominal group | | | |
| **group function** | Epithet | | | Thing |
| **complex class** | adjective complex | | | |
| **complex function** | 1 | +2 | | |
| **word class** | adjective | conjunction | adjective | common noun |

For *long glorious history* we have a sequence of two Epithets.

---

[5] Unlike *distressed*, discussed in footnote 3 above, *lifesaving* cannot be used as a Process in a clause (*they are lifesaving them*) and has no alternative verbal forms (contrast *distressed folk, distressing incident* with *lifesaving movement*, *\*lifesaved person*); because of this lack of verbal potential *lifesaving* is classified as an adjective.

[6] We will not explore complexes in detail in this book but simply draw on the analyses proposed in Halliday and Matthiessen (2014).

(9)

| Example | long | | glorious | history |
|---|---|---|---|---|
| **group class** | nominal group | | | |
| **group function** | Epithet | | Epithet | Thing |
| **word class** | adjective | | adjective | common noun |

The choice the nominal group grammar makes here is whether to add qualities at group rank via additional Epithets or at word rank by coordinated adjectives.

Comparable word complexes can be deployed to realise Classifiers and Things as well, for example *Australian and Tongan lifesavers*, or *Australian climate and weather*. The adjective complex realising the Classifier below allows us to subclassify a single entity, lifesavers, into two types.

(10)

| Example | *Australian* | *and* | *Tongan* | *lifesavers* |
|---|---|---|---|---|
| **group class** | nominal group | | | |
| **group function** | Classifier | | | Thing |
| **complex class** | adjective complex | | | |
| **complex function** | 1 | +2 | | |
| **word class** | adjective | conjunction | adjective | common noun |

The noun complex realising the Thing below, on the other hand, realises two entities (both climate and weather).

(11)

| Example | *Australian* | *climate* | *and* | *weather* |
|---|---|---|---|---|
| **group class** | nominal group | | | |
| **group function** | Classifier | Thing | | |
| **complex class** | | noun complex | | |
| **complex function** | | 1 | +2 | |
| **word class** | adjective | common noun | conjunction | common noun |

As a final step for this section, let's consider the possibility of counting the number of entities construed by a nominal group. This brings us to the final paragraph of the narrative which takes stock of the 250 people who needed rescuing.

Finally, just half an hour after the waves hit, the water was cleared of bobbing heads and waving arms, and it was time to take stock: **250 people** had needed the lifesavers to pull them out, of whom **210**[7] were OK once back on land. **Thirty-five** needed mouth to mouth to be restored to consciousness, while **five people** perished.

---

[7] The Thing function has been ellipsed in this nominal group (and in *thirty-five* following); a discussion of nominal group ellipsis and substitution in English is beyond the scope of this book; for details see Halliday and Hasan (1976).

In this stage of the narrative, a precise count of the numbers involved is provided through a Numerative function, realised by numerals (*250, 210, thirty-five, five*). Numerals cannot be intensified (\**very five*), but they can be graded in terms of precision (e.g. ***precisely** 250 people, **some** 210 survivors*); and they can be written either alphabetically (*thirty-five, five*) or numerically (*250, 210*).

(12)

| Example | five | people |
|---|---|---|
| **group class** | nominal group | |
| **group function** | Numerative | Thing |
| **word class** | numeral | common noun |

Earlier in the story there are Numeratives realised by quantifiers. These quantifiers can be intensified (e.g. *so many generations*) and can only be written alphabetically.

(13)

| Example | many | survivors |
|---|---|---|
| **group class** | nominal group | |
| **group function** | Numerative | Thing |
| **word class** | quantifier | common noun |

Numeratives precede Epithets in English nominal group structure; and there can be only one Numerative[8] per nominal group.

(14)

| Example | more | large | waves |
|---|---|---|---|
| **group class** | nominal group | | |
| **group function** | Numerative | Epithet | Thing |
| **word class** | quantifier | adjective | common noun |

Once again we see that a given function can be realised by more than one class (i.e. Numerative by numerals or quantifiers); and extrapolating from our story we could find examples of numerals playing more than one function (e.g. Classifier and then Numerative in *the **first** prize was the **third** prize handed out*).

We'll now turn our attention from ideational to textual resources and explore how entities are introduced and tracked in FitzSimons' narrative.

### 2.2.2 Textual Nominal Group Resources

The text we are focusing on here is a written text, instantiating a narrative genre – reconstruing activities that happened many decades ago. This means

---

[8] Apparent counterexamples such as *five more, many less* and *first four* would be treated as word complexes realising a single Numerative function; it is the complex as a whole that counts entities.

## 2.2 English Nominal Group Resources

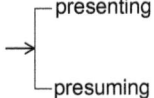
presenting
presuming

Figure 2.3 Basic IDENTIFICATION system realised by English nominal group systems

that as far as the entities involved are concerned, the text as a whole has to be relatively self-contextualising. The discourse semantic system at stake here is IDENTIFICATION; and the key choice is that of presenting an entity in terms of its identity not being recoverable by a reader on the one hand, and presuming that an entity's identity is in fact recoverable on the other (Figure 2.3).

At this point in our discussion we need to keep in mind that FitzSimons' text is a multimodal one, accompanied by a panoramic photograph of Bondi Beach, including sunbathers and swimmers. And so the first nominal group in the story proper is in fact a presuming one, the pronoun *they*, referring intermodally to the sunbathers in the photo.

And so there **they** lie, happily sweltering in the summer sun on **Australia**'s most famous beach, just as they have for so many generations past.

(15)
| Example | *they* |
|---|---|
| **group class** | nominal group |
| **group function** | Thing |
| **word class** | pronoun |

The third nominal group in the story is another presuming one, the proper noun *Australia*, designating an entity whose identity can be safely presumed given the Australian readership of FitzSimons' monthly feature article, published in Sydney. Each of these nominal groups has the same minimal structure, Thing, realised by either a pronoun or a proper name.

(16)
| Example | *Australia* |
|---|---|
| **group class** | nominal group |
| **group function** | Thing |
| **word class** | proper noun |

Several of the proper names realising the Thing function in these presuming nominal groups involve name complexes (e.g. *Peter FitzSimons, Waverly Library, "Black Sunday"*); we'll propose an activity dealing with these structures in Section 2.5.

In cases where the identity of an entity cannot be thus presumed, an expanded nominal group structure is required, beginning with a non-specific Deictic function. The first wave that hits the beach is introduced in such terms as identity unknown (***an*** *enormous wave*) before being presumed by the pronoun *it*.

*an enormous wave* suddenly rolled over the thousands in the surf, including those many standing on the large sandbank just out from the shore – knocking them all over as **it** went.

(17)

| Example | *an* | *enormous* | *wave* |
|---|---|---|---|
| **group class** | nominal group | | |
| **group function** | Deictic | Epithet | Thing |
| **word class** | determiner | adjective | common noun |

Similarly the second and third waves are introduced as presenting entities[9] (***an****other wave*, ***an****other*), before being presumed by the specific determiner *the* in ***the*** *huge waves* and then the possessive determiner *their* in ***their*** *way*.

And then *another wave* hit, and then *another*. **The huge waves**, just like that, piggy-backed **their** way further and further up the beach …

(18)

| Example | *the* | *huge* | *waves* |
|---|---|---|---|
| **group class** | nominal group | | |
| **group function** | Deictic | Epithet | Thing |
| **word class** | determiner | adjective | common noun |

(19)

| Example | *their* | *way* |
|---|---|---|
| **group class** | nominal group | |
| **group function** | Deictic | Thing |
| **word class** | determiner | common noun |

In some cases a presuming specific Deictic (i.e. *the, this, that, these, those, both, each, which*) may need the support of a prepositional phrase in order to exclusively identify an entity. The first mention of the sandbank many bathers were standing on is introduced in this way; here a Qualifier function following the Thing makes it clear which sandbank is being introduced.[10] By convention we enclose the prepositional phrase *just out from the shore* in square brackets in analysis tables to highlight that it is an embedded phrase, realising a function

---

[9] These nominal groups also include comparative reference to the first wave, which we are passing over here.
[10] Without the Qualifier a reader might be entitled to ask *Which sandbank?* The Qualifier pre-empts this question by specifying which one.

## 2.2 English Nominal Group Resources

in a structure of the same group/phrase rank.[11] It introduces an additional entity with respect to which the relevant sandbank can be identified.

**the** large sandbank **just out from the shore**

(20)

| Example | *the* | *large* | *sandbank* | *just out from the shore* |
|---|---|---|---|---|
| **group class** | nominal group | | | |
| **group function** | Deictic | Epithet | Thing | Qualifier |
| **class** | determiner | adjective | common noun | [prepositional phrase] |

And once the sandbank has been introduced, the deep channel next to it can be introduced in the same terms (Deictic: *the*, Epithet: *deep*, Thing: *channel*, Qualifier: *next to it*). Here the Qualifier specifies which deep channel Fitzsimons is writing about.

sweeping everyone off *the sandbank* and into **the** deep channel **next to it**

Where even more information is needed to identify an entity, the Qualifier can be realised by a clause. A Qualifier of this kind was used to identify the sunbathers on the beach on Black Sunday. By convention we enclose the clause *who were lying in those very spots on the afternoon of February 6, 1938* in double square brackets below to signal that it is an embedded clause, realising a function in a structure of a lower group/phrase rank.

**those** 35,000 Sydneysiders **who were lying in those very spots on the afternoon of February 6, 1938**

(21)

| Example | *those* | *35,000* | *Sydneysiders* | *who were lying in those very spots on the afternoon of February 6, 1938* |
|---|---|---|---|---|
| **group class** | nominal group | | | |
| **group function** | Deictic | Numerative | Thing | Qualifier |
| **class** | determiner | numeral | common noun | [[clause]] |

And a similar structure is used to specify a group of bathers swept away by the waves:

***those many standing on the large sandbank just out from the shore***

---

[11] Clearly, whenever we have embedding in nominal groups, the class of the embedded unit is of a higher rank than the name of its row (e.g. prepositional phrase, not word in (20)).

As we can see, the work of having to present entities and track them once there puts considerable pressure on nominal group functions when a pronoun is not enough or a recognisable proper name is not available. The role of Deictic, Thing and Qualifier functions needs to be appreciated in these identity management terms.

One final observation to make as far as textual meaning is concerned is that embedded nominal groups are also used to realise a Deictic function when a definite article, demonstrative or possessive determiner is not enough to identify the entity construed by the Thing. It is in these terms that Bondi Beach is in fact introduced in the story as *Australia's most famous beach*; the possessive morphology (*'s*) signals the embedding here.

(22)

| Example | *Australia's* | *most* | *famous* | *beach* |
|---|---|---|---|---|
| **group class** | nominal group | | | |
| **group function** | Deictic | Epithet | | Thing |
| **class** | [nominal group][12] | word complex[13] | | |
| **function** | Thing | β | α | |
| **word class** | proper noun | adverb | adjective | common noun |

In the following example the nominal group embedded in the Deictic includes its own Deictic, Classifier and Thing functions.

(23)

| Example | *the* | *Bondi* | *lifesavers'* | *reels* |
|---|---|---|---|---|
| **group class** | nominal group | | | |
| **group function** | Deictic | | | Thing |
| **word class** | [nominal group] | | | |
| **group function** | Deictic | Classifier | Thing | |
| **word class** | determiner | proper noun | common noun | common noun |

### 2.2.3 English Nominal Group Systems

In Sections 2.2.1 and 2.2.2, we have introduced the rudiments of English nominal group structure, approaching from above in terms of the discourse semantic systems of IDEATION and IDENTIFICATION, and then reasoning from around and below in terms of nominal group system and structure. To this point

---

[12] We treat *Australia's* as a nominal group here because of its potential for expansion (e.g. *the lucky country's ..., the country I love's ...*).
[13] The word complex realising the graded Epithet here is hypotactic, with an adjective head (*famous*), marked α by convention and an adverb submodifier (*most*), marked β by convention. Because the complex contains both an adjective and an adverb, we have referred to it as a word complex in the analysis. Alternatively, we could have referred to it as an adjective complex, following the convention of naming complexes with reference to the class of their head (i.e. their α function).

## 2.2 English Nominal Group Resources

we have left the systems in play relatively implicit, so let's make them explicit here. For system network conventions, see Martin, Wang and Zhu (2013) and Appendix 1 in this volume.

As a first step we'll set aside elliptical nominal groups, which we are not explicitly addressing here (i.e, 'Thing-less' groups such as *those many ⊘ standing on a large sandbank just out from the shore*). We then distinguish Thing-only nominal groups designating a presumed entity from nominal groups specifying an entity. And designating nominal groups are divided into those using a proper name to designate an entity and those using a pronoun. These systems and their interdependencies are outlined in Figure 2.4.

The realisation statements relating features in these systems to their structural consequences are compiled in Table 2.1. For realisation statement conventions, see Martin, Wang and Zhu (2013) and Appendix 1; here the '+' in Table 2.1 specifies the inclusion of a Function, the ':' specifies the realisation of a Function by a class.

The feature [specifying] opens up choices in five systems, allowing for nominal group functions which are classifying, describing, quantifying, determining and/or qualifying. As we have seen above, the features [classifying] and [describing] are in fact recursive options, since more than one Classifier or Epithet may be required; we have not taken the step of formalising this recursion in the network below. The feature [describing] is subclassified as [descriptive] or [attitudinal] as a gesture towards specifying the typical attitude-before-description sequence of Epithets in nominal groups (e.g. *the*

Table 2.1 *Realisation statements for general English nominal group features*

| non-elliptical | +Thing |
|---|---|
| naming | Thing: proper name |
| pronaming | Thing: pronoun |

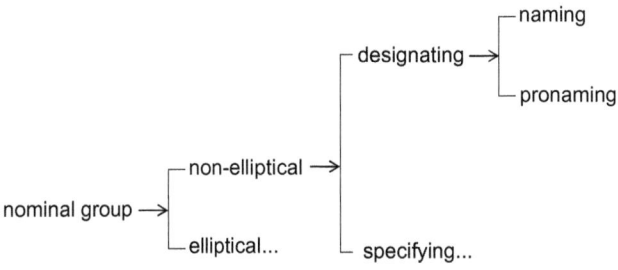

Figure 2.4 General English nominal group systems

***glorious sandy** beach*). The feature [quantifying] is subclassified as [exact] or [inexact] to distinguish digital (e.g. ***20 seconds***) from general (e.g. ***many survivors***) quantifications. The feature [determining] is subclassified as [possessive] or [general] by way of distinguishing 'possessive' nominal groups realising two entities[14] (e.g. ***their*** *popular surf carnivals,* ***Australia's*** *most famous beach*) from those realising one. The feature [qualifying] is subclassified as [phrasal] or [clausal]. These specifying systems and their interdependencies are outlined in Figure 2.5.

The realisation statements relating features in these specifying systems to their structural consequences are compiled in Table 2.2. In the structure specification column, '+' indicates the presence of a Function, '^' indicates

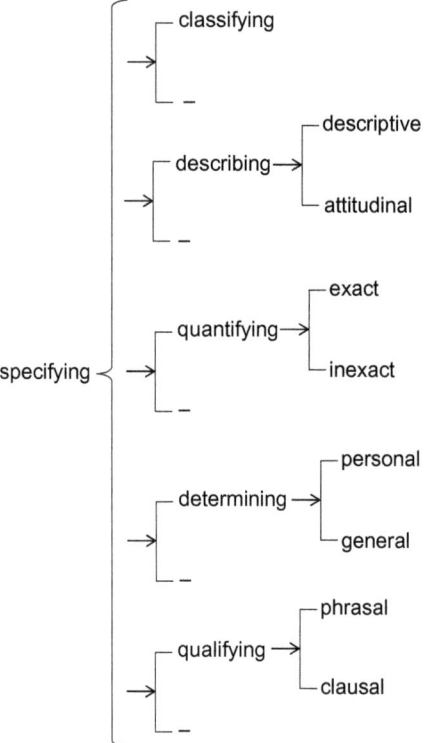

Figure 2.5 More delicate English nominal group systems

---

[14] The feature [possessive] could have been further classified to distinguish determiners distinguishing person and number (e.g. *their*) from embedded nominal groups (e.g. *Australia's*).

## 2.2 English Nominal Group Resources

Table 2.2 *Realisations statements for more delicate English nominal group features*

| classifying | +Classifier; Classifier ^ Thing |
|---|---|
| describing | +Epithet; Epithet → Classifier |
| descriptive | Epithet: descriptive adjective |
| attitudinal | Epithet: attitudinal adjective |
| quantifying | +Numerative; Numerative → Epithet |
| exact | Numerative: numeral |
| inexact | Numerative: quantifier |
| determining | +Deictic; Deictic → Numerative |
| possessive[a] | Deictic: 'possessive'[b] |
| general | Deictic: determiner: nonpronominal |
| qualifying | +Qualifier: Thing ^ Qualifier |
| phrasal | Qualifier: [prepositional phrase] |
| clausal | Qualifier: [[clause]] |

[a] Our description would have to be extended to allow for embedded nominal groups.

[b] By 'possessive' here we refer to realisation by possessive determiners (e.g. *their*, *his*) or embedded nominal groups (e.g. **Australia's** *most famous beach*, **the Australian lifesavers'** *long and glorious history*).

sequence, ':' indicates the realisation of a Function by a class and the arrows[15] '→' or '←' indicate the relative sequencing of Functions, where present.[16]

An overall look at the nominal group systems we have built up is provided in Figure 2.6. The description is, of course, just a glimpse of the English nominal group system and structure. For further in-depth analysis see Halliday and Matthiessen (2014).

### 2.2.4 Nominal Group Issue: FOCUS Systems in English

As a culminative step let's consider descriptive issues arising from the distinction English makes between count and mass nouns – e.g. the distinction between *waves* (count) and *water* (mass).

Finally, just half an hour after the **waves** hit, the **water** was cleared of bobbing heads and waving arms

---

[15] For example the Epithet → Classifier statement indicates that the Epithet will precede the Classifier when both are present.
[16] In order to simplify the realisation statements, we have used '→' to indicate the function which follows if it is present in the structure.

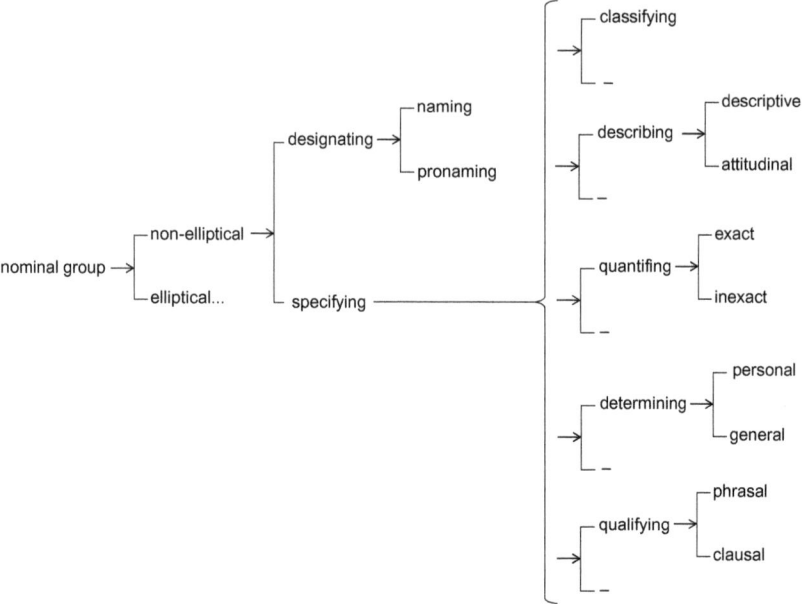

Figure 2.6 English nominal group systems

This is significant for nominal group structure since Things realised by count nouns can be quantified with a Numerative function (***35,000*** *Sydneysiders*), whereas Things realised by mass nouns cannot (***several** waters*). If we want to quantify nominal groups headed by mass nouns, we in fact need structures like the following: *two litres of water, a lot of water* and so on. And if we want to amass Things realised by count nouns, we need structures like the following: *a group of Sydneysiders, a crowd of Sydneysiders* and so on. How can we analyse structures such as these?

Reasoning from above, from a discourse semantic perspective, it is clear that we are dealing with a single entity, water. This is the entity we are talking about and the one we would track in discourse (e.g. *two litres of **water** ← **it** tasted good*). This suggests a grammatical analysis treating *water* as Thing. Martin, Matthiesssen and Painter (2010)[17] adopt this perspective and set up a Focus function realised by a quantifying nominal group as outlined below. Ultimately this means setting up a further function (a Function Marker) for postpositional nominal groups embedded in the Focus function. In the example below *of* is

---

[17] For an alternative proposal, involving separate layers of experiential and logical structure see Halliday and Matthiessen (2014).

## 2.2 English Nominal Group Resources

treated as a postposition signalling that *two litres* is embedded as a Focus function (it is not, as traditional analysis would have it, a preposition introducing a prepositional phrase Qualifier of *litres*).

(24)

| Example | *two* | *litres* | *of* | *water* |
|---|---|---|---|---|
| **group class** | nominal group | | | |
| **group function** | Focus | | | Thing |
| **word class** | [nominal group] | | | |
| **group function** | Numerative | Thing | Focus Marker | |
| **word class** | numeral | common noun | postposition | common noun |

The alternative to this analysis involves treating *litres* as the head of the nominal group (its nuclear Thing), and *of water* as its prepositional phrase Qualifier.

(25)

| Example | *two* | *litres* | *of water* |
|---|---|---|---|
| **group class** | nominal group | | |
| **group function** | Numerative | Thing | Qualifier |
| **class** | numeral | noun | [prepositional phrase] |
| | | | ... |

One problem with this traditional analysis is that we would have to restrict the kind of prepositional phrase realising the Qualifier to an 'of' phrase in just this environment (and 'possessive' ones such as *the finest hour of the Australian lifesaving movement*). It would also involve a preposition (i.e. *of*) which marks the structure but does not make any of the ideational distinctions we normally associate with prepositions (for example the distinctions in **in** *those very spots*, **as** *"Black Sunday"*, **like** *a Bondi tram*, **with** *distressed fold*, **about** *a place in Sydney*). The traditional analysis would also fail to account for why the Thing the 'of' phrase qualifies is highly unlikely to be classified or described (precisely because it is not realising an entity, but rather a dimension of one). Accordingly, we will prefer our Focus analysis here. Some further examples of Focus structures from FitzSimons' story, all exemplifying these distributional features, are presented below (their Focus function is highlighted in bold).

**one of** their popular surf competitions
**one of** the seven reels available
**one of** the lifesavers
**the lot of** them
**a kind of** emergency clearing house

We will not develop our discussion of Focus structures further here but invite readers to carefully consider the proposal presented here and elaborated in Martin, Matthiessen and Painter (2010) with the alternatives in Fawcett

(2000a, 2008), Halliday and Matthiessen (2014), Fontaine (2017) and Fontaine and Schöntal (2019). Unsettled descriptive issues of this kind are the ideal place to practise reasoning from above, around and below – honing your skills in relation to the work of SFL's leading grammarians. As you will soon discover, grammar writing is an uncertain practice involving judicious compromise, rather than a quest for truth. Ultimately what matters is that the weight given to different kinds of reasoning is made clear and that the grammar is suitable for the purpose for which it has been designed.

## 2.3 Spanish Nominal Group Resources

We now turn our attention to Spanish nominal groups, which play comparable roles in Spanish discourse as far as ideational and textual meaning are concerned. The way in which Spanish nominal groups structure these meanings, however, contrasts in several respects with their realisation in English – especially with respect to Deictic, Epithet and Classifier functions. And Spanish offers some choices English does not. We draw attention to these differences and foreshadow some of their implications as the chapter unfolds below.

### *2.3.1 Ideational Nominal Group Resources*

In this section we focus on Things realised by common nouns, setting aside Things realised by pronouns and proper names for Section 2.3.2 below.

From the perspective of field, the main taxonomies construed in the Ola Maldita text have to do with the tidal wave and its effects on people and their environs. The Things realised by nouns dealing with these taxonomies are highlighted in the sentence below.

Los **jóvenes** entraron al **hospital** sin **esperanza**. Era un **caos** de **heridos** y **muertos**. No creían que **nadie** pudiera sobrevivir a la **ola** que habían visto, pero en la **lista** de **ingresados**, el **nombre** de **Gabriel** les saltó en la **cara**.

Jonathan entró a la carrera a la **zona** de los **pacientes** y recorrió las **camillas** hasta que lo encontró. Le pegó tres **garabatos** y lo abrazó. **Gabriel** sólo tenía **heridas** en los **pies**. Tuvo la **fortuna** de que la **ola** lo llevara directo a la **orilla**.

'The **youngsters** entered the **hospital** without **hope**. It was a **chaos** of **wounded** and **dead**. One couldn't believe that **anyone** could survive the **wave** they had seen, but in the **list** of **admitted**, the **name** of **Gabriel** hit them in the **face**.

Jonathan hurriedly entered the **patient area** [literally, 'the **zone** of the **patients**'] and went through the **stretchers** until he found him. He swore at him [literally, 'he hit him with three **curses**'] and hugged him. **Gabriel** only had **injuries** in his feet. He had the **fortune** that the **wave** carried him directly to the **bank**.'

## 2.3 Spanish Nominal Group Resources

The Thing only nominal groups[18] (*esperanza* 'hope', *heridos* 'wounded', *muertos* 'dead', *nadie* 'no one', *ingresados* 'admitted', *heridas* 'injuries') would be analysed as follows for function and class.

(26)

| Example | *esperanza* |
|---|---|
| **group class** | nominal group |
| **group function** | Thing |
| **word class** | common noun |
| Gloss | hope |

For these, and the following nominal groups, the Thing function is sufficient to demarcate the entity being construed (we set aside proper names here): *el hospital* 'the **hospital**', *un caos* 'a **chaos**', *la ola* 'the **wave**', *la lista* 'the **list**', *el nombre* 'the **name**', *la cara* 'the **face**', *la zona* 'the **area**', *los pacientes* 'the **patients**', *las camillas* 'the **stretchers**', *tres garabatos* 'three **curses**', *los pies* 'the **feet**', *la fortuna* 'the **good luck**', *la ola* 'the **wave**', *la orilla* 'the **bank**'.

Elsewhere in the stories retold in this article, more than a Thing is required: for example *el bote **pesquero*** 'the **fishing** boat' and *generador **eléctrico*** '**electricity** generator'. In these examples the Classifier function is realised by an adjective,[19] and unlike in English, the Classifier follows the Thing.

(27)

| Example | *bote* | *pesquero* |
|---|---|---|
| **group class** | nominal group | |
| **group function** | Thing | Classifier |
| **word class** | common noun | adjective |
| Gloss | boat | fishing |
| Translation | 'fishing boat' | |

(28)

| Example | *generador* | *eléctrico* |
|---|---|---|
| **group class** | nominal group | |
| **group function** | Thing | Classifier |
| **word class** | common noun | adjective |
| Gloss | generator | electric |
| Translation | 'electricity generator' | |

Note that in each case the English translation is misleading, naturally deploying as it does a verb (*fishing*) to specify the kind of boat and a noun (*electricity*)

---

[18] Thing-only nominal groups in Spanish are relatively rare, as the examples used throughout this chapter show. We have picked out a few of them from our Ola Maldita text, for the sake of the discussion here.

[19] In Spanish nominal groups there is number and gender concord between adjectives and the Thing they describe or classify; we will not be dealing explicitly with concord in this chapter.

to subclassify the generator. Since they are classifying rather than describing, neither adjective realising this Classifier function, *pesquero* or *eléctrico*, is gradable; for example, \**el bote muy pesquero* 'the very fishing boat' makes no sense.

When Spanish Classifiers are realised by nouns, they are generally linked to the Thing by the particle *de*:[20] for example *silla de ruedas* 'wheelchair', *películas de guerra* 'war movies'.[21]

(29)

| Example | *silla* | *de* | *ruedas* |
|---|---|---|---|
| **group class** | nominal group | | |
| **group function** | Thing | Classifier | |
| **word class** | common noun | particle | common noun |
| Gloss | chair | 'of' | wheels |
| Translation | 'wheelchair' | | |

As the glossing perhaps suggests, a more traditional analysis would treat *de ruedas* as an embedded prepositional phrase modifying the Thing. This analysis would involve setting up *ruedas* 'wheels' as an embedded nominal group inside the prepositional phrase, with a highly restricted meaning potential (i.e. no possibility of Deictic,[22] Numerative, Epithet or Qualifier[23] specification). Were we to follow this traditional analysis, subclassification realised by adjectives (e.g. *sismológica* 'seismic' below) and subclassification realised by nouns (e.g. *Mercalli* below) would have to be treated very differently in series like the ones below.

---

[20] Other particles include *a*, as in *estufa a gas* ('gas heater'), and *con*, as in *café con leche* ('café au lait'). Classifiers realised by nouns with no particle, such as *hora punta* ('rush hour') or *coche bomba* ('car bomb') are relatively rare in Spanish.

[21] See Bartoš (1980), who specifically treats these '*de* + noun constructions' along with 'relational adjectives' (i.e. adjectives functioning as Classifiers) as resources for 'relational attribution' in Spanish. See also Hernanz and Brucart (1987), who treat both the adjectival and the '*de* + (bare) noun' configurations as subtypes of 'classifiers', and Bosque (1993), who suggests the latter configurations are doubtful as 'prepositional syntagms' and prefers analysing them as 'syntactic compounds'.

[22] The absence of deixis explains why Classifiers are rarely linked to Things by the morpheme *del* 'of the' (contracting the ungrammatical sequence \**de el*), which is used with some prepositional phrase Qualifiers (e.g. *la clase del professor* 'the professor's class').

[23] Specification of a nominal Classifier through subclassification is a possibility, if we were to argue, for example, that *eléctrica* in *el suministro de energía eléctrica* 'electrical energy supply' specifies *energía* and not the nominal group as a whole.

2.3 Spanish Nominal Group Resources 55

*la escala* 'the scale'
*la escala **sismológica*** 'the **seismic** scale'
*la escala **sismológica de Mercalli*** 'the **Mercalli seismic** scale'

*la escala* 'the scale'
*la escala **sismológica*** 'the **seismic** scale'
*la escala **sismológica de magnitud*** 'the **magnitude seismic** scale'
*la escala **sismológica de magnitud de momento*** 'the **moment magnitude seismic** scale'

In effect the traditional prepositional phrase analysis treats nominal Classifiers as Qualifiers, including the 'possessive' Qualifiers in the examples below (where the genuinely embedded nominal groups are in fact specified in various ways):

*la angustia **de ese anciano*** 'the anguish **of that old man**'
*los padres **de los otros jóvenes*** 'the parents **of the other youngsters**'
*la mente **de muchos chilenos*** 'the mind **of many Chileans**'
*los lamentos **de otras cuatro personas*** 'the moans **of four other people**'

Alongside these differences in structure potential and specification function, it is important to take into account that nominal groups with nominal Classifiers realise one entity, not more. All of *la escala* 'the scale', *la escala sismológica* 'the seismic scale' and *la escala sismológica de Mercalli* 'the Mercalli seismic scale' refer to a single scale and would be tracked as a whole in discourse (e.g. via the pronominal clitic *la*). In this respect nominal Classifiers contrast with the Qualifiers just noted; each Qualifier introduces an additional discourse semantic entity (i.e. *ese anciano* 'that old man', *los otros jóvenes* 'the other youngsters', *muchos chilenos* 'many Chileans' and *otras cuatro personas* 'four other people').

Pending further work on the structural analysis of these 'particle + noun' modifiers in Spanish (and across languages), we propose the following analysis for classifying nominal groups like *la escala sismológica de Mercalli* 'the Mercalli seismic scale'. We will introduce the Deictic function involved in examples in this section in Section 2.3.2 below.

(30)

| Example | *la* | *escala* | *sismológica* | *de* | *Mercalli* |
|---|---|---|---|---|---|
| **group class** | nominal group | | | | |
| **group function** | Deictic | Thing | Classifier | Classifier | |
| **complex class** | | | | word complex | |
| **complex function** | | | | β | α |
| **word class** | determiner | common noun | adjective | particle | proper noun |
| Gloss | the | scale | seismic | of | Mercalli |
| Translation | 'the Mercalli seismic scale' | | | | |

Turning from classification to description, the Ola Maldita text features Epithets, most of which are attitudinal. The majority of them follow the Thing – for example *un ruido ensordecedor* 'a deafening noise' in the phase of Hugo Barrera's story focused on below (Hugo is one of the survivors of the tidal wave).

Hugo Barrera la vio venir, encaramado en un eucalipto a unos siete metros de altura. Dice que era una masa **café**, **furiosa**, **veloz**, que arrastraba todo a su paso. Una masa que se extendía por todo el horizonte, que avanzaba en silencio y que cuando tocó la isla empezó a hacer un ruido **ensordecedor**, un "pac, pac, pac" **siniestro** e **imparable** que era provocado por cientos de árboles partidos como fósforos o arrancados de raíz. La ola azotó el árbol en el que Hugo estaba, lo zarandeó un rato, como si el destino aún no decidiera qué hacer con él y finalmente lo lanzó al agua. Hugo cayó a ese **furioso** torrente sabiendo que moriría.

'Hugo Barrera saw it coming, perching in a gum tree seven meters high. He says it was a **brown**, **savage**, **speedy** mass, that swept along everything in its path. A mass which extended across the whole horizon, that advanced in silence and when it reached the island began to make a **deafening** noise, an **unstoppable sinister** "pac, pac, pac" caused by hundreds of trees broken like matches or torn from their roots. The wave battered the tree where Hugo was, shaking it for a while, as if fate had still not decided what to do with him, and finally threw him into the water. Hugo fell into that **savage** torrent thinking he would die.'

(31)

| Example | *un* | *ruido* | *ensordecedor* |
|---|---|---|---|
| **group class** | nominal group | | |
| **group function** | Deictic | Thing | Epithet |
| **word class** | determiner | common noun | adjective |
| Gloss | a | noise | deafening |
| Translation | 'a deafening noise' | | |

Less commonly in our text the Epithets precede the Thing. So alongside *una masa café, furiosa, veloz* 'a **brown**, **savage**, **speedy** mass', we find *ese furioso torrente* 'that savage torrent'. There are a number of factors influencing the position of Epithets; for a useful overview see the discussion offered at the Spanish grammar website *Hispanoteca*.[24] Epithet positioning by and large involves tendencies rather than rules. Pending further intensive corpus-based research, there are no grounds for recognising distinct pre- and post-Thing functions. We will simply allow for the possibility of Epithets preceding or following the Thing here, noting as we do so that pre-Thing

---

[24] Fernández López (1999–2018) Adjetivo-posición". Hispanoteca. Retrieved on March 10 2023 from http://www.hispanoteca.eu/Gram%C3%A1ticas/Gram%C3%A1tica%20espa%C3%B1ola/Adjetivo%20-%20posici%C3%B3n%20-%20resumen.htm.

## 2.3 Spanish Nominal Group Resources

Table 2.3 *Epithet position in Spanish*

| Epithet ^ Thing | Thing ^ Epithet |
|---|---|
| *la **peor** ola* 'the **worst** wave' | *esa pared **oscura*** 'that **dark** wall' |
| *una **nueva** montaña* 'a **new** mountain' | *una isla **inundada*** 'the **flooded** island' |
| *un **buen** rato* 'a **good** while' | *una velocidad **vertiginosa*** 'a **dizzying** speed' |
| *la **gran** ola* 'the **big** wave' | *dos olas **gigantes*** 'two **giant** waves' |
| *ese **furioso** torrente* 'that **savage** torrent' | *esa noche **terrible*** 'that **terrible** night' |

Epithets do appear to be more strongly associated with interpersonal meaning, attitude and graduation in particular (Martin and White 2005). Examples of pre- and post-Thing position nominal groups from our text are presented in Table 2.3.

As *una masa **café, furiosa, veloz*** 'a **brown, savage, speedy** mass' indicates two or more Epithets are possible. And descriptions can also be expanded by word complexes realising a single Epithet. Paratactic complexes add qualities, for example *un "pac, pac, pac" **siniestro e imparable*** 'a **sinister and unstoppable** "pac, pac, pac"'.

(32)

| Example | *un* | *"pac, pac, pac"* | *siniestro* | *e* | *imparable* |
|---|---|---|---|---|---|
| group class | nominal group | | | | |
| group function | Deictic | Thing | Epithet | | |
| complex class | | | adjective complex | | |
| complex function | | | 1 | +2 | |
| word class | determiner | noise[25] | adjective | conjunction | adjective |
| Gloss | the | "pac, pac, pac" | sinister | and | unstoppable |
| Translation | 'the sinister and unstoppable "pac, pac, pac"' | | | | |

Hypotactic complexes are used to grade Epithets, for example *la mar **muy linda*** 'the **very beautiful** sea' invoked in the song Mariela Rosa sang to her children to calm them down on the island when water was rising before the actual tidal wave hit.

---

[25] We have coined the term 'noise' for the word class of this onomatopoetic sound.

(33)

| Example | la | mar | muy | linda |
|---|---|---|---|---|
| group class | nominal group | | | |
| group function | Deictic | Thing | Epithet | |
| complex class | | | word complex | |
| complex function | | | β | α |
| word class | determiner | common noun | adverb | adjective |
| Gloss | the | sea | very | beautiful |
| Translation | 'the very beautiful sea' | | | |

Quantifying entities involve a Numerative function, positioned before the Thing (and any pre-Thing Epithets). Numerals are used for digital counting (*8 metros* '**8** meters' below) and quantifiers for general measurement (*menos terror* '**less** terror' below).

Esta vez Ibarra alcanzó a "aproar" la nave y la pasaron con **menos terror**. Esta segunda ola tenía cerca de **8 metros** de altura.

This time Ibarra managed to turn the head of the ship and they passed over it with **less terror**. This second wave was about **8 metres** high.

There are two contrasts with English to point out here. One is that quantifiers can be used as Numeratives to quantify both count and mass nouns in Spanish (e.g. *muchas calorías* 'many calories' and *mucha agua* 'a lot of water'). The other has to do with comparative quantification. In English a word complex realising comparison is realised either contiguously (e.g. *four more friends*) or discontinuously (e.g. *four friends more*).

(34)

| Example | four | more | friends |
|---|---|---|---|
| group class | nominal group | | |
| group function | Numerative | | Thing |
| complex class | word complex | | |
| complex function | α | β | |
| word class | numeral | adverb | common noun |

But in Spanish the comparative adverb must be realised after the Thing (e.g. *cuatro amigos más* 'four more friends'). This structure is treated as involving a discontinuous Numerative function below, an analysis which avoids setting up a distinct comparative quantification function following the Thing and respects the discontinuous dependency relation between the numeral (*cuatro* 'four') and adverb (*más* 'more').

## 2.3 Spanish Nominal Group Resources

(35)

| Example | *cuatro* | *amigos* | *más* |
|---|---|---|---|
| **group class** | nominal group | | |
| **group function** | Numer ... | Thing | ... ative |
| **complex class** | word ... | | ... complex |
| **complex function** | α | | β |
| **word class** | numeral | common noun | adverb |
| Gloss | four | friends | more |
| Translation | 'four more friends' | | |

### 2.3.2 Textual Nominal Group Resources

The Spanish text we have been focusing on here is a written text, instantiating a number of story genres. This means that as far as the entities involved are concerned, the text as a whole has to be relatively self-contextualising. As for English, the discourse semantic system at stake here is IDENTIFICATION, with its choice of presenting an entity in terms of its identity not being recoverable by a reader and presuming that an entity's identity is in fact recoverable (Figure 2.7).

Unlike the English Bondi Beach narrative, the Ola Maldita stories presume several specific individuals by name when they are first mentioned. Just one of them would have been identifiable by most readers – *la Presidenta Bachelet* (then President of Chile). Only two of the named individuals are actually introduced through presenting reference before being named. This is exemplified for Blanca below.[26]

Encontró ahí a *una señora* que con toda calma esperaba lo que el destino le ofreciera. Se llamaba **Blanca** ... **Blanca** vivía sola y había aceptado morir sola.

'There he met *a lady* who was awaiting what fate would offer her with complete calm. She was called **Blanca** ... **Blanca** lived alone and had accepted that she would die alone.'

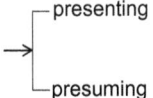

Figure 2.7 Basic IDENTIFICATION system realised by Spanish nominal group systems

---

[26] The other is Timmy, the son of Mariela Rojas. He is introduced as *uno* (understood as *uno de ellos* 'one of them', where *ellos* presumes eight children playing on the beach when Jonathan and his friends arrived on Orrego Island), and then named: *De ellos no se sabe nada, salvo de uno: Timmy, de 4 años* 'Of them nothing is known, except for one: **Timmy**, 4 years old.'

For this presenting reference a Deictic Thing structure is required, with a non-specific determiner realising the Deictic function. Once named, Blanca can be presumed by name alone.

(36)
| Example | *una señora* | |
|---|---|---|
| **group class** | nominal group | |
| **group function** | Deictic | Thing |
| **word class** | determiner | common noun |
| Gloss | a | lady |

(37)
| Example | *Blanca* |
|---|---|
| **group class** | nominal group |
| **group function** | Thing |
| **word class** | proper noun |
| Gloss | Blanca |

Like English, the Spanish Deictic function can be realised by non-specific and specific determiners, including *un/una* 'a', *el/la* 'the', demonstratives (e.g. *este/esta* 'this') and possessive determiners (e.g. *mi* 'my'). Embedded nominal groups are, however, not possible – so instead of ***the Pinita's*** *crew* (a Deictic Thing structure in English), we find *los tripulantes **del Pinita*** 'the crew **of the Pinita**' (a Spanish Deictic Thing Qualifier structure).

Several individuals who are presumed through proper names in the Ola Maldita stories are first introduced in relation to other individuals, who have been previously introduced.

*su capitán José Ibarra* '**its** captain José Ibarra'
*su hijo Jonathan Romero* '**her** son Jonathan Romero'
*su nieto de 4 años, Emilito* '**her** 4-year-old nephew, Emilito'
*su madre, Mariela Rojas* '**his** mother, Mariela Rojas'

And where this is not possible, an appositional structure is generally deployed, providing clarifying information identifying the individual.

***el pescador*** *Mario Quiroz Leal* '**fisherman** Mario Quiroz Leal'
***el contralmirante*** *Roberto* Macchiavello '**rearadmiral** Roberto Macchiavello'
***el piloto*** *Víctor González* '**pilot** Víctor González'
***el intendente de Concepción***, *Jaime Tohá* '**Concepción governor**, Jaime Tohá'
***el sargento de la Armada***, Cristián Valladares '**Navy sergeant**, Cristián Valladares'
Hugo Barrera, **un sobreviviente** 'Hugo Barrera, **a survivor**'

These strategies are more efficient than the presenting then naming strategy used for Blanca noted above, and avoid relying on a proper name alone (which would involve telling the reader they can recover the identity of someone they don't in fact know).

## 2.3 Spanish Nominal Group Resources

Once named, the proper name can, of course, be used to track the individual in question. The captain of the fishing boat caught up in the tsunami is tracked in these terms in the article.

*El bote pesquero Pinita* 'the fishing boat Pinita'
*su capitán José Ibarra* 'its captain José Ibarra'
*el capitán Ibarra* 'captain Ibarra'
*Ibarra*
*Ibarra*
*Ibarra*
*Ibarra*
*Ibarra*
*el capitán Ibarra* 'captain Ibarra'
*el capitán Ibarra* 'captain Ibarra'
*Ibarra*
*Ibarra*

As we saw above, the internal grammar of proper names in Spanish regularly includes a specific determiner when the role of the person being identified is specified (cf. *la Presidenta Bachelet* 'President Bachelet', *el sargento Valladares* 'Sergeant Valladares'). We'll touch on this again in Section 2.5 below.

(38)

| Example | *Ibarra* |
|---|---|
| **group class** | nominal group |
| **group function** | Thing |
| **word class** | proper noun |
| Gloss | Ibarra |

Although nowhere near as commonly as in English, conscious entities can be tracked by personal pronouns (as in the *Hugo Barrera, Hugo, él* 'he' sequence below):

... recuerda **Hugo Barrera, un sobreviviente** ... **Hugo** cayó a ese furioso torrente sabiendo que moriría. **Él** estaba en Orrego por trabajo.

'... remembered **Hugo Barrera, a survivor** ... **Hugo** fell into that furious torrent knowing that he would die. **He** was in Orrego for work.'

(39)

| Example | *él* |
|---|---|
| **group class** | nominal group |
| **group function** | Thing |
| **word class** | pronoun |
| Gloss | he |

Alongside proper names and pronouns, Spanish deploys a wide range of resources for tracking participants. In the story below the old man rescued by Sergeant Valladares is introduced as *un anciano* 'an old man' and tracked through two possessive determiners *sus, sus* (**sus** *familiares* 'his family', **sus** *parientes* 'his relatives'), four pronominal clitics,[27] *lo, lo, lo, lo* (**lo** *cuidaba* 'looked after him', *lo encontró* 'found him', *lo sacó* 'took him away', *lo llevó* 'left him') and two further determiners *el, ese* (*al*[28] *anciano* 'the old man', *ese anciano* 'that old man'):

En su retirada, el sargento Valladares vio que una mujer pedía ayuda. Al entrar en la casa medio derrumbada, encontró a *un anciano* en silla de ruedas que los miraba con angustia. **Sus** familiares estaban en los cerros. La señora que pedía auxilio era la mujer que **lo** cuidaba. Ella vivía en otro lugar y corrió a ver **al anciano** y **lo** encontró solo. Estaba mojado y gemía de miedo. El sargento **lo** sacó de ahí y **lo** llevó a la casa de la mujer.

El saqueo
No es difícil imaginar la angustia de **ese anciano abandonado**. Tampoco es incomprensible el miedo que deben haber sentido **sus** parientes.

'During his escape, Sergeant Valladares saw that a woman was asking for help. On entering the half-demolished house, he met **an old man** in a wheel chair who was looking at them anxiously. **His** family were in the hills. The lady who was asking for help was the woman who looked after **him**. She lived in another place and ran towards **the old man** and found **him** alone. **He** was wet and moaning with fear. The sergeant took **him** away from there and left **him** in the woman's house.

The Looting
It is not difficult to imagine the distress of **that old abandoned man**. Neither is the fear that **his** relatives must have felt incomprehensible.'

The woman looking after the old man is introduced and tracked in a comparable sequence, including the personal pronoun *ella* 'she'.

*una* mujer pedía ayuda 'a woman was asking for help'
**los** 'them'
**la** señora que pedía auxilio 'the lady who was asking for help'
**la** mujer que lo cuidaba 'the woman who looked after him'
**ella** 'she'
**la** mujer 'the woman'

An important contrast with English emerges here, since Spanish can track participants through personal pronouns functioning as participants in clauses, but more commonly through pronominal clitics functioning inside the structure of verbal groups (see Chapter 3 below for verbal group structure). As noted above, the personal pronoun nominal groups are comparatively rare.

---

[27] Spanish pronominal clitics are introduced in Chapter 3. They are non-salient elements of verbal group structure, not realisations of the Thing function in nominal groups.

[28] The words *al* and *del* in Spanish 'contract' the syntagm *a el* ('to the.MASC.SG') and *de el* ('of the.MASC.SG'), respectively.

## 2.3 Spanish Nominal Group Resources

(40)

| Example | *ella* |
|---|---|
| **group class** | nominal group |
| **group function** | Thing |
| **word class** | pronoun |
| Gloss | she |

A table of personal pronouns, which have the potential to realise participants as nominal groups at clause rank, is presented in Table 2.4[29] and can be usefully compared with the paradigm for pronominal clitics presented in Chapter 3.

Another contrast with English has to do with tracking entities realised through person and number morphology in the verbal group. This resource can be used to track participants within and between clause complexes. The woman and the sergeant are tracked in this way in the clause complexes below (presumed entity underlined, tracking suffixes in bold).

*<u>Ella</u> vivía en otro lugar y corr**ió** a ver al anciano y lo encontr**ó** solo.*
'<u>She</u> was living in another place and Ø ran towards the old man and Ø found him alone.'

*<u>El sargento</u> lo sacó de ahí y lo llev**ó** a la casa de la mujer.*
'<u>The sergeant</u> took him away from there and Ø left him in the woman's house.'

And both the sergeant and the old man are tracked between clause complexes (i.e. across sentence boundaries) in the following examples (presumed entity underlined, tracking in bold).

*Al entrar en la casa medio derrumbada, encontr**ó** a <u>un anciano</u> en silla de ruedas que los mir**aba** con angustia.*
'On entering the half-demolished house, **he** (the sergeant) met <u>an old man</u> in a wheel chair who was looking at them anxiously.'

Table 2.4 *Pronouns realising clause rank nominal groups in Chilean Spanish*

| | **Pronouns realising clause rank nominal groups** | | | |
|---|---|---|---|---|
| number | person | | non-oblique | oblique |
| singular | interactant | 1st | *yo* | *mí* |
| | | 2nd | *tú* | *ti* |
| | | 2nd (formal) | *usted* | |
| | non-interactant | 3rd | *él* (masc.), *ella* (fem.), *ello* (neut.) | |
| plural | interactant | 1st | *nosotros* | |
| | | 2nd | *ustedes* | |
| | non-interactant | 3rd | *ellos* (masc.), *ellas* (fem.) | |

[29] The use of neuter third person pronoun *ello* is quite restricted and, when used, it is only for text reference.

*Estaba mojado y gemía de miedo.*
'**He** (the old man) was wet and Ø moaning with fear.'

Tracking of this kind between clause complexes would be ungrammatical in English, which requires a Subject function in such clauses (cf. the discussion of MOOD in Chapter 5 below). The way in which the presenting and presuming reference unfolds in relation to the old man and his carer is outlined in Table 2.5 below. Compared with English a lot of work is being done in the Spanish verbal group as far as participant identification is concerned, a point we will return to in our discussion of the Spanish verbal group in Chapter 3.

Like English, Spanish deploys a Qualifier function after the Thing when extra information is needed to specify the identity of the entity being tracked. This comes in handy when Sergeant Valladares realises that a woman he has seen asking for help is the carer for the old man he is rescuing: *la señora **que pedía auxilio*** 'the lady **who was asking for help**'. The Qualifier specifies which woman (there are several female candidates mentioned earlier on in the stories) is meant.

Table 2.5 *Two instances of entity tracking in Spanish*

| presenting | presuming | | | |
|---|---|---|---|---|
| | determiners | personal pronouns | pronominal clitics | verbal group inflectional morphology |
| una mujer | | | los | |
| | la señora ... | | | |
| | = la mujer ... | | | |
| | | ella | | |
| | | | | -ió |
| | | | | -ó |
| | la mujer | | | |
| un anciano | | | | |
| | sus | | | |
| | | | lo | |
| | al anciano | | lo | |
| | | | | -aba |
| | | | | -ía |
| | | | lo | |
| | | | lo | |
| | ese anciano ... | | | |
| | sus parientes | | | |

## 2.3 Spanish Nominal Group Resources

En su retirada, el sargento Valladares vio que *una mujer pedía ayuda*. Al entrar en la casa medio derrumbada, encontró a un anciano en silla de ruedas que los miraba con angustia. Sus familiares estaban en los cerros. **La señora que pedía auxilio** era la mujer que lo cuidaba. Ella vivía en otro lugar y corrió a ver al anciano y lo encontró solo.

'During his return, Sergeant Valladares saw that a woman was asking for help. On entering the half-demolished house, he met an old man in a wheel chair who was looking at them anxiously. His family were in the hills. **The lady who was asking for help** was the woman who was looking after him. She lived in another place and ran to check on the old man and found him alone.'

(41)

| Example | *la* | *señora* | *que pedía auxilo* |
|---|---|---|---|
| **group class** | nominal group | | |
| **group function** | Deictic | Thing | Qualifier |
| **word class** | determiner | common noun | [[clause]] |
| Gloss | the | lady | who was asking for help |
| Translation | 'the lady who was asking for help' | | |

Comparable support is provided by embedded prepositional phrases, clarifying, for example, which crew members are being tracked in *los tripulantes **del Pinita*** 'the crew of the Pinita'.

(42)

| Example | *los* | *tripulantes* | *del Pinita* |
|---|---|---|---|
| **group class** | nominal group | | |
| **group function** | Deictic | Thing | Qualifier |
| **word class** | determiner | common noun | [prepositional phrase] |
| Gloss | the | crew | of the Pinita |
| Translation | 'the Pinita's crew' | | |

We close this section with two final comments on differences between Spanish and English nominal group grammar. Like English, Spanish has possessive determiners, for example *mi familia* 'my family', *tu mujer* 'your wife', *su ciudad* 'his city', *sus vidas* 'their lives', *nuestro grupo* 'our group', *nuestras costas* 'our coasts'. From a discourse semantic perspective, we have one entity referred to through a Deictic (*mi*) before the Thing and another realised by the Thing itself (*familia*).

(43)

| Example | *mi* | *familia* |
|---|---|---|
| **group class** | nominal group | |
| **group function** | Deictic | Thing |
| **word class** | determiner | common noun |
| Gloss | my | family |

The paradigm of possessive determiners functioning as Deictics in Chilean Spanish is given below (of these only the first person plural has masculine and feminine forms); in traditional terminology these are referred to as 'possessive adjectives'.

**singular : plural ::**
*mi* : *mis* :: 'my'
*tu* : *tus* :: 'your'
*su* : *sus* :: 'his/her'; 'their'
*nuestro* : *nuestros* (*nuestra* : *nuestras*) :: 'our'

But Spanish does not embed nominal groups in the Deictic function. An English nominal group such as ***the Pinita's** crew* would have to be to be translated as *los tripulantes del Pinita* 'the crew of the Pinita', as analysed above.

Non-salient possessive determiners above contrast with salient ones which follow the Thing (*el bote suyo* 'his boat') and can function as the head of a nominal group (*el suyo* 'his (one)') – for example *el bote pesquero es **suyo*** 'the fishing boat is **his (one)**'.[30] A paradigm for these possessive pronouns in Chilean Spanish is presented below. These salient possessive determiners distinguish gender in all persons.

**masculine (singular : plural) : feminine (singular : plural) ::**
(*mío* : *míos*) : (*mía* : *mías*) :: 'mine'
(*tuyo* : *tuyos*) : (*tuya* : *tuyas*) :: 'yours'
(*suyo* : *suyos*) : (*suya* : *suyas*) :: 'his/hers'; theirs'
(*nuestro* : *nuestros*) : (*nuestra* : *nuestras*) 'ours'

Salient possessive determiners are also used in structures such as *ese bote pesquero **suyo*** 'that fishing boat of his' where they further specify the group initial Deictic function. From a discourse semantic perspective, we have two entities, one realised as Thing and the other referred to after the Thing as *suyo* 'his'.

(44)

| Example | *ese* | *bote* | *pesquero* | *suyo* |
|---|---|---|---|---|
| **group class** | nominal group | | | |
| **group function** | Deictic | Thing | Classifier | Deictic |
| **word class** | determiner | common noun | adjective | possessive pronoun |
| Gloss | that | boat | fishing | his |
| Translation | 'that fishing boat of his' | | | |

---

[30] We are treating here both non-salient and salient possessives as Spanish 'determiners'; they are, however, associated with distinct patterns within the nominal group. For a review of the term determiner and its relation to these and other relevant categories in Spanish, see http://hispanoteca .eu/Lexikon%20der%20Linguistik/d/DETERMINANT%20%20Determinante%20o%20 determinativo.htm. For an in-depth exploration of possessives in Spanish, see Picallo and Rigau (1999).

## 2.3 Spanish Nominal Group Resources

This raises an issue as to how to analyse this post-Thing function and whether to analyse it in the same way we treat structures where it is head of a nominal group (as exemplified above in *el bote pesquero es **suyo*** 'the fishing boat is **his**') rather than a post-modifier. Note that unlike the Numerative *cuatro amigos más* 'four more friends' discussed above, we do not have a discontinuous constituent here. Rather, we have a specification of deixis, with the demonstrative *ese* 'that' identifying the fishing boat by position and the pronoun *suyo* 'his' identifying it through possession. And unlike English no structure marker is required to relate the possessor to the Thing (cf. ***of** his*). Accordingly, we will treat these structures as involving secondary deixis, with a second Deictic function culminating the nominal group. A comparable doubling of deixis is found with demonstrative determiners (cf. ***ese** bote pesquero* 'that fishing boat' vs *el bote pesquero **ese*** '**that** fishing boat', literally **the** boat fishing **that (one)**').[31]

(45)

| Example | el | bote | pesquero | ese |
|---|---|---|---|---|
| **group class** | nominal group | | | |
| **group function** | Deictic | Thing | Classifier | Deictic |
| **word class** | determiner | common noun | adjective | determiner |
| Gloss | the | boat | fishing | that |
| Translation | 'that fishing boat' | | | |

We close by noting that we have now suggested five different paradigms involving person used to track participants in Spanish, each with distinctive agnation. These are noted below, alongside third person exemplification for each category.

i. personal pronouns – *él*
    (realising clause rank participants, and relatively rare compared to English usage)
ii. non-salient possessive determiners – *su*
    (realising the nominal group pre-Thing Deictic function)
iii. salient possessive determiners – *suyo*
    (realising clause rank participants or a post-Thing nominal group Deictic)
iv. pronominal clitics – *lo*
    (tracking participants inside verbal groups)
v. verbal group inflectional morphology – e.g. *-aba/-ía*

These resources track participants, using the minimum amount of information required (person, number and/or case) to identify the entity they presume. Note that grammatically speaking there are no grounds for recognising a generalisable class of 'pronouns' in Spanish; each of the tracking resources in (i), (ii), (iii) and (iv) above plays a different role in grammatical structure and

---

[31] It appears that when two Deictics are deployed, the second has to be more specific than the first. For example, *ese ... suyo* 'that ... his/her' and *el ... ese* 'the ... that'.

### 2.3.3 Spanish Nominal Group Systems

We will now shift our perspective from nominal group structures to systems. As we did with English, for our first step we'll set aside elliptical nominal groups, which we are not explicitly addressing here ('Thing-less' groups such as *los ∅ de otras cuatro personas* 'those (moans) of another four people'). We then distinguish Thing-only nominal groups designating a presumed entity from nominal groups specifying an entity. And designating nominal groups are divided into those using a proper name to designate an entity and those using a personal pronoun. These systems and their interdependencies are outlined in Figure 2.8.

The realisation statements relating features in these systems to their structural consequences are compiled in Table 2.6.

As for English, the feature [specifying] opens up choices in five systems, allowing for functions which are [classifying], [describing], [quantifying], [determining] and/or [qualifying]. The features [classifying] and [describing] are in fact recursive options, since more than one Classifier or Epithet may be required; we have not taken the step of formalising this recursion in the network below (Figure 2.9).

The feature [classifying] is specified as [adjectival] or [nominal] to allow for Classifiers realised by adjectives (*generador **eléctrico*** '**electricity** generator') or word complexes (*silla **de ruedas*** '**wheel** chair'). The feature [describing] is

Table 2.6 *Realisation statements for general Spanish nominal group features*

| non-elliptical | +Thing |
|---|---|
| naming | Thing: proper name |
| pronaming | Thing: personal pronoun |

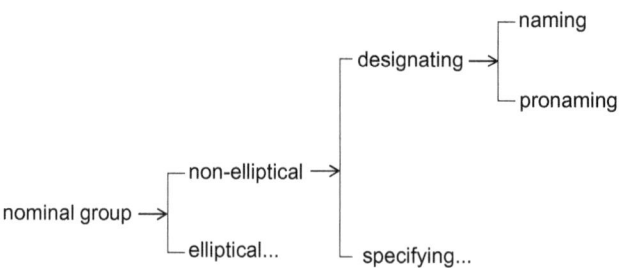

Figure 2.8 General Spanish nominal group systems

## 2.3 Spanish Nominal Group Resources

provisionally subclassified as [descriptive] or [attitudinal], reflecting the possible implications of this distinction for the interpretation of certain adjectives when sequenced before or after the Thing (e.g. feeling sorry for a friend: *un pobre amigo* 'an **unfortunate** friend' vs describing a friend as impecunious: *un amigo pobre* 'a **poor** friend').

The feature [quantifying] is subclassified as [exact] or [inexact] to distinguish digital (e.g. *8 metros* '**8** meters') from general (e.g. *menos terror* '**less** terror') quantifications. We have cross-classified this system with an optional comparative one in order to provide for the discontinuous Numeratives discussed above (*cuatro amigos más* '**four** friends **more**').

The feature [determining] is subclassified as [personal] or [general] by way of distinguishing nominal groups realising two entities (e.g. *sus familiares* '**his** family') from those realising one (*ese bote pesquero* '**that** fishing boat'). A further system dependent on the feature [determining] makes provision for nominal groups with additional personalised or demonstrative deixis following the Thing.

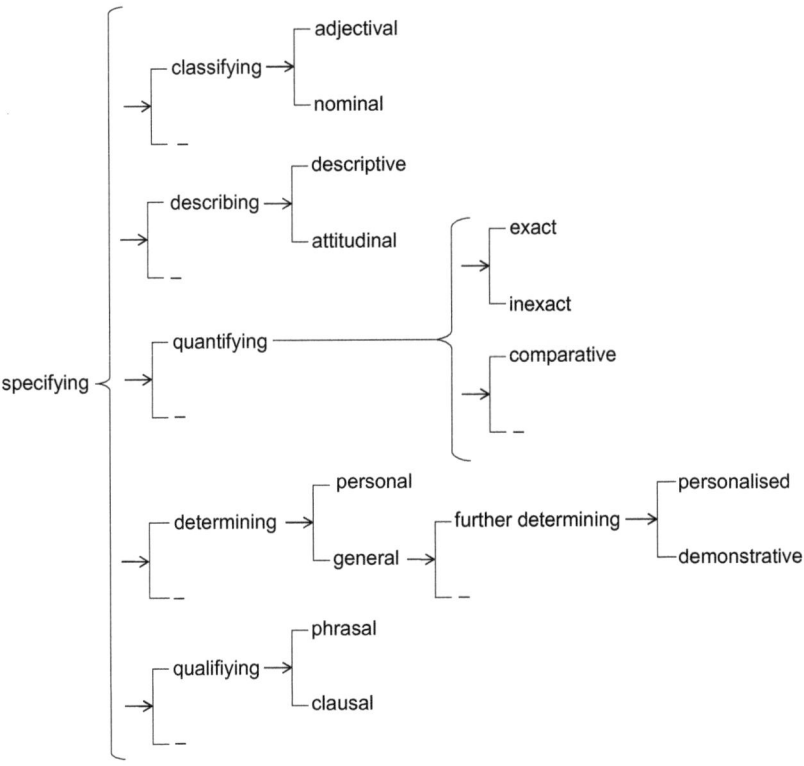

Figure 2.9 More delicate Spanish nominal group systems

70    Nominal Group

The feature [qualifying] is subclassified as [phrasal] or [clausal]. These specifying systems and their interdependencies are outlined below and illustrate the sense in which from a paradigmatic perspective the differences between English and Spanish have to do with more delicate network options (for example the [further determined] feature allowing for double deixis in nominal groups: e.g. *esa casa **tuya*** '**that** house of **yours**').

The realisation statements relating features in these specifying systems to their structural consequences are outlined in Table 2.7. These statements demonstrate that there is more difference between English and Spanish in terms of the structural realisation of nominal group systems than in the systems themselves.

## 2.4    Chinese Nominal Group Resources

In this section we describe systems and structures of Chinese nominal groups. We approach the systemic features and multivariate structures of Chinese nominal groups from an ideational perspective first and then a textual perspective.

Table 2.7 *Realisation statements for more delicate Spanish nominal group features*

| | |
|---|---|
| classifying | +Classifier; Thing ^ Classifier |
| adjectival | Classifier: adjective |
| nominal | Classifier: *de* ^ noun |
| describing | +Epithet; Epithet → Thing or Thing ← Epithet |
| descriptive | Epithet: descriptive adjective |
| attitudinal | Epithet: attitudinal adjective |
| quantifying | +Numerative; Numerative → Epithet |
| exact | Numerative: numeral |
| inexact | Numerative: quantifier |
| comparative | Numerative: word complex; Numer ... → Thing ← ... ative |
| determining | +Deictic; Deictic → Numerative |
| personal | Deictic: determiner: possessive |
| general | Deictic: determiner: non-possessive |
| further determining | +Deictic; Deictic ^ # |
| personalised | Deictic: possessive pronoun |
| demonstrative | Deictic: demonstrative |
| qualifying | +Qualifier: Thing ← Qualifier |
| phrasal | Qualifier: [prepositional phrase] |
| clausal | Qualifier: [[clause]] |

*Note*: In the structure specification column, '#' indicates the beginning or end of a nominal group, '+' indicates the presence of a Function, '^' indicates the sequence of Functions, ':' indicates the realisation of a Function by a class and the arrows '→' or '←' indicate the relative sequencing of Functions. The direction of the sequencing arrows is used here to encode the dependency relations among Functions (so X '→' Y means X dependent on Y, and vice versa).

## 2.4 Chinese Nominal Group Resources

Compared to English and Spanish, Chinese nominal groups have both commonalities and differences with respect to systemic choices and realisation statements.

### 2.4.1 Ideational Nominal Group Resources

In this section we focus on Things realised by common nouns, setting aside Things realised by pronouns and proper names for Section 2.4.2 below.

From the perspective of field, the main taxonomies construed in the Sea Lettuce text[32] have to do with the ecology of the sea near shore and the green algae that grew very quickly. The Things realised by nouns dealing with these taxonomies are highlighted in the paragraphs below.

2008 年6月,是距离第29届北京奥运会开幕仅仅两个月的日子,如果你走进中国科学院海洋研究所,你将被眼前空地上晾晒的一片绿油油的**海藻**所吸引,这些海藻就是被称为"突如其来的海洋自然**灾害**"的**主角**——浒苔。

2008 年5月31日,大面积浒苔进入青岛近岸**海域**,使滨海名城青岛的蓝**海**呈现绿色。随着时间的推移,越来越多的浒苔随**潮水**涌上**岸**,它们到达了青岛著名的**栈桥**、第一海水**浴场**和前海风景游览区一带的**沙滩**,没几天便堆起了厚厚一层,并迅速扩散,在太阳晒后更是臭气熏天,成为污染**带**。

'June 2008 was the time only two months away from the 29th Beijing Olympic Games. If you walked into the Institute of Oceanology, Chinese Academy of Sciences, you would be attracted to a mass of green **seaweed** being dried on the ground. This seaweed was known as the **protagonist** of the "unexpected ocean natural **disaster**" – sea lettuce.

On 31 May 2008, expansive sea lettuce invaded Qingdao's offshore **area**, causing the famous coastal city Qingdao's blue **sea** to turn green. As time went by, more and more sea lettuce rushed onto the shore with the **tidewater**; it reached Qingdao's famous **pier**, the First Seawater **Resort**, and the **beach** near the Qianhai scenic spot. Within just a few days a thick heap formed and spread fast. Rotting away in the sun, it stunk to high heaven and turned into a **belt** of pollution.'

For nominal groups with only one noun in this text (e.g. 海藻 *hǎizǎo* 'seaweed', 海 *hǎi* 'sea', 沙滩 *shātān* 'beach'), the noun realises the Thing function. Such nominal groups are analysed as follows for function and class.

(46)

| Examples | 海藻 |
|---|---|
| Transliteration | *hǎizǎo* |
| **group class** | nominal group |
| **group function** | Thing |
| **word class** | common noun |
| Gloss | seaweed |

---

[32] The full text can be found at: www.cas.cn/xw/yxdt/200809/t20080905_986639.shtml.

For some nominal groups, the Thing function is sufficient to demarcate the entity being construed. For many others, however, the Thing function is not sufficient, e.g. 海水浴场 *hǎishuǐ yùchǎng* 'seawater resort', 近海 *jìn hǎi* 'coastal waters', 打捞技术 *dǎlāo jìshù* 'retrieving technology'. In these examples the Thing is subclassified by a Classifier function, realised by another common noun, an adjective or a verb respectively in (47), (48) and (49) below.

(47)

| Example | 海水浴场 | |
|---|---|---|
| Transliteration | *hǎishuǐ* | *yùchǎng* |
| **group class** | nominal group | |
| **group function** | Classifier | Thing |
| **word class** | common noun | common noun |
| Gloss | seawater | resort |
| Translation | 'seawater resort' | |

(48)

| Example | 近海 | |
|---|---|---|
| Transliteration | *jìn* | *hǎi* |
| **group class** | nominal group | |
| **group function** | Classifier | Thing |
| **word class** | adjective | common noun |
| Gloss | near | sea |
| Translation | 'coastal waters' | |

(49)

| Example | 打捞技术 | |
|---|---|---|
| Transliteration | *dǎlāo* | *jìshù* |
| **group class** | nominal group | |
| **group function** | Classifier | Thing |
| **word class** | verb | common noun |
| Gloss | retrieve | Technology |
| Translation | 'retrieval technology' | |

At this point we need to note that the distinct word classes realising Classifiers have different meaning-making potential. The noun 海水 *hǎishuǐ* 'seawater' in (47) has the potential to realise a Thing itself. The adjective 近 *jìn* 'near' in (48) has the potential to describe another entity, e.g. 近路 *jìn lù* 'near road, shortcut', and to be graded, e.g. 更近 *gèng jìn* 'nearer', 特别近 *tèbié jìn* 'very near'. The adjective 近 *jìn* 'near' realises a Classifier in (48) because it demarcates the sea according to its distance from the shore, and thus construes

## 2.4 Chinese Nominal Group Resources

a taxonomic relationship rather than a property of the sea – as we do not find *更近的海 gèng jìn de hǎi* 'nearer sea' to grade the sea's nearness to the shore to establish contrast with 近海 *jìn hǎi* 'near sea, coastal waters'. The verb 打捞 *dǎlāo* 'retrieve from underwater' has the potential to construe an activity and realise a Process in a clause, as in 印尼政府将打捞"黑匣子" *yìnní zhèngfǔ jiāng dǎlāo hēixiázǐ* 'The Indonesian government will retrieve the "black box"'.[33] But in (49) it specifies a type of technology.

We can see that reasoning about function (e.g. Thing, Classifier) has to do with the role played by a unit in a given structure, whereas reasoning about class (e.g. noun, adjective, verb) has to do with the potential of a unit to play different roles in different structures. Function labels are thus about what something is doing; class labels are about what something could be. And the relationship between function and class is not one to one; we can have a function realised by more than one class (e.g. Classifier by noun or adjective or verb) and a given class can realise more than one function (e.g. noun as Classifier or Thing).

There can be more than one Classifier, as many as are needed in fact to pinpoint the entity being construed and its place in the relevant field taxonomy, e.g. 海洋自然灾害 *hǎiyáng zìrán zāihài* 'ocean natural disaster' in our text, which is analysed for function and class below.

(50)

| Example | 海洋自然灾害 | | |
|---|---|---|---|
| Transliteration | *hǎiyáng* | *zìrán* | *zāihài* |
| **group class** | nominal group | | |
| **group function** | Classifier | Classifier | Thing |
| **word class** | common noun | common noun | common noun |
| Gloss | ocean | nature | disaster |
| Translation | 'ocean natural disaster' | | |

This brings us to the third ideational nominal group function we will consider – the Epithet. From the perspective of field, this function has to do with properties we assign to items; from the perspective of discourse semantic ideation, this means attributing qualities to entities. There are several examples in the paragraphs we quoted above, highlighted in bold below.

2008年6月,是距离第29届北京奥运会开幕仅仅两个月的日子,如果你走进中国科学院海洋研究所,你将被眼前空地上晾晒的一片**绿油油的**海藻所吸引,这些海藻就是被称为"**突如其来的**海洋灾害"的主角——浒苔。

---

[33] This example is taken from a news report at Xinhuanet (www.xinhuanet.com/world/2019-01/05/c_1210030343.htm; retrieved on 19 July 2021).

2008年5月31日,大面积浒苔进入青岛近岸海域,使滨海名城青岛的**蓝**海呈现绿色。随着时间的推移,越来越多的浒苔随潮水涌上岸,它们到达了青岛**著名的**栈桥、第一海水浴场和前海风景游览区一带的沙滩,没几天便堆起了厚厚一层,并迅速扩散,在太阳晒后更是臭气熏天,成为污染带。

'June 2008 was the time only two months away from the 29th Beijing Olympic Games. If you walked into the Institute of Oceanology, Chinese Academy of Sciences, you would be attracted to a mass of **green** seaweed being dried on the ground. This seaweed was known as the protagonist of the "**unexpected** ocean natural disaster" – sea lettuce.

On 31 May 2008, expansive sea lettuce invaded Qingdao's offshore area, causing the famous coastal city Qingdao's **blue** sea to turn green. As time went by, more and more sea lettuce rushed onto the shore with the tidewater; it reached Qingdao's **famous** pier, the First Seawater Resort, and the beach near the Qianhai scenic spot. Within just a few days a thick heap formed and spread fast. Rotting away in the sun, it stunk to high heaven and turned into a belt of pollution.'

An Epithet is used to answer the question 什么样的? *Shénme yàng de?* 'What like?' and is typically realised through a word complex involving an adjective and a subsequent clitic 的 *de*. The clitic does not have any lexical meaning (and so not glossed) but only serves to link the Epithet to the Thing. Two nominal groups with Epithets are analysed for function and class below.

(51)

| Example | 著名的栈桥 | | |
|---|---|---|---|
| Transliteration | *zhùmíng* | *de* | *zhànqiáo* |
| **group class** | nominal group | | |
| **group function** | Epithet | | Thing |
| **complex class** | word complex | | |
| **complex function** | α | β | |
| **word class** | adjective | clitic | common noun |
| Gloss | famous | | pier |
| Translation | 'famous pier' | | |

(52)

| Example | 突如其来的海洋自然灾害 | | | | |
|---|---|---|---|---|---|
| Transliteration | *tūrúqílái* | *de* | *hǎiyáng* | *zìrán* | *zāihài* |
| **group class** | nominal group | | | | |
| **group function** | Epithet | | Classifier | Classifier | Thing |
| **complex class** | word complex | | | | |
| **complex function** | α | β | | | |
| **word class** | adjective | clitic | common noun | common noun | common noun |
| Gloss | unexpected | | ocean | nature | disaster |
| Translation | 'unexpected ocean natural disaster' | | | | |

The Epithet *tūrúqílái* is historically derived from a clause but has been lexicalised as an adjective in Modern Chinese. It can be graded by adverbs, e.g. 有点突如其来 *yǒudiǎn tūrúqílái* '**somewhat** unexpected', 特别突如其来 *tèbié tūrúqílái* '**very** unexpected'.

On the basis of example (52) we see once again that a class is capable of performing more than one function (i.e. adjective realising the α function in the word complex realising Epithet as well as Classifier). It can also be seen that both the Epithet and the Classifier are sequenced before the Thing if both are present in a Chinese nominal group, with the Epithet preceding the Classifier.

There can also be more than one Epithet, adding as many descriptive and attitudinal qualities as needed to an entity. There is an example from our text, 实用、高效的打捞技术 *shíyòng, gāoxiào de dǎlāo jìshù* '**practical, efficient** retrieving technology', which contains two Epithets, i.e. 实用 *shíyòng* 'practical' and 高效的 *gāoxiào de* 'efficient'. For this we have a sequence of two Epithets. Typically, it is the final Epithet that is realised by a word complex involving the α ^ β structure.

(53)

| Example | 实用、高效的打捞技术 | | | | |
|---|---|---|---|---|---|
| Transliteration | *shíyòng* | *gāoxiào* | *de* | *dǎlāo* | *jìshù* |
| **group class** | nominal group | | | | |
| **group function** | Epithet | Epithet | | Classifier | Thing |
| **complex class** | | word class | | | |
| **complex function** | | α | β | | |
| word class | adjective | adjective | clitic | common noun | common noun |
| Gloss | practical | efficient | | retrieve | technology |
| Translation | 'practical, efficient retrieving technology' | | | | |

Alternatively, if an additive conjunction is inserted between the two adjectives, e.g. 实用且高效的打捞技术 *shíyòng qiě gāoxiào de dǎlāo jìshù* 'practical **and** efficient retrieving technology', we need to expand the analysis to allow for an adjective complex realising the α function in the word complex realising the Epithet, adding qualities at the word rank. The structure of this adjective complex is 1 +2 (paratactic extension); the +2 function is realised by yet another word complex with a β ^ α structure realised through a conjunction followed by an adjective syntagm.

(54)

| Example | 实用且高效的打捞技术 | | | | | |
|---|---|---|---|---|---|---|
| Transliteration | shíyòng | qiě | gāoxiào | de | dǎlāo | jìshù |
| **group class** | nominal group | | | | | |
| **group function** | Epithet | | | | Classifier | Thing |
| **complex class** | word complex | | | | | |
| **complex function** | α | | | β | | |
| **complex class** | adjective complex | | | | | |
| **complex function** | 1 | +2 | | | | |
| **complex class** | | word complex | | | | |
| **complex function** | | β | α | | | |
| **word class** | adjective | conj. | adjective | clitic | common noun | common noun |
| Gloss | practical | and | efficient | | retrieve | technology |
| Translation | 'practical and efficient retrieving technology' | | | | | |

Apart from adjective complexes, the α function of an Epithet can also be realised by other types of word complex to describe the entity. We have an example of this kind in our text, i.e. 大面积的浒苔 *dà miànjī de hǔtái* 'expansive sea lettuce', analysed below for function and class.

(55)

| Example | 大面积的浒苔 | | | |
|---|---|---|---|---|
| Transliteration | dà | miànjī | de | hǔtái |
| **group class** | nominal group | | | |
| **group function** | Epithet | | | Thing |
| **complex class** | word complex | | | |
| **complex function** | α | | β | |
| **complex class** | word complex | | | |
| **complex function** | α | β | | |
| **word class** | adjective | noun | clitic | common noun |
| Gloss | big | area | | sea lettuce |
| Translation | 'expansive sea lettuce' | | | |

In this nominal group, the word complex 大面积 *dà miànjī*, literally 'big area', describes the expansiveness of the sea lettuce and realises the α function

## 2.4 Chinese Nominal Group Resources

in the higher-level word complex realising the Epithet. It is composed of an adjective 大 *dà* 'big' and a noun 面积 *miànjī* 'area'. From the perspective of discourse semantics, the noun realises a dimension – deployed to specify to the facet of the entity the preceding adjective is used to assign (i.e. size, weight, colour, etc.).

We can see from the above examples that the Epithet (or the rightmost Epithet if there is more than one) is always realised by a word complex in which the β function is realised by the clitic 的 *de*. However, in our focus text there is also a nominal group 大面积浒苔 *dà miànjī hŭtái* 'expansive sea lettuce', which lacks the clitic 的 *de* compared with (55). We analyse this nominal group as having a Classfier ^ Thing structure, as shown in (55') below. Thus a Classifier can also be realised by a word complex alongside the noun, verb and adjective introduced above.

(55')

| Example | 大面积浒苔 | | |
|---|---|---|---|
| Transliteration | *dà* | *miànjī* | *hŭtái* |
| **group class** | nominal group | | |
| **group function** | Classifier | | Thing |
| **complex class** | word complex | | |
| **complex function** | α | β | |
| word class | adjective | noun | common noun |
| Gloss | big | area | sea lettuce |
| Translation | 'expansive sea lettuce' | | |

Structurally, the Classifier functions are adjacent to the left of the Thing and no other function can be inserted in between. In contrast, the Epithet can be either preceded or followed by a Measurer (see examples (58) and (58') below).

As a final step for this section, let's consider the possibility of quantifying the entities construed by a nominal group. This brings us to the paragraph of our text where the ocean research institute and research staff are working to obtain scientific data for the control of the sea lettuce.

来自中国海洋大学 … … **6个科研单位**的**25名科研人员**参加了此次航行。本次航行历时**16天**,共完成了黄东海典型海域的**8个断面**、**67个站位**的观测调查,取得了**一大批基础数据和资料**,为浒苔灾害的治理提供了重要的科学依据。

'**25 researchers** from **6 research institutes** including Ocean University of China … participated in the exploration on the sea. This voyage took **16 days**, accomplishing observation on **8 sections**, **67 stations** in key areas on the Yellow Sea and East China Sea and obtaining **a big batch of basic statistics and data**, which provides important scientific basis for the control of sea lettuce disaster.'

Quantification of an entity is realised in a nominal group through a Measurer function. We do not use the function label Numerative which was deployed in the description of English and Spanish nominal groups (Sections 2.2 and 2.3 above) because the Chinese function gives rise to a different structure. The Measurer function in a Chinese nominal group is not only realised by a numeral but also involves a word whose class we refer to as 'measure', e.g. 6个科研单位 *6 gè kēyán dānwèi* '6 research institutes', 25名科研人员 *25 míng kēyán rényuán* '25 researchers' in the above paragraph. The most commonly used measure in Chinese is 个 *gè*; other measures serve to specify the shape or nature of the quantified entity; for example, 名 *míng* is used as a measure for people, 张 *zhāng* for thin objects, 辆 *liàng* for land vehicles, etc.

A function and class analysis of the nominal group 8个断面 *8 gè duànmiàn* '8 sections' is presented below as example (56). Here the Measurer function is analysed as being realised by a word complex, involving a hypotactic relationship formed by a numeral and a measure word class depending on that numeral.

(56)

| Example | 8个断面 | | |
|---|---|---|---|
| Transliteration | 8 | gè | duànmiàn |
| **group class** | nominal group | | |
| **group function** | Measurer | | Thing |
| **complex class** | word complex | | |
| **complex function** | α | β | |
| **word class** | numeral | measure | common noun |
| Gloss | 8 | | section |
| Translation | '8 sections' | | |

The Measurer function can also be realised by a word complex involving an inexact number, e.g. 30多个国家 *30 duō gè guójiā* '**more than 30** countries' in our focus text. This nominal group is analysed for function and class below, where 30多 *30 duō* 'more than 30' and the measure 个 *gè* form a hypotactic relationship (α and β); within the α, another layer of hypotaxis is added, with the quantifier 多 *duō* 'many' dependent on the numeral 30.[34] The quantifier can also appear alone without a numeral, e.g. 多个国家 *duō gè guójiā* '**many countries**' (modified from the previous example). Analysis of both examples are presented below as (57) and (57').

---

[34] In such a structure the numeral realising the α function must be a multiple of ten, e.g. 100多 *100 duō* 'more than 100'. It is ungrammatical to say e.g. *8多 *8 duō* 'more than eight', *95多 *95 duō* 'more than 95'.

## 2.4 Chinese Nominal Group Resources

(57)

| Example | 30多个国家 | | | |
|---|---|---|---|---|
| Transliteration | *30* | *duō* | *gè* | *guójiā* |
| **group class** | nominal group | | | |
| **group function** | Measurer | | | Thing |
| **complex class** | word complex | | | |
| **complex function** | α | | β | |
| **complex class** | word complex | | | |
| **complex function** | α | β | | |
| **word class** | numeral | quantifier | measure | common noun |
| Gloss | 30 | many | | country |
| Translation | 'more than 30 countries' | | | |

(57')

| Example | 多个国家 | | |
|---|---|---|---|
| Transliteration | *duō* | *gè* | *guójiā* |
| **group class** | nominal group | | |
| **group function** | Measurer | | Thing |
| **complex class** | word complex | | |
| **complex function** | α | β | |
| **word class** | quantifier | measure | common noun |
| Gloss | many | | country |
| Translation | 'many countries' | | |

A nominal group only allows for one Measurer function, which tends to precede the Epithet in structure, e.g. 一片绿油油的海藻 *yī piàn lǜyóuyóu de hǎizǎo* 'one mass of green seaweed', 一场突如其来的海洋自然灾害 *yī chǎng tūrūqílái de hǎiyáng zìrán zāihài* 'one unexpected ocean natural disaster'. The latter example is analysed below.

(58)

| Example | 一场突如其来的海洋自然灾害 | | | | | | |
|---|---|---|---|---|---|---|---|
| Transliteration | *yī* | *chǎng* | *tūrūqílái* | *de* | *hǎiyáng* | *zìrán* | *zāihài* |
| **group class** | nominal group | | | | | | |
| **group function** | Measurer | | Epithet | | Classifier | Classifier | Thing |
| **complex class** | word complex | | word complex | | | | |
| **complex function** | α | β | α | β | | | |
| **word class** | numeral | measure | adjective | clitic | c. noun | c. noun | c. noun |
| Gloss | one | | unexpected | | ocean | nature | disaster |
| Translation | 'one unexpected ocean natural disaster' | | | | | | |

However, as indicated above, the Measurer can follow the Epithet as well, e.g. 绿油油的一片海藻 *lǜyóuyóu de yī piàn hǎizǎo* 'one mass of green seaweed', 突如其来的一场海洋自然灾害 *tūrūqílái de yī chǎng hǎiyáng zìrán zāihài* 'one unexpected ocean natural disaster'. The latter example is analysed as (58').

(58')

| Example | 突如其来的一场海洋自然灾害 | | | | | | |
|---|---|---|---|---|---|---|---|
| Transliteration | *tūrūqílái* | *de* | *yī* | *chǎng* | *hǎiyáng* | *zìrán* | *zāihài* |
| **group class** | nominal group | | | | | | |
| **group function** | Epithet | | Measurer | | Classifier | Classifier | Thing |
| **complex class** | word complex | | word complex | | | | |
| **complex function** | α | β | α | β | | | |
| **word class** | adjective | clitic | numeral | measure | c. noun | c. noun | c. noun |
| Gloss | unexpected | | one | | ocean | nature | disaster |
| Translation | 'one unexpected ocean natural disaster' | | | | | | |

Finally, let's consider another kind of complex structure in relation to the Measurer function. The measure in the word complex realising the Measurer may sometimes be preceded by an adjective, e.g. 一大批基础数据和资料 *yī dà pī jīchǔ shùjù hé zīliào* 'one **big** batch of basic statistics and data' – analysed for function and class below. This reflects a similarity between a measure word and a noun in that they both can be described by an adjective. Other examples of the numeral-adjective-measure syntagm are: 一长串 *yī cháng chuàn* 'one long string', 两小块 *liǎng xiǎo kuài* 'two small chunks', 三满碗 *sān mǎn wǎn* 'three full bowls'. However, the occurrence of an adjective before a measure word is highly restricted; only a small number of monosyllabic adjectives can be thus deployed, and such an adjective cannot be graded, e.g. *一更长串 *yī gèng cháng chuàn* 'one longer string', *两很小块 *liǎng hěn xiǎo kuài* 'two very small chunks'.

(59)

| Example | 一大批基础数据和资料 | | | | | | |
|---|---|---|---|---|---|---|---|
| Transliteration | *yī* | *dà* | *pī* | *jīchǔ* | *shùjù* | *hé* | *zīliào* |
| **group class** | nominal group | | | | | | |
| **group function** | Measurer | | | Classifier | Thing | | |
| **complex class** | word complex | | | | noun complex | | |
| **complex function** | α | β | | | 1 | +2 | |
| **complex class** | | word complex | | | | word complex | |
| **complex function** | | β | α | | | β | α |
| **word class** | numeral | adjective | measure | c. noun | c. noun | conj. | c. noun |
| Gloss | one | big | batch | basis | statistics | and | data |
| Translation | 'one big batch of basic statistics and data' | | | | | | |

## 2.4 Chinese Nominal Group Resources

In (59) the Measurer function is analysed as being realised by a double-layered word complex. In the first layer, 一 *yī* 'one' and 大批 *dà pī* 'big batch' enter into a hypotactic relationship (α and β respectively); with the β, there is another layer of hypotaxis, with the adjective 大 *dà* 'big' dependent on the measure 批 *pī* 'batch'.[35]

Note in passing that this example also illustrates the realisation of the Thing function through a noun complex, i.e. 数据和资料 *shùjù hé zīliào* 'statistics and data'. This noun complex realises two entities in discourse semantics.

### 2.4.2  Textual Nominal Group Resources

The text we are focusing on here is a written text, instantiating a narrative genre – reconstruing a disastrous event that is evaluated and resolved. As far as the entities involved are concerned, the text as a whole is self-contextualising. The discourse semantic system at stake here is IDENTIFICATION; and the key choice is that of presenting an entity in terms of its identity not being recoverable by a reader on the one hand, and presuming that an entity's identity is in fact recoverable on the other (Figure 2.10).

A nominal group comprising the Thing function only, which is realised by a proper noun or a pronoun, presumes an entity. This kind of nominal group has a minimalist structure. There are a good number of these Thing-only presuming nominal groups in our focus text; two examples are given below and analysed for function and class.

2008年5月31日,大面积浒苔进入**青岛**近岸海域

'On 31 May 2008, expansive sea lettuce invaded **Qingdao**'s offshore area'

越来越多的浒苔随潮水涌上岸,**它们**到达了青岛著名的栈桥

'More and more sea lettuce rushed onto the shore with the tidewater; **they** reached Qingdao's famous pier'

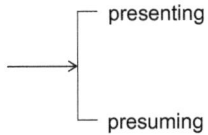

Figure 2.10  Basic IDENTIFICATION system realised by Chinese nominal group systems

---

[35] Note the difference in direction of dependency between the word complexes 大批 *dà pī* 'big batch' here and 大面积 *dà miànjī* 'big area' above: in the former 大 *dà* 'big' is dependent on 批 *pī* 'batch' and thus can be omitted, i.e. 一批基础数据和资料 *yī pī jīchǔ shùjù hé zīliào* 'one batch of basic statistics and data'; in the latter, however, 大 *dà* 'big' is the host on which 面积 *miànjī* 'area' is dependent and thus cannot be omitted. In terms of word class, 大批 *dà pī* 'big batch' represents an adjective ^ measure syntagm, whereas 大面积 *dà miànjī* 'big area' represents an adjective ^ noun syntagm.

(60)

| Examples | 青岛 |
|---|---|
| Transliteration | *Qīngdǎo* |
| **group class** | nominal group |
| **group function** | Thing |
| **word class** | proper noun |
| Gloss | Qingdao |

(61)

| Examples | 它们 |
|---|---|
| Transliteration | *tāmen* |
| **group class** | nominal group |
| **group function** | Thing |
| **word class** | pronoun |
| Gloss | they |

Like English and Spanish, several of the proper names in the Chinese focus text realising the Thing function in the presuming nominal groups involve name complexes (e.g. 孙松所长 *Sūn Sōng Suǒzhǎng* 'Director Sun Song', 第29届北京奥运会 *Dì 29 Jiè Běijīng Àoyùnhuì* 'the 29th Beijing Olympic Games', 中科院海洋所 *Zhōngkēyuàn Hǎiyángsuǒ* 'Institute of Oceanology, Chinese Academy of Sciences'). We'll touch on these structures in our proposed challenge activity in Section 2.5.

In cases where the identity of an entity cannot be thus presumed, an expanded nominal group structure is required. The sea lettuce is introduced for the first time in the text through the nominal group 一片绿油油的海藻 *yī piàn lùyóuyóu de hǎizǎo* 'a mass of green seaweed'. In terms of word class, unlike English and Spanish, Chinese does not have articles; but the presenting function is served by a Measurer involving the numeral 一 *yī* 'one'.

Once the entity is presented, it is presumed afterwards in the text as 这些海藻 *zhèxiē hǎizǎo* '**these pieces of** seaweed'.[36] In the structure of this nominal group, the presuming function is fulfilled by a Deictic, which is realised by a demonstrative determiner, as analysed in (62) below.

---

[36] 这些 *zhèxiē* 'these' is plural in Chinese. Chinese uses the plural determiner for things that exist in separable units – pieces, cubes, slices, etc. In English those things are mass nouns, e.g. *bread, ice, grass, time*. In Chinese they can all take the plural determiner. Here seaweed is seen as being composed of many pieces.

(62)

| Examples | 这些海藻 | |
|---|---|---|
| Transliteration | *zhèxiē* | *hǎizǎo* |
| **group class** | nominal group | |
| **group function** | Deictic | Thing |
| **word class** | demonstrative determiner | common noun |
| Gloss | these | seaweed |
| Translation | 'these pieces of seaweed' | |

The realisation of the Deictic function in a Chinese nominal group can involve measure; in this case the Deictic function, like Measurer one, is realised by a word complex – e.g. **本次**绿潮 *běn cì lǜcháo* 'green tide **of this time**', analysed below for function and class. In a Chinese nominal group, a measure word does not occur alone; it is always part of a word complex, depending on either a numeral or a demonstrative determiner.

(63)

| Example | 本次绿潮 | | |
|---|---|---|---|
| Transliteration | *běn* | *cì* | *lǜcháo* |
| **group class** | nominal group | | |
| **group function** | Deictic | | Thing |
| **complex class** | word complex | | |
| **complex function** | α | β | |
| **word class** | demonstrative determiner | measure | common noun |
| Gloss | this | time | green tide |
| Translation | 'green tide of this time' | | |

In addition to demonstrative determiners, possessives can also be used to realise the Deictic function. A possessive is typically realised through a complex culminating in the clitic 的 *de*, the α function on which the clitic depends can be a personal pronoun (e.g. 我 *wǒ* 'I': 我的 *wǒ de* 'my'; 他们 *tāmen* 'they': 他们的 *tāmen de* 'their'), or an embedded nominal group (e.g. **多家涉海单位**的专家 *duō jiā shè hǎi dānwèi de zhuānjiā* '**many ocean-related** institutes' experts'). The clitic 的 *de* can be omitted, thus dissolving the complex, especially when the Thing is preceded by an Epithet (itself involving such a clitic) (e.g. **青岛**著名的栈桥 *Qīngdǎo zhùmíng de zhànqiáo* '**Qingdao**'s famous pier'). The last two examples are analysed in detail below for function and class.

84    Nominal Group

(64)

| Examples | 青岛著名的栈桥 | | | |
|---|---|---|---|---|
| Transliteration | Qīngdǎo | zhùmíng | de | zhànqiáo |
| **group class** | nominal group | | | |
| **group function** | Deictic | Epithet | | Thing |
| **group/complex class** | [nominal group] | word complex | | |
| **group/complex function** | Thing | α | β | |
| **word class** | proper noun | adjective | clitic | common noun |
| Gloss | Qingdao | famous | | pier |
| Translation | 'Qingdao's famous pier' | | | |

Here the Deictic function is analysed as being realised by an embedded nominal group though it only contains a proper noun 青岛 *Qīngdǎo*; this is because it is potentially expandable, e.g. **美丽的青岛**著名的栈桥 *měilì de Qīngdǎo zhùmíng de zhànqiáo* '**beautiful Qingdao's** famous pier'. By convention we enclose the nominal group 青岛 *Qīngdǎo* in single square brackets to signal that it is an embedded group, realising a function in a structure of the same group/phrase rank.

(65)

| Examples | 多家涉海单位的专家 | | | | | |
|---|---|---|---|---|---|---|
| Transliteration | duō | jiā | shè hǎi | dānwèi | de | zhuānjiā |
| **group class** | nominal group | | | | | |
| **group function** | Deictic | | | | | Thing |
| **complex class** | complex | | | | | |
| **complex function** | α | | | | β | |
| **group class** | [nominal group] | | | | | |
| **group function** | Measurer | | Classifier | Thing | | |
| **complex class** | word complex | | | | | |
| **complex function** | α | β | | | | |
| **word class** | quantifier | measure | verb | c. noun | clitic | c. noun |
| Gloss | many | | relate-ocean | institute | | expert |
| Translation | 'many ocean-related institutes' experts' | | | | | |

In this example 多家涉海单位 *duō jiā shè hǎi dānwèi* 'many ocean-related institutes' realises the Deictic function by way of forestalling the question 'Which experts?'; it is an embedded nominal group with a complex structure, involving a Measurer (realised by a hypotactic word complex), a Classifier

## 2.4 Chinese Nominal Group Resources

(realised by a verb involving a morpheme of 'relate' and one of 'ocean') and a Thing.

Since the Measurer comes sequentially before the Thing in nominal group structure, the measure word in the Measurer plays a key role in determining whether the numeral or quantifier in the Measurer (多 *duō* 'many' in this case) is quantifying the Thing in the embedded nominal group (i.e. 单位 *dānwèi* 'institutes') or the Thing in the entire nominal group (i.e. 专家 *zhuānjiā* 'expert'). It is on the basis of the measure word 家 *jiā* that we know it is *many institutes*, not *many experts*, because this is the measure word used for institutions. Compare this with another nominal group in which the measure word 家 *jiā* is replaced by 位 *wèi*:

多**家**涉海单位的专家
*duō **jiā** shè hǎi dānwèi de zhuānjiā*
'experts from many ocean-related institutes'

多**位**涉海单位的专家
*duō **wèi** shè hǎi dānwèi de zhuānjiā*
'many experts from ocean-related institutes'

The measure word 位 *wèi* is used to refer to people (in a respectful manner), so we know that the Measurer in the latter example 多位 *duōwèi* 'many' functions in the ranking nominal group rather than the embedded one.

In some cases a nominal group needs a Qualifier function to exclusively identify an entity. The Qualifier function is always realised by a complex composed of an α function, which can be realised either by an embedded coverbal phrase[37] or by an embedded clause, and a β function realised by the clitic 的 *de*. Unlike English and Spanish, in Chinese nominal group structure, the Qualifier precedes the Thing function. Two examples from our focus text are presented below, each with a Qualifier specifying the exact identity of the entity.

**关于浒苔的**各种科学数据
***guānyú hǔtái de** gè zhǒng kēxué shùjù*
'various scientific statistics **about the sea lettuce**'

---

[37] The coverbal phrase is regarded as functionally equivalent to a prepositional phrase in English (Halliday and McDonald, 2004, p. 317; Li, 2017, p. 349), and formed by the combination of a coverb and a following nominal group. The coverb is called a 'prepositive verb' in Halliday (1956); it is a subclass of verb and functions as minor Process.

(66)

| Examples | 关于浒苔的各种科学数据 | | | | | |
|---|---|---|---|---|---|---|
| Transliteration | guānyú hǔtái | de | gè | zhǒng | kēxué | shùjù |
| group class | nominal group | | | | | |
| group function | Qualifier | | Deictic | | Classifier | Thing |
| complex class | complex | | word complex | | | |
| complex function | α | β | α | β | | |
| class | [coverbal phrase] | clitic | demonstrative pronoun | measure | c. noun | c. noun |
| Gloss | about sea lettuce | | each | kind | science | statistics |
| Translation | 'various scientific statistics about the sea lettuce' | | | | | |

**空地上晾晒的**一片绿油油的海藻
***kòngdì shàng liàngshài de** yī piàn lǜyóuyóu de hǎizǎo*
'a mass of green seaweed **that is being dried on the ground**'

(67)

| Examples | 空地上晾晒的一片绿油油的海藻 | | | | | | | |
|---|---|---|---|---|---|---|---|---|
| Transliteration | kòngdì shàng liàngshài | de | yī | piàn | lǜyóuyóu | de | hǎizǎo | |
| group class | nominal group | | | | | | | |
| group function | Qualifier | | Measurer | | Epithet | | Thing | |
| complex class | complex | | word complex | | word complex | | | |
| complex function | α | β | α | β | α | β | | |
| class | [[clause]] | clitic | numeral | measure | adjective | clitic | c. noun | |
| Gloss | dry on the ground | | one | expanse | green | | seaweed | |
| Translation | 'a mass of green seaweed that is being dried on the ground' | | | | | | | |

By convention we enclose the clause 空地上晾晒 *kòngdì shàng liàngshài* 'dry on the ground' in double square brackets to signal that it is an embedded clause, realising a function in a structure of a lower group/phrase rank.

When there is more than one Qualifier in a nominal group, typically both Qualifiers are realised by a complex structure, e.g. 科学家收集的关于浒苔的各种科学数据 *kēxuéjiā shōují de guānyú hǔtái de gè zhǒng kēxué shùjù* 'various scientific statistics about the sea lettuce that scientists collected'. This is unlike the multiple-Epithet structure where typically only the last Epithet is realised by a word complex.

## 2.4 Chinese Nominal Group Resources

Although the Qualifier function is positioned before the Thing in Chinese nominal group structure, it does not necessarily come in the initial position of the structure, as the above two examples might suggest. Either the Deictic or the Measurer function can precede the Qualifier – for example:

关于浒苔的各种科学数据 (**Qualifier** ^ Deictic)
***guānyú hǔtái de** gè zhǒng kēxué shùjù*
各种关于浒苔的科学数据 (Deictic ^ **Qualifier**)
gè zhǒng ***guānyú hǔtái** de kēxué shùjù*
'various scientific statistics **about the sea lettuce**'

在空地上晾晒的一片绿油油的海藻 (Qualifier ^ Measurer)[38]
*zài vkòngdì shàng liàngshài de **yī piàn** lùyóuyóu de hǎizǎo*
一片在空地上晾晒的绿油油的海藻 (Measurer ^ Qualifier)
***yī piàn** zài kòngdì shàng liàngshài de lùyóuyóu de hǎizǎo*
'**a mass of** green seaweed **that is being dried on the ground**'

### 2.4.3 Chinese Nominal Group Systems

In Sections 2.4.1 and 2.4.2, we have introduced a preliminary outline of Chinese nominal group structure, approaching from above in terms of the discourse semantic systems of IDEATION and IDENTIFICATION, and then reasoning from around and below in terms of nominal group system and structure. In this section we will present Chinese nominal group systems. For system network conventions see Martin, Wang and Zhu (2013) and Appendix 1 in this volume.

As we did with English and Spanish, as an initial step we set aside elliptical nominal groups ('Thing-less' groups such as 厚厚一层 ⊘ *hòuhòu yī céng* ⊘ 'a thick layer (of ⊘)'). We then distinguish Thing-only nominal groups designating a presumed entity from nominal groups specifying an entity. And designating nominal groups are divided into those using a proper name to designate an entity and those using a pronoun. These systems and their interdependencies are outlined in Figure 2.11.

The realisation statements relating features in these systems to their structural consequences are compiled in Table 2.8. For realisation statement conventions see Martin, Wang and Zhu (2013) and Appendix 1. Here the '+' specifies the inclusion of a Function; the ':' specifies the realisation of a Function by a class.

---

[38] Note that we add a coverb 在 *zài* 'in, on, at' at the beginning of nominal group in (67) to avoid ambiguity. If the Measurer in (67) is positioned before the Qualifier the nominal group would be 一片空地上晾晒的绿油油的海藻 *yī piàn kòngdì shàng liàngshài de lùyóuyóu de hǎizǎo*, where the Measurer 一片 *yī piàn* 'one expanse of' can quantify/determine either 空地 *kòngdì* 'ground' or 海藻 *hǎizǎo* 'seaweed', since the measure 片 *piàn* 'expanse' can be used for either ground or seaweed.

88  Nominal Group

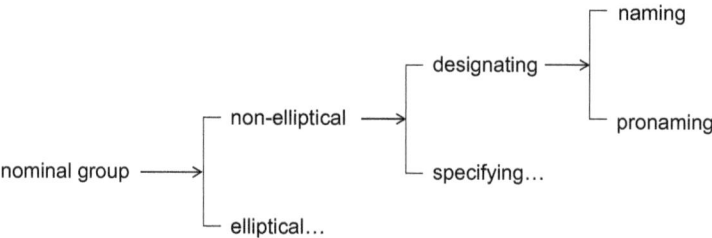

Figure 2.11  General Chinese nominal group systems

Table 2.8 *Realisation statements for general Chinese nominal group features*

| non-elliptical | +Thing |
| --- | --- |
| naming | Thing: proper name |
| pronaming | Thing: pronoun |

The feature [specifying] opens up five simultaneous systems, allowing the nominal group to optionally classify, describe, quantify, determine and/or qualify an entity. As we have seen above, the features [classifying] and [describing] are in fact recursive options, since more than one Classifier or Epithet may be required. As we did with English and Spanish, we have not taken the step of formalising this recursion in the network below.

The feature [describing] selects between [dimensioning] and not, since the adjective in such nominal groups can be optionally followed by a noun realising dimension (e.g. 大面积的浒苔 *dà miànjī de hǔtái* 'expansive sea lettuce').

The feature [quantifying] is subclassified as [exact] or [inexact] to distinguish digital (e.g. **8**个断面 *8 gè duànmiàn* '**8** sections') from general (e.g. 多位专家 *duō wèi zhuānjiā* '**many** experts') quantifications. The feature [exact] can further select between [gradable] (e.g. 一**大**批基础数据和资料 *yī dà pī jīchǔ shùjù hé zīliào* 'one **big** batch of basic statistics and data') and not. The feature [inexact] can select [numeric] where the quantifier is preceded by a numeral, e.g. **30**多个国家 *30 duō gè guójiā* '**more than 30** countries'.

The feature [determining] is subclassified as [demonstrative] and [possessive]. The [demonstrative] selects further between [measuring] and not, depending on whether a measure is used after the demonstrative determiner (e.g. 本**次**绿潮 *běn cì lùcháo* 'green tide of this **time**'). The [possessive] selects further from two simultaneous systems. One chooses between [pronominal] and [embedding], featuring a Deictic function realised by a pronoun (e.g. 我们国家 *wǒmen guójiā* '**our** country') and an embedded nominal group (e.g. [美丽的青岛]著名的栈桥 [*měilì de Qīngdǎo*] *zhùmíng de zhànqiáo* '[**beautiful Qingdao**'s] famous pier') respectively. Both subtypes can optionally involve a complex structure with the clitic 的 *de* (e.g. 我们**的**国家 *wǒmen de guójiā* 'our country', [美丽的青岛]**的**著名的栈桥 [*měilì de Qīngdǎo*] *de zhùmíng de zhànqiáo* '[beautiful Qingdao's] famous pier'), hence a simultaneous system distinguishing between [complex] and not.

The feature [qualifying] is subclassified as [phrasal] or [clausal], reflecting the realisational features of the Qualifier function in the nominal group structure. These specifying systems and their interdependencies are outlined in Figure 2.12.

The realisation statements relating features in these specifying systems to their structural consequences are compiled in Table 2.9.

An overall look at the nominal group systems we have built up is provided in Figure 2.13. The description is, of course, just a glimpse of Chinese nominal group system and structure; however, it is an improved analysis in relation to Wang (2020a).

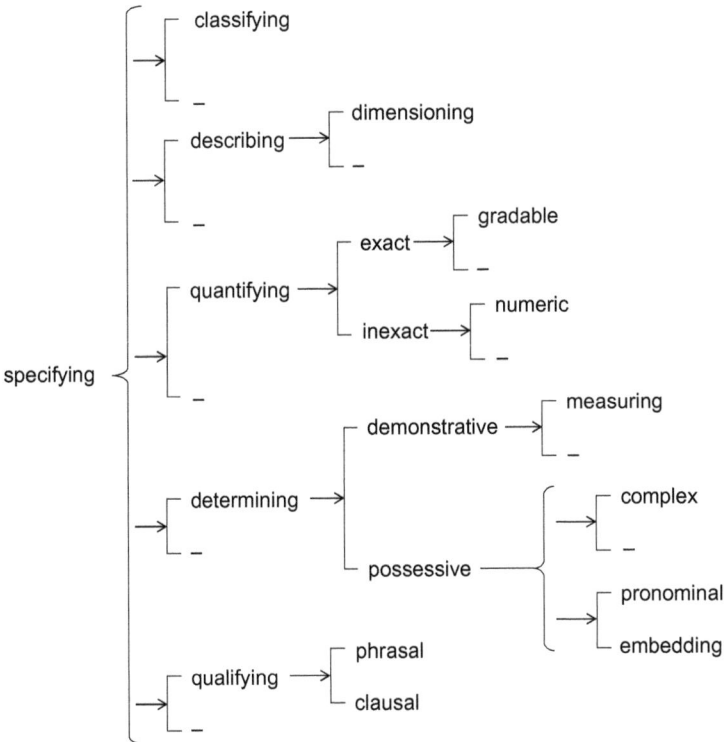

Figure 2.12 More delicate Chinese nominal group systems

Table 2.9 *Realisations statements for more delicate Chinese nominal group features*

| classifying | +Classifier; Classifier ^ Thing |
|---|---|
| describing | +Epithet; Epithet → Classifier; Epithet: word complex; β: clitic (*de*) |
| non-dimensioning | α: adjective |
| dimensioning | α: word complex (α: adjective; β: dimension noun) |
| quantifying | +Measurer; Measurer → Classifier; Measurer: word complex |
| exact | α: numeral |
| gradable | β: word complex (α: measure; β: adjective) |
| non-gradable | β: measure |
| inexact | β: measure |
| numeric | α: word complex (α: numeral; β: quantifier) |
| non-numeric | α: quantifier |
| determining | +Deictic; Deictic → Classifier |
| non-measuring demonstrative | Deictic: demonstrative determiner |
| measuring demonstrative | Deictic: word complex; α: demonstrative determiner; β: measure |
| complex pronominal possessive | Deictic: word complex; α: pronoun; β: clitic (*de*) |
| non-complex pronominal possessive | Deictic: pronoun |
| complex embedding possessive | Deictic: word complex; α: [nominal group]; β: clitic (*de*) |
| non-complex embedding possessive | Deictic: [nominal group] |
| qualifying | +Qualifier; Qualifier → Epithet; Qualifier: word complex; β: clitic (*de*) |
| phrasal | α: [coverbal phrase] |
| clausal | α: [[clause]] |

*Note*: In the structure specification column, '+' indicates the presence of a Function, '^' indicates sequence (originally for Functions, here for classes and the lexical item de as well), ':' indicates the realisation of a Function by a class, and the arrow '→' indicates the relative sequencing of Functions, where present.

## 2.5 Proper Name Challenge

For those of you familiar with other languages, we trust that we have now modelled an approach to nominal group system and structure that you will find instructive. For those of you familiar with English, Spanish or Chinese, we note that the descriptions introduced above have been provided for pedagogic

## 2.5 Proper Name Challenge

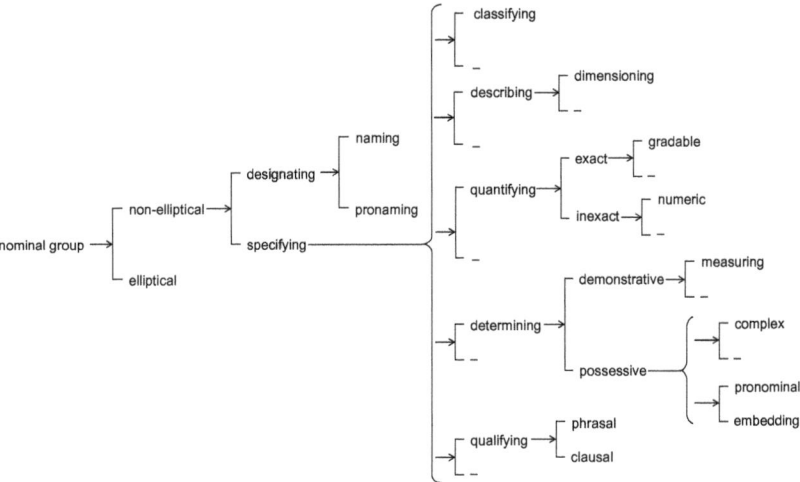

Figure 2.13 Chinese nominal group systems

purposes. They are both preliminary and provisional – SFL grammarians working in both the Sydney and Cardiff models have pushed the description of English beyond what we have presented here (see, for example, Matthiessen, 1995; Halliday and Matthiessen, 2014; Fontaine, 2017 and Fontaine and Schönthal, 2019). Spanish nominal group grammar is further explored from the perspective of SFL in Quiroz and Martin (2021); see Lavid, Arús and Zamorano-Mansilla (2010) for an alternative description to that offered here. For related descriptions of Chinese nominal groups, see Li (2017) and Fang (2022). Turning to other languages, four special issues of *Word* 67(3), 67(4), 68(1) and 68(2) are devoted to SFL descriptions of nominal groups (Doran, Martin and Zhang 2021a, 2021b, 2022a, 2022b).

One suggestion we make here as far as a hands-on engagement with system and structure is concerned has to do with the grammar of proper names, which have not been properly described from an SFL perspective for English, Spanish or Chinese. The challenge we are posing here has to do with whether the nominal group grammar we built up for English, Spanish and Chinese above can be generalised for proper names for people, places, agencies, dates and so on, or whether a specialised proper name grammar is required. Above we simply treated all proper names as realising the Thing function, no matter how many words were involved. This says nothing about their internal structure, which we have left open.

Some of the English data you will need to consider, taken from the Bondi Beach text, is presented below. As you can see there is a wide variety of structures involved, dealing with proper names for people, agencies, places (including e-mail addresses), dates and times.

Bill Jenkins
Peter FitzSimons
Diane Touzell

Waverly Library

Sydney
Sydney town
Australia

pfitzsimons@smh.com.au

February 6, 1938
"Black Sunday"

three o'clock

The Ola Maldita text is even richer as far as proper names are concerned, since it introduces so many people and places as it unfolds. A sample of its proper names for people, agencies, places and things is presented below. One interesting difference between the languages we can see at a glance is the frequency of what looks like a definite determiner (*el*, *la* 'the')[39] in the Spanish names. And there are obvious graphological differences as far as upper- and lower-case letters are concerned. In addition, although not exemplified in our Ola Maldita stories, attitudinal adjectives are more commonly found in Spanish proper names than in English (e.g. *el valiente capitán Ibarra* 'courageous Captain Ibarra'). Do Spanish proper names in fact share more of their grammar with other nominal groups than is the case for English ones?

El capitán Ibarra 'Captain Ibarra'
la Presidenta Bachelet 'President Bachelet'
el sargento Valladares 'Valladares Sergeant'
el Gringo

Mario Quiroz Leal
José Ibarra
Ibarra

Emilito

---

[39] Note that the *el/la* determiners in Spanish names do not alternate with other determiners (e.g. *un/una* 'a', *ese/esa* 'that') as they would in specifying nominal groups; this is one respect in which proper names have a relatively restricted meaning potential compared to specifying nominal groups which choose freely for meaning realised through Numerative, Epithet, Classifier and Qualifier functions.

## 2.5 Proper Name Challenge

la Armada 'The Navy'
la Capitanía de Puerto 'Harbour Master's Office'
el Servicio Hidrográfico y Oceanográfico de la Armada (SHOA)
la radio Biobío 'Biobío radio'

Concepción
San Javier
Orrego
Chile
el río Maule 'Maule river'
la isla Orrego 'Orrego island'
el cerro O'Higgins 'O'Higgins Hill'
el Maule
el Golfo de Penas
la playa de Dichato 'Dichato beach'

el Pinita

In the Sea Lettuce text there are plenty of proper names as well, including names of people, places, institutions, ships, events, slogans, etc. – with a wide variety of structures. Unlike English and Spanish, complex names of places or institutions in Chinese are arranged from general to particular, e.g. 山东省青岛市 *Shāndōng Shěng Qīngdǎo Shì* 'Shandong Province Qingdao City' (cf. proper English translation 'Qingdao City, Shandong Province'), 中科院海洋所 *Zhōngkēyuàn Hǎiyángsuǒ* 'Chinese Academy of Sciences, Institute of Oceanology' (cf. proper English translation 'Institute of Oceanology, Chinese Academy of Sciences'). Chinese zeroes in on location and institution, whereas English and Spanish moves out. In addition, some proper names involve classifying, describing or evaluating elements.

全国人大常委会副委员长、中国科学院院长路甬祥 *Quánguó Réndà Chángwěihuì Fù Wěiyuánzhǎng, Zhōngguó Kēxuéyuàn Yuànzhǎng Lù Yǒngxiáng* 'Lu Yongxiang, Vice Chairman of the National People's Congress and President of the Chinese Academy of Sciences
青岛市副市长张惠 *Qīngdǎo Shì Fù Shìzhǎng Zhāng Huì* 'Zhang Hui, deputy mayor of Qingdao City'
海洋研究所党委书记、所长孙松 *Hǎiyáng Yánjiūsuǒ Dǎngwěi Shūjì, Suǒzhǎng Sūn Sōng* 'Sun Song, Secretary of CPC Committee and Director of the Institute of Oceanology'

青岛 *Qīngdǎo* 'Qingdao'
崂山 *Láoshān* 'Mount Lao'
黄海 *Huánghǎi* 'Yellow Sea'

中国科学院海洋研究所 *Zhōngkēyuàn Hǎiyángsuǒ* 'Chinese Academy of Sciences, Institute of Oceanology'
山东省委省政府 *Shāndōng Shěngwěi Shěngzhèngfǔ* 'Shandong Provincial CPC Committee, Provincial Government'

青岛市科学技术局 *Qīngdǎo Shì Kēxué Jìshù Jú* 'Qingdao Municipal Bureau of Science and Technology'
中国海洋大学 *Zhōngguó Hǎiyáng Dàxué* 'Ocean University of China'

"科学三号"科考船 *'Kēxué sān hào' kēkǎo chuán* 'Science No. 3 scientific research ship'

第29届北京奥运会 *Dì 29 jiè Běijīng Àoyùnhuì* 'The 29th Beijing Olympic Games'

"绿色奥运" *'Lǜsè Àoyùn'* 'Green Olympics'
"平安奥运" *'Píng'ān Àoyùn'* 'Safe Olympics'

There is lots to work on here. For a serious account, of course, it is necessary to move well beyond the data considered in this chapter, and collect texts from a wide range of registers. Terms of endearment (e.g. *honey, love, darling, mate*, etc.) are completely missing from the Bondi Beach, Ola Maldita and Sea Lettuce texts, but are an essential part of a more complete picture. Also missing are titles (e.g. *señor, señora, señorita, don, doña, doctor, doctora, profesor, profesora, profe, Su Excelencia Michele Bachelet, Su Santidad Francisco*) and post-nominal letters signifying honours and roles in English (e.g. *FAHA* 'Fellow of the Australian Academy of the Humanities', *VC* 'Victoria Cross', *QC* 'Queen's Council', *JP* 'Justice of the Peace', *MP* 'Member of Parliament'). This should keep you busy for quite a while.

# 3 Verbal Group

## 3.1 Approaching from Above

In this chapter we will approach verbal groups from an ideational and then an interpersonal perspective. In terms of field (ideational context), verbal groups construe both a dynamic and a static perspective on phenomena. Dynamically speaking, they provide resources for characterising the nature of an activity and its temporal relation to other activities; statically speaking, they provide resources for construing relationships among items and properties. The outline of field in Figure 3.1 is based on Doran and Martin (2021).

As far as discourse semantics is concerned (Halliday and Matthiessen, 1999; Hao, 2015, 2020a), with reference to this ideational perspective on meaning verbal groups play a role in configuring elements in figures (the system of IDEATION) and sequencing figures in relation to one another (the system of CONNEXION). In relation to IDEATION, verbal groups take responsibility for specifying the central occurrence element in occurrence figures and specifying relationships in state figures. From a lexicogrammatical perspective, the

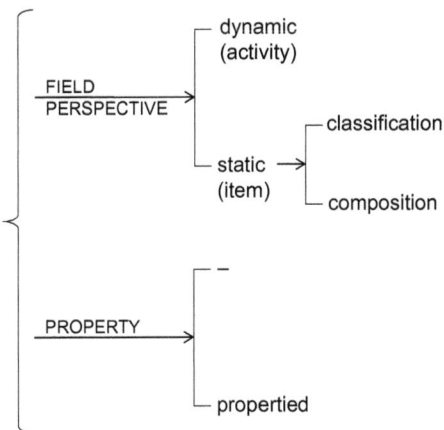

Figure 3.1 Field variables

relevant nuclear function in the structure of the verbal group is the Event. Verbal groups also tend to play a role in configuring elements within figures, including entities – as we will exemplify in Section 3.3 in terms of the lexicogrammatical realisation of entities through pronominal clitics in Spanish. In terms of CONNEXION, verbal groups contribute to the sequencing of figures by temporally positioning them in relation to one another (in co-operation with other linking resources realised through conjunctions and phrases locating goings on in time). An outline of the ideational discourse semantic resources we are flagging here is provided in Figure 3.2.

In terms of tenor (interpersonal context), verbal groups provide key resources for enacting social relations of power (status) and solidarity (contact) among interlocutors – positioning interlocutors and repositioning them as more or less involved with, and more or less on the same footing as, one another. These key dimensions are outlined in Figure 3.3.

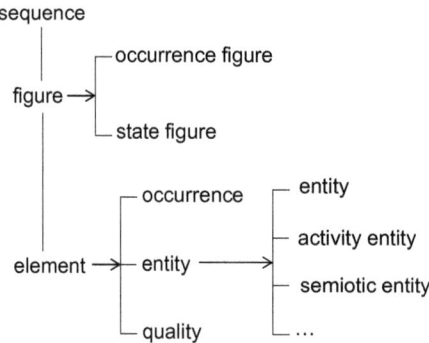

Figure 3.2  Basic ideational discourse semantic resources

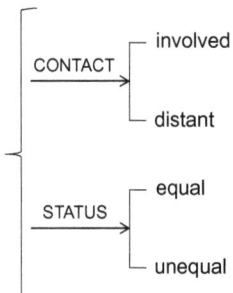

Figure 3.3  Tenor variables

As far as interpersonal discourse semantic systems are concerned, verbal groups play a role in positioning moves in dialogue and in adjusting the play of voices around these moves. NEGOTIATION is concerned with the to and fro of dialogue as speakers make moves in conversation (Martin, 1992; Martin and Rose, 2007). Verbal groups play a role in specifying the kinds of move that are made, as we explore in much more detail in relation to MOOD in Chapter 4. In addition, verbal groups make important contributions to the realisation of APPRAISAL, its subsystem of ENGAGEMENT in particular. Verbal group systems such as MODALITY, EVIDENTIALITY, POLARITY and ADDRESSEE DEFERENCE all work to adjust the play of voices implicated in the negotiation of a conversational exchange (Martin and White, 2005; Martin, Quiroz and Figueredo, 2021).

In Section 3.2 below we explore English verbal group resources, before turning to Spanish resources in Section 3.3 and Chinese resources in 3.4. In each section we first consider ideational resources, and then bring in interpersonal resources. Our focus text for English this time round is a Youtube video titled Let's Talk. | Random Chatty Vlog (https://youtu.be/YRx-zDoPbVw), which we refer to as the Chatty Vlog text (Appendix 2.2). For Spanish we continue with the stories about the famous earthquake and tidal wave in Maule and Bío-bío, Chile in 2010 (Appendix 3.1), our Ola Maldita text. For Chinese we use a journalistic interview with former curator of the Palace Museum in Beijing as our focus text, referred to as Interview with Curator text (Appendix 4.2). In Section 3.5 we present an analysis challenge in relation to using a corpus to explore recursive systems in verbal groups.

## 3.2   English Verbal Group Resources

### *3.2.1   Ideational Verbal Group Resources*

In this section we focus on finite verbal groups, setting aside discussion of non-finite verbal groups for Section 3.2.2 below. Our initial focus is on TENSE systems, exploring the way these systems locate figures in relation to the moment of speaking and sequence them in relation to one another. We begin with a consideration of PRIMARY TENSE. This system positions occurrence and state figures in relation to the time a text is spoken to be heard or written to be read – as manifested at that moment, as preceding, or as following on. We then move on to combinations of tenses in verbal groups drawing on SECONDARY TENSE. These SECONDARY TENSE selections are optional; but when selected they take PRIMARY TENSE as their point of departure and further position figures in relation to one another – as happening at the same time, as preceding, or as following on.

First, PRIMARY TENSE. From the perspective of field, the main work the Chatty Vlog text attends to has to do with sequencing goings on in the personal activities she is presenting to her followers. The vlogger's verbal groups position these activities in relation to the time she makes the vlog. She uses simple present tense for figures construing states and desires coinciding with that moment, for example *needs*, *are* and *need* in her 'outro' below.

Clock is dinging, Charlie **needs** me, kids **are** hungry so I better go. Thank you for watching guys. [break] I will see you Thursday at for a day in the life video. It will be live at two PM eastern standard time. So don't miss it. Thanks for watching guys. Bye. [child walks in] You **need** a drink. OK. [reaches to turn off camera]

She uses simple past tense for figures construing states and occurrences preceding that moment, for example *had, filmed, was, brought, started, got, was* and *thought* in her 'intro' below.

Hi everybody and I am going to do just a random chatty vlog for you guys. I **had** a video for today. I **filmed** it and I was going to edit it. It **was** a type one Tuesday. I was showing all the diabetes supplies like the extra supplies we **brought** on vacation but I had bent down like before I **started** filming and my shirt **got** caught in my bra so it was it was like sitting- it just- it's all I could see the whole time so I **was** like "I am not posting this video" because that's all people would be looking at. So this is what you get today. So many of you actually love these sit down chatty videos so I **thought** it would be kind of fun.

And she uses future tense for figures that will materialise later on, also illustrated here form her outro (*will see, will be*).

Clock is dinging, Charlie needs me, kids are hungry so I better go. Thank you for watching guys. [break] I **will see** you Thursday at for a day in the life video. It **will be** live at two PM eastern standard time. So don't miss it. Thanks for watching guys. Bye. [child walks in] You need a drink. OK. [reaches to turn off camera]

As we can see, future tense verbal groups are structured differently from present and past verbal groups. Future tense involves two verbs, while present and past tense involve just one. English future tense in other words is realised 'analytically' by a verb (*will* above) preceding the Event; present and past tenses on the other hand are realised 'synthetically' by different inflectional forms of the verb realising the Event (e.g. *had* and *filmed* above). Keep in mind that we are analysing verbal groups here, not verbs. This means we can bring both analytic and synthetic realisations of tense into the picture (i.e. both the 'syntax' of verbal groups and the morphology of the verbs constituting them are relevant). Grammarians who argue that English has no future tense[1] are basing their analysis on verb morphology, at word rank, not tense choices, at group rank, as we are doing here.

---

[1] For an in-depth discussion of this issue, see Matthiessen (1996) and Halliday and Matthiessen (1999).

3.2 English Verbal Group Resources 99

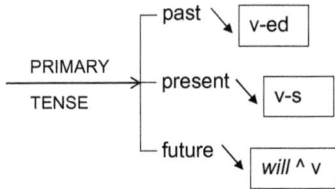

Figure 3.4 PRIMARY TENSE in English

The verbal group system we are discussing here, called PRIMARY TENSE, is shown in Figure 3.4. The realisation statements specify the form the verbs involved (v-ed for past, v-s for present and *will* ^ v for future).

Now, SECONDARY TENSE. Exploring further, we encounter several other verbal groups consisting of more than one verb. In her closing phase the vlogger notes that the clock she has primed to warn her when time is up is dinging. For this occurrence she in fact makes two tense selections. Her primary tense choice is present (cf. *will be dinging,* **is** *dinging, was dinging*); in addition, she makes a secondary tense choice of present, realised by the verb *be* (which appears in one of its v-s forms here, i.e. *is*) followed by the v-ing form of the following verb (here *dinging*). This combined 'present in present' tense selection is the favoured choice for English occurrences coinciding with the moment of speaking.

Clock **is dinging**, Charlie needs me, kids are hungry so I better go. Thank you for watching guys.

The same 'present in present' verbal group selection is present in the occurrence figure *am ... posting* in the vlogger's opening remarks.

Her intro also includes a secondary present selection combined with a primary tense past – *was showing* (cf. *will be showing, is showing,* **was showing**). This allows her to stretch out the time involved in showing the diabetes supplies she took on vacation (cf. 'past' *showed,* 'present in past' *was showing*).

It was a type one Tuesday. I **was showing** all the diabetes supplies like the extra supplies we brought on vacation ...

These opening remarks also include a verbal group combining a primary present tense with a secondary future one – *am going to do* (cf. *was going to do,* ***am going to*** *do, will be going to do*).

Hi everybody and I **am going to do** just a random chatty vlog for you guys.

This allows the vlogger to bring what she is about to do (a random chatty blog) closer to the moment of speaking (cf. the future tenses she uses in her closing, *will see* and *will be*, which are about her next vlog, still some time away, not this one). Her secondary future is realised by the word complex *be going to* followed by the v form of the following verb (here *do*).

Secondary future tense is ignored in treatments of English tense by some grammarians (e.g. Huddleston, 1988). But linguists interested in grammaticalisation (e.g. Hopper and Traugott, 2003; Taverniers, 2018) regularly treat *going* in *am going to do* as prototypical grammaticalisation – here grammaticalisation of the lexical verb *go* (which grammaticalisation in turn makes possible its colloquial articulation as *gonna*, discussed below). We will show, however, that secondary future is just as much a part of the English verbal group tense system as primary tense future is. To explore this, let's consider the other secondary future tense in the vlogger's intro:

I had a video for today. I filmed it and I **was going to edit** it.

From a discourse semantic perspective, this secondary future tense clearly positions editing the video after filming it. It works the same way as a tense sequence we might imagine if we travel into the vlogger's past and imagine her preparing for the vlog; then and there she might have said, possibly to herself: *Now I've filmed it, I'll edit it*. The primary and secondary future tense selections are precisely proportional, then as now; the secondary future simply allows the sequence of tenses to be shifted into the past.

Table 3.1 allows us to compare the primary and secondary tense selections just discussed. As a primary tense choice, future positions editing the video as something that will happen after the vlogger proposes doing it; as a secondary tense choice, future positions editing the video as something that would happen after the vlogger proposed doing it.

Reasoning from around, at the level of lexicogrammar, we can take into account the correlations between tense selection and circumstances of location in time. Thus primary future correlates with *later on* in *Now I've filmed it, I'll edit it **later on***; similarly primary past correlates with *that Tuesday* and secondary future with *later on* in *I filmed it and I **was going to edit** it **later on that Tuesday*** (primary past : *that Tuesday* :: secondary future : *later on*). These mirror image relations between primary and secondary tense selections and choices for location in time are outlined in Table 3.2.

Table 3.1 *Comparing primary and secondary future tense*

|  |  |  | moment of speaking |  |
|---|---|---|---|---|
|  | preceding |  | during | following |
|  |  |  |  | *I'll edit it* |
| preceding | during | following |  |  |
|  |  | *I was going to edit it* |  |  |

Table 3.2 *Primary and secondary tense selections in relation to location in time*

|  | tense |  |  | location in time |  |
|---|---|---|---|---|---|
| 'primary future' |  |  | future | afterwards |  |
| I'll edit it |  |  | will | later on |  |
|  |  |  |  |  |  |
| I was going to edit it | was |  | be going to | later on | that Tuesday |
| 'secondary future' |  |  | future | afterwards |  |
| 'primary past' | past |  |  |  | back then |
|  | tense |  |  | location in time |  |

Reasoning from below we can take into account the way in which English phonology reflects the grammaticalisation of the lexical verb *go* as a future tense option. As sometimes reflected in English graphology through the spelling *gonna*, secondary future has the possibility of a very contracted verbal expression:

Hi everybody and I am **gonna** do just a random chatty vlog for you guys.
I was **gonna** edit it later on that night.

This is not possible when the lexical verb *go* is used to specify the Event function in a verbal group, where *go to* is not a syntagm.

I am **going** to Melbourne.
*I am gonna Melbourne.

From various perspectives, then, secondary future is best considered as an integral part of the English tense system. Further argumentation is explored in Matthiessen (1996).

This introductory phase of the vlog also includes the combination of both a primary past and a secondary past selection – *had bent* (cf. *had bent, has bent, will have bent*).

… but I **had bent** down like before I started filming …

Here the secondary past is realised by the verb *have* followed by the v-en form of the following verb (here *bent*).[2] This allows the vlogger to reinforce the sequence of experiences involving her bending down before the start of her filming: *but I **had bent** down like before I **started** filming.* In this example the tense selection co-operates with the explicit conjunctive relation between the figures (realised by *before*); but tense can also be used to sequence figures on

---

[2] For many verbs, including *bend*, the realisation of the v-ed and v-en forms of the verb are identical (cf. **bent** *: had bent :: **showed** : had **shown**).

its own. This happens later on during the vlogger's account of a parking lot incident (sequencing getting into her car before starting to use social media to share a picture; Table 3.3).

And I met up with a Kimmy from the Dodge family and I went to- I wanted to like Instagram a picture of us and Facebook whatever. And as I was doing that I- I **had** just **got** in my car, got my phone and as I **was doing** that some guy was sitting there …

As we can see, the TENSE system does a lot of work setting figures in time and sequencing them in relation to one another. An outline of this work in the phase of text used to illustrate past tense above is provided as Table 3.4. This

Table 3.3 *Tense selection in relation to a sequence of figures*

| preceding experience | following experience |
|---|---|
| I had just got in my car | I was doing that |

Table 3.4 *Locating and sequencing figures in time through tense*

| | preceding | | now | following |
|---|---|---|---|---|
| preceding | then | following | | |
| | | | | am going to do |
| | had | | | |
| | filmed | | | |
| | | was going to edit | | |
| | was | | | |
| | ←was showing→ | | | |
| | brought | | | |
| had bent | | | | |
| | started | | | |
| | got caught | | | |
| | ←was sitting→ | | | |
| | | | 's | |
| | could see | | | |
| | was | | | |
| | "←am not posting→"* | | | |
| | | ←would be looking→ | | |
| | | | is | |
| | | | love | |
| | thought | | | |
| | | would be | | |

\* This verbal group is in a quoting clause, and so uses present tense, reflecting what the vlogger would have actually said at the time (cf. how it might have been reported: *and so I decided I* **wasn't posting** *the video*).

3.2 English Verbal Group Resources 103

phase is repeated below, with all verbal groups highlighted in bold. In the table, '←*xxx*→' is used to notate a secondary present tense selection.

Hi everybody and I **am going to do** just a random chatty vlog for you guys. I **had** a video for today. I **filmed** it and I **was going to edit** it. It **was** a type one Tuesday. I **was showing** all the diabetes supplies like the extra supplies we **brought** on vacation but I **had bent** down like before I **started** filming and my shirt **got caught** in my bra so it was it **was** like **sitting-** it just- it**'s** all I **could see** the whole time so I **was** like "I **am not posting** this video" because that**'s** all people **would be looking** at. So this **is** what you get today. So many of you actually **love** these sit down chatty videos so I **thought** it **would be** kind of fun.

Let's take a moment here to take stock of the patterns emerging from our exploration of tense choices in these phases of the vlog. Table 3.5 shows the different English verb classes involved in the realisation of tenses at word rank. We've included here the verbs *be* and *have*, which are involved in secondary tenses, and an example of a verb (*show*) with distinct v-ed and v-en forms (*showed, shown*), and a verb (*bend*) with identical v-ed and v-en forms (*bent, bent*). Except for the verb *be*, English only realises person and number in its v-s forms (distinguishing third person singular from the rest: e.g. *has/shows/bends* vs *have/show/bend*). The verb *be* makes further distinctions involving person and number for its v-s form (*I am, you are, s/he is, we are, you are, they are*) and v-ed form (*I was, you were, s/he was, we were, you were, they were*). As we can see, English verb morphology rarely provides much information about the relation of an occurrence to the entities in its figure.

We should also consolidate here the distinctive realisations of the secondary past, present and future tense selections (Figure 3.5).

Table 3.5 *English verb classes exemplified*

| v | be | have | show | bend |
|---|---|---|---|---|
| v-s | am, are, is | have, has | show, shows | bend, bends |
| v-ed | was, were | had | showed | bent |
| v-en | been | had | shown | bent |
| v-ing | being | having | showing | bending |

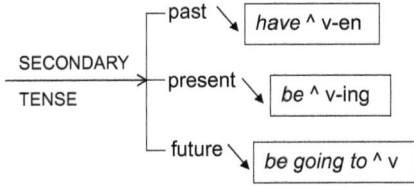

Figure 3.5 Realisation of SECONDARY TENSE choices in English

As the examples discussed above have shown, SECONDARY TENSE is optional. And as the discussion has implied, secondary tenses combine freely with primary ones. What is going on here is that English PRIMARY TENSE choices take the moment of speaking as point of departure and arrange figures as taking place before, during or after that moment. The unfolding text, in other words, shifts into the past, stays in the present or shifts into the future. Once it does so, these temporal locations in the past, present or future can themselves be taken as the point of departure for further tense selections. Tense choice in other words is always relative. The full set of possibilities introduced so far is presented below (for the verb *show*).

past: *showed*
present: *shows*
future: *will show*

past in past: *had shown*
past in present: *has shown*
past in future: *will have shown*

present in past: *was showing*
present in present: *is showing*
present in future: *will be showing*

future in past: *was going to show*
future in present: *is going to show*
future in future: *will be going to show*

Tenses are named from right to left as far as their realisation in verbal group structure is concerned. This naming better captures the sense in which secondary tenses manage time by taking as point of departure the immediately preceding selection from the verbal group network. So the tense combination in *has shown* is referred to as 'past in present' not 'present in past'; the meaning of this verbal group is that something that began in the past is impressing itself upon on the present.

The system network below, Figure 3.6 (a displayed network; Fawcett, 1988) makes room for all twelve possibilities. Each PRIMARY TENSE selection leads to a system in which a secondary tense can be chosen or not. And if a secondary tense is needed, it can be past, present or future. This network accounts for all the tense selections in the Chatty Vlog text.

What we haven't discussed yet is the possibility of additional secondary tense selections, which don't crop up in the vlog. One might have appeared early on in the vlog, which we adjust for illustrative purposes here:

Hi everybody and I am going to do just a random chatty vlog for you guys. I had a video for today. I filmed it and I **had been going to edit** it (when all of a sudden the kids rushed in).

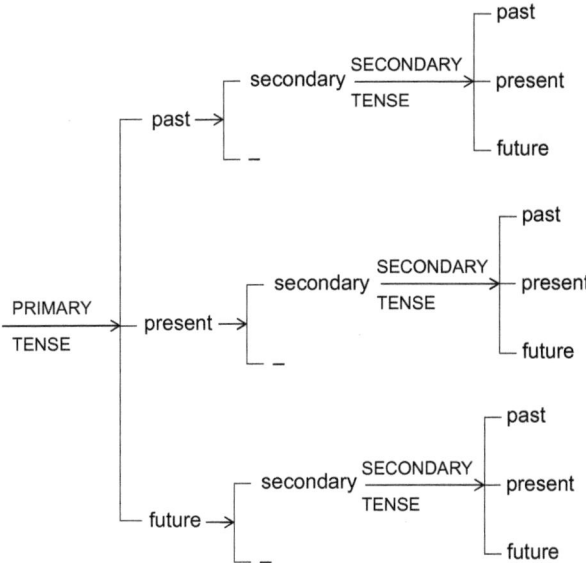

Figure 3.6 English PRIMARY TENSE system in relation to one optional SECONDARY TENSE system

This amended version of the opening involves a secondary present selection (*be going to edit*), a secondary past selection (*have been*) and a primary past selection (*had*). These choices position the vlogger's intention to edit the video in the past before the kids rushed in. We can break this verbal group down in tabular form as follows:

(1)  *had been going to edit*

| v-ed | have ^ v-en | be going to ^ v | edit |
|---|---|---|---|
| past | past | future | event |
| 'future in past in past' | | | |

Halliday and Matthiessen (2014, p. 399) include a number of attested examples involving one primary and two secondary tense selections. Four of these are presented below.

'present in past in present'
So when is this thing scheduled to produce results, Frank? – Oh, it'**s been producing** results for a long time.

'present in past in past'
When **I'd been teaching** apprentices at Vauxhall …

'present in future in present'
They never know in the long vac or in the summer what they **are going to be doing** the next year.

'present in future in future'
We live in Arizona, so they**'ll be going to be traveling** back and forth during the course of the season.

Also missing from the vlog are any examples of passive voice, some of which we need to fill out the picture here. We'll accordingly adapt here the explanations of vlogs and blogs incorporated by our colleague Michele Zappavigna in Martin and Zappavigna (2019).

A 'vlog' (the term **is derived** from 'blog') is a video in which a user recounts, or presents, some form of personal activity (e.g. a 'day in the life' vlog where highlights from their activity over a day **are shown**).

A 'blog' (truncated form of 'weblog') is a website which **is comprised** of posts which **are displayed** in reverse chronological order. Most often they involve personal diary-style entries which **are composed** by individuals; corporations and organisations may also incorporate blogs into their online material.

As we can see from these examples (*is derived, are shown, is comprised, are displayed, are composed*), passive verbal groups are formed in a very similar way to verbal groups with secondary tenses – with passive realised by the verb *be* followed by the v-en form of the following verb (e.g. *shown*).

(2)   *are shown*

| v-s | be ^ v-en | show |
|---|---|---|
| present | passive | event |
| passive 'present' | | |

These passive verbal groups allow Zappavigna to reconfigure entities in her figures to suit her information flow. We will return to the significance of this verbal group resource for clause grammar in Chapters 4, 5 and 6 below.

Passive combines freely with primary and secondary tense selections, as in *'re going to have been pulled out* below (Halliday and Matthiessen, 2014, p. 399):

I think that there's going to be some of that, but for some people they**'re going to have been pulled** back into a process in which they had not participated at all.

(3)   *'re going to have been pulled*

| v-s | be going to ^ v | have ^ v-en | be ^ v-en | pull |
|---|---|---|---|---|
| present | future | past | passive | event |
| passive 'past in future in present' | | | | |

The longer examples Halliday has noted include one primary and up to four secondary tenses. These longer groups may also include passive voice, as in the following attested example:

'present in past in future in past in future'
It'll've been going to've been being tested every day for about a fortnight soon.

(4)     *'ll've been going to've been being tested*

| will | have ^ v-en | be going to ^ v | have ^ v-en | be ^ v-ing | be ^ v-en | test |
|---|---|---|---|---|---|---|
| future | past | future | past | present | passive | event |
| passive 'present in past in future in past in future' ||||||| 

Halliday (1991/2005, p. 86) presumes a dialogic context for this example along the following lines:

Can I use that machine?
– Sorry, we use it ourselves in the mornings.
– Are you using it now?
– Yes we are.
– Are you going to be using it this afternoon?
– Well no, but it's going to be being tested.
– What! It's been going to be being tested now for ages! It'll have been going to've been being tested every day for about a fortnight soon!

The fact that in specific dialogic contexts such as this one English allows up to four secondary tenses shows that what we are in fact dealing with here is a recursive system. So instead of extending the displayed network introduced in Figure 3.6 to allow for three more rounds of secondary tense choice (and running out of screen or page width in the process), we can introduce a recursive SECONDARY TENSE system as in the network in Figure 3.7.

This representation better captures the nature of the English tense system as it has evolved over the past millennium. The choice of the feature [secondary] is much less common than not, and so verbal groups involving more than three tenses are rare, and much more likely to crop up in conversation than in written texts (Halliday and James, 1993). In addition, there are three 'stop' rules that block certain combinations of tense choice; these formalise the limits of the English system as far as the evolution of its recursive potential to this point in its history is concerned.

i. secondary future can only be chosen once
ii. secondary present can only be chosen once, as the final choice
iii. the same secondary tense cannot be chosen twice in a row

In SFL the logical component of the ideational metafunction can be defined as comprising all and only recursive systems, realised by univariate structures. This suggests that unlike our analysis of nominal groups in Chapter 2, where we

108    Verbal Group

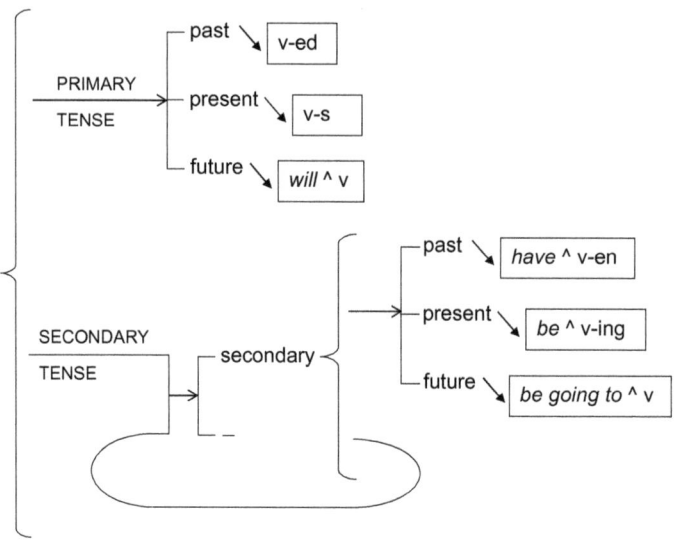

Figure 3.7 English PRIMARY TENSE and recursive SECONDARY TENSE systems

proposed multivariate structures with each function playing a distinct role, for English verbal groups we should propose univariate structures in which the same choices are realised over and over again. We introduce this approach to verbal group structure in the tables below. The Greek letters in this notation capture the dependency relations involved (α as head, β dependent on α, γ on β and so on)[3].

(5)   had been going to edit

| v-ed | have ^ v-en | be going to ^ v | edit |
|------|-------------|-----------------|------|
| past | past        | future          | event |
| α    | β           | γ               | δ    |
| 'future in past in past' ||||

To these univariate functions we can add superscripts indicating the choices from the verbal group network that have been selected: ⁰for present, ⁻ for past, ⁺ for future, ᵖᵃˢˢ for passive and ᵉᵛᵉⁿᵗ for event. This is exemplified for *'re going to have been pulled* below. In the analysis tables we have been developing, the top row records the verbal group being analysed, the second row presents the

---

[3] See Halliday (1965/1981) for an introduction to the distinction between multivariate and univariate structures in SFL, and Halliday (1966/1976, 1979/2002) for their relation to non-recursive and recursive systems, respectively. By convention function labels for hypotactic univariate structures are written in lower-case Greek letters (not upper-case ones).

## 3.2 English Verbal Group Resources

word classes realising its structure, the third row presents the verbal group features being realised, the fourth row presents its structure and the final row presents the name of the tense involved.

(6)

| Example | 're going to have been pulled | | | | |
|---|---|---|---|---|---|
| word class | v-s | be going to ^ v | have ^ v-en | be ^ v-en | pull |
| features | present | future | past | passive | event |
| structure | $\alpha^0$ | $\beta^+$ | $\gamma^-$ | $\delta^{pass}$ | $\varepsilon^{event}$ |
| tense | passive 'past in future in present' | | | | |

The ideational English verbal group systems we have developed to this point in the discussion are consolidated in Figure 3.8 below, along with their realisations in verbal group structure.

### 3.2.2 Interpersonal Verbal Group Resources

English verbal groups have a role to play as far as distinguishing moves in exchange structure is concerned. All of the examples discussed above positioned moves as giving information. And the PRIMARY TENSE selections

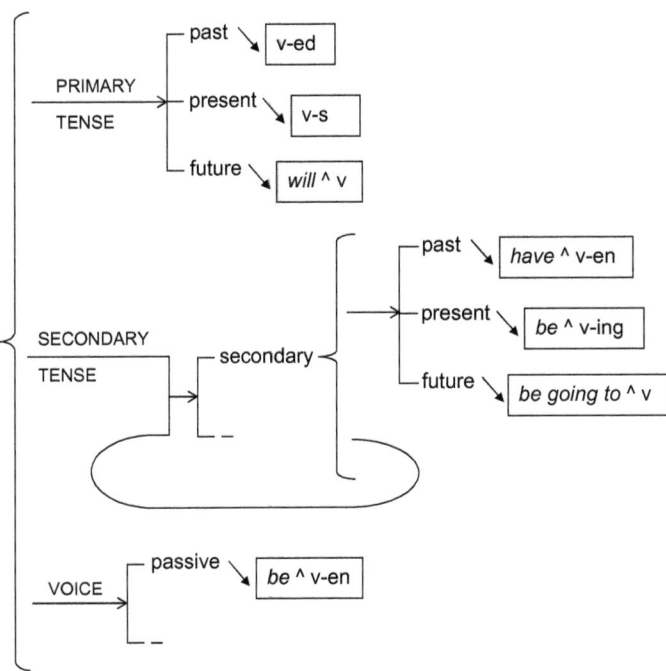

Figure 3.8 English verbal group systems – ideational resources

provided terms making these moves arguable. We can replay part of Halliday's tense example to illustrate this point, highlighting the present primary tense selections in bold:

- **Are** you using it now?
- Yes we **are**.
- **Are** you going to be using it this afternoon?
- Well no (we**'re** not), but it's going to be being tested.

This contribution of the verbal group to exchange structure will be further explored in Chapter 4.

As an alternative to giving information, verbal groups can position moves as demanding goods and services. Moves of this kind are congruently realised by imperative clauses. We had one example in our Bondi Beach text.

**Write** to Peter FitzSimons at pfitzsimons@smh.com.au

Unlike all the verbal groups we have discussed so far, *write* does not select for PRIMARY TENSE. It simply appears in one of its non-finite forms, *write* – verb class v (its other perfective form, *to write*, i.e. *to* ^ v, is introduced below). Using this verb class to realise the main verbal group in an English clause signals that it is imperative. Verbal groups of this kind used in this way favour just one secondary tense selection (Halliday, 1964/1976, p. 125) – i.e. secondary present as in *be writing by the time I get back*. We can analyse *write* and *be writing* as follows, beginning the univariate structure with a β to show that primary tense is missing, and labelling the verbal group perfective ('perf' for short).

(7) a. *write*

| write |
|---|
| event |
| β$^{perf/event}$ |
| perfective |

b. *be writing*

| be ^ v-ing | write |
|---|---|
| present | event |
| β$^{0/perf}$ | γ$^{event}$ |
| present perfective ||

Alongside signalling imperative mood in English, non-finite verbal groups are commonly deployed in dependent and embedded clauses, where their missing primary tense selection signals in effect that a clause is not negotiable. When our vlogger lodges her complaint about cars stalking her for her parking space in a parking lot, for example, she is setting up an argument about

## 3.2 English Verbal Group Resources

what drives her crazy (*It drives me crazy ... – Does it really?*). She is not arguing about whether a car is following her or not or whether she will leave or not – because these clauses involve non-finite verbal groups, *following* and *to leave*, both of which have no primary tense selection to argue with. These two non-finite verbal groups illustrate the contrast between imperfective *following* (v-ing verb class) and perfective *to leave* (*to* ^ v verbalisation); for the distinction between perfective and imperfective verbal groups in English, see Halliday and Matthiessen, 2014, pp. 405, 490ff.

It drives me crazy when a car is like sitting there **following** you and then they just wait for you **to leave**.

(8)

| *following* |
|---|
| event |
| β$^{\text{imperf/event}}$ |
| imperfective |

| *to leave* |
|---|
| event |
| β$^{\text{perf/event}}$ |
| perfective |

Non-finite verbal groups do allow a full range of SECONDARY TENSE and VOICE selections. We've amended the examples just above to illustrate this possibility and provided analyses below.

It drives me crazy when you are like sitting there **having been followed** and then they just wait for you **to be leaving**.

(9)

| *having been followed* | | |
|---|---|---|
| have ^ v-en | be ^ v-en | *follow* |
| past | passive | event |
| β$^{-\text{/imperf}}$ | γ$^{\text{pass}}$ | δ$^{\text{event}}$ |
| passive past imperfective | | |

| *to be leaving* | |
|---|---|
| be ^ v-ing | *leave* |
| present | event |
| β$^{\text{o/perf}}$ | γ$^{\text{event}}$ |
| present perfective | |

Another key role played by English verbal groups in the exchange structure has to do with nuancing the play of voices around a move. This brings MODALITY and POLARITY into the picture as realisation of what is referred to as ENGAGEMENT in the APPRAISAL system (Martin and White 2005). ENGAGEMENT is the APPRAISAL system concerned with expanding and contracting the opinions being negotiated in an exchange. To explore this, let's begin with MODALITY. As an alternative to PRIMARY TENSE and so basing the arguability of a move on its temporal relation to the moment of speaking, finite verbal groups provide resources for establishing the arguability of a move in terms of MODALITY – making probability, usuality, inclination, obligation or ability the terms of a clause's arguability. Here are two examples from the vlog.

... it's all I **could see** the whole time ...
... but the discoloration **might stay** there for a really really long time so.

Although we will not explore this rich domain of interpersonal meaning in any detail here, from the perspective of ENGAGEMENT one of its key functions is to turn a monoglossic move into a heteroglossic one, implicating relevant opinions other than the speaker's own (for heteroglossic expansion, see Martin and White, 2005). Compare the modalised examples below with their present tense counterparts – in say *you see it, don't you?* or *he stays there, does he?* For these verbal groups the first element of univariate structure is $\alpha^{modal}$ rather than $\alpha^{-/0/+}$.

(10)  *could see*

| could | see |
|---|---|
| modal | event |
| $\alpha^{modal}$ | $\beta^{event}$ |
| modalised | |

(11)  *might stay*

| might | stay |
|---|---|
| modal | event |
| $\alpha^{modal}$ | $\beta^{event}$ |
| modalised | |

As was the case for non-finite verbal groups, a full range of SECONDARY TENSE and VOICE selections is available. Another of Halliday and Matthiessen's (2014, p. 399) more complex examples is analysed below.

But long term, the tax cut will 'generally drain funds that **should have been going to be saved** for Medicare and Social Security'.

(12)  *should have been going to be saved*

| should | have ^ v-en | be going to ^ v | be ^ v-en | save |
|---|---|---|---|---|
| modal | past | future | passive | event |
| $\alpha^{modal}$ | $\beta^{-}$ | $\gamma^{+}$ | $\delta^{pass}$ | $\varepsilon^{event}$ |
| modalised passive 'future in past' | | | | |

In some traditional and formal analyses modal verbs like *could, might* and *should* are treated as 'past tense' forms of *can, may* and *shall* respectively.[4] This analysis relies on purely morphological criteria and fails to take into account the grammaticalisation processes which have redeveloped these morphological oppositions for modal, not temporal purposes. The traditional and formal analysis also doesn't make much sense from a discourse semantic perspective, since all three modals noted above (i.e. *could, might, should*) can be used to modalise experiences which will take place immediately following or simply following the moment of speaking: *I could/might/would/*

---

[4] *Could* retains an element of its original past tense meaning, as reflected in pairs such as *I could do it yesterday, but today I can't* (cf. **I can do it yesterday* ...).

*should go now/tomorrow*. It also fails to capture the subtle differences in meaning between *can* and *could*, *may* and *might*, and *shall* and *should* as far as the arguability of a move is concerned (for discussion see Halliday, 1970/2005, 1982/2002; Halliday and Matthiessen, 2014). As far as English verbal groups are concerned, MODALITY is an alternative to PRIMARY TENSE (we'll see below that this is not true for Spanish, where MODALITY does co-select for PRIMARY TENSE).

Turning to POLARITY, English verbal groups do not explicitly realise positive unless it is emphasised. Our vlogger deploys an emphatic *do want* in the example below to contrast what she doesn't want with what she does. For emphatically positive verbal groups, α is lexicalised as *do*.

I don't want this video to like ramble on. I **want** it to be kind of short. But I **do want** to start going live either on Instagram, Facebook, YouTube, I don't know.

(13)   a.  *want*        b.  *do want*

| want |
|---|
| event |
| α$^{event/0}$ |
| present |

| do | want |
|---|---|
| positive | event |
| α$^{positive}$ | β$^{event}$ |
| emphatic positive ||

Negative verbal groups in indicative clauses include the negative marker *not*, following the α. In terms of ENGAGEMENT, these are used to contract the dialogic space, eliminating an opinion bearing on the negotiation. When not emphasised negation is realised morphologically at word rank as an inflection of the verb realising the α (e.g. *wasn't* and *shouldn't* below); when emphasised it is realised separately as part of verbal group structure (as the particle *not*).

I immediately drove away but- I **wasn't** even thinking; I **shouldn't** have done that. I should **not** have done that. I should**n't** have to leave.

These contrasting structures are analysed below.

(14)   a.  *shouldn't have done*

| shouldn't | have ^ v-en | do |
|---|---|---|
| negative modal | past | event |
| α$^{modal/neg}$ | β⁻ | γ$^{event}$ |
| modalised negative 'past' |||

b.  *should not have done*

| should | not | have ^ v-en | do |
|---|---|---|---|
| modal | emphatic negative | past | event |
| α$^{modal}$ | β$^{neg}$ | γ⁻ | δ$^{event}$ |
| modalised emphatic negative 'past' ||||

In second person negative imperative clauses, negation is marked by *don't*, unless emphatic, as in *do not*.

I will see you Thursday for a day in the life video. It will be live at two PM eastern standard time. So **don't miss** it.

(15)  a.  *don't miss*

| don't | miss |
|---|---|
| negative | event |
| β$^{neg}$ | γ$^{event}$ |
| negative | |

b.  *do not miss*

| do | not | miss |
|---|---|---|
| emphasis | negative | event |
| β$^{emph}$ | γ$^{neg}$ | δ$^{event}$ |
| emphatic negative | | |

In inclusive imperatives (e.g. *Let's see if I can show you from here.*) negation is realised by *not* (e.g. *Let's **not** miss it.*).

As we can see, the beginning of the English verbal group is crucial as far as interpersonal meaning is concerned; considerations of MOOD, PRIMARY TENSE and MODALITY, and POLARITY are all realised before those of SECONDARY TENSE, VOICE and the type of Event. Verbal group structure kicks off by establishing the arguability of a move; we'll relate this predilection for 'terms first' to interpersonal clause structure in Chapter 4.

We have now explored English verbal groups from the perspective of their ideational and interpersonal contributions to discourse. Ideationally speaking, they position figures in time in relation to the moment of speaking and in relation to one another. Interpersonally speaking, they position moves and nuance their negotiability in dialogue. From the perspective of paradigmatic relations, they involve a recursive tense system – choices which from the perspective of syntagmatic relations are realised through univariate structure. In order to provide an integrated account of verbal group structure, we have treated all verbal group systems as realised through a serial structural configuration of this kind, using superscripts to index the specific choices being realised (e.g. α$^{modal}$ β$^{neg}$ γ δ$^{event}$ for *should not have done* above).

## 3.3   Spanish Verbal Group Resources[5]

### *3.3.1   Ideational Verbal Group Resources*

As for English, ideational verbal group resources in Spanish are concerned with the temporal positioning of discourse semantic figures – locating them in

---

[5] The account of Spanish verbal group resources presented in this section is largely based on the detailed work developed by Quiroz (2013).

## 3.3 Spanish Verbal Group Resources

time and sequencing them in relation to one another. Unlike English, Spanish verbal groups also include important ideational resources for configuring entities with occurrences in figures, which we pursue in relation to person/number suffixes and pronominal clitics below.

As we did in Section 3.1 above, we start with TENSE systems, exploring the way these systems locate figures in relation to the moment of speaking and sequence them in relation to one another. We begin with a consideration of PRIMARY TENSE; this system positions occurrence and state figures in relation to the time a text is spoken to be heard or written to be read – as manifested at that moment, as one preceding another or one as following on. We then move on to combinations of tenses in verbal groups drawing on SECONDARY TENSE; these SECONDARY TENSE selections are optional, but when selected they take PRIMARY TENSE as their point of departure and further position figures in relation to one another – as happening at the same time, as one preceding another, or one as following on.[6]

The introductory phase of our feature article contains two present tense verbal groups, *reconstruye* 'reconstructs' and *cuentan* 'recount', which position these events at the moment this text is read (i.e. the journalist and survivors speaking 'live' to the readers).

Se ha dicho casi todo sobre el terremoto y posterior tsunami que asoló las costas de las regiones del Maule y Biobío. En este reportaje, el periodista Juan Andrés Guzmán **reconstruye** el pavor que experimentaron quienes acampaban en la isla Orrego, en la desembocadura del Maule, mientras sentían el agua subiendo despacio hasta inundarlo todo. Aquí, los sobrevivientes **cuentan** qué vieron exactamente.

'Almost everything has been said about the earthquake and tsunami that devastated the coast of the regions of Maule and Biobío. In this article, the journalist Juan Andrés Guzmán **reconstructs** the terror which people camping on Orrego island, in the mouth of the Maule, experienced while they sensed the water slowly rising until it inundated everything. Here the survivors **recount** exactly what they saw.'

In addition, there are verbal groups sequencing experiences that took place before the article is read. These are of two kinds, traditionally referred to as 'preterite perfect' (*asoló* 'devastated', *experimentaron* 'experienced' and *vieron* 'saw') and 'preterite imperfect' (*acampaban* 'were camping' and *sentían* 'sensed'). As indicated by the glosses used here, from the perspective of English the imperfect would appear to construe a less bounded event than the perfect. And Spanish certainly uses the distinction to construe one longer duration event as encompassing a relatively shorter duration one (e.g. imperfect *acampaban* 'were camping' temporally enclosing perfect *experimentaron* 'experienced') in the Ola Maldita introduction.

En este reportaje, el periodista Juan Andrés Guzmán reconstruye el pavor que **experimentaron** quienes **acampaban** en la isla Orrego, en la desembocadura del Maule, mientras sentían el agua subiendo despacio hasta inundarlo todo.

---

[6] We will comment on conditional and subjunctive verbal groups as they become relevant in the discussion below.

'In this article, the journalist Juan Andrés Guzmán reconstructs the terror which whoever **were camping** on Orrego island, in the mouth of the Maule, **experienced** as they sensed the water slowly rising until it inundated everything.'

Note, however, that the free translation for imperfect *sentían* in the same passage, which we used above, is *sensed* (which sounds fine in this context, perhaps because to English ears the conjunction *as* already encodes temporal duration and sensing processes are in any case more stative than action ones). This is a warning that it would be misleading to interpret imperfect verbal groups from the perspective of English as simply a 'present in past' meaning realised by a single verb. We also have to take into account that in addition to the imperfect tense Spanish also has a 'present in past' tense, which it uses later on in the article for the same verb *acampar* 'to camp' (*estaban acampando* 'were camping' below);

Oficialmente **estaban acampando** cerca de casa, en San Javier, a casi 90 kilómetros, y aún tenían la esperanza de que nadie supiera la verdad.

'Officially they **were camping** close to home, in San Javier, about 90 kilometres away, and still held onto hope that no one would find out the truth.'

There has, of course, been extensive discussion of perfect/imperfect opposition in Spanish (e.g. Bull, 1960; Bosque, 1990; Camus and García, 2004; Rojo and Veiga, 1999; Veiga, 2004a, 2004b); and the precise difference in meaning and usage between imperfect (*acampaban*) and 'present in past' (*estaban acampando*) remains an outstanding issue.[7] The crucial point here is that Spanish has a different range of PRIMARY TENSE choices from English, including as it does two past tense options, not one. The PRIMARY TENSE systems in the two languages are not the same. We return to the problem of interpreting differences in agnation of this kind in our 'challenge' section at the end of the chapter.

Before proceeding further, we need to establish the verb class terminology we will use in our analyses. This is presented in Table 3.6. Following the v class (which does not mark person/number) and the v-e class (exemplified for the second person 'formal' *usted* imperative), third person singular[8] verbs are used as examples. We've included the verbs *estar* 'to be', *haber* 'to have' and *ir* 'to go' which are involved in the realisation of secondary tenses, and *ser* 'to

---

[7] Notably, Bello (1847) challenged the traditional distinction between preterite 'perfect' and 'imperfect', suggesting instead the distinction between 'preterite' proper and 'co-preterite', respectively – the latter being analogous to the Hallidayian 'past in present'. Bello's general approach to tense in terms of relative temporal frames was later re-interpreted in Bull's (1960) well-known 'vectorial' approach to verb tense. This approach in turn was later adjusted with much more specific attention to Spanish by Rojo (1974).

[8] In our texts, the -ar verbs (i.e. from the first conjugation) are more frequent, and their third person singular is more regular than in verbs from the other conjugation paradigms (-er and -ir).

3.3 Spanish Verbal Group Resources

Table 3.6 *Spanish verb classes exemplified*

| traditional term | class | 'be' | 'have' | 'go' | 'be' | -ar verb | -er/-ir verb |
|---|---|---|---|---|---|---|---|
| 'infinitive' | v | estar | haber | ir | ser | cantar | recibir |
| 'imperative' | v-e | esté | haya | vaya | sea | cante | reciba |
| 'present' | v-a | está | ha | va | es | canta | recibe |
| 'perfect' | v-ó | estuvo | hubo | fue | fue | cantó | recibió |
| 'imperfect' | v-aba | estaba | había | iba | era | cantaba | recibía |
| 'future' | v-ará | estará | habrá | irá | será | cantará | recibirá |
| 'participle' | v-ado | estado | habido | ido | sido | cantado | recibido |
| 'gerund' | v-ando | estando | habiendo | yendo | siendo | cantando | recibiendo |

be' which is used for passive voice, along with a representative -ar (*cantar* 'to sing') and -er/-ir (*recibir* 'to receive') conjugation verb. We introduce the relevant PERSON/NUMBER system in relation to our discussion of pronominal clitics below. The names of the classes (other than infinitive and imperative) are based on the third person singular realisations of -ar conjugation verbs (the conjugation most often instantiated in Spanish texts). The traditional terms[9] for these verb classes are provided in the left-most column.

The range of choices and realisation statements for Spanish primary tense are formalised in Figure 3.9.

We will not review the PERSON/NUMBER distinctions available for each of these primary tense selections and their regional variations; readily available online Spanish verb conjugators can be consulted for the choices involved (basically first, second and third person, and singular and plural number).

We now turn to a consideration of optional SECONDARY TENSE choices. With respect to these choices, the introduction to the article contains just

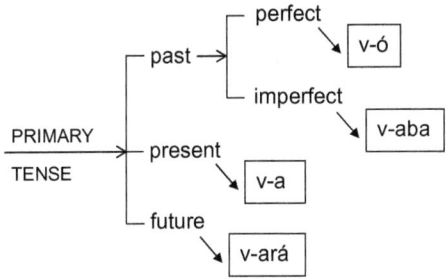

Figure 3.9 Spanish PRIMARY TENSE systems

---

[9] Note that we will not be using these traditional terms to name verb classes in this book; the terms imperative, present, perfect, imperfect and future are used here to name classes of verbal group, not word rank verb classes.

one, *ha dicho* 'has said'. The verbal group as a whole is *se ha dicho* (see Quiroz, 2013, 2017b for the [recessive: generalised] voice realised by *se* here), which invites translation as an English passive – 'has been said' (this is further evidence that we are dealing with a distinctive range of verbal group systems in Spanish). We are setting aside the choices realised by voice clitics at this point in the discussion in order to concentrate on tense selections. The 'past in present' choice, realised by the verb *haber* 'to have' followed by what is traditionally called the participle of the following verb (v-ado verb class), signals that what has been said in the past still matters at the moment of reading.

Se **ha dicho** casi todo sobre el terremoto y posterior tsunami que asoló las costas de las regiones del Maule y Biobío.

'Almost everything **has been said** about the earthquake and tsunami that devastated the coast of the regions of Maule and Biobío.'

The most common secondary tense selection in the Ola Maldita text is the 'past in past' tense realised by the imperfect (i.e. v-aba) class of the verb *haber* followed by the v-ado class of the following verb (e.g. *había dicho* 'had told', *había llevado* 'had taken') in the passage below. This secondary tense selection plays an important role in sequencing figures in the example below – for example it positions Jonathan telling his mother (*le había dicho* 'had told her') about what happened to his friend Gabriel as taking place before his mother Nora arrived in Constitución (*llegó* 'arrived') the following morning, even though it comes later in the unfolding text.

Nora llegó a Constitución a las diez de la mañana, cuando los saqueos estaban en su apogeo. Venía acompañada de la madre de Gabriel. Durante la noche Jonathan, llorando, le **había dicho** que a Gabriel se lo **había llevado** la ola y Nora se lo transmitió a la madre. Pero ella no perdía la esperanza.

'Nora arrived in Constitución at ten in the morning, when the looting was at its peak. She came accompanied by Gabriel's mother. During the night Jonathan, crying, **had told** her that the wave **had taken** Gabriel and Nora passed this on to his mother. But she did not lose[10] hope.'

The secondary past tenses, *ha dicho* 'past in present' and *había dicho* 'past in past' are analysed as univariate structures below. For Spanish we adopt the following superscripts for verbal group features: $^0$for present, $^-$ for perfect and for secondary past, $^{--}$ for imperfect, $^+$ for future and $^{event}$ for event.

---

[10] Note in relation to the discussion of the Spanish imperfect tense above, our preference for the English past tense in the translation of the Spanish imperfect *perdía*.

3.3 Spanish Verbal Group Resources         119

(16)   *ha dicho*

| v-a | *hacer* ^ v-ado | *decir* |
|---|---|---|
| present | past | event |
| α⁰ | β⁻ | γ^event |
| 'past in present' | | |
| '(s/he) has said' | | |

(17)   *había dicho*

| v-aba | *haber* ^ v-ado | *decir* |
|---|---|---|
| imperfect | past | event |
| α⁻⁻ | β⁻ | γ^event |
| 'past in past: imperfect' | | |
| '(s/he) had said' | | |

The Ola Maldita text contains one further example of a secondary present tense besides *estaban acampando* 'were camping' – namely *estuviera rascando* 'were scratching' in the crisis described below (*estuviera* is the imperfect subjunctive realisation of *estar* in one of its typical uses, in a counterfactual conditional dependent clause).

Entonces, el Pinita, de 50 toneladas, empezó a brincar como si fuera un bote a remos, o mejor, como si una ballena se **estuviera rascando** el espinazo con la quilla, según describió otro capitán que también pasó el terremoto en el mar.

'Then, the Pinita, a 50 ton boat, began to bob around as if it was an oar boat, or better, as if a whale **were scratching** its back on the keel, according to another captain that also experienced the earthquake at sea.'

(18)   *estuviera rascando*

| v-aba | *estar* ^ v-ando | *rascar* |
|---|---|---|
| imperfect | present | event |
| α⁻⁻ | β⁰ | γ^event |
| 'present in past: imperfect' | | |
| '(it) were scratching' | | |

And the text has one example of a secondary future, *iba a reventar* 'was going to break', co-textualised and analysed below. This secondary tense allows Ibarra to look forward from an occurrence that was taking place in the past.

– Venía arqueada y chispeando. Todo el tiempo parecía que nos **iba a reventar** encima.

'It was coming retching and spitting. The whole time it seemed like it **was going to break** over us.'

120    Verbal Group

(19)   *iba a reventar*

| v-aba | *iba a* ^ v | *reventar* |
|---|---|---|
| imperfect | future | event |
| α⁻⁻ | β⁺ | γ^event |
| 'future in past: imperfect' | | |
| '(it) was going to break' | | |

At this point we can consolidate the realisations of SECONDARY TENSE in Spanish as *haber* ^ v-ado 'past', *estar* ^ v-ando 'present' and *ir a* ^ v 'future' (Figure 3.10).[11]

Spanish allows for up to three secondary tenses, as outlined in Table 3.7. As with English, we have both an analytical tense pattern based on verb complexing and a synthetic one based on inflection. From the perspective of English, these resources present some challenges for translation. One example is the synthetic imperfect (*acampaba*) and analytic 'present in past' (*estaban acampando*) choices introduced above, which could both be glossed in English as 'were camping' in certain environments. In addition, there is an issue arising from the synthetic future (*acampará* 'will camp) and analytic 'future in present' (*va a acampar* 'is going to camp'), with some regions (Latin America for example) preferring the *ir a* ^ v 'future in present' realisation to position figures after the moment of speaking. These regions, at least in most spoken registers, do not use tense to distinguish between figures that will happen and those that are (relatively speaking) about to occur.[12]

In general, primary perfect and imperfect tenses seem to be in competition for secondary tense options, with imperfect tense the favoured host. So

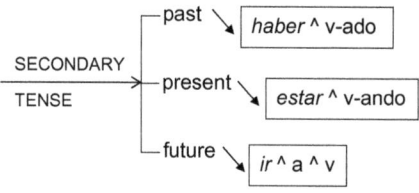

Figure 3.10  Spanish SECONDARY TENSE system

---

[11] Note that here we're not discussing the possibility that in Spanish the distinction between primary and secondary tenses may be realised by both verb simplexes (as we modelled them for English) and verbal group complexes. This discussion involves a close examination of the criteria for distinguishing simplexes from complexes at group rank, which we don't pursue here. For a useful review of possible criteria for the distinction between verb 'compounds' and 'periphrases', see Tornel Sala (2001–2).

[12] For these Spanish varieties the *ir a* ^ v realisation arguably functions like a primary future tense, not secondary future (comparable to English *will* ^ v).

## 3.3 Spanish Verbal Group Resources

Table 3.7 *Spanish primary and secondary tense choice combinations*

| primary α | secondary β | secondary γ | secondary δ |
|---|---|---|---|
| perfect: v-ó<br>*cantó* 'sang' | past: haber ^ v-ado<br>*hubo cantado*<br>'had sung' | present: estar ^ v-ando<br>*hubo estado cantando*\*<br>'had been singing' | |
| | present: estar ^ v-ando<br>*estuvo cantando* 'was singing' | | |
| imperfect: v-aba<br>*cantaba* 'was singing' | past: haber ^ v-ado<br>*había cantado*<br>'had sung' | present: estar ^ v-ando<br>*había estado cantando*<br>'had been singing' | |
| | present: estar ^ v-ando<br>*estaba cantando* 'was singing' | | |
| | future: ir a ^ v<br>*iba a cantar*<br>'was going to sing' | past: haber ^ v-ado<br>*iba a haber cantado*<br>'was going to have sung' | present: estar ^ v-ando<br>*iba a haber estado cantando* 'was going to have been singing' |
| | | present: estar ^ v-ando<br>*iba a estar cantando*<br>'was going to be singing' | |
| present: v-a<br>*canta* 'sings' | past: haber ^ v-ado<br>*ha cantado*<br>'has sung' | present: estar ^ v-ando<br>*ha estado cantando* 'has been singing' | |
| | present: estar ^ v-ando<br>*está cantando*<br>'is singing' | | |
| | future: ir *a* ^ v<br>*va a cantar*<br>'is going to sing' | past: haber ^ v-ado<br>*va a haber cantado* 'is going to have sung' | present: estar ^ v-ando<br>*va a haber estado cantando* 'is going to have been singing' |
| | | present: estar ^ v-ando<br>*va a estar cantando*<br>'is going to be singing' | |
| future: v-ará<br>*cantará* 'will sing' | past: haber ^ v-ado<br>*habrá cantado*<br>'will have sung' | present: estar ^ v-ando<br>*habrá estado cantando*<br>'will have been singing' | |
| | present: estar ^ v-ando<br>*estará cantando* 'will be singing' | | |

\* The 'present in past in perfect' form seems to appear almost exclusively in teaching materials for non-native speakers.

in Table 3.7, 'past in imperfect' is much more common that 'past in perfect';[13] and clear examples of 'future in perfect' are very doubtful.[14] This means that Spanish tends to neutralise the perfect/imperfect primary tense distinction in its complex tenses, as least as far as translation into English is concerned.[15]

The Spanish PRIMARY TENSE and SECONDARY TENSE systems are formalised systemically in Figure 3.11. For restrictions on the possibility of a second and third secondary tense selections, see Table 3.7. As far as tense is

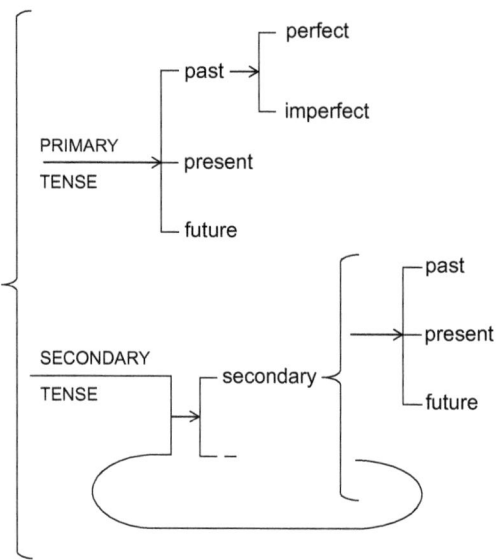

Figure 3.11 Spanish PRIMARY TENSE and recursive SECONDARY TENSE systems

[13] There is, however, at least one environment in Chilean Spanish where 'past in perfect' would be preferred over 'past in imperfect'. So we find *Apenas hubo comido, se echó a dormir una siesta* ('as soon as s/he had finished eating, s/he went to take a nap') but not \**Apenas había comido, se echó a dormir una siesta.* In fact, in contemporary (Chilean) Spanish, primary past would be by far the preferred alternative to 'past in perfect' (i.e. *Apenas comió, se echó a dormir una siesta* 'as soon as she finished eating, s/he went to take a nap'). For discussion of the (restricted) use of 'past in perfect' in Chilean Spanish, see Soto (2009).

[14] For example, *fuimos a ayudar* 'we went to help' would mean that we did go to help (with *fuimos* 'we went' realising an Event, not a secondary future tense) – not that we simply intended to; it is a verbal group complex, not a 'future in perfect' complex tense.

[15] Verbs such as *estar* and *ir* in our proposal for secondary tenses in Spanish may also realise lexical meanings in a different environment (e.g. *estar* 'be' may realise the Process in (attributive) relational clauses, and *ir* 'go' may realise the Process in material clauses). The verb *haber*, in contemporary usage, can only function as an 'auxiliary' in the realisation of secondary tense, or as the Process in existential clauses. Its original lexical 'possessive' meaning is now realised by the verb *tener* 'have' in Spanish (Fontanella de Weinberg, 1992; Penny, 2002; Hernández Díaz, 2006);. See also Chapter 5 on TRANSITIVITY.

## 3.3 Spanish Verbal Group Resources

concerned, Spanish verbal groups seem to have developed to the point where they allow for twenty-three different possibilities; this degree of recursion contrasts with that developed in English, where 'stop rules' restrict the system to thirty-six distinct selections.

Spanish stop rules are similar to the English ones, except that future tense can be chosen only once in a verbal group.

i. future can only be chosen once
ii. secondary present can only be chosen once, as the final choice
iii. the same secondary tense cannot be chosen twice in a row

All of these tense selections can be combined with passive voice, realised by *ser* ^ v-ado. This combination is, however, much less frequent in Spanish than English because of the richer voice potential of a Spanish verbal group, which we will not pursue here (see Quiroz, 2013). Our text includes an example of a passive 'present in past' verbal group, illustrated and analysed below.

Cuando los jóvenes y sus madres abandonaron Constitución, la ciudad **estaba siendo saqueada** sin piedad.

'When the youngsters and their mothers left Constitución, the city **was being looted** mercilessly.'

(20) *estaba siendo saqueada*

| v-aba | *estar* ^ v-ando | *ser* ^ v-ado | *saquear* |
|---|---|---|---|
| imperfect | present | passive | event |
| $\alpha^{--}$ | $\beta^{\circ}$ | $\gamma^{pass}$ | $\delta^{event}$ |
| passive 'present in imperfect' | | | |
| '(it) was being looted' | | | |

At this point, we'll add a short spoken text from another context to our discussion – in order to illustrate the role of a range of PRIMARY TENSE and SECONDARY TENSE selections as far as setting figures in time and sequencing them in relation to another is concerned. Verbal groups are highlighted in bold below.

Eeh el susto más grande **fue** ahora en campamento de verano. Lo que pasa es que **soy** dirigente de scout y de repente una niña **tuvo** un ataque respiratorio y claro me **tocó** correr cuatro cinco kilómetros buscando una ambulancia y en el momento **estaba** súper agotado **había caminado** todo el día, pero por el puro golpe de adrenalina al final **corrí** los cinco kilómetros y cuando ya **iba a llegar** al teléfono como que me **avisaron** ya se **había mejorado** que **había sido** algo momentáneo que en el momento **no vimos** bien la situación y **llegamos** y **actuamos** no más.[16]

---

[16] Our thanks to Dr Abelardo San Martín and Dr Silvana Guerrero, from the Universidad de Chile, who gave us full access to the sociolinguistic PRESEEA corpus from Santiago, Chile (PRESEEA, 2014–2022). The corpus is also available for consultation at http://preseea.linguas.net/Corpus.aspx.

124    Verbal Group

'ehm, the worse fright **was** now in summer camp. The thing is I **am** a scout leader and suddenly a girl **had** a breathing attack and of course I **had** to run four five kilometres looking for an ambulance and at that moment I **was** super exhausted, I **had walked** the whole day, but just because of the adrenaline rush in the end I **ran** the five kilometres and when I **was going to get** to a phone someone like **told** me she had already **recovered**, it **had been** a momentary thing, that in that moment we **didn't check** the situation properly and we just **came** and **reacted**.'

As Figure 3.12 reveals, the speaker uses perfect and imperfect tense selections to position what happened before the moment in which he recounts his story. The display has been arranged to align the main chain of unfolding goings on with one another, and position what precedes to the left and what follows to the right of this time line. Imperfect is preferred whenever there is a secondary tense selection – to sequence one figure before another (*había caminado* 'had walked', *había mejorado* 'had recovered', *había sido* 'had been') or as happening after (*iba a llegar* 'was going to get'). It would be interesting to explore, across a range of registers, whether imperfect, not perfect, is in fact the favoured host for SECONDARY TENSE selections in Spanish.

As noted in Chapter 2 (see especially Table 2.5), Spanish verbal groups may also include pronominal clitics (discussed there as resources for tracking discourse semantic entities). These clitics realise entities involved in secondary and tertiary roles in a figure (and so traditionally referred to as accusative

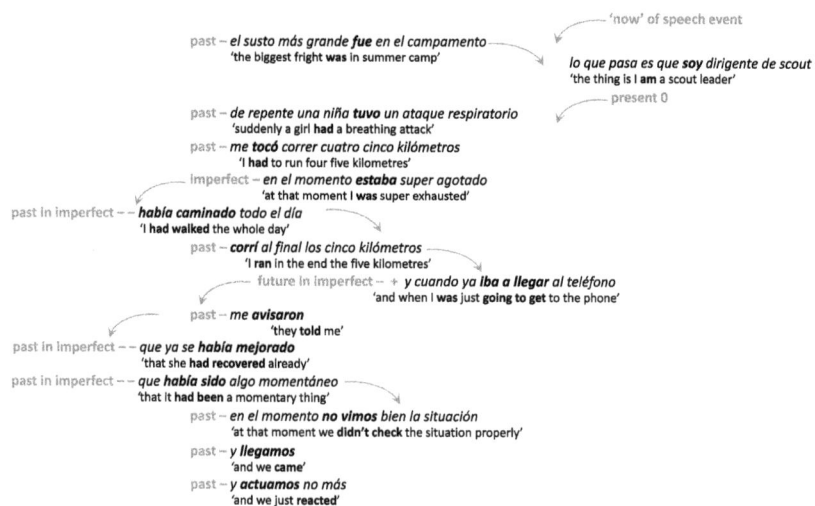

Figure 3.12  Tense choice and the temporal position of figures

3.3 Spanish Verbal Group Resources 125

or dative case). In Chapter 4 we refer to their function as that of realising P2 and P3 participant roles inside the verbal group. Taken alongside verbal group person and number affixation realising P1 participant roles, this means that Spanish verbal groups play an instrumental role as far as organising entities in figures is concerned. The way they complement nominal group realisations of participant roles or function as the sole realisation of participant roles in a clause is elaborated in Chapter 4. Here we concentrate on their realisation as part of verbal group structure.

One or two clitics of this kind may be included, as exemplified below for *le había dicho* 'had told her' and *se lo transmitió* 'passed it on to her' (we'll skip over *se lo había llevado* because the *se* clitic in this case is a non-pronominal clitic).

Durante la noche Jonathan, llorando, *le había dicho* que a Gabriel se lo había llevado la ola y Nora *se lo transmitió* a la madre. Pero ella no perdía la esperanza.

'During the night Jonathan, crying, *had told **her*** that the wave had taken Gabriel and Nora *passed **this** on* to his mother. But she did not lose hope.'

An extension to our univariate analysis of Spanish verbal groups is suggested below (using the superscript $^{tr\text{-}cl}$ to label the pronominal tracking clitic). We will critically reconsider this representation in Section 3.3.3. The second example includes two pronominal clitics, in the obligatory dative then accusative sequence; the expected *le* dative clitic is replaced here by *se* because Spanish does not permit the syntagm **le lo* 'it to him/her (cf. the grammatical *me lo transmitió* 'passed it on to me').

(21)  *le había dicho*

| le | v-aba | haber ^ v-ado | decir |
|---|---|---|---|
| pron clitic | imperfect | past | event |
| $\alpha^{tr\text{-}cl}$ | $\beta^{--}$ | $\gamma^{-}$ | $\delta^{event}$ |
| cliticised 'past in imperfect' | | | |
| '(s/he) had told (her)' | | | |

(22)  *se lo transmitió*

| se | lo | v-ó | transmitir |
|---|---|---|---|
| pron clitic | pron clitic | perfect | event |
| $\alpha^{tr\text{-}cl}$ | $\beta^{tr\text{-}cl}$ | $\gamma^{-}$ | $\delta^{event}$ |
| bi-cliticised 'perfect' | | | |
| '(s/he) passed it on (to her)' | | | |

The clitic *se* is also used to mark a range of voice options, as illustrated below for *se le ha dicho* 'he has been told' (using superscript $^{v\text{-}cl}$ to specify the function of the *se* clitic as having a voice clitic function).[17] This leaves room for only one entity tracking clitic function (*le* below).

Se le ha dicho casi todo sobre el terremoto.

'He has been told almost everything about the earthquake.'

(23)     *se le ha dicho*

| se | le | v-a | *haber* ^ v-ado | *decir* |
|---|---|---|---|---|
| se clitic | pron clitic | present | past | event |
| α$^{v\text{-cl}}$ | β$^{tr\text{-cl}}$ | γ° | δ⁻ | ε$^{event}$ |
| bi-cliticised 'past in present' | | | | |
| 'he has been told' | | | | |

As exemplified above, clitics are regularly sequenced before the verb realising PRIMARY TENSE in indicative clauses.[18] The *se* clitic always comes first, followed by either a dative or an accusative clitic; elsewhere the 'accusative' clitic always follows the 'dative' one if both are present.

Table 3.8 displays the pronominal clitics used in Chilean Spanish. As a tracking resource they are less restricted than the personal pronouns introduced in Chapter 2, since they are used to track all types of entity (including non-conscious entities, activity entities and semiotic entities), not just conscious ones.

Table 3.8 *Pronominal clitics in Chilean Spanish*

| Pronominal clitics (group rank) in Chilean Spanish | | | | |
|---|---|---|---|---|
| number | person | | accusative | dative |
| singular | interactant | 1st | me | |
| | | 2nd | te | |
| | | 2nd (formal) | *lo* (masc.), *la* (fem.) | *le* / *se*[19] |
| | non-interactant | 3rd | *lo* (masc.), *la* (fem.) | *le* / *se* |
| plural | interactant | 1st | nos | |
| | | 2nd | *los* (masc.), *las* (fem.) | *les* / *se* |
| | non-interactant | 3rd | *los* (masc.), *las* (fem.) | *les* / *se* |

---

[17] Note that the Spanish verbal group *se le ha dicho* is not passive; see Quiroz (2013) for a systemic sketch of the Spanish VOICE system at group rank.

[18] For discussion of (pronominal and non-pronominal) clitic placement in Spanish, see Fernández Soriano (1999a).

[19] *Se* here is the third person dative pronominal clitic used before an accusative pronominal clitic: e.g. *se lo dio* ('s/he gave it to him/her').

3.3 Spanish Verbal Group Resources    127

To this outline we need to add the accusative neuter clitic *lo*, which is used for text reference (to preceding discourse) and the Attribute and Value functions in Spanish relational clauses (see Chapter 5 on TRANSITIVITY for discussion) and any meta-phenomenon (whether projected or embedded).[20] This clitic does not distinguish number or gender; in terms of clitic placement, it can be considered accusative, since it always follows a dative tracking clitic or voice clitic where one is present.

Durante la noche Jonathan, llorando, le había dicho que a Gabriel se lo había llevado la ola y Nora *se lo transmitió* a la madre.

'During the night, Jonathan, crying, had told her that Gabriel had been taken by the wave and Nora *had passed it on* to his mother.'

The following short phase of our Ola Maldita text illustrates the role of these clitics as far as organising entities in figures and tracking them in discourse is concerned.

Los jóvenes entraron al hospital sin esperanza. Era un caos de heridos y muertos. No creían que nadie pudiera sobrevivir a la ola que habían visto, pero en la lista de ingresados, el nombre de Gabriel **les** saltó en la cara.
Jonathan entró a la carrera a la zona de los pacientes y recorrió las camillas hasta que **lo** encontró. **Le** pegó tres garabatos y **lo** abrazó. Gabriel sólo tenía heridas en los pies. Tuvo la fortuna de que la ola **lo** llevara directo a la orilla.

'The youngsters entered the hospital without hope. It was a chaos of wounded and dead. One couldn't believe that anyone could survive the wave they had seen, but in the list of admitted, the name of Gabriel hit **them** in the face.
Jonathan hurriedly entered the patient area [literally "the zone of the patients"] and went through [literally "toured"] the stretchers until he found **him**. He swore at him [literally "hit **him** with three curses"] and hugged **him**. Gabriel only had injuries in his feet. He had the fortune that the wave carried **him** directly to the bank.'

As highlighted in Table 3.9, the friends, minus Gabriel, are realised by a nominal group in the first clause (*los jóvenes* 'the youngsters') and then tracked twice through verbal group morphology (*creían* '**they** believed' and *habían visto* '**they** had seen') and once through the dative clitic *les* (*les saltó* 'hit **them**'). Their friend Gabriel is realised twice by name, once indirectly (*los pies* 'the feet'),[21] once through morphology (*tuvo* 'he had') and four times by clitics (*lo encontró* 'found **him**', *le pegó tres garabatos* 'hit

---

[20] See Chapter 5 on TRANSITIVITY for discussion of meta-phenomena in relation to mental and relational clauses.
[21] In terms of IDENTIFICATION, the specificity of this nominal group depends on what is termed bridging (Martin 1992) – between Gabriel and an inalienable part of his body. See also our discussion of this way of construing 'in/alienable possession' in Spanish, particularly in relation to perception mental clauses, in Chapter 5 on TRANSITIVITY.

Table 3.9 *Participant roles and entity tracking as Gabriel's friends find him alive*

| proper name | determiners | personal pronouns | pronominal clitics | inflectional morphology |
|---|---|---|---|---|
| | *los jóvenes* 'the youngsters' | | | *creían* 'they believed' *habían visto* 'they had seen' |
| | *la cara* 'the face' | | *les* 'them' | |
| Gabriel | | | *lo* 'him' *le* 'him' *lo* 'him' | |
| Gabriel | *los pies* 'the feet' | | | *tuvo* 'he had' |
| | | | *lo* 'him' | |
| Jonathan | | | | *recorrió* 'he toured' *encontró* 'he found' *pegó* 'he hit' *abrazó* 'he hugged' |

**him** with three curses', *lo abrazó* 'hugged **him**' and *lo llevara* 'took **him**'). And Jonathan is realised once by name and four times through morphology (*recorrió* 'he toured', *lo encontró* 'he found him', *le pegó tres garabatos* '**he** hit him with three curses' and *lo abrazó* '**he** hugged him'. As we can see, in only four of the clauses are the participant roles played by the friends realised by nominal groups; in the other twelve clauses the verbal group registers their roles on its own.

3.3 Spanish Verbal Group Resources                                      129

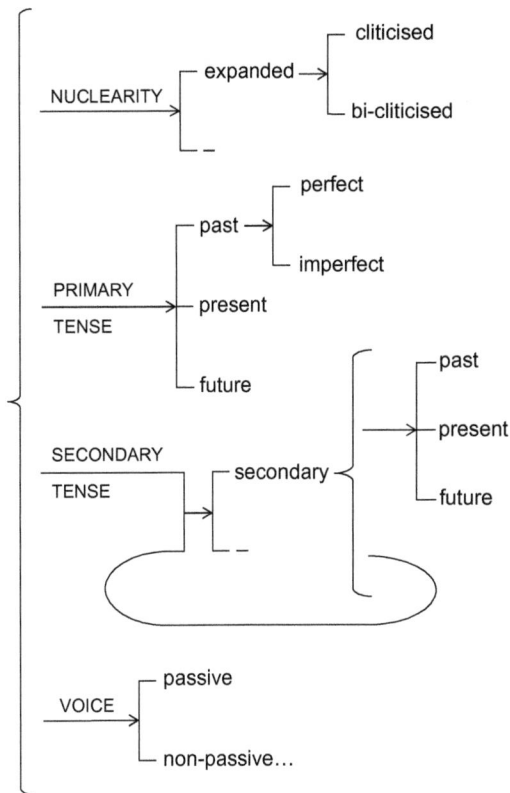

Figure 3.13 Spanish verbal group NUCLEARITY, PRIMARY TENSE, SECONDARY TENSE and VOICE[22] systems

The verbal group systems introduced in this section are outlined in Figure 3.13. The system introducing pronominal tracking clitics is referred to as NUCLEARITY, and opens up the possibility of one (cliticised) or two (bi-cliticised) clitic positions. The PERSON, NUMBER and GENDER (and CASE for third person clitics) distinctions for Chilean Spanish pronominal clitics were outlined in Table 3.8 above; they have not been incorporated into the network below (as systems dependent on the feature [expanded]).

We will problematise this univariate interpretation of Spanish verbal group structure in Section 3.3.3 below.

---

[22] We have not been explicit about the interdependency of the NUCLEARITY and VOICE systems in this network; in addition, non-passive verbal groups, classified by Quiroz (2013) as [active], [recessive] and [reflexive] have not been distinguished.

### 3.3.2 Interpersonal Verbal Group Resources

We now turn to the role played by Spanish verbal groups in distinguishing moves in exchange structure (NEGOTIATION) and nuancing the play of voices around a move (ENGAGEMENT). We'll deal first with verbal group resources expanding and contracting the range of opinions being negotiated in an exchange.

This brings the systems of MODALITY and POLARITY into the picture, as realisations of what is referred to as ENGAGEMENT in the APPRAISAL system (Martin and White, 2005). ENGAGEMENT is the APPRAISAL system concerned with expanding and contracting the opinions being negotiated in an exchange. We begin with MODALITY, which in Spanish is not an alternative to PRIMARY TENSE but is chosen along with PRIMARY TENSE to provide resources for establishing the arguability of a move in dialogue – adding probability, usuality, inclination, obligation or ability to the terms of a clause's arguability. We focus here on MODALITY as it is enacted through modal verbs.[23]

Verbal group MODALITY of this type is realised by a modal verb followed by the v class of the following verb – as for *pudo volver* 'could return' below.

Cuando lo hizo y **pudo volver** a la ribera, ya no habían embarcaciones.

'When it did and he **could return** to the riverbank, there weren't any vessels anymore.'

Some verbs expanding the play of voices around a move in this way are *poder* 'can', *deber* 'should/must', *tener* 'should/must' and *soler* 'tend to'. As noted above, Spanish modal verbs choose from a full range of primary tenses. For example, for *poder* 'can', we find *pudo* 'past', *podía* 'imperfect', *puede* 'present', *podrá* 'future' (illustrated for past above, imperfect below and present further along).

Eran las 11 de la mañana del 27 de febrero y el piloto Víctor González los transportó al único lugar donde **se podía aterrizar**: el estadio de Constitución.

'It was 11 in the morning of February 27 and the pilot, Victor González carried them to the only place **one could land** on: Constitución's Stadium.'

In terms of the univariate structural analysis we have been developing above, modalised verbal groups could be incorporated as follows (the slash in the superscript means that *pudo* 'could' is modalised and past tense):[24]

---

[23] MODALITY in Spanish may be realised by modal verbs and/or morphological distinctions (particularly 'subjunctive' and 'conditional' morphology). For a very general and updated review of the interactions between modal verbs and verb morphology in Spanish, see Laca (2005).

[24] Group-by-group glosses provided in tables do not necessarily match the more fully contextualised translation shown after each Spanish example.

(24)   *pudo volver*

| poder | v-ó | volver |
|---|---|---|
| modal | perfect | event |
| α<sup>modal/–</sup> | | β<sup>event</sup> |
| modalised 'perfect' | | |
| '(he) could return' | | |

When obligation is realised by *tener* 'should/must', it is connected to its following v class verb by *que* (for a historical perspective on verbal groups realising modality in Spanish, see Garachana, 2017).

Quiroz sabía que **tenían que escapar**.

'Quiroz knew that **they had to escape**.'

(25)   *tenían que escaper*

| tener que | v-ía | escaper |
|---|---|---|
| modal | imperfect | event |
| α<sup>modal/– –</sup> | | β<sup>event</sup> |
| modalised 'imperfect' | | |
| '(they) had to escape' | | |

In modalised verbal groups clitics tend to either come before the modal verb or follow the Event, as exemplified below. Spanish graphology treats clitics as separate words when they precede the Event and as part of the Event when they follow; this reflects the fact that secondary tenses and/or passive voice can interrupt the clitic and verb syntagm when they precede the Event but cannot interrupt the verb and clitic syntagm when they follow.

Jonathan decidió que tenía que avisar**le** a su madre …
Jonathan decidió que **le** tenía que avisar a su madre …
'Jonathan decided he had to warn his mother and tell **her** the truth.'

(26)   *le tenía que avisar*

| le | tener que | v-aba | avisar |
|---|---|---|---|
| pron clitic | modal | imperfect | event |
| α<sup>tr-cl</sup> | β<sup>modal/– –</sup> | | γ<sup>event</sup> |
| cliticised modalised 'imperfect' | | | |
| '(he) had to warn (her)' | | | |

(27)   *tenía que avisarle*

| tener que | v-aba | avisar | le |
|---|---|---|---|
| modal | imperfect | event | pron clitic |
| α<sup>modal/– –</sup> | | β<sup>event</sup> | γ<sup>tr-cl</sup> |
| modalised 'imperfect' cliticised | | | |
| '(he) had to warn (her)' | | | |

132    Verbal Group

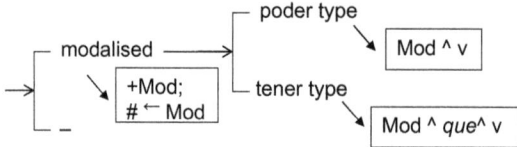

Figure 3.14  Spanish verbal group MODALITY systems

These analyses call into question the appropriateness of extending our univariate analysis of verbal groups to include clitics. We return to this issue in Section 3.3.3 immediately below. Verbal group MODALITY systems and realisation statements are presented in Figure 3.14.

Modalised verbal groups can also select for secondary tense, as exemplified and analysed below.

Tampoco es incomprensible el miedo que **deben haber sentido** sus parientes.

'Neither is the fear that his relatives **must have felt** incomprehensible.'

(28)    *deben haber sentido*

| deber | v-a | haber ^ v-ado | sentir |
|---|---|---|---|
| modal | present | past | event |
| $\alpha^{modal/0}$ | | $\beta^{-}$ | $\gamma^{event}$ |
| modalised 'past in present' | | | |
| '(they) must have felt' | | | |

The fact Spanish modal verbs select for PRIMARY TENSE means that there are two ways in which a secondary tense can be realised – by either conflating the secondary tense with the modal (as below) or not (as above). So instead of *deben haber sentido* '(they) must have felt' in (28) above we might have had *han debido sentir* '(they) must have felt' as in (29). We suggest the following representation for the alternative.

(29)    *han debido sentir*

| v-a | haber ^ v-ado | deber | sentir |
|---|---|---|---|
| present | past | modal | event |
| $\alpha^0$ | $\beta^{modal/-}$ | | $\gamma^{event}$ |
| 'past in present' modalised | | | |
| '(they) must have felt' | | | |

The difference in meaning has not, as far as we are aware, been previously explored. The MODALITY and SECONDARY TENSE choices we have been considering here are outlined systemically in Figure 3.15 and exemplified for a

3.3 Spanish Verbal Group Resources

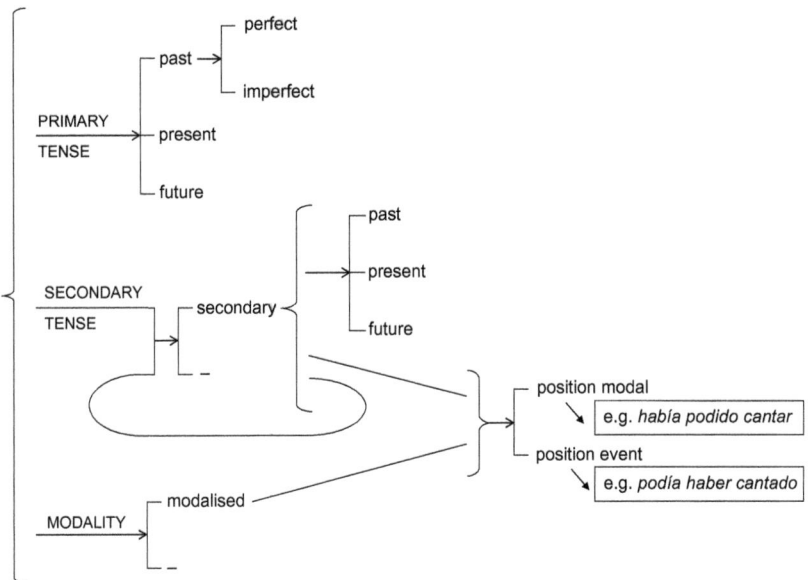

Figure 3.15 Alternative realisations of SECONDARY TENSE in modalised verbal groups

'past in imperfect' tense selection (*había podido cantar* vs *podía haber cantado*, 'could have been singing').

Another verbal group system in Spanish that is relevant to the discourse semantic ENGAGEMENT system is POLARITY. Verbal group POLARITY is realised in first position in the Spanish verbal group by the particles *no* or *sí* (e.g. Carbonero, 1980; Dumitrescu, 1973). Negative polarity allows speakers to challenge opinions at odds with a discourse move.

Nora **no** lo podía creer.

'Nora could**n't** believe it.'

(30)   *no lo podía creer*

| no | lo | v-aba | poder | creer |
|---|---|---|---|---|
| negative | pron clitic | imperfect | modal | event |
| $\alpha^{neg}$ | $\beta^{tr\text{-}cl}$ | $\gamma^{--}$ | $\delta^{modal}$ | $\varepsilon^{event}$ |
| negative cliticised modalised 'imperfect' | | | | |
| '(she) could not believe it' | | | | |

A marker of positive polarity, *sí*, can be included in verbal groups when the dialogic space around a move needs to be contracted not by denying an opinion but by strongly asserting one.

134    Verbal Group

(31)    *sí le había dicho*

| sí | le | v-aba | haber ^ v-ado | decir |
|---|---|---|---|---|
| positive | pron clitic | imperfect | past | event |
| α^pos | β^tr-cl | γ⁻ | δ⁻ | ε^event |
| positive cliticised 'past in imperfect' ||||||
| '(s/he) had indeed told (her)' ||||||

These contracting POLARITY resources and their realisations are outlined in Figure 3.16.

At this point we return to our discussion of MOOD systems. So far we have only considered verbal group resources realising indicative moods – in moves exchanging information. As an alternative to negotiating information, verbal groups can position moves as demanding goods and services. Moves of this kind are congruently realised in Spanish through a range of verb inflections,

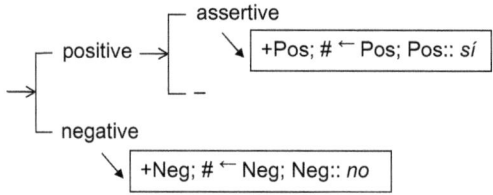

Figure 3.16  Spanish POLARITY systems

Table 3.10  *Verbal inflections used in congruent moves requesting goods & services*

| imperative 'person' | verbal group type | examples |
|---|---|---|
| addressee (informal) | 2nd person singular imperative | *(tú) transmit-**e*** '(you) pass on' |
| addressee (formal) | 3nd person singular present subjunctive | *(usted) transmit-**a*** '(you) pass on' |
| non-interlocutor | 3rd person singular present subjunctive | *que (ella) transmit-**a*** '(she) pass on' |
| speaker/addressee | 1st person plural present subjunctive | *(nosotras) transmit-**amos*** 'let's pass on' |
| addressee plus | 3nd person plural present subjunctive | *(ustedes) transmit-**an*** '(you) pass on' |
| non-interlocutors | 3rd person plural present subjunctive | *que (ellas) transmit-**an*** 'let (them) pass on'[25] |

[25] The appropriate rhythm for the rather archaic English third person imperative would be //^ let / them /pass on the /news//, to discourage a reading in which *let* is salient, realising permission: // let them /pass on the /news//. See Chapter 1.

3.3 Spanish Verbal Group Resources                                    135

exemplified for the verb *transmitir* 'pass on' in Table 3.10. All of these are present subjunctive inflections, except for the distinctive informal jussive imperative *transmit-e* (see Chapter 4 on MOOD).

These verbal groups never select for MODALITY or SECONDARY TENSE. And clitics follow the Event in these verbal groups (traditionally termed 'enclisis'), if they are positive; but in negative verbal groups of this kind, clitics precede the Event (traditionally termed 'proclisis'). Once again pushing our univariate analysis a little too far, we can analyse verbal groups realising imperative mood as exemplified below (beginning with β to reflect the absence of PRIMARY TENSE and MODALITY in these verbal groups).

(32)     *transmítaselo*

| v-e | *transmitir* | *se* | *lo* |
|---|---|---|---|
| subjunctive | event | pron clitic | pron clitic |
| β°/subjunctive | γ event | δ tr-cl | ε tr-cl |
| negative bi-cliticised present subjunctive ||||
| 'pass it on to her' ||||

(33)     *no se lo transmita*

| *no* | *se* | *lo* | v-e | *transmitir* |
|---|---|---|---|---|
| negative | pron clitic | pron clitic | subjunctive | event |
| β neg | γ tr-cl | δ tr-cl | ε°/subjunctive | ζ event |
| negative bi-cliticised present subjunctive |||||
| 'don't pass it on to her' |||||

An overview of Spanish verbal group systems is presented in Figure 3.17 setting aside the non-indicative groups just reviewed and using the superscript $^n$ to designate the recursive nature of the SECONDARY TENSE system to simplify the presentation. From the perspective of discourse semantics, we have two lexicogrammatical interpersonal systems realising APPRAISAL (ENGAGEMENT in particular) and positioning moves as interacts: POLARITY and MODALITY. And there are four ideational systems, temporally positioning figures in relation to the moment of speaking and one another, and configuring entities with events as figures: PRIMARY TENSE and SECONDARY TENSE, VOICE and NUCLEARITY.

### 3.3.3   The Limits of Univariate Structure

At this point we need to shift gears and look critically at the structural analysis we have been deploying for Spanish verbal groups, which we have pursued here for pedagogic purposes. We were concerned, in other words, to introduce a range of Spanish resources in terms comparable to those used for English verbal groups, and to delay discussion of issues bearing on this analysis until

136    Verbal Group

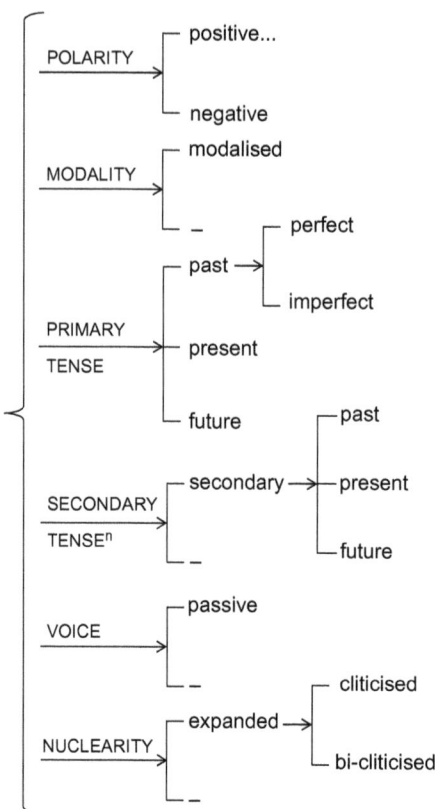

Figure 3.17 Spanish verbal group systems

a reasonable coverage of Spanish resources had been achieved. Essentially what we have done is to treat the whole verbal group as a progressive hypotactic word complex (as we did for English in Section 3.2), headed by its leftmost realisation (the α or β elements of univariate structure above). From a discourse semantic perspective, this implies that the interpretation of each element of structure depends on the element before. While this is clearly the case for tense choices, realisations of POLARITY, MODALITY, VOICE, NUCLEARITY and PERSON/NUMBER are not necessarily dependent on preceding elements of structure. The presence of tracking clitics, for example, has nothing to do with whether the verbal group is positive or negative, whether modalised or not, or whether past, present or future. And as we have seen, in some types of verbal groups the clitics precede the Event and in others they follow. As tabled above, this means treating their relation to other elements of verbal group structure

3.3 Spanish Verbal Group Resources 137

very differently depending simply on their position. But regardless of their position, their function in verbal groups is identical insofar as positioning entities in figures and tracking them in discourse is concerned.

From a lexicogrammatical perspective, the univariate structure analysis also raises serious concerns. For one thing, with regard to the logical component of the ideational metafunction in SFL, univariate structures are meant to realise recursive systems; and in Spanish only the TENSE system involves recursion. For another, the univariate analysis fails to show that the relation of the Event function to pronominal clitics is different from its relation to other elements of verbal group structure. The person/number inflection of the verbal group, along with accusative and dative pronominal clitics, in fact construes the participant roles involved in a given process type – participant roles which in Spanish may or may not be realised as constituents at clause rank (see Chapter 5 on TRANSITIVITY). The finite verbal groups highlighted in bold below, for example, share responsibility with clause structure as far as construing what went on is concerned.

Durante la noche Jonathan, llorando, **le había dicho** que a Gabriel **se lo había llevado** la ola y Nora **se lo transmitió** a la madre. Pero ella **no perdía** la esperanza.

'During the night Jonathon, crying, **had told her** that the wave **had taken** Gabriel and Nora **passed this** on to his mother. But she **did not lose** hope.'

We outline this co-operation in the Table 3.11, which specifies the realisation of Process and Participant functions at clause and group rank. The column headings necessarily anticipate our analysis of TRANSITIVITY in Chapter 5; they can be understood here in simple terms as Participant 1 (undertaking

Table 3.11 *Spanish verbal groups in relation to Process and Participant structure*

| verbal group | Process | Participant 1 | Participant 2 | Participant 3 |
|---|---|---|---|---|
| *le había dicho* '(he) had told (her)' | *decir* 'say' | Jonathan, 'Jonathan' 3SG (v-aba) | | *le* 'to her' |
| *se lo había llevado* '(it) had taken (him)' | *llevar* 'take' | la ola, 'the wave' 3SG (v-aba) | a Gabriel, 'Gabriel' *lo* 'him' | |
| *se lo transmitió* '(she) passed it on (to her)' | *transmitir* 'pass on' | Nora, 'Nora' 3SG (v-ó) | *lo* 'it' | a la madre, 'to the mother' *se* 'her' |
| *no perdía* '(she) didn't lose' | *perder* 'lose' | ella 'she', 3SG (v-aba) | | |

the Process), Participant 2 (undertaken by the Process) and Participant 3 (less directly affected by the Process). For this phase of the story, Participant 1 is realised at both clause and groups ranks (e.g. *Jonathan* as an explicit clause Participant and as the third person singular imperfect realisation of *decir*). Participant 2 is similarly realised at clause and group ranks[26] in the second example (i.e. *a Gabriel* 'Gabriel' and *lo* 'him'), but only at group rank in the third (as *lo* 'it'). And Participant 3 is realised only at group rank in the first example (as *le* 'her') but at clause and group ranks in the third (*a la madre* 'to the mother' and *se* 'to her') (Quiroz, in press).

In short our univariate structure analysis fails to distinguish the dependency relation among tenses from the dependency relation among clitics and the Event function as they construe the ideational structure of the clause (see Chapter 5 on TRANSITIVITY).

Of the remaining verbal group systems, VOICE is the one most closely connected to the realisation of participant roles, since, for example, it creates the possibility of what is usually referred to as an 'agentless passive' (an optional Participant 1 in our terms). Those responsible for looting the city are thereby left implicit in the example below.

Cuando los jóvenes y sus madres abandonaron Constitución, la ciudad **estaba siendo saqueada** sin piedad.

'When the young men and their mothers left Constitución, the city **was being looted** mercilessly.'

Pushing further, with respect to verbal group structure, the interpersonal systems of MODALITY and POLARITY operate independently of the TENSE, NUCLEARITY and VOICE systems discussed above. Both systems establish a heteroglossic stance for the verbal group as a whole (realising ENGAGEMENT, as discussed above). Our univariate structure analysis fails to capture the prosodic scope of these systems.

All of this suggests that a multi-tiered analysis is needed, involving a combination of univariate structure alongside multivariate structure we used to analyse nominal groups in Chapter 2. This will allow us to better capture both the serial tense dimension and the more orbital nucleus/satellite dimension of Spanish verbal groups (Martin, 1996, 2018c; Quiroz 2017b). For the serial tense structure, we can maintain the univariate analyses developed above, as exemplified below.

---

[26] Realisation of Participants 2 and 3 at both clause and group ranks in Spanish is traditionally referred to as 'clitic doubling'. More recent corpus-based work has suggested analysing this phenomenon as a manifestation of 'object agreement', thus pointing to the 'affix-like' nature of Spanish pronominal clitics (Enrique-Arias, 2003; Vázquez & García, 2012). See further discussion in Chapter 5 on TRANSITIVITY.

(34) *siente*

| v-a | *sentir* |
|---|---|
| α⁰ | |
| '(s/he) feels' | |

(35) *ha sentido*

| v-a | *haber* ^ v-ado | *sentir* |
|---|---|---|
| α⁰ | β⁻ | |
| '(s/he) has felt' | | |

(36) *ha estado sintiendo*

| v-a | *haber* ^ v-ado | *estar* ^ v-ando | *sentir* |
|---|---|---|---|
| α⁰ | β⁻ | γ⁰ | |
| '(s/he) has been feeling' | | | |

Setting TENSE aside for the moment, for the orbital event and participant clitic structure we can deploy a multivariate structure analysis with four functions (Finite, Event, P2cl and P3cl), each playing a distinctive complementary role. We'll refer to the multivariate nucleus of the verbal group as Event. Finite verbal groups include an additional function Finite, realised through inflections distinguishing PERSON and NUMBER (and TENSE in verbal groups in indicative clauses). Analysis of examples (34)–(36) could then be extended as follows.

(37) *siente*

| v-a | *sentir* |
|---|---|
| α⁰ | |
| Finite/Event | |
| '(s/he) feels' | |

(38) *ha sentido*

| v-a | *haber* ^ v-ado | *sentir* |
|---|---|---|
| α⁰ | β⁻ | |
| Finite | | Event |
| '(s/he) has felt' | | |

(39) *ha estado sintiendo*

| v-a | *haber* ^ v-ado | *estar* ^ v-ando | *sentir* |
|---|---|---|---|
| α⁰ | β⁻ | γ⁰ | |
| Finite | | | Event |
| '(s/he) has been feeling' | | | |

As modelled above, where no passive voice, SECONDARY TENSE nor MODALITY is involved, we conflate Finite with the Event function (reflecting its realisation via inflection, e.g. third person singular below).

(40)

| transmitió | |
|---|---|
| 3SG v-a | transmitir |
| Finite/Event | |
| '(s/he) passed on' | |

Where passive voice, SECONDARY TENSE or MODALITY is indeed involved, the Finite can be treated as a separate unconflated function (realised by the person/number of the primary tense).

(41)

| ha transmitido | | |
|---|---|---|
| 3SG v-a | haber ^ v-ado | transmitir |
| Finite | – | Event |
| '(s/he) has passed on' | | |

Verbal groups involving one or two pronominal clitics would be analysed as follows (using P2cl and P3cl as verbal group function labels). The terms reflect the labelling used in Table 3.10 to distinguish different types of participant role in Spanish clauses (as discussed in more detail in Chapter 5 on TRANSITIVITY) (Quiroz, 2017b, in press).

(42)

| lo transmitió | | |
|---|---|---|
| lo | 3sg v-a | transmitir |
| P2cl | Finite/Event | |
| it | passed on | |
| '(s/he) passed it on' | | |

(43)

| se lo transmitió | | | |
|---|---|---|---|
| se | lo | 3sg v-a | transmitir |
| P3cl | P2cl | Finite/Event | |
| to her | it | passed on | |
| '(s/he) passed it on to her' | | | |

The scoping relation of both MODALITY and POLARITY to the verbal group as a whole invites an analysis with additional tiers of structure to capture the prosody (Martin 2004, 2008b). We are using the term prosody here to refer to interpersonal structure that in effect scopes over what would be treated as separate segments from an ideational point of view (i.e. our univariate tense and multivariate Finite, Event and clitic functions). It is the whole of a verbal group that is modalised, asserted or negated, not just the unit enacting MODALITY or POLARITY.

## 3.3 Spanish Verbal Group Resources

(44) *se lo explicará*

| se | lo | 3SG v-ará | *explicar* |
|---|---|---|---|
| P3cl | P2cl | Finite/Event | |
| to her | it | explain | |
| '(s/he) will explain (it) (to her)' | | | |

(45) *podrá explicárselo*

| 3sg v-ará | *poder* | *explicár* | se | lo |
|---|---|---|---|---|
| Modal | ⇒ | | | |
| Finite | | Event | P3cl[27] | P2cl |
| will be able | | explain | to her | it |
| '(s/he) will be able to explain (it) (to her)' | | | | |

(46) *sí podrá explicárselo*

| sí | 3sg v-ará | *poder* | *explicár* | se | lo |
|---|---|---|---|---|---|
| Pos | ⇒ | | | | |
| | Modal | ⇒ | | | |
| | Finite | | Event | P3cl | P2cl |
| | will be able | | explain | to her | it |
| '(s/he) **will** be able to explain (it) (to her)' | | | | | |

(47) *no podrá explicárselo*

| no | 3sg v-ará | *poder* | *explicár* | se | lo |
|---|---|---|---|---|---|
| Neg | ⇒ | | | | |
| | Modal | ⇒ | | | |
| | Finite | | Event | P3cl | P2cl |
| | will be able | | explain | to her | it |
| '(s/he) won't be able to explain (it) (to her)' | | | | | |

An example of a three-tier analysis is presented below (including a Vcl function for the verbal group voice function realised by the *se* clitic in example (48)).

no se le había dicho casi nada
'He had hardly been told almost anything'

---

[27] In analysing P3cl and P2cl as unconflated multivariate functions, we are treating the realisation of the Event and P3cl and P2cl functions as one written word as an arbitrary graphological convention; *se lo explicó, explíqueselo, explicárselo* and *explicándoselo* are treated, in other words, as involving the same experiential Event and participant role relations.

142    Verbal Group

(48)    *no se le había dicho*

| no | se | le | 3sg v-aba *haber* | | v-ado *decir* |
|---|---|---|---|---|---|
| Neg | ⇒ | | | | |
| | Vcl | P3cl | Finite | | Event |
| | | | α⁻⁻ | β⁻ | |
| no | se | le | v-aba | *haber* ^ v-ado | *decir* |
| | | to him | | | tell |
| '(he) had hardly been told' | | | | | |

At this point you might find it useful to go back and reconsider the analysis of the English verbal group presented in Section 3.2 – asking whether a two-tier or three-tier structural analysis would be more appropriate. The arguments we just made about MODALITY and POLARITY are also relevant there. As ever in grammar description, we have to weigh up the cost of complicating the analysis in relation to representational integrity.

Pushing further back you are now in a position to reconsider the multivariate analysis of nominal groups deployed in Chapter 2. Would multivariate Classifier Thing structures with multiple Classifiers be better analysed as a univariate word complex realising the Thing function (e.g. *Australian surf lifesaving competition* or *la escala sismológica de magnitud de momento* 'the moment magnitude seismic scale')? Comparable univariate structures might also be considered for recursive Focus and Qualifier systems:

that kind of beer
the last of that kind of beer
a bottle of the last of that kind of beer
the bottom of a bottle of the last of that kind of beer

[el fondo de una botella del último de ese tipo de cerveza]

the trip from Santiago
the trip from Santiago through La Serena
the trip from Santiago through La Serena via Iquique
the trip from Santiago through La Serena via Iquique to Arica

[el viaje desde Santiago pasando por la Serena pasando por Iquique hasta Arica]

We have now explored Spanish verbal groups from the perspective of their ideational and interpersonal contributions to discourse. Ideationally speaking, they position figures in time in relation to the moment of speaking and in relation to one another. Interpersonally speaking, they position moves and nuance their negotiability in dialogue. From the perspective of paradigmatic relations, they include a recursive tense system – choices which, from the perspective of syntagmatic relations, are realised through univariate structure. In order to provide an integrated account of verbal group structure comparable to our English analysis, we began by treating all Spanish verbal group systems as realised through a serial structural configuration of this kind, using superscripts to index the specific choices being realised (e.g. $\alpha^{neg} \beta^{tr-cl} \gamma^{-} \delta^{modal} \varepsilon^{event}$ for *no lo podía creer* 's/he could not believe it' above). We then problematised this analysis with respect to:

i. the difference between the serial interdependency relations among tenses, on the one hand, and the orbital 'nucleus and satellite' dependency relations between P2cl and P3cl functions and the Event on the other and
ii. the scoping relations of modality and polarity functions with respect to the verbal group as a whole.

In light of these differences, we suggested a multi-tiered analysis distinguishing interpersonal, experiential and logical layers of structure.

## 3.4 Chinese Verbal Group Resources

As mentioned at the beginning of this chapter, verbal groups construe both a dynamic and a static perspective on phenomena. Statically, verbal groups provide resources for construing relationships among items and properties. This is true of both English and Spanish, but the situation in Chinese needs to be qualified. In Chinese, relationships among items and properties can be construed by verbal groups; but not always. Below are a few examples from our Interview with Curator text which lack Processes realised by verbal groups.

所以我对故宫并**不陌生**
*suǒyǐ wǒ duì Gùgōng bìng **bù mòshēng***
'so I (am) **not unfamiliar** with the Forbidden City'

故宫的文化底蕴**深不可测**
*Gùgōng de wénhuà dǐyùn **shēnbùkěcè***
'the cultural background of the Forbidden City (is) **profound beyond measure**'

我打70分绝对**高**了
*wǒ dǎ qīshí fēn juéduì **gāo** le*
'I give it 70 points – it (is) absolutely **high**'

In these examples, there are no verbal groups construing the relationships between items and properties; rather, word groups headed by adjectives (in bold above) directly realise properties of items. In the MOOD structure of a clause, these word groups realise the Predicator function that is closely associated with MOOD types of Chinese (see Chapter 4). Seen from below, these adjectival groups bear strong similarities to verbal groups – they can both be marked with aspect (e.g. 了 *le*), polarity (e.g. 不 *bù* for the negative) and modality (e.g. 可能 *kěnéng* 'can'). For this reason Chao (1948, p. 52) maintains that 'Chinese adjectives are verbs.' And Zhu (1982, p. 55) groups Chinese verbs and adjectives together under the category 谓词 *wèicí* 'predicate'.

That said, verbs and adjectives in Chinese are two distinguishable word classes. They have structural differences with regard to gradability and complementation with objects. Here we focus on the systems and structures of verbal groups with verbs as head – from the perspectives of ideational resources and interpersonal resources.

Generally speaking, the central function of a verbal group in Chinese is Event, realised by a verb. The verbal group can be expanded both after and before the Event. Functions after the Event are mainly responsible for ideational meaning (i.e. aspect and phase) and functions before the Event are mainly responsible for interpersonal meaning (i.e. polarity and modality); see Halliday and McDonald (2004: 314–15) for discussion.

### 3.4.1   Ideational Verbal Group Resources

When positioning a figure in relation to the time a text is spoken or written, Chinese does not make use of a TENSE system realised in a verbal group – unlike English and Spanish. So Chinese is 'not a tense language' (Norman, 1988, p. 163). The positioning of a figure in relation to time is mainly realised by Circumstances of location in time (for which see Chapter 5). What Chinese verbal groups do is construe figures as completed or ongoing in relation to a certain reference point in time; alternatively, they construe figures as habitual or repetitive occurrences or states. These meanings are realised lexicogrammatically through the system of ASPECT. The reference point in time, unlike that in tense languages like English and Spanish, is not the moment of speaking (i.e. 'interpersonal' time), but rather a moment in time established ideationally in discourse.

A Chinese verbal group may take no overt aspectual marker, in which case it realises a general, habitual occurrence or state. In our Interview with Curator text, the journalist opens with an introduction to International Museum Day and the exhibitions held at the Palace Museum, before moving on to the transcription of her interview with Mr Shan Jixiang (then curator of the Palace Museum).

今天**是**5.18国际博物馆日,这一天,故宫箭亭广场上,高科技艺术互动展演《清明上河图》惊艳**亮相**,人们**可以**"**走入**"画中,**穿越到**繁华的北宋都城,**一睹**宋代人文生活图景,**感受**宋代艺术之美。像这样生动有趣的高品质展览,故宫每年大概**要举办**40个。 …… 在国际博物馆日,人民网记者**走进**故宫博物院,独家**专访**院长单霁翔。

'Today **is** May 18, International Museum Day. On this day, on the Jianting Square of Palace Museum, a high-tech interactive exhibition *Along the River during the Qingming Festival* **makes its public appearance**. People **can "walk into"** the painting, **time-travel** to the bustling capital of the Northern Song Dynasty, **have a glimpse at** Song's culture and life, and **feel** the beauty of Song's art. Lively, interesting and high-class exhibitions like this one, the Palace Museum **would hold** around 40 every year.

… … On International Museum Day, the journalist of *People* **steps into** the Palace Museum, and exclusively **interviews** Curator Shan Jixiang.'

Verbal groups in Chinese (and their rough equivalent in English) are in bold above. In this excerpt there are nominal groups and a coverbal phrase indicating time – including 今天 *jīntiān* 'today', 这一天 *zhè yī tiān* 'this day', 每年 *měinián* 'every year' and 在国际博物馆日 *zài Guójì Bówùguǎn Rì* 'on International Museum Day'. Verbal groups, however, are not deployed to position figures in time.

The verbal groups in this excerpt are not marked as completed or ongoing either. They involve neutral aspect. In analysing the structure of verbal groups with neutral aspect, we introduce an Aspect function and conflate it with the Event, as illustrated in (49) and (50).

(49)

| Example | 亮相 |
|---|---|
| Transliteration | *liàngxiàng* |
| **group class** | verbal group |
| **group function** | Event/Aspect |
| **word class** | verb |
| Translation | 'strike a pose, make a public appearance' |

(50)

| Example | 感受 |
|---|---|
| Transliteration | *gǎnshòu* |
| **group class** | verbal group |
| **group function** | Event/Aspect |
| **word class** | verb |
| Translation | 'feel' |

This conflation allows us to distinguish between indicative clauses like (49) and (50) with neutral aspect and imperative clauses; the latter cannot access the ASPECT system (see Section 4.4.1 for discussion of imperative mood in Chinese). Indicative causes, on the other hand, make ASPECT choices, although neutral aspect has zero marking in verbal groups.

Chinese verbal groups explicitly mark perfective aspect (for completed occurrences) through the clitic 了 *le*; it is positioned at the end of the verbal group (in bold below).

住了很多四合院
*zhù le hěn duō sìhéyuàn*
'**lived** in many courtyard houses'

故宫近年来**策划了**一系列高品质展览
*Gùgōng jìnniánlái **cèhuà le** yī xìliè gāo pǐnzhì zhǎnlǎn*
'the Palace Museum **arranged** a series of high-quality exhibitions in recent years'

去年年底,故宫已经**研发了**10500种文创产品
*qùnián niándǐ, Gùgōng yǐjīng **yánfā le** 10500 zhǒng wénchuàng chǎnpǐn*
'(by) the end of last year, the Palace Museum **had developed** 10,500 kinds of cultural products'[28]

As mentioned at the beginning of this section, the reference point in time for the completedness of the occurrence is 'ideational' time. The completion of occurrences in the first two examples above, 住了 *zhù le* 'lived' and 策划了 *cèhuà le* 'arranged', is based on the present time – either left implicit or specified by 近年来 *jìnniánlái* 'in recent years'. Accordingly, these verbal groups are translated as simple past tense in English. In the third example, it is still the clitic 了 *le* that marks the completion of the occurrence 研发 *yánfā* 'develop'. But the time reference here is based on past time in discourse (specified ideationally as 去年年底 *qùnián niándǐ* '(by) the end of last year'). So this verbal group is translated as 'past-in-past' in English – 'had developed'.

Structurally these verbal groups are composed of an Event, realised by a verb, and an Aspect function realised by the postpositional clitic 了 *le*. Two examples are analysed for function and class in (51) and (52). The position of verbal groups in these examples is important because the word 了 *le* can be either an element of group structure (i.e. a clitic) or an element of clause structure (i.e. a particle). In traditional Chinese grammar the two classes are known as *le*₁ and *le*₂, or 'word-final *le*' and 'sentence-final *le*' (e.g. Liu 2002). 了 *le* functions as a verbal group clitic below.

(51)

| 住了 | | 很多四合院 |
|---|---|---|
| *zhù* | *le* | *hěnduō sìhéyuàn* |
| verbal group | | |
| Event | Aspect | |
| verb | clitic | |
| live | | many courtyard houses |
| 'lived in many courtyard houses' | | | |

(52)

| 故宫已经**研发了**10500种文创产品 | | | | |
|---|---|---|---|---|
| *Gùgōng* | *yǐjīng* | ***yánfā*** | *le* | *10500 zhǒng wénchuàng chǎnpǐn* |
| | | verbal group | | |
| | | Event | Aspect | |
| | | verb | clitic | |
| Palace Museum | already | develop | | 10,500 kinds of cultural products |
| 'the Palace Museum had developed 10,500 kinds of cultural products' | | | | |

---

[28] In Chinese there are a range of aspectual adverbs that cooperate with aspectual features in verbal groups, e.g. 已经 *yǐjīng* 'already' construing completedness, 正在 *zhèngzài* 'in process' construing ongoingness, 曾经 *céngjīng* 'ever' construing a figure as experienced.

## 3.4 Chinese Verbal Group Resources

We now move on to another subtype of the perfective aspect. The head verb realising the Event in a verbal group can also be followed by the clitic 过 *guo*,[29] meaning that an occurrence has been experienced at least once and that the discourse is dealing with implications of that experience. The contrast between 'completed' and 'experienced' can be usefully illustrated by the following pair of examples.

Completed:  我见了那些人
 *wǒ **jiàn le** nà xiē rén*
 'I **met** those people' (sometime in the past)

Experienced:  我见过那些人
 *wǒ **jiàn guo** nà xiē rén*
 'I **have met** those people' (so now I know something about them)

As with completed aspect, the reference point in time for experienced aspect is also 'ideational' time – either the past, the present or the future. An example retrieved from Peking University's modern Chinese corpus is provided below, with time set in the future; in this example what is implicated by the experience is made explicit ('you'll know I didn't lie').

下次我带你回家,你见过我的父母,就知道我没有说谎
*xiàcì wǒ dài nǐ huí jiā, nǐ **jiàn guo** wǒ de fùmǔ, jiù zhīdào wǒ méiyǒu shuōhuǎng*
'next time I take you home, you **will have met** my parents, and you'll know I didn't lie'

The following two examples with 'experienced' aspect, are from our focus text. The first sets time in the past, the second in the present.

我到故宫博物院之前,曾在北京市文物局及国家文物局**工作过**
*wǒ dào Gùgōng Bówùyuàn zhíqián, céng zài Běijīng Shì Wénwù Jú jí Guójiā Wénwù Jú **gōngzuò guo***
'Before I came to the Palace Museum, I **had worked** at Beijing Municipal Cultural Heritage Bureau and National Cultural Heritage Administration'

您**说过**改革开放带来的巨大变化是 … …
*nín **shuō guo** gǎigé kāifàng dài lái de jùdà biànhuà shì …*
'You **have said** that a great change brought by China's opening and reform was … '

The structural configurations of verbal groups containing the clitic 过 *guo* and those with 了 *le* are identical – the Event function realised by verb followed by the Aspect function realised by clitic.

---

[29] 过 *guo* as clitic takes the neutral tone and therefore does not have phonological salience. With the falling tone, 过 *guò* is a verb meaning 'cross', 'pass', 'spend', etc.

148    Verbal Group

(53)

| 曾在北京市文物局及国家文物局**工作过** | | |
|---|---|---|
| céng zài Běijīng Shì Wénwù Jú jí Guójiā Wénwù Jú | **gōngzuò** | **guo** |
| | verbal group | |
| | Event | Aspect |
| | verb | clitic |
| ever   at Beijing Municipal Cultural Heritage Bureau and National Cultural Heritage Administration | work | |
| '(I) had worked at Beijing Municipal Cultural Heritage Bureau and National Cultural Heritage Administration' | | |

(54)

| 您**说过** | | |
|---|---|---|
| nín | **shuō** | **guo** |
| | verbal group | |
| | Event | Aspect |
| | verb | clitic |
| you (respect form) | say | |
| 'you have said' | | |

To this point we have introduced neutral, completed and experienced aspect. In Figure 3.18 we group [completed] and [experienced] choices together as subtypes of perfective, as opposed to the neutral aspect. This grouping is supported by evidence both from above and from below. From above, they both realise the meaning that an occurrence or state involved in a figure has finished in relation to some reference point in time, as against an occurrence or state that is habitual or whose completion is unspecified. From below, both completed and experienced aspects are realised by the post-Event function Aspect, as against conflated Aspect/Event functions realising the neutral aspect. The relevant system network and realisation statements is provided in Figure 3.18.

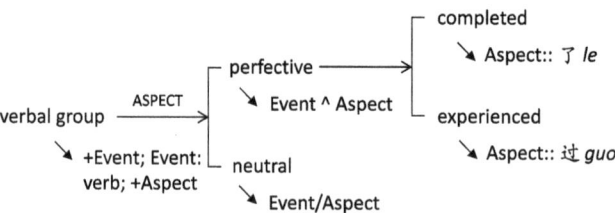

Figure 3.18  Basic Chinese verbal group ASPECT systems

## 3.4 Chinese Verbal Group Resources

The major difference between [completed] and [experienced] aspect is that completed aspect construes an occurrence or state as having taken place, whereas experienced aspect construes an occurrence or state as having become part of some participant's experience. In the following example,[30] the first emboldened verbal group, 参加过 *cānjiā guo* 'had participated', construes the occurrence of participating in fire fighting as the worker's experience; the other emboldened verbal groups, 烧掉了 *shāo diào le* 'burnt away', 昏了 *hūn le* 'fainted' and 爬上了 *pá shàng le* 'climbed up', simply construe individual occurrences that took place in the process of fire fighting.

一位**参加过**扑火的工人告诉我们,当时的战士**烧掉了**头发和眉毛,有的战士被浓烟呛得**昏了过去**,但醒来后又**爬上了**楼顶……

'A worker who **had participated** in the fire fighting told us that the soldiers had their hair and eyebrows **burnt away**, and some soldiers were choked by the heavy smoke and **fainted**, but **climbed up** the building upon awakening …'

Now we move on to additional choices in the ASPECT system. Chinese verbal groups take progressive aspect when the occurrence or state is ongoing in relation to some reference point in time. Again, this time can be set in the past, present or future as the discourse unfolds. Our focus text only has ongoing aspect in relation to the present time – as reflected in 'present-in-present' translations into English.

故宫**有着**600年历史
*Gùgōng yǒu zhe liùbǎi nián lìshǐ*
'The Forbidden City **is having** (has) 600 years of history'

故宫博物院开展每一项工作,往往都深刻而多样地**交织着**"两难"的问题
*Gùgōng Bówùyuàn kāizhǎn měi yī xiàng gōngzuò, wǎngwǎng dōu shēnkè ér duōyàng de jiāozhī zhe 'liǎngnán' de wèntí*
'A lot of work at the Palace Museum **is being mingled with** (involves) "dilemmas"'

我**保持着**对文化遗产事业的执着和专一
*wǒ bǎochí zhe duì wénhuà yíchǎn shìyè de zhízhuó hé zhuānyī*
'**I am keeping** my perseverance and dedication to the work of cultural heritage'

In this group of examples, the Event function in the verbal group is also followed by an Aspect function – lexicalised by the clitic 着 *zhe*. We provide an analysis of two examples below.[31]

---

[30] This example is retrieved from the corpus of Centre for Chinese Linguistics, Peking University.
[31] Note that 故宫 *Gùgōng* (lit. 'Ancient Palace') in (55) is glossed as 'Forbidden City'. In (52) the same word is glossed 'Palace Museum'. It depends on the context which gloss to use: 'Forbidden City' if it refers to the imperial palace complex that was China's political and ritual centre; 'Palace Museum' if it refers to museums that are housed in former royal palaces.

(55)

| 故宫**有着**600年历史 | | | |
|---|---|---|---|
| Gùgōng | **yǒu** | **zhe** | liùbǎi nián lìshǐ |
| | verbal group | | |
| | Event | Aspect | |
| | verb | clitic | |
| Forbidden City | have | | 600 years of history |
| 'The Forbidden City is having (has) 600 years of history' | | | |

(56)

| 我**保持着**对文化遗产事业的执着和专一 | | | |
|---|---|---|---|
| wǒ | **bǎochí** | **zhe** | duì wénhuà yíchǎn shìyè de zhízhuó hé zhuānyī |
| | verbal group | | |
| | Event | Aspect | |
| | verb | clitic | |
| I | keep | | perseverance and dedication to the work of cultural heritage |
| 'I am keeping my perseverance and dedication to the work of cultural heritage' | | | |

Another marker of an ongoing occurrence is (正)在 (zhèng)zài. Some studies (e.g. Halliday and McDonald, 2004; Li and Thompson, 1981; McDonald, 1996, 1998; Zuo, 1999) treat it as marking the progressive aspect, whereas others (e.g. Hu, 2011, p. 286) do not list it among aspect markers of verbs. In our focus text we have examples that use (正)在 (zhèng)zài to mark ongoing occurrences.

故宫博物院一直**在思考**故宫文化如何与今天的人们生活顺畅对话的问题
Gùgōng Bówùyuàn yīzhí **zài sīkǎo** Gùgōng wénhuà rúhé yǔ jīntiān de rénmen shēnghuó shùnchàng duìhuà de wèntí
'the Palace Museum **has been pondering** over the question as to how the Forbidden City culture can interact smoothly with modern people's life'

所以观众看到的是今天故宫**正在走向**世界一流博物馆
suǒyǐ guānzhòng kàn dào de shì jīntiān Gùgōng **zhèngzài zǒuxiàng** shìjiè yīliú bówùguǎn
'so visitors can see that the Palace Museum today **is rising** to the rank of the world's first-rate museums'

我们**正在实施**两项工程
wǒmen **zhèngzài shíshī** liǎng xiàng gōngchéng
'we **are implementing** two projects'

We do not analyse (正)在 (zhèng)zài as functioning in the system of ASPECT (i.e. realising the Aspect) because it has many differences in terms of structure and class from the clitics that realised the Aspect function. Firstly, (正)

## 3.4 Chinese Verbal Group Resources

在 (*zhèng*)*zài* appears before the verb realising the Event – this is unlike Aspect clitics (and words realising the other ideational function Phase in verbal groups), which are positioned after the Event. Secondly, between (正)在 (*zhèng*)*zài* and the Event a clause rank element can be inserted – e.g. 正在以各种鲜活生动的方式**走**出紫禁城 ***zhèngzài*** *yǐ gèzhǒng xiānhuó de fāngshì **zǒu chū Zǐjìnchéng*** '(our products) are going out of the Forbidden City in various lively ways'; but no clause rank element can be inserted between the Event and the post-verb Aspect clitic. Thirdly, even if (正)在 (*zhèng*)*zài* is present in a clause, the verbal group can still use the clitic 着 *zhe* to mark progressive aspect – e.g. 他**在**躺着呢 *tā zài tǎng zhe ne* 'he is lying (assuming a horizontal resting position)'. Fourthly, in terms of class, the Aspect clitics 着 *zhe*, 了 *le*, 过 *guo* are clitics, while 在 *zài* and 正在 *zhèngzài*, when denoting an ongoing occurrence or state, are treated as adverbs in traditional Chinese grammar. 在 *zài* is essentially a coverb.[32] Zhu (1982, pp. 184–5) suggests that a clause that expresses an ongoing action, e.g. 他**在**躺着呢 *tā **zài** tǎng zhe ne* 'he is lying (assuming a horizontal resting position)', has evolved from the ellipsis of a location, e.g. 他**在那儿**躺着呢 *tā **zài nàr** tǎng zhe ne* 'he is lying **there**'.[33] Fifthly, from below, the clitics 着 *zhe*, 了 *le*, 过 *guo* take the neutral tone and are phonologically non-salient, whereas (正)在 (*zhèng*)*zài* can be made phonologically salient.

Our description of the ASPECT system for Chinese verbal groups is summarised in the system network in Figure 3.19. In this system network, we take into consideration the aspectless choice for a verbal group (see Section 4.4 in Chapter 4 for discussion of the imperative mood in Chinese). We also bring into the system network a distinction between [progressive] and [perfective], which together are opposed to [neutral].

Structurally, our generalisation of [completed] and [experienced] as [perfective] in opposition to [progressive] can be supported by the fact that a verbal group in the progressive aspect can co-exist with the adverb (正)在 (*zhèng*)*zài* in the same clause, while a verbal group in the perfective aspect cannot. In addition, the realisations of POLARITY in verbal groups with perfective and progressive aspects are different (see discussion below); this provides cryptogrammatical motivation for our distinction between [perfective] and [progressive].

---

[32] As mentioned in Section 2.4, in Chinese, a coverb is a subclass of verb. By itself, 在 *zài* can realise the Process of a clause, e.g. 新馆**在**海淀上庄地区 *xīn guǎn **zài** Hǎidiàn Shàngzhuāng dìxū* 'the new museum site **is at** Shangzhuang, Haidian'. Its use as a coverb is grammaticalised from its use as a full verb.

[33] It would be interesting to compare verbal groups featuring 在 *zài* ... 着 *zhe* with the archaic or dialectal use of English 'present in present' in the form of *a-* ... *-ing*, e.g. *I remembered it was the twenty-seventh and came **a-running*** (Shirley Jackson, *The Lottery*). The prefix *a-* is said to derive from Early Middle English preposition *an/on* (Montgomery, 2009).

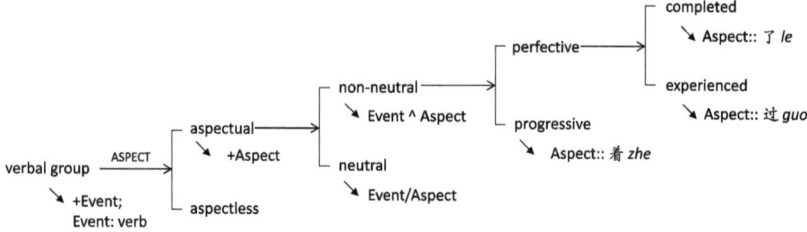

Figure 3.19 Chinese verbal group ASPECT systems

We now turn to the second type of ideational resource in Chinese verbal groups. According to Halliday and Matthiessen (1999, p. 307), in a Chinese verbal group it is often the case that the verb itself does not imply completion of an occurrence; this contrasts with English, where 'the meaning of a process typically includes its completion'. For example, the English verb 'cut' indicates the completion of the act of cutting; in Chinese, however, we have to use 剪断 *jiǎn duàn* 'cut off' or 切开 *qiē kāi* 'cut open' to culminate the cutting. A simple verb 剪 *jiǎn* or 切 *qiē* would not make it clear whether the cutting was successfully accomplished or not. The additional element attached subsequently to the verb, expressing the result or direction of the verb meaning is known as a 补语 *bǔyǔ* 'complement' in traditional Chinese grammar; and the syntagm as a whole is called 'verb–complement structure' or 'predicate–complement structure'. In our focus text there are many examples of verbal groups involving the expression of result or direction of occurrences.

**保护好**故宫世界文化遗产
***bǎohù hǎo*** *Gùgōng shìjiè wénhuà yíchǎn*
'**protect** the Forbidden City's world cultural heritage **well**'

**研发出**故宫元素文化创意产品
***yánfā chū*** *Gùgōng yuánsù wénhuà chuàngyì chǎnpǐn*
'**develop** cultural products with elements of the Forbidden City'

很多观众**进到**故宫后一直往前走
*hěn duō guānzhòng* ***jìn dào*** *Gùgōng yīzhí wǎng qián zǒu*
'many visitors keep walking straight after they **enter** the Palace Museum'

改革开放四十年,对您个人而言,**带来了**哪些影响
*gǎigé kāifàng sìshí nián, duì nín gèrén éryán,* ***dài lái le*** *nǎxiē yǐngxiǎng*
'what influences **did** 40 years' opening and reform **bring** to you'

In SFL, the complementary element after the Event verb has been described in terms of the system of PHASE (see also McDonald, 1994, 1996, 1998;

## 3.4 Chinese Verbal Group Resources

Halliday and McDonald, 2004), which alongside ASPECT is also an ideational system at the rank of verbal group. The system gives rise to presence of a Phase function, positioned after the Event and realised by verb or adjective. Analyses of two examples for function and class are provided below.

(57)

| 很多观众**进到**故宫 | | | |
|---|---|---|---|
| hěn duō guānzhòng | **jìn** | **dào** | Gùgōng |
| | verbal group | | |
| | Event | Phase | |
| | verb | verb | |
| many visitors | enter | arrive | Palace Museum |
| 'many visitors **enter** the Palace Museum' | | | |

(58)

| **保护好**故宫世界文化遗产 | | |
|---|---|---|
| **bǎohù** | **hǎo** | Gùgōng shìjiè wénhuà yíchǎn |
| verbal group | | |
| Event | Phase | |
| verb | adjective | |
| protect | good | Forbidden City's world cultural heritage |
| 'protect the Forbidden City's world cultural heritage well' | | |

Although both are realised after the Event, the Phase and Aspect functions have a major difference in their realisations. The Aspect function is realised by a clitic, whereas the Phase function realising result of occurrence is realised by a verb or an adjective.

The phases of a verbal group can be divided into two types: resultative and directional (Halliday and McDonald, 2004). Examples (57) and (58) above illustrate resultative phase. The two examples below illustrate directional phase.

(59)

| 人民网记者**走进**故宫博物院 | | | |
|---|---|---|---|
| Rénmínwǎng jìzhě | **zǒu** | **jìn** | Gùgōng Bówùyuàn |
| | verbal group | | |
| | Event | Phase | |
| | verb | verb | |
| journalist of *People* | walk | go in | Palace Museum |
| 'the journalist of *People* steps into the Palace Museum' | | | |

(60)

| 故宫文物**走出**红墙 | | | |
|---|---|---|---|
| Gùgōng wénwù | zǒu | chū | hóng qiáng |
| | verbal group | | |
| | Event | Phase | |
| | verb | verb | |
| cultural relics of the Palace Museum | walk | go out | red wall |
| 'cultural relics of the Palace Museum go out of the red walls' | | | |

The verb 进 *jìn* 'go in' in (59) and the verb 出 *chū* 'go out' in (60) are known in traditional Chinese grammar as 'directional verbs'; they are attached to a main verb (usually one indicating movement) to express the direction of that movement. Besides 进 *jìn* 'go in' and 出 *chū* 'go out', other commonly used 'directional verbs' in Chinese include 上 *shàng* 'go up', 下 *xià* 'go down', 来 *lái* 'come near', 去 *qù* 'go away' – or combinations of them, e.g. 上来 *shàng lái* 'come up', 下来 *xià lái* 'come down', 进来 *jìn lái* 'come in', 进去 *jìn qù* 'go in'. Chao (1968, p. 458) presents a more detailed account.

It is worth noting that the same verb form may realise both resultative and directional phases. For example, the verb 出 *chū* 'go out' in (60) realises the directional phase, construing the outward direction of walking. It can also realise the resultative phase, as shown in (61) below, construing the successful result of development of cultural products.

(61)

| **研发出**故宫元素文化创意产品 | | |
|---|---|---|
| yánfā | chū | Gùgōng yuánsù wénhuà chuàngyì chǎnpǐn |
| verbal group | | |
| Event | Phase | |
| verb | verb | |
| develop | go out | cultural products with elements of the Forbidden City |
| 'develop cultural products with elements of the Forbidden City' | | |

What reasons do we have for analysing the 'verb–complement' units such as 走出 *zǒu chū* 'walk out' and 看懂 *kàn dǒng* 'understand by seeing' as verbal groups rather than single verbs? There are words in Chinese that apparently have the same structure, but we will treat them as verbs rather than verbal groups – e.g. 说明 *shuōmíng* 'explain (lit. "speak-clear")', 改正 *gǎizhèng* 'rectify (lit. "change-correct")'. One probe that helps to distinguish between the two categories is to see whether a modality marker 得 *de* (positive) or 不 *bù* (negative) can be inserted in between. Verbal groups with Event ^ Phase structure can be interrupted by such markers, whereas single verbs cannot.

## 3.4 Chinese Verbal Group Resources

走出 *zǒu chū* 'walk out'
走**得**出 *zǒu **de** chū* 'can walk out'
走**不**出 *zǒu **bù** chū* 'cannot walk out'

看懂 *kàn dǒng* 'understand by seeing'
看**得**懂 *kàn **de** dǒng* 'can understand by seeing'
看**不**懂 *kàn **bù** dǒng* 'cannot understand by seeing'

说明 *shuōmíng* 'explain'
*说**得**明 *shuō **de** míng* 'can explain'
*说**不**明 *shuō **bù** míng* 'cannot explain'

改正 *gǎizhèng* 'rectify'
*改**得**正 *gǎi **de** zhèng* 'can rectify'
*改**不**正 *gǎi **bù** zhèng* 'cannot rectify'

As stated earlier, the Phase function realising the resultative meaning can be realised either by a verb or by an adjective; accordingly, we distinguish between two subtypes of resultative phase: verbal and adjectival. We thus arrive at a system network (with realisation statements) that outlines the system of PHASE for Chinese verbal groups (Figure 3.20).

When both Phase and Aspect functions are present in the verbal group structure, Phase is positioned before Aspect. Two examples are analysed below.

(62)

| 走遍了故宫的9371间房间 | | | |
|---|---|---|---|
| ***zǒu*** | ***biàn*** | ***le*** | *Gùgōng de jiǔqiān sānbǎi qīshí yī jiān fángjiān* |
| verbal group | | | |
| Event | Phase | Aspect | |
| verb | verb | clitic | |
| walk | be everywhere | | 9371 rooms of the Forbidden City |
| 'have been to all the 9371 rooms of the Forbidden City' | | | |

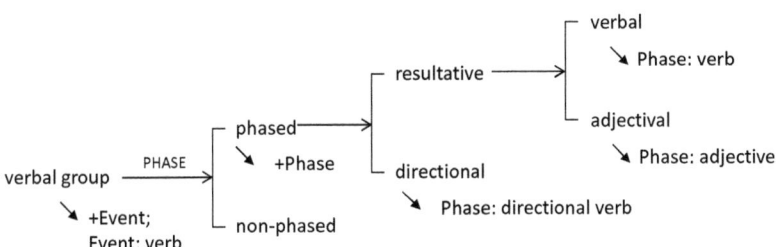

Figure 3.20 Chinese verbal group PHASE systems

(63)

| 带来了哪些影响 | | | |
|---|---|---|---|
| *dài* | *lái* | *le* | *nǎxiē yǐngxiǎng* |
| verbal group | | | |
| Event | Phase | Aspect | |
| verb | verb | clitic | |
| take | come | | what influences |
| 'what influences did (they) bring' | | | |

Taking into account the systems of PHASE and ASPECT as simultaneous systems, we need to make an adjustment to the realisation statement for the feature [non-neutral]. Specifically, we need to replace the sequencing symbol ^ in Event ^ Aspect with an arrow superscript ←; this indicates the relative positions of the two functions, without requiring them to be adjacent to each other. When both Aspect and Phase are present, the structure is Event ^ Phase ^ Aspect. The consolidated system network and adjusted realisation statements are presented in Figure 3.21.[34]

Finally in this section, we take a closer look at the verb ^ verb/adjective syntagm noted above (a 'verb–complement structure' in traditional grammar) with the positive modality marker 得 *de* in between. The verb ^ 得 *de* ^ verb/adjective syntagm actually realises two types of structure: one enacts probability or ability (e.g. 走得出 *zǒu de chū* 'can walk out') while the other

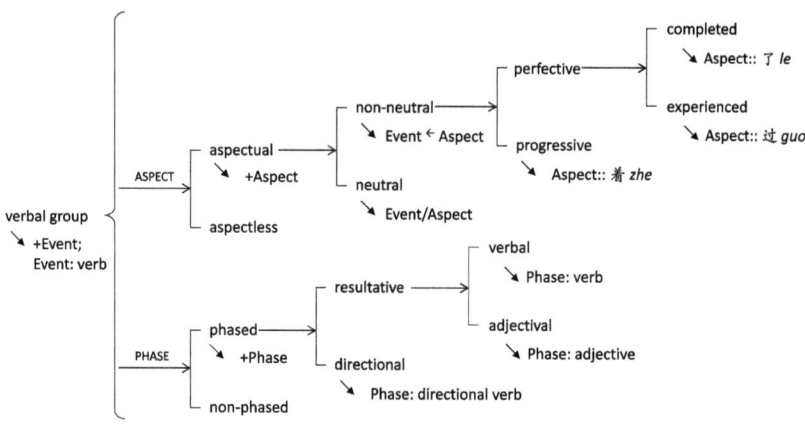

Figure 3.21 Chinese verbal group ASPECT and PHASE systems

[34] Not all features in the ASPECT system can be co-selected with all features in the PHASE system. However, we do not discuss specific conditions and restrictions here. For further discussion see Guo (1993) and Ma (2005).

## 3.4 Chinese Verbal Group Resources

construes an attribute (e.g. 长得漂亮 *zhǎng de piàoliàng* 'be beautiful', lit. 'grow *de* beautiful').

The first type realises the Event ^ Mod ^ Phase structure in our analysis of Chinese verbal groups (see Section 3.4.2 for discussion of MODALITY). If the modality marker 得 *de* is removed, the verbal group still bears the Event ^ Phase structure discussed above (as shown in (60)). The word that realises Phase cannot be expanded and its meaning is not negotiable. What is negotiable rests with the entire Predicator realised by the verbal group as a whole (see Chapter 4 for discussion of negotiability and the Predicator function in Chinese clauses). That is to say, if a question is raised in relation to the proposition, the response must be based on the entire verbal group, not just on the word that realises Phase.

Question: 走得出吗? *zǒu de chū ma* 'can (someone) walk out?'
Response (positive): 走得出 *zǒu de chū* '(someone) can walk out'
Response (negative): 走不出 *zǒu bù chū* '(someone) cannot walk out'

Question: 走得出吗? *zǒu de chū ma* 'can (someone) walk out?'
Response (ungrammatical): *出 *chū* 'go out' / *不出 *bù chū* 'not go out'

The second type, however, cannot have the word 得 *de* removed. In addition, the unit after 得 *de* can be expanded and its meaning is negotiable.

长得漂亮 *zhǎng de piàoliàng* 'be beautiful' (lit. 'grow *de* beautiful')

Note the ungrammaticality if 得 *de* is removed:

*长漂亮 *zhǎng piàoliàng* lit. 'grow beautiful'

Compare expandability:

长得**真**漂亮 *zhǎng de **zhēn** piàoliàng* 'be **really** beautiful'
长得**比她妈妈**还漂亮 *zhǎng de **bǐ tā māma** piàoliàng* 'be **more** beautiful **than her mum**'

Compare negotiability:

Question: 长得漂亮吗? *zhǎng de piàoliàng ma* 'is (she) beautiful?'
Response (positive): 漂亮 *piàoliàng* 'beautiful'
Response (negative): 不漂亮 *bù piàoliàng* 'not beautiful'

When adjectives are used in this syntagm, the same form can realise both the first and the second type of structure. The difference can be explored through reactances, as illustrated in Table 3.12.

Based on the above analysis, we can conclude that only the first type is relevant to the verbal group structure discussed in this section. The adjective in the second type of structure realises the Attribute function at clause rank (we will return to discussion of this structure in Chapter 5 on Transitivity).

Table 3.12 *Contrasting structures involving modality vs attribution*

| | Type 1: modality | Type 2: attribution |
|---|---|---|
| **positive** | 说得清楚<br>*shuō de qīngchǔ*<br>lit. 'speak *de* clear'<br>'can explain clearly' | 说得清楚<br>*shuō de qīngchǔ*<br>lit. 'speak *de* clear'<br>'can explain something so that it is clear' |
| **negative** | 说不清楚<br>*shuō bù qīngchǔ*<br>'cannot explain clearly' | 说得不清楚<br>*shuō de bù qīngchǔ*<br>'explain something but it is not clear' |
| **expandability** | | 说得十分清楚<br>*shuō de shífēn qīngchǔ*<br>'explain something so that it is very clear' |
| **negotiability** | 说得清楚吗?<br>*shuō de qīngchǔ ma*<br>'can (someone) explain clearly?'<br>–说得清楚<br>*shuō de qīngchǔ*<br>'(someone) can explain clearly'<br>–说不清楚<br>*shuō bù qīngchǔ*<br>'(someone) cannot explain clearly' | 说得清楚吗?<br>*shuō de qīngchǔ ma*<br>'is (something) clear after being explained?'<br>–清楚<br>*qīngchǔ*<br>'(it is) clear'<br>–不清楚<br>*bù qīngchǔ*<br>'(it is) not clear' |
| **proposition-oriented interrogative**[35] | 说不说得清楚?<br>*shuō bù shuō de qīngchǔ*<br>'(does someone) explain clearly or not?' | 说得清楚不清楚?<br>*shuō de qīngchǔ bù qīngchǔ*<br>'(is something) clear or not after being explained?' |

### 3.4.2 Interpersonal Verbal Group Resources

The interpersonal resources involved in Chinese verbal groups are POLARITY and MODALITY; these are grammatical systems realising the ENGAGEMENT subsystem of the discourse semantic system of APPRAISAL (Martin and White, 2005). The system of ENGAGEMENT concerns the expansion or contraction of dialogic space in relation to the position under negotiation.

First, POLARITY. This system offers two choices: [positive] and [negative]. Like English and Spanish, Chinese does not have explicit marking for the positive polarity on the verbal group, except for emphasis. Negative polarity is explicitly realised by a Neg function, which in turn is realised by an adverb enacting negation. From the perspective of discourse semantics, negation contracts dialogic space, pushing aside the position being negated.

---

[35] See Chapter 4, Section 4.4 on Mood.

## 3.4 Chinese Verbal Group Resources

Our Interview with Curator text features two negation adverbs: 不 *bù* and 没 (有) *méi(yǒu)*.[36] When the Event verb in the verbal group is 有 *yǒu* 'have, there be' (construing possession or existence), negative polarity is realised by putting 没 *méi* before the verb – i.e. forming the verbal group 没有 *méi yǒu* 'not have, there not be'.[37] This is illustrated by example (64).

(64)

| 这些大家具**没有**空间修复 | | | | |
|---|---|---|---|---|
| *zhèxiē dà jiājù* | ***méi*** | ***yǒu*** | *kōngjiān* | *xiūfù* |
| | verbal group | | | |
| | Neg | Event | | |
| | adverb | verb | | |
| these large pieces of furniture | not | there be | space | repair |
| 'there is no space to repair these large pieces of furniture' | | | | |

With other verbs, the negation adverbs 不 *bù* and 没(有) *méi(yǒu)* are used for neutral aspect and non-neutral aspect respectively. We provide some examples from our focus text below, analysed for function and class.

我**不是**段子手
*wǒ **bù shì** duànzishǒu*
'I **am not** a joke teller'

我**不讲**段子
*wǒ **bù jiǎng** duànzi*
'I **don't tell** jokes'

**没想到**最后一个岗位是在北京最大的四合院看门
***méi xiǎng dào*** *zuìhòu yī gè gǎngwèi shì zài Běijīng zuì dà de sìhéyuàn kān mén*
'(I) **didn't expect** that (my) last post is looking after Beijing's biggest courtyard house'

80%的观众**没有看到**故宫博物院的展览就出去了
*bǎifēnzhī bāshí de guānzhòng **méiyǒu kàn dào** Gùgōng Bówùyuàn de zhǎnlǎn jiù chū qù le*
'80% of the visitors go out of the Palace Museum, **not having seen** its exhibition'

(65)

| 我**不讲**段子 | | | |
|---|---|---|---|
| *wǒ* | ***bù*** | ***jiǎng*** | *duànzi* |
| | verbal group | | |
| | Neg | Event | |
| | adverb | verb | |
| I | not | tell | joke |
| 'I don't tell jokes' | | | |

[36] In this chapter we mainly discuss negation in verbal groups in declarative clauses. Negation adverbs 别 *bié* and 不要 *bùyào* in imperative clauses are discussed in Chapter 4, Section 4.4.

[37] In colloquial usage the verb 有 *yǒu* 'have, there be' can be omitted from the verbal group 没有 *méi yǒu* 'not have, there not be'. In formal contexts, the negative verb 无 *wú* 'not have, there not be' can also be used.

(66)

| 没想到最后一个岗位是在北京最大的四合院看门 | | | |
|---|---|---|---|
| *méi* | *xiǎng* | *dào* | *zuìhòu yī gè gǎngwèi shì zaì Běijīng zuì dà de sìhéyuàn kān mén* |
| verbal group | | | |
| Neg | Event | Phase | |
| verb | verb | verb | |
| not | think | arrive | last post is looking after Beijing's biggest courtyard house |
| '(I) didn't expect that (my) last post is looking after Beijing's biggest courtyard house' | | | |

(67)

| 没有看到故宫博物院的展览 | | | |
|---|---|---|---|
| *méiyǒu* | *kàn* | *dào* | *Gùgōng Bówùyuàn de zhǎnlǎn* |
| verbal group | | | |
| Neg | Event | Phase | |
| verb | verb | verb | |
| not | look | arrive | exhibition of the Palace Museum |
| '(they) didn't see the exhibition of the Palace Museum' | | | |

In verbal groups with completed aspect, when the verbal group takes a Neg function lexicalised as 没(有) *méi(yǒu)*, then the clitic 了 *le* which would have realised the Aspect function in a positive clause is not present in the structure.

Positive:  看到了故宫博物院的展览
*kàn dào le Gùgōng Bówùyuàn de zhǎnlǎn*
'**saw** the exhibition of the Palace Museum'

Negative:  没(有)看到故宫博物院的展览
*méi(yǒu) kàn dào Gùgōng Bówùyuàn de zhǎnlǎn*
'**didn't see** the exhibition of the Palace Museum'

In case of experienced aspect, the clitic 过 *guo* is included. The following example is slightly modified from (67).

Positive:  看到过故宫博物院的展览
*kàn dào guo Gùgōng Bówùyuàn de zhǎnlǎn*
'**have seen** the exhibition of the Palace Museum'

Negative:  没(有)看到过故宫博物院的展览
*méi(yǒu) kàn dāo guo Gùgōng Bówùyuàn de zhǎnlǎn*
'**haven't seen** the exhibition of the Palace Museum'

When negation is enacted in verbal groups with progressive aspect realised by the clitic 着 *zhe*, the Neg function is lexicalised as 没(有) *méi(yǒu)* and

## 3.4 Chinese Verbal Group Resources

positioned before the Event ^ Aspect structure.[38] The following examples involve slight modifications of our focus text.

**没(有)交织着**"两难"的问题
*méi(yǒu) jiāozhī zhe liǎngnán de wèntí*
'**not being mingled with** "dilemmas"'

我**没(有)保持着**对文化遗产事业的执着和专一
*wǒ méi(yǒu) bǎochí zhe duì wénhuà yíchǎn shìyè de zhízhuó hé zhuānyī*
'I **am not keeping** my perseverance and dedication to the work of cultural heritage'

Next, MODALITY. As introduced in Sections 3.2.2 and 3.3.2 above, the MODALITY resources include probability, usuality, inclination, obligation and ability. The realisation of MODALITY in Chinese verbal groups is the Mod function, realised by modal verbs and modal adverbs. As mentioned earlier, the interpersonal resources of Chinese verbal groups are placed before the Event verb in structure. The following examples are from our focus text, with verbal groups emboldened, and modal verbs and adverbs underlined.

人们**可以"走入"**画中
*rénmen <u>kěyǐ</u> 'zǒu rù' huà zhōng*
'people <u>can</u> "**walk into**" the painting'

观众还**能"走进"**画中
*guānzhòng hái <u>néng</u> 'zǒu jìn' huà zhōng*
'visitors also <u>can</u> "**walk into**" the painting'

今年故宫开放面积**将超过**80%
*jīnnián Gùgōng kāifàng miànjī <u>jiāng</u> chāo guò bǎifēnzhī bāshí*
'opening area of the Palace Museum this year <u>will</u> **exceed** 80%'

像这样生动有趣的高品质展览,故宫每年大概**要举办**40个
*xiàng zhèyàng shēngdòng yǒuqù de gāo pǐnzhì zhǎnlǎn, Gùgōng měinián dàgài <u>yào</u> jǔbàn sìshí gè*
'lively, interesting and high-class exhibitions like this one, the Palace Museum <u>would</u> **hold** around 40 every year'

**能够领略到**故宫文物藏品的丰富多样
*<u>nénggòu</u> lǐnglüè dào Gùgōng wénwù cángpǐn de fēngfù duōyàng*
'<u>can</u> **appreciate** the great variety of the Palace Museum's collection articles of cultural relics'

---

[38] Li and Thompson (1981: 437) suggest that 着 *zhe* marks a durative state of an activity, and denial of that state is to negate its existence through negating the existential verb 有 *yǒu* 'there be' with 没 *méi* 'not'.

解读经典的文化,就**需要用**一种生动的、喜闻乐见的形式来加以表达
*jiědú jīngdiǎn de wénhuà, jiù **xūyào** yòng yī zhǒng shēngdòng de, xǐwénlèjiàn de xíng-shì lái jiāyǐ biǎodá*
'explanation of classic culture **needs to** use lively, popular expressions'

我不仅是一个看门人,还**应该是**一个讲解员
*wǒ bùjǐn shì yī gè kānménrén, hái **yīnggāi shì** yī gè jiǎngjiěyuán*
'I'm not only a doorkeeper, but also **should** be an interpreter'

**必须承认**,故宫博物院院长是一个风险很大的岗位
***bìxū** chéngrèn, Gùgōng Bówùyuàn yuànzhǎng shì yī gè fēngxiǎn hěn dà de gǎngwèi*
'(we) **must admit** that the curator of Palace Museum is a post of high risks'

Below we provide detailed analysis of two verbal groups enacting probability and two enacting obligation, with one modal verb and one modal adverb for each pair.

(68)

| 观众还**能**"走进"画中 | | | | | |
|---|---|---|---|---|---|
| *guānzhòng* | *hái* | ***néng*** | ***zǒu*** | ***jìn*** | *huà zhōng* |
| | | verbal group | | | |
| | | Mod | Event | Phase | |
| | | modal verb | verb | verb | |
| visitor | also | can | walk | go in | inside of painting |
| 'visitors also can "walk into" the painting' | | | | | |

(69)

| 今年故宫开放面积**将超过**80% | | | | | |
|---|---|---|---|---|---|
| *jīnnián* | *Gùgōng kāifàng miànjī* | ***jiāng*** | ***chāo*** | ***guò*** | *bǎifēnzhī bāshí* |
| | | verbal group | | | |
| | | Mod | Event | Phase | |
| | | modal adverb | verb | verb | |
| this year | Palace Museum's opening area | will | exceed | pass | 80% |
| 'opening area of the Palace Museum this year will exceed 80%' | | | | | |

(70)

| 还**应该是**一个讲解员 | | | |
|---|---|---|---|
| *hái* | ***yīnggāi*** | ***shì*** | *yī gè jiǎngjiěyuán* |
| | verbal group | | |
| | Mod | Event | |
| | modal verb | verb | |
| also | should | be | an interpreter |
| '(I) also should be an interpreter' | | | |

(71)

| 必须承认 | |
|---|---|
| **bìxū** | **chéngrèn** |
| verbal group | |
| Mod | Event |
| modal adverb | verb |
| must | admit |
| '(we) must admit' | |

Modal verbs and modal adverbs can be differentiated in relation to the possibility of a 'V not V' syntagm. Modal verbs can enter into such a syntagm (e.g. 能不能 *néng bù néng* 'can or cannot', 应该不应该 *yīnggāi bù yīnggāi* 'should or should not'); but modal adverbs cannot (e.g. *将不将 *jiāng bù jiāng* 'will or will not', *必须不必须 *bìxū bù bìxū* 'must or not').

Modality in Chinese verbal groups can also be realised through discontinuous structures, with other clause rank elements inserted between Mod and Event, as illustrated by the following examples.

能准确**记得**
***néng** zhǔnquè **jìdé***
'**can** accurately **remember**'

必须心怀敬意地**研究**
***bìxū** xīnhuáijìngyì de **yánjiū***
'**must** reverently **study**'

可以在新馆气势恢宏地**布置出来**
***kěyǐ** zài xīn guǎn qìshìhuīhóng de **bùzhì chūlái***
'**can** at the new museum magnificently **put on exhibition**'

In the previous section when we introduced the system of PHASE as an ideational resource for Chinese verbal groups, we mentioned another way of enacting MODALITY. For positive verbal groups, the clitic 得 *de* is inserted between the Event verb and the Phase verb or adjective (e.g. 走得出 *zǒu de chū* 'can walk out', 看得懂 *kàn de dǒng* 'can understand by seeing'). For negative verbal groups, the adverb 不 *bù* is inserted in the same position (e.g. 走不进 *zǒu bù jìn* 'cannot walk in', 看不完 *kàn bù wán* 'cannot finish seeing'). In both cases the MODALITY bears on the phase rather than on the verbal group as a whole.[39] Detailed analysis for two examples is provided below.

---

[39] When the MODALITY bears on the phase, it modalises only the phase. For example, 走得进 *zǒu de jìn* 'can walk in' means one can walk and can also walk into a place; and 走不进 *zǒu bù jìn* 'cannot walk in' means one can walk but cannot walk into a place. In contrast, when the MODALITY bears on the verbal group as a whole, it modalises the entire verbal group: 能走进 *néng zǒu jìn* 'can walk in' means one can enter a place; and 不能走进 *bù néng zǒu jìn* 'cannot walk in' means one cannot enter a place.

(72)

| 看**得**懂 | | |
|---|---|---|
| kàn | ***de*** | *dǒng* |
| verbal group | | |
| Event | Mod | Phase |
| verb | clitic | verb |
| see | | understand |
| 'can understand by seeing' | | |

(73)

| 看**不**完 | | |
|---|---|---|
| kàn | ***bù*** | *wán* |
| verbal group | | |
| Event | Mod/Neg | Phase |
| verb | adverb | verb |
| see | not | understand |
| 'cannot finish seeing' | | |

When the verbal group has both a Neg function and a Mod function before the Event, both Neg ^ Mod and Mod ^ Neg structures are possible. In the Neg ^ Mod structure, the negative polarity contracts dialogic space by dismissing the modalised proposition as a whole; for example, 不可以走进 ***bù** kěyǐ zǒu jìn* '**can't** enter' invalidates the proposition established by 可以走进 *kěyǐ zǒu jìn* 'can enter'.

(74)

| 不可以走进 | | | |
|---|---|---|---|
| *bù* | *kěyǐ* | *zǒu* | *jìn* |
| verbal group | | | |
| Neg | Mod | Event | Phase |
| adverb | modal verb | verb | verb |
| not | can | walk | go in |
| 'can't enter' | | | |

In the Mod ^ Neg structure, e.g. 可以**不**走进 *kěyǐ **bù** zǒu jìn* 'can **not** enter (can stay outside)', the Neg function also plays an ideational role. In this case the interpersonal meaning enacted through modality scopes over the rest of the verbal group, expanding dialogic space. We analyse the example in (75) by following the tiered model proposed for the Spanish verbal group – using an arrow ⇒ to denote the scope of the prosody. Example (74) is reanalysed below as (76) in order to make the scope of the prosodies more explicit.

3.4 Chinese Verbal Group Resources    165

(75)

| 可以不走进 | | | |
|---|---|---|---|
| kěyǐ | bù | zǒu | jìn |
| verbal group | | | |
| Mod | ⇒ | | |
| | Neg | ⇒ | |
| | | Event | Phase |
| modal verb | adverb | verb | verb |
| can | not | walk | go in |
| 'can not enter (can stay outside)' | | | |

(76)

| 不可以走进 | | | |
|---|---|---|---|
| bù | kěyǐ | zǒu | jìn |
| verbal group | | | |
| Neg | ⇒ | | |
| | Mod | ⇒ | |
| | | Event | Phase |
| adverb | modal verb | verb | verb |
| not | can | walk | go in |
| 'can't enter' | | | |

Before we close this section, let's consider a more complex modality resource. Some Chinese modal verbs and modal adverbs can be used conjointly, as illustrated in the following examples.[40]

这些东西**应该可以**卖个好价钱
*zhèxiē dōngxī **yīnggāi kěyǐ** mài ge hǎo jiàqián*
'these things **should be able to** be sold at a good price'
probability ^ ability; modal verb ^ modal verb

我不相信有任何人**会愿意**出面帮我的忙
*wǒ bù xiāngxìn rènhé rén **huì yuànyì** chūmiàn bāng wǒ de máng*
'I don't believe anyone **will be willing** to help me'
probability ^ inclination; modal verb ^ modal verb

**可能要**花较多的时间
***kěnéng yào** huā jiào duō de shíjiān*
'**probably will** take more time'
probability ^ obligation; modal verb ^ modal verb

---

[40] There are no double modals in our focus text. These examples are retrieved from the corpus of Centre for Chinese Linguistics, Peking University.

我们**或许应该**怀着体贴和同情来看待这段历史
*wǒmen **huòxǔ yīnggāi** huái zhe tǐtiē hé tóngqíng lái kàndài zhè duàn lìshǐ*
'We **probably should** look at the history with compassion and sympathy'
probability ^ obligation; modal adverb ^ modal verb

**要能够**充分理解这些资料
*yào nénggòu chōngfèn lǐjiě zhèxiē zīliào*
'**should be** able to fully understand these materials'
obligation ^ ability; modal verb ^ modal verb

Consecutive modals appear to unfold with modalisation (probability, usuality) preceding modulation (inclination, obligation), which in turn precedes ability. And modal adverbs precede modal verbs. For detailed discussion on double and multiple modals in Chinese, see Ma (2005).[41]

### 3.5 Verbal Group Corpus Challenge

For those of you familiar with other languages, we trust that we have now modelled an approach to verbal group system and structure that you will find instructive. For those of you familiar with English, Spanish or Chinese, we reiterate as a reminder here that the descriptions introduced above have been provided for pedagogic purposes. They are both preliminary and provisional.

We took time to challenge our univariate analysis of Spanish verbal groups and make suggestions about an alternative metafunctionally diversified tiered approach more respectful of the different kinds of structure involved. We also showed that Chinese verbal groups have a basic multivariate structure, not a univariate one, with ideational and interpersonal components placed on the right and left sides of the Event function respectively. SFL grammarians working in both the Sydney (e.g. Matthiessen, 1996) and the Cardiff (e.g. Fawcett, 2000b, 2000c) models have already pushed the discussion of English beyond what we have presented here; and Bache (2008) both extends the debate and proposes an alternative model. For Spanish, our proposals here have been largely based on Quiroz (2013, 2017b) and can be usefully compared with those in Lavid, Arús and Zamorano-Mansilla (2010). As Quiroz (2017b) has emphasised, when monitoring these discussions it is crucial to keep in mind the foundational role played by axis, rank, metafunction and stratification in analyses. For Chinese, our analysis can serve as a useful complement to McDonald (1998), Halliday and McDonald (2004) and Li (2007). Different theoretical foundations inevitably lead to different analyses, a point that is far too often lost sight of in descriptive debates. Just to be clear, we have assumed the axial

---

[41] Interestingly, double modal verbs are used in some varieties of English, for example in the southern United States – e.g. *might could, might should*, as reported in Di Paolo (1989). These also follow a modalisation then modulation sequence.

foundations outlined in Matthiessen and Halliday (1997/2009) and Martin, Wang and Zhu (2013) here.

As noted above some languages do all or most of the work discussed in this chapter at word rather than group rank, via verb morphology. People working on languages of this kind will find Matthiessen's (2004) discussion of descriptive motifs and generalisations across languages helpful; and they will also need to consult Matthiessen (2015c) for an introduction to modelling morphology in SFL. Kim et al. (2023) deal explicitly with verb morphology in their grammar of Korean.

For readers familiar with English, Spanish or Chinese, the main challenge we would like to put to you here is a corpus one. For pedagogic purposes we have mainly relied for examples on just three key texts in this chapter; this is obviously an extremely limited sample as far as exploring the instantiation and genesis of verbal groups systems is concerned.

One important research question for both English and Spanish is the extent to which their recursive tense systems are still developing, and in which registers. How many examples can we find of the more complex verbal groups introduced above and where do they arise? Unfortunately, the large corpora of informal conversational registers we need to answer many of our questions are still being developed; data of this kind is relatively expensive to collect and still relatively scarce – more so for Spanish than English, and more so again for less well documented languages. Meanwhile we can all practise learning to keep our ears open, as telling examples sweep by.

In our discussion of Spanish verbal groups above, we also noted in passing a number of apparent alternatives with respect to the temporal positioning of figures – including the following:

i. the perfect and imperfect primary 'past' tenses
ii. imperfect primary tense vs 'present in perfect'
iii. future primary tense vs 'future in present'
iv. an apparent blurring of the perfect/imperfect distinction once secondary tenses are deployed (with 'secondary tense in imperfect' preferred to the 'secondary tense in perfect' option)
v. the alternative realisations of secondary tenses in modalised verbal groups

In part it is as if the development of the analytic recursive tense system alongside synthetic tense resources might be seen as giving rise to grammatical resources competing for a comparable discourse niche. To find out more about how Spanish is managing this 'competition', we need intensive register analysis, looking for significant patterns of co-textualised variation. As we know from Caffarel's work on TENSE systems in French (e.g. 1992), the meaning potential of the system can show considerable variation across registers. And to this we need to add the possibility of regional dialectal variation as well (the Latin American preference for 'future in present' over primary future being a case in point).

For readers familiar with Chinese, the challenge we propose is also related to the use of a corpus. Our description of Chinese verbal groups for pedagogical purposes focuses mainly on the multivariate structure of verbal groups; however, Chinese verbal groups may also involve univariate structures realising MODALITY, as briefly touched upon at the end of Section 3.4. Corpus-based studies can reveal more detail about such structures: what are the possible combinations of modal verbs and modal adverbs? How many examples can we find involving more than two or three Mod functions? What are the limits to recursion in univariate structure? What are the possible co-occurrences of modality bearing on the verbal group as a whole and modality bearing only on the phase?

We look forward to hearing from those of you taking up our corpus challenge.

# 4 Mood

## 4.1 Approaching from Above

In this chapter we will approach clauses from an interpersonal perspective. In terms of tenor (interpersonal context), clauses provide key resources for enacting social relations of power (status) and solidarity (contact) among interlocutors – positioning and repositioning interlocutors as more or less involved with and more or less on the same footing as one another (Figure 4.1).

In terms of interpersonal discourse semantics, the systems of NEGOTIATION and APPRAISAL, in particular, clauses, play a key role in positioning moves in dialogue and in adjusting the play of voices around these moves.

In order to better co-textualise our analysis of interpersonal grammar, we begin this chapter by introducing the discourse semantic system of NEGOTIATION. This system allows for exchanges consisting of between 1 and 5 moves, in addition to tracking and challenging options. In terms of rank (SFL's constituency hierarchy), NEGOTIATION is thus realised by Halliday's system SPEECH FUNCTION (e.g. Halliday, 1985). Our examples are sourced and adapted from our Youth Justice Conference text and involve the Convenor (who organises the conference), the Young Person (charged with an offence) and an Ethnic Community Liaison Officer (abbreviated ECLO), a policeman who works with young people in the Muslim community.

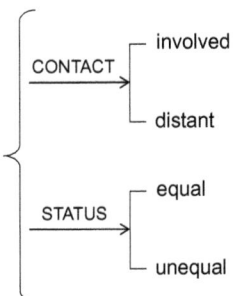

Figure 4.1 Tenor variables

Following Berry (1981a, 1981b) this system distinguishes between exchanges negotiating proposals (action exchanges involving an exchange of goods & services) and exchanges negotiating propositions (knowledge exchanges involving an exchange of information). Action exchanges have an obligatory move whereby goods are exchanged or a service undertaken by the primary actor (an A1 move):

(1)

| Convenor: | A1 | Here's some water (handing it over). |
|---|---|---|

Information exchanges have a corresponding obligatory move whereby information is provided by the primary knower (a K1 move):

(2)

| Young Person: | K1 | My mum wears a scarf. |
|---|---|---|

Alternatively, an exchange can be initiated by a secondary actor (an A2 move) or a secondary knower (a K2 move). Below the secondary actor requests a drink:

(3)

| Young Person: | A2 | Can I have some water please? |
|---|---|---|
| Convenor: | A1 | – Here you go. |

In the next example a secondary knower (an Ethnic Community Liaison Officer) requests information relating to the young person's mother's religion:

(4)

| ECLO: | K2 | Does your mum wear a scarf? |
|---|---|---|
| Young Person: | K1 | – Yeah. |

A third possibility is for an exchange to be initiated by a primary actor or knower (as in the first two examples above), but this time checking first whether the goods & services are desired by the secondary actor (a delay A1 move), or to highlight information of special pertinence for the secondary knower (a delay K1 move).

(5)

| Convenor: | Da1 | Would you like some water? |
|---|---|---|
| Young Person: | A2 | – Yes please. |
| Convenor: | A1 | – Here you go. |

(6)

| ECLO: | Dk1 | Mate, what's your mum wearing on her head?[1] |
|---|---|---|
| Young Person: | K2 | – Scarf. |
| ECLO: | K1 | – Yeah. |

The obligatory A1/K1 moves in these exchanges can be optionally followed up by the secondary actor or knower. The discourse function of follow-up moves is to consolidate the successful negotiation of the nuclear A1 or K1 moves in an exchange.

---

[1] The Young Person's mother is present at this conference and wearing a headscarf (hijab).

## 4.1 Approaching from Above

(7)

| Convenor: | A2 | I need you to speak a bit louder. |
|---|---|---|
| Young Person: | A1 | – OK. |
| Convenor: | A2f | – Thanks. |

(8)

| ECLO: | K2 | How does that make our community look? |
|---|---|---|
| Young Person: | K1 | – Worse. |
| ECLO: | K2f | – It does, doesn't it? |

Ventola's service encounter data (1987) drew attention to the possibility of a further follow-up move by the primary actor or knower, extending Berry's model.

(9)

| Convenor: | A2 | I need you to speak a bit louder. |
|---|---|---|
| Young Person: | A1 | – OK. |
| Convenor: | A2f | – Thanks. |
| Young Person: | A1f | – No problem. |

(10)

| ECLO: | K2 | How does that make our community look? |
|---|---|---|
| Young Person: | K1 | – Worse. |
| ECLO: | K2f | It does, doesn't it? |
| Young Person: | K1f | – Yes. |

From a syntagmatic perspective, the structure for each exchange type can be expressed as a structure potential (with optional moves in parentheses, and '^' specifying sequence):

action exchanges: $((Da1) \wedge A2) \wedge A1 \wedge (A2f \wedge (A1f))$
knowledge exchanges: $((Dk1) \wedge K2) \wedge K1 \wedge (K2f \wedge (K1f))$

Martin (1992) further extended this description to allow for calling, greeting and exclaiming exchanges. The discourse semantic meaning potential developed to this point can be formalised as a system network (including the relevant paradigmatic oppositions and interdependencies, and their structural consequences). The key systems and realisation statements are presented in Figure 4.2[2] (for an accessible introduction to this model see Martin and Rose 2007).

Provision also has to be made for what are referred to as tracking and challenging moves, extending Burton's (1980, 1981) and Berry's (1981a) concern with uncooperative responses. Tracking moves clarify information that has

---

[2] In the realisation statements, Cl stands for Call, Rcl for Response to Call (e.g. *Ahmar. – What?*), Gr stands for Greeting, Rgr for Response to greeting (*Hi. – Hi.*) and Ex stands for Exclamation and Rex for Response to Exclamation (*Amazing! – Yeah!*); immediate action A1 moves are realised non-verbally, optionally accompanied by verbalisation (e.g. *Can I have some water? – Here you go.* [while pouring]), whereas postponed action A1 moves are realised verbally, optionally followed by action (e.g. *Can I have some water? – I'll see if I can get you some.*).

172    Mood

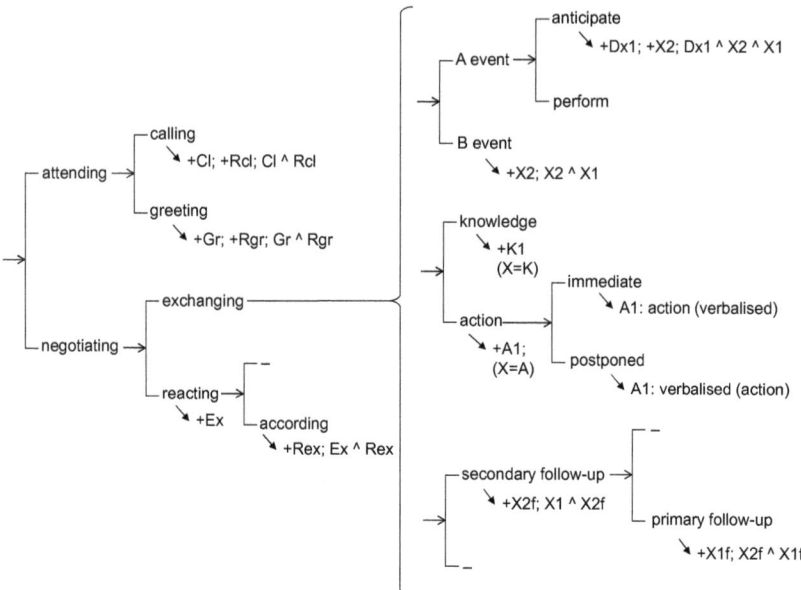

Figure 4.2 NEGOTIATION systems

not been confidently interpreted from a preceding move (an ideational focus); challenging moves resist the complaint positioning which a preceding move has presumed (an interpersonal focus). In the tracking example below 'tr' stands for 'track', and 'rtr' for 'response to 'track'.

(11)
| ECLO: | K2 | Any of your friends go? |
| Young Person: | tr | – At the police station? |
| ECLO: | rtr | – Yeah. |
| Young Person: | K1 | – No. |

More significant disruptions arise when the addressee is not comfortable with the way they have been positioned by a move in an exchange and challenge this positioning. In information exchanges, for example, the addressee may not know the answer to a K2 request for information and refuse the primary knower role which has been assigned to them. Non-compliant moves of this kind are referred to as challenges, notated as 'ch' in the analyses below.

In goods & services exchanges, an example of non-compliance would involve an addressee's disinclination or inability to enable an A1 move. A challenge to an Da1 move is illustrated below.

(12)
| Convenor: | Da1 | Would you like some water? |
| Young Person: | ch | – No thanks. |

## 4.1 Approaching from Above

Subtypes of tracking and challenging moves (e.g. backchannels, checks and invites) will not be reviewed here but introduced where needed for text analysis below (for overviews see Martin, 1992; Ventola, 1987; Zappavigna and Martin, 2018). Tracking and challenging moves enter into dependency relations with immediately preceding moves in exchange structure,[3] including other tracking or challenging moves and all the moves realising the NEGOTIATION system (Martin, 1992).

The other discourse semantic concepts we need to introduce have to do with the arguability of a move – namely its nub and terms. The nub of a move is the entity that is most at risk in an exchange; the terms is the temporal or modal grounding of the exchange. In the following exchanges, for example, the nub shifts from the young person to the Koran, while the terms stay grounded in the moment of the interaction (i.e. not before or after, nor are the moves modalised). The parts of the moves realising the nub and terms are noted in Table 4.1 (with parentheses enclosing implicit realisations).

In the following moves (Table 4.2), both the nub and the terms shift around. The nub of the first move is the problem the conference is dealing with; in the

Table 4.1 *Nub and terms exemplified in English dialogue*

|  |  |  | nub | terms |
|---|---|---|---|---|
| ECLO: | A2 | You show me where in the Koran it says we can do things like that. | you | show |
|  | A2 | You show me where. | you | show |
|  | A2 | Tell me where. | (you) | tell |
|  | Dk1 | Does it? | it | does |
| Young Person: | K2 | – No. | (it) | (doesn't) |
| ECLO: | K1 | – It doesn't, does it? | it | doesn't |
| Young Person: | K2f | – No. | (it) | (doesn't) |

Table 4.2 *Nub and terms (further examples)*

|  |  |  | nub | terms |
|---|---|---|---|---|
| Young Person: | K1 | It's me. | it | 's |
|  | K1 | Sometimes I can think, | I | sometimes, can |
|  | K1 | sometimes I can't. | I | sometimes, can't |
|  | K1 | That's why I'm here. | that | 's |

---

[3] For development of the analysis of exchange structure in relation to Ventola's (1987) notion of 'linguistic service', see Zappavigna and Martin (2018); for discussion of a manoeuvre rank consisting of one or more exchanges in classroom discourse, see Martin and Dreyfus (2015).

174    Mood

second and third it is the young person and in the fourth it's the young person's ability to think or not. The terms shift in line with these changes, from grounding in the moment of the interaction, to modalities of usuality and ability and back to the moment of interaction again.

In the following exchanges (Table 4.3), the nub of the argument, the young offender, is held constant until the final move when it shifts to the ethic community liaison officer. The terms shift from the moment of the interaction to involve modalities of probability on the part of the liaison officer (expressed as the metaphorical modality *I don't think*)[4] before culminating in the final move in the moment of interaction again.

As the chapter unfolds we will attend carefully to the grammatical resources English, Spanish and Chinese deploy to make moves arguable, including their resources for establishing the nub and terms of an exchange.

In Section 4.2 below we explore English MOOD, before turning to Spanish resources in Section 4.3 and Chinese resources in Section 4.4. Our focus text for English is drawn from research on Youth Justice Conferencing, a restorative justice programme in New South Wales, Australia (Zappavigna and Martin, 2018). Since the offence it deals with is affray (the use or threatened use of physical force to harm another person), we'll refer to it as the Affray text. Our focus texts for Spanish are call centre ones, one attempting to change a satellite TV plan (El Plan 'the plan'), the other getting a set-top box working again (El Decodificador 'the set-top box'). Our focus text for Chinese is based on the interaction in the courtroom trial of a reckless driving case; we'll refer to it as the Reckless Driving text. In Section 4.5 we present an analysis challenge.

Table 4.3 *Nub and terms (additional examples)*

|  |  |  | nub | terms |
|---|---|---|---|---|
| ECLO: | K2 | Do you understand what I'm saying to you? | you | do |
| Young Person: | K1 | Yes. | I | do |
| ECLO: | ch | Do you really understand? | you | do |
|  | ch | Because I don't really … I honestly don't think you do. | you | I don't think … do |
| Young Person: | rch | I do. | I | do |
| ECLO: | ch | I don't think you do. | you | I don't think … do |
|  | ch | I don't think you do. | you | I don't think … do |
|  | K1 | I'm being honest with you. | I | 'm |

[4] Metaphorical modalities were introduced in Chapter 1, Section 1.4 (see also Halliday and Matthiessen, 2014, pp. 686ff); the reference to the speaker, *I*, is part of this metaphorical modality and does not therefore encode the nub of the argument (which remains focused on the Young Person).

## 4.2 English MOOD Resources

In this section we begin with three main types of clause in the Affray text that are used to negotiate exchanges of information or of goods & services, zeroing in on the resources English uses to realise the nub and terms of its moves. First, clauses in information exchanges. Early in the affray conference, the Convenor, a private citizen trained to manage conferencing, makes some essential conference moves. She begins by declaring one of the conditions of a conference.

(13)

| Convenor | K1 | Ok, Aatif, one of the conditions of a juvenile conference is that you admit to the offence in front of all of us here today and that you tell us that you are here of your own free will. |
|---|---|---|

The conditions are then confirmed through a pair of K2 ^ K1 exchanges.

(14)

| Convenor | K2 | So did you commit the offences you were charged with? |
|---|---|---|
| YP | K1 | – Yes. |

(15)

| Convenor | K2 | And are you here of your own free will? |
|---|---|---|
| YP | K1 | – Yes. |

In order to explore the grammar of these moves, let's add a tag to the Convenor's K1 move.

(16)

| Convenor | K1 | Ok, Aatif, one of the conditions of a juvenile conference is that you admit to the offence in front of all of us here today and that you tell us that you are here of your own free will, isn't it? |
|---|---|---|

And let's make the YP's K1 moves less elliptical.

(17)

| Convenor | K2 | So did you commit the offences you were charged with? |
|---|---|---|
| YP | K1 | – Yes, I did. |

(18)

| Convenor | K2 | And are you here of your own free will? |
|---|---|---|
| YP | K1 | – Yes, I am. |

And now let's make them not elliptical at all.

(19)

| Convenor | K2 | So did you commit the offences you were charged with? |
|---|---|---|
| YP | K1 | – Yes, I did commit the offences I was charged with. |

(20)

| Convenor | K2 | And are you here of your own free will? |
| YP | K1 | – Yes, I am here of my own free will. |

Finally let's add some tags to the YP's K1 moves.

(21)

| Convenor | K2 | So did you commit the offences you were charged with? |
| YP | K1 | – Yes, I did, didn't I? |

(22)

| Convenor | K2 | And are you here of your own free will? |
| YP | K1 | – Yes, I am, aren't I? |

(23)

| Convenor | K2 | So did you commit the offences you were charged with? |
| YP | K1 | – Yes, I did commit the offences I was charged with, didn't I? |

(24)

| Convenor | K2 | And are you here of your own free will? |
| YP | K1 | – Yes, I am here of my own free will, aren't I? |

The point of making these alternations is to focus attention on two matters. One is the way in which English grammar deals with the nub and terms of an argument, foregrounding them in tags and elliptical responses (*I did, I am, didn't I, aren't I* above). The other is the way English positions the moves in an exchange through the sequence of these elements. In play here are two multivariate clause functions, Subject and Finite. Not only do these functions demarcate the nub and terms of a clause, but their sequencing encodes the kind of move it is making in an exchange (the distinction between a declarative and an interrogative, as tabled below).

(25)

|    |               | Finite  | Subject |                                            |
|----|---------------|---------|---------|--------------------------------------------|
| K2 | interrogative | Did     | you     | commit the offences you were charged with? |
| K1 | declarative   | – I     | did.    |                                            |
|    |               | Subject | Finite  |                                            |

The fact that Subject and Finite functions are replayed in English tags (notated Finite' and Subject' below) makes tags a valuable resource for identifying Subject and Finite functions in any English declarative clause.

(26)

|             | Subject | Finite | Finite' | Subject' |
|-------------|---------|--------|---------|----------|
| declarative | I       | did,   | didn't  | I?       |

Only a few dialects of English (Australian English for example) allow tags in interrogatives.

## 4.2 English MOOD Resources

(27)

|  | Finite | Subject |  | Finite' | Subject' |
|---|---|---|---|---|---|
| interrogative | Did | you | have a knife, | did | you? |

And so for most speakers using a tag to identify the Subject and Finite functions means turning an interrogative clause back into a corresponding declarative (holding all other meaning constant).

(28)

|  | Finite | Subject |  | Finite' | Subject' |
|---|---|---|---|---|---|
| interrogative | Did | you | have a knife? |  |  |
| declarative | I | did | have a knife, | didn't | I? |
|  | Subject | Finite |  | Finite' | Subject' |

Let's step back at this point and think paradigmatically about what is going on. As networked in Figure 4.3, we have a SUBJECT PERSON[5] system realised through a Subject function, and realising the nub of the clause; it allows speakers to position the speaker, an addressee or a non-interlocutor as the entity most at risk in relation to any other entities realised in the clause. The speaker and

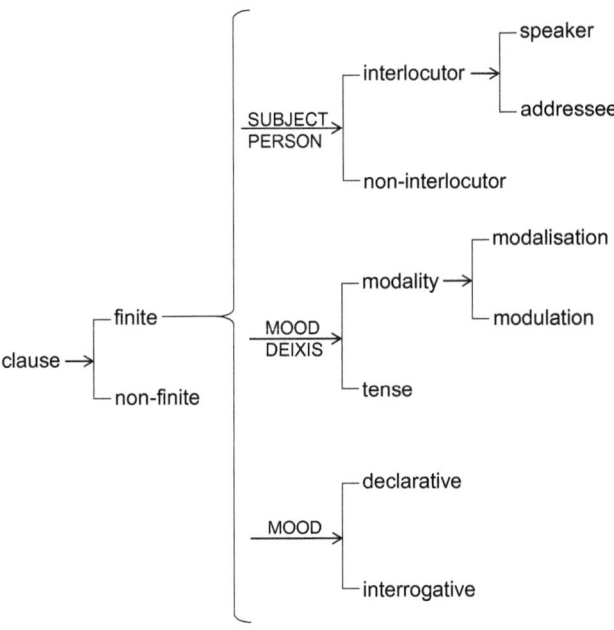

Figure 4.3 Basic English MOOD systems

---

[5] Although we will not develop the interaction of SUBJECT PERSON and MOOD DEIXIS in this book, English tag systems depend on choices from these systems, and there is also some NUMBER and PERSON agreement to coordinate (for present tense for most verbs).

addressee are grouped together as interlocutors. We also have a MOOD DEIXIS system, realised through a Finite function, and realising the terms of the clause; it allows speakers to ground the argument in tense or modality. In addition, we have a MOOD system, at this stage distinguishing declaratives from interrogatives, realised through the sequence of the Subject and Finite functions and positioning the clause as a move in an exchange. These three systems cross-classify finite clauses. Non-finite clauses are not negotiable and so don't select options from these systems.

In conferences YPs have to provide a full recount of their offence. In our affray conference the YP in fact initially leaves out various pieces of information that the Convenor feels are relevant to the conference process. She explores these through interrogatives asking for specific details.

(29)
| Convenor | K2 | … what did he actually say to you? |
|---|---|---|
| YP | K1 | - He was going to see Misbah. |

(30)
| Convenor | K2 | And why was he going to see Misbah? |
|---|---|---|
| YP | K1 | – Because Misbah offered him out.[6] |

(31)
| Convenor | K2 | (… you had something on your person) What was that? |
|---|---|---|
| YP | K1 | – The knife. |

These K2 moves involve a different type of interrogative. The Finite function still comes before the Subject, reflecting the demand for information. But in addition, the clauses include a Wh function in clause-initial position (realised by *why* and *what* above) soliciting specific experiential meaning – what the YP's friend said in the first example, why his friend was going to see Misbah in the second and what the YP took with him in the third. This kind of interrogative cannot be tagged, and so confirming their Subject and Finite function depends once again on finding the nearest possible declarative alternative. This generally involves replacing wh group or phrase realising the Wh function with a non-specific realisation and sequencing it appropriately in declarative clause structure. Alternatives for the wh-interrogatives exemplified above are suggested below.[7]

He actually said **something** to you, didn't he?

He was going to see Misbah **for some reason**, wasn't he?

The thing you had on your person was …?[8]

---

[6] A colloquial expression meaning that Misbah has challenged the YP's friend to a fight, one-on-one.
[7] In some languages, for example Korean, these indefinite expressions are used in place of a special class of 'wh' words (Kim et al., 2023).
[8] Non-specificity is realised by withholding the tonic syllable in this example and thus creating an information gap for a K1 move to fill in.

4.2 English MOOD Resources 179

The first of the wh clauses exemplified above could be analysed as follows – limiting ourselves to the SUBJECT PERSON (Subject), MOOD DEIXIS (Finite) and MOOD (Subject and Finite sequence) systems introduced so far.

(32)
| | Wh | Finite | Subject | |
|---|---|---|---|---|
| wh-interrogative | What | did | he | actually say to you? |

At this point we'll focus our attention on paradigmatic relations, and elaborate the simple declarative/interrogative MOOD system introduced above (including structure building realisation statements).[9] From the perspective of MOOD, the knowledge exchanges we've been analysing involve indicative clauses (Figure 4.4). As the realisation statement for indicative specifies, they include a Subject function and a Finite function. In declarative clauses the Subject precedes the Finite; in interrogative clauses it follows. Interrogative clauses are then divided into polar and wh classes; for wh clauses it is necessary to insert a Wh function, position it first in the clause (the # ^ Wh notation) and sequence it before the Finite.

Let's now problematise this description. At one point in the conference, the ECLO challenges the YP's relationship with his mates, asking if any of them came to visit him when he served time in juvenile detention earlier on in life for another offence.

(33)
| ECLO | Who went and visited you? |
|---|---|
| | Who went to see you there? |

In these examples the ECLO is looking for information about the Subject of the clauses (i.e. trying to find out which entity is nub). And this creates a

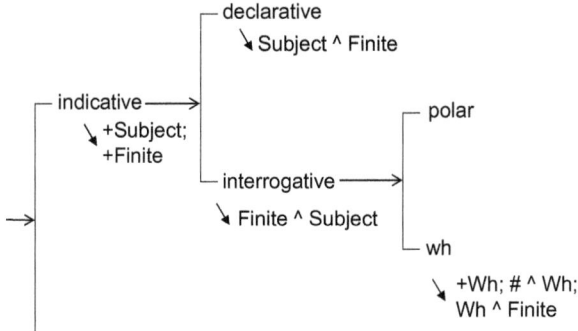

Figure 4.4 English indicative systems

[9] For an introduction to this formalism, see Matthiessen and Halliday (1997/2009); Martin, Wang and Zhu (2013).

problem for the network and realisation statements just reviewed. The realisation statement there says that in all interrogatives Finite precedes Subject; but the statement for wh-interrogatives says that the Wh function comes first in the clause. When English asks for information about the Subject, thereby conflating the Wh function with the Subject one, then the realisation statements conflict with one another; both cannot be true. English, in other words, has to choose between saying *Did who go and visit you?* (following its Finite before Subject in interrogatives pattern) or *Who went and visited you?* (following its Wh function first pattern). The latter wins out.

This means we have to adjust our description as follows, distinguishing between the two types of wh-interrogative (wh subject vs wh other), and restricting the Finite before Subject realisation statement to polar and wh other clauses (Figure 4.5). Since the realisation statement for wh-interrogatives in general specifies that the Wh function precedes Finite, we don't need a separate sequencing rule for wh subject interrogatives; it is enough to conflate the Subject function with the Wh function to achieve the sequence Wh/Subject ^ Finite structure we need.

This immediately raises a question as to whether the feature [interrogative] is now simply motivated from above, as a congruent realisation of exchange initiating K2 moves, or whether there are grammatical patterns depending on this feature. One piece of evidence we can point to has to do with what Halliday and Matthiessen (2014) call Comment Adjuncts. Attitudinal ones, such as *sadly, unfortunately, regrettably* etc., can only be used in declarative clauses (e.g. *Sadly he didn't apologise* but not \**Sadly, did he apologise?*). Another group, including *honestly, frankly, confidentially*, etc., can be used in either declaratives or interrogatives (e.g. *Frankly, he doesn't sound sincere* and *Frankly, does he sound sincere?*). In declaratives this group realises the

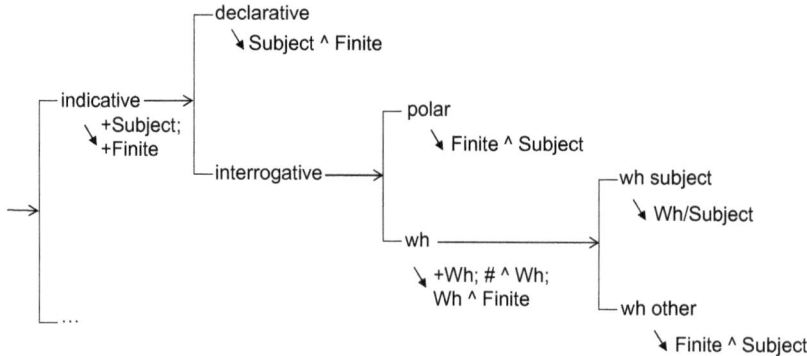

Figure 4.5 Adjusted English indicative systems

## 4.2 English MOOD Resources

speaker's stance on what he is saying, whereas in interrogatives they position the addressee to answer in terms of how they feel.

Now let's extend our description a little, imagining that the ECLO intensifies his intervention with exclamations of the following kind. How should we treat these clauses?

(34) 
| ECLO | What a follower you are! |
|---|---|
| | What a mess you got yourself into! |

In terms of exchange structure, these are exclamations (reacting moves). They bring intensified attitude (APPRAISAL resources) into play, alongside the nub and terms of the negotiation. Like declaratives, they sequence Subject before Finite. Unlike the declaratives we have seen so far, they begin with what looks like a wh phrase. But we need to be careful here. This is clearly not the Wh function that is realised by information-seeking expressions such as *who, what, when, where, why* and *how*. Here the wh word is part of a syntagm in a nominal group with non-specific deixis (e.g. *what a follower, what followers*). And the function of the syntagm is to intensify the ECLO's attitude to the YP; this clause type cannot initiate a K2 ^ K1 exchange structure.[10]

(35)
| ECLO | K2 | What a follower you are! |
|---|---|---|
| YP | *K1 | ... |

Compare an exchange initiated by a wh clause.

(36)
| ELCO | K2 | What kind of follower are you? |
|---|---|---|
| YP | K1 | – A dumb kind. |

We accordingly propose the following structural analysis for this clause type, introducing a Whex function for the wh phrase.

(37)
| | **Whex** | **Subject** | **Finite** |
|---|---|---|---|
| exclamative | What a follower | you | are! |

We have now reasoned from above, around and below about this clause type – with respect to exchange structure (from above), with respect to which clause type it is most alike (from around) and with respect to its realisation at a lower rank (from below). We Accordingly need to adjust our paradigmatic description as Figure 4.6, grouping exclamative clauses together with declarative ones as informative (both realised by Subject ^ Finite sequence), and specifying the insertion and sequencing of a Whex function for exclamatives. More specifically, the realisation statement for exclamatives inserts the Whex function and positions it in clause-initial position, followed by the Subject.

---

[10] Exclamatives intensifying manner are also possible: *How easily she won!*

182  Mood

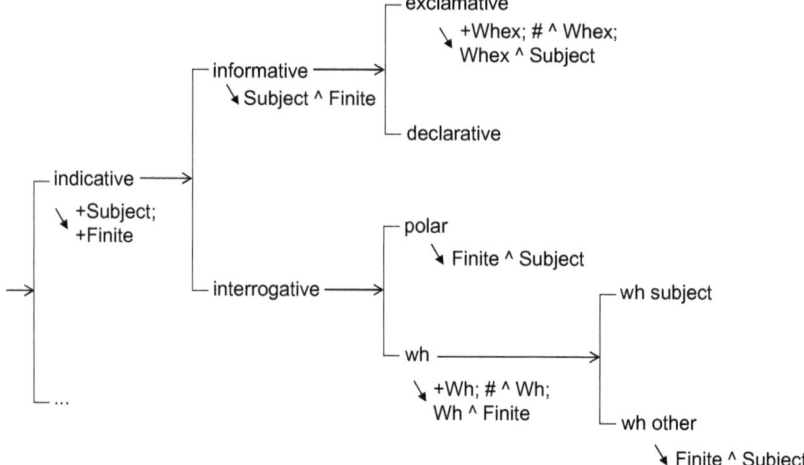

Figure 4.6 Further adjusted English indicative systems

Let's turn now to goods & services exchanges. These are mainly used in the affray conference to control the YP's behaviour. Here are some examples of A2 moves from the Convenor and the ECLO (these are not exchange structures; just a list of examples).

(38)

| Convenor | Hang on a sec. |
|---|---|
|  | And speak up for us. |
| ECLO | Have a look across. |
|  | Look at me as your older brother, man. |

These English clauses are very different from the ones we've focused on above. Not only do they feature in action exchanges rather than knowledge ones, but their nub, terms and exchange function are all in effect realised together through the choice of MOOD (SUBJECT PERSON and MOOD DEIXIS systems are not involved). From the MOOD selection itself, we know that nub of the bare imperative is the addressee; its terms are harder to specify but could perhaps be glossed as 'action now'.

(39)

|  |  |  | nub | terms |
|---|---|---|---|---|
| ECLO: | A2 | You show me where in the Koran it says we can do things like that. | you | action now |
|  | A2 | You show me where. | you | action now |
|  | A2 | Tell me where. | (you) | action now |

## 4.2 English MOOD Resources

If we want to involve the SUBJECT PERSON and MOOD DEIXIS systems in the realisation of the nub and terms of these moves, then we need to explore some further choices alongside imperative mood – e.g. the addition of a tag (*will you?* or *won't you?*) or a range of likely compliant and non-compliant responses (e.g. *OK I will, Sure I can, No I won't, Do I have to?*). Modalities of modulation (i.e. inclination, obligation and ability) feature in these extensions. It is revealing to note that grammatical metaphors for this MOOD type tend to involve comparable explicit modulations (e.g. ***Can** you show me?*, *You **must** show me.*)

(40)

|  |  |  | nub | terms |
|---|---|---|---|---|
| ECLO: | A2 | Show me, won't you? | (you) | won't |
| Young Person: | A1 | OK I will. | I | will |

As we can see, these imperative clauses distinguish themselves from indicative ones (declaratives, interrogatives and exclamatives) through the general absence[11] of both a Subject and a Finite function. This is already reflected in the network above, through the specification of the insertion of these functions for the feature indicative, but not for imperative. What is not made explicit there is one implication of this, namely that indicative clauses involve finite verbal groups and imperative clauses involve perfective non-finite ones (see Chapter 3, Section 3.2.2 for non-finite verbal groups).

All the examples of imperative clauses introduced so far position the addressee to provide the service being negotiated. But the nub of these moves may involve both the speaker and the addressee, in which case it has to be made explicit. In the example below the ECLO imagines what the YP should have said to his mate when he was invited out to back him up in a fight. For this type of imperative, the Subject function is explicit and realised by the pronoun *let's*.

(41)

| ELCO for YP | A2 | "Mate, **let's** let it go. |
|---|---|---|
|  | K1 | It's not worth it." |

These imperative options and additional realisation statements are added to our description in Figure 4.7. The network also allows for an informationally prominent Subject in exclusive imperatives (e.g. ***You** show me where.* in one of the ECLO's moves introduced above).

The realisation statements insert a Predicator function for all clauses, condition the realisation of the verbal group realising the Predicator in imperatives (as a non-finite verbal group) and the realisation of the Finite Predicator

---

[11] A Subject function is sometimes present, necessarily so in the case of the inclusive imperatives introduced below (e.g. ***Let's** go.*) and optionally to give informational prominence to the nub of the move (e.g. ***You** show me where.* in the preceding examples.).

184  Mood

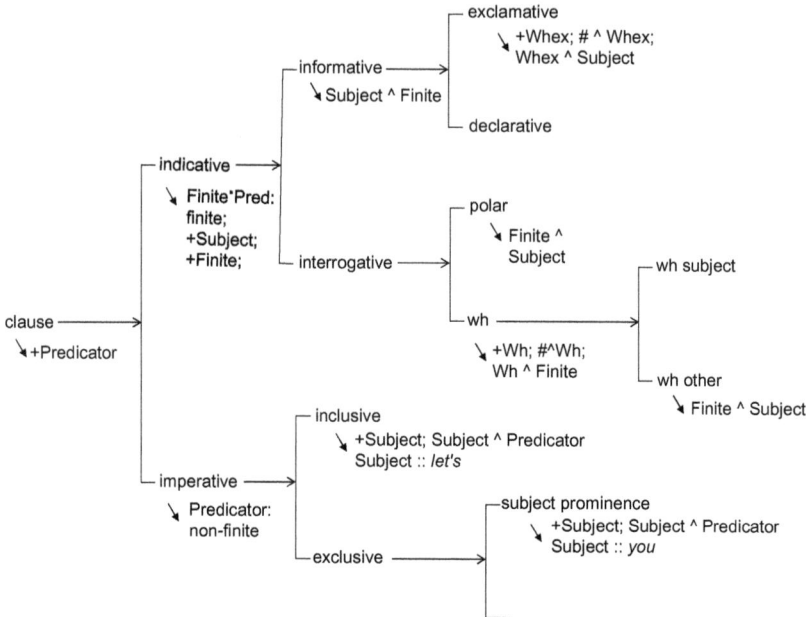

Figure 4.7 English MOOD including imperative systems[12]

structure in indicatives (as a finite verbal group), and specify the insertion of a Subject function in imperatives when it needs to be made explicit.

At this point we will shift our focus from the kinds of move made in exchanges to the negotiation of opinions in those moves (from the system of NEGOTIATION to the system of APPRAISAL in discourse semantic terms). This allows us to focus in more detail on the terms of a negotiation. In the following exchanges, the YP and Convenor are debating the extent to which the YP really cares about what comes out of the affray conference. He claims he does care, and the Convenor challenges him with respect to his behaviour when he arrived late for the meeting.

| (42) | Convenor | K2 | Well why did you **not** care when you walked in that door, about what I said about you being late and the effect that it has on everybody sitting here? |
|---|---|---|---|
|  | YP | K1 | – You were telling me off. |

| (43) | Convenor | K2 | You do**n't** like being told off? |
|---|---|---|---|
|  | YP | K1 | – **No**, I don't. |

[12] Realisation statements conflating Wh with Subject, Complement or Adjunct functions have not been specified in this figure.

## 4.2 English MOOD Resources

In the first exchange the Convenor uses negative polarity to challenge any presumption that the YP cared about what she said when he arrived. In the second exchange negative polarity is used to dismiss the idea that the YP likes being told off.

Just before these exchanges, the Convenor sums up a point the ECLO has been pushing about the impact the YP's behaviour is having on perceptions of the Muslim community. What people might think is modalised on three occasions (***may** have a perception,* ***may** think,* ***might** think*) and contrasted with what they will think if the YP carries on.

(44) | Convenor | So people's perceptions, Aatif, that's what Amir's getting at. Because the rest of us sitting around this table **may** have a perception and you are holding that perception up. You are allowing us to keep thinking that, aren't you? Because of your behaviour. Some people **may** think, "Well, Muslims are this". Just like they **might** think Asians are this or Australians are this. But if you keep doing it and you keep behaving that way, the people **will** think that way. Some people, **won't** they?

From the perspective of discourse semantics what is going on here is that the grammatical resources of POLARITY and MODALITY are being used to close down and open up the play of opinions around the information being negotiated. The bare bones of this ENGAGEMENT system are outlined in Figure 4.8. The monogloss option means that speakers assert their position authoritatively without reference to other possibilities. The contract feature acknowledges other positions but shuts them down (via negative polarity and concession); the expand feature brings additional voices into play (via MODALITY and PROJECTION).[13] In this respect the pair of exchanges debating whether the YP cares about what is going on are basically contracting; the Convenor's summation of the ECLO's intervention on the other hand is basically expanding.

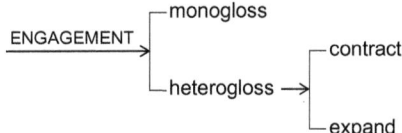

Figure 4.8 Basic ENGAGEMENT systems

---

[13] From the perspective of ENGAGEMENT, then, the monogloss option makes tense the terms of a move, whereas heterogloss opens up the possibility of modalised terms.

We'll deal first here with one key grammatical resource for contracting opinions – POLARITY. We'll base our examples on the following exchanges, which include a negative indicative and a negative imperative clause.

(45)

| ECLO | K2 | Do you really understand, because I **don't** really, I honestly **don't** think you do, man. |
|---|---|---|
| YP | K1 | – I do. |

(46)

| Convenor | K2 | And how do you think you're gonna become a better person? |
|---|---|---|
| YP | K1 | – **Don't** hang around with people that used to make trouble with me. |

From these we can extrapolate the following possibilities. Both indicative and imperative clauses can be positive or negative.

I understand
I don't understand
hang around with them
don't hang around with them

And both positive and negative can be emphatic or not, with POLARITY foregrounded through the phonological system of tonicity.[14]

//^ I / **do** under/stand//
//^ I do /**not** under/stand//
//**do** /hang a/round with them//
//^ do /**not** /hang a/round with them//

In English the implications of these oppositions for mood structure are relatively complex. It's not enough to simply insert a Neg function realised by *not*, as we can do for non-finite clauses.

**not** understanding (was a problem)
(she warned him) **not** to hang around

Both negative and emphatic finite clauses (whether indicative or imperative) involve what looks to be a Finite function, which is not conflated with the Predicator. In clauses where interrogative mood, MODALITY, SECONDARY TENSE or passive voice options do not give rise to the presence of a non-conflated Finite function,[15] then the general verb *do* is brought into play to

---

[14] For the rhythm and intonation analysis of English used here, see Halliday and Greaves 2008; '//' represents a tone group boundary, '/' a foot boundary, '^' a silent beat, '.' a syllable boundary within a foot, and bold the tonic syllable.

[15] In clauses like **Did** *he hang around with them?* (interrogative), *He* **shouldn't** *hang around with them.* (modalised), *He* **was** *hanging around with them.* (secondary present), *He* **was** *misled by them.* (passive).

'verbalise' the function (e.g. *I don't understand, I do understand, don't hang around, do hang around*).[16] We won't attempt to formalise the fine details of these patterns in a system network and realisation statements here (if you are inclined to do so, review Martin, Wang and Zhu, 2013).

Let's turn now to the MODALITY system, which expands the play of voices in a heteroglossic exchange. As illustrated above, and introduced in Chapter 3 (Section 3.3.2), MODALITY can be realised through a modalised verbal group.

Because the rest of us sitting around this table **may** have a perception

Some people **may** think, "Well, Muslims are this".

Just like they **might** think Asians are this or Australians are this.

This kind of MODALITY, which realises probability, can be alternatively realised adverbially. Here are two examples.

(47)
| Convenor | K2 | Did they say anything to you about the fact that it, you know, as a panel beater you **probably** don't need a knife? |
|---|---|---|
| YP | K1 | – Yes. |

(48)
| Convenor | K2 | Did you say you tried to walk away? |
|---|---|---|
| YP | K1 | – **Maybe**. |

For examples like these we need to add an additional interpersonal function to mood structure. We'll call it Modal; it is realised by an adverbial group headed by a modal adverb (e.g. *perhaps, quite probably, almost certainly*, etc.).

| you | probably | don't | need | a knife |
|---|---|---|---|---|
| Subject | Modal | Finite | Predicator | |

As formalised in the system network below, imperative clauses cannot be modalised; this kind of dialogic expansion is a feature of indicative clauses. To the network in Figure 4.9, we have also added $^{\text{I/T}}$ (if/then) superscripts coordinating the choice of exclamative clauses with positive polarity, since they are never negative (*\*What a follower you aren't!*).[17]

---

[16] Referring to this function as Finite is arguably inappropriate in negative or emphatic imperative clauses, since it is not replayed in the tag: e.g. ***Don't*** *hang around with them,* ***will*** *you?* ***Do*** *avoid them,* ***won't*** *you?*

[17] Verbal and adjunctival realisations of modality can be combined (e.g. *He possibly might win.*), a possibility not developed in this network.

188  Mood

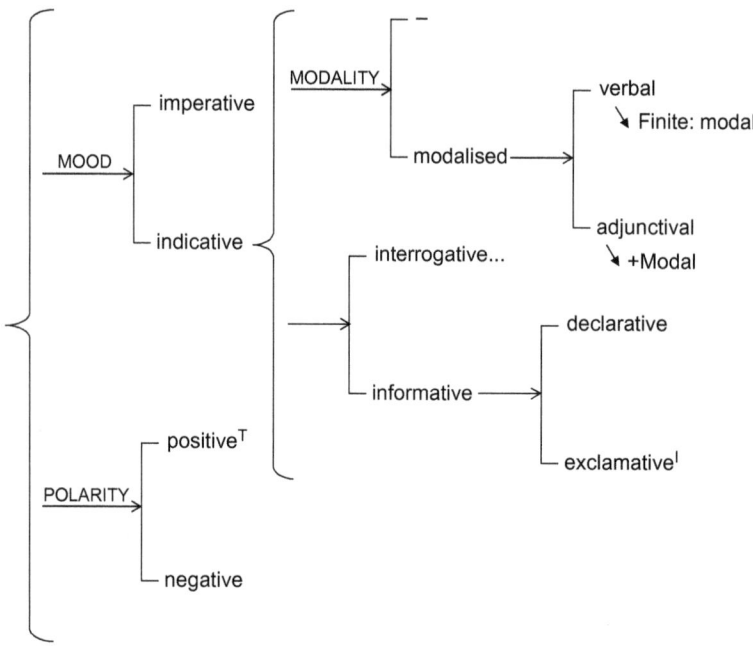

Figure 4.9 English MOOD, MODALITY and POLARITY systems

We will not focus English's tag systems in detail here. But it is important to note in passing that they interact in significant ways with both MOOD and POLARITY options. As suggested above, for most English speakers only declarative and imperative clauses can be tagged. And the option of reversing polarity or not in tags is restricted to positive clauses. The K1 move initiating the exchange below, for example, could have been alternatively tagged positively (*A knife is included, is it?*), in a context where the Convenor is checking on something she has just learned. But below a negative tag is deployed, because she is positioning the YP to confirm something she knows they both know.

(49)

| Convenor | K1  | A knife is included, isn't it? |
|----------|-----|-------------------------------|
| YP       | K2f | – Yeah.                       |

The negative clause in the following exchange, however, can only be tagged with reversed polarity. The ECLO is positioning the YP to agree that his mate didn't have to take up the offer of a showdown.

(50)

| ECLO | K1  | Your mate didn't have to go to town, did he? |
|------|-----|----------------------------------------------|
| YP   | K2f | – No.                                        |

These examples show that tags play an important role, not just in terms of explicitly positioning the addressee to respond, but positioning them to respond in a particular way as far as ENGAGEMENT is concerned. They both reinforce the terms of a move and influence the way it will be negotiated in exchange structure. It is clear below that the YP has been positioned to agree to the Convenor's modalised summation of the ECLO's intervention introduced above.

(51)

| Convenor | So people's perceptions, Aatif, that's what Amir's getting at. Because the rest of us sitting around this table may have a perception and you are holding that perception up. You are allowing us to keep thinking that, aren't you? Because of your behaviour. Some people may think, "Well, Muslims are this". Just like they might think Asians are this or Australians are this. But if you keep doing it and you keep behaving that way, the people will think that way. Some people, won't they? |
|---|---|
| YP | – Yes. |

As a final step in our exploration of English MOOD, let's look at another way in which APPRAISAL can be realised through MOOD structure – with respect to what Halliday and Matthiessen, 2014 call Comment Adjuncts. They are mainly realised by adverbial groups headed by an adverb encoding speakers' attitudes to the proposition or proposal they are negotiating. Three examples are presented below.

(52)

| Convenor | A2 | **Please** sign it just there for me. |
|---|---|---|
| YP | A1 | – [signs] |

(53)

| Convenor | K2 | At any point when any of this happened did you think about the impact that it would have on any of your family? |
|---|---|---|
| YP | K1 | – Yeah, **of course**. |

(54)

| ECLO | K1 | When I see someone of my own background bringing their mum in wearing a hijab, OK, **honestly**, man, I feel sick inside. |
|---|---|---|

Although assigned the same structural label by Halliday and Matthiessen, there are actually three different systems in play here. First, there is the tiny set of adverbs used in polite A2 moves (i.e. requests for goods & services) – generally realised by *please* (and very occasionally by virtually archaic alternatives like *kindly*). Second, there is a relatively large set that is found only in informative clauses, and concerned with encoding a speaker's attitude to what they are saying (*obviously, surprisingly, luckily, importantly, stupidly*, etc.).

190    Mood

Third, there is a comparatively smaller set that is deployed across indicative clauses – providing the speaker's comment on what they are saying in informatives or inviting the addressee to comment in interrogatives. Compare the following example with the third example just above. Above, in the informative clause *honestly* realises the speaker's attitude; below it solicits the attitude of the addressee.

(55)

| ECLO | K2 | When you see someone of our own background bringing their mum in wearing a hijab, OK, **honestly**, doesn't it make you feel sick inside? |
|---|---|---|
| Convenor | K1 | – It does. |

The systems providing these options are positioned in relation to MOOD options in Figure 4.10. The feature [proposal commentary] allows for the addition of *please* to A2 moves, whether these moves are realised in imperative, interrogative or declarative mood – as illustrated from a range of conference data below.[18]

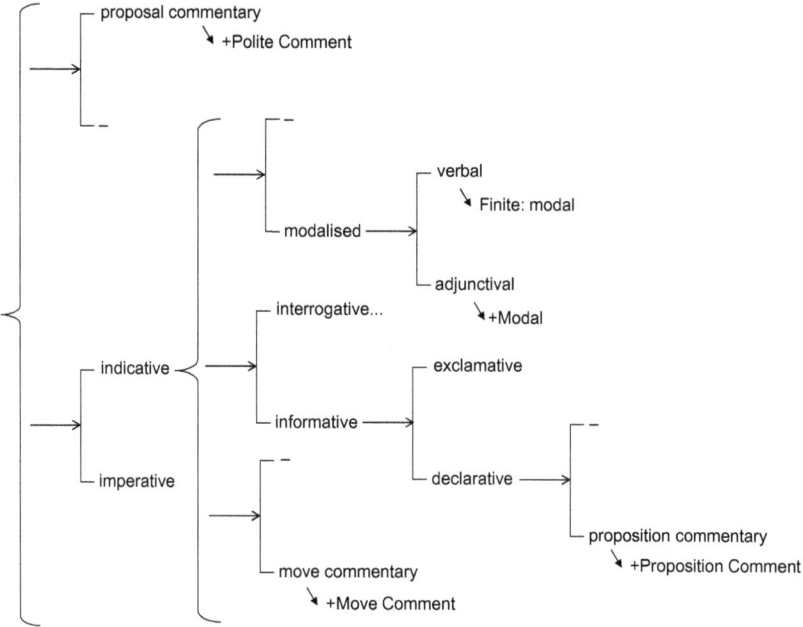

Figure 4.10  English MOOD in relation to Comment Adjuncts

---

[18] We will not be dealing with grammatical metaphors of MOOD or MODALITY in any detail in this chapter; for discussion see Martin, Wang and Zhu (2013).

## 4.2 English MOOD Resources

While we complete some important paperwork after the conference, **please** stay and join us for refreshments. [imperative]

... before we go any further can I just ask that everybody has their mobile phones turned off, or on silent ... **please**. [interrogative]

So if I could **please** have you sign it Jeff, just there where it says 'Young Person', for me ... [declarative]

The feature [move commentary] allows interlocutors to express or invite a comment on the knowledge move being negotiated (in informative or interrogative clauses respectively). The feature [proposition commentary] allows speakers to comment on the knowledge move they are enacting.

The realisation statements in this network provide for three different structural functions, depending on the system being realised: Polite Comment realising [proposal commentary], Move Comment realising [move commentary] and Proposition Comment realising [proposition commentary]. Reasoning from above in terms of their role in exchange structure and from around in terms of their relation to MOOD systems, there is no justification for treating these three types of comment as realised by the same structural function. Reasoning from below, one might argue that all three are realised by comparably structured adverbial groups. But on these grounds, they would be impossible to distinguish from adverbial groups realising the Modal function (e.g. *usually*, *just perhaps*), which in terms of systemic dependency and their role realising expanding engagement have a completely different grammatical and discourse semantic function (as we have seen above).

Let's now take stock of the English MOOD systems and structures we have been exploring in this section by looking at a phase of interaction between the ECLO and the YP. Our focus here is on the work done at the front of an English clause as far as MOOD, POLARITY and MODALITY are concerned. The arguability of the first exchange (i.e. its mood and realisation of its nub and terms) is highlighted in bold below, as enacted by its MOOD and POLARITY. This brings our Subject, Finite and Neg functions into play, alongside a realisation of POLARITY not discussed above – namely as a distinct response adjunct realised by *yes* or *no* and their colloquial alternatives (*yeah*, *nope*, etc.) in clause-initial or clause-final position.

| (56) | ECLO | When you went down to that railway station, **did you** think at any stage of saying to your mate, "Mate, let's let it go. It's not worth it."? |
|---|---|---|
| | YP | **No.** |
| | ECLO | **No, you didn't.** |

The typical English ellipsis patterns we find in dialogue are well illustrated here. The basic principle is to make the clause's arguability explicit, and ellipse the rest (for details see Halliday and Hasan, 1976, chapters 3 and 4). The YP's second move manifests simply the negative polarity of his response; in the third move, the ECLO in addition replays the relevant Subject and Finite/Neg functions. The general point here is that English invests most of the negotiability of a move at the beginning of a clause, and that the Predicator function is not central (and so can be ellipsed in responding moves along with further elements of experiential clause structure).[19] For analysis of a language which invests most of the negotiability of a move at the end of the clause, see Kim et al. (2023) grammar of Korean.

In the next section we turn our attention to Spanish resources for positioning moves in exchanges, and realising their nub and terms.

## 4.3 Spanish MOOD Resources

The texts we have chosen as the basis for this exploration of Spanish MOOD are call centre ones (from data analysed by Castro, 2010).[20] In one, the client is trying to change their satellite television plan; but they are informed by the server that they cannot do so until they have paid money owing from a service that has been cut off for non-payment. In the other, the client is seeking help to get his television set-top box working. Accordingly, the 'change of plan' text features knowledge exchanges – such as the negotiation of information about service charges below. As for English we begin with a discussion of MOOD systems, before turning our attention to POLARITY and MODALITY options. Again, as for English, our examples are set out to display the role played by Spanish grammar as far as enacting moves in exchange structure is concerned.

(57)

| Client | K2 | ¿*Pero ahí no me siguen cobrando más?* <br> 'But then you don't keep charging me anymore?' |
|---|---|---|
| Server | K1 | – *Mientras esté cortado, no se le está cobrando, porque está cortado.* <br> – 'While it's cut off, it's not costing you, because it's cut off.' |
| Client | K2f | – *Ya.* <br> – 'Right.' |

And the 'set-top box' exchange features action exchanges – such as the negotiation of a step towards getting the set-top box working below.

---

[19] We are not extending our analysis of English MOOD structure to include what Halliday and Matthiessen (2014) refer to as Complement and Adjunct functions, since neither are immediately relevant to the negotiability of a move in English conversation.

[20] The account of Spanish interpersonal resources presented in this section is largely based on work by Quiroz (2013, 2015, 2017a, 2018).

(58)

| Server | A2 | *Saque la tarjeta del decodificador.*<br>'Remove the card from the set-top box.' |
|---|---|---|
| Client | A1 | *– Ah, nunca he hecho eso.*<br>– 'Ah, I've never done that.' |

In dialogic texts of this kind, languages need to keep track of who is speaking to who as opposed to who or what is being talked about. We'll refer once more to the interlocutor roles as speaker and addressee, and the other role as non-interlocutor. In Spanish clauses with finite verbal groups, one of these interpersonal roles is foregrounded as the key entity at stake in the negotiation – its nub. It is realised by a PERSON and NUMBER inflection in the verbal group (realising the Spanish verbal group Finite function introduced in Chapter 3).

In Spanish, the PERSON and NUMBER inflections in the verbal group can also realise TENSE (a portmanteau realisation of three systems); this means that these inflections not only realise the nub of the move but also contribute to its terms.

The basic INTERLOCUTION system for indicative clauses in Chilean Spanish is exemplified in Table 4.4 (for present tense), with portmanteau inflections for PERSON, NUMBER and TENSE highlighted in bold. In this table, and Tables 4.5 and 4.6, the left-hand column specifies the relevant INTERLOCUTION choice at

Table 4.4 *Spanish INTERLOCUTION system and verbal group inflections realising indicative mood exemplified*

| indicative mood INTERLOCUTION | verbal group PERSON and NUMBER | examples (verb inflection in bold)* |
|---|---|---|
| speaker | 1st person singular | *necesit-o el RUT del titular por favor*<br>'**I need** the ID of the account holder please' |
| addressee (informal) | 2nd person, singular | *tien-es que cancelar la deuda*<br>'**you have to** pay off the debt' |
| addressee (formal) | 3nd person singular | *tien-e que cancelar la deuda*<br>'**you have to** pay the debt' |
| non-interlocutor | 3rd person singular | *si no est-á cancelado*<br>'if **it's** not paid off' |
| speaker plus | 1st person plural | *no ten-emos ninguno de diecisiete y fracción*<br>'**we don't have** any seventeen and a fraction' |
| addressee plus | 3nd person plural | *¿pero ahí no me sigu-en cobrando más?*<br>'But then **you don't keep** charging me anymore?' |
| non-interlocutors | 3rd person plural | *le cort-an por no pago*<br>'**they cut** you off for not paying' |

\* The inflections included in tables and highlighted in examples in this chapter are for illustrative purposes only. There are various verb conjugations in play – for -ar, -er/-ir and irregular verbs. We do not attempt exhaustive coverage here. A helpful conjugator can be found at www.wordreference.com/conj/EsVerbs.aspx?

clause rank, and the second column specifies the PERSON and NUMBER choice at group rank (which is in turn realised by inflection at word rank, as highlighted in bold in the examples).

Note that there are two choices for a single addressee – informal (*tien-es*) and formal (*tien-e*), but only one for more than one addressee (*sigu-en*).[21] This means that as far as inflectional morphology is concerned, the distinction between 2nd person singular formal and 3rd person singular, and the distinction between 2nd and 3rd person plural has 'collapsed' in Chilean Spanish (and most Latin American dialects). So formal addressee and addressee plus interlocution is actually realised by 3rd person inflections in the verbal group, not 2nd person ones.

In Spanish conversation, the key entity at stake in the negotiation (the nub) is normally foregrounded simply by inflection; nominal groups showing agreement relations with this inflection are not necessarily deployed. In our 'change of plan' text there are, however, several examples of the marked pattern, which include a nominal group agreeing in PERSON and NUMBER with the verbal group. Relevant examples of this marked pattern in indicative clauses from the text are presented in Table 4.5 (including an adaptation of the second person plural example above, since *ustedes* 'you-pl' is not found in our texts). Note

Table 4.5 *Spanish nominal groups agreeing with verbal group inflection exemplified*

| indicative mood INTERLOCUTION | verbal group PERSON and NUMBER | examples (including agreeing pronouns and verb inflection in bold) |
|---|---|---|
| speaker | 1st person singular | *yo teng-o dos – dos decodificadores* '**I have** two – two set-top boxes' |
| addressee (informal) | 2nd person singular | *¿qué folleto est-ás viendo tú?* 'what leaflet **are you** looking at?' |
| addressee (formal) | 3rd person singular | *¿qué folleto est-á viendo usted?* 'what leaflet **are you** looking at?' |
| non-interlocutor | 3rd person singular | *porque el sistema no me lo permit-e* 'because **the system won't** allow (me) it' |
| speaker plus | 1st person plural | **nosotros** *no ten-emos ningún plan de diecisiete mil ...* '**we don't** have any plan costing seventeen thousand' |
| addressee plus | 3rd person plural | *¿pero ustedes ahí no me sigu-en cobrando más?* 'But then **you don't** keep charging me anymore?' |
| non-interlocutors | 3rd person plural | *cuando a mí me di-eron el papel – el folleto las niñas ...* 'When **the girls gave** me the paper – the leaflet ... ' |

---

[21] However, Peninsular Spanish (here understood as the variety spoken mostly in Madrid, Spain, and considered 'standard' for speakers of the Iberian Peninsula) also admits choices in 'formality' for more than one addressee, since in this variety 'imperative verb mood' allows for such a distinction (Lavid, Arús and Zamorano-Mansilla, 2010).

## 4.3 Spanish MOOD Resources

that in the addressee formal and addressee plus interlocution rows in Table 4.5, the 2nd person addressee pronoun *usted/ustedes* agrees with 3rd person inflection (since historically speaking, *usted/ustedes* has evolved from *vuestra merced/vuestras mercedes* 'your grace/s', respectful terms of address correlating with 3rd person inflection).

In summary then, the nub of a move is realised by verbal group inflection in Spanish;[22] it may or may not be additionally encoded through a nominal group whose number and person agrees with the number and person of the verbal group inflection.

Turning to imperative clauses in goods & services exchanges, the nub of a move is also realised through verbal group inflection. In the example moves below, the verbal group inflection earmarks the entity responsible for performing a service or providing goods. The Server instructs the Client to open the lid of the set-top box and replace the card they have previously removed; the verbal group inflections position the Client as responsible for these steps in the repair activity.

| (59) | Server | A2 | *abr-a la tapita*<br>'open the lid' |
|---|---|---|---|
| | | A2 | *ingres-e la tarjeta con el chip hacia abajo y hacia el fondo*<br>'insert the card with the chip down and to the back' |

The inflections here are third person singular subjunctive suffixes realising formal addressee interlocution (and would thus agree with *usted* had the addressee been included in the move as a nominal group – e.g. **usted** *abr-a la tapita* 'you open the lid'). Present subjunctive morphology, distinguishing the person and number of the modally responsible entity, is used for all imperative clause interlocution except informal single addressee interlocution in positive imperatives, which has the distinctive imperative morphology exemplified in (60) below.

| (60) | Server | A2 | *abr-e la tapita*<br>'open the lid' |
|---|---|---|---|
| | | A2 | *ingres-a la tarjeta con el chip hacia abajo y hacia el fondo*<br>'insert the card with the chip down and to the back' |

Alongside this morphology imperative clauses have additional distinguishing features. They never select for either TENSE or MODALITY (although they do select for PERSON). In addition, as noted in Chapter 3, as long as their POLARITY is positive, pronominal clitics follow the Event function in the

---

[22] In a responding move, a verbal group without clitics is sufficient to negotiate an exchange, even when responding to a transitive or ditransitive clause; this suggests that it is verb inflection which realises the nub of a move.

verbal group in imperative clauses. The example above is adapted to reflect this pattern below.

(61)
| Server | A2 | *ábre***la**<br>'open **it**' |
|---|---|---|
| | A2 | *ingrésa***la** *con el chip hacia abajo y hacia el fondo*<br>'insert **it** with the chip down and to the back' |

A full paradigm for Spanish imperative clauses is presented in Table 4.6, expanding on the *abra la tapita* 'open the lid' clause from our text.[23]

The relevant INTERLOCUTION systems for Chilean Spanish imperative clauses are formalised systemically in Figure 4.11. The realisation statements specify the person and number of the present subjunctive verbal group morphology realising features, in addition to the distinctive imperative morphology for informal addressee interlocution in positive imperative clauses.[24] The pronouns agreeing with this morphology are included in parentheses for addressee selections.

Table 4.6 *Spanish* INTERLOCUTION *system and verbal group inflections realising imperative mood exemplified*

| imperative mood INTERLOCUTION[a] | verbal group PERSON and NUMBER | examples (agreeing pronouns in parentheses, verb inflection in bold) |
|---|---|---|
| addressee (informal) | 2nd person singular imperative | *(tú) abr-***e** *la tapita*<br>'**(you)** open the lid' |
| addressee (formal) | 3nd person singular subjunctive | *(usted) abr-***a** *la tapita*<br>'**(you)** open the lid' |
| non-interlocutor | 3rd person singular subjunctive | *que (ella) abr-***a** *la tapita*<br>'**(she)** open the lid' |
| speaker/addressee | 1st person plural subjunctive | *(nosotras) abr-***amos** *la tapita*<br>'**let's** open the lid' |
| addressee plus | 3nd person plural subjunctive | *(ustedes) abr-***an** *la tapita*<br>'**(you)** open the lid' |
| non-interlocutors | 3rd person plural subjunctive | *que (ellas) abr-***an** *la tapita*<br>'let **them** open the lid'[b] |

[a] There is no distinctive first person imperative interlocution; for Da1 moves (offers) a first person, present tense, indicative interrogative clause could be used: *¿abr-o la tapita?* 'do I open the lid?'

[b] The appropriate rhythm for the rather archaic English third person imperative would be //^ let /them o/pen the /lid//, to discourage a reading in which *let* is salient, realising permission: //let them o/pen the /lid//.

[23] The non-interlocutor options have evolved from projected optative clauses with subjunctive morphology (e.g. *espero que abr-an la tapita* 'I hope they open the lid') (Bello, 1847, pp. 444–5), and retain the linker *que* from that history (Gili, 1958/2000).

[24] One reason for grouping the distinctive imperative informal addressee option with the others (which are all subjective) is enclisis – i.e. clitics follow the Event in these, as in other positive imperative clauses.

## 4.3 Spanish MOOD Resources

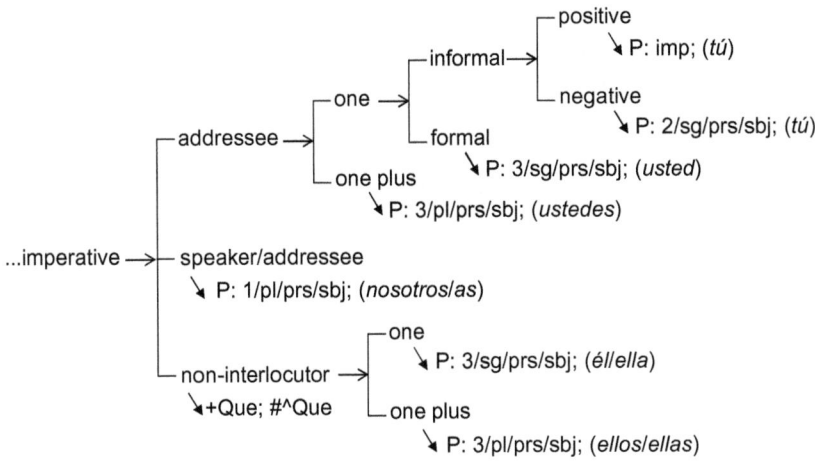

Figure 4.11 Spanish imperative INTERLOCUTION systems[25]

Let's return our attention now to knowledge exchanges, where indicative clauses play a key role in realising Dk1, K2 and K1 moves. The knowledge exchange with which we opened this section is repeated below. As with imperatives, the nub is realised through inflectional verb morphology, highlighted in bold below; but because of the third person plural morphology it is a very non-specific nub, which could be variously glossed in English as 'you' (respectful reference to the addressee) or generalised 'they'.

| (62) | Client | K2 | ¿*Pero ahí no me sigu-**en** cobrando más?*<br>'But then you/they don't keep charging me anymore?' |
|---|---|---|---|
| | Server | K1 | – *Mientras est-**é** cortado, no se le est-**á** cobrando, porque est-**á** cortado.*<br>– 'While it's cut off, no-one is charging you (i.e. it's not costing you) because it's cut off.' |
| | Client | K2f | – *Ya.*<br>– 'Ok.' |

Let's remove the dependent clauses from this exchange to concentrate on the heart of the negotiation. As we can see, the nub shifts from the question to its response – from the non-specific third person plural affix to something even

---

[25] We have provisionally included a [positive] or [negative] system for singular informal addressee reference in this network in order to restrict the imperative inflection option – pending our introduction of the POLARITY system in general below.

less determinant (a third person singular verbal group with the voice clitic *se*). The Client asks whether you/they is still collecting a fee from him (3rd person plural present *sigu-en*); the Server replies that it's not happening (via impersonal *se* and 3rd person singular present *est-á*).²⁶

| (63) | Client | K2 | ¿*Pero ahí no me sigu-en cobrando más?*<br>'But then you/they don't keep charging me anymore?' |
|---|---|---|---|
| | Server | K1 | – *No se le est-á cobrando.*<br>– 'No-one is charging you.' (i.e. it's not costing you.)' |
| | Client | K2f | – *Ya.*<br>– 'Right.' |

If the server had directly negotiated the Client's question, he would have argued that 'they' (interpretable as the company, or alternatively as generalised reference) won't keep charging him (*no le sigu-en cobrando*), as in the revised exchange below.

| (64) | Client | K2 | ¿*Pero ahí no me sigu-en cobrando más?*<br>'But there you/they don't keep charging me anymore?' |
|---|---|---|---|
| | Server | K1 | – *No le sigu-en cobrando.*<br>– 'They don't keep charging you anymore.' |

An elliptical response, with polarity negotiated through an adjunct, would have had the same effect – sustaining a degree of responsibility.

| (65) | Client | K2 | ¿*Pero ahí no me sigu-en cobrando más?*<br>'But then you/they don't keep charging me anymore?' |
|---|---|---|---|
| | Server | K1 | – *No.*<br>– 'No.' |

But the Server's job in general is to deflect responsibility whenever it might reflect negatively on his company. His shift of gears, via the impersonal *se* verbal group (repeated in an abbreviated version of the exchange below) is a significant one.

| (66) | Client | K2 | ¿*Pero ahí no me sigu-en cobrando más?*<br>'But then you/they don't charge me anymore?' |
|---|---|---|---|
| | Server | K1 | – *No se le est-á cobrando.*<br>– 'No-one is charging you.' (i.e. it's not costing you.)' |

---

²⁶ Compare the following exchange initiated by a Chilean female, and the possible reply by a Chilean male friend (not her boyfriend): *Te extrañ-o* 'I miss you.' – *Se te extrañ-a* 'You are missed.' The male friend may feel he needs to shift to second person formal interlocution in order not to imply an intimate relationship. Note that the Spanish original and English translation are using different resources here for a comparable effect – Spanish shifts from a personal to an 'impersonal' construction, where English shifts from active voice to an 'agent-less' passive.

## 4.3 Spanish MOOD Resources

Unlike English, which depends on its Subject and Finite functions to shift responsibility along these lines, in Spanish the verbal group alone is up to the job. Compare the following exchange, in which the Server reminds the Client that although he has paid his bill up to January 13, they are now in February.

(67)

| Server | K1  | Est-**amos** en febrero, señor. 'We're in February, sir.' |
|--------|-----|-----------------------------------------------------------|
| Client | K2f | – Sí po, est-**amos** en febrero. – 'Yes, we are in February.' |

The follow-up move by the Client could have been realised by a verbal group alone – in this case sustaining the nub.[27]

(68)

| Server | K1  | Est-**amos** en febrero, señor. 'We're in February, sir.' |
|--------|-----|-----------------------------------------------------------|
| Client | K2f | – Est-**amos**. – 'We are.' |

Or simply by a polarity adjunct, resuming the rest of the proposition being negotiated.

(69)

| Server | K1  | Est-**amos** en febrero, señor. 'We're in February, sir.' |
|--------|-----|-----------------------------------------------------------|
| Client | K2f | – Sí po. – 'Yes.' |

We'll refer to the function of the verbal group in MOOD structure as Predicator.

The Predicator's inflectional morphology plays a key role in distinguishing imperative from indicative clauses in Spanish. As we have seen, informal 2nd person positive imperatives have their own distinguishing morphology; and the present subjunctive morphology does the job elsewhere.[28]

The Spanish Predicator does not, however, play a role in distinguishing declarative from interrogative moods. Returning once again to our knowledge exchange, we can see that there is nothing in the verbal group telling us whether a move is demanding or providing information. For polar interrogatives in Spanish, this is accomplished through intonation, with rising intonation used to signal the interrogative mood of the K2 move (contrasting with the falling intonation of the K1). Compared to English, we can see that there is no need to propose a Subject and Finite function and worry about their sequencing in so far as distinguishing informative from interrogative mood is concerned.

---

[27] Another example of a verbal group only response would be ¿Vamos a mi casa? 'Shall we go to my place?' – Vamos 'Let's go'.

[28] Subjunctive morphology is elsewhere a feature associated with dependent and embedded clauses, not ranking independent ones (and is also triggered by some MODALITY selections).

(70)

| Client | K2 | ¿*Pero ahí no me siguen cobrando más?*↑<br>'But then you don't keep charging me any longer?' |
|---|---|---|
| Server | K1 | – *Mientras esté cortado, no se le está cobrando, porque está cortado.*↓<br>– 'While it's cut off, no-one is charging you (i.e. it's not costing you) because it's cut off.' |
| Client | K2f | – *Ya.*↓<br>– 'Right' |

Elemental interrogatives, which ask for specific pieces of information, involve a group or phrase involving one of the following words: *qué* 'what', *cuál/cuáles* 'which', *quién/quiénes* 'who', *cómo* 'how', *cuándo* 'when' *cuánto/cuántos/cuánta/cuántas* 'how much, how many' and *dónde/adónde* 'where/where to'. Spanish graphology uses a tilde (e.g. *qué*)[29] for these words when they are seeking information in elemental interrogatives. For these clauses we propose a Qint function, which comes first in the clause (e.g. *qué folleto* 'what leaflet' below).

(71)

| Client | K2 | ¿***Qué folleto*** *está viendo usted?*<br>'what leaflet are you looking at?' |
|---|---|---|
| Server | K1 | – *Eh, o sea, es del Chile Cable.*<br>– 'Um, I mean, it's the one from Chile Cable' |

The final MOOD distinction we will explore is between declarative and exclamative informative clauses. Exclamatives intensify the grading of occurrences and qualities of entities. They include an exclamative nominal or adverbial group, the function of which we refer to as Qex, positioned at the front of the clause. Two examples are presented below.

(72)

| Server | K1 | ¡***Cómo peleaba ese cliente!***<br>'How that client argued!' |
|---|---|---|

(73)

| Server | K1 | ¡***Qué persistente*** *era!*<br>'How persistent s/he was!' |
|---|---|---|

The INTERLOCUTION and MOOD systems for Chilean Spanish indicative clauses are formalised systemically in Figure 4.12. The realisation statements specify the PERSON and NUMBER of the verbal group morphology realising features. The pronouns showing agreement relations with this morphology are included in parentheses for interlocutor features. As for English, the network can be used to help generalise the distribution of comment adverbials – with attitudinal comments such as *lamentablemente* 'sadly' restricted to declarative clauses and stance comments such as *de verdad* 'honestly' found

---

[29] The term *tilde* is used in Spanish to refer to the 'diacritics' in both *qué* and *niña*.

4.3 Spanish MOOD Resources

in both informative and interrogative clauses (cf. 'ideational' versus 'speech functional' adjuncts respectively, as described for English by Halliday and Matthiessen, 2014, pp. 190ff.). In addition, from the perspective of exchange structure, responding to an informative clause is optional, whereas responding to an interrogative clause is not.

At this point let's shift our gaze from grammatical resources for positioning moves in an exchange to resources for opening up and closing down the play of voices around a proposition or proposal (i.e. resources for extending the terms of a move) – POLARITY and MODALITY in particular. As we saw in Chapter 3, the Spanish verbal group provides resources for negotiating both expanding and contracting ENGAGEMENT.

We'll begin with indicative clauses. The following exchange includes a number of positive and negative clauses. In this example the positive clauses have no special polarity marking, but the Predicators in the negative clauses

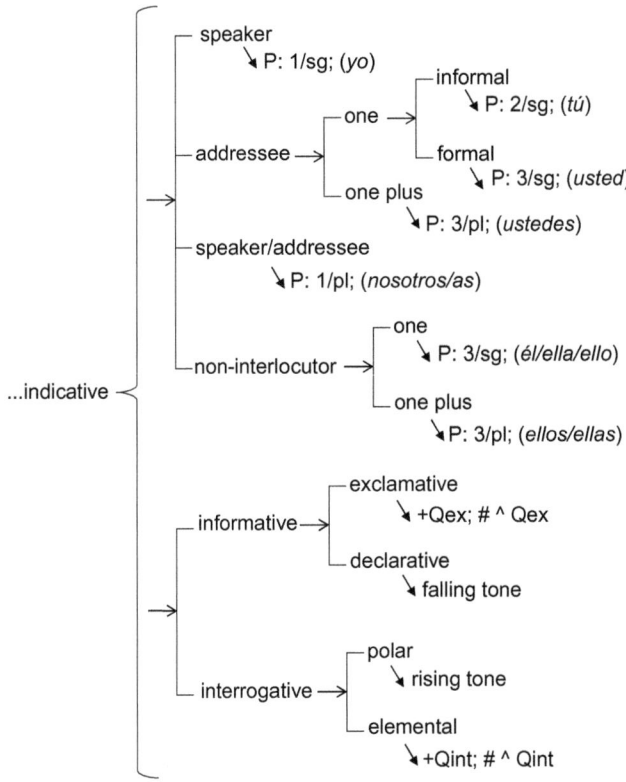

Figure 4.12 Spanish indicative clause INTERLOCUTION and MOOD systems

all begin with the negative particle *no*. The last move, by the Client, reinforces its negative polarity with three clause-initial adjuncts (*no, no, no*). We'll refer to these adjuncts, and their positive counterpart *sí*, as Polar Adjuncts. Unlike polarity markers in verbal groups, they are realised on a separate tone group (and demarcated with a comma in writing). Verbal groups are underlined in the examples illustrating POLARITY below.

| (74) | Server | K1 | *Si usted <u>me indica</u> que **no** <u>lo está viendo</u> <u>es</u> porque **no** <u>está pagado</u>*<br>'if you are indicating to me that you aren't watching it it's because it isn't paid' |
|---|---|---|---|
| | | K1 | *por eso **no** <u>lo está viendo</u>*<br>'that is why you aren't watching it' |
| | | K1 | ***no** <u>es</u> porque <u>tenga</u> algún problema con la señal.*<br>'it's not because you have any problem with the signal' |
| | Client | ch | *– **No, no, no**, yo **no** <u>le estoy diciendo</u> por señal.*<br>'No, no, no, I am not saying it's because of the signal' |

As noted in Chapter 3, positive polarity can be explicitly marked in verbal groups, realised by *sí* in place of *no*. The Server's K1 move below includes a Predicator of this kind, along with a positive Polar Adjunct (also realised by *sí*) (Carbonero, 1980; Dumitrescu, 1973, 1979).

| (75) | Client | K2 | *¿O sea <u>tengo que pagarle</u> esa deuda primero?*<br>'that is, do I have to pay you that debt first?' |
|---|---|---|---|
| | Server | K1 | ***Sí**, usted **sí** <u>tiene que pagarla</u>.*<br>– 'Yes, you indeed have to pay it.' |

In Chilean Spanish Polar Adjuncts can be colloquially expanded as *sí po* and *no po* (as illustrated in the Client's move in the second example below);[30] this is not possible within verbal groups (e.g. in the Client's verbal group *sí pagué* 'I did pay'). Compare the following examples.

| (76) | Server | K1 | <u>Le cortaron</u> porque <u>no pagó</u>.<br>'They cut you off because you didn't pay.' |
|---|---|---|---|
| | Client | ch | *- <u>Sí pagué</u>.*<br>'I did pay.' |

| (77) | Server | K1 | <u>Le cortaron</u> porque <u>no pagó</u>.<br>'They cut you off because you didn't pay.' |
|---|---|---|---|
| | Client | ch | *– No po, <u>sí pagué</u>.*<br>'No, I did pay.' |

---

[30] *Sí po* and *no po* are distinctive features of Chilean Spanish and serve as strong markers of identity in colloquial registers. They can be associated with Andean Spanish *sí pues* and *no pues* (Zavala, 2001). A full SFL account of their discourse function depends on further research (see Fuentes-Rodríguez, Placencia and Palma-Fahey, 2016).

## 4.3 Spanish MOOD Resources

As illustrated above (examples repeated below), these Polar Adjuncts can be used to negotiate polarity on their own in elliptical responses.

(78)
| Client | K2 | ¿Pero ahí <u>no me siguen cobrando</u> más?<br>'But then you/they don't keep charging me more?' |
|---|---|---|
| Server | K1 | – ***No***.<br>– 'No.' |

(79)
| Server | K1 | <u>Estamos</u> en febrero, señor.<br>'We're in February, sir.' |
|---|---|---|
| Client | K2f | – ***Sí po***.<br>– 'Yes.' |

In negative clauses, non-specific groups and phrases following a negative Predicator spread the negation prosodically across the clause in a pattern referred to by some grammarians as 'polarity concord' (following Mathesius, 1933; see, for example, Camus, 1992). The groups and phrases affected include the following negative words: *ninguno* 'none', *nada* 'nothing', *nadie* 'no one', *nunca* 'never', *jamás* 'never', *tampoco* 'neither'. To illustrate this pattern, let's adjust one of the moves introduced above. The original clause is repeated below.

(80)
| Server | K1 | <u>No es</u> porque <u>tenga</u> algún problema con la señal.<br>'It's **not** because you have **any** problem with the signal.' |
|---|---|---|

Let's turn the embedded clause (i.e. *porque tenga algún problema con la señal*) into a ranking one, and make it negative, as follows.

(81)
| Server | K1 | <u>No tiene</u> **ningún** problema con la señal.<br>'You do**n't** have **any** problem with the signal.'[31] |
|---|---|---|

Note that to do this we had to adjust both its Predicator (now *no tiene*)[32] and the following non-specific nominal group (now *ningún problema*, not *algún problema*). This prosodic negation pattern[33] affects all non-specific groups and phrases following the Predicator, as illustrated below.

(82)
| Server | K1 | <u>No tiene</u> **ningún** problema con **nada**.<br>'You do**n't** have **any** problem with **anything**.' |
|---|---|---|

(83)
| Server | K1 | <u>No tiene</u> **nunca ningún** problema con **nada**.<br>'You do**n't ever** have **any** problem with **anything**.' |
|---|---|---|

---

[31] This could be more literally glossed in non-standard English as 'You do**n't** have **no** problem with the signal.'

[32] The verb inflection has also shifted from subjunctive *teng-a* to indicative *tien-e*.

[33] The same pattern is found in English, manifested in standard English by *anyone, anybody, anything, anywhere, anytime, ever*), and in non-standard English by *no one, nobody, nothing, nowhere, never* (cf. *I didn't see **anyone anywhere**/I didn't see **no one nowhere**.*).

204    Mood

(84) | Server | K1 | <u>No tiene</u> **nunca ningún** problema con **nada tampoco**.<br>'You do**n't ever** have **any** problem with **anything either**.'

It may be helpful to compare the positive and negative groups and phrases we are focusing on here.

**positive : negative ::**
*algún/alguno* 'some/any' : *ningún/ninguno* 'no/no one/not … any' ::
*alguien* 'somebody/anybody' : *nadie* 'nobody/not … anybody' ::
*algo* 'something/anything' : *nada* 'nothing/not … anything' ::
*siempre* 'always' : *nunca/jamás* 'never/not ever' ::
*también* 'also/too' : *tampoco* 'neither/not … either'

When positioned before the Predicator the negative groups and phrases can be used to launch a comparable negative prosody, as illustrated below.

(85) | Server | K1 | **Nunca** <u>tiene</u> **ningún** problema con **nada tampoco**.<br>'You do**n't ever** have **any** problem with **anything either**.'

(86) | Server | K1 | **Con nada** <u>tiene</u> **nunca ningún** problema **tampoco**.<br>'You do**n't ever** have **any** problem with **anything either**.'

(87) | Server | K1 | **Tampoco** <u>tiene</u> **nunca ningún** problema con **nada**.<br>'You do**n't ever** have **any** problem with **anything either**.'

Note that in these three examples the verbal group realising the Predicator is not negative. Realising negation through a group or phrase before the Predicator is an alternative way of making the clause negative (so we do not find \**Porque* **nunca no** *tiene problema con la señal* meaning 'Because you never have a problem with the signal.').

(88) | Server | K1 | **Nunca** <u>tiene</u> problemas con la señal.<br>'You do**n't ever** have problems with the signal.'

If we were to combine clause negation of this kind with Predicator negation, we would in effect undo the negation. So the example below would mean 'you never don't have a problem with someone', not 'you never have any problem with anyone' (for a detailed review of these possibilities in Spanish, see Camus, 1992).

(89) | Server | K1 | **Nunca no** <u>tiene</u> **ningún** problema con **nadie**.<br>'You do**n't never** have **any** problem with **someone**.'

As a penultimate step let's turn from the contracting ENGAGEMENT resources realised through POLARITY to expanding resources realised through MODALITY. In our 'set-top box' text, MODALITY is realised through verbal groups and concerned with obligation and ability. In the examples below, the Server

## 4.3 Spanish MOOD Resources

indicates that the responsibility he assigns to the Client (in the first example) and to himself (in the second) has a source elsewhere – the voice of the company and its regulations is brought into play; the modality implicates the company as the source of the onus on the Client voiced by the Server.

(90)
| Server | A2 | ***Tiene que cancelar*** la deuda. |
|---|---|---|
|  |  | '**You have to pay off** the debt.' |

(91)
| Server | K1 | ***No puedo darle*** ninguna información acá en Sistema. |
|---|---|---|
|  |  | '**I can't give you** any information here in the system.' |

These verbal group realisations of MODALITY were discussed in Chapter 3. MODALITY can be alternatively realised as a Modal Adjunct, through adverbial groups including *quizá* 'maybe', *tal vez* 'perhaps', *probablemente* 'probably', etc. Alternative verbal group and adverbial group realisations are illustrated below.

(92)
| Client | K2 | ¿Hasta cuándo ***tengo que pagar*** eso? |
|---|---|---|
|  |  | 'By when do **I have to pay** that?' |
| Server | K1 | – Usted ***lo puede pagar*** cuando quiera. |
|  |  | – '**You can pay** it whenever.' |
| Client | K1 | ***Quizá*** lo puedo pagar mañana. |
|  |  | '**Maybe** I can pay it tomorrow.' |

These expanding resources are only found in indicative clauses, as networked in Figure 4.13.

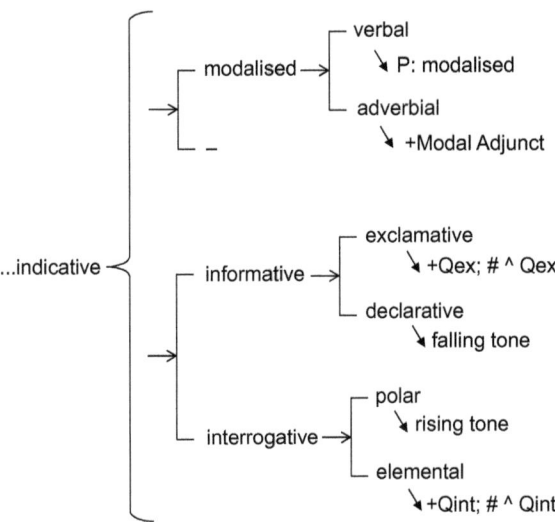

Figure 4.13  Spanish indicative MOOD and MODALITY systems

POLARITY, on the other hand, combines freely with indicative and imperative clauses, as networked below. The exception is exclamative clauses which must be positive (as conditioned by the $^{I/T}$ superscript marking in the network, which is interpreted as 'if [exclamative] is selected then [positive] is selected as well'). The POLARITY system included in Figure 4.14 needs to be expanded to account for realisations inside and alongside the Predicator, and to make provision for the prosodic realisations exemplified above. We won't take these steps in this chapter.

This brings our discussion of MOOD, MODALITY, POLARITY and INTERLOCUTION systems in Spanish to a close. Before posing a challenge, we will review the structures we have introduced realising these systems. We have introduced the following mood functions:

        Predicator
        Qint
        Qex

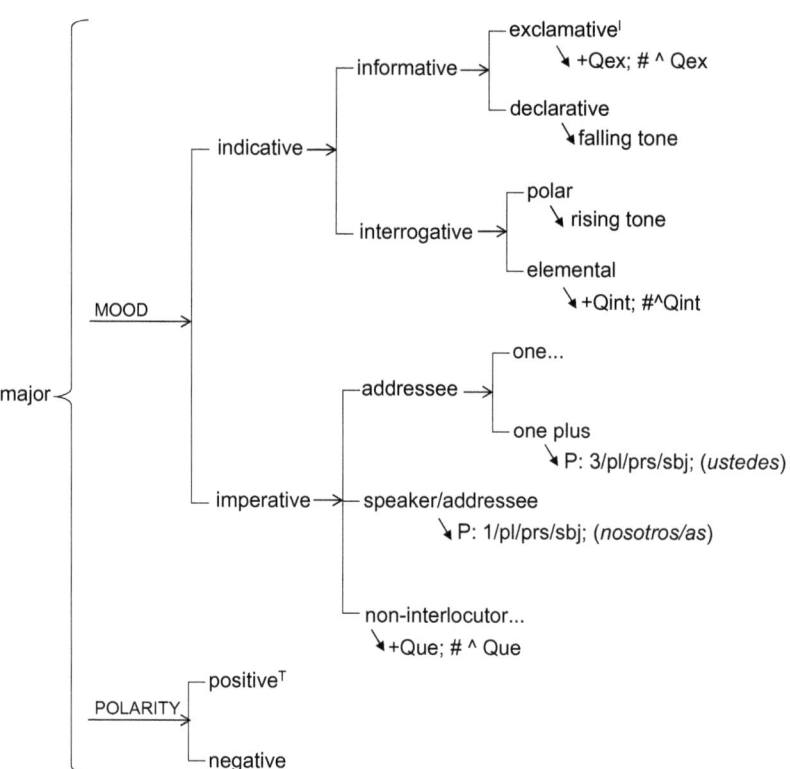

Figure 4.14 Spanish MOOD and POLARITY

## 4.3 Spanish MOOD Resources

Polar Adjunct
Modal Adjunct

To complete the picture for our call centre texts we would need to add a Vocative function, realised by *señor* 'sir' in the example below.

(93)

| Server | K1  | *Estamos en febrero, **señor**.*<br>'We're in February, sir.' |
|--------|-----|---------------------------------------------------------------|
| Client | K2f | – *Sí po, estamos en febrero.*<br>– 'Yes, we are in February.' |

Returning for a moment to the Ola Maldita text, we would also need to recognise a Comment Adjunct function – realised by *oficialmente* 'officially' in the recount of what the friends camping on the island were hiding from their parents.

**Oficialmente** estaban acampando cerca de casa, en San Javier ...
'Officially they were camping near home, in San Javier ... '

We'll now review a number of our examples, analysing them in terms of the structural functions we have proposed (Predicator, Qint, Qex, Polar Adjunct and Comment Adjunct). By doing so we hope to draw attention to the role being played by the Predicator function as far as positioning a move in an exchange and realising its nub and terms are concerned – drawing more explicitly on our analysis of verbal groups in Chapter 3 to display PRIMARY TENSE along with PERSON and MOOD distinctions. Recall from Chapter 3 that PRIMARY TENSE choices are designated as follows – perfect '$\alpha^-$', imperfect '$\alpha^{--}$', present '$\alpha^\circ$' and future '$\alpha^+$' (in addition we have added person and number specifications to the superscripts to distinguish first, second and third person, singular or plural, as '$\alpha^{--/1/sg}$', '$\alpha^{--/2/sg}$', '$\alpha^{--/3/sg}$', '$\alpha^{--/1/pl}$', '$\alpha^{--/2/pl}$', '$\alpha^{--/3/pl}$'). We also include a suggestion for modelling negation as a prosody in our description of Spanish clauses. We begin with the following information exchange.

(94)

| Client | K2 | *¿Pero ahí no me sigu-**en** cobrando más?*<br>'But then **you** don't keep charging me anymore?' |
|--------|----|---------------------------------------------------------------------------------------------------|
| Server | K1 | – *No se le est-**á** cobrando.*<br>– 'No-one is charging **you** (i.e. it's not costing you).' |

The mood structure of each move is tabled below.

(94a)  *pero  ahí  no me sigu-**en** cobrando  más*

|     |      | Predicator                    |         |
|-----|------|-------------------------------|---------|
| but | then | **you** don't keep charging me | anymore |

(94b)  *no se le est-**á** cobrando*

| Predicator |
|------------|
| is not charging you (i.e. 'is not costing you') |

208   Mood

Let's now extend the analysis of the Predicator down a rank, bringing in the structure we developed in Chapter 3.

(94c)  *pero   ahí   no me sigu-**en** cobrando              más*

| Predicator | | | |
|---|---|---|---|
| verbal group complex | | | |
| α | | | β |
| verbal group | | | verbal group |
| Neg ⇒ | | | |
| | P2cl | Finite/Even | Event |
| | | $\alpha^{0/3/pl}$ | $\beta^{imperfective}$ |
| not | me | keep | charging |

'but then **you** don't keep charging me anymore'

(94d)  *no se le est-**á** cobrando*

| Predicator | | | | |
|---|---|---|---|---|
| verbal group | | | | |
| Neg ⇒ | | | | |
| | Vcl | P2cl | Finite | Event |
| | | | $\alpha^{0/3/sg}$  $\beta^0$ | |
| not | | you | is   be -ing | charge |
| 'is not charging you' (i.e. 'is not costing you') | | | | |

An example of a formal second person singular imperative involving a subjunctive verb class is tabled below.

(95)  *abra          la tapita*

| Predicator | |
|---|---|
| verbal group | |
| Finite/Event | |
| $\alpha^{0/3/sg/subj}$ | |
| open | the lid |
| 'open the lid.' | |

An example of an elemental interrogative structure and its declarative response:

(96)

| Client | K2 | *¿**Qué folleto** está viendo usted?*<br>'**What leaflet** are you looking at?' |
|---|---|---|
| Server | K1 | *– Eh, o sea, es del Chile Cable*<br>– 'Um, I mean, it's the one from Chile Cable' |

(96a)  *qué folleto    está viendo      usted*

| Qint | Predicator | |
|---|---|---|
| what leaflet | are looking at | you |

## 4.3 Spanish MOOD Resources

(96b)

| o sea | es | del Chile Cable |
|---|---|---|
| | Predicator | |
| that is | is | from Chile Cable |

An example of an exclamative structure:

(97)

| | Server | Ex | ¡*Qué persistente* era!<br>'**How persistent** s/he was!' |
|---|---|---|---|

(97a)

| qué persistente | era |
|---|---|
| Qex | Predicator |
| how persistent | s/he was |

An example with POLARITY realised by a Polar Adjunct:

(98)

| | Client | K2 | ¿*o sea tengo que pagarle esa deuda primero?*<br>'that is do I have to pay them that debt first?' |
|---|---|---|---|
| | Server | K1 | – *Sí, usted sí tiene que pagár-se-la.*<br>– '**Yes**, you **indeed** have to pay it to them.' |

(98a)

| ¿o sea | tengo que pagarle | esa deuda | primero? |
|---|---|---|---|
| | Predicator | | |
| that is | I have to pay them | this debt | first |

(98b)

| Sí | | usted | sí tiene que pagár-se-la | | | | |
|---|---|---|---|---|---|---|---|
| Polar Adjunct | | | Predicator | | | | |
| | | | verbal group | | | | |
| | | | Pos | ⇒ | | | |
| | | | | Modal | ⇒ | | |
| | | | | Finite | Event | P3cl | P2cl |
| | | | | α$^{modal/0/2/sg}$ | | | |
| Yes, | | you | | have to | pay | them | it |

An example with MODALITY realised by a Modal Adjunct:

(99)

| | Client | K2 | ¿*Hasta cuándo tengo que pagar eso?*<br>'When do **I have to pay** that?' |
|---|---|---|---|
| | Server | K1 | – *Usted lo puede pagar cuando quiera.*<br>– 'You **can pay it** whenever.' |
| | Client | K1 | *Quizá lo puedo pagar mañana.*<br>'**Maybe** I can pay it tomorrow.' |

(99a)

| Quizá | lo puedo pagar | mañana |
|---|---|---|
| Modal Adjunct | Predicator | |
| Maybe | I can pay it | tomorrow |

An example with a Vocative:

(100)
| Server | K1 | *Estamos en febrero, señor.*<br>'We're in February, sir.' |
|---|---|---|
| Client | K2f | – *Sí po, estamos en febrero.*<br>– 'Yes, we are in February.' |

(100a)
| *Estamos* | *en febrero* | *señor* |
|---|---|---|
| Predicator | | Vocative |
| we are | in February | sir |

An example with a Comment Adjunct:

**Oficialmente** estaban acampando cerca de casa, en San Javier …

'**Officially** they were camping near home, in San Javier …'

(101)
| *oficialmente* | *estaban acampando* | *cerca de casa* | *en San Javier* |
|---|---|---|---|
| Comment Adjunct | Predicator | | |
| officially | they were camping | near home | in San Javier |

Modelling a prosody of negation at clause rank would involve setting up a Negation function to launch the prosody; this function can be realised by a negative Predicator (first example below).

(102)
| Server | K1 | **no** tiene **nunca ningún** problema con la señal.<br>'you **don't ever** have **any** problem with the signal.' |
|---|---|---|

(102a)
| **no** *tiene* | | ***ningún*** *problema* | *con la señal* | ***jamás*** |
|---|---|---|---|---|
| Negation | ⇒ | | | ⇒ |
| Predicator | | | | |
| verbal group | | | | |
| Neg | ⇒ | | | |
| | Finite/Event | | | |
| | α$^{0/3/sg}$ | | | |
| You **don't** have | | **no** problem | with the signal | **never** |

'You don't have any problem with the signal'

A negative prosody can also be launched by a negative group or phrase before the Predicator (*nunca* 'never' in the examples below).

(103)
| Server | K1 | **nunca** tiene **ningún** problema con la señal.<br>'you **never** have **any** problem with the signal.' |
|---|---|---|

(104)
| Server | K1 | **nunca** tiene **ningún** problema **con ninguna señal.**<br>'you **never** have **any** problem with **any** signal.' |
|---|---|---|

This way of modelling prosodic structure at clause rank is based on our modelling of prosody in verbal groups in Chapter 3, as reviewed below.

(105) *no podrá explicárselo*

| Neg | ⇒ | | | |
|---|---|---|---|---|
| | Modal | ⇒ | | |
| | Finite | Event | P3cl | P2cl |

's/he won't be able to explain it to her'

## 4.4 Chinese MOOD Resources

The description of Chinese MOOD developed in this section is based on discourse taken from a courtroom trial in China about a reckless driving case. This discourse involves spontaneous dialogue among various parties at the trial, including the judge (JU), two prosecutors (PR), two defendants (DE) and their respective defence lawyers (DL), and a court police officer (CP). In grammatical analysis below, these parties are labelled using the shortened forms provided in the parentheses.

As for English and Spanish MOOD resources, the grammatical system of MOOD in Chinese is responsible for realising the discourse semantic system of NEGOTIATION. Chinese MOOD is involved with the discourse semantic system of APPRAISAL; and within APPRAISAL, the subsystem of ENGAGEMENT is especially relevant. The POLARITY system that is associated with this ENGAGEMENT subsystem interacts in significant ways with MOOD.

The primary contrast in dialogic exchanges is between action exchanges and knowledge exchanges. It is realised lexicogrammatically by distinguishing between MOOD options. Major moves involving action exchanges, i.e. A2 and A1, behave differently in their grammatical realisations in that A2 moves are congruently realised by the imperative MOOD, whereas A1 moves are typically performed non-linguistically, or on some occasions realised through minor clauses consenting to delivery of goods or services, e.g. 好的 *hǎode* 'OK', 行 *xíng* 'OK', 没问题 *méi wèntí* 'no problem'. Knowledge exchanges, on the other hand, are congruently realised in grammar through the indicative MOOD type. This primary contrast in the grammatical system of MOOD is represented in Figure 4.15.

At this low level of delicacy, the layout of MOOD choices is similar across many languages, and the primary distinction between indicative and imperative is widely recognised (Quiroz, 2008, p. 54). However, their structural realisations are varied. To motivate the systemic distinction, we must determine how elements in clause structure engage the clause in different types of negotiation.

212   Mood

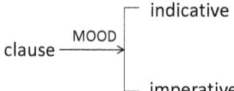

Figure 4.15 Basic Chinese MOOD system

We have seen in Section 4.2 that in English the structural motivation of the distinction between the indicative and imperative clauses rests on the presence or absence of clause functions Subject and Finite. For Spanish, as introduced in Section 4.3, the distinction between indicative and imperative is determined by verb inflection. For Chinese, we propose that the clause function Predicator plays an essential role and serves as the functionally motivated focus for the realisation of MOOD systems; other important functions include the Inquirer and the Moderator. Below we will explore how the distinction between the imperative and indicative MOOD types is motivated through structural configurations, overtly and covertly, in relation to the Predicator of a Chinese clause.

*4.4.1   Imperative Mood*

The imperative clause, as the congruent realisation of the A2 move in an exchange of action, typically features a Predicator realised by a word group without any aspectual marking via a clitic dependent on its head word. When the primary actor is the addressee, it is often left implicit. Optionally, a Modal Adjunct 请 *qǐng* 'please' can precede the Predicator to show politeness. Examples (106) and (107) are from our Reckless Driving text, analysed in terms of functions and classes that are pertinent to imperative mood. Elements that are not relevant to the MOOD structure are not labelled for either function or class.

| (106) | CP | A2 | 全体起立 | |
|---|---|---|---|---|
| | | | *quántǐ* | *qǐlì* |
| | | | | Predicator |
| | | | | word group |
| | | | | Event |
| | | | | verb |
| | | | all | stand up |
| | | | 'All rise.' | |

(107)

| JU | A2 | 请坐下 | |
|---|---|---|---|
| | | qǐng | zuòxià |
| | | Modal Adjunct | Predicator |
| | | | word group |
| | | | Event |
| | | | verb |
| | | please | sit down |
| | | 'Please sit down.' | |

A third person imperative clause requires that the entity responsible for undertaking the action (the primary actor) is made grammatically explicit and positioned before the Predicator, as in examples (108) and (109) below.

(108)

| CP | A2 | 请辩护人和公诉人入庭 | | | | |
|---|---|---|---|---|---|---|
| | | qǐng | biànhùrén | hé | gōngsùrén | rù | tíng |
| | | Modal Adjunct | | | | Predicator | |
| | | | | | | word group | |
| | | | | | | Event | |
| | | | | | | verb | |
| | | please | defence lawyer | and | prosecutor | enter | court |
| | | 'Defence lawyers and prosecutors please enter the courtroom.' | | | | | |

(109)

| JU | A2 | 说话声音大一点 | | |
|---|---|---|---|---|
| | | shuōhuà | shēngyīn | dà | yīdiǎn |
| | | | | Predicator | |
| | | | | word group | |
| | | | | Event | |
| | | | | adjective | |
| | | speak | sound | big | a little |
| | | '(Let your) voice rise a little.' | | | |

In Chinese, the group rank function Event can be realised by either a verb or an adjective; these words function as the head of a word group that realises the Predicator. For this reason, we label the class that realises the Predicator function as 'word group' (instead of specifying whether it is a verbal or adjectival group). The difference in class at word rank is based on their grammatical potential. For instance, an adjective can function as the Epithet in a nominal group, whereas a verb cannot; and an adjective is gradable, whereas a verb is not.

To capture the aspectual feature of the word group that realises the Predicator, we can use the agnation and enation patterns below – the neutral-tone clitic 了 *le* marks the perfective aspect in the indicative mood, whereas there is no aspect marking in the imperative mood.

| Imperative **(no aspect)** | Indicative **(perfective aspect)** |
|---|---|
| 全体起立： *quántǐ qǐlì* 'All rise.' | 全体起立了:: *quántǐ qǐlì **le*** 'All rose.' |
| 坐下： *zuòxià* 'Sit down.' | 坐下了:: *zuòxià **le*** '(Someone) sat down.' |
| 说话声音大一点： *shuōhuà shēngyīn dà yīdiǎn* '(Let your) voice rise a little.' | 说话声音大了一点 *shuōhuà shēngyīn dà **le** yīdiǎn* '(Someone's) voice rose a little.' |

It is worth noting that the word group realising the Predicator in an indicative clause takes no explicit marker if the aspect is general or habitual (i.e. imperfective). Minus a Modal Adjunct like 请 *qǐng* 'please', an indicative clause and an imperative clause have identical forms. To see the difference between mood types, we need to consider perfective aspect, since it is a possible choice for indicative clauses but not for imperatives. This is where the notion of cryptogrammar comes into play (see Section 1.3 in Chapter 1).

One cryptogrammatical characteristic of imperative clauses in Chinese can be explored by subjecting the clause to a negative probe. The negation marker for imperatives is 不要 *bùyào* or 别 *bié* 'don't', whereas the negation marker for indicatives is 不 *bù* 'not' (for the imperfective aspect) or 没(有) *méi(yǒu)* 'have not' (for the perfective aspect). Compare the pattern below, which shows how imperative mood interacts with the ideational system of ASPECT and the interpersonal system of POLARITY.

| Positive imperative | Negative imperative |
|---|---|
| 审判员入庭 *shěnpànyuán rù tíng* 'Judges enter the courtroom!' | 审判员**不要/别**入庭 *shěnpànyuán **bùyào**/**bié** rù tíng* 'Judges not to enter the courtroom!' |
| Positive indicative (imperfective) 审判员入庭 *shěnpànyuán rù tíng* 'Judges enter the courtroom.' | Negative indicative (imperfective) 审判员**不**入庭 *shěnpànyuán **bù** rù tíng* 'Judges do not enter the courtroom.' |
| Positive indicative (perfective) 审判员入庭了 *shěnpànyuán rù tíng le* 'Judges entered the courtroom.' | Negative indicative (perfective) 审判员**没(有)**入庭 *shěnpànyuán **méi**(**yǒu**) rù tíng* 'Judges did not enter the courtroom.' |

## 4.4 Chinese MOOD Resources

Sometimes an imperative clause has a particle 吧 *ba* in final position to express a tentative suggestion or wish (i.e. an optative MOOD type), as illustrated in example (110). We give the particle 吧 *ba* the function label Moderator; its function is to encourage agreement from the addressee. In (110), one of the defendants suggests to the other that they'd better call the police; but he leaves this suggestion open to negotiation by attaching the Moderator to tone down the proposal.

(110)

| DE1 | A2 | 咱们报警吧 | | | |
|---|---|---|---|---|---|
| | | *zánmen* | *bào* | *jǐng* | *ba* |
| | | | Predicator | | Moderator |
| | | | verbal group | | particle |
| | | we (inclusive) | report | police | |
| | | 'Shall call the police.' | | | |

The system network in Figure 4.16 outlines the imperative MOOD types and the structural motivation for differentiating it from the indicative. The feature [imperative] is realised by having an aspectless Predicator;[34] it is further split into two options – [jussive] giving a direct command and [optative] expressing a desire or wish. For the optative imperative to be realised, the Moderator function at the clause rank must be inserted in clause-final position. This function is realised by a particle, which is lexicalised as 吧 *ba*.

### 4.4.2 Declarative Mood

Clauses in the declarative mood function as the congruent realisation of K1 moves. They usually lack a specific structural marker and have relatively high frequency in discourse (Huang and Liao, 2002, p. 110; Li, 2007, p. 127). As Halliday and McDonald (2004, p. 332) suggest, in Chinese a Subject function plays no part in signalling declarative mood. The only obligatory function in a non-elliptical declarative clause in Chinese is the Predicator. Below are two

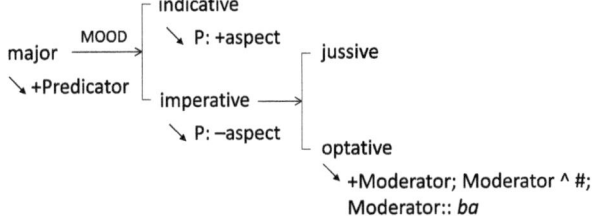

Figure 4.16 Chinese imperative MOOD systems

---

[34] Strictly speaking, ASPECT is a system not a system of the clause, but of the word group realising the Predicator (see Chapter 3, Section 3.4). The realisation statements for [indicative] and [imperative] in the system network are only shorthand ones.

examples of declarative clauses from our Reckless Driving text. The unanalysed part in (112) plays no part in the realisation of the declarative mood; it specifies the Participant or Circumstance involved in the clause.

(111)

| DL | K1 | 同意 |
|---|---|---|
| | | *tóngyì* |
| | | Predicator |
| | | word group |
| | | Event |
| | | verb |
| | | agree |
| | | '(I) agree.' |

(112)

| CP | K1 | 开庭前准备工作已经就绪 | | | | | |
|---|---|---|---|---|---|---|---|
| | | *kāi* | *tíng* | *qián* | *zhǔnbèi* | *gōngzuò* | *yǐjīng* | *jiùxù* |
| | | | | | | | | Predicator |
| | | | | | | | | word group |
| | | | | | | | | Event |
| | | | | | | | | adjective |
| | | open | court | before | prepare | work | already | ready |
| | | 'The preparatory work before the opening of court session is done.' |

We have introduced above the clause-final particle 吧 *ba* which functions as Moderator in imperative mood. The same particle can also be used in a declarative clause, in which case it denotes the speaker's uncertainty with respect to the proposition they are negotiating. In our focus text there is an exchange in which the K1 move is realised by an elliptical clause ending with the particle 吧 *ba*. Its meaning is represented by *would have been* in the free translation. In subsequent detailed analysis in (114), we provide in parentheses the elided part that would be used in a full major clause.

(113)

| PR2 | K2 | 你去医院的时间是什么时候？ |
|---|---|---|
| | | *nǐ qù yīyuàn de shíjiān shì shénme shíhòu* |
| | | 'When did you go to the hospital?' |
| DE1 | K1 | 下午两点左右吧。 |
| | | *xiàwǔ liǎng diǎn zuǒyòu **ba*** |
| | | '**Would have been** around 2 p.m.' |

4.4 Chinese MOOD Resources 217

(114)

| DE1 | K1 | (时间是)下午两点左右吧 | | | | | |
|---|---|---|---|---|---|---|---|
| | | *(shíjiān* | *shì)* | *xiàwǔ* | *liǎng* | *diǎn* | *zuǒyòu* | *ba* |
| | | | Predicator | | | | | Moderator |
| | | | word group | | | | | particle |
| | | | Event | | | | | |
| | | | verb | | | | | |
| | | time | be | afternoon | two | o'clock | around | |
| | | '(The time) would have been around 2 p.m.' | | | | | | |

At this stage we can see that the particle 吧 *ba* doesn't help distinguish between imperative and declarative clauses. The key function that distinguishes the imperative from the declarative is, in fact, the Predicator. This is the function that is realised through a word group with the potential negation and aspect markers that can be used to distinguish moods.

### 4.4.3 Interrogative Mood

As the congruent realisation of a K2 move in a knowledge exchange, a clause in the interrogative mood seeks information, thereby inviting a declarative clause that realises a K1 move as a response. The question can solicit knowledge of various kinds – it can ask for a piece of missing information in a proposition that the addressee is expected to provide; it can comprise a complete proposition, which the addressee is asked to confirm or not; it can also provide two or more alternatives for the addressee to select from in their response.

Given the variety of interrogatives and their structural configurations in Chinese, several ways of classifying them have been suggested by grammarians. In traditional terms it is generally agreed that there are four kinds of questions (e.g. Huang, 1984; Huang and Liao, 2002):

(1) 特指 *tèzhǐ* 'refer in particular' question;
(2) 是非 *shìfēi* 'right–wrong' question;
(3) 正反 *zhèngfǎn* 'face–reverse' question;
(4) 选择 *xuǎnzé* 'select' question.

Note that we refer to these as 'questions' rather than 'interrogatives' because not all of them are treated as features in the system of interrogative MOOD in the description developed below. Here they simply serve as a point of departure, drawing on the description of Chinese interrogative MOOD types in traditional Chinese grammar.

There have also been classifications of Chinese interrogatives from a functional perspective – e.g. Halliday and McDonald (2004), Li (2007) and Li and Thompson (1981). Table 4.7 compares these classifications. From the table

Table 4.7 *Functional classifications of interrogatives in Chinese*

|  | Li & Thompson (1981) | Halliday & McDonald (2004); Li (2007) |
|---|---|---|
| 特指 *tèzhǐ* 'refer in particular' | question-word question | elemental |
| 是非 *shìfēi* 'right–wrong' | particle question | polar: biased |
| 正反 *zhèngfǎn* 'face–reverse' | disjunctive question: A-not-A type | polar: unbiased |
| 选择 *xuǎnzé* 'select' | disjunctive question: constituents connected by 还是 *háishì* | |

we can see that *shìfēi* 'right–wrong' and *zhèngfǎn* 'face–reverse' questions are grouped together by Halliday and McDonald (2004) and Li (2007) as polar interrogative, which category is in turn subdivided into 'biassed' and 'unbiassed'; Li and Thompson (1981), on the other hand, group *zhèngfǎn* 'face–reverse' and *xuǎnzé* 'select' together as disjunctive questions.[35]

By observing the congruent realisations of K2 moves and their responses in our data, we now explore the systemic contrasts and structural realisations of Chinese interrogatives.

We call the first type of interrogative in Chinese an elemental interrogative, comparable to the wh-interrogative in English (see Section 4.2 above) and elemental interrogative in Spanish (see Section 4.3 above); it solicits missing ideational information. In all existing classifications of Chinese interrogative types, elemental interrogatives are treated as a distinct class. An elemental interrogative clause in Chinese involves the insertion of an interrogative function that we call Inquirer – typically realised by lexical items such as 什么 *shénme* 'what', 谁 *shuí* 'who', 哪个 *nǎge* 'which', 哪里 *nǎlǐ* 'where', 怎样 *zěnyàng* 'how', 多少 *duōshǎo* 'how many/much', 为什么 *wèishénme* 'why', etc. Many of the Inquirers that are realised by nominal groups share a common word 什么 *shénme* 'what' (e.g. 什么时候 *shénme shíhòu* 'what time, when', 什么地方 *shénme dìfāng* 'what place, where', 什么人 *shénme rén* 'what person, who', etc.). In fact, the interrogative word 什么 *shénme* 'what' can combine with any noun to form a nominal group realising the Inquirer function. Below is an example from our Reckless Driving text.

---

[35] Li and Thompson (1981, p. 546) mention the 'tag question' as another type of question. However, their tag question always involves two clauses, the first of which is a declarative, the second (the 'tag') an 'A-not-A' disjunctive in their terminology.

(115)

| JU | K2 | 此次涉嫌什么罪名 | | | |
|---|---|---|---|---|---|
| | | *cǐcì* | *shèxián* | *shénme* | *zuìmíng* |
| | | | Predicator | Inquirer | |
| | | | verbal group | nominal group | |
| | | | | Deictic | Thing |
| | | | | pronoun | noun |
| | | this time | suspected | what | crime |
| | | 'What crime (are you) suspected of this time?' | | | |

The structural realisation of an elemental interrogative in Chinese is different from that in English and Spanish. In Chinese, the Inquirer function is not positioned at the beginning of a clause, but remains *in situ* – i.e. where the missing piece of ideational information would be in a declarative clause. This is illustrated in the example below, in which we expand the actual response to (115) to its full clausal form.

(116)

| DE1 | K1 | (此次涉嫌)危险驾驶(罪名) | | | | |
|---|---|---|---|---|---|---|
| | | (*cǐcì* | *shèxián*) | *wēixiǎn* | *jiàshǐ* | (*zuìmíng*) |
| | | | Predicator | | | |
| | | | verbal group | nominal group | | |
| | | this time | suspected | danger | drive | crime |
| | | '(I am suspected of the crime of) reckless driving (this time).' | | | | |

The two examples below from the Reckless Driving text further illustrate an elemental interrogative and its response. In (117) the Inquirer is realised by the nominal group 何时 *héshí* 'when', which is a more literary, refined version of 什么时候 *shénme shíhòu* 'what time' and is thus an appropriate choice for the courtroom context (in general terms it is favoured by people with higher social status).

(117)

| JU | K2 | 何时被羁押 | | |
|---|---|---|---|---|
| | | *héshí* | *bèi* | *jīyā* |
| | | Inquirer | Predicator | |
| | | nominal group | verbal group | |
| | | when | PASS | detain |
| | | 'When were (you) detained?' | | |

(118)

| DE1 | K1 | 4月12号被羁押 | | | | | |
|---|---|---|---|---|---|---|---|
| | | *sì* | *yuè* | *shí'èr* | *hào* | (*bèi* | *jīyā*) |
| | | | | | | Predicator | |
| | | nominal group | | | | verbal group | |
| | | 4 | month | 12 | number | PASS | detain |
| | | '(I was detained on) 12 April.' | | | | | |

Note that in the above examples, the ideational function which the Inquirer is conflated with has not been labelled, nor has the function realised by the nominal group in declarative clauses; neither are relevant to the realisation of MOOD in Chinese. It is sufficient at this stage simply to recognise that the position of the Inquirer function depends on these ideational components.

A second type of Chinese interrogative is realised structurally by adding a clause-rank particle at the end of the declarative clause; it has the function of checking whether the knowledge proposed in the K2 move is correct or not. This type of interrogative is known in traditional Chinese grammar as *shìfēi* 'right–wrong' question. Halliday and McDonald (2004) and Li (2007) call it 'biassed polar' – termed 'biassed' probably because only one polarity choice, either positive or negative, is provided in the clause. This does not imply that all such interrogatives presuppose or expect an answer that is either positive or negative. To avoid such misunderstanding, we do not use the term 'biassed' or 'unbiassed' in our analysis.

In our description we term this type of interrogative an 'addressee-oriented' interrogative. The function realised by the clausal-final particle is again labelled Moderator. The most frequently used particle realising this Moderator is 吗 *ma*, a non-salient syllable spoken on a neutral tone. The *ma* interrogative does not presume either a positive or a negative answer. What follows are two exchanges from our data, each containing a *ma* interrogative clause realising the K2 move and a declarative clause realising the K1 move in response.

(119)

| JU | K2 | 同起诉书载明的信息一致吗 | | | | | |
|---|---|---|---|---|---|---|---|
| | | *tóng* | *qǐsùshū* | *zàimíng* | *de* | *xìnxī* | *yīzhì* | *ma* |
| | | | | | | | Predicator | Moderator |
| | | | | | | | word group | particle |
| | | with | indictment | record | | information | consistent | |
| | | '(Is it) consistent with the information recorded in the indictment?' | | | | | | |

(120)

| DE1 | K1 | 一致 |
|---|---|---|
| | | *yīzhì* |
| | | Predicator |
| | | word group |
| | | consistent |
| | | '(It is) consistent.' |

## 4.4 Chinese MOOD Resources

(121)

| JU | K2 | 检察院的起诉书副本你收到了吗 | | | | | | |
|----|----|----|----|----|----|----|----|----|
| | | *jiǎncháyuàn* | *de* | *qǐsùshū* | *fùběn* | *nǐ* | *shōudào* | *le* | *ma* |
| | | | | | | | Predicator | | Moderator |
| | | | | | | | word group | | particle |
| | | procuratorate | | indictment | copy | you | receive | PF | |
| | | 'Have you received a copy of the indictment of the procuratorate?' | | | | | | |

(122)

| DE1 | K1 | 收到了 | |
|-----|----|----|----|
| | | *shōudào* | *le* |
| | | Predicator | |
| | | word group | |
| | | receive | PF |
| | | '(I) have received (it).' | |

The Moderator happens to appear immediately after the Predicator in both examples (119) and (121) because in the former the standard of comparison must precede the word group (一致 *yīzhì* 'consistent') and in the latter 检察院的起诉书副本 *jiǎncháyuàn de qǐsùshū fùběn* 'a copy of the indictment of the procuratorate' is thematised textually. Example (121) can be rewritten with an alternative thematic arrangement below as (123).

(123)

| JU | K2 | 你收到了检察院的起诉书副本吗 | | | | | | |
|----|----|----|----|----|----|----|----|----|
| | | *nǐ* | *shōudào* | *le* | *jiǎncháyuàn* | *de* | *qǐsùshū* | *fùběn* | *ma* |
| | | | Predicator | | | | | | Moderator |
| | | | word group | | | | | | particle |
| | | you | receive | PF | procuratorate | | indictment | copy | |
| | | 'Have you received a copy of the indictment of the procuratorate?' | | | | | | |

In (120) and (122), both K1 response moves repeat the Predicator to affirm the proposition in their preceding K2 moves, affirming that in Chinese the Predicator is the key interpersonal function in a declarative clause.[36] The response move may also include a Polarity Adjunct 是的 *shìde*, affirming the proposition, or 不 *bù*, contradicting the proposition.

(124)

| JU | K2 | 同起诉书载明的信息一致吗? |
|-----|----|----|
| | | *tóng qǐsùshū zàimíng de xìnxī yīzhì ma* |
| | | '(Is it) consistent with the information recorded in the indictment?' |
| DE1 | K1 | 是的,一致。 |
| | | *shìde, yīzhì* |
| | | '**Yes**, (it is) consistent.' |

---

[36] Compare this with discussion in Section 4.2 above. The Predicator function does not play a central role in an English declarative, and it can be elided, along with with other experiential elements, in a response move.

| (125) | JU | K2 | 同起诉书载明的信息一致吗？<br>*tóng qǐsùshū zàimíng de xìnxī yīzhì ma*<br>'(Is it) consistent with the information recorded in the indictment?' |
|---|---|---|---|
| | DE1 | K1 | 不,不一致。<br>**bù**, *bù yīzhì*<br>'**No**, (it is) not consistent.' |

| (126) | JU | K2 | 检察院的起诉书副本你收到了吗？<br>*jiǎncháyuàn de qǐsùshū fùběn nǐ shōudào le ma*<br>'Have you received a copy of the indictment of the procuratorate?' |
|---|---|---|---|
| | DE1 | K1 | 是的,收到了。<br>**shìde**, *shōudào le*<br>'**Yes**, (I) have received (it).' |

| (127) | JU | K2 | 检察院的起诉书副本你收到了吗？<br>*jiǎncháyuàn de qǐsùshū fùběn nǐ shōudào le ma*<br>'Have you received a copy of the indictment of the procuratorate?' |
|---|---|---|---|
| | DE1 | K1 | 不,没收到。<br>**bù**, *méi shōudào*<br>'**No**, (I) haven't received (it).' |

It is also worth noting that if the interrogative move is negative, the Polarity Adjuncts 是的 *shìde* and 不 *bù* work differently from English *yes* and *no*. The examples below (modified on the basis of (119)) illustrate the use of 是的 *shìde* and 不 *bù* in affirming and denying a proposition.

(128)

| JU | K2 | 同起诉书载明的信息不一致吗 | | | | | |
|---|---|---|---|---|---|---|---|
| | | *tóng* | *qǐsùshū* | *zàimíng* | *de* | *xìnxī* | **bù** | *yīzhì* | *ma* |
| | | | | | | | Predicator | | Moderator |
| | | | | | | | word group | | particle |
| | | with | indictment | record | | information | not | consistent | |
| | | '(Is it) not consistent with the information recorded in the indictment?' | | | | | | | |

(129)

| DE1 | K1 | 是的,不一致 | | |
|---|---|---|---|---|
| | | ***shìde*** | *bù* | *yīzhì* |
| | | Polarity Adjunct | Predicator | |
| | | | word group | |
| | | right | not | consistent |
| | | 'Right, (it is) not consistent.' | | |

## 4.4 Chinese MOOD Resources

(130)

| DE1 | K1 | 不,一致 | |
|---|---|---|---|
| | | **bù** | **yīzhì** |
| | | Polarity Adjunct | Predicator |
| | | | word group |
| | | no | consistent |
| | | 'No, (it is) consistent.' | |

In English, if we want to agree with the proposition that something is not consistent with the information recorded in the indictment, the Polarity Adjunct in the response would be *no*, as in ***No**, it is not*. If we want to contradict the proposition, the Polarity Adjunct in the response would be *yes*, as in ***Yes**, it is*.

In our description of Chinese, we treat negation as realised inside the word group realising the Predicator, since the form of its realisation is conditioned by aspect (see Section 4.4.1 above). This is in contrast with the possible realisation of negation in English as Neg in Section 1.2 above – as a distinct part of clause structure (*not*) or conflated with Finite (e.g. *didn't*).

(131)

| K2 | Is | it | not | consistent with the information recorded in the indictment? |
|---|---|---|---|---|
| | Finite | Subject | Neg | |

Taking this into account we can reason that Chinese Polarity Adjuncts 是的 *shìde* and 不 *bù* affirm or contradict the Predicator (which may be either positive or negative), whereas English polarity and Adjuncts *yes* and *no* affirm or contradict the proposition as a whole.

In an address-oriented interrogative clause, the clause-final particle can be 吧 *ba*. Unlike 吗 *ma*, the particle 吧 *ba* marks an interrogative that involves the speaker's expectation that the proposition being negotiated is true and that the addressee will confirm the proposition. We provide below analysis of an interrogative of this kind in a K2 move, along with its response.

(132)

| JU | K2 | 都没有意见吧 | | | | |
|---|---|---|---|---|---|---|
| | | *dōu* | *méi* | *yǒu* | *yìjiàn* | *ba* |
| | | | Predicator | | | Moderator |
| | | | word group | | | particle |
| | | all | not | have | objection | |
| | | '(You) all do not have (any) objection, do you?' | | | | |

(133)

| DE1 | K1 | 没有 | |
|---|---|---|---|
| | | *méi* | *yǒu* |
| | | Predicator | |
| | | word group | |
| | | not | have |
| | | '(We) do not have (any) objection.' | |

Here we analyse the clause with the final particle 吧 *ba* as interrogative rather than declarative because it congruently realises a K2 move soliciting a responding K1 move and expecting an affirmative response. Nevertheless, the K1 move can either affirm or deny the proposition, using a clause centring on the Predicator – optionally with the Polarity Adjunct 是的 *shìde* or 不 *bù* (just like the responses elicited by an interrogative clause with the particle 吗 *ma*).

(134)

| JU | K2 | 都没有意见吧? <br> *dōu méi yǒu yìjiàn ba* <br> 'You don't have any objection, do you?' |
|---|---|---|
| DE1 | K1 | 是的,没有。 <br> *shìde, méi yǒu* <br> 'Right, we don't have any.' |

(135)

| JU | K2 | 都没有意见吧? <br> *dōu méi yǒu yìjiàn ba* <br> 'You don't have any objection, do you?' |
|---|---|---|
| DE1 | K1 | 不,有意见。 <br> *bù, yǒu yìjiàn* <br> 'No, we do have some objection.' |

The third type of interrogative in Chinese we call a proposition-oriented interrogative, which is traditionally described in traditional Chinese grammar as *zhèngfǎn* 'face–reverse' question. In such an interrogative both the positive and the negative sides of the proposition are provided in the K2 move, and the addressee needs to choose between them in the K1 move. The response contains either a positive or a negative version of the proposition, hence the name of the interrogative – 'proposition-oriented'. Halliday and McDonald (2004) and Li (2007) treat this type of interrogative as 'polar', and they subclassify it as 'unbiassed' (probably because both sides of the proposition are made explicit in the interrogative).

The proposition-oriented interrogative features a Predicator realised by a word group complex in which a word group first appears in the positive and is then followed by a word group in the negative with the same Event (realised by either a verb or an adjective). We analyse below a proposition-oriented interrogative from our focus text, where two word groups 有 *yǒu* 'have' and 没有 *méiyǒu* 'not have' are juxtaposed and the second word group extends the first one, and a negative response to this interrogative. We treat this complex as paratactic, signalled by the 1 +2 notation.

## 4.4 Chinese MOOD Resources

(136)

| JU | K2 | 你有没有意见 | | | | |
|----|----|----|----|----|----|----|
| | | *nǐ* | *yǒu* | *méi* | *yǒu* | *yìjiàn* |
| | | | Predicator | | | |
| | | | word group complex | | | |
| | | | 1 | +2 | | |
| | | | word group | word group | | |
| | | | Event | Neg | Event | |
| | | | verb | adverb | verb | |
| | | you | have | not | have | objection |
| | | 'Do you have (any) objection?' | | | | |

(137)

| DE1 | K1 | 没有 | |
|-----|----|----|----|
| | | *méi* | *yǒu* |
| | | Predicator | |
| | | word group | |
| | | Neg | Event |
| | | adverb | verb |
| | | not | have |
| | | '(I) do not have (any) objection.' | |

The proposition-oriented interrogative allows for the word group complex realising the Predicator to be discontinuous. The example below is adjusted from (136); there in (138) the second component of the word group complex is placed after the nominal group 意见 *yìjiàn* 'objection'.

(138)

| JU | K2 | 你有意见没有 | | | | |
|----|----|----|----|----|----|----|
| | | *nǐ* | *yǒu* | *yìjiàn* | *méi* | *yǒu* |
| | | | Predi ... | | ... cator | |
| | | | word ... | | ... group complex | |
| | | | 1 | | +2 | |
| | | | word group | | word group | |
| | | | Event | | Neg | Event |
| | | | verb | | adverb | verb |
| | | you | have | objection | not | have |
| | | 'Do you have (any) objection?' | | | | |

Note that there is optional phonological conditioning at play when the word group in the positive polarity comprises two or more syllables. The first word group in the word group complex realising the Predicator in a proposition-oriented interrogative may be reduced to its first syllable, thus rendering the first word group phonologically incomplete. This is illustrated in the example below, where 记得 *jìdé* 'remember' is reduced to 记 *jì* in the first word group.

(139)

| JU | K2 | 你记不记得 …… | | | |
|---|---|---|---|---|---|
| | | *nǐ* | *jì* | *bù* | *jìdé* | … |
| | | | Predicator | | | |
| | | | word group complex | | | |
| | | | 1 | +2 | | |
| | | | word group | word group | | |
| | | | Event | Neg | Event | |
| | | | verb | adverb | verb | |
| | | you | remember | not | remember | … |
| | | 'Do you remember … ?' | | | | |

In contrast to addressee-oriented interrogatives, proposition-oriented interrogatives cannot be responded to with the Polarity Adjunct 是的 *shìde* or 不 *bù*. The response can only be realised by a declarative clause with either a positive or a negative Predicator, as in (137).

A special kind of proposition-oriented interrogative uses the verb 是 *shì* 'be right' to form the verbal group complex 是不是 *shì bù shì* 'be right or not right'. This verbal group complex forms a clause on its own. Adjacent to this clause is another clause that contains the proposition that the addressee is asked to confirm or contradict. An example, slightly modified from our focus text, is analysed below.

(140)

| JU | K2 | 被告人辩护人**是不是**都听清楚了 | | | | | | | |
|---|---|---|---|---|---|---|---|---|---|
| | | *bèigàorén* | *biànhùrén* | *shì* | *bù* | *shì* | *dōu* | *tīng* | *qīngchǔ* | *le* |
| | | 1 … | | <<=2>> | | | … 1 | | | |
| | | cl … | | <<clause>> | | | … ause | | | |
| | | | | Predicator | | | Predicator | | | |
| | | | | verbal group complex | | | word group | | | |
| | | | | 1 | +2 | | | | | |
| | | | | verb group | verb group | | | | | |
| | | | | Event | Neg | Event | | | | |
| | | | | verb | adverb | verb | | | | |
| | | defendant | defence lawyer | be right | not | be right | all | hear | clearly | PF |
| | | 'The defendants and defence lawyers have all heard clearly, yes or no?' | | | | | | | | |

Here the 是不是 *shì bù shì* 'be right or not right' clause realises the interrogative MOOD type of the K2 move, and the other clause, a declarative one,

## 4.4 Chinese MOOD Resources

establishes the proposition. This kind of question in a sense splits the interpersonal and ideational meaning into two clauses in a paratactic relationship – in which the *shì bù shì* clause is responsible for realising the interrogative mood of the K2 move and the enclosing clause is responsible for establishing its content.

In the response move for this question type, the addressee can respond either with a choice between positive and negative based on the proposition-oriented interrogative (i.e. the 是不是 *shì bù shì* 'be right or not right' clause) or with the Predicator from the declarative clause (with positive or negative polarity). The actual Predicator response from our data is provided below.

(141)

| DE, DL | K1 | 听清楚了 | | |
|---|---|---|---|---|
| | | *tīng* | *qīngchǔ* | *le* |
| | | Predicator | | |
| | | word group | | |
| | | Event | Phase | Asp |
| | | verb | adverb | clitic |
| | | hear | clearly | PF |
| | | '(We) have heard clearly.' | | |

Some Chinese grammarians treat the 是不是 *shì bù shì* 'be right or not right' interrogative as a separate type of interrogative (e.g. Tao, 1998; Ding, 1999). Their arguments are largely based on the practice in traditional Chinese grammar of analysing MOOD at sentence level rather than clause level.

Our analysis of 是不是 *shì bù shì* 'be right or not right' as a clause paratactically related to another clause is also supported by the fact that the position of 是不是 *shì bù shì* 'be right or not right' is rather flexible – it can appear before or after the declarative clause presenting the proposition being negotiated, as well as being inserted in the middle (as in (140)). The example below is from our focus text, with 是不是 *shì bù shì* 'be right or not right' following the declarative; its response picks up its Predicator from the declarative clause in the clause complex realising the K2 move.

(142)

| JU | K2 | 需要讯问**是不是** | | | | |
|---|---|---|---|---|---|---|
| | | *xūyào* | *xùnwèn* | *shì* | *bù* | *shì* |
| | | 1 | | <<=2>> | | |
| | | Predicator | | Predicator | | |
| | | word group | | verbal group complex | | |
| | | | | 1 | +2 | |
| | | Mod | Event | Event | Neg | Event |
| | | modal verb | verb | verb | adverb | verb |
| | | need | interrogate | be right | not | be right |
| | | '(You) need to interrogate (the defendants), yes or no?' | | | | |

(143)

| PR1 | K1 | 需要 |
|---|---|---|
| | | xūyào |
| | | Predicator |
| | | word group |
| | | Mod |
| | | modal verb |
| | | need |
| | | '(I) need to.' |

The classification of Chinese interrogatives in traditional grammar presented above, included a *xuǎnzé* 'select' question. In our description, however, we do not treat this as part of the MOOD system. It is realised not by a clause, but by a complex structure involving at least two clauses, providing two or more alternatives for the addressee to choose from. The two alternatives are connected by the conjunction 还是 *háishì* 'or'. Below is an example comprising two clauses in an extending paratactic relationship. Taken together they realise a K2 move. But neither of the clauses realise interrogative mood on their own.

(144)

| K2 | 你吃饭 | | | 还是吃面 | | |
|---|---|---|---|---|---|---|
| | nǐ | chī | fàn | háishì | chī | miàn |
| | 1 | | | +2 | | |
| | you | eat | rice | or | eat | noodle |
| | 'Do you eat rice or eat noodle?' | | | | | |

In summary, there are three types of clause-level interrogatives in Chinese that congruently realise a K2 move – elemental, addressee-oriented and proposition-oriented interrogatives. Halliday and McDonald (2004) and Li (2007) group addressee-oriented and proposition-oriented interrogatives together as polar interrogatives, as they both solicit either a positive or a negative response to the proposition in question, as opposed to elemental interrogatives that demand missing ideational information.

Reasoning from below, we can see that the structure of MOOD elements of the three types of interrogatives are distinct from one another. The clause-rank functions that realise elemental, addressee-oriented and proposition-oriented interrogatives are Inquirer, Moderator and Predicator respectively. The Predicator in a proposition-oriented interrogative needs to be realised by a word group complex with both positive and negative components. The response to an addressee-oriented or proposition-oriented interrogative typically picks up the Predicator from the interrogative and gives it positive or

## 4.4 Chinese MOOD Resources

negative polarity. The Polarity Adjunct 是的 *shìde* or 不 *bù* can be used in response to addressee-oriented interrogatives only. These features are summarised in Table 4.8.

We can now propose the system network for the interrogative MOOD in Chinese shown in Figure 4.17. The elemental interrogative is set apart at primary delicacy from the others since the addressee-oriented and proposition-oriented interrogatives are cryptogrammatically related – both solicit a response replaying the Predicator in the interrogative. The elemental interrogative requires the insertion of the Inquirer function and its conflation with whatever function the interrogative inquires about. The addressee-oriented interrogative inserts the Moderator function and places it at the end of the clause. The Moderator can be lexicalised as 吗 *ma* (querying the addressee about the truthfulness of the proposition) or 吧 *ba* (seeking from the addressee confirmation of the proposition), realising features [querying] and [confirming] respectively. The proposition-oriented interrogative requires the Predicator to be realised by word group complexing with the positive polarity

Table 4.8 *Three types of interrogative in Chinese*

|  | elemental | addressee-oriented | proposition-oriented |
|---|---|---|---|
| clause-rank functions realising mood | Inquirer | Moderator | Predicator |
| Predicator realised by word group complex |  |  | + |
| response using Predicator from interrogative |  | + | + |
| response using Polarity Adjunct |  | + |  |

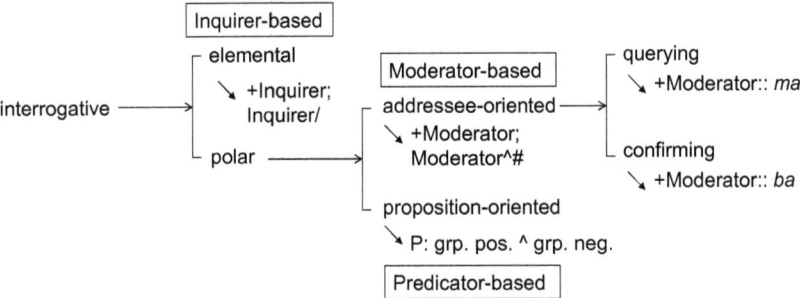

Figure 4.17 Chinese interrogative MOOD systems

preceding the negative. The different 'orientations' of these interrogative types are annotated in boxes in the figure.

### 4.4.4 MOOD in Chinese: An Alternative Perspective

Based on the discussion above, we can consolidate the MOOD system in Chinese in a system network (Figure 4.18). This system network is oriented to the realisation of the discourse semantic system NEGOTIATION. The major problem with this classification of Chinese MOOD is that if we reason from around and below it is impossible to find structural evidence, either phenotypical or cryptotypical, for the feature [interrogative] that justifies its opposition to [declarative].

From an alternative perspective, the discourse semantic system of ENGAGEMENT (a subsystem of APPRAISAL) (Martin and White, 2005) might be accorded greater relevance as far as MOOD choices in Chinese are concerned. The system of ENGAGEMENT allows for individual subjectivity to be expressed when presenting a proposition or proposal for negotiation. In Chinese, this can be foregrounded by setting up a simultaneous system alongside the primary MOOD distinction between [indicative] and [imperative]. Both indicative and imperative clause would choose from this system, as shown in Figure 4.19. In this alternative way of analysis, we do not distinguish between [declarative] and [interrogative].

The system oriented to ENGAGEMENT has two options: [pose] and [tender]. The feature [pose] means that we present a proposition or proposal for modal assessment, opening up dialogic space; [tender] indicates that we proffer the proposition or proposal as non-negotiable. The [pose] option is realised by a modal element (Moderator realised by a particle) at the end of a clause, i.e. 吗 *ma* or 吧 *ba*.

For imperative clauses, the [pose] type is optative, which opens up negotiating space around the obligation; the [tender] type, on the other hand, is jussive and enacts a direct demand for action. We reproduce and modify example (110) to illustrate this opposition.

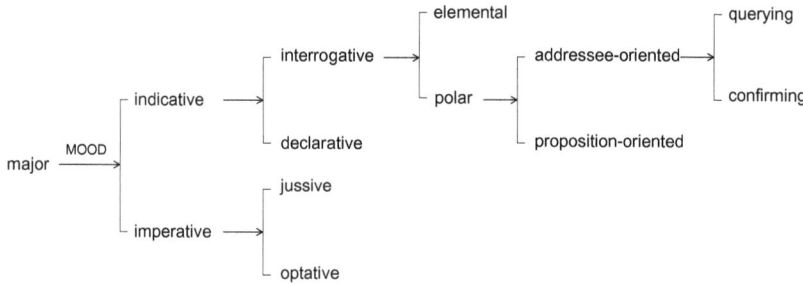

Figure 4.18 Chinese MOOD systems (oriented to NEGOTIATION)

## 4.4 Chinese MOOD Resources

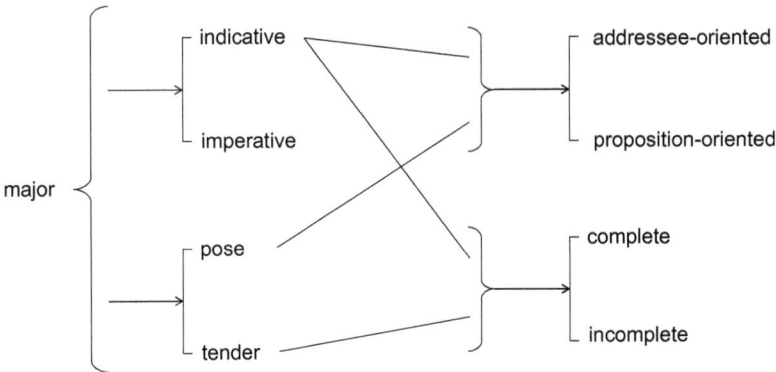

Figure 4.19 Alternative Chinese MOOD systems (oriented to both NEGOTIATION and ENGAGEMENT)

(145)

| [imperative/pose] | | | |
|---|---|---|---|
| 咱们报警吧 | | | |
| zánmen | bào | jǐng | ba |
| | Predicator | | Moderator |
| | verbal group | | particle |
| we (inclusive) | report | police | |
| 'Let's call the police.' | | | |

(146)

| [imperative/tender] | | |
|---|---|---|
| 咱们报警 | | |
| zánmen | bào | jǐng |
| | Predicator | |
| | verbal group | |
| we (inclusive) | report | police |
| 'Let's call the police.' | | |

An indicative clause can also select between [pose] and [tender]; either choice will lead to further MOOD options. For [indicative] and [pose], Chinese has a fairly broad range of resources for assessment of the probability of a proposition. On the one hand, a Moderator can be put at the end of an indicative clause, realised by a variety of particles fine-tuning modal assessment (e.g. 吗 *ma*, 吧 *ba* in our analysis). We have seen in the previous section that both declarative and addressee-oriented interrogative clauses can have the particle 吧 *ba*; from the perspective of ENGAGEMENT, both can be viewed as posing the probability of the proposition for negotiation with the addressee. Thus, they are grouped with interrogatives featuring the particle 吗 *ma* together as [addressee-oriented]. We reproduce example (132) below with this alternative analysis. Taken out of context, an [indicative] and [pose]: [addressee-oriented] clause with the particle 吧 *ba* can realise either a K2 or a K1 move in a dialogic exchange.

(147)

| [indicative/pose:addressee-oriented] | | | | |
|---|---|---|---|---|
| 都没有意见吧 | | | | |
| *dōu* | *méi* | *yǒu* | *yìjiàn* | *ba* |
| | Predicator | | | Moderator |
| | word group | | | particle |
| all | not | have | objection | |
| '(You) all do not have (any) objection, do you?' | | | | |

On the other hand, the [indicative] and [pose] can be realised by having a word group complex in the realisation of the Predicator and juxtaposing the positive and negative polarities. Here we continue to the use the feature name [proposition-oriented]. Example (136) is reproduced below with the alternative analysis.

(148)

| [indicative/pose:proposition-oriented] | | | | |
|---|---|---|---|---|
| 你有没有意见 | | | | |
| *nǐ* | *yǒu* | *méi* | *yǒu* | *yìjiàn* |
| | Predicator | | | |
| | word group complex | | | |
| | 1 | +2 | | |
| | Event | Neg | Event | |
| | verb | adverb | verb | |
| you | have | not | have | objection |
| 'Do you have (any) objection?' | | | | |

For [indicative] and [tender], the clause is more oriented towards the experiential dimension of the proposition. A further choice is made between [complete] and [incomplete] depending on whether the experiential meaning in the clause is complete. The [indicative] and [tender]: [complete] clauses are analysed as declarative in the previous section, and [indicative] and [tender]: [incomplete] ones as elemental interrogatives. The two examples below, reproduced from (116) and (115) respectively, illustrate this distinction. In (150), an Inquirer is used to sort out the incomplete experiential meaning that is complete in (149).

## 4.5 Mood Challenge

(149)

| [indicative/tender:complete] | | | | |
|---|---|---|---|---|
| 此次涉嫌危险驾驶罪名 | | | | |
| *cǐcì* | *shèxián* | *wēixiǎn* | *jiàshǐ* | *zuìmíng* |
| | Predicator | | | |
| | verbal group | nominal group | | |
| this time | suspected | danger | drive | crime |
| '(I am suspected of the crime of) reckless driving this time.' | | | | |

(150)

| [indicative/tender:incomplete] | | | |
|---|---|---|---|
| 此次涉嫌什么罪名 | | | |
| *cǐcì* | *shèxián* | *shénme* | *zuìmíng* |
| | Predicator | Inquirer | |
| | verbal group | nominal group | |
| | | Deictic | Thing |
| | | pronoun | noun |
| this time | suspected | what | crime |
| 'What crime (are you) suspected of this time?' | | | |

When we bring Figures 4.18 and 4.19 together, we can see that the congruent grammatical realisations of various moves in the system of NEGOTIATION are scattered across the system networks and oriented to both NEGOTIATION and ENGAGEMENT. Taking ENGAGEMENT into account in the description of Chinese MOOD types is mainly motivated by structural considerations. Here, the perspectives 'from above' and 'from below' are complementary perspectives. Wang (2021) provides a comparable analysis of Chinese MOOD types, with a more detailed account of its theoretical basis and comparison with other languages.

## 4.5 Mood Challenge

For those of you familiar with other languages, we hope that we have now modelled an approach to MOOD system and structure that you will find helpful. For those of you familiar with English, Spanish or Chinese, we reiterate as a reminder here that the descriptions introduced above have been provided for pedagogic purposes. That said we have done our best to develop descriptions based on the distinctive systemic oppositions and structural resources of English, Spanish and Chinese. Our approach to Spanish interpersonal resources is largely based on Quiroz (2013, 2015, 2017a, 2021). We have provided an alternative analysis of Chinese which is strongly oriented to the discourse semantic system of ENGAGEMENT (rather than NEGOTIATION). For an alternative analysis of Spanish, see Lavid, Arús and Zamorano-Mansilla (2010); and for Chinese see Li (2007). For descriptions of MOOD in other languages, see Wang (2020b), Martin (2018a) and Martin, Quiroz and Figueredo (2021).

In Chapter 1 we noted that there is no one-to-one mapping of discourse semantic systems onto lexicogrammatical ones. Discourse semantic features can be realised in different ways just as lexicogrammatical options can participate in the realisation of different discourse semantic ones. And we noted in passing that one of the payoffs of this diversification is the possibility that lexicogrammar might symbolise rather than directly encode discourse semantics – the phenomenon referred to in SFL as grammatical metaphor.

In this chapter we have concentrated on congruent relations between discourse semantics (NEGOTIATION and APPRAISAL) and lexicogrammar (MOOD). Our challenge to you is to extend the discussion, taking non-congruent metaphorical realisations into account. These are discussed in Halliday and Matthiessen (2014) as grammatical metaphors of MOOD and MODALITY.

Let's begin with metaphors of MOOD. Halliday and Matthiessen's model of the congruent realisations of what they refer to as speech functions is tabled and exemplified in Table 4.9, alongside corresponding exchange structure moves. Their proposals do not include suggestions for congruent and metaphorical realisations of Dk1 or exchange initial A1 moves.

Some examples of alternative metaphorical realisations are given in Table 4.10. The basic idea is that congruent realisations work fine for some kinds of tenor relations but not others. The mood metaphors provide additional resources for negotiating tenor as the grammar symbolises rather than directly encodes discourse semantics. These indirect realisations are referred to as metaphorical because there are two meanings involved (one lexicogrammatical and the other discourse semantic), they are layered (in a figure/ground relationship with lexicogrammar on the surface and discourse semantics behind) and the lexicogrammatical meaning is symbolising the discourse semantic one (the source to target relation we are familiar with from studies of lexical metaphor).

Table 4.9 *Congruent realisations of* SPEECH FUNCTION *in English*

| NEGOTIATION | SPEECH FUNCTION | congruent MOOD | example |
|---|---|---|---|
| Dk1 | – | – | |
| K2 (initiating) | question | interrogative | *Did he leave?* |
| K1 (initiating) | statement | declarative | *He left.* |
| Da1 | offer | (no congruent realisation) | |
| A2 (initiating) | command | imperative | *Leave.* |
| A1 (initiating) | – | – | |

## 4.5 Mood Challenge

Table 4.10 *Metaphorical realisations of speech function in English*

| NEGOTIATION | SPEECH FUNCTION | metaphorical MOOD | example |
|---|---|---|---|
| Dk1 | – | – | |
| K2 (initiating) | question | declarative | *He left?* |
| | | imperative | *Tell me if he left.* |
| K1 (initiating) | statement | interrogative | *How could he have left?* |
| | | imperative | *Notice that he left.* |
| Da1 | offer | (no congruent realisation) | |
| A2 (initiating) | command | declarative | *I need you to leave.* |
| | | interrogative | *Would you please leave?* |
| A1 (initiating) | – | – | |

Table 4.11 *Congruent and metaphorical modality in realising* ENGAGEMENT *in English*

| ENGAGEMENT | congruent MODALITY | metaphorical MODALITY | example |
|---|---|---|---|
| expand: entertain | | explicit subjective | *I think I'm the best.* |
| | implicit subjective | | *I may be the best.* |
| | implicit objective | | *Maybe I'm the best.* |
| | | explicit objective | *It's possible I'm the best.* |

The fact that there are two layers of meanings involved creates the potential for misunderstanding and verbal play. In the following exchange a Server in a bakery rejects as un-Australian the tenor relationship implied by an expat's mood metaphor – by interpreting it literally (i.e. lexicogrammatically) instead of negotiating the intended A2 move.

CLIENT: I was wondering if I could have one of those ...
SERVER: Why do you wonder? It's right there in front of you.

Comparable metaphors of MODALITY were introduced in Chapter 1 in the course of our discussion of stratification. Halliday and Matthiessen's proposals for congruent and metaphorical realisations of MODALITY are presented in Table 4.11 in relation to the heteroglossic expanding ENGAGEMENT option they realise.

Once again, because there are two layers of meaning involved, possibilities for misunderstanding and verbal play arise. The following joke depends on the lie detector negotiating what the rugby centre and front-rower say, and interpreting it as metaphorically modalised. But what the second-rower says is interpreted literally as a statement about his thought processes. This would not be possible if there were not two meanings involved, in a figure/ground relationship, with the first person present tense mental cognition clause (*I think*) intended to symbolise heteroglossic expansion.

When laughter can be the best medicine

This was followed by Kapokie Tapokie from Pukekohe's phone message: "Hey bro. Heard the one about a lie detector being installed on the Wallabies bus? A centre hooked himself up and said, '**I think we have the best defence in the world**.' The detector went off. A front-rower then hooked himself up and said, '**I think I'm the best player in the world.**' The detector went off. A second-rower said, '**I think ...**' and the detector went off. Good one, eh! Eh! You there?"

(Monday Maul Greg Crowden *SMH* 14/5/2007)

Our challenge to you is to explore comparable phenomena in Spanish and Chinese. Are there grammatical metaphors of MOOD? Are there grammatical metaphors of MODALITY? For metaphorical realisations, what lexicogrammatical resources are used to symbolise discourse semantics rather than realising it directly? Are grammatical metaphors used as resources for negotiating tenor relations? Do you sense they are used more frequently or less frequently than in English? Are they used more by one social group in your community than another? Lots to explore!

# 5 Transitivity

## 5.1 Approaching from Above

In this chapter we will approach clauses from an ideational perspective. In terms of field (ideational context), TRANSITIVITY construes either a dynamic or a static perspective on phenomena. In addition, it may associate spatio-temporal and qualitative properties with activity and with items. Figure 5.1 presents an outline of these options.

In terms of IDEATION (ideational discourse semantics), TRANSITIVITY construes either occurrence or state figures. Occurrence figures configure entities and occurrences in relation to changes we perceive through our senses or consciousness; state figures configure entities with respect to relationships they have with one another and with qualities. Both occurrence and state figures may be additionally configured in terms of locations in space and time (Hao, 2020a).

In English and Spanish the clauses construing discourse semantic figures regularly include a verbal group realising a nuclear clause function we will refer to as Process; this is less true of Chinese, where certain types of state figure configure entities and qualities without a Process. With the exception of a small set of meteorological experience figures in English and Spanish (e.g. *it's raining, llueve* 'it's raining'),[1] the Process is closely associated with 1, 2 or 3 Participants; and there may be 1 or more associated Circumstances as well.

In Section 5.2 below we explore English TRANSITIVITY resources, before turning to Spanish resources in Section 5.3 and Chinese resources in Section 5.4. Our focus text for English remains the YouTube video titled Let's Talk. | Random Chatty Vlog (https://youtu.be/YRx-zDoPbVw), which we refer to as the Chatty Vlog text (Appendix 2.2). Our focus text for Spanish once again comprises stories about a famous earthquake and tidal wave in Maule and Biobío, Chile, in 2010 (Guzmán, 2010), which we refer to as the Ola Maldita

---

[1] In Chinese the meteorological experience involves a Process ^ Participant structure, e.g. 下雨 *xià yǔ* (lit. 'falls rain').

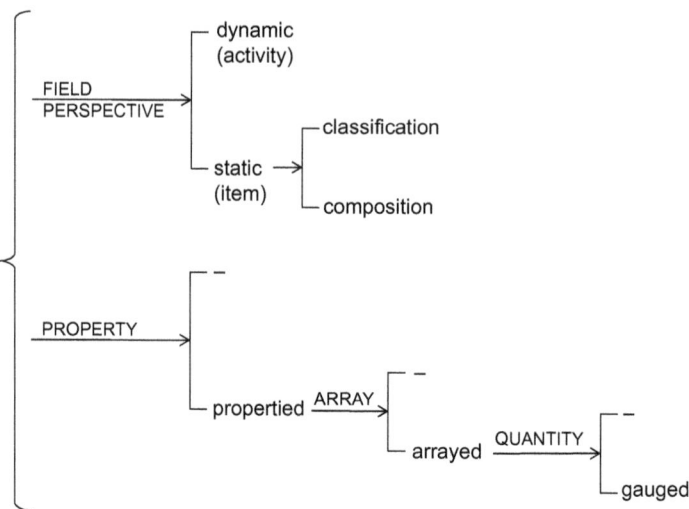

Figure 5.1 Field variables

('the hellish wave') text (Appendix 3.1). Our focus text for Chinese is still the journalistic interview with Mr Shan Jixiang, then curator of the Palace Museum, which we refer to as Interview with Curator text (Appendix 4.2). In Section 5.5 we present an analysis challenge.

## 5.2 English TRANSITIVITY Resources

### 5.2.1 Three Kinds of Clause in English

In this section we begin by focusing on the three main types of clause found in the Chatty Vlog text. The most frequently instantiated type construes the various activities the vlogger recounts for her viewers. The vlogger uses several of clauses to explain why she isn't showing a video she had made (their nuclear Processes in bold below).

I **was showing** all the diabetes supplies like the extra supplies we **brought** on vacation but I **had bent** down like before I **started filming** and my shirt **got caught** in my bra …

The other two types of clause have about half as many instantiations each. One of these types construes the perceptions, thoughts and feelings of the vlogger. Examples include clauses used to intensify how much the vlogger hates her new hair colour.

I **hate** it. I **hate** it. I **hate** the- the colour of it …

## 5.2 English TRANSITIVITY Resources

The third type of clause deals with a range of relations among entities, qualities and locations in time and space. Clauses of this kind are used to describe the granuloma inflammation on her feet.

I **have that** mark and then there's another one and then another one and then on my other feet and it **was** all like bumpy and stuff.

If you have studied SFL before, you will not be surprised by a pattern of this kind in the vlogger's personal recounts – lots of material, mental and relational clauses respectively. But where does the idea of 'three main types of clause' come from? What is the grammatical justification for a classification of this kind?

### 5.2.2   Experiential Clause Typology

Before getting into our classification per se, let's back up a little now and make some simple observations about the English examples introduced above, drawing on our work on nominal groups and verbal groups in Chapters 2 and 3. In these terms, one recurring pattern in the examples is that of nominal group followed by verbal group, followed by another nominal group. If you've studied a little grammar, you will probably recognise this pattern, often referred to as a 'transitive' clause (Table 5.1).

As we can see, as far as the sequence of classes of group is concerned, the clauses are all the same. And we can substitute shorter or longer groups for each of those tabled above (Table 5.2).

Recurrent sequences of classes of the kind we are considering here are referred to in linguistics as syntagms (as discussed in Chapter 1, Section 1.3).

Table 5.1 *Transitive clause syntagms in English*

| nominal group | verbal group | nominal group |
|---|---|---|
| I | was showing | all the diabetes supplies |
| I | hate | it |
| I | have | that mark |

Table 5.2 *More transitive clause syntagms in English*

| nominal group | verbal group | nominal group |
|---|---|---|
| the vlogger | showed | them |
| the vlogger | was going to hate | her hair colour |
| the vlogger | will have | it |

Table 5.3 *Sample syntagms for different types of clause*

| syntagm | nominal group | verbal group | nominal group |
|---|---|---|---|
| examples | *I* | *was showing* | *all the diabetes supplies* |
| | *the vlogger* | *showed* | *them* |
| | *Andy* | *will show* | *the film* |
| examples | *I* | *hate* | *it* |
| | *the vlogger* | *was going to hate* | *her hair colour* |
| | *Andy* | *had hated* | *Target* |
| examples | *I* | *have* | *that mark* |
| | *the vlogger* | *will have* | *it* |
| | *Andy* | *didn't have* | *Chex Mix* |

These clause syntagms recur in the vlog, construing activity, feeling and relations (Table 5.3).

When exploring syntagms there are a number of kinds of evidence linguists take into account. One is the sequence of classes, which may or may not be significant. Another is distinctive morphology (i.e. inflections of various kinds) which may or may not distinguish one class in the syntagm from another, and which may or may not show a relationship between classes – via agreement (e.g. in PERSON, NUMBER or GENDER) or government (e.g. in terms of CASE). In the English syntagms above, the verbal groups have the distinctive verb morphology outlined in Chapter 3; and some of the pronominal nominal groups have distinctive realisations depending on their relationship to the verbal group (*I* vs *them* above). In many traditions of linguistic analysis, sequence and morphological distinctions of this kind are the main focus of inquiry. And the clauses in our vlog might be analysed as either intransitive or transitive, simply depending on whether there is a nominal group following the verbal group (with different morphology when it precedes than when it follows if the nominal group in question was a pronoun). Whorf (1945) described analysis of this kind as based on phenotypes – i.e. based on categories marked by sequence or distinctive word morphology in the examples to hand.

Whorf's own position was that a deeper analysis than one based simply on phenotypes was required if linguists were to come to grips with the grammar of a language, and SFL follows strongly in this tradition. This means bringing cryptotypes into the picture, by which Whorf meant categories that become apparent only when a syntagm is considered in terms of its distinctive oppositions to related syntagms. Let's look at several examples of reasoning of this kind.

## 5.2 English TRANSITIVITY Resources

In her parking lot exemplum, the vlogger tells how she got up, put her phone down and drove away when harassed by the guy waiting for her parking space. She then twice comments *I should not have done that.*

Like I **immediately** got up, put my phone down. I immediately drove away but- I wasn't even thinking. I **shouldn't have done** that. I **should not have done** that.

Her castigations involve the general English verb *do*, which can be used in place of action Processes like *get*, *put* and *drive*. Note that she could not have used this verb to refer to her feelings about being harassed in this way; *I cannot do that* cannot work as a less explicit version of *I cannot stand that* (i.e. *do* cannot substitute for the feeling verb *stand*).[2]

I **cannot stand** that.
*I **cannot do** that.

So while there is nothing overtly present in the syntagm distinguishing *I cannot film that* from *I cannot stand that* as far as phenotypes are concerned (i.e. sequence and morphology), the two clauses are clearly different once the possibility of substitution by a general verb is brought into the picture (these general verbs are often referred to as 'pro-verbs'). Let's push this further, taking into account the consciousness of one of the key Participants in action and feeling clauses. As far as an action like filming is concerned, the Participant undertaking the filming can be either human or a machine (i.e. the vlogger or a camera).

I filmed it ...
**A camera** set up in National Park of Abruzzo, Lazio and Molise, Italy, filmed a tree for 365 days.

And as a general rule we can say that both conscious and non-conscious Participants undertake Processes in action clauses – *the dermatologist* vs *it* (referring to the steroid injected into the bumps) below.

And so **the dermatologist** took like this needle and under each like bump and injected this like steroid and **it** all bubbled up.

But a Participant sensing feelings has to be conscious (and so can be referred to anaphorically with personal pronouns like *I*, *we*, *you*, *she* and *he*).

I hate it. I hate it. I hate the- the colour of it ...
I cannot stand that

*A camera hates it.
*A camera cannot stand that.

---

[2] Compare clauses where *stand* used as an action verb and can be substituted by *do*: *You can stand on one leg for hours but I can't **do** that for long.*

If, on the other hand, we consider phenomena affected by the Process, we see that action clauses are more restricted than sensing ones. In action clauses the affected Participant is typically realised by a nominal group construing an entity of some kind (a 'micro-phenomenon').

I filmed **it** ...
if they follow **me** ...

This is also possible in sensing clauses.

I hate **the- the colour of it** ...

But in sensing clauses the Participant perceived may be more than an entity; it may be an entity involved with an occurrence – a discourse semantic figure in fact. English uses a non-finite embedded clause to construe phenomena of this kind (as a macro-phenomenon).[3]

I hear [[**children coming**]].

And a sensing Process may in fact be used to position a figure – not as something going-on which is being processed but rather as something brought into existence by being felt or thought (as a meta-phenomenon).[4]

I don't care **if they follow me around the whole parking lot to get to my car**.

Thinking clauses are used several times in our vlog to position figures realised by finite clauses.

so I thought ⇒ **it would be kind of fun.**
so I don't know ⇒ **if people like hated it** ...
I feel ⇒ **like so many of you would miss out.**

One further step we can take as far as Participants configured with the Process is concerned is to note that action clauses in English may involve up to three Participants, as bold underlined below (all realised by nominal groups[5]).

**I** am not moving.
and **I** was going to edit **it**.
**I** just gave **them Chex Mix and applesauce squeezes**.

---

[3] Macro-phenomena are also found in English action clauses, e.g. [[*losing that match*]] *stopped their winning streak at nine games.*
[4] For an in-depth exploration of English grammatical resources distinguishing macro-phenomena ('acts') and meta-phenomena (embedded 'facts' and projected 'ideas/locutions'), see Halliday and Matthiessen (2014, pp. 503ff.).
[5] And with the potential to be made Subject of the clause (see Chapter 4).

English sensing clauses on the other hand never have more than two Participants.

**I** hate **it**. **I** hate **it**. **I** hate **the- the colour of it** ...
**I** cannot stand **that**.

Another difference between action and sensing clauses has to do with the way Participants are related to one another. In action clauses the Participant undertaking a going-on impacts on the Participant undertaken. The vlogger recounts preparing for the neighbourhood gathering in these terms.

and **I** just put **some makeup** on ...
and **I** put **a fancy shirt** on.
**I** like never wear **this** ...
**I** have worn **this** one time ...
since **I** got **it**.

Sensing clauses, however, can construe the relationship between the sensing Participant and the Participant encoding what is sensed in two directions. In her vlog, the vlogger consistently construes the sensing Participant as processing a phenomenon.

**I** hear [[**children coming**]].
... if **you** can see **that**.
**I** cannot stand **that**.
so I don't know ⇒ if **people** like hated **it** or I was really annoying.

In the last of these, she also construes feeling as a relationship (*I was really annoying*) – between herself and the feeling involved (the grading shows that *really annoying* is a nominal group here, not a verbal group, and so is comparable to groups like *quite angry, rather unpleasant*, etc.). But she might have used an additional sensing clause for this feeling too: *I was really annoying people.* In this case she herself would have been the phenomenon impacting on a sensing Participant.

The ability to construe what is going on as either emanating from the sensing Participant (the first example) or impinging on this participant role (the second example) is a feature of sensing clauses, not action ones.[6]

−emanating type

| sensing Participant | Process | Participant reacted to |
|---|---|---|
| *people* | *hated* | *it* |

[6] Note that the verbal groups in both *people **hated** it* and *I **was annoying** people* are active not passive (cf. the passive verbal groups in *it **was hated** by people* and *people **were annoyed** by her*).

–impinging type

| Participant reacted to | Process | sensing Participant |
|---|---|---|
| I | was annoying | people |

Possibly influenced by his training in chemical engineering, Whorf (1945) referred to distinguishing features of this kind we are reviewing here as reactances – i.e. differences that appear only when a syntagm's distinctive oppositions are brought into the picture. To this point we have reviewed a number of reactances reflecting the difference between action and sensing clauses. The reactances show that what looks like the same syntagm may turn out to behave rather differently when adjusted in particular ways. Let's consider now a further reactance emerging when we adjust the tense of action and sensing clauses. As far as past and future tense are concerned, nothing distinctive emerges.

The clock **donged**.
The clock **will ding**.

I **hated** it.
I **will hate** it.

But when we bring present time into the picture, we see that the unmarked tense for action concurrent with the moment of speaking is 'present in present', while that for sensing clauses is 'present'.

The clock **is dinging**,
I **hate** it. I **hate** it. I **hate** the- the colour of it ...

In action clauses simple present tense is typically not used for things going on 'right now' but rather for habitual activities; the vlogger uses present tense in this way to describe what happens at the annual neighbourhood national day gathering.

But it is national night out like I said and our neighbourhood **gathers** together and we **have** like a pot luck and the police **come** and the fire truck **come** ...

The reactances distinguishing action from sensing clauses are summarised in Table 5.4 below. The terms micro-phenomenon (bold), macro-phenomenon (enclosed in square brackets) and meta-phenomenon (italics) are illustrated below.

**Messi** ruined **their season**
[[Losing **that match**]] ruined **their season**

I saw **Messi**.
I saw [[**Messi** ruin **their season**]].
I think ⇒ **Messi** *ruined their season*.

## 5.2 English TRANSITIVITY Resources

Table 5.4 *Reactances distinguishing action from sensing clauses*

|  | action clauses | sensing clauses |
|---|---|---|
| **general verbs** | do, happen | none |
| **consciousness** | unrestricted | sensing Participant |
| **phenomena** | micro-/macro-phenomena | micro-/macro-/meta-phenomena |
| **Participant/s**[a] | 1, 2 or 3 | 1[b] or 2 |
| **directionality** | one-way | two-way |
| **present time** | 'present in present' tense | 'present' tense |

[a] We are not considering 'extra Agents' (i.e. Initiator, Inducer, Attributor, Assigner) at this point in the discussion, nor the possibility of a resultative or depictive Attribute (e.g. *He arrived **happy**, he painted the fence **green***).

[b] Here we are following Halliday and Matthiessen (2014) who treat the projection in examples such as *I thought* ⇒ ***that would be really good for the kids*** as a separate ranking dependent clause, not a clause embedded as Phenomenon; for them the projecting clause, *I thought*, has a single Participant (i.e. Senser).

For Whorf (1945), adjusting syntagms and exploring reactances along these lines is a strategy for uncovering what he called cryptotypes. The action and sensing clause classes we are motivating here are canonical cryptotypes – 'hidden' in the nominal group, verbal group, nominal group syntagm we began with, but emerging as we ask questions about the range of oppositions this syntagm can enter into. So when we say that in English there is a class of material clauses and a class of mental ones, we are setting up categories based on the distinctive patterns of reactances reviewed above. We are not simply setting up notional categories based on an interpretation of the meaning of a verb.[7]

For purposes of text analysis, and to clearly encode the distinction between material and mental clauses in structure, different functions can be proposed for the two clause types. Since the structures we are dealing with here involve a finite number of elements, each playing a distinctive role, multivariate structures such as those we developed in our nominal group analyses in Chapter 2 are appropriate (we are not dealing with the recursive systems realised by univariate structures outlined in Chapter 3 as far as basic transitivity systems and structures are concerned). For two Participant material clauses mainstream SFL uses the terms Actor, Process and Goal (Table 5.5).

For mental clauses, the terms Senser, Process and Phenomenon are deployed. Tables showing the structure for the two types of sensing clause discussed above are presented below. In the first example the occurrence emanates from a Senser processing a Phenomenon (Table 5.6); in the second the Phenomenon impinges on the Senser (Table 5.7).

---

[7] See Davidse (1998) for an in-depth exploration of Whorf's and Halliday's contribution to the account of grammatical meaning, particularly in relation to the analysis of the verb classes.

Table 5.5 *Structure and syntagm analysis of English material clauses*

| structure | Actor | Process | Goal |
|---|---|---|---|
| syntagm | nominal group | verbal group | nominal group |
| examples | I | was showing | all the diabetes supplies |
| | the vlogger | showed | them |
| | Andy | will show | the film |

Table 5.6 *Structure and syntagm analysis of English 'emanating' mental clauses*

| structure | Senser | Process | Phenomenon |
|---|---|---|---|
| syntagm | nominal group | verbal group | nominal group |
| examples | I | hate | it |
| | the vlogger | was going to hate | her hair colour |
| | Andy | had hated | Target |

Table 5.7 *Structure and syntagm analysis of English 'impinging' mental clauses*

| structure | Phenomenon | Process | Senser |
|---|---|---|---|
| syntagm | nominal group | verbal group | nominal group |
| examples | I | was annoying | people |
| | that | reminds | me |
| | the solution | struck | him |

The structural analysis now encodes what our exploration of patterns of reactances revealed. We have one syntagm (i.e. the same nominal group followed by verbal group followed by nominal group sequence), but two different structures.

What about the third major set of clauses in the vlog, which deals with relationships among entities and qualities and their location in space and time? This relational clause set shares certain features with material clauses, certain features with mental clauses and has some distinctive features of its own. Compared with material and mental clauses relatively few verbs are deployed in the Process in clauses of this kind, and of these, *be* and *have* are much more common than the others. Our vlogger uses mainly *be*, along with few instances of *have* (and one each of *look, stay, drive* and *call*). She in fact uses three times as many different verbs in mental clauses:

see, hear; think, know, realise, feel, forget, remember; like, love, want, hate, attract, stand, care, like, need

And there are several times as many verbs again used in material clauses (examples from its opening phases below):

do, film, edit, show, bring, bent, catch, sit, post, get, put, wear, gather, come, walk, bring, go ...

In terms of prosodic phonology one very common feature of this third clause class is the weak accentuation of the verbs realising the Process. They are typically non-salient, like *are* in the tone group below.[8]

// kids.are /**hung**.ry //

And they are regularly contracted with a preceding Subject pronoun, thereby losing phonological status as a separate syllable (e.g. *'s* below).

// ^ so /that'<u>s</u> /kind.of.ex /**cit**.ing //

And in some English clauses there is no Process at all (compare the clause *her kids were in another room* with its non-finite alternative below).

She was vlogging, **with her kids ∅ in another room**.[9]

As far as the kind of Participants involved is concerned, relational clauses are fairly open. Like material clauses, both conscious and non-conscious entities are construed.

... since **I**'m a picky eater.
... and **it**'s a busy place.

And like mental clauses, entities (micro-phenomena), entities configured with occurrences (macro-phenomena) and figures positioned as thoughts and feelings (meta-phenomena) may be involved.

| | |
|---|---|
| **Twenty-thousand subscribers** is her goal. | micro-phenomenon |
| **[[Getting twenty-thousand subscribers]]** is her goal. | macro-phenomenon |
| It disturbed her **[[that she lost thirty-eight subscribers]]**. | meta-phenomenon |

Relational clauses are also similar to mental clauses in having two Participants.[10]

... since **I**'m **a picky eater.**
**Twenty-thousand subscribers** is **her goal.**

---

[8] For the English rhythm and intonation analysis used here, see Halliday and Greaves 2008; '//' represents a tone group boundary, '/' a foot boundary, '^' a silent beat, '.' a syllable boundary within a foot, and bold the tonic syllable.

[9] Compare the non-finite relational clause here with material or mental alternatives, which do have an explicit Process: *with her kids playing in another room, with her kids annoying one another in another room*. The prepositional phrase *in another room* in *with her kids in another room* is not a Qualifier of *her kids* (note we cannot say \**it was with her kids in another room she was vlogging*, treating *her kids in another room* as a nominal group in a prepositional phrase).

[10] We are not dealing with existential clauses at this point in the discussion, nor with clauses including the 'agentive' functions Attributor and Assigner.

And they are similar to mental clauses in taking 'present' tense to refer to relationships obtaining at the moment of speaking.

… since I**'m** a picky eater.
Twenty-thousand subscribers **is** her goal.

The reactances discussed to this point are summarised in Table 5.8. Our account is by no means complete (for further details see Davidse, 1991/1999; Halliday and Matthiessen, 2014; Matthiessen, 1995). We have simply pushed it as far as we needed to illustrate SFL's articulation of Whorf's perspective on grammatical reasoning, drawing on a range of phenotypic and cryptotypic evidence.[11]

As we can see, there is no single reactance distinguishing one type of clause from another; less still is there any special sequencing of groups and phrases or word morphology differentiating clauses into just these three types and not others. What we encounter instead is an array of contributing factors, and classification ultimately depends on the weight given to one reactance or set of reactances or another, and to further evidence from above, around and below. We'll propose material, mental and relational clause classes as the best fit classification at this stage, as formalised in the system network in Figure 5.2. We return to this issue after some further discussion of relational clauses and the structures we will propose for them.

Table 5.8 *Reactances for English material, mental and relational clauses*

|  | material clauses | mental clauses | relational clauses |
|---|---|---|---|
| **general verbs** | *do, happen* | none | none |
| **verb classes** | open | relatively open | relatively closed |
| **consciousness** | unrestricted | sensing Participant | unrestricted |
| **phenomena** | micro-/macro- | micro-/macro-/meta- | micro-/macro-/meta-* |
| **Participant/s** | 1, 2 or 3 | 1 or 2 | 2 |
| **directionality** | one-way | two-way ('emanating' & 'impinging') | one-way |
| **present time** | 'present in present' | 'present' | 'present' |
| **accentuation** | salient | salient | non-salient *be, have* |
| **syllabification** | necessary | necessary | contractable *be, have* |
| **explicit Process** | required | required | non-finite elision of *be* |

* It is sometimes argued that relational clauses involve facts (i.e. pre-projected meta-phenomena) but cannot project; counterexamples would include clause complexes like the following in which the projections are arguably not facts: *I was hopeful they'd leave*, *I had an idea they'd come*.

[11] For a fuller exploration of the contribution of Whorf's ideas to grammatical description in SFL, see Quiroz (2020).

## 5.2 English TRANSITIVITY Resources

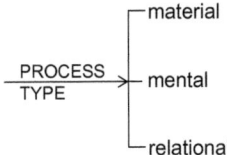

Figure 5.2 Basic English PROCESS TYPE system (types of clause)

### 5.2.3 Further Delicacy

Earlier on we suggested general structures for roles in material (Actor and Goal) and mental (Senser and Phenomenon) clauses in English. For relational clauses, however, we are going to push our classification one further step in delicacy before setting up Participant structures. From a discourse semantic perspective, this relates to the difference between figures involving generalisation and those involving abstraction. With generalisation an entity is related to a quality or class membership (e.g. *I'm picky*, *I'm a picky eater*); with abstraction, a relatively concrete entity is related to something less concrete (e.g. *Andy is the vlogger's husband*).

This distinction between generalisation and abstraction underlies the different voice potential of what we'll call attributive and identifying clauses. Attributive clauses, which ascribe qualities and class membership to entities are always active.

That was kind of exciting./That looked kind of exciting.
I am a picky eater./I became a picky eater.

We cannot turn these clauses around; they have no passive.

*Kind of exciting was that./Kind of exciting was looked by that.
*A picky eater was me./A picky eater was become by me.

Identifying clauses, on the other hand, can be turned around; they have 'active' and 'passive' alternatives.[12]

So this is what you get today : so what you get today is this ::
20,000 subscribers is my goal : my goal is 20 thousand subscribers

Somewhat unhelpfully (given the frequency of its usage in this clause type), verbal groups with the verb *be* as their Event are always active (we do not say \**what you get today **is beed** by this*). One pertinent reactance involves

---

[12] Halliday (1969/1976, pp. 161ff.) in fact reserves the terms 'active' and 'passive' for verbal group 'voice' options in English (which are not available for the verb *be*) and uses the terms 'operative' and 'receptive' at clause rank.

substituting another verb to help make the voice distinction clear (e.g. active *encapsulates* vs passive *is encapsulated* below).

20,000 subscribers **encapsulates** my goal : my goal **is encapsulated** by 20 thousand subscribers

In order to encode this subclassification of relational processes in structure, we will follow Halliday and Matthiessen (2014), using the labels Carrier and Attribute for attributive clauses and Token and Value for identifying ones (Table 5.9 and 5.10 respectively).

The Carrier is always the Subject function in English (see Chapter 4) and is realised by a nominal group headed by a Thing; the Attribute is realised by a nominal group[13] headed by either a Thing or an Epithet, and typically with non-specific deixis.[14]

Turning to identifying clauses, the Token is the Subject in the active voice (and so the Value is Subject in the passive). Both functions are realised by nominal groups headed by a Thing, and both functions typically involve presuming reference.[15]

Table 5.9 *Structure and syntagm analysis for English attributive relational clauses*

| structure | Carrier | Process | Attribute |
|---|---|---|---|
| syntagm | nominal group | verbal group | nominal group |
| examples | that | looks | kind of exciting |
| | I | became | a picky eater |
| | it | 's | a busy place |

Table 5.10 *Structure and syntagm analysis for English identifying relational clauses*

| structure | Token | Process | Value |
|---|---|---|---|
| syntagm | nominal group | verbal group | nominal group |
| examples | this | is | [[what you get today]] |
| | 20,000 subscribers | encapsulates | my goal |
| | it | is | national night out |

[13] We do not deal with possessive or circumstantial relational clauses in this chapter.
[14] Nominal groups headed by Epithets are sometimes referred to as adjectival groups (which we treat as a subtype of nominal group here, with Epithet rather than Thing as head).
[15] We can make the presuming reference more transparent by adjusting the Values to make room for a specific determiner: *the vlog you get today, the goal I've set for myself, the Fourth of July*.

Our subclassification of relational clauses as attributive or identifying raises the issue of why stop at this point in delicacy when assigning Participant functions. The Attributes in attributive clauses are of two distinct types, reflecting the fact that Epithet-headed Attributes describe the Carrier (configuring an entity with a quality) while Thing-headed ones classify it (configuring two entities in terms of hyponymy). This distinction could be added to our classification of types of clause by subclassifying attributive clauses as [describing] or [classifying] (as in Figure 5.3 below); this subclassification could then be encoded in structure by terming the function of the Epithet-headed nominal groups Description and the Thing-headed nominal groups Classification.

| Carrier | Process | Description |
|---|---|---|
| nominal group | verbal group | nominal group (Epithet headed) |
| that | looks | kind of exciting |

| Carrier | Process | Classification |
|---|---|---|
| nominal group | verbal group | nominal group (Thing headed) |
| I | became | a picky eater |

This raises a further issue of why stop here. Some Epithet-headed nominal groups in this clause type describe Carriers in terms of ideational properties (*wet, dark, light*, etc.) and others involve evaluation (*gross, upset, weird*, etc.).

… well, one it's wet,
… and it's so dark …
It's lighter than it was a few days ago …

It was really gross …
And I was so upset.
… it's kind of weird,

Should we therefore push our subclassification further and replace the Description function proposed above with an ideational function such as Depiction; and should we label those with an attitudinal function as Evaluation? Were we to do so, what grammatical criteria could we find to support this distinction? And if we can't find any grammatical reactances, could we justify further subclassification simply on the basis of a difference in meaning, drawing, for example, on the discourse semantic system of APPRAISAL (Martin and White, 2005)? Should participant role structure reflect all of the classes we have noted to this point in the chapter, as formalised as a system network below?

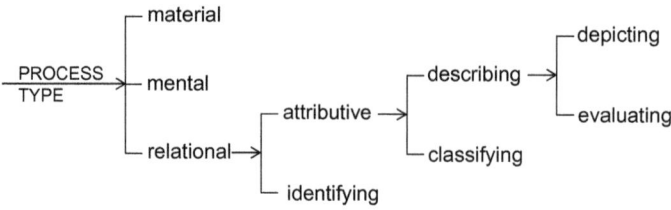

Figure 5.3 English relational clause systems

Earlier we proposed function structures for material and mental clauses at the first stage of delicacy in this network (Tables 5.5 to 5.7). For relational clauses we have just explored the possibility of setting up function structures for secondary (Carrier, Attribute), tertiary (Description, Classification) and quaternary (Depiction, Evaluation) delicacy. As we can see, the specificity of our structure labels is tied absolutely to the delicacy of our systems (in SFL you can't have a structural distinction that does not reflect a systemic one). But we can choose, if we wish, to make our structural functions more general than our systemic account. In Halliday and Matthiessen's (2014) account of English TRANSITIVITY, function structures are proposed for their more general systems.

Ultimately the answer to the question of how far we push delicacy, with respect to both system and structure, has to be a pragmatic one. In a project focusing on scientific discourse, for example, where classifying and describing entities, where depicting entities and evaluating research, and where giving examples and defining terms was fundamental to an understanding of the discourse, then further delicacy would be warranted – and pushed up to the point where criteria for reliably recognising categories cannot be established. For other projects, either more or less delicacy might be required. In order to function effectively as appliable linguistics, this kind of flexibility in our descriptions is a critical resource.

As a final illustration of this interplay between system delicacy and function structure specificity, let's return to the description of material clauses proposed above. Adjusting that account, we need to distinguish intransitive clauses (with Actor and Process structure), from transitive ones (with Actor, Process and Goal functions). A set of intransitive and then transitive clauses is presented below, with Participant/s highlighted in bold and the Process underlined.

… like before **I** started filming …
… and **the police** come …
**Clock** is dinging,

## 5.2 English TRANSITIVITY Resources

... if **they** <u>follow</u> **me** around the whole parking lot ...
... **I'**<u>d posted</u> like **four little clips of videos** ...
**I** for some reason <u>deleted</u> **them all**.

In traditional and school grammars, which tend to be built up around phenotypical patterns, the following clauses would also be treated as transitive (because a nominal group follows the Process).

... and **I** <u>am going to do</u> just **a random chatty vlog** for you guys.
... **they** <u>had</u> **a big lunch**.
And as **I** <u>was doing</u> **that** ...

This would imply treating *a random chatty vlog, a big lunch* and *that* in the examples just above as Goals. But nominal groups like these are neither created by nor affected by the Process. We would not ask what the vlogger was going to do to or do with *a random chatty vlog* or *a big lunch* (in other words, a reactance involving a query with a general verb doesn't work for this syntagm). From a discourse semantics perspective, *doing a vlog* and *having lunch* realise occurrences; and *a vlog* and *lunch* are not entities impacted on by the occurrence. The Process in fact gives us very little information about what is going on (it is realised by what is sometimes referred to as a 'light verb'); specification is rather redistributed to the following nominal group (cf. *do some work, have a bath, make a mistake, take a look, give a damn,* etc.). Taking this and other reactances into account, Halliday and Matthiessen (2014) in fact treat this third set of material clauses as intransitive and set up a more delicate system allowing intransitive clauses to be structured with a relatively non-specific Process, along with a relatively specific nominal group – which they refer to as Scope.[16] The relevant system network is elaborated Figure 5.4.

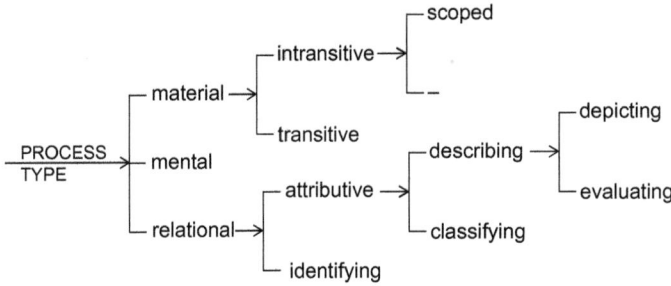

Figure 5.4 Extended English PROCESS TYPE systems

---

[16] The first and second editions of Halliday's *An Introduction to Functional Grammar* (1985, 1994) refer to this function as Range, a label restricted in later editions to an ergative interpretation of English (alongside Agent, Medium and Beneficiary).

254   Transitivity

Table 5.11 *Structure and syntagm analysis for English scoped intransitive material clauses*

| structure | Actor | Process | Scope |
|---|---|---|---|
| syntagm | nominal group | verbal group | nominal group |
| enate clauses | I | am going to do | a random chatty vlog |
| | they | had | a big lunch |
| | I | was doing | that |

And these structures would be analysed as in Table 5.11 (not as Actor Process Goal).

Our general point here then is that function structures can be specified at different degrees of delicacy in system networks, and that reasoning based on cryptotypes, alongside phenotypes, allows for a much finer-grained analysis than is possible in phenotype-based descriptions alone.

All of this, of course, takes us back to the question of classifying clause types raised above. Why material, mental and relational and not classification of other kinds? The answer is still 'It depends'. In terms of reactances, as with any classification process, we are looking to maximise differences between and minimise differences within categories. For English, categorisation into material, mental and relational clause types gives us the best differentiation of this kind. We also have to take into account the degree of responsibility taken by a grammar with respect to higher strata: is our TRANSITIVITY analysis revealing as far as ideational discourse semantics and ultimately field are concerned? In addition, with regard to considerations of structure, there is the question of appliability in relation to register specificity. Across registers, material, mental and relational clauses may, of course, have more and less work to do. But in general terms, the trilogy gives us a productive grip on data as we move from one register to another[17] – in the sense that most of the data can be grouped into one or another of these three categories and the reactances surveyed above can be used as criteria to ensure replicability from one SFL-trained analyst to another.

### 5.2.4   Other Types of Clause

"Most of the data" we just claimed. What else might we find? Space is limited here so we will simply mention in passing three additional types of clause that may or may not require attention as we describe the TRANSITIVITY system of different languages. These are generally considered to be less central

---

[17] As we will see below, this is also true as we move from one language to another.

## 5.2 English TRANSITIVITY Resources

categories because they share reactances with material, mental and relational processes, because they are realised relatively infrequently across registers (as they are in our vlog) and because they are not clearly distinguishable subtypes that have to be recognised across all languages. A useful guide to clause type frequencies for TRANSITIVITY choices in English is provided by Matthiessen (1999, 2006).

First existential clauses; a set of examples of this clause type is presented below. As for the relational clauses introduced above, the Event in the verbal group realising the Process is also overwhelmingly the verb *be* (similarly non-salient and contractible); and these clauses are positioned as concurrent with the moment of speaking through present tense. For these reasons existential clauses are sometimes treated as a type of relational clause.

... and there are **neighbours that I see like once a year** ...
... and there was **a whole stack of them** ...
... because there's **like feet people** ≪out there≫ **that like are obsessed with feet** ...

In English, however, they have distinctive properties: (i) there is only one Participant (in bold above), termed Existent; (ii) their Subject is non-salient[18] *there*; and (iii) when a clause-initial Circumstance of location is present, the Subject may be elided (e.g. *Behind him ∅ were cars, weren't there?*). Our vlogger uses several structures of this kind, which from a discourse semantic perspective introduce entities in her stories. As displayed in Table 5.12, the *there* Subject is not assigned a transitivity function, since it is not a Process, Participant or Circumstance in this clause structure.

Next verbal clauses, which encode figures of communication. These resemble material processes in terms of the possibility of a general verb (*What did they do? – Asked for food.*) and tense selection (*They're asking for more food.*). And they allow for a third Participant (added in parentheses to the examples below), although in this clause type it receives (or is positioned to give) information rather than goods or services. On the other hand, unlike material

Table 5.12 *Structure and syntagm analysis for English existential clauses*

| structure | | Process | Existent |
|---|---|---|---|
| **syntagm** | *there* | verbal group | nominal group |
| examples | *there* | *are* | *neighbours that I see like once a year* |
| | *there* | *was* | *a whole stack of them* |
| | *there* | *'s* | *feet people ... that are obsessed with feet* |

[18] The rhythm of the third example is thus //^ be/cause there's like /feet /people out /there that like /^ are ob/sessed with /feet //, with first 'existential' *there* non-salient and the second 'locative' *there* salient.

processes and like mental ones, they can project meta-phenomena (e.g. *not to film it* below).[19]

They're going to ask (me) for more food.
... if I can show you (the marks) from here.
... so Andy said (to me) ⇒ not to film it ...
... what I was just saying (to you).

Finally behavioural clauses. This clause type construes a physiological interpretation of figures realised by mental or verbal clauses, as exemplified below.

... all people would be looking at.
Thank you for watching guys.

What else can we talk about?
... to like ramble on.

These clauses share some reactances with material processes (e.g. substitution with a general verb and 'present in present' tense usage) and others with mental or verbal clauses (e.g. restrictions on the entity involved as the behaving participant, as conscious or a source of information). Their ability to project is limited, with examples mainly found in story genres; they quote (paratactically, as 'direct speech') rather than report (hypotactically, as 'indirect speech') meta-phenomena. When paratactic projection is involved, the behavioural clause follows the quote and is typically deployed to characterise the manner in which something was said or thought (e.g. *"I might lose more followers"*, ⇐ ***she frowned***).

The presence of intermediate categories of this kind has prompted some grammarians to pursue topological alongside typological analysis of TRANSITIVITY systems. This has typically involved designing diagrams configuring material, behavioural, verbal, mental, relational and existential processes as more or less like one another – along one or another cline. Well-known examples include Figure 17 in Martin and Matthiessen (1991), the front cover of Halliday (1994), Figure 4.12 in Matthiessen (1995), Figure 5.3 in Halliday and Matthiessen (2014) and Figure 4.4 in Martin, Matthiessen and Painter (2010). Unfortunately these diagrams are inexplicit about the precise phenotypic and cryptotypic features making clause classes more or less alike. In this respect a tabular representation such as that in Table 5.13 is more informative and can be usefully compared with the corresponding table for material, mental and relational processes above (Table 5.8).

---

[19] The source of this information is typically a conscious Participant, a similarity with mental clauses; but it can also be a non-conscious Participant such as books, radios and text messages (e.g. *the message told me I was late*), a difference from mental clauses.

5.3 Spanish TRANSITIVITY Resources                                                257

Table 5.13 *Reactances for English behavioural, verbal and existential clauses*

|  | behavioural clauses | verbal clauses | existential clauses |
|---|---|---|---|
| **general verbs** | *do, happen* | *do, happen* | none |
| **consciousness** | restricted | relatively restricted | unrestricted |
| **phenomena** | micro-/macro-/meta- | micro-/meta- | micro-/macro- |
| **Participant/s** | 1 or 2 | 1, 2 or 3 | 1 |
| **directionality** | one-way | one-way | – |
| **present time** | 'present in present' | 'present in present' | 'present' |
| **accentuation** | salient | salient | non-salient *be* |
| **syllabification** | necessary | necessary | contractable *be* |
| **explicit Process** | required | required | required[a] |

[a] As noted above, under certain conditions the *there* Subject in existential clauses is elided.

At this point we move on from our glimpse of English clause types to Spanish. Once again we will concentrate on reactances in relation to classification; but for Spanish we will focus on additional delicacy for mental clauses, complementing our more detailed pursuit of English relational clauses above.

## 5.3 Spanish TRANSITIVITY Resources

### 5.3.1 Three Kinds of Clause

One of the major challenges in language description, and certainly the most dangerous one, lies in striking a balance between pretending that one has no expectations about the phenomena one is investigating and making use of the expectations one in fact has in mind. We'll accordingly begin cautiously here, by looking to see if the material, mental and relational classification of clause types in English explored above helps us work our way into Spanish TRANSITIVITY resources. If we pick up the story of the Pinita 10 minutes after the earthquake has woken the crew up, we can certainly find candidates for each clause type.

Los tripulantes del Pinita se quedaron especulando sobre cómo estaría su ciudad. Pero entonces, a 10 minutos del terremoto, ocurrió algo que nunca habían visto. El mar empezó a succionarlos, a llevarlos aguas adentro con tal fuerza que cortó de un tirón la soga de 10 centímetros de diámetro que los ataba al ancla.
   Lo que los absorbía era una ola de 15 metros de alto que cerraba el horizonte. Estaba a 200 metros y se acercaba a toda velocidad por el costado de la nave.

'The crew of the Pinita were left speculating about how their city would be. But then, 10 minutes after the earthquake, something happened that they had never seen. The sea started to suck them, to take them into open waters with such force that it cut in a jerk the 10-centimeter-diameter rope that tied them to the anchor.
   What was absorbing them was a 15-meter-high wave that was blocking the horizon. It was 200 meters away and was approaching the side of the boat at full speed.'

258    Transitivity

There's a lot going on in this phase of discourse, and we can pick out a set of clauses dealing with what happened. The verbal group (or verbal group complex) realising the Process in each Spanish clause is in bold (as is its English translation).

Pero entonces, a 10 minutos del terremoto, **ocurrió** algo …
'But then, 10 minutes after the earthquake, something **happened** …'

El mar **empezó a succionarlos**,
'The sea **started to suck them**,'

… a **llevarlos** aguas adentro con tal fuerza …
'… to **take them** into open waters with such force …'

… que **cortó** de un tirón la soga de 10 centímetros de diámetro …
'… that it **cut** in a jerk the 10-centimeter-diameter rope …'

… que **los ataba** al ancla.
'… that **tied them** to the anchor.'

… lo que **los absorbía** …
'What **was absorbing them** …'

… que **cerraba** el horizonte.
'… that **was blocking** the horizon.'

… y **se acercaba** a toda velocidad por el costado de la nave.
'… and **was approaching** the side of the boat at full speed.'

There is just one clause touching on the fishermen's perceptions.

… que nunca **habían visto**.
'… that they **had** never **seen**.'

And there are three clauses that focus on relationships – description, classification and location in space respectively below.

… cómo **estaría** su ciudad.
'… how their city **would be**.'

Lo que los absorbía **era** una ola de 15 metros de alto …
'What was absorbing them **was** a 15-meter-high wave …'

**Estaba** a 200 metros …
'It **was** 200 meters away …'

For the likes of these, proceeding rather less cautiously than we did for English above, we might propose distinctive function structures at clause rank of the following kind.

## 5.3 Spanish TRANSITIVITY Resources

(1)
| una ola | cerraba | el horizonte |
|---|---|---|
| Actor | Process | Goal |
| | verbal group | |
| | Finite/Event | |
| a wave | close.IMPF.3SG | the horizon |
| 'a wave was blocking the horizon' | | |

(2)
| los tripulantes | vieron | la ola |
|---|---|---|
| Senser | Process | Phenomenon |
| | verbal group | |
| | Finite/Event | |
| the crew | see.PST.3PL | the wave |
| 'the crew saw the wave' | | |

(3)
| lo que vieron | era | una ola |
|---|---|---|
| Carrier | Process | Attribute |
| | verbal group | |
| | Finite/Event | |
| what they saw | be.IMPF.3SG | a wave |
| 'what they saw was a wave' | | |

Before considering the reactances supporting a classification and structural analysis of this kind, we need to remind ourselves that Spanish verbal groups include inflectional and pronominal clitic resources which help for sorting out participant roles. The verb realising the Event, in the verbal group realising the Process of the material clause analysed above, for example, is inflected as 3rd person singular, 'agreeing' with the Actor (verbal group inflection and agreeing Participant, where present, are in bold in examples from this point on). In Chapter 3 we suggested conflating a Finite function with the Event in the verbal group structure for clauses of this kind.

(1)
| **una ola** | **cerraba** | el horizonte |
|---|---|---|
| Actor | Process | Goal |
| | verbal group | |
| | Finite/Event | |
| a wave | close.PST.3SG | the horizon |
| 'a wave was blocking the horizon' | | |

Part of our motivation for doing this is that participant roles in Spanish may not be realised as distinct constituents realised as nominal groups. In our third relational clause example above, for example, there is no nominal group realising a Carrier in clause structure. The clause consists of a Process realised by a verbal group and an Attribute realised by a nominal group. But the verb realising the Event, in the verbal group realising the Process, is inflected as third person singular, thereby encoding the Carrier. Structures of this kind can be treated as involving a conflation of the Carrier with the Process at clause rank, as outlined below.[20]

(4)

| *estaba* | *a 200 metros* |
|---|---|
| Process/Carrier | Attribute |
| verbal group | |
| Finite/Event | |
| be.PST.3SG | at 200 metres |
| 'it was 200 metres away' | |

Pronominal clitics in the verbal group structure can also be used to encode a Participant that is not realised through a distinct constituent by a nominal group in clause structure. The Goal is realised in this way by a P2cl verbal group function in the analysis below (and so conflated with the Process).

(5)

| *la ola* | *los* | *absorbía* |
|---|---|---|
| Actor | Goal/Process | |
| | verbal group | |
| | P2cl | Finite/Event |
| the wave | ACC.3pl | absorb.IMPF.3SG |
| 'the wave was absorbing them' | | |

To simplify the presentation, we will adopt the convention (deployed above) of conflating a clause rank Participant function with the Process only when it is not realised by a separate constituent realised by a nominal group at clause rank. Thus, in those cases where a participant role is realised both by a separate nominal group clause constituent and by inflection or a pronominal clitic at group rank (the latter is traditionally referred to as 'clitic doubling' by Spanish grammarians[21]), then the participant role will not be conflated with the Process. Our convention is exemplified below.

(6)

| *al bote* | *la ola* | *lo* | *absorbía* |
|---|---|---|---|
| Goal | Actor | Process | |
| | | verbal group | |
| | | P2cl | Finite/Event |
| the boat | the wave | ACC.3SG.MASC | absorb.IMPF.3SG |
| 'the wave was absorbing the boat' | | | |

[20] Our English translations construe these conflated Participants as unconflated clause rank pronouns.
[21] See Vázquez and García (2012) for a discourse-oriented overview of 'clitic doubling' in Spanish (which the authors also consider as a kind of agreement relation), based on (synchronic and diachronic) corpora across varieties.

Clitic doubling may also involve a P3 participant role, as illustrated below for *le* and *a su madre*. (for more details on the structural realisation of experiential funciona in Spanish, see Quiroz 2023).

(7)

| **Jonathan** | le | ocultó | todo eso | a su madre |
|---|---|---|---|---|
| Actor | Process | | Goal | Beneficiary[22] |
| | verbal group | | | |
| | P3cl | Finite/Event | | |
| Jonathan | DAT.3SG | hide.PST.3SG | all that | his mother |
| 'Jonathan hid all that from his mother' | | | | |

### 5.3.2  Experiential Clause Typology

As far as reactances distinguishing one clause type from another are concerned, there are a number of relevant parameters to take into account; several are included in Table 5.14.

As Table 5.14 suggests, there is a large class of verbs realising material clauses, all of which can be substituted by the general verbs *pasar* 'happen' or *hacer* 'do' (e.g. *¿Que **hacían** las mujeres? – Vendían dulces.* 'What were the women doing? – Selling sweets.'). Both conscious and non-conscious Participants are involved (e.g. *el Pinita* 'the Pinita', *las mujeres* 'the women' respectively); Participants can be things or acts (i.e. micro- or macro-phenomena – *la ola* 'the wave', *aproar la nave* 'directing the ship's prow' respectively); there can be one, two or three Participants (1, 10, 12 respectively); both P2 and P3 can be cliticised (11 and 12 respectively); and the figures involved are uni-directional.

Table 5.14 *Reactances for Spanish material, mental and relational clauses*

| | material clauses | mental clauses | relational clauses |
|---|---|---|---|
| **general verbs** | *pasar* 'happen', *hacer* 'do' | *hacer* 'do' (restricted) | none |
| **verb classes** | open | relatively open | relatively closed |
| **consciousness** | unrestricted | sensing Participant | unrestricted |
| **Participant/s**[a] | 1, 2 or 3 | 1, 2 or 3 | 2 or 3 |
| **clitic potential** | P2, P3 | P2, P3 | P2 (neuter *lo*),[b] P3 |
| **directionality** | one-way | two-way (reaction) | one-way |

[a]  As for English, we are not considering additional 'agentive' Participants such as Initiator, Inducer, Attributor or Assigner.

[b]  The neuter clitic lo is used for Attribute and Value only in relational clauses with *ser/estar/parecer* 'copulas'; regular number and gender distinctions obtained elsewhere.

[22] The Spanish Beneficiary function involves both positively and adversely affected Participants ('Maleficiaries'); we follow Quiroz (2013) in our use of this term (which is not to be confused with Halliday and Matthiessen's (e.g. 2014) use of the term in their ergative analysis of English.

(8)

| *el Pinita* | *empezó* | | *a brincar* |
|---|---|---|---|
| Actor | Process | | |
| | verbal group complex | | |
| | α | | β |
| | verbal group | | |
| | Finite/Event | | |
| the Pinita | started.PST.3SG | | to jump.INF |
| 'the Pinita started to skip up and down' | | | |

(9)

| *las mujeres* | *vendían* | *dulces* |
|---|---|---|
| Actor | Process | Goal |
| | verbal group | |
| | Finite/Event | |
| the women | sell.IMPF.3PL | sweets |
| 'the women sold sweets' | | |

(10)

| [[*aproar la nave*]] | *salvará* | *la vida de los tripulantes* |
|---|---|---|
| Actor | Process | Goal |
| | verbal group | |
| | Finite/Event | |
| [[direct.prow.of the ship]] | save.FUT.3SG | the life of the crew |
| 'directing the ship's prow will save the lives of the crew' | | |

(11)

| *la ola* | *lo* | *llevó* | *a Gabriel* | *a la orilla* |
|---|---|---|---|---|
| Actor | Process | | Goal | Location |
| | verbal group | | | |
| | P2cl | Finite/Event | | |
| the wave | ACC.3SG | take.PST.3SG | to Gabriel | |
| 'the wave took Gabriel to the bank' | | | | |

(12)

| *Jonathan* | *le* | *ocultó* | *todo eso* | *a su madre* |
|---|---|---|---|---|
| | Actor | Process | Goal | Beneficiary |
| | | verbal group | | |
| | | P3cl | Finite/Event | |
| Jonathan | DAT.3SG | hide.PST.3SG | all that | to his mother |
| 'Jonathan hid all that from his mother' | | | | |

Turning to mental clauses, there is a relatively large class of verbs involved; the Process in two of the subtypes (i.e. perception and most reaction clauses) can be substituted with *hacer* 'do'. One of the Participants most closely

5.3 Spanish TRANSITIVITY Resources          263

associated with the Process must be conscious (the Senser below). In Spanish this conscious Participant is referred to through personal pronouns at clause rank (unlike non-conscious Participants, which tend to be referred to through demonstratives; see Chapter 2, Section 2.3.2); and the clause can also involve a thing (micro-phenomenon), a happening (macro-phenomenon) or an idea or fact (meta-phenomenon).[23] Micro-phenomena and macro-phenomena (both non-finite in (14) and finite in (15)) are illustrated below.

(13)

| *los tripulantes* | *vieron* | *la ola* |
|---|---|---|
| Senser | Process | Phenomenon |
|  | verbal group |  |
|  | Finite/Event |  |
| the.PL crew.PL | see.PST.3PL | the wave |
| 'the crew saw the wave' | | |

(14)

| *los tripulantes* | *vieron* | [[*la ola acercándose*]][24] |
|---|---|---|
| Senser | Process | Phenomenon |
|  | verbal group |  |
|  | Finite/Event |  |
| the.PL crew.PL | see.PST.3PL | the wave approaching |
| 'the crew saw the wave moving closer' | | |

(15)

| *los tripulantes* | *vieron* | [[*que la ola se acercara*]] |
|---|---|---|
| Senser | Process | Phenomenon[25] |
|  | verbal group |  |
|  | Finite/Event |  |
| the.PL crew.PL | see.PST.3PL | that the wave was approaching |
| 'the crew saw that the wave was moving closer' | | |

Mental clauses of the reaction subtype may construe emotional experiences 'bi-directionally' as well, that is, either as emanating from the Senser or as impinging thereupon. In example (16) below the Senser, Captain Ibarra, is negatively appraising the Phenomenon (the wave); in example (17), it's the other way around – the Phenomenon (the wave) is triggering the Senser's (Captain Ibarra's) emotions. The latter type, with Phenomenon impinging on Senser,

---

[23] Although their distribution is a critical factor in distinguishing subtypes of mental clause, we will not deal with ideas and facts in any detail in this chapter – in part because the relevant research has not been completed, and in part because we are not dealing with clause complexing in this book.
[24] We will problematise the inclusion of *la ola* in this embedded clause below.
[25] We are treating *que la ola se acercaba* 'that the wave was approaching' as an embedded, finite macro-phenomenal clause in this analysis; see Quiroz (2013) for discussion.

is in fact the favoured construal of reaction clauses in Spanish. Note in the examples that the agreeing Participant is *el capitán Ibarra* (singular) 'Captain Ibarra' in the first example, but *las olas* (plural) 'the waves' in the second; the verbal groups in both clauses are active voice, not passive.

(16)

| ***el capitán Ibarra*** | ***temió*** | *las olas* |
|---|---|---|
| Senser | Process | Phenomenon |
| | verbal group | |
| | Finite/Event | |
| the Captain Ibarra | fear.PST.3SG | the waves |
| 'Captain Ibarra feared the wave' | | |

(17)

| *al capitán Ibarra* | *le* | | ***asustaron*** | ***las olas*** |
|---|---|---|---|---|
| Senser | Process | | | Phenomenon |
| | verbal group | | | |
| | P3cl | Finite/Event | | |
| to Captain Ibarra | DAT.3SG | frighten.PST.3PL | | the waves |
| 'the wave frightened Captain Ibarra' | | | | |

Mental clauses also accommodate a full range of phenomena (micro-, macro- and meta-phenomena) that require future research, building on Quiroz (2013, 2020) and drawing on corpora of Spanish discourse.[26]

Relational clauses involve a small relatively closed set of verbs, most commonly *ser* 'be' and *estar* 'be', and also *tener* 'have' (*ser* is used in both attributive and identifying relational clauses, but *estar* and *parecer* only in attributive ones). They cannot be probed by the general verbs *pasar* 'happen' or *hacer* 'do'. Alongside micro-phenomena realised by nominal groups and macro-phenomena realised by embedded non-finite clauses, they allow for meta-phenomena, especially embedded facts – i.e. embedded clauses that can be prefaced by *el hecho (de) que* 'the fact that').

---

[26] When the Phenomenon impinges on the Senser it can also be realised by an embedded fact clause (an embedded meta-phenomenon), as exemplified below (these fact clauses have subjunctive verbal groups).

| *al capitán Ibarra* | *le* | *asustó* | [[*que las olas se acercaran*]] |
|---|---|---|---|
| Senser | Process | | Phenomenon |
| | verbal group | | |
| | P3cl | Finite/Event | |
| to Captain Ibarra | DAT.3SG | frighten.PST.3SG | the waves were approaching |
| 'it frightened Captain Ibarra that the waves were approaching' | | | |

5.3 Spanish TRANSITIVITY Resources

(18)

| esta ola | era | distinta |
|---|---|---|
| Carrier | Process | Attribute |
|  | verbal group |  |
|  | Finite/Event |  |
| this wave | be.IMPF.3SG | different |
| 'this wave was different' | | |

(19)

| Ricardo | es | radioaficionado local |
|---|---|---|
| Carrier | Process | Attribute |
|  | verbal group |  |
|  | Finite/Event |  |
| Ricardo | be.PRS.3SG | local ham.radio.operator |
| 'Ricardo is a local ham radio operator' | | | |

(20)

| no | es | difícil | [[imaginar la angustia de ese anciano]] |
|---|---|---|---|
| Process | | Attribute | Carrier |
| verbal group | | | |
| Neg | Finite/Event | | |
| not | be.PRS.3SG | difficult | [[imagine.INF the anguish of that old.man]] |
| 'it is not difficult [[to imagine the distress of that old man]]' | | | |

(21)

| lo cierto | es | el hecho [[de que sí los veían]] |
|---|---|---|
| Value | Process | Token |
|  | verbal group |  |
|  | Finite/Event |  |
| the certain.thing | be.PRS.3SG | the fact [[of that see.IMPF.3PL them indeed]] |
| 'what is certain is the fact that they indeed saw them' | | |

A distinctive feature of relational clauses (with *ser*, *estar* or *parecer*) is that their P2 (i.e. Attribute or Value) can only be realised inside verbal groups by the neuter clitic *lo* (and clitic doubling is not possible). Thus the wave (feminine gender) is tracked by the clitic *lo* (neuter), not *la* (feminine), in the K2f move below (cf. the Token in both K1 moves, *esa*, which is a feminine determiner).

(22)

| K1 | esa | fue | la peor ola [[que había visto]] |
|---|---|---|---|
|  | Token | Process | Value |
|  |  | verbal group |  |
|  |  | Finite/Event |  |
|  | 'that was the worst wave he had seen' | | |
| K2f | - lo fue | | |
|  | Value/Process/Token | | |
|  | verbal group | | |
|  | P2cl | Finite/Event | |
|  | 'that it was' | | |

Correspondingly, the only way to track a P2 at clause rank in this type of clause is through a neuter demonstrative. Thus, *la ola* 'the wave' (feminine gender) is tracked by the demonstrative *eso* (neuter), not *esa* (feminine), in the K2f move below (a fairly marked structure implying some kind of contrast between the wave in question and some other one).

(23)

| | K1 | *esa* | *fue* | | *la peor ola* [[*que había visto*]] |
|---|---|---|---|---|---|
| | | Token | Process | | Value |
| | | | verbal group | | |
| | | | Finite/Event | | |
| | | 'that was the worst wave he had seen' | | | |
| | K2f | *fue* | | | *eso* |
| | | Token/Process | | | Value |
| | | verbal group | | | |
| | | Finite/Event | | | |
| | | 'that it was (the worst)' | | | |

Accentuation is not a distinctive feature of relational clauses in Spanish. All of them involve one salient syllable. Spanish has often been positioned as a syllable-timed, not a stress-timed language (Abercrombie, 1967; Catford, 1977; Pike, 1945), which might be taken to explain why it does not foster fast speech processes that diminish accentuation. Pamies (1999), however, challenges the distinction on acoustic grounds. More recently Nespor, Shukla and Mehler (2011) suggest that it is more accurate to distinguish languages favouring syllable reduction (e.g. English) from those which don't (e.g. Spanish). This might also explain the lack of diminished accentuation for Processes in Spanish relational clauses.

As far as intermediate types of clause are concerned, the Ola Maldita text features a number of clauses which might be interpretable as existential and behavioural clauses, and a relatively large number of verbal ones. Existential clauses involve third person realisations of the verb *haber* 'have',[27] an Existent and optional circumstantiation. There is no agreeing Participant in the present tense example below (although in spoken mode, in other than present tense, speakers do tend to treat the Existent as an agreeing Participant).

(24)

| | *no **hay*** | | *lugar* | *aquí* |
|---|---|---|---|---|
| | Process | | Existent | Location |
| | verbal group | | | |
| | Neg | Finite/Event | | |
| | not | have.PRS.3SG | place | here |
| | 'there is no room here' | | | |

---

[27] In existential clauses, the distinctive verb form *hay* is used for third person singular, present tense (in place of *ha*). See Fernández-Soriano (1999b) and Melis and Flores (2007) for an account of other '(pseudo)impersonal verbs' that may be realising existential clauses in Spanish.

(25)

| había | un cuerpo | en el río |
|---|---|---|
| Process | Existent | Location |
| verbal group | | |
| Finite/Event | | |
| have.IMPF.3SG | a body | in the river |
| 'there was a body in the river' | | |

In Spanish, tense choice ('present' vs 'present in present') is not a relevant reactance distinguishing behavioural from mental or verbal clauses. The most effective test is projection: can the clause report another clause (involving indirect speech or thought)? As in English there are several pairs of verbs which construe comparable experiences but from either a behavioural or a mental/verbal perspective. These include pairs like the following:

**behavioural : mental ::**
*conocer* 'be familiar/acquainted with' : *saber* 'know' ::
*estudiar* 'study': *aprender* 'learn' ::
*hablar* 'speak' : *decir* 'say' ::
*interrogar* 'interrogate' : *preguntar* 'ask' ::
*rugir* 'bellow': *gritar* 'shout'

The following example opposes behavioural *conocer* ('be familiar/acquainted with') to mental *saber* ('know') along these lines (with *sabía* 'I knew' projecting *que era el capitán* 'that he was the captain').

sab**ía** ⇒ que **era** el capitán, porque conoc**í** a los tripulantes
'I knew ⇒ he was the captain because I was acquainted with the crew'

Our Ola Maldita text includes the contrast between verbal *gritar* 'shout' (projecting what the crew yelled below) and behavioural *rugir* 'bellow' (which cannot project hypotactically, and in fact personifies the wave – since behavioural processes involve a conscious P1).

– ¡Tsunami, tsunami! ¡Apróate!, ¡apróate! – ⇐ le grit**aron** los tripulantes al capitán.
'"Tsunami, tsunami! Turn into the wind! Turn into the wind!" ⇐ shouted the crew to the captain.'

esa pared oscura que rug**ía** como si estuviera a punto de desmoronarse sobre ellos
'that dark wall that bellowed as if it was on the point of collapsing on them'

Verbal processes typically play a key role in journalism, a field in which the sourcing of information is critical. They accordingly involve a Process, a Participant realising the source of information (usually conscious, but also including print and electronic media), the Participant realising the information itself and potentially a Participant realising the recipient of that information.

These possibilities are exemplified below, using the terms Sayer, Verbiage and Receiver, respectively, for the relevant participant roles.

(26)

| *Nora* | *rogaba* |
|---|---|
| Sayer | Process |
|  | verbal group |
|  | Finite/Event |
| Nora | plead.IMPF.3SG |
| 'Nora was pleading' | |

(27)

| *Tohá* | *repitió* | *ese anuncio* | *a todos* |
|---|---|---|---|
| Sayer | Process | Verbiage | Receiver |
|  | verbal group | | |
|  | Finite/Event | | |
| Tohá | repeat.PST.3SG | that announcement | to all |
| 'Tohá repeated that announcement to everyone' | | | |

(28)

| *Tohá* | *repitió* | [[*lo que había asegurado el contralmirante*]] |
|---|---|---|
| Sayer | Process | Verbiage |
|  | verbal group | |
|  | Finite/Event | |
| Tohá | repeat.PST.3SG | [[what have.IMPF.3SG assure.PTCP the rear admiral]] |
| 'Tohá repeated what the rear admiral had assured' | | |

Verbal clauses are also commonly used to project what was said, either directly (i.e. quoting) or indirectly (i.e. reporting). Examples of direct speech, involving exclamations, commands, a question and a statement are presented below:

– ¡Tsunami, tsunami! ¡Apróate!, ¡apróate! – ⇐ le **gritaron los tripulantes** al capitán.
'"Tsunami, tsunami! Turn into the wind! Turn into the wind!" ⇐ shouted the crew to the captain.'

–¿Ah, **era** tu mujer?– ⇐ le preguntó.
'Ah, was she your wife? – ⇐ he asked him.'

–**Ése fue** el momento más terrible– ⇐ sintetiza Jonathan.
'That was the most terrible moment– ⇐ sums up Jonathan.'

Indirect alternatives for commands, questions and statements are illustrated below.

**El joven de 18 años** le contestó a su madre ⇒ que no se preocupara
'The 18-year-old youth replied to his mother ⇒ that she was not to worry'

## 5.3 Spanish TRANSITIVITY Resources

se preguntó ⇒ si habría un bote con qué ir a buscar a la gente
'he asked himself ⇒ if there would be a boat with which to go to pick people up'

**sus amigos** no habían dicho a sus padres ⇒ que irían a la playa
'his friends had not told their parents ⇒ that they would go to the beach'

Neither the quoting and reporting clause type are treated as involving Verbiage (realised by an embedded clause). They are rather analysed as a complex of two clauses, as tabled below. Logical relations between clauses are beyond the scope of this book, so we will not pursue justification of this analysis here; for discussion see Halliday and Matthiessen (1999, 2014).

(29)

| **sus amigos** | no | habían dicho | | a sus padres | ⇒ que irían a la playa |
|---|---|---|---|---|---|
| Sayer | Process | | | Receiver | projected clause |
| | verbal group | | | | |
| | Neg | Finite | Event | | |
| his friends | not | have.IMPF.3PL | say.PRCTP | to their parents | that they.would.go to the beach |
| 'his friends had not told their parents ⇒ that they would go to the beach' ||||||

The key reactances touched on above for behavioural, verbal and existential clauses in Spanish are summarised in Table 5.15. As we have been highlighting throughout this chapter, the classification does not depend on any one pattern, but rather on configurations of patterns which taken together establish a clause class.

These clusters of reactances can be usefully compared at this point with the clusters coordinated as material, mental and relational clauses above (Table 5.14 is extended as Table 5.16 below for convenience of comparison).

As we can see, the reactances position behavioural clauses as an intermediate category, especially if we compare them with mental clauses of perception. In Spanish many Processes in mental clauses of this kind are 'active' enough that they can be substituted by the general verb *hacer* 'do', as exemplified in the question–answer sequence below.

Table 5.15 *Reactances for Spanish behavioural, verbal and existential clauses*

| | behavioural clauses | verbal clauses | existential clauses |
|---|---|---|---|
| **general verb** | *hacer* 'do' | *hacer* 'do' | none |
| **verb classes** | relatively open | relatively open | *haber* (3rd person) |
| **consciousness** | sensing/saying P1 | relatively restricted P1 | unrestricted |
| **deixis** | unrestricted | unrestricted | non-specific Existent |
| **Participant/s** | 1 or 2 | 1, 2 or 3 | 1 |
| **directionality** | one way | one-way | – |

Table 5.16 *Extended reactances for Spanish material, mental and relational clauses*

|  | material clauses | mental clauses | relational clauses |
|---|---|---|---|
| general verbs | *pasar* 'happen', *hacer* 'do' | *hacer* 'do' (restricted) | none |
| verb classes | open | relatively open | relatively closed |
| consciousness | unrestricted | sensing Participant | unrestricted |
| deixis | unrestricted | unrestricted | typically non-specific Attribute |
| Participant/s | 1, 2 or 3 | 1, 2 or 3 | 2 or 3 |
| clitic potential | P2 and/or P3 | P2 and/or P3 | P2 (neuter *lo*) and/or P3 |
| directionality | one-way | two-way (reaction) | one-way |

¿Qué **hicieron** las miles de personas?
'What did the thousands of people do?'

– **Observaron** la isla iluminada.
– 'Observed the illuminated island.'

Perception clauses, which we discuss in more detail below, also resemble behavioural ones in that they cannot project thought (i.e. they are not involved in clause complexes like those illustrated for verbal clauses above). A useful test for embedding vs projection in Spanish is to see if the clause in question can be negotiated (since embedded clauses cannot be negotiated). The POLARITY of the projected *que* clause (i.e. *que las familias pedían ayuda* 'the families were asking for help'), projected by a mental clause of cognition, is negotiated successfully below.

¿Crees ⇒ que **las familias** pedían ayuda?
'Do you believe ⇒ the families were asking for help?'

– Creo ⇒ que sí/Creo ⇒ que no/**Creo** ⇒ que quizás.
'I believe ⇒ so/I believe ⇒ not/I believe ⇒ perhaps.'

This is not possible with a mental perception process, since the relevant *que* clause (i.e. *que las familias pedían ayuda* 'that the families were asking for help') is embedded not projected. If the clause with *vieron* below is interpreted as a perception clause, projection is not possible:[28]

¿Vieron (con el catalejo) que **las familias** pedían ayuda?
'Did they see (with a telescope) that the families were asking for help?'

– *Vieron que sí.
'They saw that, yes.'

---

[28] However, projection is possible when the verb *ver* realises the Process in a cognition mental clause, in which case a macro-phenomenal non-finite embedded clause would not be possible.

In terms of PROJECTION, then, mental perception clauses differ from mental cognition ones, which do clearly project ideas – typically indirectly, as exemplified below.

**Quiroz** sabía ⇒ que tenían que escapar.
'Quiroz knew ⇒ he had to escape.'

**Los marinos** querían saber ⇒ si veía olas.
'The sailors wanted to know ⇒ if he saw waves.'

**Mariela** no sabe ⇒ cómo lograron salvarse.[29]
'Mariela doesn't know ⇒ how they escaped.'

Mental perception clauses also project directly by, in effect, 'quoting' thought:

– Era terrorífica, negra. Era fea la hueá de ola, fea – recuerda **el capitán**.

'"It was terrifying, black. That bugger of a wave was ugly, ugly." recalls the captain.'

As we can see reactances having to do with different kinds of phenomena (micro-phenomena, embedded macro-phenomena and projected or embedded meta-phenomena) are as crucial to the interpretation of Spanish mental clauses as they are for English ones. To date, however, questions remain about the recognition criteria distinguishing one type of phenomenon from another in Spanish, and thus about their role as we develop an appropriate subclassification of Spanish mental clauses. As noted above, corpus-based research drawing on Quiroz's (2013) foundational study is urgently required.

### 5.3.3  Further Delicacy

The play of reactances around behavioural and subtypes of mental clauses discussed above shows the importance of pushing the delicacy of our analysis – beyond the material, mental, relational classification we used as a starting point for Spanish, and on to prospective intermediate categories such as behavioural, verbal and existential. It also shows the importance of exploring the generality of the clusters of reactances we summarised in Tables 5.15 and 5.16 above. We haven't however explored the reactances distinguishing subtypes of mental clause in Spanish in detail here (for which see Quiroz, 2013, 2020). A summary of some of the relevant criteria is presented in Table 5.17. The perception type is associated with a small set of verbs including *ver* ('see'), *oír* ('hear'), *escuchar* ('listen'), *oler* ('smell') and *sentir* ('feel', 'sense'). The cognition type is associated with a larger set

---

[29] For examples of projected wh clauses in English, see Halliday and Matthiessen (2014, p. 521); cf. *he wondered* ⇒ *why (on earth) they'd left?* vs *he understood [[what(ever) they did]]* (the latter is agnate to *he understood the things they did* and involves an embedded wh clause).

Table 5.17 *Summary of reactances for subtypes of Spanish mental clauses*

|  | perception | cognition | reaction |
|---|---|---|---|
| **general verbs** | *hacer* (many) | none | *pasar/hacer*, mostly impinging |
| **verb classes** | relatively open | relatively open | relatively open |
| **consciousness** | sensing P1 | sensing P1 | sensing P1, P2 or P3 |
| **Participant/s** | 1, 2 or 3 | 1, 2 or 3 | 1, 2 or 3 |
| **clitic potential** | P2 and/or P3 | P2 and/or P3 (restricted) | P2 and/or P3 |
| **directionality** | one-way | one-way | two-way |

of verbs including *pensar* 'think', *saber* 'know', *creer* 'believe', *entender* 'understand', *comprender* 'understand', *recordar* 'remember/remind' and *olvidar* 'forget'. And the reaction type is associated with verbs like *gustar* 'like', *encantar* 'please', *amar* 'love', *adorar* 'adore', *odiar* 'hate', *fascinar* 'fascinate', *asustar* 'scare' and *molestar* 'upset'.

In the discussion that follows we will focus on just one subtype, perception. We do this for two reasons. One is that this clause type poses a challenge for current approaches to TRANSITIVITY analysis in SFL – namely that of a participant role which is in some sense 'shared' between an embedded clause (a macro-phenomenon or 'act') and the clause that it is embedded in. The other is that this clause type includes a third participant role (which we call Ensemble here),[30] which is not found in English.

The most common perception verbs in the Ola Maldita stories are *ver* 'see' and *oír* 'hear'. They are used to construe the firsthand experiences of the victims of the earthquake and tsunamis.

(30)
| *durante esa noche* | ***vieron*** | *a otros cuatro más* |
|---|---|---|
| Location | Process/Senser | Phenomenon |
|  | verbal group |  |
|  | Finite/Event |  |
| during that night | see.PST.3PL | to other four more |
| 'during that night they saw four more' ||||

(31)
| ***los jóvenes*** | *oyeron* | *su grito desesperado* |
|---|---|---|
| Senser | Process | Phenomenon |
|  | verbal group |  |
|  | Finite/Event |  |
| the youngsters | hear.PST.3PL | his desperate scream |
| 'the youngsters heard his desperate scream' ||||

[30] See Quiroz (2013), where the term Implicated is preferred for this perceptive clause function and some structurally comparable functions in other clause types.

## 5.3 Spanish TRANSITIVITY Resources

This is consistent with literature on Spanish 'perception verbs', which tends to agree that these are the two verbs involved in most of the key clause patterns distinguishing perception clauses from other mental clause types (e.g. Di Tullio, 1998; Suñer, 1978). Additional 'perception verbs' are mentioned in the discussion of relevant clause patterns, including *sentir* 'feel', *escuchar* 'listen' and *mirar* 'look' (e.g. Rodríguez Espiñeira, 2000). Further analysis is needed to clarify whether these verbs are best treated as realising perception clauses and/or behavioural ones.

As illustrated in examples given above, the Phenomenon in this clause type may construe an entity (a micro-phenomenon such as *la ola* 'wave' or *más cantos de niños* 'more children's songs' in the examples below).

(32)

| *los tripulantes* | *vieron* | | | *la ola* |
|---|---|---|---|---|
| Senser | Process | | | Phenomenon |
| | verbal group | | | |
| | Finite/Event | | | |
| the crew | see.PST.3PL | | | the wave |
| 'the crew saw the wave' | | | | |

(33)

| *en la isla* | *no se escucharon* | | | *más cantos de niños* |
|---|---|---|---|---|
| Location | Process | | | Phenomenon |
| | verbal group | | | |
| | Neg | Vcl | Finite/Event | |
| in the island | | | hear.PST.3PL | more songs of children |
| 'in the island one didn't hear any more children's songs' | | | | |

Alternatively, the Phenomenon may construe a figure (a macro-phenomenon such as *la ola acercándose* 'the wave moving closer', configured around an occurrence).[31]

(34)

| *los tripulantes* | *vieron* | [[*la ola acercándose*]] |
|---|---|---|
| Senser | Process | Phenomenon |
| | verbal group | |
| | Finite/Event | |
| the crew | see.PST.3PL | [[the wave approaching]] |
| 'the crew saw the wave moving closer' | | |

Here are three examples of macro-phenomenal perception clauses from our Ola Maldita text. As highlighted in bold, the Process of the macro-phenomenon

---

[31] For discussion of types of phenomena in English (micro-, macro- and meta-), see Halliday and Matthiessen (1999, 2014).

can be realised by either an infinitive non-finite verbal group (*venir* 'come', *volar* 'fly' below) or a gerundive non-finite verbal group (*entrando* 'entering', *escarbando* 'digging' below). The non-finite verbs in these clauses are in italics below.

**Hugo Barrera** la vio *venir*,
'Hugo Barrera saw it come.'

… y luego sint**ió** el mar *entrando* en su casa y *escarbando* en el piso de abajo.
'and later felt the sea entering into her house and digging into the floor below.'

A los pocos minutos se escuch**ó** el helicóptero de la empresa *volar* rumbo a la isla.
'In a few minutes one heard the company helicopter fly towards the island.'

The first of these is the one that needs to give us pause. There are two verbal groups in this clause: *la vio* 'saw it' and *venir* 'come'. The first, *la vio* 'saw it', construes the Process/Phenomenon of the main perception clause; the second, *venir* 'come', construes the Process of the embedded material clause realising the Phenomenon in the main clause. Notice, however, that the first verbal group includes the clitic *la* 'it'. The feminine singular class of this clitic reveals that it is actually tracking *la ola* 'the wave', not the whole macro-phenomenon involved in the embedded clause (including the second verbal group). The interesting thing about this is that Spanish usually deploys neuter clitic *lo* 'it' to recover embedded or projected clauses (e.g. meta-phenomena in reaction and cognition processes), which doesn't seem to be the case in this perception clause. The verbal group realising the Process/Phenomenon of the example we are discussing here is highlighted in bold in (35):

(35)

| Hugo Barrera | *la vio* | | *venir* |
|---|---|---|---|
| | Phenomenon/Process | | |
| | verbal group | | |
| | P2cl | Finite/Event | |
| Hugo Barrera | ACC.3SG.FEM | see.PST.3SG | come.INF |
| 'Hugo Barrera saw it come' | | | |

A second important thing to note is that the example we are working on here would be ungrammatical without the clitic. We cannot say \**Hugo Barrera vio venir* 'Hugo Barrera saw coming', which lacks reference to *la ola* 'the wave', because this element has to be made explicit, via a clitic (*la* 'it' in the first example below), or a full nominal group (*la ola* 'the wave' in the second example below), or both (via clitic doubling – *la* 'it' and *la ola* 'the wave' in the third example below) – as exemplified below.

**Hugo Barrera** *la* vio venir.
'Hugo Barrera saw *it* coming'

5.3 Spanish TRANSITIVITY Resources 275

**Hugo Barrera** vio *la ola* venir.
'Hugo Barrera saw *the wave* coming'

**Hugo Barrera** *la ola la* vio venir.
'Hugo Barrera saw *the wave* coming'

This means that this element is treated by the grammar of Spanish as a separate clause constituent. If it is realised by a nominal group (as *la ola* 'the wave'), its position is variable, as it is generally the case in Spanish with clause constituents realising Participants. This potential variation in position is illustrated below.

**Hugo Barrera** *la* vio venir *la ola*
'Hugo Barrera saw *the wave* coming'

**Hugo Barrera** vio *la ola* venir
'Hugo Barrera saw *the wave* coming'

**Hugo Barrera** *la ola la* vio venir
'Hugo Barrera saw *the wave* coming'

*la ola* la vio venir **Hugo Barrera**
'Hugo Barrera saw *the wave* coming'

Another pattern showing this element needs to be treated as a separate Participant is that it can be cliticised separately also when there is a change of voice at group rank (which involves the clitic *se*).[32]

se *la* vio venir
'**It** was seen coming'

Summing up, we can see not only that these macro-phenomenal perception structures in Spanish involve two clauses (one embedded in the other) with Processes, but that these two clauses somehow 'share' a Participant (the wave, realised as a nominal group and/or a clitic, in the examples above). The shared dependency is outlined in Figure 5.5 below.

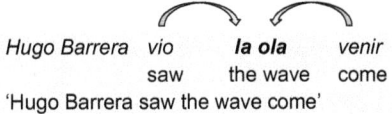

Hugo Barrera  vio    **la ola**    venir
                  saw    the wave  come
'Hugo Barrera saw the wave come'

Figure 5.5 Shared participant function in Spanish macro-phenomenal perception clauses

---

[32] For a full review of the VOICE system at group rank in Spanish, see Quiroz (2013).

This means that we cannot simply analyse such a perception clause as involving a Phenomenon realised by an embedded clause, including *la ola* 'the wave' as its Actor, as in the following example:

(36)

| *Hugo Barrera* | *vio* | *la ola venir* | |
|---|---|---|---|
| Senser | Process | Phenomenon | |
| | verbal group | [[clause]] | |
| | Finite/Event | Actor | Process |
| | see.PST.3SG | the wave | come.INF |
| 'Hugo Barrera saw the wave come' | | | |

This analysis misses the fact that the wave is also playing a participant role on its own as a Phenomenon in the perception clause.

By way of an alternative, let's aim for an analysis of the following slightly expanded example.

**Hugo Barrera** vio la ola venir hacia su eucalipto
'Hugo Barrera saw the wave coming towards his gum tree'

In order to systematically build up the analysis we present below, it is instructive to begin with a perception clause involving just a micro-phenomenon realised by a nominal group (*la ola* 'the wave').

(37)

| *Hugo Barrera* | *vio* | *la ola* |
|---|---|---|
| Senser | Process | Phenomenon |
| | verbal group | |
| | Finite/Event | |
| | see.PST.3SG | the wave |
| 'Hugo Barrera saw the wave' | | |

The Phenomenon can be alternatively realised as a pronominal clitic, and thus conflated with the Process.

(38)

| *Hugo Barrera* | *la* | *vio* |
|---|---|---|
| Senser | Phenomenon/Process | |
| | verbal group | |
| | P2cl | Finite/Event |
| | ACC.3SG.FEM | see.PST.3SG |
| 'Hugo Barrera saw it' | | |

Let's now expand this clause so what Hugo is seeing is a macro-phenomenon (i.e. something happening) rather than a simple phenomenon (i.e. *la ola* 'the wave'). We indicate this expansion with an arrow in the table below.

5.3 Spanish TRANSITIVITY Resources                                    277

(39)
| **Hugo Barrera** | *vio* | *la ola* | *venir hacia su eucalipto* |
|---|---|---|---|
| Senser | Process | Phenom …→ | … enon |
| | see.PST.3SG | the wave | come.INF towards his gum tree |
| 'Hugo Barrera saw the wave coming towards his gum tree' ||||

Having expanded the perception clause along these lines, we might then view the macro-phenomenon as a kind of additional Phenomenon, in which the wave (*la ola*) also plays a part. So what was the Phenomenon in a microphenomenal perception clause (*Hugo Barrera vio la ola* 'Huga Barrera saw the wave') takes on an additional participant role (as Actor) in the macrophenomenal perception clause (*la ola venir hacia su eucalito* 'the wave come towards his gum tree') – it is in fact a Participant that is shared between the two Processes (conflating the Phenomenon and Actor roles). Using traditional function labels, we might say that *la ola* 'the wave' is both the Object of the verb *vio* 'saw' and the Subject of the verb *venir* 'come'.

There is no standard way of displaying structures of this kind in SFL. The idea that a constituent can play a participant role in both an embedded clause (Actor above) and the clause it is embedded in (Phenomenon above) has not yet been properly addressed. Spanish poses the challenge,[33] and we offer a suggestion below. Our suggestion treats *la ola* 'the wave' as primarily a Phenomenon of the Process *vio* 'saw' (termed Phenomenon 1), since most of the evidence flagged above points in this direction (e.g. it has to be realised as part of the perception clause and can function as a P2 clitic in its Process). It then treats *venir hacia su eucalipto* 'coming towards his gum tree' as a secondary Phenomenon (termed Phenomenon 2 below).[34] Finally it conflates the Phenomenon 1 role played by *la ola* 'the wave' in the perception clause with its Actor role in the embedded material clause (adding parentheses by way of indicating that this role is of secondary importance as far as the structure as a whole is concerned).

(40)
| **Hugo Barrera** | *vio* | *la ola* | *venir* | *hacia su eucalipto* |
|---|---|---|---|---|
| Senser | Process | Phenomenon 1/ | Phenomenon 2 | |
| | | | [[clause]] | |
| | | (Actor) | Process | Location |
| Hugo Barrera | see.PST.3SG | the wave | come.INF | towards his gum tree |
| 'Hugo Barrera saw the wave come towards his gum tree' |||||

---

[33] Although not addressed in Section 5.2 above, English perception clauses with embedded macrophenomena present a comparable challenge. Compare *Hugo saw the wave coming* with *the wave was seen coming (by Hugo)*; the voice potential, with *the wave* now the Subject of the perception clause, indicates *the wave* is playing a role in both the perception clause and the embedded material one.

[34] Rodríguez Espiñeira (2000), in fact, treats these 'infinitive clauses' as 'secondary predications' (Phenomenon 2) of the 'nominal complement' (Phenomenon 1) in perception clauses (p. 34).

A system network underlying an approach of this kind is presented in Figure 5.6. Setting aside intermediate clause types, it first distinguishes among material, relational and mental clauses. Choosing mental involves inserting a Senser. Mental clauses are then subclassified as cognition, reaction or perception types. For the feature perception, a Phenomenon 1 is inserted. Perception also opens up choices in two systems. The [group] or [clause] system allows for Phenomenon 1 to be realised through a clitic or a clause constituent, and then, if realised as a clause constituent to be further realised as a clitic as well (via clitic doubling). There is some awkwardness here which stems from the fact that system network notation has no standard way of representing the possibility of [a] or [b], or both [a] and [b], but not neither [a] nor [b].[35]

The upper system, allowing for [macro-phenomenal] or not, makes room for the optional addition of a macro-phenomenon in which Phenomenon1 also plays a role. The relevant realisation statement triggers the insertion of a Phenomenon 2, its realisation by an embedded clause, and the conflation of Phenomenon 1 with an unspecified participant role (Px) in the embedded clause.

As we can see, Spanish perception clauses with macro-phenomenal Phenomena create challenges for description and representation in SFL. And this is exactly what we want description to do as we move from one language to another, testing the assumptions about system and structure that are either inherent in SFL theory or customary in its practice – its habit, for example, of avoiding discussion of English perception clauses in which a macro-phenomenal Participant is made Subject (cf. *Hugo saw the wave coming*/***the wave** was seen coming*).

We'll take one more step before closing this section, dealing with a further challenge that Spanish perception clauses have in store. Let's imagine that

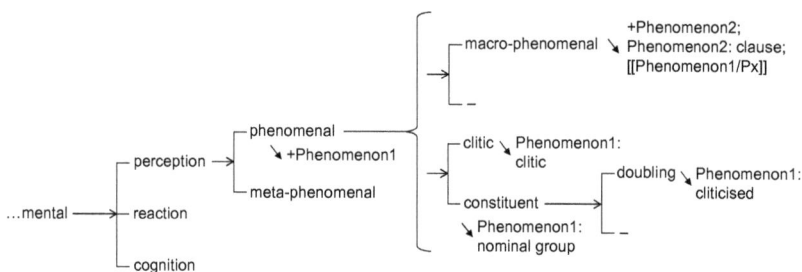

Figure 5.6 Spanish mental clause systems[36]

---

[35] In other words, system network notation allows for a system with options [a] or [b], or two systems, one with options [a] or nothing and one with or [b] nothing – but the latter allows [–] to be selected twice (i.e nothing); standard notation does not allow for and and/or bracket.

[36] For an alternative approach to description of this structure and the underpinning reasoning, see Quiroz (2013).

Jonathan Romero saw the look on Hugo Barrera's face as he was swept away. In example (41) below the part/whole relation between Hugo and his face is construed as a nominal group (*la cara de Hugo* 'Hugo's face'); this Phenomenon is cliticised in the example (42) (as *la* 'it').

(41)

| ***Jonathan*** | *vio* | *la cara de Hugo* |
|---|---|---|
| Senser | Process | Phenomenon |
| | verbal group | |
| | Finite/Event | |
| Jonathan | see.PST.3SG | the face of Hugo |
| 'Jonathan saw Hugo's face' | | |

(42)

| ***Jonathan*** | *la* | *vio* |
|---|---|---|
| Senser | Phenomenon/Process | |
| | verbal group | |
| | P2cl | Finite/Event |
| Jonathan | ACC.3SG | see.PST.3SG |
| 'Jonathan saw it' | | | |

In the next example, however, the relation between Hugo and his face is construed in clause structure rather than through a nominal group. Here the Phenomenon is realised simply by *la cara* 'the face'. And Hugo is realised as an additional Participant (a P3) through an adpositional nominal group (*a Hugo*). Clitic doubling is required in a structure of this kind, which means that the P3 clitic *le* is needed, co-referencing *Hugo*. What the English translation construes as one participant role (*Hugo's face* as Phenomenon), Spanish construes as two distinct participant roles (*la cara* 'face' and *a Hugo* 'Hugo').

(43)

| ***Jonathan*** | *le vio* | | *la cara* | *a Hugo* |
|---|---|---|---|---|
| Senser | Process | | Phenomenon | ? |
| | verbal group | | | |
| | P3cl | Finite/Event | | |
| Jonathan | DAT.3SG | see.PST.3SG | the face | to Hugo |
| 'Jonathan saw Hugo's face' | | | | |

In this respect Spanish offers a choice that English does not have. Like English, it can construe Hugo's face as a Phenomenon in a perception clause (i.e. *Jonathan vio **la cara de Hugo*** 'Jonathan saw Hugo's face').[37] Unlike English it can alternatively construe Hugo and his face separately, as distinct Participants (as in the example just above).

---

[37] In this case it cannot use a dative clitic to refer to Hugo (\**le vio the cara de Hugo*).

Since they are distinct Participants, both *la cara* and *Hugo* can be cliticised separately (as *se la* since the clitic sequence **le la* does not occur in Spanish).

(44)

| Jonathan | se | la | vio |
|---|---|---|---|
| Senser | ?/Phenomenon/Process | | |
| | verbal group | | |
| | P3cl | P2cl | Finite/Event |
| | DAT.3SG | ACC.3SG | see.PST.3SG |
| 'Jonathan saw it'[38] | | | |

It remains to propose a term for this third participant role in perception clause structure. A range of 'possessive' relationships are involved (including alienable and inalienable possession and relations of kith and kin);[39] accordingly we are proposing the relatively neutral term Ensemble for this encompassing clause function. The structural analysis for perception clauses of this kind would then proceed as follows.

(45)

| Jonathan | le | vio | la cara | a Hugo |
|---|---|---|---|---|
| Senser | Process | | Phenomenon | Ensemble |
| | verbal group | | | |
| | P3cl | Finite/Event | | |
| Jonathan | DAT.3SG | see.PST.3SG | the face | to Hugo |
| 'Jonathan saw Hugo's face' | | | | |

(46)

| Jonathan | se | la | vio | a Hugo |
|---|---|---|---|---|
| Senser | Phenomenon/Process | | | Ensemble |
| | verbal group | | | |
| | P3cl | P2cl | Finite/Event | |
| Jonathan | DAT.3SG | ACC.3SG | see.PST.3SG | to Hugo |
| 'Jonathan saw Hugo's face' | | | | |

(47)

| Jonathan | se la vio | | |
|---|---|---|---|
| Senser | Ensemble/Phenomenon/Process | | |
| | verbal group | | |
| | P3cl | P2cl | Finite/Event |
| | DAT.3SG | ACC.3SG | see.PST.3SG |
| 'Jonathan saw it' | | | |

[38] These perception clauses are literally untranslatable. There is no way in English to construe the possessive relation in play here in a perception clause, so the translation is inevitably misleading.

[39] Cf. *Jonathan le vio el auto a Hugo* 'Jonathan saw Hugo's car', an example involving alienable possession. A comparable structure is found in material clauses too: **Le chocó el auto a Jonathan** ('He crashed Jonathan's car'), **Le golpeó la cara a Jonathan** ('He hit Jonathan's face').

## 5.3 Spanish TRANSITIVITY Resources

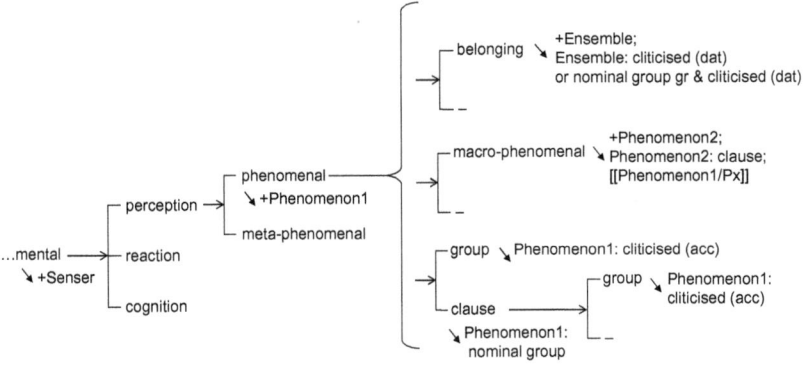

Figure 5.7 Spanish mental clause systems extended

Our systemic description of perception clauses is expanded in Figure 5.7 to allow for this third Ensemble function.[40] The additional system (with the choice of [belonging] or not) allows for perception clauses to optionally construe some kind of 'possessive' relation between Phenomenon 1 and its Ensemble. The associated realisation statement (for the feature [belonging]) inserts this function and specifies its realisation by a P3 clitic or by nominal group and an accompanying P3 clitic.[41]

Our discussion of Spanish perception clauses here highlights the importance of exploring subtypes of both major and minor clause types as far as TRANSITIVITY is concerned. This is important for checking whether generalisations formalised in realisation statements for less delicate features hold for more delicate ones. And it draws attention to potentially significant differences in structure from one subtype to another. Spanish perception clauses distinguish themselves with respect to at least the 'shared' Participant and 'possessive' Ensemble patterns reviewed above. Ultimately it is important to push delicacy to the point where grammatical distinctions cannot be found, and to push in fact beyond this point, with reference to discourse semantics, where the needs of register and genre analysis call for a finer-grained description.

---

[40] Note that network allows for an Ensemble function in embedded macro-phenomenal clauses such as *Paola le vio la cámara caer a Hugo* 'Paula saw Hugo's camera fall', *Paola le vió la cámara caer* 'Paula saw his camera fall' or *se la vio caer* 'She saw it fall', which we have not discussed here (for analysis, see Quiroz, 2013).

[41] We have not made these realisation statements as explicit as they would need to be for computational implementation, a task beyond the scope of this book.

282  Transitivity

## 5.4 Chinese TRANSITIVITY Resources

### 5.4.1 Four Kinds of Clause

In our Chinese focus text, we can also find three main types of clause comparable to those in English and Spanish (i.e. material clause, mental clause and relational clause) construing different types of phenomena which we experience. In addition, at the lowest level of delicacy, we can identify a fourth type of clause for Chinese – an existential clause.

Material clauses are the most frequently instantiated type of clause in our focus text, construing various occurrences, as exemplified below by a few clauses from the beginning of the focus text.

像这样生动有趣的高品质展览,故宫每年大概**要举办**40个
'lively, interesting and high-class exhibitions like this one, the Palace Museum **would host** around 40 every year'

自2012年单霁翔**执掌**故宫博物院以来
'since Shan Jixiang **took over** the Palace Museum in 2012'

开放面积不断**扩大**
'the opening area **is expanding** constantly'

人民网记者**走进**故宫博物院
'the journalist of *People* **enters** the Palace Museum'

Mental clauses construe perceptions, feelings and thoughts of sentient beings, as illustrated by the following clauses, which are also taken from the beginning of our focus text.

(人们)**一睹**宋代人文生活图景
'(people) **see** the scene of cultural life of the Song Dynasty'

(人们)**感受**宋代艺术之美
'(people) **feel** the beauty of art of the Song Dynasty'

Relational clauses construe the relationships that entities have with one another or with qualities. In the three examples below, the first construes relationship between entities, and the second and third construe relationships between an entity and a quality.

今天**是**5.18国际博物馆日
'today **is** May 18, International Museum Day'

故宫的文化底蕴深不可测
'the cultural background of the Forbidden City (is) profound beyond measure'

文化资源博大精深
'the cultural resource (is) substantial and expansive'

Existential clauses, as the term suggests, construe the existence of entities, often in relation to circumstances.

**有**多款文创产品
'**there are** many cultural products'

**有**哪些规划
'what plans **are there**'

在故宫博物院**有**看不完的展览
'**there are** countless exhibitions at the Palace Museum'

We mentioned in Section 5.2 that differentiating clause types often needs to rely on cryptotypic evidence. So clause syntagms comprising the same types of group (e.g. nominal group and verbal group) need to be explored in terms of reactances, so that their differences can be revealed. In the next section, we will explore grammatical justifications for our four types of clause.

### 5.4.2   Experiential Clause Typology

Based on our discussions about Chinese nominal groups in Chapter 2 and verbal groups in Chapter 3, we can observe the general features of the four types of clause introduced above in terms of number and type of nominal group and verbal group. Material and mental clauses contain a verbal group and one or more nominal groups. Relational clauses do not necessarily involve a verbal group; and one Participant is not necessarily realised by a nominal group but can be realised by an adjectival group.[42] Existential clauses contain a verbal group followed by a nominal group. We consolidate the clause syntagms of some of the examples in Table 5.18 below, showing the configuration of groups (but with circumstantial elements omitted).

From the perspective of clause structure, Chinese clauses have different configurations from English and Spanish clauses. The MOOD structure of English indicative clauses requires the presence of a Participant before the Process. Inflection and pronominal clitics in Spanish verbal groups encode Participants, so Participants do not have to be realised by nominal groups in Spanish clauses. In contrast, Chinese verbal groups do not feature inflectional morphology or clitics, nor does realisation of mood types involve functions realised by nominal groups. One consequence of this is that when Participants can be retrieved from context, they can be omitted from clause structure. For pedagogic purposes, we will make explicit such Participants whenever they are

---

[42] Chinese adjectives have many common features with verbs; but they are still a word class distinct from verbs (see Section 3.4 for a brief discussion); in this section we treat groups headed by adjectives in Chinese as a separate type of group – i.e. adjectival group.

Table 5.18 *Chinese clause syntagms*

| nominal group | verbal group | nominal group | adjectival group | |
|---|---|---|---|---|
| 开放面积<br>*kāifàng miànjī*<br>'opening area' | 扩大<br>*kuòdà*<br>'expand' | | | material clause |
| 人民网记者<br>*Rénmínwǎng jìzhě*<br>'journalist of People' | 走进<br>*zǒu jìn*<br>'enter' | 故宫博物院<br>*Gùgōng Bówùyuàn*<br>'Palace Museum' | | |
| (人们)<br>*rénmen*<br>'people' | 一睹<br>*yīdǔ*<br>'see' | 宋代人文生活图景<br>*Sòngdài rénwén shēnghuó tújǐng*<br>'scene of cultural life of the Song Dynasty' | | mental clause |
| (人们)<br>*rénmen*<br>'people' | 感受<br>*gǎnshòu*<br>'feel' | 宋代艺术之美<br>*Sòngdài yìshù zhī měi*<br>'beauty of art of the Song Dynasty' | | |
| 今天<br>*jīntiān*<br>'today' | 是<br>*shì*<br>'be' | 5.18国际博物馆日<br>*5.18 Guójì Bówùguǎn Rì*<br>'5.18 International Museum Day' | | relational clause |
| 故宫的文化底蕴<br>*Gùgōng de wénhuà dǐyùn*<br>'cultural background of the Forbidden City' | | | 深不可测<br>*shēnbùkěcè*<br>'profound beyond measure' | |
| | 有<br>*yǒu*<br>'there be' | 多款文创产品<br>*duō kuǎn wénchuàng chǎnpǐn*<br>'many cultural products' | | existential clause |
| | 有<br>*yǒu*<br>'there be' | 哪些规划<br>*nǎxiē guīhuà*<br>'what plans' | | |

needed to clarify our analysis (as we did for the mental clauses in Table 5.18 where we added 人们 *rénmen* 'people' to the clauses).

In Chinese we can explore clause types from the perspectives of the possibility of general verbs, the number of Participants, the consciousness of Participants, types of phenomena, directionality and the possibility of projection. In addition, differentiation of Chinese clause types may also involve reactances such as aspect, phase and negation in the verbal group that realises Process.

Let's first take a look at existential clauses, which are relatively easy to identify. The Process in existential clauses is lexicalised as 有 *yǒu* 'there be', which is the most prominent feature of this type of clause as opposed to other types (except for possessive relational clauses; see Section 5.4.2). Existential clauses have only one Participant; it realises either a micro-phenomenon (realised by a nominal group) or a meta-phenomenon (realised by an embedded clause). This Participant is labelled Existent. Optionally there can be a Circumstance before the Process. The three examples below illustrate existential clauses in Chinese – (48) is without a Circumstance, (49) has one and (50) has a Participant realised by an embedded clause.

(48)

| 有 | 多款文创产品 |
|---|---|
| *yǒu* | *duō kuǎn wénchuàng chǎnpǐn* |
| Process | Existent |
| verbal group | nominal group |
| there be | many cultural products |
| 'there are many cultural products' | |

(49)

| 在故宫博物院 | 有 | 看不完的展览 |
|---|---|---|
| *zài Gùgōng Bówùyuàn* | *yǒu* | *kànbùwán de zhǎnlǎn* |
| Circumstance | Process | Existent |
| coverbal phrase | verbal group | nominal group |
| in the Palace Museum | there be | countless exhibitions |
| 'there are countless exhibitions in the Palace Museum' | | |

(50)

| 有 | [[哪些新改变值得我们期待]] |
|---|---|
| *yǒu* | [[*nǎxiē xīn gǎibiàn zhídé wǒmen qīdài*]] |
| Process | Existent |
| verbal group | [[clause]] |
| there be | what new changes deserve our expectation |
| 'what new changes deserving our expectation are there?' | |

Another distinctive feature of existential clauses is the negation used in the verbal group. Existential clauses always use the adverb 没 *méi* to deny the existence of something, whereas other types of clause (except for possessive relational clauses) restrict the use of the negation adverb 没 *méi* to the non-neutral aspect (for details see Section 3.4.2). The negative existential clauses versions of (48) and (49) are realised as follows (verbal groups in bold):

**没有**多款文创产品
***méi yǒu*** *duō kuǎn wénchuàng chǎnpǐn*
'**there aren't** many cultural products'

在故宫博物馆**没有**看不完的展览
*zài Gùgōng Bówùyuàn **méi yǒu** kànbùwán de zhǎnlǎn*
'**there aren't** countless exhibitions in the Palace Museum'

The verbal group realising the Event 有 *yǒu* 'there be' in existential clauses does not select for PHASE, either directional or resultative. However, aspect clitics are possible – 着 *zhe* construing an ongoing state of existence, 了 *le* construing existence that has finished and 过 *guo* construing existence as an experience that has happened at least once – as illustrated by the following examples:[43]

Progressive aspect:

父母与子女之间**有着**特殊的情感关系
*fùmǔ yǔ zǐnǚ zhījiān **yǒu zhe** tèshū de qínggǎn guānxì*
'a special emotional relationship **is existing** between parents and children'

信息接收者和信息输出者的心目中**有着**共同的语法规则
*xìnxī jiēshōuzhě hé xìnxī shūchūzhě de xīnmù zhōng **yǒu zhe** gòngtóng de yǔfǎ guīzé*
'common grammatical rules **are existing** in the minds of information receivers and information givers'

Completed aspect:

**有了**先进的生产工具和生产方法
***yǒu le*** *xiānjìn de shēngchǎn gōngjù hé shēngchǎn fāngfǎ*
'**there were** advanced production tools and production methods'

比前一年**有了**很大的提高
*bǐ qián yī nián **yǒu le** hěn dà de tígāo*
'**there was** a big increase compared with the previous year'

Experienced aspect:

17部美剧里都**有过**类似桥段
*shíqī bù měijù lǐ dōu **yǒu guo** lèisì qiáoduàn*
'**there have been** similar scenes in seventeen American TV dramas'

---

[43] These examples are retrieved from the corpus of the Centre for Chinese Linguistics, Peking University.

## 5.4 Chinese TRANSITIVITY Resources

这在中国曾经**有过**[44]
*zhè zài Zhōngguó céngjīng **yǒu guo***
'this **has** ever **existed** in China'

We now turn to material clauses. Material clauses provide grammatical resources for construing figures related to doing and happening. The various occurrences realised by the Process in material clauses can mostly be queried with general verbs 做 *zuò* 'do' and 发生 *fāshēng* 'happen'. According to Long and Peng (2012, p. 5), material clauses can be queried with interrogatives like 做什么 *zuò shénme* 'do what' and 怎么了 *zěnme le* 'what happened':

开放面积**怎么了**?
*kāifàng miànjī **zěnme le***
'What happened to the opening area?'

开放面积扩大了。
*kāifàng miànjī kuòdà le*
'The opening area expanded.'

人民网记者**做什么**?
*Rénmínwǎng jìzhě **zuò shénme***
'What is the journalist of *People* doing?'

人民网记者走进故宫博物院。
*Rénmínwǎng jìzhě zǒu jìn Gùgōng Bówùyuàn*
'The journalist of *People* is entering the Palace Museum.'

Participants in material clauses can be either conscious – e.g. 人民网记者走进故宫博物院 ***Rénmínwǎng jìzhě zǒu jìn Gùgōng Bówùyuàn* 'the journalist of *People* enters the Palace Museum'** or unconscious – e.g. 开放面积扩大了 ***kāifàng miànjī* *kuòdà le* 'the opening area** expanded'. Participants can be a thing (micro-phenomenon) or a happening (macro-phenomenon) – e.g. 担任故宫博物院院长挑战了我的能力、学识、经验 *dānrèn Gùgōng Bówùyuàn yuànzhǎng tiǎozhàn le wǒ de nénglì, xuéshí, jīngyàn* '**holding the post of curator of the Palace Museum** challenged my ability, knowledge and experience'.

A material clause can involve one Participant, or two Participants, as illustrated by examples (51) and (52) below. The Participant initiating the Process is known as Actor, and the Participant affected by the Process is Goal.

(51)

| 开放面积 | 扩大 |
|---|---|
| *kāifàng miànjī* | *kuòdà* |
| Actor | Process |
| nominal group | verbal group |
| opening area | expands |
| 'the opening area expands' | |

---

[44] In this example the Existent 这 *zhè* 'this' is placed at the beginning of the clause to gain textual prominence.

(52)

| 故宫研发了10500种文创产品 | | |
|---|---|---|
| *Gùgōng* | *yánfā le* | *yīwàn líng wǔbǎi zhǒng wénchuàng chǎnpǐn* |
| Actor | Process | Goal |
| nominal group | verbal group | nominal group |
| Palace Museum | developed | 10,500 cultural products |
| 'the Palace Museum developed 10,500 cultural products' | | |

In (53) below, however, the Participant 故宫博物院 *Gùgōng Bówùyuàn* 'Palace Museum' is neither created nor affected by the occurrence in the Process 走进 *zǒu jìn* 'enter'; therefore, it does not realise the Goal function but realises Scope (see Section 5.2 above).

(53)

| 人民网记者走进故宫博物院 | | |
|---|---|---|
| *Rénmínwǎng jìzhě* | *zǒu jìn* | *Gùgōng Bówùyuàn* |
| Actor | Process | Scope |
| nominal group | verbal group | nominal group |
| journalist of *People* | enter | Palace Museum |
| 'the journalist of *People* enters the Palace Museum' | | |

A material clause may also involve three Participants, as illustrated by example (54) below. The unit realising the Goal function is known in traditional Chinese grammar as 把字结构 *bǎ zì jiégòu* '*bǎ*-structure'. Here we analyse it as a nominal group, in which 把 *bǎ* is treated as structure marker. If the Goal is given information, it can be positioned before the Process in the clause as a *bǎ*-group. The Scope, however, cannot be realised by a *bǎ*-group, e.g. *人民网记者**把故宫博物院**走进 *Rénmínwǎng jìzhě bǎ Gùgōng Bówùyuàn zǒu jìn* (modified from (53)).

(54)

| (您)要**把紫禁城**完整地交给下一个六百年 | | | | | |
|---|---|---|---|---|---|
| *nín* | *yào* | ***bǎ Zǐjìnchéng*** | *wánzhěng de* | *jiāogěi* | *xià yī gè liùbǎi nián* |
| Actor | Pro ... | Goal | Circumstance | ... cess | Recipient |
| nominal group | verbal ... | nominal group | adverbial group | ... group | nominal group |
| you (polite form) | would | Forbidden City | intactly | hand over | next six hundred years |
| '(you) would hand over the Forbidden City intactly to the next six hundred years' | | | | | |

## 5.4 Chinese TRANSITIVITY Resources

Table 5.19 *Reactances distinguishing material from existential clauses*

|  | material clause | existential clauses |
|---|---|---|
| general verbs | 做 *zuò* 'do'<br>发生 *fāshēng* 'happen' | none |
| verb class | open | 有 *yǒu* 'there be' |
| Participant/s | 1, 2 or 3 | 1 |
| phenomena | micro-/macro- | micro-/meta- |
| bǎ-group | possible | not possible |
| phase | possible | not possible |
| neutral aspect negation | 不 *bù* | 没 *méi* |

Verbal groups realising Process in material clauses can select for ASPECT and PHASE. The choice of negative polarity is conditioned by aspect and mood type (for detailed discussion see Sections 3.4 and 4.4). In neutral aspect, the adverb that realises the Neg function is 不 *bù*. Thus far, we can summarise the major reactances for material clauses and existential clauses in Chinese as outlined in Table 5.19.[45]

We now turn to mental clauses. Mental clauses construe our experience of perception, cognition, desire and emotion. The verb class in the verbal group that realises Process is relatively open, but not as open as that in material clauses. A mental clause requires two Participants, one of which must be a conscious being and realised through the Senser function. The other Participant is the target of sensing and realises the Phenomenon function. The Phenomenon can realise an entity (i.e. micro-phenomenon), entities configured with occurrences (i.e. macro-phenomena) and figures positioned as thoughts and feelings (i.e. meta-phenomena). Configurations involving these three types of phenomena are illustrated by examples (55–57) below.

(55) micro-phenomenon

| 您喜欢这样的评价吗 | | | |
|---|---|---|---|
| *nín* | *xǐhuān* | *zhèyàng de píngjià* | *ma* |
| Senser | Process | Phenomenon | |
| nominal group | verbal group | nominal group | |
| *you* (polite form) | *like* | *such remarks* | |
| 'Do you like such remarks?' | | | |

---

[45] As in our discussions of English and Spanish, for the number of Participants we are not considering 'extra Agents' (i.e. Initiator, Inducer, Attributor, Assigner) at this point, nor the possibility of a resultative or depictive Attribute.

(56)   macro-phenomenon

| 人们喜欢[[听历史和文物藏品背后的故事]] | | |
|---|---|---|
| rénmen | xǐhuān | [[tīng lìshǐ hé wénwù cángpǐn bèihòu de gùshì]] |
| Senser | Process | Phenomenon |
| nominal group | verbal group | [[clause]] |
| people | like | listening to stories behind historical and cultural collections |
| 'people like listening to stories behind our historical and cultural collections' ||| 

(57)   meta-phenomenon

| 我深刻地感受到故宫的文化底蕴深不可测 | | | |
|---|---|---|---|
| wǒ | shēnkè de | gǎnshòu dào | [[Gùgōng de wénhuà dǐyùn shēnbùkěcè]] |
| Senser | Circumstance | Process | Phenomenon |
| nominal group | adverbial group | verbal group | [[clause]] |
| I | deeply | feel | the cultural background of the Forbidden City is profound beyond measure |
| 'I deeply feel that the cultural background of the Forbidden City is profound beyond measure' ||||

Mental clauses can be divided into four subtypes: perceptive, cognitive, desiderative and affective (see Halliday and McDonald, 2004; Martin, Matthiessen and Painter, 2010). Affective clauses feature two-way directionality (i.e. 'impinging' and 'emanating') between Senser and Phenomenon, as exemplified below. There is no impinging affective clause in our focus text, so some examples are added from the Modern Chinese corpus of Beijing Language and Culture University.Impinging (Phenomenon ^ Process ^ Senser):

我的发型没有**吓到**你
wǒ de fàxíng méiyǒu **xià dào** nǐ
'my hairstyle didn't **frighten** you'

我教的课**吸引了**学生
wǒ jiāo de kè **xīyǐn le** xuéshēng
'the course I taught **attracted** students'

Emanating (Senser ^ Process ^ Phenomenon):

她**害怕**大街上的俄国兵
tā **hàipà** dàjiē shàng de Éguó bīng
'she **fears** the Russian soldiers on the street'

## 5.4 Chinese TRANSITIVITY Resources

您**喜欢**这样的评价吗
nín **xǐhuān** zhèyàng de píngjià ma
'Do you **like** such remarks?'

In impinging mental clauses, the Phenomenon can be realised by a *bǎ*-phrase, whereas the Phenomenon in emanating mental clauses cannot – e.g. 我教的课**把学生**吸引了 *wǒ jiāo de kè **bǎ xuéshēng** xīyǐn le* 'the course I taught attracted **students**', *她**把大街上的俄国兵**害怕 *tā **bǎ dàjiē shàng de Éguó bīng** hàipà* 'she fears **the Russian soldiers on the street**'. In cognitive mental clauses, the use of *bǎ*-phrase is restricted; for example, we cannot say *把 … … 知道 *bǎ … zhīdào* 'know … ', *把 … … 思考 *bǎ … sīkǎo* 'ponder … ', etc., but 把 … … 忘记 *bǎ … wàngjì* 'forget about … ' is grammatical (e.g. 很多人**把亏损**忘记了 *hěn duō rén **bǎ kuīsǔn** wàngjì le* 'many people forgot about **their loss**'). Some perceptive mental clauses involving a phase can have their Phenomenon realised by the *bǎ*-phrase, e.g. **把剩下10集**看完 ***bǎ shèngxià shí jí** kàn wán* 'finish seeing **the remaining 10 episodes**' (for Phase realised by the verb 完 *wán* 'finish', see example (73) in Chapter 3).

In mental clauses, choices in the ASPECT system are not as free as in material clauses. The restriction has mainly to do with ongoing aspect. Verbal groups realising the Process in some perceptive and cognitive mental clauses cannot select ongoing aspect – i.e. the clitic 着 *zhe* is not possible (e.g. *看见着 *kàn jiàn zhe* 'seeing', *知道着 *zhīdào zhe* 'knowing').

Selection from the PHASE system is not as free either. The use of resultative phase is relatively less restrictive, e.g. 看见 *kàn jiàn* 'see' (lit. 'look + see'), 忘光 *wàng guāng* 'forget all about' (lit. 'forget + nothing left'), 想好 *xiǎng hǎo* 'decide' (lit. 'think + good'), 恨死 *hèn sǐ* 'loathe' (lit. 'hate + dead'); however, the use of directional phase is impossible in in mental clauses, since mental clauses construe sensing rather than action.[46]

As in material clauses, the use of a negative adverb in mental clauses is conditioned by aspect and mood. In neutral aspect and indicative mood, 不 *bù* is used for negation, e.g. 不看 *bù kàn* 'not look', 不听 *bù tīng* 'not listen', 不想 *bù xiǎng* 'not think', 不喜欢 *bù xīhuān* 'not like'. When the verbal group contains a Phase element, negation is realised by 没(有) *méi(yǒu)*, as illustrated by the following two examples from our focus text:

**没想到**最后一个岗位是在北京最大的四合院看门
***méi xiǎng dào** zuìhòu yī gè gǎngwèi shì zài Běijīng zuì dà de sìhéyuàn kān mén*
'(I) **didn't expect** that (my) last post is looking after Beijing's biggest courtyard house'

---

[46] Verbal groups like 想出 *xiǎng chū* 'think out' (lit. 'think + go out'), 看出来 *kàn chūlái* 'find, realise, perceive' (lit. 'look + come out') appear to contain directional verbs, but the Phase that is realised is result, not direction.

**没有看到**故宫博物院的展览
*méiyǒu kàn dào Gùgōng Bówùyuàn de zhǎnlǎn*
'(they) **didn't see** the exhibition of the Palace Museum'

Another important characteristic of cognitive and desiderative mental clauses is that they can project another clause. What is projected is a dependent clause, not an embedded clause that realises Phenomenon.[47] The projecting and projected clauses form a clause complex, in which the projecting clause has only one Participant.

我**觉得** ⇒ 最重要的一点,就是一切工作要以观众方便为中心
'I **think** ⇒ the most important thing is that all our work should be centred on bringing convenience to visitors'

(我们)**希望** ⇒ 到2020年能有8%左右的文物展出来
'(we) **hope** ⇒ around 8% of our collections will be put on exhibition by 2020'

Table 5.20 provides a summary of reactances distinguishing among material, mental and existential clauses in Chinese.

Finally for this section, we discuss relational clauses, which construe relationships between entities or between entity and quality. Relational clauses

Table 5.20 *Reactances for Chinese material, mental and existential clauses*

|  | material clauses | mental clauses | existential clauses |
| --- | --- | --- | --- |
| **general verbs** | 做 *zuò* 'do'<br>发生 *fāshēng* 'happen' | none | none |
| **verb class** | open | relatively open | 有 *yǒu* 'there be' |
| **Participant/s** | 1, 2 or 3 | 1 or 2 | 1 |
| **consciousness** | unrestricted | sensing Participant | unrestricted |
| **phenomena** | micro-/macro- | micro-/macro-/meta- | micro-/meta- |
| **directionality** | one-way | two-way | not applicable |
| **bǎ-group** | unrestricted | restricted (impinging) | not possible |
| **ongoing aspect** | unrestricted | restricted (perceptive, cognitive) | unrestricted |
| **phase** | unrestricted | restricted (resultative) | not possible |
| **neutral aspect negation** | 不 *bù* | 不 *bù* (without phase)<br>没(有) *méi (yǒu)* (with phase) | 没 *méi* |
| **projection** | not possible | possible (cognitive, desiderative) | not possible |

[47] An embedded clause realising Phenomenon can be alternatively realised as a nominal group, e.g. 我深刻地感受到[[故宫的文化底蕴深不可测]]**这个事实** *wǒ shēnkè de gǎnshòu dào [[Gùgōng de wénhuà dǐyùn shēnbùkěcè]] zhègè shìshí* 'I deeply feel **the fact** that the cultural background of the Forbidden City is profound beyond measure' (modified from (57)), whereas a projected clause cannot.

feature a relatively closed verb class, mainly involving verbs such as 是 *shì* 'be', 有 *yǒu* 'have', 在 *zài* 'be at', or verbs with related meanings. Some relational clauses do not involve verbs and we treat them as having no Process function – as illustrated in example (58) below.

(58)

| 故宫的文化底蕴深不可测 | |
|---|---|
| *Gùgōng de wénhuà dǐyùn* | *shēnbùkěcè* |
| Participant | Participant |
| nominal group | adjectival group |
| cultural background of the Forbidden City | profound beyond measure |
| 'the cultural background of the Forbidden City is profound beyond measure' | |

In terms of the number of Participants, since relational clauses construe relationships between two entities or between one entity and its quality, they necessarily involve two Participants. There is no restriction as to whether Participants are conscious or not.

As in mental clauses, Participants in relational clauses can be micro-phenomena, macro-phenomena or meta-phenomena, as shown in the examples below. Note, however that the meta-phenomena are not projected but realised in grammar as embedded.[48]

Micro-phenomenon:

我不仅是**一个看门人**,还应该是**一个讲解员**
'I'm not only **a doorkeeper**, but also should be **an interpreter**'

Macro-phenomenon:

最后一个岗位是[[在北京最大的四合院看门]]
'(my) last post is **looking after Beijing's biggest courtyard house**'

Meta-phenomenon:

最重要的一点,就是[[一切工作要以观众方便为中心]]
'the most important point is **that all our work should be centred on bringing convenience to visitors**'

Some relational clauses can have one of their Participants positioned before the Process through the use of a *bǎ*-group, as illustrated by the two examples below. The use of *bǎ*-group is restricted to the cases where an extra Participant – i.e.

---

[48] Embedded clauses realising meta-phenomena can be alternatively realised as nominal groups involving the embedding, e.g. 最重要的一点就是[[一切工作要以观众方便为中心]]**这件事** *zuì zhòngyào de yī diǎn jiù shì* [[*yīqiè gōngzuò yào yǐ fāngbiàn guānzhòng wéi zhōngxīn*]] *zhè jiàn shì* 'the most important point is **the thing** that all our work should be centred on bringing convenience to visitors'.

Assigner or Attributor (see 5.5 below) – is present or can be inferred from the co-text or context.

(我们)**把它们**作为保管、陈列的对象
(*wǒmen*) **bǎ tāmen** *zuòwéi bǎoguǎn, chénliè de duìxiàng*
'(we) treat **them** as objects for maintenance and exhibition'

(展演)**把原本隐藏在作品中不易被了解的细节**变成观众能看懂的故事
(*zhǎnyǎn*) **bǎ yuánběn yǐncáng zài zuòpǐn zhōng bù yì bèi liǎojiě de xìjié** *biànchéng guānzhòng néng kàn dǒng de gùshì*
'(the exhibition) turns **elusive details hidden in the works** into stories that viewers can understand'

In relational clauses that contain verbal groups, the selection for ASPECT and PHASE is highly restricted. The mostly commonly used verbs, 是 *shì* 'be', 有 *yǒu* 'have' and 在 *zài* 'be at', cannot select freely from the PHASE system; their aspect is always neutral. Other verbs (e.g. 体现 *tǐxiàn* 'embody', 表示 *biǎoshì* 'mean', 代表 *dàibiǎo* 'represent', 包括 *bāokuò* 'include') can make restricted selections in the systems of ASPECT and PHASE, which we will not elaborate here. For the ASPECT and PHASE selections of specific verbs, see Lü (1999).

When it comes to negation for neutral aspect, the verb 有 *yǒu* 'have' realising possession (see Section 5.4.3 below) uses the adverb 没 *méi* (e.g. 没有时间 *méi yǒu shíjiān* 'not have time'); other verbs take the adverb 不 *bù* (e.g. 不是段子手 *bù shì duànzǐshǒu* 'not be a joke teller'). The adjectival group (see Section 3.4) in attributive relational clauses can have the adverb 不 *bù* realising the Neg function in its structure, e.g. 不陌生 *bù mòshēng* 'not strange' in example (59) analysed below.

(59)

| 我对故宫不陌生 | | | |
|---|---|---|---|
| *wǒ* | *duì Gùgōng* | *bù mòshēng* | |
| Carrier | Process | Attribute | |
| nominal group | verbal group | adjective group | |
| | | Neg | |
| I | to Palace Museum | not | strange |
| 'I am not strange to the Palace Museum' | | | |

In phonology, the verb 是 *shì* 'be' used in relational clauses usually involves a deletion of its initial consonant [ʂ] and only the vowel [ɿ] is audible. This is common in northern dialects which form the basis of the standard variety of Chinese. Even when the initial consonant is retained, the syllable is very much weakened in tone. This means that the falling tone contour is not as salient as that in other verbs that have a falling tone syllable, e.g. 他是叛徒 *tā shì pàntú* 'he is a traitor' (relational clause, 是 *shì* 'be' weakened) vs. 他恨叛徒 *tā hèn pàntú* 'he hates traitors' (mental clause, 恨 *hèn* 'hate' salient).

## 5.4 Chinese TRANSITIVITY Resources

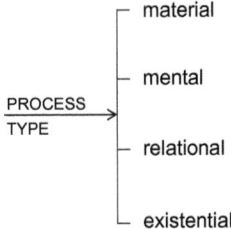

Figure 5.8 Basic Chinese PROCESS TYPE system (types of clause)

Based on the discussion above, we summarise the four major types of clause in Chinese with the system network in Figure 5.8; relevant reactances are provided in Table 5.21.

Table 5.21 *Reactances for Chinese material, mental, relational and existential clauses*

|  | material clause | mental clause | relational clause | existential clause |
|---|---|---|---|---|
| **general verbs** | 做 *zuò* 'do' 发生 *fāshēng* 'happen' | none | none | none |
| **verb class** | open | relatively open | relatively closed | 有 *yǒu* 'there be' |
| **explicit Process** | required | required | optional (attributive) | required |
| **Participant/s** | 1, 2 or 3 | 1 or 2 | 2 | 1 |
| **consciousness** | unrestricted | sensing Participant | unrestricted | unrestricted |
| **phenomena** | micro-/macro- | micro-/macro-/meta- | micro-/macro-/meta- | micro-/meta- |
| **directionality** | one-way | two-way | one-way | not applicable |
| **bǎ-group** | unrestricted | restricted (impinging) | restricted (involving Assigner) | not possible |
| **ongoing aspect** | unrestricted | restricted (perceptive, cognitive) | highly restricted | unrestricted |
| **perfective aspect** | unrestricted | unrestricted | highly restricted | unrestricted |
| **phase** | unrestricted | restricted (resultative) | highly restricted | not possible |
| **neutral aspect negation** | 不 *bù* | 不 *bù* (without phase) 没(有) *méi(yǒu)* (with phase) | 没 *méi* (possessive) 不 *bù* (others) | 没 *méi* |
| **projection** | not possible | possible (cognitive, desiderative) | not possible | not possible |
| **weakening of verb** | not possible | not possible | possible for 是 *shì* 'be' | not possible |

### 5.4.3 Further Delicacy

In the previous section, we specified the Participants in material, mental and existential clauses as Actor, Goal, Scope, Recipient; Senser, Phenomenon and Existent. But we have not specified them for relational clauses. To do so we need to push our classification of relational clauses further in delicacy.

From the perspective of discourse semantics, the classification of relational clauses relates to the difference among figures construing relationships between an entity and its temporal or spatial position, between an entity and its quality or between entities in terms of class membership, composition or possession.

To begin we consider relational clauses that position one entity in relation to another entity that construes time or space. The Process in such clauses is typically 在 *zài* 'be at'. Here is an example from our focus text:

新馆**在**海淀上庄地区
*xīnguǎn **zài** Hǎidiàn Shàngzhuāng dìqū*
'the new museum site **is at** Shangzhuang, Haidian'

We refer to this type of relational clause as a circumstantial clause. There are two Participants – the entity being positioned is labelled Positioned and the entity realising placement in time or space is labelled Position.

(60)  relational: circumstantial

| 新馆在海淀上庄地区 | | |
|---|---|---|
| *xīnguǎn* | *zài* | *Hǎidiàn Shàngzhuāng dìqū* |
| Positioned | Process | Position |
| nominal group | verbal group | nominal group |
| new museum | be at | Shangzhuang, Haidian area |
| 'the new museum site is at Shangzhuang, Haidian' | | |

The second type of relational clause attributes a quality to an entity – an attributive clause. Attributive clauses involve Carrier and Attribute functions. Attributive clauses in Chinese can be subclassified into a describing type and a classifying type. The descriptive type either has a Process or does not have one, while the classifying type always has a Process. Two examples are provided below for analysis of function and class.[49]

---

[49] Example (61) is a descriptive relational clause without a Process. A Process can be added to it to produce 故宫的文化底蕴**变得**深不可测 *Gùgōng de wénhuà dǐyùn **biànde** shēnbùkěcè* 'the cultural background of the Forbidden City **has become** profound beyond measure'.

(61) relational: attributive: descriptive

| 故宫的文化底蕴深不可测 | |
|---|---|
| Gùgōng de wénhuà dǐyùn | shēnbùkěcè |
| Carrier | Attribute |
| nominal group | adjectival group |
| cultural background of the Forbidden City | profound beyond measure |
| 'the cultural background of the Forbidden City is profound beyond measure' | |

(62) relational: attributive: classifying

| 故宫博物院院长是一个风险很大的岗位 | | |
|---|---|---|
| Gùgōng Bówùyuàn yuànzhǎng | shì | yī gè fēngxiǎn hěn dà de gǎngwèi |
| Carrier | Process | Attribute |
| nominal group | verbal group | nominal group |
| curator of Palace Museum | be | a post of high risks |
| 'the curator of Palace Museum is a post of high risks' | | |

The unmarked sequence of the two Participants in attributive clauses is Carrier ^ Attribute. Normally they cannot be reversed (e.g. *深不可测故宫的文化底蕴 shēnbùkěcè Gùgōng de wénhuà dǐyùn 'profound beyond measure is the cultural background of the Forbidden City', *一个风险很大的岗位是故宫博物院院长 yī gè fēngxiǎn hěn dà de gǎngwèi shì Gùgōng Bówùyuàn yuànzhǎng 'a post of high risks is the curator of Palace Museum').[50]

The third type of relational clause involves degrees of abstraction, as a relatively concrete entity is related to something less concrete. We refer to this clause type as identifying; its Participants are specified as Token and Value. The Value is conferred upon the Token via the Process. We provide two examples from our data below.

今天**是**5.18国际博物馆日
*jīntiān* **shì** *5.18 Guójì Bówùguǎn Rì*
'today **is** May 18, International Museum Day'

北院区**包括**文物修复与展示中心、故宫文化传播中心、宫廷园艺中心等
*běi yuànqū* **bāokuò** *wénwù xiūfù yǔ zhǎnshì zhōngxīn, Gùgōng wénhuà chuánbō zhōngxīn, gōngtíng yuányì zhōngxīn děng*
'the north section **comprises** cultural relics restoration and exhibition centre, Forbidden City culture publicity centre, palace horticulture centre, etc.'

---

[50] Attribute ^ Carrier structure can be used as a highly marked sequence, typically in poems and lyrics, to create a stylistic effect, e.g. 温暖是你的拥抱, 红色是你的围巾 *wēnnuǎn shì nǐ de yōngbào, hóngsè shì nǐ de wéijīn* 'warm is your embrace, red is your scarf' (lyrics of a pop song).

More detailed analyses are provided below. Identifying clauses in Chinese can use the general verb 是 *shì* 'be' to realise the Process. For example, the second clause above can be rewritten as 北院区**是**文物修复与展示中心、故宫文化传播中心、宫廷园艺中心等 *běi yuànqū* **shì** *wénwù xiūfù yǔ zhǎnshì zhōngxīn, Gùgōng wénhuà chuánbō zhōngxīn, gōngtíng yuányì zhōngxīn děng* 'the north section **is** cultural relics restoration and exhibition centre, Forbidden City culture publicity centre, palace horticulture centre, etc.' In addition, the sequence of Token and Value in identifying clauses is flexible – as exemplified in (63) and (64) – though Token ^ Value is the unmarked sequence.

(63) relational: identifying

| 今天是5.18国际博物馆日 | | |
|---|---|---|
| *jīntiān* | *shì* | *5.18 Guójì Bówùguǎn Rì* |
| Token | Process | Value |
| nominal group | verbal group | nominal group |
| today | be | May 18, International Museum Day |
| 'today is May 18, International Museum Day' | | |

(64) relational: identifying (reversed)

| 5.18国际博物馆日是今天 | | |
|---|---|---|
| *5.18 Guójì Bówùguǎn Rì* | *shì* | *jīntiān* |
| Value | Process | Token |
| nominal group | verbal group | nominal group |
| May 18, International Museum Day | be | today |
| 'May 18, International Museum Day is today' | | |

Different sequences may implicate different verbs (cf. 包括 *bāokuò* 'comprise' and 构成 *gòuchéng* 'constitute' in examples (65) and (66) below).

(65) relational: identifying

| 北院区包括文物修复与展示中心、故宫文化传播中心、宫廷园艺中心等 | | |
|---|---|---|
| *běi yuànqū* | *bāokuò* | *wénwù xiūfù yǔ zhǎnshì zhōngxīn, Gùgōng wénhuà chuánbō zhōngxīn, gōngtíng yuányì zhōngxīn děng* |
| Token | Process | Value |
| nominal group | verbal group | nominal group |
| north section | comprise | cultural relics restoration and exhibition centre, Forbidden City culture publicity centre, palace horticulture centre, etc. |
| 'the north section comprises cultural relics restoration and exhibition centre, Forbidden City culture publicity centre, palace horticulture centre, etc.' | | |

(66) relational: identifying (reversed)

| 文物修复与展示中心、故宫文化传播中心、宫廷园艺中心等构成北院区 | | |
|---|---|---|
| wénwù xiūfù yǔ zhǎnshì zhōngxīn, Gùgōng wénhuà chuánbō zhōngxīn, gōngtíng yuányì zhōngxīn děng | gòuchéng | běi yuànqū |
| Value | Process | Token |
| nominal group | verbal group | nominal group |
| cultural relics restoration and exhibition centre, Forbidden City culture publicity centre, palace horticulture centre, etc. | constitute | north section |
| 'cultural relics restoration and exhibition centre, Forbidden City culture publicity centre, palace horticulture centre, etc. constitute the north section' | | |

The fourth type of relational clause in Chinese construes a possessive relationship between two entities. The Participants in possessive clauses are labelled Possessor and Possessed. The most common lexical realisation of the Process is the verb 有 *yǒu* 'have'. Note that we translate this verb as 'there be' in existential clauses, where there is only one Participant (Existent). Possessive relational clauses involve two Participants (Possessor and Possessed). Analysis of an example is given below.

(67) relational: possessive

| 中华传统文化有辉煌的过去 | | |
|---|---|---|
| Zhōnghuá chuántǒng wénhuà | yǒu | huīhuáng de guòqù |
| Possessor | Process | Possessed |
| nominal group | verbal group | nominal group |
| Chinese traditional culture | have | glorious past |
| 'Chinese traditional culture has a glorious past' | | |

The discussion above has pushed our analysis of Chinese relational clauses further in delicacy, as outlined by the system network in Figure 5.9. This is followed by an extended table of reactances (Table 5.22). As indicated in Section 5.2.3, the question of how far we push delicacy with respect to both system and structure has to be a pragmatic one, depending on the appliable linguistics focus of the analysis.

300   Transitivity

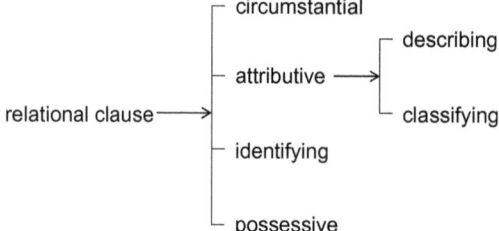

Figure 5.9 Extended Chinese RELATIONAL CLAUSE TYPE systems

Table 5.22 *Reactances for subtypes of Chinese relational clauses*

| subtypes | circumstantial | attributive | | identifying | possessive |
| --- | --- | --- | --- | --- | --- |
| | | describing | classifying | | |
| participants | Located, Location | Carrier, Attribute | | Token, Value | Possessor, Possessed |
| main verb | 在 *zài* 'be at' | none | 是 *shì* 'be' | 是 *shì* 'be' | 有 *yǒu* 'have' |
| explicit Process | required | not required | required | required | required |
| bǎ-phrase | not allowed | not allowed | | restricted | not allowed |
| ongoing aspect | not allowed | not allowed | | restricted | unrestricted |
| perfective aspect | restricted | not allowed | | restricted | unrestricted |
| phase | not allowed | not allowed | | restricted | not allowed |
| neutral aspect negation | 不 *bù* | 不 *bù* | | 不 *bù* | 没 *méi* |
| reversibility | no | no | | yes | no |

### 5.4.4   Verbal Clauses

In our account for English and Spanish, we recognised two other types of clause – verbal and behavioural. These two types of clause have some reactances in common with material and mental clauses. For Chinese we need only to recognise verbal clauses.

Verbal clauses construe figures about communication, with the Process most frequently realised by a verbal group headed by 说 *shuō* 'say'; it is illustrated below with the two examples from our focus text. Like mental clauses, verbal clauses can project another clause realising a meta-phenomenon (in this case a locution rather than an idea).

您说"要把紫禁城完整地交给下一个600年"
*nín **shuō** 'yào bǎ Zǐjìnchéng wánzhěng de jiāogěi xià yī gè 600 nián'*
'you **say** "(we) should hand over the Forbidden City intactly to the next six hundred years"'

## 5.4 Chinese TRANSITIVITY Resources

您**说过**改革开放带来的巨大变化是使人们的能力在为社会做贡献时得到巨大的提升

nín **shuō guo** gǎigé kāifàng dài lái de jùdà biànhuà shì shǐ rénmen de nénglì zài wèi shèhuì zuò gòngxiàn shí dédào jùdà de tíshēng

'you **have said** that the big change brought by (China's) reform and opening up (policy) is the big increase in people's ability of contributing to the society'

Verbal clauses may have only one Participant, which is the source of the speech – a Sayer. The Sayer is not necessarily a conscious being but can be another source of information (e.g. 天气预报说明天会下雨 *tiānqì yùbào shuō míngtiān huì xià yǔ* '**the weather forecast** says it will rain tomorrow'). Verbal clauses can also have additional Participants, i.e. Verbiage[51] and Receiver, as exemplified below. Verbal clauses are thus like material clauses in that they both can have up to three Participants.

(66)

| 记者问了院长一些问题 | | | |
|---|---|---|---|
| jìzhě | wèn le | yuànzhǎng | yīxiē wèntí |
| Sayer | Process | Receiver | Verbiage |
| nominal group | verbal group | nominal group | nominal group |
| journalist | asked | curator | some questions |
| 'the journalist asked the curator some questions' | | | |

Table 5.23 provides a summary of similarities and differences between verbal clauses on the one hand, and material and mental clauses on the other.

There seems to be no grammatical evidence that can distinguish behavioural clauses as a separate clause type in Chinese. Halliday and McDonald (2004, p. 376) treat behavioural clauses as a subset of intransitive material clauses for Chinese.

This means that we can treat conscious being's physiological or social behaviour as realised by material or verbal clauses. Processes involving verbs like 哭 *kū* 'cry', 笑 *xiào* 'laugh', 坐 *zuò* 'sit', 看 *kàn* 'look', 听 *tīng* 'listen', 盯 *dīng* 'stare', 观察 *guānchá* 'observe', 考虑 *kǎolǜ* 'ponder', 咳嗽 *késòu* 'cough', 呼吸 *hūxī* 'breathe' (which can be queried with 做什么 *zuò shénme* 'do what' or 怎么了 *zěnme le* 'what happened' and cannot project) can be treated as material. Processes involving verbs construing various manners of speaking, e.g. 谈 *tán* 'talk', 聊 *liáo* 'chat', 讲 *jiǎng* 'tell', 倾诉 *qīngsù* 'pour out (words, feelings)', 埋怨 *mányuàn* 'complain' (which can involve Receiver and/or Verbiage but cannot project), can be treated as borderline cases between material and verbal.

This concludes our exploration of Chinese clause types as far as TRANSITIVITY is concerned. In the next section, we pose some challenges for TRANSITIVITY analysis, which we invite readers to pursue.

---

[51] Projected clauses are not considered as Verbiage, but as dependent clauses – e.g. 明天会下雨 *míngtiān huì xià yǔ* 'it will rain tomorrow' in the previous example.

Table 5.23 *Reactance for Chinese material, verbal and mentals clauses*

|  | material clause | verbal clause | mental clause |
|---|---|---|---|
| general verbs | 做 *zuò* 'do'<br>发生 *fāshēng* 'happen' | 说 *shuō* 'say' | none |
| verbal class | open | relatively closed | relatively open |
| Participant/s | 1, 2 or 3 | 1, 2 or 3 | 1 or 2 |
| consciousness | unrestricted | speaking Participant | sensing Participant |
| phenomenon | micro-/macro- | micro-/meta- | micro-/macro-/meta- |
| directionality | one-way | one-way | two-way |
| projection | not possible | possible | possible |

## 5.5 TRANSITIVITY Challenge

For those of you familiar with other languages, we trust that we have now modelled an approach to TRANSITIVITY that you will find instructive. We have deliberately designed it to be challenging, especially with respect to Spanish perception clauses – raising important issues that need to be addressed from the perspective of SFL theory and description. Our SFL perspective can be usefully compared with work on argument structure (sometimes discussed in terms of thematic relations, semantic roles or cases in other traditions). When doing so, try and make explicit the classification criteria deployed in these traditions, comparing them with the reactances concentrated on above. For those of you familiar with English, Spanish or Chinese, we reiterate here that the descriptions introduced above have been provided for pedagogic purposes. They are both preliminary and provisional. SFL grammarians working in both the Sydney (e.g. Matthiessen, 1995) and Cardiff (as reviewed in Neale, 2017) registers of SFL have already pushed the discussion of English far beyond what we have presented here. For Spanish, our proposals here can be usefully compared with those in Lavid, Arús and Zamorano-Mansilla (2010); and they are much further developed in Quiroz (2013, 2020, in press). For Chinese, our description in this chapter can be compared with Halliday and McDonald (2004), Long and Peng (2012), McDonald (1998) and Zhou (1997) – particularly in terms of which reactances are given more weight in distinguishing between clause types. And we reiterate that we have assumed the foundations of SFL theory and description outlined in Matthiessen and Halliday (1997/2009) and Martin, Wang and Zhu (2013) here.

The challenge we suggest for this chapter has to do with pushing the description of TRANSITIVITY beyond the focus on P1 and P2 functions we have concentrated on here. From an SFL perspective, this has meant that we have dwelt for the most part on the most general systems; this is reflected in our proposals for function structures realising very general features (Actor and Goal, Senser and Phenomenon, Carrier and Attribute and so on). At one point we showed how a more delicate description might be reflected in more specific structures (e.g. Classification and Description in place of Attribute in English attributive clauses). At two others we showed how additional Participants can be brought into the picture (in passing for the Receiver in verbal clauses and in a little more detail for the Ensemble function in Spanish perception clauses).

Our challenge, then, is for you to take one of the clause types in a language you are working on (categories like material, mental or relational as a good starting point, or behavioural, verbal or existential if you prefer) and push your description – pushing delicacy from the perspective of system and pushing specificity from the perspective of structure. For this, of course, you will need to select data from registers the are relatively rich in terms of the clause class you are working on (recall in this respect the foregrounding of verbal processes in the Ola Maldita journalism register compared to the personal Random Chatty Vlog and Interview with Curator register where they were relatively rare).

The rich detail of Halliday and Matthiessen (2014) shows us the kinds of things we need to watch out for. Additional participant roles will emerge, such as those they refer to as Recipient, Client, Depictive Attribute and Resultative Attribute in English material clauses (e.g. *they gave **her** the prize, they cooked **her** the cake, she left **happy**, they painted it **red***). And as Quiroz (2013) explores, there are additional Participants to consider in Spanish mental clauses (under the scope of a generalised Implicated function).

Another set of roles to watch out for is the set of agentive ones, which in some sense instigate the basic clause patterns introduced in this chapter – functions sometimes referred to as Initiator, Inducer, Attributor and Assigner in English (e.g. ***they** made them help, **they** persuaded them to come, **they** drove her mad, **they** elected her President* respectively) and are often generalised as Agents (especially where an ergative perspective is brought into play). Hao (2018, 2020a), working from a discourse semantic perspective, refers to this domain of meaning as INSTIGATION.

Finally, keep in mind that questions about the border between Participants and Circumstances will soon arise. Certain kinds of Circumstance will show themselves to be strongly associated with one clause type or another – Circumstances of Manner with reaction clauses (e.g. *love madly*), Circumstances of Matter with behavioural clauses (e.g. *talk about it*), Circumstances of Location in space with dispositive material clauses (e.g. *move it there*) and so on. This will force you to think carefully about the orbital structure of clauses and how this can be reflected in system networks and function labelling or by other means altogether (perhaps in discourse semantics or beyond).

It's a huge world out there and inside us. Across languages, TRANSITIVITY manages it all. We have our work cut out for us.

# 6 Theme

## 6.1 Approaching from Above

In this chapter we will approach clauses from a textual perspective. In terms of mode (textual context), clauses provide key resources for managing information flow in ways that suit the immediacy of aural and visual feedback among interlocutors and the context dependency of discourse. The key mode variables are monologue vs dialogue, and language in action vs language as reflection (Figure 6.1; Martin, 1992; Martin and Rose, 2008)

These variables are better conceived of as clines rather than oppositions. So we can ask how monologic or dialogic a text is – i.e. to what extent do the interlocutors take turns of roughly equal length? And we can ask how context dependent the language is – i.e. is it part of or accompanying what is going on, or is it recreating and commenting on what has already happened? A topology reflecting these intersecting clines is presented in Figure 6.2, including canonical examples of the text types implicating different kinds of information flow.

In terms of textual discourse semantics, the key system framing our discussion for this chapter is PERIODICITY,[1] which organises discourse as a hierarchy of waves of information (Martin and Rose, 2007). Clauses and tone groups play a key role in managing the smallest of these waves in relation to longer wavelength ones managing phases of discourse.

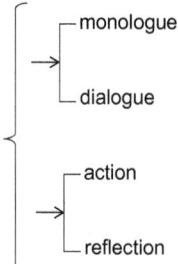

Figure 6.1 Mode variables

[1] The other relevant discourse semantic system, IDENTIFICATION, was flagged in Chapter 2.

6.2  English Information Flow 305

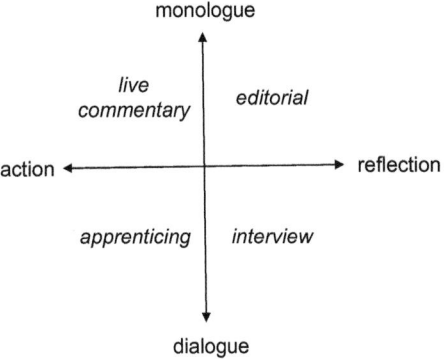

Figure 6.2  Mode topology (with exemplary text types)

In Section 6.2 below we explore English THEME and INFORMATION, before turning to Spanish and Chinese resources in Sections 6.3 and 6.4. For English we return to FitzSimons' (2005) story about the famous beach rescue at Bondi Beach, our Bondi Beach text (Appendix 2.1). Our focus text for Spanish once again comprises stories about a famous earthquake and tidal wave in Maule and Biobío, Chile, in 2010 (Guzmán, 2010), which we refer to as the Ola Maldita ('the hellish wave') text (Appendix 3.1). For Chinese we go back to the news story about controlling the sea lettuce near China's coastal city of Qingdao in 2008, which we refer to as the Sea Lettuce text (Appendix 4.1). In Section 6.5 we present an analysis challenge.

## 6.2  English Information Flow

In terms of mode, FitzSimons' text is virtually monologic (he does, however, make a couple of interactive gestures towards his readers at the end of the feature – *With thanks to Waverly Library and reader Diane Touzell; Do you have a historical anecdote about a place in Sydney?*; and it is almost all language as reflection (except for his intermodal reference to the picture of Bondi Beach in his opening paragraph – *And so **there they** lie ...*). Taking into account these shifts in mode, alongside the field and tenor transitions in the text, we can propose a generic structure unfolding in stages as follows: Kicker, Localisation, Orientation, Complication, Evaluation, Resolution, Coda, Thanks, Solicitation. As argued in Martin (2008a) and Martin, Matthiessen and Painter (2010), the Bondi Beach text is a narrative (its Orientation, Complication, Evaluation, Resolution, Coda staging), recontextualised as one of FitzSimons' 'Place in Time' feature articles (thus its Kicker, Localisation, Thanks, Solicitation staging). This genre staging is presented below.

**Kicker**
Big waves and Bondi Beach have always gone together, writes Peter FitzSimons, but no one had ever seen the ocean rise up with a strength such as this …

**Localisation**
And so there they lie, happily sweltering in the summer sun on Australia's most famous beach, just as they have for so many generations past. It is such a wonderfully peaceful scene – of people and nature as a happy whole – that it is simply unimaginable that nature could ever rear up and savage the lot of them.

**Orientation**
Ah, but those 35,000 Sydneysiders who were lying in those very spots on the afternoon of February 6, 1938, surely felt equally at peace. The day was, in the vernacular of the time, a "stinker", and some thought it was in fact a record turnout on the beach, with the numbers perhaps swelled by the fact that those bronzed boys of the Bondi Surf Bathers' Life Saving Club had turned up in force to have one of their popular surf competitions.

**Complication**
At three o'clock there was still not the slightest clue that this afternoon would forever be known as "Black Sunday" in the annals of Sydney. Then it happened. With a roar like a Bondi tram running amok, an enormous wave suddenly rolled over the thousands in the surf, including those many standing on the large sandbank just out from the shore – knocking them all over as it went. And then another wave hit, and then another. The huge waves, just like that, piggy-backed their way further and further up the beach and grabbed everything they could along the way – from babies to toddlers to adolescents to beach umbrellas, to old blokes and young sheilas alike, and then made a mad dash for the open sea again, carrying all before it and sweeping everyone off the sandbank and into the deep channel next to it in the process. In no more than 20 seconds, that peaceful scene had been tragically transformed into utter chaos. Now, the boiling surf, with yet more large waves continuing to roll over, was filled with distressed folk waving for help.

**Evaluation**
In their long and glorious history, this still stands as the finest hour of the Australian lifesaving movement.

**Resolution**
For, ignoring their own possible peril, the Bondi boys now charged into the surf, some attached to one of the seven reels available, some relying only on their own strength. As one, they began pulling the people out. On the shore, many survivors were resuscitated, as the Bondi clubhouse was turned into a kind of emergency clearing house, and ambulances from all over Sydney town descended and carried the victims away. Finally, just half an hour after the waves hit, the water was cleared of bobbing heads and waving arms, …

**Coda**
… and it was time to take stock: 250 people had needed the lifesavers to pull them out, of whom 210 were OK once back on land. Thirty-five needed mouth to mouth to be restored to consciousness, while five people perished.

## 6.2 English Information Flow

**Thanks**
With thanks to Waverly Library and reader Diane Touzell, whose grandfather, Bill Jenkins, was one of the lifesavers.

**Solicitation**
Do you have a historical anecdote about a place in Sydney?

One distinctive feature of FitzSimons' adaptation of the genre (in the service of this popular history) is its tendency to foreshadow what happened before it tells us what happened. The Kicker of course functions in this way, since its purpose is to get us to read the article (we use the symbols '⇒' below to indicate that following information has been anticipated and '⇐' to indicate that preceding information is being consolidated).

Big waves and Bondi Beach have always gone together, writes Peter FitzSimons, but no one had ever seen the ocean rise up with a strength such as this … ⇒

But foreshadowing also takes place several times within the article itself – once to foreshadow the waves' inundation, once for the lifesavers' rescue and once for taking stock:

At three o'clock there was still not the slightest clue that this afternoon would forever be known as "Black Sunday" in the annals of Sydney. Then it happened. ⇒

In their long and glorious history, this still stands as the finest hour of the Australian lifesaving movement. ⇒

… and it was time to take stock: ⇒

This foreshadowing is complemented on one occasion by a retrospective comment on the impact of the waves:

⇐ Now, the boiling surf, with yet more large waves continuing to roll over, was filled with distressed folk waving for help.

FitzSimons' account of the inundation is thus book-ended by sentences that look forward and look back – a kind of rhetorical sandwich as outlined below.

At three o'clock there was still not the slightest clue that this afternoon would forever be known as "Black Sunday" in the annals of Sydney. Then it happened. ⇒
With a roar like a Bondi tram running amok, an enormous wave suddenly rolled over the thousands in the surf, including those many standing on the large sandbank just out from the shore – knocking them all over as it went. And then another wave hit, and then another. The huge waves, just like that, piggy-backed their way further and further up the beach and grabbed everything they could along the way – from babies to toddlers to adolescents to beach umbrellas, to old blokes and young sheilas alike, and then made a mad dash for the open sea again, carrying all before it and sweeping everyone off the sandbank and into the deep channel next to it in the process. In no more than 20 seconds, that peaceful scene had been tragically transformed into utter chaos.

⇐ In no more than 20 seconds, that peaceful scene had been tragically transformed into utter chaos. Now, the boiling surf, with yet more large waves continuing to roll over, was filled with distressed folk waving for help.

This brings us down to the shorter wavelengths of information, which the grammar of languages has evolved to compose. We're going to work our way slowly into our analysis here, drawing at first on our analysis of MOOD in Chapter 4. Our Subject function is once again going to play a critical role; and we need to look carefully at how it is realised in different types of clause and from one clause to the next as a text unfolds. Let's begin with the meat in the rhetorical sandwich just replayed. Graphologically speaking we can divide this into sentences as follows.

With a roar like a Bondi tram running amok, an enormous wave suddenly rolled over the thousands in the surf, including those many standing on the large sandbank just out from the shore – knocking them all over as it went.

And then another wave hit, and then another.

The huge waves, just like that, piggy-backed their way further and further up the beach and grabbed everything they could along the way – from babies to toddlers to adolescents to beach umbrellas, to old blokes and young sheilas alike, and then made a mad dash for the open sea again, carrying all before it and sweeping everyone off the sandbank and into the deep channel next to it in the process.

Grammatically speaking we have finite clauses (which we can tag), and non-finite clauses (which we cannot tag); the latter are indented below.

With a roar like a Bondi tram running amok, an enormous wave suddenly rolled over the thousands in the surf,

> including those many standing on the large sandbank just out from the shore
> – knocking them all over
> as it went.[2]

And then another wave hit,

and then another.

The huge waves, just like that, piggy-backed their way further and further up the beach

and grabbed everything they could along the way – from babies to toddlers to adolescents to beach umbrellas, to old blokes and young sheilas alike,

and then made a mad dash for the open sea again,

> carrying all before it
>
> and sweeping everyone off the sandbank and into the deep channel next to it in the process.

And there are three embedded clauses, enclosed in double square brackets below.

With a roar like [[a Bondi tram running amok]], an enormous wave suddenly rolled over the thousands in the surf,

---

[2] This clause is indented because it is dependent on the preceding non-finite clause.

## 6.2 English Information Flow

including those many [[standing on the large sandbank just out from the shore]]

and grabbed everything [[they could]] along the way – from babies to toddlers to adolescents to beach umbrellas, to old blokes and young sheilas alike,

We'll set aside the embedded clauses for the moment (they are not small waves of information[3] but rather part of the small waves in which they are embedded). From the perspective of MOOD, we can note that our non-finite clauses lack explicit Subjects. This is a typical pattern in English clauses of this type, since they are not negotiable (as reflected in the fact they can't be tagged). Being in a sense 'moodless', they don't need a Subject and a Finite to separate indicative from imperative, or informative from interrogative. Or, to put this in discourse semantic terms, they can't be moves in exchange structure (they are always part of other moves).

including those many [[standing on the large sandbank just out from the shore]]

– knocking them all over

carrying all before it

and sweeping everyone off the sandback and into the deep channel next to it in the process.

It is clear, however, what the relevant Participant would be if it had been made explicit (*the thousands in the surf*, *an enormous wave*, *the huge waves* and *the huge waves* respectively in the non-finite clauses above). We can confirm this by turning these clauses into immediately related finite ones, as illustrated below.

**the thousands in the surf** included those many [[standing on the large sandbank just out from the shore]] (*didn't they?*)

– **an enormous wave** knocked them all over (*didn't it?*)

**the huge waves** carried all before it[4] (*didn't they?*)

and **the huge waves** swept everyone off the sandbank and into the deep channel next to it in the process. (*didn't they?*)

We've focused on the analysis of these English non-finite clauses for a moment here because it bears critically on their contribution to our analysis of information flow below as far as identifying Themes is concerned.

Turning to our finite non-embedded clauses, the first five have explicit Subjects, highlighted in bold below.

With a roar like [[a Bondi tram running amok]], **an enormous wave** suddenly rolled over the thousands in the surf,

---

[3] Accordingly, they would not be spoken on their own tone group (and so are not set apart from the rest of their sentence with special punctuation).

[4] As far as presuming reference is concerned, FitzSimons' should have written *them*, not *it*, to agree in number with *the waves* (in both this clause and the next one); the dense intervening ideation has presumably distracted him (and his editors).

as **it** went

And then **another wave** hit,

and then **another**.

**The huge waves**, just like that, piggy-backed their way further and further up the beach

and grabbed everything [[they could]] along the way – from babies to toddlers to adolescents to beach umbrellas, to old blokes and young sheilas alike,

and then made a mad dash for the open sea again,

The last two involve branching parataxis, meaning their Subject is ellipsed – presumed from the first clause in the sentence. Once again, we can reliably make the Subject of these clauses explicit.

**The huge waves**, just like that, piggy-backed their way further and further up the beach (didn't they?)

and **the huge waves** grabbed everything [[they could]] along the way – from babies to toddlers to adolescents to beach umbrellas, to old blokes and young sheilas alike, (didn't they?)

and then **the huge waves** made a mad dash for the open sea again, (didn't they?)

We're now in a position to highlight all the Subject functions, whether explicit, implicit (in non-finite clauses) or ellipsed (in finite ones).

With a roar like [[a Bondi tram running amok]], **an enormous wave** suddenly rolled over the thousands in the surf,

**(the thousands in the surf)** including those many [[standing on the large sandbank just out from the shore]]

– **(an enormous wave)** knocking them all over

as **it** went.[5]

And then **another wave** hit,

and then **another**.

**The huge waves**, just like that, piggy-backed their way further and further up the beach

and **(the huge waves)** grabbed everything [[they could]] along the way – from babies to toddlers to adolescents to beach umbrellas, to old blokes and young sheilas alike,

and then **(the huge waves)** made a mad dash for the open sea again,

**(the huge waves)** carrying all before it

and **(the huge waves)** sweeping everyone off the sandbank and into the deep channel next to it in the process.

And as a final observation before embarking on an analysis of information flow proper, we can note that in the first of these clauses the Subject does not come

---

[5] This clause is indented because it is dependent on the preceding non-finite clause.

## 6.2 English Information Flow

first but is preceded by a Circumstance of Manner – *With a roar like* [[*a Bondi tram running amok*]].

Now let's stand back a little from this phase of discourse and consider how information unfolds clause by clause. As outlined in the Table 6.1, six clauses begin with conjunctions, linking them additively and temporally to clauses before. The first of the clauses, as just noted, begins by characterising the sound of the first wave; it then proceeds, like every other clause in this phase except one, with reference to the waves. The remainder of each clause deals with the impact of the waves on the people at the beach. In Table 6.1 'implicit' Subjects are made explicit in parentheses, drawing on the discussion of non-finite and branching paratactic structures above.

Table 6.1 *Information flow in the 'waves attack' phase of the Bondi Beach text*

| linker[a] | pre-Subject | Subject | post-Subject |
|---|---|---|---|
| | With a roar like [[a Bondi tram running amok]] | an enormous wave | suddenly rolled over the thousands in the surf, |
| | | (the thousands in the surf) | including those many [[standing on the large sandbank just out from the shore]] |
| | | – (an enormous wave) | knocking them all over |
| as | | it | went |
| And then | | another wave | hit, |
| and then | | another. | (hit)[b] |
| | | The huge waves, | just like that, piggy-backed their way further and further up the beach |
| and | | (the huge waves) | grabbed everything [[they could]] along the way – from babies to toddlers to adolescents to beach umbrellas, to old blokes and young sheilas alike, |
| and then | | (the huge waves) | made a mad dash for the open sea again, |
| | | (the huge waves) | carrying all before it |
| and | | (the huge waves) | sweeping everyone off the sandbank and into the deep channel next to it in the process. |

[a] We deploy the general term 'linker' here to cover what are traditionally referred to as conjunctions (e.g. *and, so; that, whether*), adverbs (e.g. *however, therefore*) and relative pronouns (e.g. *that, who*) – i.e. what in Halliday and Matthiessen (2014) are treated as textual Themes.

[b] Ideation presumed from the preceding clause has been inserted here.

As an exercise, let's now, as far as possible, turn most of these clauses around – using a change of VOICE to make people rather than the waves Subject (Table 6.2). This change has a number of effects. One is that the choices for Subject are less consistent than before. Not all of the clauses could be turned around, so both people and the waves occupy the Subject position. Another is that two of the Subjects are much longer than before, including detailed information about the people affected by the waves; concomitantly, the information following the Subject is less dense, since these details have been moved to Subject position, and there are several repetitive references to the waves.

As we can see, English is flexible in terms of the sequence of the presentation of information in a clause. VOICE (active vs passive) is obviously a key

Table 6.2 *Reworking information flow in the 'waves attack' phase of the Bondi Beach text*

| linker | pre-Subject | Subject | post-Subject |
|---|---|---|---|
| | With a roar like [[a Bondi tram running amok]] | the thousands in the surf | were suddenly rolled over by an enormous wave, |
| | | those many [[standing on the large sandbank just out from the shore]] | included |
| | | – all of them | being knocking over |
| as | | it | went |
| And then | | they[a] | were hit by another wave, |
| and then | | (they) | (were hit) by another. |
| | | The huge waves, | just like that, piggy-backed their way further and further up the beach |
| and | | everything [[they could]] along the way – from babies to toddlers to adolescents to beach umbrellas, to old blokes and young sheilas alike, | was grabbed |
| and then | | the huge waves | made a mad dash for the open sea again, |
| | | all | being carried before it |
| and | | everyone | being swept off the sandbank and into the deep channel next to it in the process. |

[a] This clause and the next were actually intransitive in FitzSimons' original text (and then another wave hit and then another); we have taken the liberty of reformulating them as transitive here in order to turn the information flow around.

## 6.2 English Information Flow

resource; and as the first clause indicates, Circumstances can be moved around. We could, for example, further adjust the information flow in the table by rewriting certain clauses as follows:

further and further up the beach, just like that, the huge waves piggy-backed their way

and then for the open sea again (the huge waves) made a mad dash,

Some of these changes, you might reasonably object, make the text sound awkward. But what exactly do we mean when we say that?

There are two textual variables in play here as far as clause grammar is concerned. One has to do with establishing an ideational anchor for what we want to say. The anchor in Table 6.1 was the waves; in Table 6.2 it was the people affected by the waves. The anchor confirms a redundant jumping off point for ideational meaning. In English, in declarative clauses, it is realised through the Subject function; this is why we zoomed in on the Subject function as our point of departure for our analyses above. This anchor is referred to in SFL as Theme. The function of Subject/Theme conflations in English is to hold steady our gaze on the field; the Theme, in other words, aims a discourse sensitive camera at an ideational hub in a field and fixes our gaze there as a phase of text unfolds.

The other variable, complementing Theme, is New. Unlike Theme, which is realised grammatically, New is realised by intonation.[6] At stake here is the prosodic phonology of English tone groups (Halliday, 1967, 1970; Halliday and Greaves, 2008). The basic idea is that like grammar, phonology also organises discourse as waves of information. The unit we are interested in here is called a tone group, and in the unmarked case it has the same wavelength as a clause (one tone group per clause in other words). In tone groups one salient syllable, in the unmarked case the final one, carries the major pitch movement in the tone group. This 'super-salient' tonic syllable highlights the most prominent information in the tone group and can be used to recognise the New function in the grammar of a clause – minimally the clause constituent containing the tonic syllable.

In the clauses below, '//' stands for a tone group boundary, '/' for a foot boundary (which always begins with a salient syllable or a silent beat), '^' stands for a silent beat, and bold highlights the tonic syllable (featuring the major pitch movement of the tone group). And we are basing our analysis of these written clauses on the way we feel they would be most naturally read aloud. In the first clause, *hit* is the tonic syllable, and the minimal New of this clause is thus the Process (*hit*). In the second clause, the tonic syllable is *noth*,

---

[6] For pedagogic purposes we will not be setting up distinct INFORMATION systems at the level of lexicogrammar and TONALITY and TONICITY systems in phonology (as they are distinguished in Halliday and Greaves, 2008).

and the minimal New of this elliptical clause is thus the Participant *another (wave)*.

//^ and /then a/nother /wave /**hit**//
//^ and /then a/**noth**er//

Why do we write 'minimal New'? This is because when the tonic syllable is the final salient syllable in a tone group, English intonation does not tell us how much information to treat as New. But it does tell us how little; in the following clause the minimal New is *the thousands in the surf* (the constituent of the clause containing the tonic syllable).

//^ an e/normous /wave /suddenly /rolled over the /thousands in the /**surf**//

Maximal New might be extended to include *rolled over*, or *suddenly rolled over*, moving left until we reach the clause's Theme. Determining maximal New depends on a range of discourse factors that are beyond the scope of this book. Here we will restrict ourselves to a consideration of minimal New.

Tone groups tend to correspond to the small wavelengths organised by grammar (i.e. clauses). There may be one tone group per clause (as for the intonation examples above); but there can also be more than one (as indicated by the comma in the punctuation below).

With a roar like a Bondi tram running amok, an enormous wave rolled over the thousands in the surf.

//^ with a /roar like a /Bondi /tram /running a/**mok** //^ an e/normous /wave /suddenly / rolled /over the /thousands in the /**surf**//.

And there may be more than one clause per tone group (*and some thought* and *it was a record turnout on the beach* below).

//^ and /some /thought it was in /fact a /record /turnout on the /**beach**//

The cases where clause and tone group wavelengths do not correspond (i.e. more than one clause per tone group or more than one tone group per clause) are referred to as involving marked tonality.

We're now in position to replay the first table we introduced above (6.1), setting up columns for Theme and minimal New functions. The Themes anchor our gaze on the field, creating a discourse semantic pattern referred to by Fries (1981) as a text's method of development (anchored here on the waves). The minimal News then extend our gaze, creating a complementary discourse semantic pattern referred to by Fries as a text's point (here the impact of the waves). The complementarity Table 6.3 can be usefully contrasted with that in Table 6.2. There the change of voice meant that the text's method of development is people; and the text's point is less elaborated and includes repeated references to the waves, which once introduced are not really news.

6.2 English Information Flow

Table 6.3 *Theme and New in the 'waves attack' phase of the Bondi Beach text*

| linker | pre-Subject | Theme | minimal New (bold) |
|---|---|---|---|
| | With a roar like [[a Bondi tram running amok,]] | an enormous wave | **over the thousands in the surf,** |
| | | (the thousands in the surf) | **those many [[standing on the large sandbank just out from the shore]]** |
| | | – (an enormous wave) | **over** |
| as | | it | **went** |
| And then | | another wave | **hit,** |
| and then | | a … | **… nother**[a] |
| | | The huge waves, | **further and further up the beach** |
| and | | (the huge waves) | **along the way** – **from babies to toddlers to adolescents to beach umbrellas, to old blokes and young sheilas alike,**[b] |
| and then | | (the huge waves) | **for the open sea again,** |
| | | (the huge waves) | **before it** |
| and | | (the huge waves) | **in the process.** |

[a] The ellipsis arguably positions *another* as both unmarked Theme and minimal New (with ***noth*** as the tonic syllable).

[b] As indicated by the dash, there are actually two tone groups for this clause, *and grabbed everything they could along the way* and *from babies to toddlers to adolescents to beach umbrellas, to old blokes and young sheilas alike*; we've accordingly recognised two segments of minimal New.

At this point we need to qualify the picture of information flow introduced above, which was based on unmarked choices for Theme and New. Bringing marked choices into the picture means that we shift in a sense from discourse continuity to discontinuity – i.e. scaffolding changes in a text's method of development and local contrasts in its news.

First, Marked Theme. In declarative clauses, Marked Theme is the term used to refer to ideational meaning coming before the Subject. *With a roar like a Bondi tram running amok* is thus a Marked Theme in the first clause of the tables above. The function of Marked Theme is to shift our gaze on the field. In FitzSimons' text this Marked Theme signals a shift from the anchor of the preceding phase (whose ideational hub was the people on the beach) to a new phase in which the waves which are breaking on the beach anchor our gaze on the field.

Marked New is much less relevant to written than spoken modes, but we'll introduce it here to fill out our account of information flow. Marked New is realised by means of a tonic syllable that is not the final salient syllable in its tone group. Let's return to the intonation examples we used above, but make the second clause non-elliptical. In this case, as analysed below, the tonic syllable of the second tone group would fall naturally on *noth*, since what is news is that yet another wave rolled in. With Marked New, the boundedness of the New is delimited – to just that clause constituent containing the tonic syllable (*another wave* in the second clause below), no more.

/^ and /then a/nother /wave /**hit**//
//^ and /then a/**not**her /wave /hit//

Marked News are often found in dialogue, to correct misunderstandings. In the following exchange, the first speaker's misunderstanding is rectified.

//^ so /no one /**died**//
- // no// **five** /people //died//

In light of its contrastive function, the Marked New in our wave example above might sound more natural if we add an explicit marker of counter-expectancy to the clause (i.e. *yet* below).

//^ and /then yet a/**not**her /wave /hit//

Let's now replay Table 6.1 one more time, setting up columns for Marked Theme, Theme and minimal New functions. The left-hand column involves what are referred to in SFL as textual Themes (for linkers of various kinds preceding the Subject). Both Marked Themes and Themes are referred to as topical Themes (realising ideational meaning). Interpersonal Themes are also possible (for comment, vocation, modality and mood functions before the Subject) but are not used in this phase of the Bondi Beach text.[7]

As we have been doing all along, we've included implicit and elliptical Themes in our table. In doing so we are reflecting a general trend across languages, more widely deployed in some languages than in others – namely that of establishing a thematic orientation to a field and then sustaining it via implicit and elliptical unmarked Themes rather than through nominal group repetition.

---

[7] FitzSimons uses just one interpersonal Theme in his article, the sigh initiating *Ah, but those 35,000 Sydneysiders who were lying in those very spots on the afternoon of February 6, 1938, surely felt equally at peace*; for Halliday and Matthiessen (2014), the category of interpersonal Themes covers a range of interpersonal functions, including Vocatives, Expletives, Comment Adjuncts and Modal Adjuncts.

## 6.2 English Information Flow

The implicit and ellipsed Themes have been included in parentheses in the tables, as a reminder about how our gaze on the field is being sustained. English is less implicit and elliptical than many languages in this respect – because unmarked Theme is conflated with its Subject function and English relies on its Subject and Finite functions to distinguish mood types (as seen in Chapter 4).

Note that for English Table 6.4 reflects the unmarked sequential complementarity of unmarked Theme and unmarked New, namely Theme early in the clause and New late. This complementarity is reinforced for Themes in

Table 6.4 *Marked Theme, Theme and minimal New in the 'waves attack' phase of the Bondi Beach text*

| linker | Marked Theme | Theme | minimal New |
|---|---|---|---|
| | With a roar like a Bondi tram running **amok**,[a] | an enormous wave | **the thousands in the surf,** |
| | | (the thousands in the surf) | **those many standing on the large sandbank just out from the shore** |
| | | – (an enormous wave) | over |
| as | | it | went |
| And then | | another wave | **hit,** |
| and then | | a ... | **... nother**[b] |
| | | The huge waves, | **just like that,**[c] **further and further up the beach** |
| and | | (the huge waves) | **along the way**[d] **– from babies to toddlers to adolescents to beach umbrellas, to old blokes and young sheilas alike,** |
| and then | | (the huge waves) | **for the open sea again,** |
| | | (the huge waves) | **before it** |
| and | | (the huge waves) | **in the process.** |

[a] As indicated by the comma, this marked Theme would be spoken on its own tone group, and thus include amok as minimal New.

[b] *Another* is both Theme and New in this elliptical clause, so listed in both columns.

[c] The commas indicate that there are two pieces of News here (i.e. two tone groups), **just like that** and **further and further up the beach**; so more than one clause constituent is treated as minimal New (this a further example of marked tonality, with one clause but two tone groups).

[d] The dash indicates that there are two pieces of news here (i.e. two tone groups), **along the way** and **from babies to toddlers to adolescents to beach umbrellas, to old blokes and young sheilas alike**; so more than one clause constituent is treated as minimal New (another example of marked tonality – i.e. non-coalescence of clause and tone group wave-lengths).

general, since textual Themes, interpersonal Themes and Marked Themes are all identifiable as realised before the Subject.

In some SFL accounts of Theme, an unmarked Theme function is not recognised after a Marked Theme function (e.g. Halliday and Matthiessen, 2014). In such analyses the basic rule is to analyse Theme up to and including the first topical Theme and stop. However, since Marked Themes and unmarked Themes have different discourse functions, the former shifting our gaze on the field and the latter establishing and sustaining it, we allow here for both a Marked Theme and an unmarked Theme in the same clause (following Martin and Rose, 2007).

At this point we are going to push upwards in our discussion to consider longer wavelengths of information flow. This means making room for higher-level Theme function, called Hyper-Theme, which foreshadows a phase of discourse about to unfold; and it also means making room for a higher-level New function, called Hyper-New, which consolidates and perhaps interprets what has gone before (Table 6.5). In traditional composition studies in the English-speaking world, Hyper-Themes are referred to as 'topic sentences'. The SFL term is preferred here, to make it clear that we are dealing with information flow one wavelength up from the shorter wavelength coalescing clause with tone group. In many texts, though not below, the Hyper-Theme

Table 6.5 *Two wavelengths of periodicity in the 'wave attack' phase of the Bondi Beach text*

| Hyper-Theme | | | |
|---|---|---|---|
| At three o'clock there was still not the slightest clue that this afternoon would forever be known as "Black Sunday" in the annals of Sydney. Then it happened. ⇒ | | | |
| linker | Marked Theme | Theme | minimal New (in bold) |
|  | With a roar like [[a Bondi tram running amok]] | an enormous wave | **the thousands in the surf,** |
|  |  | (the thousands in the surf) | **those many [[standing on the large sandbank just out from the shore]]** |
|  |  | – (an enormous wave) | **over** |
| as |  | it | **went** |
| And then |  | another wave | **hit,** |
| and then |  | a … | **… nother** |
|  |  | The huge waves, | **just like that, further and further up the beach** |
| and |  | (the huge waves) | **along the way – from babies to toddlers to adolescents to beach umbrellas, to old blokes and young sheilas alike,** |

## 6.2 English Information Flow

Table 6.5 (*Cont.*)

| and then | | (the huge waves) | **for the open sea again,** |
| --- | --- | --- | --- |
| | | (the huge waves) | **before it** |
| and | | (the huge waves) | **off the sandbank and into the deep channel next to it in the process.** |
| ⇐ In no more than 20 seconds, that peaceful scene had been tragically transformed into utter chaos. Now, the boiling surf, with yet more large waves continuing to roll over, was filled with distressed folk waving for help. | | | |
| | | | **Hyper-New** |

specifically predicts the pattern of unmarked Themes in a phase of discourse (i.e. its method of development). The Hyper-New, on the other hand, aggregates the point of a phase. The Hyper-New is typically more than a summary; in many texts it evaluates the significance of the ideation expanded as New (for FitzSimons the chaos and distress resulting from the waves' incursion).

Let's now examine how the text deals with the rest of what went on that day (Table 6.6). The next phase recounts the lifesaver's rescue. It has a Hyper-Theme introducing its method of development, and a Marked Theme reinforcing its shift of gaze. For this analysis we are following the practice of treating dependent clauses (here *ignoring their own possible peril*) positioned before the clause they depend on as Marked Themes. This practice is based on the similarity in discourse function of clauses of this type and Marked Themes realised by Circumstances of various kinds; both the dependent clauses and the Circumstances shift our gaze on the field. The method of development of this phase is the lifesavers; its point is what they accomplished.

Table 6.6 *Information flow in the 'rescue' phase of the Bondi Beach text*

| **Hyper-Theme** | | | |
| --- | --- | --- | --- |
| In their long and glorious history, this still stands as the finest hour of the Australian lifesaving movement. ⇒ | | | |
| linker | **Marked Theme** | **Theme** | **minimal New** (in bold) |
| For, | ignoring their own possible **peril**,[a] | the Bondi boys | now charged **into the surf,** |
| | | some | attached **to one of the seven reels available** |
| | | some | relying **only on their own strength.** |
| | As one, | they | began pulling the people **out.** |

[a] Once again we have a Marked Theme, but it would be spoken as a distinct tone group and thus can be analysed as including its own minimal New (in bold).

The next phase begins with a Marked Theme shifting our gaze on shore. Its pattern of Themes is less repetitive than that in the previous two phases. It anchors our gaze on entities involved once the water was cleared. And the point of this phase is how these entities were affected and what they did.

The final phase we will consider in this chapter has a Hyper-Theme announcing that it was time to take stock (Table 6.8). Its pattern of Themes fulfils this announcement by tallying up the numbers of people involved in the rescue; its point is how they fared. The textual Theme *finally*, initiating this phase, signals that FitzSimons' account of what happened is drawing to a close.

As a final comment on these phases, note that each Hyper-Theme itself begins with a Marked Theme (*at three o'clock, in their long and glorious history* and *just half an hour after the waves hit*). This reinforces their role in moving the text along from one phase to the next.

Table 6.7 *Information flow in the 'medical response' phase of the Bondi Beach text*

| linkers | Marked Theme | Theme | minimal New (in bold) |
|---|---|---|---|
|  | On the shore | many survivors | were resuscitated |
| as |  | the Bondi clubhouse | was turned **into a kind of emergency clearing house**, |
| and |  | ambulances from all over Sydney town | descended |
| and |  | (ambulances from all over Sydney town) | carried the victims **away**. |

Table 6.8 *Information flow in the 'taking stock' phase of the Bondi Beach text*

| Hyper-Theme | | | |
|---|---|---|---|
| Finally, just half an hour after the waves hit, the water was cleared of bobbing heads and waving arms, and it was time to take stock: ⇒ | | | |
| linker | Marked Theme | Theme | minimal **New** (in bold) |
|  |  | 250 people | had needed the lifesavers to pull them **out**, |
| of whom* |  | 210 (of whom) | were **OK** |
| once |  | (210) | back **on land**. |
|  |  | thirty-five | needed **mouth to mouth** |
| in order to |  | (thirty-five) | to be restored **to consciousness**, |
| while |  | five people | **perished**. |

* The nominal group Qualifier *of whom* is treated as a textual Theme because it links the non-restrictive relative clause *of whom 210 were OK once back on land* to the preceding clause on which it depends. It is not a Marked Theme because it has to precede part of the Subject for these structural reasons, not because it is shifting our gaze in terms of information flow; but it is simultaneously a topical Theme because it is part of the Participant *210 (of whom)*.

## 6.2 English Information Flow

The information flow resources we have introduced above are formalised as system networks below. We are proposing two theme systems. The top system, called THEME, first allows for the possibility of clauses fixing our gaze on the field by having an unmarked Theme or not. If not, we have Theme-less clauses (for example, meteorological clauses such as *it's snowing*). The next option allows for unmarked Themes to be explicitly realised as a nominal group (or embedded clause), or implicitly (as is common in non-finite and branching paratactic clauses).

The second system, called MARKED THEME, allows for the possibility of clauses shifting our gaze on the field by having a Marked Theme or not. It then allows for different types of Marked Theme, including non-Subject Participants and Circumstances. Circumstantial Marked Themes tend to scaffold shifts from one phase of discourse to another. Participant Marked Themes, on the other hand, tend to involve localised shifts of meaning, often between adjacent clauses (e.g. *the lifesavers rescued 250 people but **five victims** they couldn't reach in time*). Circumstantial Marked Themes, especially those of time and place, tend to involve more global shifts of meaning – from one phase of a text to another as it unfolds. Spatio-temporal Circumstances are thus separated from others in the network below.

We recognise two THEME systems in Figure 6.3 because unmarked Theme and Marked Theme have different functions. Unmarked Themes sustain our gaze on the field while Marked Themes adjust it.

We are also proposing two information systems (Figure 6.4). The TONICITY system allows for the major pitch movement in a tone group to fall on its final salient syllable or an earlier one. This conditions our interpretation of which clause constituents are presented as New. The TONALITY system first allows for tone groups of the same wavelength as a clause as opposed to cases where they involve longer or shorter wavelengths than a clause (i.e. marked tonality). This conditions our interpretation of the number of New elements per clause (one, more than one or less than one).

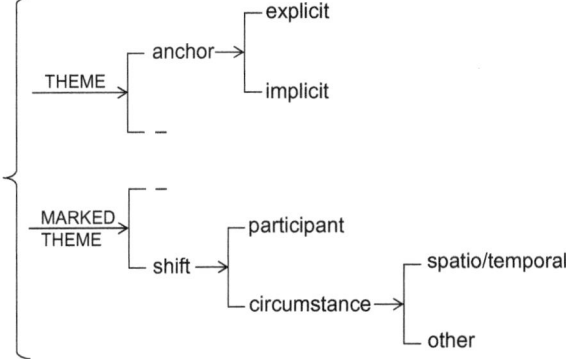

Figure 6.3 English THEME systems (for clauses)

322    Theme

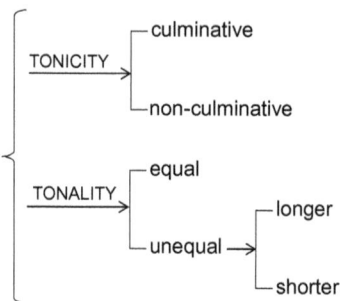

Figure 6.4  English INFORMATION systems (for tone groups)

This has been a very preliminary account of textual meaning in the English clause. We have only considered declarative mood. And we haven't had space to deal with predicated Themes (e.g. *it was the lifesavers who saved the day*) or thematic equatives (e.g. *what they did was charge into the surf*). What we have tried to do is show how patterns of Theme and New can be interpreted from a discourse perspective, as realising the method of development and the point of a phase of discourse. Crucially, it is the pattern of Themes and the pattern of News that matters. We can only make sense of information flow in a clause by interpreting that clause in relation to its co-text. It is in this sense that analysis of Theme and New functions as a kind of bridge from the analysis of lexicogrammar to the analysis of discourse semantics – reminding us that lexicogrammar is there to make meaning, but equally importantly that the fundamental unit of meaning in any language is the text, not the tone group or the clause.

## 6.3  Spanish Information Flow

In terms of mode, the Ola Maldita text is basically monologic, although some of the interaction among survivors is quoted directly (initiating moves only, no dialogue). And the text is relatively context independent, making no intermodal reference to the photos of the Pinita, key survivors, Orrego Island and damage arising from the disaster which were published with the article. The main reflective mode shift takes place when the journalist, Juan Andrés Guzmán, reviews the choices faced by the Chileans affected on that fateful day – a few sentences introducing the looting of Constitución, in a more abstract generalising mode than his recounting of what went on elsewhere.

In terms of graphology, the feature is composed of a kicker and seven sections (as outlined in Table 6.9). From the point of view of genre, it's a macro-genre (Martin, 2002; Zappavigna and Martin, 2018) consisting of nine major story genres (Martin and Rose, 2008), three of them unfolding across more than one section.

6.3 Spanish Information Flow

Table 6.9 *The macro-generic structure of the Ola Maldita text*

| **La ola maldita** (kicker)<br>'The hellish wave' | Introduction to Guzman's report |
|---|---|
| [untitled] | Captain Ibarra and crew survive the tsunami at sea |
| **Sin permiso**<br>'Without permission' | Four friends are stranded on Orrego Island |
| **El canto de los niños**<br>'The childrens' singing' | Families and the four friends struggle with rising water on the island |
| **La ola**<br>'The wave' | The wave sweeps across the island |
| **No hay lugar para los débiles**<br>'There is no place for the weak' | The fate of those left behind in Constitución when their families flee to the hills |
| **El saqueo**<br>'The looting' | The looting of Constitución after the tsunami and the survival of the four friends |
| **El capitán regresa**<br>'The captain returns' | Captain Ibarra and crew return to Constitución |

We will concentrate on the *No hay lugar para los débiles* 'There is no place for the weak' section, the stories of Hugo Barrera and Cristián Valladares in particular. Both stories open with a Hyper-Theme establishing their angle on the field – Barrera's escape from the river and Valladares' rescue of an old man respectively.

Hugo Barrera salió del río más o menos cuando la Presidenta negaba el maremoto. ⇒
'Hugo Barrera got out of the river more or less when the President was dismissing the tidal wave. ⇒'

Otros ancianos, en cambio, vieron cómo sus familias escapaban y los dejaban botados. El sargento de la Armada, Cristián Valladares, se encontró con uno de ellos cuando intentaba llegar a la Capitanía de Puerto para ayudar. ⇒
'Other old people, however, saw how their families escaped and left them abandoned. Navy Sergeant, Cristián Valladares, met one of them when he tried to reach the Harbour Command to help. ⇒'

The 'There is no place for the weak' section begins with a review of some further misleading announcements made by authorities, reassuring Chileans that there had not been and would not be a tsunami. It then picks up the narrative of Hugo Barrera, which in fact began in the previous section and ended there with him being swept off the tree he was clinging to by the huge wave. Then the Resolution of this Complication unfolds. The text is set out below in ranking clauses (i.e. clauses that are not embedded as Participants in other clauses); any embedded clauses are placed in double square brackets ('[[…]]'). For reasons we're going to explain below, the finite verbal groups in these clauses are formatted in italics; and any nominal groups showing agreement relations in PERSON and NUMBER with a finite verbal group are formatted in bold (as is the affixation registering this agreement).

**Hugo Barrera** *salió* del río
'**Hugo Barrera** *got out* of the river'

más o menos cuando **la Presidenta** *negaba* el maremoto.
'more or less when **the President** *was dismissing* the tidal wave'

*Notó* desesperado
'(*He*) *noted* in desperation'

que **la resaca** *lo llevaba* hacia el mar
'that **the undertow** *was taking him* towards the sea'

y *nadó* con todas sus fuerzas
'and (*he*) *swam* with all his strength'

para no terminar en el océano.
'in order not to end up in the ocean.'

*Alcanzó* la orilla con su último aliento
'(*He*) *reached* the bank with his last breath'

y temblando de frío y de miedo,
'and trembling from cold and fear'

*caminó* [[por lo que quedaba de la costanera de Constitución]]
'(*he*) *walked* along [[what remained of the waterfront of Constitución]]'

buscando una edificación alta,
'looking for a high building'

pues *estaba* convencido [[de que la tragedia no había terminado]].
'since (*he*) *was* convinced [[that the tragedy had not ended.]]'

*Descubrió* una casa de dos pisos [[donde protegerse]].
'(*He*) *discovered* a house with two floors [[(where) to protect himself]].'

*Se metió* en ella
'(*He*) *went in* it'

gritando "¡Aló!"
shouting "Hello!"

y *subió* al segundo piso.
'and *went up* to the second floor.'

*Encontró* ahí a una señora [[que con toda calma *esperaba* lo que el destino le ofreciera]].
'There (*he*) *found* a lady [[who with complete calm *was waiting* for what fate would offer her.]]'

*Se llamaba* **Blanca**.
'(*She*) *was called* Blanca.'

*Tenía* unos 70 años
'(*She*) *was* about 70 years old'

### 6.3 Spanish Information Flow

y *necesitaba* muletas
'and *(she) needed* crutches'

para moverse.
'to move.'

*No intentó huir.*
'*(She) didn't try to flee.*'

Estoicamente *resistió* el sismo
'Stoically *(she) waited out* the earthquake

y luego *sintió* el mar [[entrando en su casa y escarbando en el piso de abajo]].
and later *(she) sensed* the sea [[entering her house and scratching around on the floor below]].'

**Blanca** *vivía* sola
'**Blanca** *lived* alone'

y *había* aceptado [[morir sola]].
and *(she) was resigned* [[to dying alone]].'

The reason we have highlighted the finite verbal groups in this text is that they realise the Spanish Predicator function – and as we explained in Chapter 4, it is this function which makes a Spanish clause negotiable. The key aspect of this negotiability we need to highlight here is the specification of PERSON and NUMBER in verbal group morphology. This not only contributes to making a clause arguable but, in addition, draws attention to one clause Participant that has special significance as far as textual meaning is concerned. The textual significance of this Participant is developed below.

As we can see the Spanish has just five nominal groups that are co-referential with the inflectional morphology in the Predicator (for details see Chapter 3, Section 3.3). For the remainder of this chapter, we will refer to these simply as co-referential nominal groups.[8] Three occur in the first four clauses of the Resolution (repeated below), as Hugo Barrera is reintroduced, the President's dismissal of the tsunami is reiterated and the undertow dragging him back to sea is noted (*Hugo Barrera, la Presidenta* 'the President', *la resaca* 'the undertow').

**Hugo Barrera** *salió* del río
'**Hugo Barrera** *got out* of the river'

más o menos cuando **la Presidenta** *negaba* el maremoto.
'more or less when **the President** *was dismissing* the tidal wave.'

---

[8] We are simplifying here, since P2 and P3 Participants realised at clause rank by nominal groups can also be co-referential – to clitics in a verbal group. What matters for this chapter is co-referentiality with the Finite function (i.e. with the verbal group PERSON and NUMBER morphology presented in Chapter 4).

*Notó* desesperado
'(*He*) *noted* in desperation'

que **la resaca** *lo llevaba* hacia el mar
'that **the undertow** *was taking him* towards the sea'

The other co-referential nominal groups refer to Blanca, the lady Hugo meets in the house in which he sought refuge once he'd managed to swim to the bank of the river and climb out.

*Se llamaba* **Blanca**.
'(*She*) *was called* **Blanca**.'

**Blanca** *vivía* sola
'**Blanca** *lived* alone'

In the other finite ranking clauses, the Predicator realises the potentially co-referential Participant on its own. Four of the five co-referential nominal groups precede the Predicator (*Hugo Barrera, la Presidenta* 'the President', *la resaca* 'the undertow' and the second mention of *Blanca*) and one follows (the introduction of *Blanca*). In two clauses there is additional ideational information before the Predicator (the Circumstance of Manner, *estoicamente* 'stoically', and the Circumstance of Location, *luego* 'later'; underlined below).

Estoicamente *resistió* el sismo
'Stoically (*she*) *waited out* the earthquake'

y luego *sintió* el mar [[entrando en su casa y escarbando en el piso de abajo]].
'and later (*she*) *sensed* the sea [[entering her house and scratching around on the floor below]].'

This pattern is presented in Table 6.10, including a column for linking material at the front of the clause. For the sake of completeness, we also include in the Predicator column non-finite verbal groups (*no terminar, temblando, buscando, gritando* and *moverse*). Unlike finite verbal groups they do not realise MOOD and do not distinguish PERSON and NUMBER, and so they do not enter into agreement relations with nominal groups. The nominal groups they would have agreed with had they been finite are, however, readily 'recoverable' from the co-text – as readily one might argue as any of the 'recoverable' nominal groups in clauses with finite verbal groups. We are accordingly reluctant to exclude them from our consideration of information flow in Spanish at this time.[9]

---

[9] Halliday and Matthiessen (2014, p. 127) recognise a topical Theme in non-finite English clauses when they include a Subject (e.g. *with **all the doors** being locked*), but not when there is no Subject. We are not prepared at this time to argue from the perspective of a text's information flow that comparable Spanish clauses lack topical Themes.

## 6.3 Spanish Information Flow

As Table 6.10 makes clear, Spanish deploys relatively few co-referential nominal groups. In addition, like English, nominal groups that might have been co-referential in agnate finite clauses are seldom used in non-finite ones (Table 6.11).

Table 6.10 *Information flow in the 'Barrera escape' phase of the Ola Maldita text*

| linker | pre-Predicator ideation | co-referential nominal group | Predicator | co-referential nominal group |
|---|---|---|---|---|
|  |  | **Hugo Barrera** | sal**ió** |  |
| cuando |  | **la Presidenta** | neg**aba** |  |
|  |  |  | Not**ó** |  |
| que |  | **la resaca** | lo llev**aba** |  |
| y |  |  | nad**ó** |  |
| para |  |  | no terminar |  |
|  |  |  | Alcanz**ó** |  |
| y |  |  | tembl**ando** |  |
|  |  |  | camin**ó** |  |
|  |  |  | busc**ando** |  |
| pues |  |  | est**aba** |  |
|  |  |  | Descubri**ó** |  |
|  |  |  | Se meti**ó** |  |
|  |  |  | grit**ando** |  |
| y |  |  | subi**ó** |  |
|  |  |  | Encontr**ó** |  |
|  |  |  | Se llam**aba** | **Blanca**[a] |
|  |  |  | Ten**ía** |  |
| y |  |  | necesit**aba** |  |
| para |  |  | moverse |  |
|  |  |  | No intentó huir |  |
|  | Estoicamente |  | resist**ió** |  |
| y | luego |  | sint**ió** |  |
|  |  | **Blanca** | viv**ía** |  |
| y |  |  | había aceptado |  |

[a] The English translation ('She was called Blanca') is misleading here; the nominal group Blanca is co-referential with the person selection in the verb morphology, in a verbal group selecting for recessive:ergative voice, that is, where the voice clitic se is realising that selection (see Quiroz, 2013, and also Chapter 3 on the verbal group).

And again, as for English Subjects, co-referential nominal groups are not used in continuing clauses – in a branching paratactic clause complex which has a co-referential nominal group in its initiating clause (such as the example from our text in Table 6.12).

Table 6.11 *Absence of co-referential nominal groups in non-finite clauses*

| linker | pre-Predicator ideation | 'recoverable' nominal group | Predicator |
|---|---|---|---|
| *para* 'in order to' | | | *no terminar* 'not to end up'* |
| *y* 'and' | | | *temblando* 'trembling' |
| | | | *buscando* 'looking for' |
| | | | *gritando* 'shouting' |
| *para* 'in order to' | | | *moverse* 'to move' |

* Group-by-group translations (rather than clause by clause translations) are provided in table columns throughout.

Table 6.12 *Absence of co-referential nominal group in the continuing clause of a branching paratactic clause complex*

| linker | pre-Predicator ideation | co-referential nominal group | Predicator | co-referential nominal group |
|---|---|---|---|---|
| | | **Blanca** | *vivía* 'lived' | |
| *y* 'and' | | | *había aceptado* 'had accepted' | |

Unlike English, Spanish often does not deploy a co-referential nominal group in clause complex initial clauses (such as those in tabled below in Table 6.13).

Table 6.13 *Absence of co-referential nominal groups in clause complex initial clause*

| linker | pre-Predicator ideation | co-referential nominal group | Predicator | co-referential nominal group |
|---|---|---|---|---|
| | | | *notó* 'noted' | |
| | | | *alcanzó* 'reached' | |
| | | | *descubrió* 'discovered' | |

### 6.3 Spanish Information Flow

Table 6.13 (*Cont.*)

| linker | pre-Predicator ideation | co-referential nominal group | Predicator | co-referential nominal group |
|---|---|---|---|---|
| | | | *se metió* 'went in' | |
| | | | *encontró* 'met' | |
| | | | *tenía* 'had' | |
| | | | *no intentó huir* 'didn't try to flee' | |

The overall trend is a familiar one for languages around the world – namely to anchor a phase of text in its field and sustain that orientation to the field as implicitly as practicable until that gaze needs to be reinforced or changed. In these terms the Resolution of the Barrera narrative reintroduces Hugo in a co-referential nominal group in its initial clause (picking up on the Complication of the narrative in the preceding section); but it doesn't realise him again as a co-referential nominal group thereafter. The spots where this might have been done are noted as *(Barrera)* in Table 6.14.[10]

Table 6.14 *Absence of co-referential nominal groups referring to Barrera*

| linker | pre-Predicator ideation | co-referential nominal group | Predicator | co-referential nominal group |
|---|---|---|---|---|
| | | **Hugo Barrera** | *salió* 'went out' | |
| *cuando* 'when' | | **la Presidenta** | *negaba* 'was dismissing' | |
| | | (Barrera) | *Notó* 'noted' | |
| *que* 'that' | | **la resaca** | *lo llevaba* 'was taking him' | |
| *y* 'and' | | (Barrera) | *nadó* 'swam' | |
| *para* 'in order to' | | (Barrera) | *no terminar\** 'not to end up' | |
| | | (Barrera) | *Alcanzó* 'reached' | |
| *y* 'and' | | (Barrera) | *temblando* 'trembling' | |

---

[10] Once again, for the sake of completeness, we include non-finite clauses in our analysis.

Table 6.14 *(Cont.)*

| linker | pre-Predicator ideation | co-referential nominal group | Predicator | co-referential nominal group |
|---|---|---|---|---|
| | | (Barrera) | *caminó* 'walked along' | |
| | | (Barrera) | *buscando* 'looking for' | |
| *pues* 'since' | | (Barrera) | *estaba* 'was' | |
| | | (Barrera) | *Descubrió* 'discovered' | |
| | | (Barrera) | *Se metió* 'went in' | |
| | | (Barrera) | *gritando* 'shouting' | |
| *y* 'and' | | (Barrera) | *subió* 'went up' | |
| | | (Barrera) | *Encontró* 'found' | |

* Non-finite verbal groups do not realise PERSON or NUMBER features; the co-referential nominal group in such clauses has to be inferred from a corresponding finite clause, a strategy we follow in this chapter.

Similarly, Blanca is introduced as a co-referential nominal group, and referred to in this way just once thereafter; in the Table 6.15 (*Blanca*) notes the spots where she might have been realised as a co-referential nominal group.[11]

In light of these patterns, we're now in a position to suggest that the Participant potentially realised as a nominal group co-referential with the

Table 6.15 *Absence of co-referential nominal groups referring to Blanca*

| linker | pre-Predicator ideation | co-referential nominal group | Predicator | co-referential nominal group |
|---|---|---|---|---|
| | | | *Se llamaba* 'was called' | *Blanca* |
| | | (Blanca) | *Tenía* 'had' | |
| *y* 'and' | | (Blanca) | *necesitaba* 'needed' | |
| *para* 'in order to' | | (Blanca) | *moverse* 'to move' | |
| | | (Blanca) | *No intentó huir* 'didn't try to flee' | |

[11] Once again, for the sake of completeness, we include non-finite clauses in our analysis.

6.3 Spanish Information Flow       331

Table 6.15 (*Cont.*)

| linker | pre-Predicator ideation | co-referential nominal group | Predicator | co-referential nominal group |
|---|---|---|---|---|
| | *Estoicamente* 'stoically' | (Blanca) | *resistió* 'waited out' | |
| *y* 'and' | *luego* 'later' | (Blanca) | *sintió* 'sensed' | |
| | | Blanca | *vivía* 'lived' | |
| *y* 'and' | | (Blanca) | *había aceptado* 'had accepted' | |

PERSON and NUMBER morphology of the Spanish Predicator functions as unmarked Theme in Spanish. And by way of maintaining our orientation to the field (Hugo, then Blanca above), an unmarked Theme is usually left implicit (i.e. the potential to be realised by a nominal group is usually not taken up). Let's explore this now in the next phase of the section, an exemplum dealing with Sergeant Cristián Valladares's experiences on the day (co-referential nominal groups and the verb affixation showing NUMBER and PERSON distinctions are in bold from this point on in this section).

**Otros ancianos**, en cambio, **vieron** [[cómo sus familias escapaban y los dejaban botados]].
'**Other old people**, however, *saw* how their families escaped and left them abandoned.'

**El sargento de la Armada, Cristián Valladares**, *se encontró* con uno de ellos
'**Navy Sergeant Cristián Valladares** *encountered* one of them'

cuando *intentaba llegar* a la Capitanía de Puerto
'when (*he*) *tried* to reach the Harbour Command

para ayudar.
'to help.'

*Eran* **las seis de la mañana**,
'It *was* **six in the morning**,'

ya *estaba clareando*.
'(and) (*it*) *was* already clearing' (≈ it was already growing light)

Mientras *se acercaba* a la costa
'While (*he*) *was approaching* the coast'

*oyó* los gritos de la isla Orrego
'(*he*) *heard* the cries from Orrego island'

y *se preguntó*
'and (*he*) *wondered*'

si *habría* un bote [[con qué ir a buscar a la gente]].
'if *there were* a boat [[with which to go to pick up the people]].'

Entonces *vio* [[cómo el río se recogía y se formaba otra ola gigantesca]].
'Then (*he*) *saw* [[how the river receded and formed another giant wave]].'

Mientras *huía*
'While (*he*) *was escaping*'

*vio* [[que esa ola tapaba los árboles]],
'(*he*) *saw* [[that wave cover the trees]],'

por lo que *calcula*
'so *(he) estimates*'

que *tendría* unos 10 metros.
'that *(it) would be* about 10 meters high.'

*Debe haber sido* la tercera o cuarta gran ola [[que azotó Constitución]].
'*(It) must have been* the third or fourth biggest wave [[that hit Constitución]].'

En su retirada, **el sargento Valladares** *vio* [[que una mujer pedía ayuda]].
'In his retreat **Sergeant Valladares** *saw* [[a woman asking for help]].'

Al entrar en la casa medio derrumbada,
'On entering the half-disintegrating house,'

*encontró* a un anciano en silla de ruedas [[que los miraba con angustia]].
'(*he*) *encountered* an old man in a wheel chair [[that was watching them in anguish]].'

**Sus familiares** *estaban* en los cerros.
'**His relatives** *were* in the hills.'

**La señora [[que pedía auxilio]]** *era* la mujer [[que lo cuidaba]].
'**The lady [[asking for help]]** *was* the woman [[who looked after him]].'

**Ella** *vivía* en otro lugar
'**She** *lived* in another place'

y *corrió a ver* al anciano
and (*she*) *ran* to check on the old man'

y *lo encontró* solo.
'and (*she*) *found him* alone.'

*Estaba* mojado y gemía de miedo.
'(*He*) *was* wet and (he) was moaning from fear.'

**El sargento** *lo sacó* de ahí
'**The sergeant** *took him out* from there'

y *lo llevó* a la casa de la mujer.
'and (*he*) *left him* at the woman's house.'

The pattern of Themes in this text is presented in Table 6.16. There are seven explicit Themes (*otros ancianos* 'other old people', *El sargento de la Armada, Cristián Valladares* 'Navy Sergeant Cristián Valladares', *el sargento Valladares* 'Sergeant Valladares', *sus familiares* 'his relatives', *La señora que pedía auxilio* 'the woman asking for help', *ella* 'she' and *el sargento* 'the sergeant'). Unlike Barrera, who was never realised explicitly as a nominal group once introduced, Sergeant Valladares is reintroduced twice in the story – once to return our gaze to him following consideration of the size of the wave, and once to return our gaze following consideration of the old man he rescued and his carer. Elsewhere our gaze is fixed on the field through implicit Themes, both within and between clause complexes (i.e. within and between sentences).

There are no explicit Themes following the Predicator in this story (like *Blanca* in *se llamaba Blanca* 'she was called Blanca' above)[12] and just one piece of non-co-referential ideation in pre-Predicator position (*en su retirada* 'in his retreat').[13]

For three of the clauses we have not recognised a Theme. The first is a time clause, with agreement between the Predicator (*eran* 'was') and a co-referential nominal group (*las seis* 'six'); cf. singular *era la una* 'it was one o'clock').

*Eran* **las seis** de la mañana,
'It *was* **six** in the morning,'

The second is a meteorological clause, with a Predicator realising modal responsibility (*estaba clareando* 'was growing light'); but from an ideational perspective, it is assigning responsibility to no entity in particular. We can't have a Participant realised by a co-referential nominal group in clauses of this kind.

ya *estaba clareando*.
'(and) *was* already *growing* light.'

The third is what is traditionally viewed as an existential clause, with agreement assigning modal responsibility[14] to the Existent.

si *habría* **un bote [[con qué ir a buscar a la gente]].**
'if there *were* **a boat with which to go to pick up the people**'.

---

[12] We will deal with the *Eran las seis de la mañana* 'it was six in the morning' clause below, arguing that it does not have a Theme.
[13] Once again, for the sake of completeness, we include non-finite clauses in our analysis.
[14] Traditionally, Spanish grammarians have argued that existential clauses with *hay* are impersonal and that there should therefore be no agreement between the Process and the Existent. Their 'subjectless' nature is backed up by the fact that the Existent in these clauses may be tracked with the neuter accusative clitic *lo*. There is, however, a clear example of agreement in our text: *ya no habían embarcaciones* 'there weren't any boats any longer'.

Table 6.16 *Theme in the 'Valladares to the rescue' phase of the Ola Maldita text*

| linker | pre-Predicator ideation | nominal group Theme | Predicator | nominal group Theme |
|---|---|---|---|---|
| | | ***Otros ancianos*** 'other old people' | *vieron* 'saw' | |
| | | ***... Cristián Valladares*** | *se encontró* 'encountered' | |
| *cuando* 'when' | | (Valladares) | *intent**aba** llegar* 'tried to return' | |
| *para* 'in order to' | | (Valladares) | *ayudar* 'to help' | |
| | | - | *Eran* 'were' | |
| | | - | *est**aba** clareando* 'was clearing' | |
| *mientras* 'while' | | (Valladares) | *se acerc**aba*** 'was approaching' | |
| | | (Valladares) | *oyó* 'heard' | |
| *y* 'and' | | (Valladares) | *se preguntó* 'asked himself' | |
| *si* 'if' | | - | *habría* 'there were' | |
| *entonces* 'then' | | (Valladares) | *vio* 'saw' | |
| *mientras* 'while' | | (Valladares) | *huía* 'was escaping' | |
| | | (Valladares) | *vio* 'saw' | |
| *por lo que* 'so that' | | (Valladares) | *calcula* 'estimates' | |
| *que* 'that' | | (esa ola) 'that wave' | *tendría* 'would be' | |
| | | (esa ola) 'that wave' | *Debe haber sido* 'must have been' | |
| | *en su retirada* 'in his retreat' | *el sargento Valladares* 'sergeant Valladares' | *vio* 'saw' | |
| *al* 'on' | | (Valladares) | *entrar* 'to enter' | |
| | | (Valladares) | *encontró* 'encountered' | |
| | | ***Sus familiares*** 'his family' | *estaban* 'were' | |
| | | ***La señora ...*** 'the lady ...' | *era* 'was' | |

6.3 Spanish Information Flow            335

Table 6.16 *(Cont.)*

| linker | pre-Predicator ideation | nominal group Theme | Predicator | nominal group Theme |
|---|---|---|---|---|
| | | ***Ella***<br>'she' | *vivía*<br>'lived' | |
| *y*<br>'and' | | (la señora)<br>'the lady' | *corrió*<br>'ran' | |
| *y*<br>'and' | | (la señora)<br>'the lady' | *lo encontró*<br>'found him' | |
| | | (el anciano)<br>'the old man' | *Estaba*<br>'was' | |
| | | ***El sargento***<br>'the sergeant' | *lo sacó*<br>'took him out' | |
| *y*<br>'and' | | (Valladares) | *lo llevó*<br>'took him' | |

Our reasoning for not recognising a Theme in these clauses is partly grammatical, based on the restricted meaning potential of these clauses as far as information flow is concerned. The co-referential nominal group in these clause types is either necessarily missing or fairly fixed in final position. So these clauses cannot readily adjust information flow by realising Participants in different positions. And a co-referential nominal group has to either be there or not. Unlike the clauses in which we recognise a Theme, there is no explicit Theme vs implicit Theme choice available.

These limitations on the meaning potential of these co-referential nominal groups reflect their discourse semantics. These clauses are not involved in sustaining our gaze on the field. Existential clauses typically initiate an orientation to the field by introducing a new entity, which is thereafter sustained by other clause types. And both time and weather clauses add occasional information about the ambient setting of a phase of discourse; they do not contribute to its overall method of development. We are not going to attempt an exhaustive treatment of Theme-less clauses here; but we would encourage readers to consider clause types carefully as candidates arise,[15] in relation to the grammatical and discourse semantic reasoning just reviewed (and additional reasoning they consider relevant).

We'll now propose the following network for unmarked Theme in Spanish clauses (Figure 6.5). Move from left to right in delicacy, the first system allows

---

[15] Modalised clauses beginning with the verbs *ser* 'be' or *parecer* 'seem' warrant further consideration (e.g. *era imposible que* ... 'it was impossible that ...', *es probable que* ... 'it's probable that ...', *es posible que* ... 'it's possible that ...' in the Ola Maldita text). Their embedded *que* clause agree with the Predicator; but is this enough to argue that they are Theme?

336  Theme

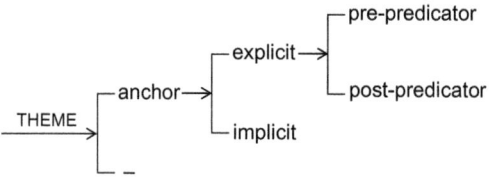

Figure 6.5 Spanish THEME systems (for clauses)

for the possibility of having a Theme or not; the second offers the choice of realising the Theme explicitly as a nominal group, or implicitly (with its ideation recoverable anaphorically from the preceding co-text or exophorically from outside the text); the third system allows for the realisation of an explicit Theme before or after the Predicator (which we distinguish as pre-predication vs post-predication options).

Spanish is sometimes referred to as a 'free word order' language, especially in contrast to English, which is often taken as a canonical 'fixed word order' exemplar (see Greenberg, 1966). As the tables in this chapter show, this dramatically overstates the difference between the two languages as far as information flow is concerned – since the same kinds of meaning are in fact arranged early and late in a clause. More to the point is English's predisposition to realise Theme implicitly within clause complexes but not between, a restraint Spanish does not share (as the many clause complex initial clauses with an implicit Theme tabled above demonstrate). Behind this predisposition is English's dependence on Subject and Finite sequence to realise MOOD, a realisation pattern not deployed in Spanish (as we have outlined in Chapter 4 on MOOD). This means that English more regularly needs to maintain an explicit unmarked Theme in order to also indicate mood by way of its Subject and Finite functions. As Spanish does not have this constraint, it is possible, as allowed for in the system network above, for Theme to be realised after the Predicator in Spanish clauses.[16]

Let's pursue this a little further here by exploring examples of Themes following the Predicator. The first point we need to make is that from the perspective of TRANSITIVITY, several Spanish clause types actually favour the realisation of Theme after the Predicator.

In our Ola Maldita text, for example, when a verbal or mental process projects a clause that follows (i.e. when it projects speech or thought), the Sayer or

---

[16] It is simplistic to suggest that the reason Spanish can realise co-referential nominal groups before or after the Predicator is that it has person and number agreement. Comparable flexibility is found in many languages without such agreement, as we will illustrate in the Chinese section of this chapter.

## 6.3 Spanish Information Flow

Senser is realised before the Predicator (e.g. *los jóvenes* 'the youngsters' below – Sayer and Senser, and PERSON and NUMBER verb morphology are in bold, Predicator in italics).

**Los jóvenes** *decidieron* ver
'**The youngsters** *decided* to see'

si, por alguna casualidad, **su amigo** *había llegado* al hospital.
'if, by any chance, **their friend** *had arrived* at the hospital.'

But when speech or thought is quoted in a preceding clause, the Sayer or Senser (*Jonathan* below) can be realised after the Predicator (and it always is in Old Maldita).

–Ése fue el momento más terrible– *sintetiza* **Jonathan**.
'"That was the most terrible moment," *summarises* **Jonathan**'

A second post-Predicator pattern involves impersonal *se* clauses. A series of such clauses is used in the *La ola* 'The wave' section of our text, foregrounding the silencing of the people swept off the island by the wave. This is not done in terms of what someone in particular could or couldn't hear; there are no Sensers in the clauses below. Rather, an impersonal construal is preferred, which has the effect of realising the Phenomena as a co-referential nominal group. There is no equivalent structure in English, which makes translation awkward. Clauses with a generalised Senser *one* are used below; an alternative translation might offer a passive clause (e.g. 'until the dawn nothing was heard on that island' for the third example). Both translations are somewhat misleading as far as the Spanish 'impersonality' of the option is concerned.

Pero debajo de ellos ya *no se oyó* **otro ruido humano fuera de sus lamentos y los de otras cuatro personas también aferradas a las copas de los árboles**.
'But below them *one couldn't* any *longer* hear **any other human sounds besides their lamentations and those of the other four people also clinging to the tops of the trees**.'

Después de esa ola, en la isla *no se escucharon* **más cantos de niños ni gritos de padres**.
'After that wave, in the island *one didn't hear* **more children's songs or parents' screams**.'

Hasta el amanecer << ... >> en esa isla *no se oyó* **nada**.
'Until the dawn on that island *one didn't hear* **anything**.'

A third post-Predicator pattern which we will simply note in passing here (as it does not occur in the Ola Maldita text) involves impacting mental processes of reaction. In this clause type the Phenomenon is the co-referential nominal group and is regularly realised after the Predicator. The example of this clause type we used in Chapter 5 is repeated below.

| al capitán Ibarra | no le gustó | **la ola** |
|---|---|---|
| Senser | Process | Phenomenon |
| nominal group | verbal group | nominal group |
| to Captain Ibarra | not him please.PST.3SG | the wave |
| 'the wave displeased Captain Ibarra' ||||

The final clause type we will review here favouring the realisation of Theme after the Predicator is attributive clauses with Carriers realised by lexically dense nominal groups or embedded clauses. Two examples from the beginning of the *El saqueo* 'The looting' section of the text are presented below. In clauses of this kind, the Attributes (*difícil* 'difficult' and *incomprensible* 'incomprehensible' below) establish an attitudinal stance towards the experiences which follow.

No *es* difícil [[imaginar la angustia de ese anciano abandonado]].
'It *is* not difficult [[to imagine the anguish of those old abandoned people]].'

Tampoco *es* incomprensible **el miedo [[que deben haber sentido sus parientes]]**.
'Neither is it incomprehensible **the fear [[that their relatives must have felt]]**.'

Modalising attributive clauses could be treated as part of this group.

*Era* imposible [[que nadie los viera]].
'It *was* impossible that [[no-one had seen them]].'

¿Cómo *es* posible [[que toda esa belleza guardara algo tan feroz, tan demencial]]?
'How *is* it possible [[that all that beauty harboured something so ferocious, so nonsensical?]]'

What this review of post-Predicator Theme patterns reveals is that TRANSITIVITY is an important influence on the distribution of information in a Spanish clause. Several ideational clause types favour the realisation of Theme after the Predicator. That said, most of the examples reviewed above would allow for a pre-predication Theme in alternative contexts. And there are several examples in the Ola Maldita text where what would normally be realised before the Predicator follows it. We review these below (excluding the time, weather, existential, projection, *se* recessive, impacting mental and lexically dense Attribute clauses discussed above).

Four examples involve attributive clauses, with post-Predicator Carriers. Each of these features an attitudinally loaded Attribute, amplified by repetition in the first two examples. The *ahí* 'there' in the third example is referring to the island where Mario Quiroz's family died, and the *así* 'like this' in the fourth is referring to Captain Ibarra and his family having to flee another earthquake in 1985; both presuming items are thus attitudinally charged in this context.

*Era* fea **la hueá de ola**, fea
'It *was* ugly **the shit of a wave**, ugly'

*Está* linda **la mar**, muy linda
'it *is* pretty **the sea**, very pretty'

Ahí *estaba* **mi familia**.
'There *was* **my family**'

Bueno, así *es* **Chile**.
'Well, like that *is* **Chile**'

At this point, since information flow is realised through both lexicogrammatical and phonological resources, we need to bring prosodic phonology into the picture and consider the way in which Spanish foregrounds information as news. Unfortunately, there is as yet no systematic SFL informed description of Spanish intonation to draw on here. We're going to stick our necks out and assume that the system is comparable to that of English. Several Spanish studies (e.g. Navarro 1944; Quilis 1988) are consistent with this position. But our analysis needs to be treated with caution, pending the results of the yet to be undertaken investigations we badly need.

Let's assume, then, the following. Spanish intonation organises small wavelengths of information called tone groups, which tend to correspond to the small wavelengths organised by grammar (i.e. clauses). There may be one tone group per clause (the first example below), but also more than one (as reflected in the comma used in the original punctuation of the second example).

// ahí estaba mi familia //
'//there was my family//'

// era fea la hueá de ola // fea //
'//it was ugly the shit of a wave// ugly//'

And there may be more than one clause per tone group *–le ocultó todo eso* 'he hid all that from her' and *para no preocuparla* 'in order not to worry her' below (clause boundaries are marked by '||').

// || Le ocultó todo eso || para no preocuparla || //
'//|| he hid all that from her || in order not to worry her ||//'

Each tone group contains one extra-prominent syllable (the tonic) – typically the final salient syllable (in bold below) and carrying the major pitch movement for the tone group (e.g. falling in the first example below, and rising in the middle clause of the second example – *era tu mujer* 'was she your wife').

// ahí estaba mi fam**i**lia ↓//
'//there was my **fam**ily//'

// **ah** // era tu mu**jer** ↑// le preg**un**tó //
'//**ah**//was she your **wife** //he asked **him**//'

Non-final salient syllables can be made tonic, as context demands (as exemplified by the countering salience on *fea* 'ugly' in the responding move below).

// era **lind**a //
'//was it **pret**ty//'

– // era **fea** la hueá de ola // no **lind**a //
– '//it was **ugly** the shit of a wave// not **pret**ty//'

From a grammatical perspective, the clause constituent containing the tonic syllable will be treated as minimal New. The leftward extent of the New is not determined by the phonology when the tonic falls on the final salient syllable of a tone group; when the tonic falls on a non-final syllable, the clause constituent containing that salient syllable is demarcated as New (e.g. the Attribute *fea* 'ugly' in the initiation response example just above).

The INFORMATION system options are systemicised in Figure 6.6. The TONICITY system allows for culminative tonic syllables on the final salient syllable of a tone group, or non-culminative ones on earlier salient syllables. The TONALITY system allows matching clause and tone group wavelengths of information (equal) or non-matching ones (unequal); the unequal then allows for more than one clause per tone group (longer) or conversely for more than one tone group per clause (shorter).

We're now in a position to propose that in the attributive clauses we are focusing on here, Theme is realised after the Predicator in order to be conflated with New. Our analysis is presented in Table 6.17, setting aside the tone groups that realise less than a clause (i.e. // *fea* // 'ugly', // *muy* **linda** // 'very pretty' and // **buen**o // 'well') as these do not select for Theme. Our examples are simplified below, and then tabled.

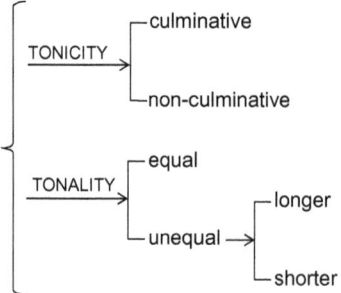

Figure 6.6 Spanish INFORMATION systems (for tone groups)

## 6.3 Spanish Information Flow

*era* fea **la hueá de ola**
'it *was* ugly **the shit of a wave**'

*está* linda **la mar**
'it *is* pretty **the sea**'

ahí *estaba* **mi familia**
'there *was* **my family**'

así *es* **Chile**
'like that *is* **Chile**'

The remaining examples of post-Predicator Theme in Ola Maldita are listed below, in the order in which they occur in the text.

cuando *comenzó* **el terremoto**
'when **the earthquake** *started*'

–¡*Viene* **otra**!–
'**Another** (wave) *is coming*'

Al igual que miles de chilenos, apenas *se detuvo* **el terremoto**
'Like thousands of Chileans, as soon as **the earthquake** *stopped*'

Entonces *empezó* a subir **el agua**
'Then **the water** *started* to rise'

Para entonces ya *había pasado* **media hora del sismo**.
'By then a half hour had already passed since the earthquake'

justo cuando *entraba* **la ola**.
'just when **the wave** *entered*'

cuando *se detuvieron* **las olas**.
'when **the waves** *stopped*'

que a él *lo saquearon* **personas con dinero que venían en grandes camionetas**.
'that **people with money who came in big pick-up trucks** *looted him*'

Table 6.17 *Post-Predicator Themes in attributive relational clauses*

| linker | pre-Predicator ideation | Theme | Predicator | Theme/minimal New |
|---|---|---|---|---|
| | | | *era* 'was' | *la hueá de ola* 'the shit of a wave' |
| | | | *está* 'was' | *la mar* 'the sea' |
| | *ahí* 'there' | | *estaba* 'was' | *mi familia* 'my family' |
| | *así* 'like this' | | *es* 'is' | *Chile* |

que a Gabriel *se lo había llevado* **la ola**
'that **the wave** *had taken* Gabriel'

porque *podía venir* **otra ola**.
'because **another wave** *could come*'

Por ello *le tocó* a él **dar aviso a los bomberos de que dos olas** gigantes **se acercaban a la costa**.
'Because of this it *fell to him* **to warn the firemen that two giant waves were approaching the coast**'

These are analysed for unmarked Theme and unmarked New in Table 6.18.

Table 6.18 *Further examples of post-Predicator Theme*

| linkers | pre-Predicator ideation | Theme | Predicator | Theme/minimal New |
|---|---|---|---|---|
| *cuando* 'when' | | | *comenzó* 'started' | **el terremoto** 'the earthquake' |
| | | | *Viene* 'came' | **otra** 'other' |
| | *Al igual que miles de chilenos* 'like thousands of Chileans' | | *se detuvo* 'stopped' | **el terremoto** 'the earthquake' |
| *Entonces* 'then' | | | *empezó a subir* 'started to rise' | **el agua** 'the water' |
| | *Para entonces* 'by then' | | *había pasado* 'had passed' | **media hora del sismo** 'half an hour from the earthquake' |
| *justo cuando* 'just when' | | | *entraba* 'entered' | **la ola** 'the wave' |
| *cuando* 'when' | | | *se detuvieron* 'stopped' | **las olas** 'the waves' |
| *que* 'that' | *a él* 'him' | | *lo saquearon* 'looted him' | **personas con dinero que venían en grandes camionetas** 'people with money who came in big pick-up trucks' |
| *que* 'that' | *a Gabriel* 'Gabriel' | | *se lo había llevado* 'had taken him' | **la ola** 'the wave' |
| *porque* 'because' | | | *podía venir* 'could come' | **otra ola** 'another wave' |
| | *Por ello* 'because of this' | | *le tocó* 'fell to him' | **dar aviso a los bomberos de que dos olas gigantes se acercaban a la costa** 'to warn the firefighters that two giant waves were approaching the coast' |

## 6.3 Spanish Information Flow

One striking pattern here is that all but one of the realisations of Theme/New refers to the earthquake or the tsunami. The apparent exception is the people with money who came in vans to loot Concepción. But these people have in fact just been characterised metaphorically as a human tsunami/earthquake by the Mayor of Lota, a community about 40 kilometres south of Concepción.

**personas que no habían sufrido daño** *se transformaban* en una nueva ola, en un terremoto humano,
'people who had not suffered harm *transformed* into a **new wave, a human earthquake**'

como *lo llamó* **el alcalde de Lota**,
'as **the mayor of Lota** *named it*'

If we were to extend our analysis from minimal to extended New, to take into account the Predicators in these clauses, we could safely generalise that what is being foregrounded as Theme and New is the comings and goings of the earthquake and tsunami as the text unfolds from one phase of the disaster to another (*comenzó* 'began', *viene* 'is coming', *detuvo* 'stopped', *empezó a subir* 'started to rise', *había pasado* 'had passed', *entraba* 'entered', *detuvieron* 'stopped', *saquearon* 'looted', *había llevado* 'had taken', *podía venir* 'could come', *se acercaban* 'were approaching'). It is quite appropriate that Theme and New are being conflated with one another in relation to momentous phases of activity.

We have now dealt with pre-Predicator and post-Predicator Themes, taking into account the conflation of Theme with New in post-Predicator position. We now turn our attention to non-agreeing Participants (P2 and P3) and Circumstances, which can also be realised before or after the Predicator.

Table 6.18 includes five examples of pre-Predicator ideation (in bold below) in post-Predicator Theme clauses. There are three Circumstances (*al igual que miles de chilenos* 'like thousands of Chileans', *para entonces* 'by then', *por ello* 'because of this') and two Participants (*a él* 'him' and *a Gabriel* 'Gabriel').

**Al igual que miles de chilenos**, apenas se detuvo el terremoto
'**Like thousands of Chileans**, as soon as the earthquake stopped'

**Para entonces** ya había pasado media hora del sismo.
'**By then** a half hour since the earthquake had already passed by'

que **a él** lo saquearon personas con dinero que venían en grandes camionetas.
'that people with money who came in big vans looted **him**'

que **a Gabriel** se lo había llevado la ola
'that **Gabriel** the wave had taken

**Por ello** le tocó a él dar aviso a los bomberos de que dos olas gigantes se acercaban a la costa.

'**Because of this** it fell to him to warn the firemen that two giant waves were approaching the coast.'

To interpret these we'll have to put them back into their co-text and see what is going on (highlighting in bold just these five examples of pre-Predicator ideation). The fifth, *por ello* 'because of this' can arguably be treated as a textual Theme (like other linkers) and so will be set aside here. The first occurs at the beginning of the *Sin permiso* 'without permission' section of the article as it turns its attention from Captain Ibarra and his crew at sea to the people camping on Orrego Island.

Sin permiso
'Without permission'

**Al igual que miles de chilenos**, apenas se detuvo el terremoto[17]
'**Like thousands of Chileans**, as soon as the earthquake stopped'

Nora Jara llamó a su hijo Jonathan Romero
'Nora Jara called her son Jonathan Romero'

para saber cómo estaba.
'to find out how he was'

The second begins the final paragraph of the *El canto de los niños* 'The children's song' section of the article, as it shifts its attention from what was happening on the island as the water twice rose and subsided to the response of the authorities.

**Para entonces** ya había pasado media hora del sismo.
'**By then** a half hour since the earthquake had already passed.'

En todo Chile los servicios de emergencia intentaban restablecer las comunicaciones.
'In all of Chile emergency services tried to re-establish communications.'

El fantasma del maremoto rondaba la mente de muchos chilenos.
'The spectre of a tsunami circled around the mind of many Chileans.'

A las 4:07 hrs, el Servicio Hidrográfico y Oceanográfico de la Armada (SHOA) trajo calma.
'At 4:07, the Hydrography and Oceanography Service of the Navy (HOSN) brought calm.'

The third references the supermarket owner, who is the only specific person affected by the looting singled out in the feature.

---

[17] In SFL descriptions of English, dependent clauses are often treated as Marked Themes in their own right, since their discourse function is comparable to that of pre-Predicator Circumstances; we agree for Spanish but do not have space to pursue argumentation for this analysis here.

## 6.3 Spanish Information Flow

El dueño de un supermercado que prefiere mantenerse anónimo cuenta
'The owner of a supermarket who prefers to remain anonymous relates'

que **a él** lo saquearon personas con dinero que venían en grandes camionetas.
'that people with money who came in big pick-up trucks looted **him**.'

"Les pagaban a los pelusas
'they paid the street kids'

para que les cargaran el vehículo.
'to fill the vehicle.'

Para abrirse paso,
'To open the way,'

aceleraban
'they accelerated'

y se iban gritando
'and left shouting'

'¡Tsunami!, ¡tsunami!',
'Tsunami! tsunami!'

y tocando la bocina.
'and honking the horn.'

Así se llevaron todo."
'In that way they took everything.'

The fourth references Gabriel, who was the only one of the four friends to be taken by the wave.

Nora llegó a Constitución a las diez de la mañana,
'Nora arrived in Constitución at 10 in the morning,'

cuando los saqueos estaban en su apogeo.
'when the looting was at its peak.'

Venía acompañada de la madre de Gabriel.
'She came accompanied by Gabriel's mother.'

Durante la noche Jonathan, llorando, le había dicho
'During the night Jonathan, crying, had told her'

que **a Gabriel** se lo había llevado la ola
'that **Gabriel** the wave had taken'

y Nora se lo transmitió a la madre.
'and Nora passed this on to his mother.'

Pero ella no perdía la esperanza.
'But she did not lose hope.'

He is singled out in the same way earlier on in the article when he is first taken.

La ola no pudo con los árboles donde estaban Jonathan y sus dos amigos.
'The wave couldn't with the trees where Jonathan and his friends were.'

Pero **a Gabriel Jaque**, que esperaba abajo, se lo tragó.
'But **Gabriel Jaque**, who was waiting below, (it) swallowed (him).'

The same pre-Predicator pattern is used to single out the parents with children who could not climb up into the trees.

Algunos se habían encaramado en los árboles,
'Some had climbed up into the trees,'

pero **a los que tenían niños** les fue imposible hacer eso.
'but **for those who had children** it was impossible to do that.'

What patterns do we see emerging here? As far as Circumstances are concerned, there seems to be an association with movements from one phase of the article to another as it unfolds; they regularly function as signposts as the text shifts gears. This is especially the case for Circumstances of time and space. Temporal Circumstances are the largest set of pre-Predicator Circumstances in the text. There are about four dozen of them punctuating the stories as they unfold. Circumstances of Location in space are the next biggest group (more than a dozen), repositioning what goes on. And there is a miscellaneous group (over a dozen) dealing with manner, matter, means, cause and angle.

Non-co-referential pre-Predicator Participants are far fewer in number (just five) and tend to manage local contrasts (e.g. Gabriel vs his three friends).

Information flow in the clauses with pre-Predicator ideation discussed above is presented in Table 6.19. The Circumstances and P2 and P3 Participants realised before the Predicator are designated in the table as Marked Themes,[18] following traditional SFL terminology. Their function is to shift our gaze on the field, either more globally (as with Circumstances) or more locally (as with Participants).

A term more attuned to their discourse semantic function might be Shifting Theme (after Moyano, 2010, 2016, 2021), as reflected in the MARKED THEME network (Figure 6.7). In purely grammatical terms, they are Circumstances and P2 or P3 Participants realised before the Predicator rather than after.

---

[18] As it does for post-Predicator Themes, TRANSITIVITY influences the positioning of pre-Predicator ideation. For example, the Senser in impinging mental clauses almost always comes before the Predicator (e.g. *Al capitán ya nada lo sorprendía.* 'Nothing would surprise **the captain** anymore.'). If research shows that local contrast is not involved for these and other pre-Predicator P3 participant roles, then a case should be made for not treating them as Marked Themes.

6.3 Spanish Information Flow

Table 6.19 *Marked Theme (Circumstances and P2/P3 Participants)*

| linkers | Marked Theme (Cir, P2, P3) | Theme | Predicator | Theme/minimal New |
|---|---|---|---|---|
| | al igual que miles de chilenos 'like thousands of Chileans' | | se detuvo 'stopped' | el terremoto 'the earthquake' |
| | para entonces 'by then' | | había pasado 'had passed' | media hora del sismo 'a half hour since the earthquake' |
| que | a él 'him' | | saquearon 'looted' | personas con dinero que venían en grandes camionetas 'people with money who came in big pick-up trucks' |
| que | a Gabriel 'Gabriel' | | se lo había llevado 'had taken him' | la ola 'the wave' |
| pero 'but' | a Gabriel Jaque 'Gabriel Jaque' | | se lo tragó 'swallowed him' | |
| pero 'but' | a los que tenían niños 'for those who had children' | | les fue 'was for them' | imposible hacer eso 'impossible to do that' |

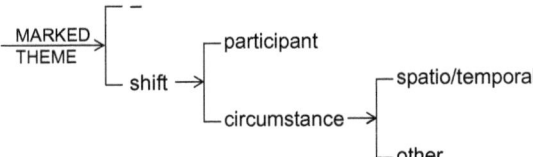

Figure 6.7 Spanish MARKED THEME systems

Note that for Spanish THEME, just as for English, we are proposing two simultaneous systems, one for each type of Theme (Figure 6.8). We do this because they are relatively independent grammatical choices with complementary discourse functions.

As for our discussion of English above, we have only been able to provide a preliminary account of information flow in the Spanish clause. We have only considered declarative mood, and we haven't had space to deal with Theme predication (e.g. *fue Valladares que llevó el anciano a la casa de la mujer* 'it was Valladares who took the old man to the woman's house') or thematic equatives (e.g. *lo que hizo Valladares fue llevar el anciano a la casa de la mujer*

347

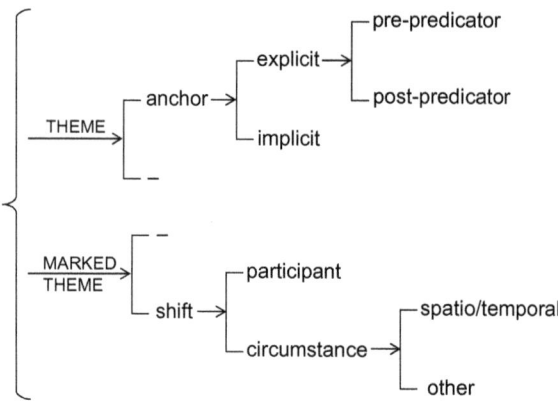

Figure 6.8 Spanish THEME and MARKED THEME systems (for clauses)

'what Valladares did was take the old man to the woman's house'). And the interaction between THEME and INFORMATION systems as far as TONALITY and TONICITY are concerned has not been properly addressed. Our goal has simply been to model the reasoning relevant to a description of these and related patterns of textual meaning.

One closing comment we will make has to do with reasoning about Theme from a paradigmatic perspective – with particular reference to the pre-predication vs post-predication options in the network above. As we have seen, this choice interacts in significant ways in Spanish with both ideational and interpersonal meaning. We saw above that TRANSITIVITY choices having to do with temporally and meteorologically oriented clauses, existential clauses, verbal projecting clauses, *se* impersonal clauses, impacting mental clauses and lexically dense attributive clauses all condition the realisation of the co-referential nominal group in post-Predicator position – some requiring post-Predicator position (e.g. existentials) and some strongly favouring it (e.g. *se* impersonal clauses). And we noted in passing that from the perspective of interpersonal meaning, certain types of evaluation have a role to play as far as post-Predicator co-referential nominal groups are concerned (e.g. attributive clauses with modalised or attitudinal Attributes and embedded clause Carriers: *es posible [[que ...]]* 'it's possible that ...', *no es difícil [[...]]* 'it's not difficult to ...'). The idea of meaning as choice is a basic tenet of SFL theory and description. Strictly speaking, as grammarians, we might argue therefore that whenever a choice in a textual system is in effect pre-empted by a choice in an ideational or interpersonal system, then in such cases assigning Theme and New functions is not relevant. Or should we perhaps back off a stratum, as discourse analysts, and argue the other way around – that the choice of a particular TRANSITIVITY or MOOD structure is being conditioned by textual considerations (e.g. the choice of a *se* recessive clause being conditioned by the need to conflate Theme and New at the end of clause)? As is so often the case, our proposed analyses will depend on how much weight we place on reasoning from above, around or below.

## 6.4 Chinese Information Flow

In terms of mode, the Sea Lettuce text is basically monologic, with only a small number of quotations from people who were interviewed by the reporter. Most of the text is 'language as reflection' mode, except for the beginning where the text involves some imagined commentary (如果你走进中国科学院海洋研究所, 你将被眼前空地上晾晒的一片绿油油的海藻所吸引| *rúguǒ nǐ zǒu jìn Zhōngguó Kēxuéyuàn Hǎiyáng Yánjiūsuǒ, nǐ jiāng bèi yǎnqián kòngdì shàng liàngshài de yī piàn lǜyóuyóu de hǎizǎo suǒ xīyǐn* 'If you walked into the Institute of Oceanology, Chinese Academy of Sciences, you would be attracted to a mass of green seaweed being dried on the ground.'). Taking into account these characteristics of its mode, alongside the field and tenor transitions in the text, we can propose that this text is an instance of a narrative genre (Martin and Rose 2008), unfolding through the following stages – Orientation, Complication, Evaluation, Resolution and Coda. Because of space limitations we cannot present the whole text here but, rather, refer you to Appendix 4.1.

Like the English Bondi Beach text, our Sea Lettuce text also foreshadows what happened before it tells us what happened. The very first paragraph of the text predicts the seaweed disaster.

2008年6月, 是距离第29届北京奥运会开幕仅仅两个月的日子, 如果你走进中国科学院海洋研究所, 你将被眼前空地上晾晒的一片绿油油的海藻所吸引, 这些海藻就是被称为"突如其来的海洋自然灾害"的主角——浒苔。 ⇒

'June 2008 was the time only two months away from the 29th Beijing Olympic Games. If you walked into the Institute of Oceanology, Chinese Academy of Sciences, you would be attracted to a mass of green seaweed being dried on the ground. This seaweed was known as the protagonist of the "unexpected ocean natural disaster" – sea lettuce.' ⇒

Subsequently three subtitles are used to foreshadow the main events in each section:

浒苔:突如其来的海洋自然灾害 ⇒
'Sea lettuce: unexpected ocean natural disaster' ⇒

五所联合:抗浒苔保奥运 ⇒
'Five institutions united: control sea lettuce, safeguard Olympic Games' ⇒

为奥运"保驾护航" 服务国家重大需求 ⇒
'Safeguarding Olympics, serving the country's major need' ⇒

Apart from these, foreshadowing also takes place several times within the text – for experts' advice, for their important contributions and for the scientists' hard work in combatting the seaweed:

根据研究情况,中国科学院专家组迅速提出建议表示 ⇒
'Based on the research results, the expert team of China Academy of Sciences promptly made the suggestions' ⇒

中国科学院的专家在委员会中发挥了重要作用 ⇒
'The experts of China Academy of Sciences played an important part in the Committee' ⇒

在采访中,记者还得知了许多关于海洋研究所与浒苔"不得不说的故事" ⇒
'During the interview, the reporter learned many "newsworthy stories" about the Institute of Oceanology and the sea lettuce' ⇒

In the analysis of grammatical resources for Chinese THEME and INFORMATION systems, we need to draw on TRANSITIVITY analysis to determine the Participants, Processes and Circumstances in clauses. The Participant before the Process plays a crucial role in the information structure; and so we need to look at how it is realised in different types of clause and from one clause to the next as the text unfolds. Note that our description of English draws on the interpersonal function of Subject for analysis; however, as is discussed in Chapter 4, there is no such function as Subject in Chinese MOOD structure. Accordingly, we refer to the system of TRANSITIVITY to locate the key element in Chinese information structure.

To analyse the grammatical resources for information flow in Chinese, we first take a look at one of the beginning paragraphs of our focus text that introduces how the sea lettuce caused severe pollution.

2008年5月31日,大面积浒苔进入青岛近岸海域,使滨海名城青岛的蓝海呈现绿色。随着时间的推移,越来越多的浒苔随潮水涌上岸,它们到达了青岛著名的栈桥、第一海水浴场和前海风景游览区一带的沙滩,没几天便堆起了厚厚一层,并迅速扩散,在太阳晒后更是臭气熏天,成为污染带。

'On 31 May 2008, expansive sea lettuce invaded Qingdao's offshore area, causing the famous coastal city Qingdao's blue sea to turn green. As time went by, more and more sea lettuce rushed onto the shore with the tidewater; it reached Qingdao's famous pier, the First Seawater Resort, and the beach near the Qianhai scenic spot. Within just a few days a thick heap formed and spread fast. Rotting away in the sun, it even stunk to high heaven and turned into a belt of pollution.'

Then we divide the paragraph up into clauses and show the Participants preceding Processes in bold.

2008年5月31日,**大面积浒苔**进入青岛近岸海域,
*èrlínglíngbā nián wǔ yuè sānshíyī rì,* **dà miànjī hǔtái** *jìnrù Qīngdǎo jìn àn hǎiyù,*
'on 31 May 2008, **expansive sea lettuce** invaded Qingdao's offshore area,'

使滨海名城青岛的蓝海呈现绿色。
shǐ bīnhǎi míngchéng Qīngdǎo de lán hǎi chéngxiàn lǜsè.
'causing the famous coastal city Qingdao's blue sea to turn green.'

随着时间的推移,**越来越多的浒苔**随潮水涌上岸,
suízhe shíjiān de tuīyí, **yuè lái yuè duō de hǔtái** suí cháoshuǐ yǒng shàng àn,
'with the passage of time, **more and more sea lettuce** rushed with the tidewater onto the shore,'

**它们**到达了青岛著名的栈桥、第一海水浴场和前海风景游览区一带的沙滩,
**tāmen** dàodá le Qīngdǎo zhùmíng de zhànqiáo, dìyī hǎishuǐ yùchǎng hé qiánhǎi fēngjǐng yóulǎn qū yīdài de shātān,
'**it** reached Qingdao's famous pier, the First Seawater Resort, and the beach near the Qianhai scenic spot,'

没几天便堆起了厚厚一层,
méi jǐ tiān biàn duī qǐ le hòuhòu yī céng,
'within just a few days formed a thick heap,'

并迅速扩散,
bìng xùnsù kuòsàn,
'and quickly spread,'

在太阳晒后更是臭气熏天,
zài tàiyáng shài hòu gèng shì chòuqìxūntiān,
'after drying of the sun, even stunk to high heaven,'

成为污染带。
chéngwéi wūrǎn dài.
'turned into a belt of pollution.'[19]

In Chinese, when the first Participant of a clause could also be realised explicitly before the Process in subsequent clauses, that Participant is often left implicit there. This is known as ellipsis of 主语 zhǔyǔ 'subject' in traditional Chinese grammar (Hu, 2011, p. 355; Wang, 2011, p. 341), or anaphoric ellipsis of 起词 qǐcí 'initial word' (Lü, 2014, p. 40). We can make such Participants explicit in each clause (marked by parentheses below).

2008年5月31日,**大面积浒苔**进入青岛近岸海域,
èrlínglíngbā nián wǔ yuè sānshíyī rì, **dà miànjī hǔtái** jìnrù Qīngdǎo jìn àn hǎiyù,
'on 31 May 2008, **expansive sea lettuce** invaded Qingdao's offshore area,'

(**大面积浒苔**)使滨海名城青岛的蓝海呈现绿色。
(**dà miànjī hǔtái**) shǐ bīnhǎi míngchéng Qīngdǎo de lán hǎi chéngxiàn lǜsè.
'(**expansive sea lettuce**) causing the famous coastal city Qingdao's blue sea to turn green.'

---

[19] To facilitate analysis, we provide a more literal translation for these clauses. The free translation attached to the paragraph above is oriented more towards idiomatic English.

随着时间的推移,**越来越多的浒苔**随潮水涌上岸,
*suízhe shíjiān de tuīyí, **yuè lái yuè duō de hǔtái** suí cháoshuǐ yǒng shàng àn,*
'with the passage of time, **more and more sea lettuce** rushed with the tidewater onto the shore,'

**它们**到达了青岛著名的栈桥、第一海水浴场和前海风景游览区一带的沙滩,
***tāmen** dàodá le Qīngdǎo zhùmíng de zhànqiáo, dìyī hǎishuǐ yùchǎng hé qiánhǎi fēngjǐng yóulǎn qū yīdài de shātān,*
'**it** reached Qingdao's famous pier, the First Seawater Resort, and the beach near the Qianhai scenic spot,'

没几天(**它们**)便堆起了厚厚一层,
*méi jǐ tiān (**tāmen**) biàn duī qǐ le hòuhòu yī céng,*
'within just a few days (**it**) formed a thick heap,'

并且[20](**它们**)迅速扩散,
*bìngqiě (**tāmen**) xùnsù kuòsàn,*
'and (***it***) quickly spread,'

在太阳晒后(**它们**)更是臭气熏天,
*zài tàiyáng shài hòu (**tāmen**) gèng shì chòuqìxūntiān,*
'after drying of the sun, (***it***) even stunk to high heaven,'

(**它们**)成为污染带。
*(**tāmen**) chéngwéi wūrǎn dài.*
'(***it***) turned into a belt of pollution.'

We can also see that in this excerpt there are four Circumstances before the first Participant in their respective clauses (2008年5月31日 *èrlínglíngbā nián wǔ yuè sānshíyī rì* 'on 31 May 2008', 随着时间的推移 *suízhe shíjiān de tuīyí* 'with the passage of time', 没几天 *méi jǐ tiān* 'within just a few days' and 在太阳晒后 *zài tàiyáng shài hòu* 'after drying of the sun'); and we can see that one clause begins with a conjunction 并且 *bìngqiě* 'and', linking neighbouring clauses additively. This is outlined in Table 6.20 below.

Now let's consider how information unfolds clause by clause. The first of the clauses introduces the Participant 大面积浒苔 *dà miànjī hǔtái* 'expansive sea lettuce'; and then each of the following clauses has the sea lettuce as its first Participant (realised explicitly or implicitly). What comes after the first Participant in these clauses deals with the extent of the sea lettuce invasion, the state of its growth and the impact it caused to the environment. We can think of this as the excerpt's 'news'.

As far as textual grammar is concerned, the first Participant of each clause establishes an ideational anchor for what we want to say in that clause. The

---

[20] The original clause begins with the conjunction 并 *bìng* 'and', which is only used when the first Participant is implicit (Lü, 1999, p. 86). When we make that Participant explicit, we need to change the conjunction into 并且 *bìngqiě* 'and'.

6.4 Chinese Information Flow

Table 6.20 *Information flow in the 'invasion of seaweed' phase of the Sea Lettuce text*

| linker | Circumstance before first Participant | first Participant | following first Participant |
|---|---|---|---|
| | 2008年5月31日<br>*èrlínglíngbā nián wǔ yuè sānshíyī rì*<br>'on 31 May 2008' | 大面积浒苔<br>*dà miànjī hǔtái*<br>'expansive sea lettuce' | 进入青岛近岸海域<br>*jìnrù Qīngdǎo jìn àn hǎiyù*<br>'invaded Qingdao's offshore area' |
| | | (大面积浒苔)<br>*(dà miànjī hǔtái)*<br>'(expansive sea lettuce)' | 使滨海名城青岛的蓝海呈现绿色<br>*shǐ bīnhǎi míngchéng Qīngdǎo de lán hǎi chéngxiàn lǜsè*<br>'causing the famous coastal city Qingdao's blue sea to turn green' |
| | 随着时间的推移<br>*suízhe shíjiān de tuīyí*<br>'with the passage of time' | 越来越多的浒苔<br>*yuè lái yuè duō de hǔtái*<br>'more and more sea lettuce' | 随潮水涌上岸<br>*suí cháoshuǐ yǒng shàng àn*<br>'rushed with the tidewater onto the shore' |
| | | 它们<br>*tāmen*<br>'it' | 到达了青岛著名的栈桥、第一海水浴场和前海风景游览区一带的沙滩<br>*dàodá le Qīngdǎo zhùmíng de zhànqiáo, dìyī hǎishuǐ yùchǎng hé qiánhǎi fēngjǐng yóulǎn qū yīdài de shātān*<br>'reached Qingdao's famous pier, the First Seawater Resort, and the beach near the Qianhai scenic spot' |
| | 没几天<br>*méi jǐ tiān*<br>'within just a few days' | (它们)<br>*(tāmen)*<br>'(it)' | 便堆起了厚厚一层<br>*biàn duī qǐ le hòuhòu yī céng*<br>'formed a thick heap' |
| 并且<br>*bìngqiě*<br>'and' | | (它们)<br>*(tāmen)*<br>'(it)' | 迅速扩散<br>*xùnsù kuòsàn*<br>'quickly spread' |
| | 在太阳晒后<br>*zài tàiyáng shài hòu*<br>'after drying of the sun' | (它们)<br>*(tāmen)*<br>'(it)' | 更是臭气熏天<br>*gèng shì chòuqìxūntiān*<br>'even stunk to high heaven' |
| | | (它们)<br>*(tāmen)*<br>'(it)' | 成为污染带<br>*chéngwéi wūrǎn dài*<br>'turned into a belt of pollution' |

ideational anchor of this phase of text is the sea lettuce; from a textual perspective it functions as the Theme of each clause. The function of Theme is to hold steady our gaze on the field as a phase of text unfolds. Chinese also displays the general crosslinguistic tendency that once the ideational anchor is established through an explicit Theme, it can be maintained through ellipsis in subsequent clauses.

Note that the first Participant that we look for in our analysis is the one before the Process; this realises the Theme of a clause. If no such Participant is found (or can be made explicit) before the Process, then this clause does not have a Theme. For example, in the meteorological clause 下雨 *xià yǔ* 'it rains', there is no Participant before the Process 下 *xià* 'fall'; the Participant after 雨 *yǔ* 'rain' does not have to do with choice in the THEME system. As a result, the clause does not have an anchor point in the field.[21]

At this point we can outline the THEME system of Chinese as Figure 6.9. The system first allows for the possibility of clauses fixing our gaze on the field by establishing an anchor or not. When [anchor] is selected, it is realised by a Theme function in the clause; otherwise, the clause does not have a Theme function. Where there is a Theme, it is conflated with the first Participant before the Process, realised either explicitly or implicitly.

The other textual variable, which complements Theme, is New. Like English and Spanish, Chinese also realises its New via intonation. The unit at stake here is tone group, and in the unmarked case it corresponds to a clause (one tone group per clause in other words). In tone groups one salient syllable, in the unmarked case the final one, carries the major pitch movement in the tone group. This 'super-salient' tonic syllable highlights the most prominent information in the tone group and can be used to recognise the New function in the grammar of a clause – minimally the clause constituent containing the tonic syllable. Since most syllables in Chinese have lexical tone, the salience is produced by 'maximal pitch movement on the relevant tone' (Halliday and McDonald 2004, p. 325).

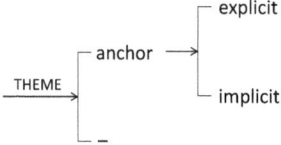

Figure 6.9 Chinese THEME systems (for clauses)

---

[21] LaPolla (2009) views the sequential position of a thing in relation to the verb as having to do with topicality. If the reference to the thing is not topical, it appears after the verb.

In the two clauses below, we use '//' to mark tone group boundaries and bold to highlight the tonic syllable.[22] We are basing our analysis of these written clauses on the way we feel they would be read aloud. In the first clause, 海 *hǎi* is the tonic syllable, and the minimal New of this clause is thus the second Participant 青岛近岸海域 *Qīngdǎo jìn àn hǎiyù* 'Qingdao's offshore area'. In the second clause, the tonic syllable is 绿 *lǜ*, and the minimal New of this elliptical clause is thus the Attribute 绿色 *lǜsè* 'green'.

//大面积浒苔进入青岛近岸**海域**//
*dà miànjī hǔtái jìnrù Qīngdǎo jìn àn **hǎi**yù*
'expansive sea lettuce invaded Qingdao's offshore area'

//使滨海名城青岛的蓝海呈现**绿**色//
*shǐ bīnhǎi míngchéng Qīngdǎo de lán hǎi chéngxiàn **lǜ**sè*
'causing the famous coastal city Qingdao's blue sea to turn green'

The reason why we call it 'minimal New' is that when the tonic syllable in a tone group falls on the final clause rank constituent, Chinese intonation does not tell us how much information to treat as New. For example, the maximal New of the first clause above can be extended to include the Process 进入 *jìnrù* 'invaded'.

As indicated above, in the unmarked case a tone group corresponds to a clause. However, there may be more than one tone group per clause (as indicated by the comma in the punctuation below).

//2008年5月31日,//大面积浒苔进入青岛近岸**海域**//
*èrlínglíngbā nián wǔ yuè **sān**shíyī rì, dà miànjī hǔtái jìnrù Qīngdǎo jìn àn **hǎi**yù,*
'on 31 May 2008, expansive sea lettuce invaded Qingdao's offshore area,'

And there may be more than one clause per tone group. In the example below, two clauses, 已有30多个国家的运动员驻扎青岛 *yǐ yǒu sānshí duō gè guójiā de yùndòngyuán zhùzhā Qīngdǎo* 'players from more than 30 countries have already settled in Qingdao' and 并开始了奥帆赛的赛前训练 *bìng kāishǐ le Àofānsài de sàiqián xùnliàn* 'and started their pre-game training for the Olympic sailing events', would be naturally read aloud as one tone group.

//已有30多个国家的运动员驻扎青岛并开始了奥帆赛的赛前**训**练//
*yǐ yǒu sānshí duō gè guójiā de yùndòngyuán zhùzhā Qīngdǎo bìng kāishǐ le Àofānsài de sàiqián **xùn**liàn//*
'players from more than 30 countries have already settled in Qingdao and started their pre-game training for the Olympic sailing events'

---

[22] In Chinese we do not use '/' to mark foot boundaries because the phonological unit of foot is not applicable to syllable-timed languages like Chinese.

356  Theme

In cases where clause and tone group wavelengths do not correspond (i.e. more than one tone group per clause or more than one clause per tone group), we have what is referred to as marked TONALITY.

We're now in a position to replay Table 6.20, setting up columns for Theme and minimal New functions. The Themes anchor our gaze on the field, creating a discourse semantic pattern anchored here on the sea lettuce. The minimal News then extend our gaze, creating a complementary discourse semantic pattern in relation to the impact of the sea lettuce.

The analysis in Table 6.21 is based on unmarked choices for Theme and New. Bringing marked choices into the picture means that we shift from discourse continuity to discontinuity – i.e. scaffolding changes in a text's anchor on the field and local contrasts in its news.

Table 6.21 *Theme and minimal New in the 'invasion of seaweed' phase of the Sea Lettuce text*

| linker | Circumstance before first Participant | Theme | minimal New (in bold) |
|---|---|---|---|
| | 2008年5月31日<br>èrlínglíngbā nián wǔ yuè sānshíyī rì<br>'on 31 May 2008' | 大面积浒苔<br>dà miànjī hǔtái<br>'expansive sea lettuce' | 进入**青岛近岸海域**<br>jìnrù **Qīngdǎo jìn àn hǎiyù**<br>'invaded **Qingdao's offshore area**' |
| | | (大面积浒苔)<br>(dà miànjī hǔtái)<br>'(expansive sea lettuce)' | 使滨海名城青岛的蓝海呈现**绿色**<br>shǐ bīnhǎi míngchéng Qīngdǎo de lán hǎi chéngxiàn **lǜsè**<br>'causing the famous coastal city Qingdao's blue sea to turn **green**' |
| | 随着时间的推移<br>suízhe shíjiān de tuīyí<br>'with the passage of time' | 越来越多的浒苔<br>yuè lái yuè duō de hǔtái<br>'more and more sea lettuce' | 随潮水涌上**岸**<br>suí cháoshuǐ yǒng shàng **àn**<br>'rushed with the tidewater onto **the shore**' |
| | | 它们<br>tāmen<br>'it' | 到达了**青岛著名的栈桥、第一海水浴场和前海风景游览区一带的沙滩**<br>dàodá le **Qīngdǎo zhùmíng de zhànqiáo, dìyī hǎishuǐ yùchǎng hé qiánhǎi fēngjǐng yóulǎn qū yīdài de shātān**<br>'reached **Qingdao's famous pier, the First Seawater Resort, and the beach near the Qianhai scenic spot**' |
| | 没几天<br>méi jǐ tiān<br>'within just a few days' | (它们)<br>(tāmen)<br>'(it)' | 便堆起了**厚厚一层**<br>biàn duī qǐ le **hòuhòu yī céng**<br>'formed **a thick heap**' |

Table 6.21 *(Cont.)*

| linker | Circumstance before first Participant | Theme | minimal New (in bold) |
|---|---|---|---|
| 并且<br>*bìngqiě*<br>'and' | | (它们)<br>(*tāmen*)<br>'(it)' | 迅速**扩散**<br>*xùnsù* **kuòsàn**<br>'quickly **spread**' |
| | 在太阳晒后<br>*zài tàiyáng shài hòu*<br>'after drying of the sun' | (它们)<br>(*tāmen*)<br>'(it)' | 更是**臭气熏天**<br>*gèng shì* **chòuqìxūntiān**<br>'even **stunk to high heaven**' |
| | | (它们)<br>(*tāmen*)<br>'(it)' | 成为**污染带**<br>*chéngwéi* **wūrǎn dài**<br>'turned into **a belt of pollution**' |

First, Marked Theme. Structurally, marked Theme is conflated with one or more ideational functions preceding the first Participant, which are normally Circumstances. The function of Marked Theme is to shift our gaze on the field. The first, third, fifth and seventh clauses of our excerpt each begin with a Circumstance of location in time (i.e. 2008年5月31日 *èrlínglíngbā nián wǔ yuè sānshíyī rì* 'on 31 May 2008', 随着时间的推移 *suízhe shíjiān de tuīyí* 'with the passage of time', 没几天 *méi jǐ tiān* 'within just a few days' and 在太阳晒后 *zài tàiyáng shài hòu* 'after drying of the sun'); they signal shifts of perspective in time and thus break the text up into four parts.

Next, Marked New. Much less relevant to written than spoken modes, Marked New is realised by means of a tonic syllable that is not the final salient syllable in the final clause rank constituent in its tone group. This is illustrated below, where the Marked New falls on the clause constituent (随潮水 *suí cháoshuǐ* 'with the tidewater') that contains the tonic syllable (潮 *cháo*).

随着时间的推移,越来越多的浒苔随**潮**水涌上岸
*suízhe shíjiān de tuīyí, yuè lái yuè duō de hǔtái suí* **cháo**shuǐ yǒng shàng àn
'with the passage of time, more and more sea lettuce rushed **with the tidewater** onto the shore'

Now we can replay Table 6.20 again, setting up columns for Marked Theme, Theme and minimal New functions. As we have been doing all along, both explicit and implicit Themes are included in the Table 6.22, by way of noting how our gaze on the field is being sustained. Marked Themes and unmarked Themes have different discourse functions, the former shifting our gaze on the field and the latter establishing and sustaining it. Accordingly, we allow here for both a Marked Theme and an unmarked Theme in the same clause (following Martin and Rose 2007).

Table 6.22 *Marked Theme, Theme and minimal New in the 'invasion of seaweed' phase of the Sea Lettuce text*

| linker | Marked Theme | Theme | minimal New (in bold) |
|---|---|---|---|
| | 2008年5月31日<br>èrlínglíngbā nián wǔ yuè sānshíyī rì<br>'on 31 May 2008' | 大面积浒苔<br>dà miànjī hǔtái<br>'expansive sea lettuce' | 进入**青岛近岸海域**<br>jìnrù **Qīngdǎo jìn àn hǎiyù**<br>'invaded **Qingdao's offshore area**' |
| | | (大面积浒苔)<br>(dà miànjī hǔtái)<br>'(expansive sea lettuce)' | 使滨海名城青岛的蓝海呈现**绿色**<br>shǐ bīnhǎi míngchéng Qīngdǎo de lán hǎi chéngxiàn **lǜsè**<br>'causing the famous coastal city Qingdao's blue sea to turn **green**' |
| | 随着时间的推移<br>suízhe shíjiān de tuīyí<br>'with the passage of time' | 越来越多的浒苔<br>yuè lái yuè duō de hǔtái<br>'more and more sea lettuce' | 随潮水涌上**岸**<br>suí cháoshuǐ yǒng shàng **àn**<br>'rushed with the tidewater onto **the shore**' |
| | | 它们<br>tāmen<br>'it' | 到达了**青岛著名的栈桥、第一海水浴场和前海风景游览区一带的沙滩**<br>dàodá le **Qīngdǎo zhùmíng de zhànqiáo, dìyī hǎishuǐ yùchǎng hé qiánhǎi fēngjǐng yóulǎn qū yīdài de shātān**<br>'reached **Qingdao's famous pier, the First Seawater Resort, and the beach near the Qianhai scenic spot**' |
| | 没几天<br>méi jǐ tiān<br>'within just a few days' | (它们)<br>(tāmen)<br>'(it)' | 便堆起了**厚厚一层**<br>biàn duī qǐ le **hòuhòu yī céng**<br>'formed **a thick heap**' |
| 并且<br>bìngqiě<br>'and' | | (它们)<br>(tāmen)<br>'(it)' | 迅速**扩散**<br>xùnsù **kuòsàn**<br>'quickly **spread**' |
| | 在太阳晒后<br>zài tàiyáng shài hòu<br>'after drying of the sun' | (它们)<br>(tāmen)<br>'(it)' | 更是**臭气熏天**<br>gèng shì **chòuqìxūntiān**<br>'even **stunk to high heaven**' |
| | | (它们)<br>(tāmen)<br>'(it)' | 成为**污染带**<br>chéngwéi **wūrǎn dài**<br>'turned into **a belt of pollution**' |

At this point we can formalise the information resources we have introduced above as system networks. We have drawn a network for the THEME system above in Figure 6.9. Here we supplement it with another system called MARKED THEME (Figure 6.10), which allows for the possibility of clauses shifting our gaze on the field by having a Marked Theme or not. It then allows for different types of Marked Theme. Participant Marked Themes tend to involve localised shifts of meaning, often between adjacent clauses. In the following example[23] (Table 6.23), the participant Marked Theme of the fourth clause refers to a Participant (畜牧人员 *xùmù rényuán* 'stock farmers') other than the first Participant (他 *tā* 'he') before the Process. Likewise, the final clause has another participant Marked Theme (真正懂养鹿技术的专家 *zhēnzhèng dǒng yǎng lù jìshù de zhuānjiā* 'experts who really knew how to raise deer'), which marks another shift of meaning.

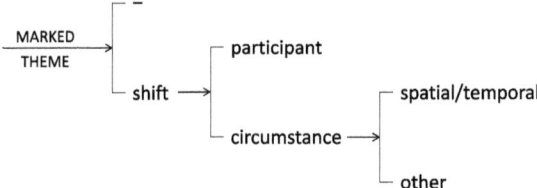

Figure 6.10 Chinese MARKED THEME systems (for clauses)

Table 6.23 *Participant Marked Themes*

| linker | Marked Theme | Theme | minimal New (in bold) |
|---|---|---|---|
| | | 他<br>*tā*<br>'he' | 食不甘味<br>*shíbùgānwèi*<br>'had no appetite for food' |
| | | (他)<br>(*tā*)<br>('he') | 寝不安席<br>*qǐnbù'ānxí*<br>'was unable to sleep' |
| | | (他)<br>(*tā*)<br>('he') | 几乎跑遍了**整个石家庄地区**<br>*jīhū pǎo biàn le zhěnggè Shíjiāzhuāng dìqū*<br>'almost went throughout **the whole Zhijiazhuang area**' |
| | 畜牧人员<br>*xùmù rényuán*<br>'stock farmers' | (他)<br>(*tā*)<br>('he') | 虽访了**不少**<br>*suī fǎng le **bùshǎo***<br>'visited **many**' |
| 但<br>*dàn*<br>'but' | 真正懂养鹿技术的专家<br>*zhēnzhèng dǒng yǎng lù jìshù de zhuānjiā*<br>'experts who really knew how to raise deer' | (他)<br>(*tā*)<br>('he') | 却**没找到**<br>*què **méi zhǎo dào***<br>'**didn't find any**' |

[23] Retrieved from the corpus of Centre for Chinese Linguistics, Peking University.

Circumstantial Marked Themes, especially those of time and place, tend to involve more global shifts of meaning. Thus, we separate the spatio-temporal Circumstances from others in the network.

When we combined the systems of THEME and MARKED THEME, we arrive at the simultaneous systems shown in Figure 6.11.

We also propose two simultaneous information systems for Chinese (Figure 6.12). The TONICITY system allows for the major pitch movement in a tone group to fall on the final salient syllable in the final clause constituent or an earlier one. This conditions our interpretation of which clause constituent is presented as New. The TONALITY system first allows for tone groups of the same wavelength as a clause as opposed to cases where they involve longer or shorter wavelengths than a clause (i.e. marked tonality). This conditions our interpretation of the number of New elements per clause. When a tone group

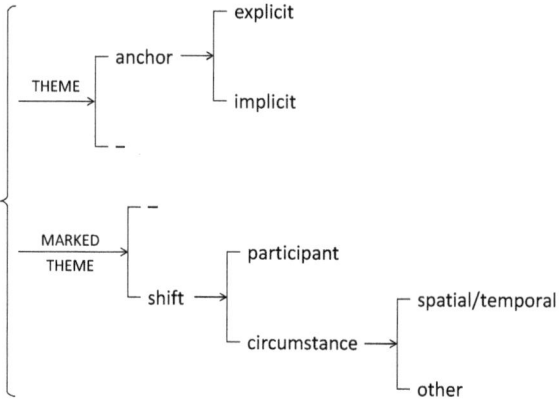

Figure 6.11 General Chinese THEME systems (for clauses)

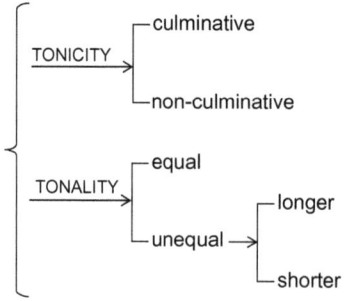

Figure 6.12 Chinese information systems (for tone groups)

shares the same wavelength as a clause, there is one New element in the clause. When a tone group has a longer wavelength than the clause, there is less than one New element per clause. When a tone group has a shorter wavelength than the clause, there is more than one New element per clause.

At this point we are going to push upwards in our discussion to consider longer wavelengths of information flow. This means making room for the possibility of a higher-level Theme function, called Hyper-Theme, which foreshadows a phase of discourse about to unfold; and in addition it makes room for the possibility of a higher-level New function, called Hyper-New, which consolidates or interprets what has gone before. In many texts, though not in our example below, the Hyper-Theme specifically predicts the pattern of unmarked Themes in a phase of discourse. The Hyper-New, on the other hand, aggregates the point of a phase (its News). The Hyper-New is typically more than a summary; in many texts it evaluates the significance of the ideation expanded as New. Below we outline the information flow in the 'experts' advice' phase of the Sea Lettuce text (Table 6.24).

Table 6.24 *Information flow in the 'experts' advice' phase of the Sea Lettuce text*

| 根据研究情况,中国科学院专家组迅速提出建议表示⇒ |||||
|---|---|---|---|
| *gēnjù yánjiū qíngkuàng, Zhōngguó Kēxuéyuàn zhuānjiā zǔ xùnsù tí chū jiànyì biǎoshì*⇒ |||| 
| 'based on the research results, the expert team of China Academy of Sciences promptly made the suggestions'⇒ ||||
| **linker** | **Marked Theme** | **Theme** | **minimal New** (in bold) |
| 第一<br>*dìyī*<br>'first' | 在当前阶段<br>*zài dāngqián jiēduàn*<br>'at the present stage' | | 需要进一步加强**监测与预警**<br>*xūyào jìnyībù jiāqiáng **jiāncè yǔ yùjǐng***<br>'need to further strengthen **monitoring and early warning**' |
| 第二<br>*dì'èr*<br>'second' | 针对奥帆赛所在时间段<br>*zhēnduì Àofānsài suǒzài shíjiānduàn*<br>'in accordance with the schedule of Olympic sailing events' | | 加强**对奥帆赛及周边海域灾害性浒苔或其他藻类暴发事件的预警、预报**工作<br>*jiāqiáng **duì Àofānsài jí zhōubiān hǎiyù zāihàixìng hǔtái huò qítā zǎolèi bàofā shìjiàn de yùjǐng, yùbào** gōngzuò*<br>'strengthen **early warning and forecasting of the outbreak of sea lettuce or other algae in and near sea areas for the Olympic sailing events**' |

Table 6.24 (Cont.)

| | | | | 为预防和治理争取**时间** <br> *wèi yùfáng hé zhìlǐ zhēngqǔ **shíjiān*** <br> 'for the sake of prevent and control, race against **time**' |
|---|---|---|---|---|
| | | | | 确保**奥帆赛顺利进行** <br> *quèbǎo **Àofānsài shùnlì jìnxíng*** <br> 'ensure **smooth progress of the Olympic sailing events**' |
| 第三 <br> *dìsān* <br> 'third' | | | | 加强**实用性技术手段的研究、示范、推广** <br> *jiāqiáng **shíyòngxìng jìshù shǒuduàn de yánjiū, shìfàn, tuīguǎng*** <br> 'strengthen **the development, demonstration and promotion of practical technological methods**' |
| | | | | 提高**打捞浒苔的效率** <br> *tígāo **dǎlāo hǔtái de xiàolǜ*** <br> 'raise **the efficiency of getting sea lettuce out of water**' |
| | | | | 达到**尽快清除比赛海域浒苔的目的** <br> *dádào **jǐnkuài qīngchú bǐsài hǎiyù hǔtái de mùdì*** <br> 'reach **the goal of removing sea lettuce from the gaming sea area as quickly as possible**' |
| | 其中 <br> *qízhōng* <br> 'among them' | 实用、高效的打捞技术、装置研发应用 <br> *shíyòng, gāoxiào de dǎlāo jìshù, zhuāngzhì yánfā yìngyòng* <br> 'practical, efficient retrieving technology, equipment development and application' | | 尤其重要 <br> *yóuqí zhòngyào* <br> '(were) **particularly important**' |
| ⇐ 专家组的建议得到了山东省青岛市的高度重视 <br> ⇐ *zhuānjiā zǔ de jiànyì dé dào le Shāndōng Shěng Qīngdǎo Shì de gāodù zhòngshì* <br> ⇐ 'the advice of the expert team was greatly valued by Qingdao City, Shangdong Province' ||||| 
| | | | | **Hyper-New** |

6.4 Chinese Information Flow 363

As Table 6.24 displays, in this phase of the text, the Hyper-Theme foreshadows the advice put forward by the expert team of China Academy of Sciences. The three Marked Themes are circumstantial elements that serve to shift our gaze on the field – the first two marking the time periods the experts' advice is applicable to and the third singling out the advice that is particularly important. Seven clauses do not contain an unmarked Theme (i.e. a Participant realised before the Process), because there is no need to establish and sustain in the field an anchor point realised by an entity. The New provides the specific content of the experts' advice. Subsequently, the nominal group 实用、高效的打捞技术、装置研发应用 *shíyòng, gāoxiào de dǎlāo jìshù, zhuāngzhì yánfā yìngyōng* 'practical, efficient retrieving technology, equipment development and application' realises Theme, positioning this Participant as the focal point of the clause information. Finally in this phase, the Hyper-New evaluates the experts' advice, 得到了 … … 高度重视 *dé dào le ... gāodù zhòngshì* 'were greatly valued', inscribing positive appreciation towards the expert team's advice.

Let's now examine how the text deals with the rest of the narrative. The next phase introduces members in the expert team (Table 6.25). The Hyper-Theme predicts the pattern of unmarked Themes in this phase of discourse, turning our

Table 6.25 *Information flow in the 'members of the expert team' phase of the Sea Lettuce text*

| Hyper-Theme | | | |
|---|---|---|---|
| 中国科学院的专家在委员会中发挥了重要作用⇒ *Zhōngguó Kēxuéyuàn de zhuānjiā zài wěiyuánhuì*⇒ 'experts from China Academy of Sciences played an important role in the committee'⇒ | | | |
| linker | Marked Theme | Theme | minimal New (in bold) |
| | | 海洋所研究员、海洋环境学家周名江 *Hǎiyángsuǒ yánjiūyuán, hǎiyáng huánjìng xuéjiā Zhōu Míngjiāng* 'Zhou Mingjiang, research fellow of the Institute of Oceanology, expert in ocean environmental studies' | 担任**专家委员会副主任委员** *dānrèn zhuānjiā wěiyuánhuì fù zhǔrèn wěiyuán* 'was appointed **deputy chairman of the expert committee**' |
| | | 海洋研究所党委书记、所长孙松 *Hǎiyáng Yánjiūsuǒ dǎngwěi shūjì, suǒzhǎng Sūn Sōng* 'Sun Song, Secretary of CPC Committee and Director of the Institute of Oceanology' | 担任**生态组组长** *dānrèn shēngtài zǔ zǔzhǎng* 'was appointed **leader of the ecology panel**' |

Table 6.25 *(Cont.)*

| | | 海洋研究所所长助理王凡和研究员李鹏程<br>*Hǎiyáng Yánjiūsuǒ suǒzhǎng zhùlǐ Wáng Fán hé yánjiūyuán Lǐ Péngchéng*<br>'Wang Fan, assistant director, and Li Pengcheng, research fellow of the Institute of Oceanology' | 分别担任**监测预警组和处置组副组长**<br>*fēnbié dānrèn **jiāncè yùjǐng zǔ hé chǔzhì zǔ fù zǔzhǎng***<br>'were respectively appointed **deputy leaders of monitoring and warning group and disposal group**' |
|---|---|---|---|
| 此外<br>*cǐwài*<br>'in addition' | | 中国科学院生态环境中心、水生生物研究所、南京地理与湖泊所、遥感应用研究所的专家<br>*Zhōngguó Kēxuéyuàn Shēngtài Huánjìng Zhōngxīn, Shuǐshēng Shēngwù Yánjiūsuǒ, Nánjīng Dìlǐ yǔ Húpō Suǒ, Yáogǎn Yìngyòng Yánjiūsuǒ de zhuānjiā*<br>'experts from China Academy of Sciences' Centre of Ecological Environment, Institute of Hydrobiology, Nanjing Geography and Lake Institute, Institute of Remote Sensing Application' | 都分别进入**专家委员会**<br>*dōu fēnbié jìn rù **zhuānjiā wěiyuánhuì***<br>'all entered **the expert committee**' |

gaze to the experts from China Academy of Sciences. The New in each clause specifies the role each expert plays in the committee.

In the next example, there is no Hyper-Theme predicting information flow; but there is a Hyper-New evaluating the significance of the ideation expanded as New in each preceding clause (also positive appreciation). There are two Circumstances of location in time serving as Marked Theme, shifting our gaze on the field with respect to time. Before the first Circumstance of location in time, there is a Circumstance of Angle introducing the source of information. In terms of Theme and New, the Theme in the first clause brings our attention to the amount of sea lettuce in the sea area for Olympic sailing events, and the New lets us know the result of sea lettuce control. The Theme in the second clause is concerned with the competing teams and their sailboats, and the New tells us they had started training. The Theme in the third clause sustains this orientation, and the New brings in further information about the teams' uninterrupted training.

What we have offered here is a preliminary account of textual meaning in the Chinese clause. From the above examples, we can see that some phases

Table 6.26 *Information flow in the 'victory over sea lettuce' phase of the Sea Lettuce text*

| linker | Marked Theme | Theme | minimal New (in bold) |
|---|---|---|---|
| | 据监测数据显示,截至7月9日<br>*jù jiāncè shùjù xiǎnshì, jiézhì qī yuè jiǔ ri*<br>'according to monitoring data, as of July 9<sup>th</sup>' | 奥帆赛竞赛水域内警戒水域浒苔面积<br>*Àofānsài jìngsài shuǐyù nèi jǐngjiè shuǐyù hǔtái miànjī*<br>'the area of sea lettuce in the sea area for Olympic sailing events' | 由最初占总面积的32.04%降到了**2.8%左右**<br>*yóu zuìchū zhàn zǒng miànjī de bǎifēnzhī sānshí'èr diǎn líng sì jiàng dào le **bǎifēnzhī èr diǎn bā zuǒyòu***<br>'decrease from the original 32.04% of the total sea area to **around 2.8%**' |
| | 7月6日<br>*qī yuè liù ri*<br>'July 6<sup>th</sup>' | 奥帆赛参赛队伍绝大多数帆船<br>*Àofānsài cānsài duìwǔ juédàduōshù fānchuán*<br>'most of the sailboats of competing teams in the Olympic sailing events' | 已**下水训练**<br>*yǐ **xià shuǐ xùnliàn***<br>'already **had started training**' |
| | | 没有队伍<br>*méiyǒu duìwǔ*<br>'no team' | 因为浒苔干扰而**中断训练**<br>*yīnwèi hǔtái gānrǎo ér zhōngduàn xùnliàn*<br>'because of disturbance by sea lettuce, **stopped training**' |
| | ⇐ 美丽的青岛奥帆中心最终迎来了成功的第29届奥帆赛<br>⇐ *měilì de Qīngdǎo Àofān Zhōngxīn zuìzhōng yíng lái le chénggōng de dì èrshíjiǔ jiè Àofānsài*<br>⇐ 'the beautiful Qingdao Olympic Sailing Centre finally greeted the successful 29th Olympic sailing events' | | |
| | | | **Hyper-New** |

of the text involve foreshadowing, some summarisation and evaluation, some both. We have revealed through our description how the patterns of Theme and New organise information flow in discourse. Making sense of information flow in a clause is only possible by interpreting that clause in relation to its co-text. This reminds us once again that lexicogrammar is there to make meaning, but equally importantly that the fundamental unit of meaning in any language is the text, not the tone group or the clause.

## 6.5 Information Flow Challenge

For those of you familiar with other languages, we trust that we have now modelled an approach to THEME and INFORMATION systems that you will find instructive, and in part challenging. Our SFL perspective can be usefully compared with work on information flow in other traditions (with reference to terms such as Topic and Focus). When doing so, try and make explicit the reasoning deployed in these traditions, comparing it with that introduced above. For those of you familiar with English, Spanish or Chinese, we reiterate as a reminder here that the descriptions introduced above have been provided for pedagogic purposes. They are both preliminary and provisional. SFL grammarians working in the Sydney register of SFL (e.g. Halliday and Matthiessen, 2014) have developed more comprehensive descriptions of English than we have offered here. For Spanish, our proposals here can be usefully contrasted with those in Taboada (1995), Arús (2010) and Lavid, Arús and Zamorano-Mansilla (2010), our approach has been strongly influenced by Moyano (2010, 2016, 2021). For Chinese, our description can be compared with SFL-informed work such as Fang, McDonald and Cheng (1995), Halliday and McDonald (2004) and Li (2007), and other discussions of Chinese topic/theme – e.g. Chao (1968), Lü (1979), Tsao (1980), Li and Thompson (1981), LaPolla (2009). And finally, we note that we have assumed the foundations of SFL theory and description outlined in Matthiessen and Halliday (1997/2009) and Martin, Wang and Zhu (2013) here, as well as drawing on the discourse semantic descriptions of periodicity in Martin (1992) and Martin and Rose (2007).

Our challenge for this chapter involves a shift of genre, from the story family to procedures (Martin and Rose, 2008). At stake here is the question of whether or not to allow for Predicator Themes. We pose the challenge for the following recipe in Spanish (Appendix 3.5). Co-referential nominal groups and potentially co-referential verb morphology are highlighted in bold face, and Predicators in italics below.

Sopaipillas
'fritters'

Por Centro de Cocina Paula
'by the Paula Kitchen Centre'

En los días invernales y fríos, *olvídate* de las cremas y chocolates. *Date* un gusto con esta receta de antaño.
'In these wintry and cold days, forget the custards and chocolates. Give yourself a treat with this recipe from old times.'

Personas
'persons'
6–8 personas
'6–8 persons'

Ingredientes
'ingredients'

1 taza de zapallo molido
'1 cup of mashed pumpkin'
2 tazas de harina
'2 cups of flour'
2 cucharadas de manteca o grasa
'2 spoons of butter or lard'
Manteca para la fritura
'butter for the frying'
Sal
'salt'

Preparación
'preparation'
1. Todos estos ingredientes *se revuelven*, pero *no se amasan*.
'**All these ingredients** are stirred, but not kneaded.'
2. Si **la masa** *no se despega, se le incorpora* **un poco más de harina**.
'If **the dough** doesn't come away, **a little more flour** is added.'
3. *Se uslerea* y *se corta* en discos.
'(The dough) is rolled out and cut into disks'
*Se pican* para que *no se inflen* y *se fríen* en manteca o grasa muy caliente.
'(The disks) are pricked so that they don't rise and are fried in very hot butter or lard.'
4. *Se sirve* con salsa de chancaca caliente.
'(The dish) is served with hot brown sugar sauce'

The introduction to this procedure comprises two A2 moves (commands), suggesting that readers give up their custards and chocolates in favour of this traditional *sopaipillas* 'fritters' dessert; both deploy an informal 2nd person, imperative mood, active voice verbal group to realise these moves (*olvída-te* 'forget', *da-te*[24] 'give yourself'). Once the preparation stage is under way, this realisation gives way to a series of clauses included with what Quiroz (2013) calls recessive *se* voice verbal groups.[25] In terms of the analysis developed above, the ranking clauses in the recipe could be analysed as follows (we've added the heading Textual Theme to Table 6.27, using the standard SFL label for these clause initial linkers).

As was the case for our Ola Maldita analyses above, the recipe favours implicit unmarked Themes. It opens with implicit reference to the reader – notated with the informal second person pronoun as (*tú*) above. Once the recessive *se* instructions get under way, an explicit pre-Predicator Theme is used to

---

[24] Unlike *olvída-te, da-te* is reflexive.
[25] Many Spanish recipes use a non-finite 'infinitive' verbal group rather than a finite one in this genre – with *revolver* in place of *se revuelven*, *amasar* in place of *se amasan* and so on (*incorporar* for *se incorpora*, *uslerea* for *se uslerea*, *cortar* for *se corta*, *picar* for *se pican*, *freír* for *se fríen*, *servir* for *se sirve*); these verbal groups do not assign modal responsibility and so unmarked Theme would have to be inferred from a corresponding finite verbal group (such as those used in our recipe above).

Table 6.27 *Information flow in the sopaipillas recipe*

| linker | Marked Theme (Cir, P2, P3) | Theme | Predicator | Theme/New |
|---|---|---|---|---|
| | *En los días ...* 'in the days ...' | (tú) 'you' | *olvídate* 'forget' | |
| | | (tú) 'you' | *date* 'give yourself' | |
| *1* | | *Todos estos ingredientes* 'all these ingredients' | *se revuelven* 'are stirred' | |
| *pero* 'but' | | *la masa* 'the dough' | *no se amasan* 'are not kneaded' | |
| *2, Si* 'if' | | (la masa) 'the dough' | *no se despega* 'doesn't come away' | |
| | | | *se le incorpora* 'is added' | *un poco más de harina* 'a little more flour' |
| *3* | | (la masa) 'the dough' | *Se uslerea* 'is rolled out' | |
| *y* | | (la masa) 'the dough' | *se corta* 'is cut' | |
| | | (los discos) 'the disks' | *se pican* 'are pricked' | |
| *para que* 'so that' | | (los discos) 'the disks' | *no se inflen* 'don't rise' | |
| *y* 'and' | | (los discos) 'the disks' | *se fríen* 'are fried' | |
| *4* | | (el plato) 'the dish' | *Se sirve* 'is served' | |

reference the ingredients (*todos los ingredientes* 'all the ingredients') and the dough (*la masa* 'the dough'), and an explicit post-Predicator Theme for added flour (*un poco más de harina* 'a little more flour'). The rest of the *se* clause Themes are implicit, sustaining our gaze on the preparation – notated in Table 6.20 as (*la masa* 'the dough'), (*los discos* 'the disks') and (*el plato* 'the dish') as the fritters emerge.[26] There is one Marked Theme, in the opening clause (*En los días invernales y fríos* 'in these wintry and cold days'), signposting the beginning of the genre.

---

[26] The change in person from singular *se corta* 'cut' (for *la masa*), to plural *se pican* 'prick' (for *los discos*) and back to singular *se sirve* 'serve' (for *el plato*) reflects the fact that the dough (singular) is transforming into disks (plural) which are then served as a dish (singular again). The procedure's method of development tracks this transformation, adjusting our gaze on the field as the text unfolds.

## 6.5 Information Flow Challenge

As far as this analysis is concerned, one might object that most of the clauses begin as far as ideation is concerned with a Predicator, and that in terms of method of development it might make sense to say that in procedural genres our gaze is fixed on occurrences as they unfold, not the entities involved. After all, this genre adopts a dynamic perspective on field (as activity), not a static one (i.e. field as items).

In relation to this objection, we will allow ourselves two comments. First, the objection assumes that first position in a Spanish clause is privileged in so far as the realisation of the method of development of a text is concerned. Our analyses in this chapter follow a different assumption. We have assumed that unmarked Themes in Spanish are realised through agreement with the Predicator (not position in the clause) and sustain our gaze on the field regardless of their position in the clause. Second, we would ask about the meaning potential of THEME systems in Spanish. What is the system that makes the Predicator the unmarked Theme in procedures of this kind, but not unmarked Theme elsewhere. What is the system? What is its entry condition? What are its features? What are the realisation statements associated with its features? Is it the case that the Predicators in clause sequences of this kind are clause initial by default – as a result of choices in other systems, not because there is a system making them unmarked Theme?

As a final caveat we need to remind ourselves that with respect to types of structure, SFL predicts that textual meaning will be realised by wave-like structures rather than particulate ones (Halliday, 1979/2002; Martin, 1996) and that informational prominence (both thematicity and newsworthiness) might be better treated as a matter of degree (as waves merge into troughs). This would mean establishing criteria for assigning degrees of thematicity or newsworthiness to interpersonal and ideational grammatical functions (a challenging task associated with the work of the Prague School on degrees of communicative dynamism (Firbas, 1966; Daneš, 1974). Needless to say, we have not addressed this issue here.

Our challenge? Try out some networks. Analyse some more procedural texts in relation to texts of other kinds. Position yourself in this debate. The references in Moyano (2010, 2016, 2021) will give you plenty to chew on, if we haven't already provided you with enough stimulus here. And have a go at some recipes and other types of procedural text in English and Chinese.

# 7 Envoi

## 7.1 Our Goal

As proposed in Chapter 1, the goal of this book has been to model the way in which grammatical descriptions can be most effectively developed in SFG, based on the basic principles of SFL. We have written this book because we believe that descriptions of different languages are important. In many regions around the world, people first bump into SFL in relation to one or another of its more 'marketable' dimensions – for example cohesion in the 1970s, genre in the 1980s, multimodal discourse analysis in the 1990s, appraisal in the first decade of the twenty-first century and perhaps identity in the 2020s. These fragments of SFL are often adopted and deployed, in descriptions and applications, in a way that leaves behind the theory as a whole. This becomes especially problematic when what is marketable was originally designed for one language, English, and is taken up and tacked onto another language without due consideration for how it needs to be recontextualised for that language, if in fact it fits at all. Borrowing from SFL is great; it's something we of course want to encourage. But we would also strongly encourage borrowers to get directly involved in the language they are in fact working with and start producing descriptions of their own. Such work will inevitably enrich applications, as a holistic integrated account of the meaning-making resources of a given language evolves. We have written this book to foster descriptive developments of this kind.

That said, our pedagogic exercise has imposed a number of limitations on what we could achieve. In this culminative chapter, we will review several of these and make some suggestions about steps that need to be taken as readers undertake fully fledged functional grammar descriptions of their own.

## 7.2 Methodology

Methodological concerns are at the heart of this volume and so need to be carefully framed here. In Chapter 1 we foregrounded three critical dimensions of methodology (i.e. data, appliability and axial argumentation), to which we return in this section.

## 7.2 Methodology

First data. In a pedagogic book of this kind, we have only been able to mimic the kind of responsibility functional grammars bear as far as basing analyses on instances of language use is concerned. We used very few texts; at times we used constructed examples to simplify the presentation; at other times we adjusted examples from the texts we used to make a point; and at all times we limited our discussion to examples from English, Chilean Spanish and Chinese. These are serious limitations. Finding examples of everything we want to describe is of course a major challenge. The functional grammar of English first published as Halliday (1985) has now gone through four editions (1985, 1994; Halliday and Matthiessen, 2004, 2014) and is still being enriched with corpus examples as more data becomes available and computational tools for retrieving grammatical structures improve. In the absence of extant corpora, every effort should be made to collect texts that are in some sense representative of a register and genre. Perhaps the best advice we can give is to suggest that data needs to comprise a range of registers and genres, and that the potential limitations of this range be carefully considered.

Another comment we would make is that the model of genre and register we use needs to be based as far as possible on a linguistically informed theory of register and genre. Canonical SFL exemplars of language-based theories include Halliday and Martin (1993), Christie and Martin (1997) and Martin and Rose (2008). Theories of this kind make predictions about recurrent patterns of meaning. It is only through models of this kind that we can be sure that we are enriching our coverage of grammar by introducing more data. And it is only through models of this kind that we can select data on the basis of what we hope to find.

Unfortunately most corpora are organised not on the basis of linguistic categories but in terms of common-sense notions of uses of language (explaining, arguing, recommending, instructing, reviewing, narrating, etc.), workplace categories (media discourse, academic discourse, medical discourse, legal discourse, etc.) or professional rhetoric of various kinds (a journalist's news story, a manager's report, an administrator's memo, a secondary school teacher's essay, an academic's research article and so on). These common-sense, workplace and professional categories do not make reliable predictions about recurrent patterns of meaning, because from a linguistic perspective they are mixed-bag categories, each involving a variety of registers and genres. Sometimes this seems harmless enough; people apparently get on perfectly well with the everyday categories they have evolved. In other cases the results are disastrous, as has been the case in western education where a wide range of very different genres involving very different patterns of meaning are referred to as stories in primary school, as essays in secondary school or as research articles in tertiary institutions. The educational linguists of the so-called Sydney

School have been struggling against these mixed-bag categorisations and the pernicious confusions they entail for decades (Rose and Martin, 2012).

The challenge then, for functional grammarians, is to organise data in such a way that as full a spectrum of grammatical resources as possible is revealed. SFL's register and genre theory and the predictions it makes about the linguistic resources differentiating registers and genres is a key resource for pursuing this goal.

The final point we will make about data has to do with quantitative studies and SFG. Very often throughout this book we have used modalities of usuality to temper our remarks (*general, often, typical, usually* we write in Chapter 6 alone). Each occasion we do so prompts the question – what statistical probability are we referring to with respect to what corpus of texts? Halliday (e.g. Halliday, 2008; see Webster, 2005) has suggested that all grammatical systems centre on either equal probability (0.5 and 0.5) or a 0.9 to 0.1 skew, and that this is a basic property of their learnability. In Halliday and James (1993) he backs this up with a quantitative study of POLARITY and PRIMARY TENSE in English (with reference to 18 million words of written text in the original Cobuild corpus) and presents results supporting his predictions. This probabilistic approach to choice in systems is the foundation of SFL studies of register and genre, since context systems are realised by adjusting the inherent probabilities of language systems – genre by genre, stage by stage within a genre, and phase by phase within a stage. Nesbitt and Plum (1988) explore this contextual dimension of quantitative studies, focusing on clause complex relations in a corpus organised by genre. Their study highlights the significance of co-patterning among systems, with choices in the systems of TAXIS and LOGICO-SEMANTICS affecting one another. This quantitative dimension of SFG is currently being developed by Giacomo Figueredo with special reference to Brazilian Portuguese (Figueredo, 2014; Figueredo and Figueredo, 2020).

As a note of caution, at this point we should emphasise that for pedagogic reasons we have not modelled this rigorous approach to managing data in this book. Rather our approach has been opportunistic, focusing on as few texts as possible to introduce the approaches to grammar description we were intent on foregrounding. Responsible language description requires a different methodology, respecting the strategies we are outlining here. Cummings (2021) and Figueredo (2021) provide models of how to move forward, in their corpus-based studies of nominal groups.

Next appliability. Our reference to educational linguistics in the previous paragraphs draws attention to the fact that we have not been able to address regions of application in this book. This means that as far as this volume is concerned, the idea that functional grammars of the kind we are modelling here (namely the idea that such grammars provide a crucial foundation for applications in educational linguistics, forensic linguistics, clinical linguistics, translation studies and beyond) has to be taken as a matter of faith. Beyond this volume there are of course many projects we can point to, where functional grammars of English have played a pivotal role. The literacy programs of the Sydney School are one outstanding exemplar (reviewed in Rose and Martin, 2012). Zappavigna and Martin's (2018) study of diversionary justice is another. Caldwell, Knox and Martin (2022) provides a survey of interventions across a wide range of applications. Our critical point here is that applications depend on an analysis of meaning making in the texts constituting communication in any site of intervention. Rich functional descriptions of grammar conceived as a meaning-making resource are fundamental in studies of this kind. Without them, discourse semantic analyses of meaning beyond the clause such as those presented in Martin (1992), Martin and White (2005) and Martin and Rose (2007) cannot be developed.[1] And in the absence of descriptions of both lexicogrammar and discourse semantics as meaning-making resources, models of register and genre as recurrent patterns of meaning cannot be conceived.

It is helpful to think about this in ecological terms. Holistic models of language are far more powerful than fragmented ones. And the most powerful thing about SFL's holistic approach to modelling language and context is that it dissolves the need for the linguistics/applied linguistics schism that so debilitates theory, description and application around the world. SFL can be used not only to describe existing registers and genres but also to design and study the implementation of changes to social practice. This is what makes SFL appliable linguistics, not linguistics or applied linguistics. And rich functional grammars are a key component in a holistic model of language of this kind.

Next argumentation. We have to be very careful here. In this book we have considered only three languages, which we selected because they are arguably three major world languages (and so address a worldwide readership) and because they reflect our personal expertise. They are different from one another, as we have shown. But we have to be modest. They are hardly representative of the range of grammatical patterns that have evolved in languages around the world. This is clear from the SFG studies of eight different languages in Caffarel, Martin and Matthieseen (2004), alongside Matthiessen's

---

[1] It is instructive in this regard to compare the strategy favoured by linguists assuming a formal model of morphology and syntax as they turn their attention to semantics and pragmatics – namely abdication. Instead of developing semantics as linguists, they draw insightfully on philosophy (e.g. truth functional semantics or speech act theory); instead of developing pragmatics as linguists, they draw insightfully on sociology (e.g. conversation analysis, aka CA), anthropology (e.g. ethnography of communication), cultural studies (e.g. critical theory) or cognitive psychology (models of mind). SFL, on the other hand, models language as an integrated meaning-making resource, thus affording a sovereign approach to discourse semantics, register and genre – i.e. a holistic analysis of co-text and context informed by linguistic theory and description.

(2004) wide-ranging culminative chapter in that book. Mwinlaaru and Xuan (2016) survey a fairly comprehensive collection of SFG work, across language families. For collections of recent studies, see the special issue of the journal *Functions of Language* focusing on interpersonal grammar (Martin, 2018c); Martin, Doran and Figueredo, 2020; Martin, Quiroz and Figueredo, 2021; and four special issues of *Word* edited by Doran, Martin and Zhang over 2021 and 2022 – 67(3), 67(4), 68(1) and 68(2). Among the work that we have found most inspirational are Caffarel's (2006) grammar of French and Rose's (2001) grammar of Western Desert (Pitjantjatjara). The grammar of Korean developed by Kim et al. (2023) implements the kind of description we hope to inspire in this book. All we can really do given the limitations of our coverage of languages in this volume is to advise caution. We have modelled developing SFL informed grammar for just three languages here; we all have a great deal more to learn.

Following the methodological advice we are giving here involves compiling data, undertaking and recording analyses, drawing system networks and writing realisation statements. Fortunately, Mick O'Donnell of the Universidad Autónoma de Madrid (UAM) has developed a very helpful workbench called Corpus Tool to help with work of this kind. It can be downloaded free at the following URL: www.corpustool.com/.

John Bateman of the University of Bremen has also designed an open access system, KPML, which he describes as "a graphically-based development environment for the construction, maintenance, and use of large-scale grammars written with the framework of Systemic-Functional Linguistics (SFL)". His site has been particularly designed to support multilingual grammar development and natural language generation: www.fb10.uni-bremen.de/anglistik/langpro/kpml/README.html.

## 7.3 Functional Language Typology

Comparing languages is a problematic enterprise, but one which few linguists are able to resist. The privileging of paradigmatic relations in SFG makes language comparison a more challenging enterprise still. As linguists influenced by Saussure have long acknowledged, the meaning of any linguistic choice lies in its valeur. And if the valeur of a choice in one language is different from its valeur in another, because it enters into different oppositions, then the meaning of that choice is not the same. One only has to review the pronoun systems for English, Spanish and Chinese discussed in this volume to realise the challenge posed by differences in valeur; and languages are seldom completely consistent with themselves. Spanish, for example, has a distinct set of oppositions for clause rank personal pronouns and verbal group pronominal clitics (not to mention its salient and non-salient possessive determiners and the variations

## 7.3 Functional Language Typology

from one dialect of Spanish to another).[2] What does it mean to compare pronoun systems in Spanish, with one another, or to pronoun systems in English, or Chinese? If the valeur is different, what is the common ground?

Let's explore this problem of common ground step by step to see where it takes us. Pronoun systems we confidently wrote above, as if it was clear what we were talking about. Was it? Consider the following Spanish clauses (everyday invitations to the cinema). The Circumstance of Accompaniment in the first example is a phrase, with the pronoun *nosotras* as complement – *con nosotras* 'with us'; in the second example the Circumstance is a word, *conmigo* 'with me', whose morphological analysis we will set aside here (cf. *contigo* 'with you', *consigo* 'with himself/herself', but not \**connosotrosigo*, \**conellosigo* etc.). Is *conmigo* a pronoun?

¿Quieres ir **con nosotras** al cine?
'Would you like to go to the movies with us?'

¿Quieres ir **conmigo** al cine?
'Would you like to go to the movies with me?'

Of interest here is the fact that we have what appears to be the same meaning but divergent structural realisations. In SFL we can bring axis into play at this point and argue that as far as paradigmatic relations are concerned, we have the same systems in play – the same ACCOMPANIMENT system at clause rank and the same PERSON system at group rank. The contrast between *con nosotras* and *conmigo* is not systemic but structural. In the first example the same choices are realised as a phrase and in the second as a word. This example shows how the dimension of axis, with its complementarity of paradigmatic and syntagmatic relations (the latter realising the former), can be used to explore similarity and differences between languages. For example, as the glosses above reveal, English always realises comparable choices as phrases (*with us*, *with me*), not single words.

Consider now the following Chilean Spanish clauses, recounting a moment in a trip to the cinema. In both we have three Participants realised by nominal groups.[3] In the first example all three nominal groups have nouns realising Thing (*niña* 'girl', *entrada* 'ticket', *amigo* 'friend'); in the second the first and third of these Things is realised by a pronoun (*ella* 'she', *él* 'him').

---

[2] The four types of 'pronoun' referred to here are illustrated in the following sentence (in sequence, personal pronoun *ella* 'she', pronominal clitic *le* 'for her', non-salient possessive determiner *su* 'her', salient possessive determiner *mía* 'mine'): *la entrada que* ***ella le*** *compró a* ***su*** *amiga no es* ***mía*** 'the ticket she bought her friend isn't mine'. The main dialectal variation has to do with 2nd person (the use or not of *os, vos, vosotros, vosotras, vuestro, vuestra*).

[3] We are treating *a un amigo* 'for a friend' as an adpositional nominal group here, on the grounds that it can be alternatively realised or additionally realised inside the verbal group as a pronominal clitic (examples follow). See Quiroz (2013) for the detailed reasoning distinguishing adpositional nominal groups from prepositional phrases.

La niña le compró una entrada a un amigo.
'The girl bought a ticket for a friend.'

**Ella** le compró una entrada a **él**.
'She bought him a ticket.'

As we saw in Chapter 5, Spanish Participants can be realised inside verbal groups by pronominal clitics and inflectional morphology. All three Participants are conflated with the Process in realisations of this kind, exemplified below (Quiroz in press).

**Se la** compró.
'She bought it for him.'

And clitic doubling means that Participants can be realised both ways, both inside and alongside a verbal group.[4]

La entrada, la niña **se la** compró a un amigo.
'The girl bought a ticket for a friend.'

La entrada, ella **se la** compró a él.
'The girl bought a ticket for him.'

Of interest here, then, is the fact that in Spanish Participants can be realised by nominal groups at clause rank, or inside verbal groups, or both – whereas English, lacking pronominal clitics, is restricted to realising Participants as nominal groups at clause rank. In SFL the concept of rank can be used to generalise across these two realisation systems, with TRANSITIVITY systems at clause rank showing how the languages are similar, and realisation statements potentially diversifying the realisation of the Chilean Spanish system across clause and group ranks structures (bringing verbal group systems into the picture where required).

Consider now the following Spanish clause, which uses the demonstrative *esa* 'that' to refer to the ticket.

La niña le compró **esa** a un amigo.
'The girl bought that one for/from a friend.'

Spanish uses a demonstrative rather than a pronoun here because personal pronouns are rarely used to realise unconscious entities in nominal groups. The ticket participant can, on the other hand, be alternatively realised or 'doubled' as a pronominal clitic (*la* 'it' below); consciousness is not an issue for pronominal clitics.

---

[4] The specific conditions favouring P2 doubling vary across Spanish varieties. See, e.g., Silva-Corvalán (1980–1981, 1981), Bogard (1999), Fernández Soriano (1999a), Enrique-Arias (2003), Belloro (2007, 2009), Vázquez Rozas & García Salido (2012), among others, for more detail.

La niña se **la** compró a un amigo.
'The girl bought it for a friend.'

This brings another system into the picture, the system of demonstratives, which is used to realise a Deictic in nominal group structure (e.g. *esa entrada* 'that ticket' or *esa* 'that'). This system involves a very different set of oppositions to those for the Spanish salient and non-salient possessive determiner, personal pronoun and pronominal clitic systems we discussed in Chapters 2 to 6.

| number | singular | | plural | |
|---|---|---|---|---|
| gender | masculine | feminine | masculine | feminine |
| near speaker | este | esta | estos | estas |
| near interlocutors | ese | esa | esos | esas |
| near neither | aquel | aquella | aquellos | aquellas |

Our point here is that in nominal groups referring to non-conscious entities, demonstratives play the same role as pronouns. We have two systems, but the same role. The 'same role' we just wrote; what did that mean? In SFL the concept of stratification can be used to make explicit what we mean. The relevant discourse semantic system is IDENTIFICATION (Martin, 1992; Martin and Rose, 2007), whose presuming options track entities in discourse. These options can be used to generalise across a range of lexicogrammatical realisations, including Spanish personal pronoun, pronominal clitic and demonstrative systems just reviewed. They also provide us with a comparable vantage point from which to explore differences in participant tracking resources and their use across languages. Unlike Spanish, for example, English pronouns can track non-conscious entities (e.g. *the wave toppled the trees/it toppled **them***). And as we saw in Chapter 6, unlike English, Spanish is comfortable tracking entities with implicit unmarked Themes between clause complexes (there are no Spanish personal pronouns tracking entities in the sequence below).

La niña le compró una entrada a un amigo.
'the girl bought a ticket for a friend'

Disfrutaron la película
'(they) enjoyed the movie'

y volvieron a casa.
'and (they) returned home'

The general rule of thumb we are developing here is that when things look different, move 'up' and look again. From the point of view of axis, different structures may be realising comparable systems; from the point of view of constituency, structures at different ranks may be realising comparable systems; and from the point of view of stratification, an array of lexicogrammatical resources may perform comparable discourse semantic functions. In SFL we can, in principle, push this two steps further on, asking (i) how different discourse semantic systems realise comparable field, mode and tenor variables, and (ii) how different combinations of register variables cooperate to realise the comparable genre systems. As far as functional language typology is concerned, what is important is to be explicit about the perspective we are comparing languages from – which stratum, which rank, which axis? We also need to keep in mind that any generalisations we make will have to be treated as defeasible, since what looks the same or different from one vantage point can look rather different from another.

This brings us to the important question of which languages and parts of languages to study and why. How should we invest our time? Let's think about this briefly here from the perspective of SFL, foregrounding methodology – data, appliability and argumentation. For a discussion of this kind it is important to separate languages into two groups, which we'll refer to as 'robust' and 'endangered' here. Robust languages are learned by significant numbers of children as their first language and are likely to be so for generations to come; endangered languages are learned by relatively few, if any, children and are unlikely to be learned once these children have children of their own.

As far as robust languages are concerned, having plenty of data around to work on is not an issue. There will be a range of registers and genres to consider, even if many communicative functions have been assumed by dominant national and/or international languages in the region. Argumentation is less problematic in the sense that there may be extant descriptions to build on and there are generations of time available for functional linguists to work their way deeply into the language; and ideally there is enough social mobility in regions where the language is mainly used outside of the workplace and education for native speakers of that language to be trained as researchers. The main selective force as far as research on robust languages is concerned is rather appliability. Where will the funding come from for linguists to work developing functional grammars? Purely academic resources are by nature limited (involving teaching and research positions in tertiary institutions, PhD students and personnel funded by grants). Much more funding, and increasingly this includes grant funding, scholarships and appointments, is available where linguists can convince people they can make a substantial contribution to solving communication problems in regions of practice (educational linguistics, forensic linguistics, clinical linguistics, translation studies and so on). SFL is well positioned to make arguments of this kind by drawing on ongoing achievements and pointing out future possibilities.

Turning to endangered languages, currently there is a sense of urgency among descriptive linguists around the world as they are confronted with the phenomenon of language 'death'. Languages are disappearing before they can be described, with neo-liberal capitalism and climate change marching hand-in-hand to accelerate the genocide. There aren't enough linguists to keep pace, in spite of the committed efforts of field workers around the world.

By way of addressing this grim reality, we would offer three comments. In terms of data, for which languages can we explore a range of registers and genres that could provide us with a reasonable picture of the phonological, lexicogrammatical and discourse semantic resources of that language? Endangered languages experience a fast-diminishing reservoir of registers and genres as these functions are taken over by the languages replacing them.

In terms of appliability, the pressing challenge is language maintenance, and where hope for this is forlorn, the challenge lies in developing descriptions that might serve the needs of language revitalisation in generations to come. For which languages, we can ask, is a maintenance intervention practicable; and for which languages is a revitalisation intervention foreseeable? Maintenance and revitalisation are enormous challenges – challenges that cannot be met through descriptions limited in scope to the segmental phonology, morphology and some of the syntax of endangered languages.

Finally, in terms of argumentation, we should stress that it takes a long time for linguists to become familiar enough with a language to explore covert categories and their reactances (Quiroz, 2020). This is probably not something that can be pushed very far in PhD work on undescribed languages, since time and funding constraints generally limit research to several months in the field, with perhaps a follow-up trip later on; and the more threatened the language, the less likelihood there will be accessible native speakers around back home. Ideally, of course, we'd like linguistically trained native speakers of dying languages to emerge; but once again, the more endangered the language, the less likely this is to happen. What is probably more likely is that the linguist or linguists involved will end up as the last speakers of the language, with no one else left to talk to.

Taking all this into account, we would argue from the perspective of SFL that for a maintenance intervention to be practicable, then compiling a corpus of texts across a range of extant registers and genres must be a priority, both in terms of profiling the resources of the language and in terms of providing models of meaningful uses of these resources for maintenance purposes. There are challenges here in so far as access to speakers, aging speakers and missing registers and genres are concerned (in some cases it may prove useful to document comparable registers and genres in affine communities where a different, perhaps unrelated, language is spoken but cultural practices are shared). It then falls to the functional linguists involved, however limited the data, to work their way into the grammars of these languages as quickly as possible in order to document how meaning beyond the clause is grammaticalised. Realistically speaking, it is only through research of this kind that endangered languages

380  Envoi

have any hope of being maintained and, where this fails, have some hope, however faint, of being revitalised, however partially, down the line.

Note that in arguing along these lines we are deliberately not prioritising our discipline's concern with archiving descriptions of as many languages as possible before they stop being learned by children. This research trajectory diverts attention from maintenance and revitalisation projects that could serve the needs of the speakers concerned and towards the academic careers of linguists who are worried about language death because of all the things they'll never know.[5] From the perspective of appliable linguistics, the needs of speakers of endangered languages should come first. Social responsibility, in other words, should be privileged over purely academic concerns.

## 7.4  Off You Go

Academic research is a social enterprise, however monastic we might sometimes feel. As you embark on functional grammar description, whether for purposes of renovating existing descriptions, extending them or developing new ones of your own, remember you have friends around. There is an international English SFL e-mail list you can join (SYSFLING) and several regional lists (e.g. ASFLAnet and ALSFAL-lista). You can find out how to join these and other lists (involving various languages) and learn more about work going on around the world at the website of the International Systemic Functional Linguistics Association (maintained by Mick O'Donnell): www.isfla.org/Systemics/index.html.

There you can also find out about international SFL meetings, which rotate annually around the world (in what is currently a Europe, Asia, Australia, North America and Latin America cycle). In addition, there are annual regional conferences held in several parts of the world, including Australia, Europe, Scandinavia, Latin America, China and Japan. Each meeting has a different flavour, in general reflecting the research interests of organisers. News about meetings and calls for papers are usually posted on SYSFLING. Our experience of these meetings is that they are welcoming events – for several reasons. One is that many colleagues, although this is far more true of some parts of the world than others, work in research and practice environments where there

---

[5] In this regard it is salutary to keep in mind that languages have been disappearing throughout human history, as hunter/gatherer communities are overwhelmed by urban/farming ones, and these in turn by industrialised capitalism, and these in turn by web-based neo-liberalism (and these in turn, we can now confidently predict, by 'growth'-driven climate change). The languages that remain are only a fragment of the languages that ever were, so we can never build anywhere near a complete picture even if we could document all the languages that remain. It's far too late in other words to panic; linguistics has more to learn from deeper descriptions of languages across a wider range of registers and genres than shallow accounts across a smaller range.

## 7.4 Off You Go

aren't many other systemic functional linguists to talk to; so they are glad to meet colleagues they can talk to about SFL. Another is that many colleagues work in fields of application where they are strongly committed to changing practice, and they have an appetite for finding out how others are addressing similar concerns. One more factor we expect is that many of us, until Halliday came along, had never realised what language was. Sure we'd studied language and some of its structures. But we had never appreciated language as the meaning-making resource that defines our humanity and enacts our social practice. That was irresistible news!

Come along, in person or online; we look forward to meeting you and hearing about your work. We do hope this book has in some part helped you on your way.

Onward!
Adelante!
加油!
;-)

# Afterword: Describing Languages Systemic-Functionally

*Christian M. I. M. Matthiessen*

**Three Steps**

This book is an important step in the engagement with the lexicogrammatical system of language viewed and interpreted ecologically in its semiotic environment (between semantics and phonology or graphology or sign). It is the third step in a series of books focused largely on systemic functional theory of language as a general human semiotic system operating within the domain of lexicogrammar and manifested in the description of the lexicogrammatical systems of particular languages.

The first step was taken by Michael Halliday and me in a short monograph, originally drafted in the 1990s as part of a large-scale publication project planned by our friend and colleague Fred Peng and later published in English with a Chinese translation and additional material in Chinese by Huang Guowen and Wang Hongyang as Matthiessen and Halliday (2009). In this monograph, we foregrounded the theoretical aspect of the approach to lexicogrammar in SFL, conceiving of it as a stand-alone complement to Halliday's *Introduction to Functional Grammar* (IFG) – which by then had come to be supported by other publications of a more introductory nature (e.g. Thompson's *Introducing Functional Grammar*, Martin, Matthiessen and Painter's *Deploying Functional Grammar*, and Bloor and Bloor's *Functional Analysis of English*), leaving room for IFG to grow in size and coverage, and my own *Lexicogrammatical Cartography* (LexCart), which is not introductory but which foregrounds systems as the way into the description of lexicogrammar.

These books all interleave theory and description. The descriptions they present are focused on English (although I included typological outlooks in LexCart); but, in our *First Step*, Halliday and I decided to include examples not only from English but also from Chinese and Japanese in order to illustrate the descriptive application of the theory to languages from different language families and also to languages with different typological profiles. Halliday had, of course, worked extensively on Chinese since the late 1940s, and I had done some work on Japanese (learning from John Bateman, see Matthiessen and

Bateman, 1991 – although the languages I had engaged with more as a linguist by the early 1990s included (Modern Standard) Arabic and Akan. And since we began the work on the monograph, Kazuhiro Teruya had started his long-term research programme concerned with the development of a comprehensive systemic functional description of Japanese (1998, 2007), which has been used extensively in further work on Japanese and used as a model in the development of descriptions of other languages.

While our *First Step* was, in a sense, excerpted from Peng's publication project and was part of a series of steps we had planned, it was J. R. Martin who took the second step with his *Systemic Functional Grammar: A Next Step into the Theory – Axial Relations* (Martin, Wang and Zhu, 2013). Here it is actually essential to include the full title of his book, because the focus on axial relations is absolutely crucial – as the current volume demonstrates throughout in the engagement with the languages under description. Halliday (e.g. 1966) had given priority to paradigmatic relations, deriving syntagmatic relations from them (through realisation statements[1]).

This turned out to be crucial, also to the success of the development of a computational model of systemic functional grammar as part of text generation systems (e.g. Matthiessen and Bateman, 1991); and I used the paradigmatic axis – that is, systemic organisation – as the principle for organising my account of the resources of English lexicogrammar in LexCart (Matthiessen 1995), and thus as a navigational instrument for readers. (When Halliday and I started on the third edition of his IFG, he wanted to include system networks; but we kept the overall orientation in our presentation to structures that realise meaning in text.)

The focus on paradigmatic organisation also turned out to be absolutely necessary as we developed the theory of a multilingual meaning potential (e.g. Bateman et al., 1991; Bateman, Matthiessen and Zeng, 1999; Matthiessen, 2018; see also Matthiessen et al., 2022) – a theory that is highly relevant to the present book and one which could be explored in another step as a way of comparing and contrasting the lexicogrammatical descriptions in relation to their semantic and contextual environments.

In language description, comparison and typology, the focus on paradigmatic relations can play a fundamental role in identifying **cryptogrammatical categories and reactances**, as has been shown in the work by Halliday and other systemic functional linguists (with references to B. L. Whorf's pioneering work). Arguably, most attention has been paid to ideational cryptogrammar and reactances (specifically in relation to the experiential system of transitivity), as in the work by Halliday, Martin and Davidse; but these more hidden

---

[1] Theoretically but also representationally, it is important to emphasise that these are 'statements' – so declarative, not 'rules' – so not procedural.

aspects of grammar are also relevant when we explore the interpersonal and textual resources of grammar and try to bring out interpersonal cryptogrammar and textual cryptogrammar in our descriptions.

Here one example of a challenge is to return to Subject as a function long mistakenly assumed to be present in the description of any language due to the inertia of tradition and considerations from 'below' such as concord, case and sequence, in a helical move where it can then be viewed and reinterpreted as part of the more cryptic patterns of the interpersonal grammar of the clause as a move in dialogic exchanges in terms of interpersonal elevation of one element taking interpersonal reactances into consideration (see Matthiessen, 2004, and, for Japanese, see Teruya, 2007). One important general point is that there will be variation across languages in what categories are more overt and what categories are more covert or cryptic, and this variation may be related to metafunction (which may show up when one explores which metafunctions 'control' marking of 'dependents' by adpositions or cases or of 'head' marking).

The Second Step, Martin, Wang and Zhu (2013), is well documented in the present book since it provides an essential part of the foundation for engaging with different languages not only syntagmatically but also paradigmatically – in fact, paradigmatically in the first instance. Nevertheless, the importance of this approach needs to be emphasised clearly and repeatedly because while there is a well-recognised extended family of functional approaches to language covering a wide range of traditions and concerns, SFL is still the only member of this family giving clear priority to the paradigmatic axis.[2] This fact highlights the unique value of the present volume: there is nothing comparable in the linguistic literature.

**The Third Step**

Martin, Wang and Zhu's *Second Step* was thus concerned with foregrounding the importance of axial relations and the priority given in SFL to the paradigmatic axis, using English as the language of illustration. This feeds directly into the present volume, which extends the descriptive base; it brings out a way of reasoning in the development of descriptions of the lexicogrammatical systems of the languages spoken around the world that has typically remained in the background even when leading linguists have devoted enormous energy to syntagmatically oriented descriptions of a growing range of languages.

---

[2] In the Prague School, both axes have been in view – resonating with Saussure and later Hjelmslev; and this is perhaps most in evidence in Trubetzkoy's (1939) posthumous work on phonology, but, in my opinion, Jakobson (1949) undermined this insight into the balance between the two axes by reinterpreting paradigmatic values in accounts of phoneme 'spaces' as syntagmatic components of phonemes ('distinctive features'), which was then taken up in early generative phonology (see Matthiessen, forthcoming).

Afterword by Christian M. I. M. Matthiessen 385

This *Third Step* is certainly important in that it sheds light on paradigmatic reasoning (including centrally the use of proportionalities); but it does much more than that: it shows how Halliday's trinocular vision can – and actually must – inform the development of descriptions of languages around the world. His original articulation of trinocular vision (e.g. Halliday, 1978) was focused on the hierarchy of stratification: lexicogrammar can be viewed 'from above' – most immediately from the vantage point of semantics, and by another step from the vantage point of context, and 'from below' – from the vantage point of phonology (or alternatively, graphology or sign); and it can be viewed 'from roundabout', from the vantage point of its own stratum of lexicogrammar (the stratum of meaning created as wording). But this trinocular vision extends to the other semiotic dimensions defining the 'architecture' of language in context (see Matthiessen, 2007, forthcoming; Matthiessen and Teruya, forthcoming) – the hierarchies of rank and axis (organising lexicogrammar locally), the spectrum of metafunction (permeating the content plane and the highest ranks of the expression plane, recognised as 'prosody'), the cline of delicacy, and the cline of instantiation (like stratification a completely global semiotic dimension).

As Martin, Quiroz and Wang present the descriptions of English, Spanish and Chinese, they make extensive use of Halliday's trinocular vision, showing again and again how we can reason about phenomena in different languages 'from above', 'from below' and 'from roundabout'. Traditionally, the view 'from below' – in terms of rank, and also in terms of stratification – has tended to be foregrounded because it includes the most 'exposed' parts of any language, i.e. the parts that are the easiest to observe and engage with as overt categories (see Halliday, 1977/2003, 1984/2002). The nature of the most exposed part of language will, obviously, vary from one language to another (as does the nature of the more cryptic, covert aspects of the language); in Ancient Greek, in Latin and in Sanskrit, it was essentially the grammar of the word since it is easy to observe that words have different forms, like the case forms of nouns – but the situation was very different in Classical Chinese; so these languages 'invited' the construction of different linguistic traditions focused on partly different aspects of the total system of language.

In SFL, Halliday's trinocular vision ensures that we always keep shunting (see Halliday, 1961/2002) along semiotic dimensions from one vantage point to another in order to ensure that we do not get locked into a single point of view. The methodology of shunting is illustrated throughout this volume. Very often, the three views adopted along any one semiotic dimension will resonate with one another (at the risk of overusing the term, we might say that they are congruent with one another); but sometimes they do not – and this is significant, partly because this lack of resonance (or 'incongruence') may indicate an internal tension in the system suggesting change in progress, which is of course an integral feature of all linguistic change (as shown by Ellegård's, 1953, pioneering corpus-based quantitative study of the gradual appearance and disappearance of the auxiliary *do* in the interpersonal environments of the systems of MOOD and POLARITY in English over a period of roughly 250 years).

**Comprehensive Descriptions**

So the power of a holistic theory of language in context is very much in evidence in this book – as a resource for developing comprehensive descriptions of particular languages; and the methodology of shunting is part of the kind of relational theory that systemic functional linguists have been constructing since the 1960s (and in the decades before, since J. R. Firth's system-structure theory was also a relational theory of language in context). The authors of this book show how this holistic theory empowers them to present descriptions of English, Spanish and Chinese – systematically and systemically, step by step; and these descriptions are on the path towards comprehensive descriptions.

In Chapter 6, the authors comment on the state of their descriptions: "For those of you familiar with English, Spanish or Chinese, we reiterate as a reminder here that the descriptions introduced above have been provided for pedagogic purposes. They are both preliminary and provisional. SFL grammarians working in the Sydney register of SFL (e.g. Halliday and Matthiessen, 2014) have developed more comprehensive descriptions of English than we have offered here." They then provide some additional references.

This raises the question of what would constitute a comprehensive description of a particular language. We can, of course, review book-length systemic functional descriptions that have been published (including PhD theses). None of them have been designed as reference grammars; rather, the typical measure of comprehensiveness can be related to the degree to which they can support analysis of texts from a wide range of registers,[3] and in many cases, this has involved going 'into the field' to record and then transcribe a significant range of spoken texts in their community settings (see Rose, 2001; Akerejola, 2005; Kumar, 2009; Mwinlaaru, 2017; see also Matthiessen and Teruya, forthcoming).

---

[3] Patpong's (2005) systemic functional description of the lexicogrammar of Thai is an interesting exception. She made the informed choice to start her long-term work on Thai with a corpus of traditional Thai folk tales, and then she checked her findings against a smaller but registerially more varied corpus. More generally, systemic functional descriptions of the lexicogrammatical systems of particular languages are typically based on contextually informed corpora containing what Gu (2002) calls "situated discourse" – rather than the tradition of corpora of American and British English launched in the 1960s (Brown, LOB, and their successors). The context-informed approach to the selection of registers from which to sample texts is, quite naturally, essential to the development of descriptions of the kind presented in this book – descriptions where the view 'from above' is part of the descriptive project from the start.

More generally, we can reason about comprehensiveness in terms of the semiotic dimensions of systemic functional theory; thus a comprehensive description should be geared towards:
- coverage of all metafunctions;
- coverage of all ranks;
- coverage of both axes (paradigmatic and syntagmatic patterns);
- coverage of a number of steps in paradigmatic delicacy, the elaboration in delicacy being an ongoing project;
- coverage of a number of 'phases' along the cline of instantiation from instances towards the total wording potential of a language, the expansion in coverage being a matter of extending the range of registers (functional varieties) accounted for.

Naturally, since the approach to lexicogrammar is ecological in SFL, coverage can also be measured 'from above' (semantics, and by another step context) and from below (phonology, graphology or sign): the description of the lexicogrammar of a language must be accountable to the neighbouring strata.

The first two dimensions from the list above, metafunction and rank, have been used by Halliday in designing function-rank matrices, as in Halliday (1970). In such matrices, the metafunctions are set out horizontally as column headings, and the ranks vertically as row headings, with primary classes being distinguished for each rank. The cells defined by metafunctions and ranks (and primary classes) constitute the locations of all the lexicogrammatical systems of a given language. Such matrices have now been proposed for a number of different languages, and one can compare these and experiment with generalised ones (see Caffarel, Martin and Matthiessen, 2004). For example, if we compare the matrices of the lexicogrammatical systems of Chinese and English, we can see quickly that they differ in terms of grammaticalised process time – ASPECT and TENSE, respectively (see Matthiessen, 2015b).

**Characterology**

Based on a comprehensive description of a given language, we can also begin to develop a profile of the language, identifying properties that seem to go together – not in causal relationships but rather in relationships of semiotic correlation. This is along the lines of Mathesius' notion of the characterology of a language, an important contribution within the Prague School; and such correlations may of course be picked up in the formulation of implicational universals of the kind Greenberg (1966) proposed.

Halliday (2014) proposes seventeen features of Mandarin lexicogrammar and phonology as a basis of a characterology of the language; and he shows how sets of features correlate so that if one visualises these correlations (as I have done), they form a kind of connected graph. Such characterologies based on comprehensive descriptions can be very helpful in the further development of existing descriptions and also in the development of new descriptions of other languages.

They are a central part of systemic functional comparison and typology, and can, as just noted, support descriptive work. For example, as hinted at above, we can contrast the construal in Chinese of the actualisation of the process with the model in Spanish and English, and relate the Chinese construal not only to the system of ASPECT (as opposed to TENSE), but also to the system of PHASE. In Chinese, the actualisation of a process unfolding in time does not imply its completion – so completive phase plays an important role; in English and Spanish, the actualisation of a process unfolding in time does imply its completion (see further Halliday and Matthiessen, 1999, pp. 306–8).

## Choice of Languages

The orientation of this book is, of course, pedagogic – an *invitation to explore* the languages under description; it is part of a contribution to the enormously challenging task of instructing researchers in how to describe a particular language.[4] The languages the authors have chosen are three 'major' languages (however we define 'major' languages; but they are all included in Comrie's edited series of sketches of the major languages of the world and come with long traditions of extensive linguistic descriptions couched in various theoretical frameworks[5]), and one of them is the first – and so far only – global

---

[4] This is, quite naturally, a greater challenge than the task of using an existing description as the basis for text analysis (see Matthiessen, 2014).
[5] From the point of view of politics and economics, 'major languages' tend to be supported by deep pocket books, so research is likely to be fairly abundant; and access to both primary and secondary sources is much more straightforward than with 'minor' languages – in particular, with languages whose speakers have been pushed to the margins of modern nation-states that promote their standard languages. As is well known, in terms of the estimated number of speakers, languages cluster, the largest clusters being (from the 2019 edition of the *Ethnologue*): (1) Mandarin, Spanish, English, Hindi, and Arabic (over 300 million native speakers); (2) Bengali, Russian, Portuguese (between 150 and 230 million speakers); (3) Japanese (around 130 million speakers); and then (4) quite a large number of languages with tens of millions of speakers, the largest one being Punjabi, Marathi, Telugu, Wu, Malay, Turkish, Korean, French, German, Vietnamese and Tamil – but unlike the other groups this group is fairly continuous down to and even below around 10 million speakers. However, the number of speakers is of course only one measure; importantly, languages differ significantly in terms of the geographical distribution of their speakers (see Ostler, 2005). For example, in this respect, Japanese is a fairly 'compact' language, whereas Arabic covers a much larger area (of course, with widespread diglossia). It is not only the number of speakers that determines the presence of a language as a major one – its dispersal around the world and its status in the communities where it is spoken also play an important part. Overall, when we map numbers of speakers against languages, we find an inverted pyramid: a relatively small number of the languages of the world are spoken by the vast majority of people, and a very large number of languages are spoken by very few people (see Harrison, 2007). There are thus not only a large number of languages with fairly few speakers but also many endangered languages.

language, namely English (see Halliday, 2003). They are all standard languages, so they embody – are aggregates of – the very wide range of registers (in Halliday's sense of functional varieties) characteristic of standard languages, including those that have emerged as part of the evolution of institutions of administration, government, the law, education and science & technology. At the same time, they may have gradually shed registers characteristic of languages of small close-knit communities sustained by hunting and gathering or small-scale farming (e.g. Wiessner, 2014[6]; see Rose, 2001, 2005; Halliday, 2010/2013). And while personal and communal multilinguality is likely to have been the norm in human speech fellowships for most of our history (as emphasised by both Halliday and Evans, e.g. Evans, 2010), the users of standard languages are often effectively monolingual (but as standard languages get 'exported' around the world, they may be influenced by the mother tongues of substrate languages overrun by colonisers, as in the case of, e.g., Spanish and Mapuche in Chile or English and Celtic languages).

Regarding the choice of languages, the authors write in the final chapter: "In this book we have considered only three languages, which we selected because they are arguably three major world languages (and so address a worldwide readership) and because they reflect our personal expertise." These two considerations are very good reasons – although I would have increased the number 'three' in "three major world" languages to ensure that a few other languages had been included, certainly Arabic (and Hindi is another good candidate, though of the same language family as English and Spanish); but it is up to those of us who are in a position to add to the descriptive pool presented in this book to expand the range of pedagogic models of how to reason in the development of descriptions of particular languages – including relatively minor ones that have been illuminated through systemic functional descriptions in the work by David Rose (Western Desert), Ernest Akerejola (Oko) and Isaac Mwinlaaru (Dagaare).

The expansion of the pool of pedagogically presented developments of language descriptions is an important task to undertake in order to support

---

[6] There do not appear to be many studies of the registerial ranges of small hunter-gatherer communities (see Wilson, 2019); anthropological studies tend to foreground maps of social activities rather than of semiotic (so also social) ones. But Wiessner's (2014) study of the !Kung is a pioneering exception. She emphasises the importance of the invention of managed fire creating the material condition of campfires that (in addition to changing diets) extended the daily opportunities for, and circumstances of, semiosis. She differentiates 'day talk' and 'night talk', and provides charts of the two in terms of topic / register categories: (1) day talk: complaint, economic, joking, land rights, stories, inter-ethnic; and (2) night talk: stories, complaint, economic, myth, interethnic, land. Motifs that emerge during the day reappear during night talk, but in more generalised and symbolic form. In this way, day time and night time registers complement one another as opportunities for members of the community to process life semiotically. Night time semiosis includes 'trance healing', song and dance.

researchers wanting to develop systemic functional descriptions of particular lexicogrammatical systems – especially since, when viewed against the background of the rich or even exuberant lexicogrammatical variation around the languages of the world, English, Spanish and Chinese are not dramatically different; they are all modern standard languages (serving as the semiotic vehicles of a number of natio- states) and they are all (originally) Eurasian languages – which is significant even if one doesn't subscribe to Joseph Greenberg's account of macro-families.

English and Spanish are, in many ways, typical of languages of western Eurasia (allowing for changes since they began to spread around the world half a millennium ago as part of European colonisation) and Chinese is a fairly typical language of (South-)East Asia (with the exception of, e.g., Korean, Ainu and Japanese). This is how Halliday (2014) characterises Mandarin Chinese within the area of East Asian languages:

> For a start, we could describe Mandarin as a fairly typical East Asian language, part of – perhaps at one end of – a continuum formed, in terms of major languages, by Mandarin, Wu, Hokkien, Cantonese, Vietnamese, Khmer (Cambodian), perhaps Thai, and Malay. These languages have invariant word forms, without morphological variation; they have a constant syllabic structure in the morpheme, generally monosyllabic but disyllabic in Malay; and they have a fixed order of modification, the modifier preceding the modified throughout Sinitic, the other way round in Vietnamese and further south. In representing time, all these languages share a general preference for locating the process by aspect rather than by tense. Aspect is the contrast between latent or ongoing (grammaticalised as imperfective) and actualised or complete (grammaticalised as perfective); tense is deictic time, past, present or future by reference to the here-&-now. In these languages aspect is grammaticalised, while deictic time is unspecified, or realised lexically. Like all such broad generalisations in 'areal linguistics' (the comparative study of languages within a given region), this one begs a number of relevant questions; but it will serve as a starting point for the present discussion.

Thus, if we consider the grammatical model of process time in English, Spanish and Chinese, we can note that English and Spanish construe process time grammatically in terms its location relative to the now of speaking, the basic choice being past vs present vs future – in terms of logical TENSE systems potentially involving intermediate reference times between the now of speaking and the time of the process itself (serial tense construing serial time; cf. Chapter 3, Section 3.2.1 on English and Section 3.3.1 on Spanish), and we find similar tendencies in other languages in western Eurasia. In contrast, Chinese construes process time grammatically in terms of the boundedness of the unfolding of the process in time, the basic distinction being 'perfective' (actualisation of process bounded in time) vs 'imperfective' (actualisation of process unbounded in time) – in terms of experiential ASPECT systems; and in this respect Chinese is like a number of other languages of South-East Asia, including ones from different genetic families such as Tagalog, Vietnamese and Thai.

These two models of process time – the TENSE model and the ASPECT model – would appear to be incompatible alternatives, but it turns out that they are complementary perspectives on process time (see Halliday, 2008, on the fundamental importance of recognising complementarities both in languages and in linguistics), and there are languages between the outer poles of Eurasia with mixed tense-aspect systems, including members of Slavic languages, Indo-Aryan languages and (in my view) Classical and Modern Standard Arabic. (And when we move to other parts of the world of languages, we can expect to find yet other models, including tense systems of an experiential rather than logical nature where time is not serialised but rather taxonomised and the different system of Hopi, as described by Whorf.) Other such systemic complementarities we can expect in different 'mixtures' include the models for construing participation in the process (the complementarity of the transitive and ergative models) and 'protocols' for assessing information (the complementarity of modality: modalisation and evidentiality). Such complementarities are important to look for and identify, since systems are often labelled 'from below', where the complementarities may not be clearly discernible.

When we move to other lexicogrammatical systems, English, Spanish and Chinese will group themselves in other different ways. For example, all three languages have highly grammaticalised pronominal systems – in contrast with languages such as Thai (see Iwasaki and Ingkaphirom, 2005), which tend towards lexical or lexicogrammatical rather than grammatical systems. Naturally, they differ in particular details, as do pronominal systems of different varieties of Spanish (even within particular regions as in Colombia); but on a 'global' scale they are fairly similar.

The general point is, of course, that the lexicogrammatical resources of any particular language embody many lexicogrammatical systems, and each system can be taken as a reference point when we compare, contrast and typologise languages. This is indeed why Halliday has always pointed out that language typology should be focused on systems within languages rather than on whole languages (e.g. Halliday, 1959/60), and I think the consensus around this view has grown considerably over the decades of empirical language typology. In other words, we have to recognise that the nineteenth-century attempts to typologise languages based on a single 'feature' of word grammar is quite unhelpful (see already Sapir's, 1921, contribution to the separation of different aspects of the standard nineteenth-century typologies).

**Paradigmatic Orientation; Metafunctions**

Here, as in the present book, the notion of system is foregrounded – i.e. we give priority to the paradigmatic axis over the syntagmatic axis (see Halliday, 1966/2002; and see Matthiessen, 2015a). This has been important in systemic functional language description, comparison and typology. The primacy of systemic organisation makes it possible to bring out patterns of similarity and difference when we move around the languages of the world that might otherwise not have been highlighted.

At the same time, this means that syntagmatic patterns are shown to serve as realisations of terms in systems, and they are thus always 'contextualised' systemically (paradigmatically). One consequence of this is that terms in one and the same system may be realised syntagmatically at different ranks (or even by either grammatical items or phonological features); and it becomes possible to discern the continuity in comparison of different languages (or different historical phases of one language or language family, as in the well-known case of Romance languages) between syntagmatic patterns that might at first seem very different – e.g. the realisation of participants (transitivity) as nominal groups (or adpositional phrases) serving as elements in the clause (whether pronominal or non-pronominal), as pronominal clitics partially 'integrated' in the structures of lower-ranking units such as verbal groups or as pronominal affixes serving within the structure of units at word rank such as verbs. So in this area it is possible to see a cline from, say, English and German to French, Spanish and Portuguese to Mapuche, Panare and Inuit. (And while it is significant that, e.g., personal references may be realised pronominally as pronominal nominal group serving as elements of the clause, or as pronominal 'clitics' that are in a sense halfway down the rank scale from clause to group function, or as pronominal affixes serving at word rank, one should not exaggerate such differences. Indeed, they often represent different phases in the evolution of a particular language or family of languages; and there is often uncertainty among linguists reflected, e.g. in the orthographies they propose, as in the case of a number of languages spoken in West Africa where pronominal Subjects are written as separate orthographic words in some languages and as prefixes in other languages even where there are no linguistic differences.)

Many contributions *outside* SFL to language typology are, of course, focused on *syntagmatic* patterns. One reason for this is theoretical in the sense that researchers outside SFL work with syntagmatically oriented conceptions of language. Another reason – which is directly related – is that when we examine the literature, it is much easier to find observations about syntagmatic patterns; paradigmatic patterns tend not to be in focus outside phonology and morphology. One obvious example is the extensive work on 'word order typology' based on observations about the sequence of elements in different grammatical units, perhaps primarily the clause, the nominal group and the adpositional phrase, starting with Greenberg (1966) and continued (and corrected) by Matthew Dryer and many other scholars. Some early generalisations have been confirmed (like the 'resonance' between V • O and sequence in adpositional phrases) but others have now been rejected as it became possible to consult larger more representative samples of languages – like Greenberg's early correlation between the sequence of elements in the clause and of elements in the nominal group (adjective and noun) – predictably, from a systemic functional point of view since clauses and phrases are both exocentric constructions but groups are endocentric rather than exocentric.

In explorations of 'word order', metafunctional considerations are crucial: the myth of 'fixed word order languages' vs 'free word order languages' has turned out to be remarkably resilient despite the increasing evidence that the fundamental issue is not whether the 'word order' is 'fixed' or 'free' but rather how the sequence of elements is deployed as a mode of realisation in any given particular language by the different metafunctions (see Matthiessen, 2004). Halliday wrote a paper designed to demolish the myth, "It's a fixed word order language is English" (1985/2005); any linguist who reads it could be expected to question the distinction between 'free' and 'fixed'.

Most commonly, it's the textual metafunction that's ignored when linguists make claims about 'free word order', which is a consequence of relying on (elicited or constructed) clauses deprived of their discursive environment (i.e. a non-ecological approach to the investigation of grammar). This is one of many areas where the present volume makes an important metafunctional contribution. For example in Chapter 6, which is concerned with the textual metafunction, the authors write:

Spanish is sometimes referred to as a 'free word order' language, especially in contrast to English, which is often taken as a canonical 'fixed word order' exemplar (cf. Greenberg 1966). As the tables in this chapter show, this dramatically overstates the difference between the two languages as far as information flow is concerned – the same kinds of meaning are arranged early and late in a clause.

(I would add to the insightful discussion in this chapter that 'Themes' appearing after the Predicator of a clause might be interpreted as thematic Reprises or Afterthoughts.)

This is one of many areas where it's crucially important to distinguish between the general theory of language and specific descriptions of particular languages – a distinction that can be found already in Firth's work (theoretical and descriptive terms are distinguished clearly in Matthiessen, Teruya and Lam, 2010). Various frameworks used in the description of particular languages and in linguistic comparison and typology such as LFG, FG and RRG would include as part of the 'theory' notions like Subject or Pivot, Object, Predicate, Topic, Undergoer, Patient and many other categories that would be posited in SFL in the course of the description of particular languages based on empirical evidence derived trinocularly – as in this volume for English, Spanish and Chinese. The fact that such categories are not part of systemic functional *theory* is not a *bug* but rather a *feature* – one informed by extensive engagement in the Firth–Halliday tradition with a very wide range of languages. Linguists are encouraged to do the hard work of showing that the descriptive categories they posit in their interpretation of any particular languages can actually be motivated empirically based on weighty evidence coming from the examination of registerially varied corpora of texts in context.

The theory of language is designed to *empower* linguists to *imagine* a wide range of possible languages, guiding them in their approach to particular languages by providing them with a general conception of human language as it must have evolved together with AMHs (Anatomically Modern Humans) – *Homo Sapiens Sapiens* – on the order of 150,000 to 200,000 years ago, and as it emerges when young children make the transition from the protolanguages they have constructed in interaction with their immediate caregivers starting around the age of 5 to 8 months to the mother tongue(s) spoken around them somewhere halfway into their second year of life (see Halliday, in Webster, 2004).

**Parallels and Descriptive Generalisations**

Empowered by the general theory of language provided by SFL, researchers can develop descriptions of particular languages, reasoning in the way illustrated in this book as the authors develop the descriptions of English, Spanish and Chinese – always deploying Halliday's trinocular vision. In addition to such theoretical guidance, one might also draw on descriptive generalisations of the kind put forward in Matthiessen (2004), Teruya et al. (2007), Arús-Hita et al. (2018) and, with an areal focus on West Africa, in Mwinlaaru, Matthiessen and Akerejola (2018).

If one is interested in contributing descriptions of Spanish or languages like Spanish, it makes sense to consult the book-length systemic functional description of Spanish by Lavid, Arús and Zamorano-Mansilla (2010) and in addition other accounts of specific areas of Spanish lexicogrammar by Estela Moyano, Anne McCabe and other SFL scholars mentioned in this book. Also relevant is the work on French by Alice Caffarel, including her 2006 book and her engagement with the challenge of interpreting tense in Romance languages in Caffarel (1992). See in particular Chapter 3, Section 3.4 in her book – on the role of a corpus in the investigation of verbal groups; see Benveniste (1966). Systemic functional descriptions of areas of Portuguese would also be relevant, although there is as yet no book-length overview. Taking account of these different Romance languages and the systemic functional descriptions developed so far would shed light on the verbal group in relation to the clause – and the rank-related changes since Latin. These illustrate a common phenomenon around the languages of the world – namely that of cycles along the rank scale, with realisational items drifting down (as recognised in studies of grammaticalisation) and gradually being replaced as new items 'drift' at higher ranks along the cline of delicacy from lexis to grammar.

Similarly, if one is interested in contributing descriptions of Chinese or languages like Chinese, one can now consult a number of book-length systemic functional accounts in English (not to mention the ever-growing systemic functional literature in Chinese), including Li (2007) on Mandarin and Tam (2004) on Cantonese, and accounts of particular systems of Chinese, including McDonald (1994, 1998), Fang, McDonald and Cheng (1995), Fung (2018). But systemic functional work on Vietnamese (e.g. Thai, 2004) is also relevant, as is work on Thai (e.g. Patpong, 2005) – for example, in the interpretation of interpersonal particles serving as realisational resources in systems of MOOD and MODAL ASSESSMENT (including MODALITY and EVIDENTIALITY) at the end of the clause, the construal of ASPECT, and the location of so-called serial verb constructions metafunctionally in relation to experiential transitivity and logical complexing.

But, of course, helpful linguistic descriptions are not limited to languages that are genetically related to the language under description or spoken in the same linguistic area. There may be particular systems or syntagmatic patterns that are illuminated in the descriptions of languages which are at some or several removes from one another historically or geographically. This is brought out at various points in this book; for example, in Chapter 6, the authors note: "It is simplistic to suggest that the reason Spanish can realise co-referential nominal groups before or after the Predicator is that it has person and number agreement. Comparable flexibility is found in many languages without such agreement, as we will illustrate in the Chinese section of this chapter."

Similarly, in exploring the system of PHASE in Chinese, I find it helpful not only to consider so-called 'serial verb constructions' common in languages spoken in South-East Asia but also to compare them with such constructions in languages spoken in West Africa such as Akan, Dagaare, Yoruba and Oko. Likewise, at some point after I had begun to try to learn Spanish and (Modern Standard) Arabic (MSA) in the 1970s and was moving into linguistics, it struck me how helpful it was to use (descriptions of) these two languages to illuminate one another. Thus when systemic functional linguists have discussed and debated the demarcation of Theme in Spanish, I have realised that comparison with MSA would be quite helpful (and not only with MSA, obviously). For instance, when one approaches the clause grammar of MSA registerially, it becomes clear that the classification of the language as 'VSO' includes a typical pattern in narrative texts (often simply VO or V), but under other registerial conditions, SV or SVO is motivated, as in taxonomic reports. The value of register-sensitive description, comparison and typology has been brought out in a number of SFL studies, including Teich (1999), Lavid (2000) and Rose (2005); see also Matthiessen, Arús-Hita and Teruya (2021).

**Comparison and Typology: Etic Pools**

Naturally, one should not limit oneself to languages one happens to be familiar with (as a systemic functional linguist), but the exploration needs to become more systematic. Here the long-term project of developing systemic functional comparison and typology is directly relevant. In Teruya and Matthiessen (2015), we provide a brief overview of systemic functional descriptions of various languages, and Mwinlaaru and Xuan (2016) report on a systematic review undertaken by them of systemic functional typological work, with Kashyap (2019) adding another overview (see also Matthiessen et al., 2022, chapter 7); and in Matthiessen (2004), I try to provide links to relevant work in other traditions – though a decade and a half later, this now needs updating (a task I'm working on: a multilingual version of IFG).

Complementing systemic functional theory of language as an empowering resource, typologically oriented generalisations provide further help – minimally, to put it in Tagmemic Linguistic terms, as an etic pool.[7] In working on different languages and in 'supervising' research by doctoral students, I have always thought that we need to be nudged to *expand* the horizon of our imagination – to think more creatively in an informed way about the various ways in which language may evolve in different eco-social environments (I think this was one of the points Whorf tried to get across to us). So we need holistic theories of language and we need to accumulate and process and profile comprehensive descriptions of particular languages. (Developing etic pools based on descriptions of the expression planes of languages is, naturally, much easier than doing the same for their content planes; but the contributions by two British phoneticians who had been influenced by Abercrombie in Edinburgh and moved to the USA – J. C. Catford and Peter Ladefoged – still stand out as

---

[7] From a systemic functional point of view, this is the focus of a great deal of functional typology – including Dixon's encyclopaedic three volumes of 'basic' theory and the very informative books on different grammatical areas edited by Aikhenvald and him. These are very important contributions, but they do not present a general theory of language (in context) – basic or otherwise; they contribute generalisations based on descriptions of many languages. Thus, they do not provide us with the kind of theoretical guidance needed to begin to develop a comprehensive description of a particular language; there is nothing analogous to the theoretical notion of a function-rank matrix – one that could serve as an index into the 'etic pool' of observations drawn from comprehensive descriptions. This is, of course, directly related to the issue of appliability that the authors of this book raise. To be appliable, the account of a particular language must be descriptively comprehensive and theoretically holistic; otherwise, any attempt to apply it will be very limited. This may not be an issue for all typological linguists, but it is a fundamental issue for linguists whose work embodies a sense of social accountability (cf. Halliday, 1984b).

remarkable achievements; they give an indication of what systemic functional phonetics might be (cf. Matthiessen, (2021)) and can serve as good models for thinking with also when we turn our attention to the content plane and try to conceptualise and develop etic pools within that plane[8].)

## Insiders and Outsiders

Rich holistic theory supported by descriptive aggregation and generalisation can help us as we develop descriptions of particular languages whether we have mastered these languages as insiders, members of the relevant speech fellowship, or approach them as outsiders. The descriptions of English, Spanish and Chinese presented in this book have, of course, been undertaken by 'native speakers' (I have added the quotes since the notion of native speaker has been problematised in the last couple of decades – importantly by leaders in applied linguistics, including Alan Davies and Lourdes Ortega), and they are able to enrich their accounts, not only by analysing and interpreting texts in contexts, but also by probing paradigms without the intermediate step of working through elicitation with language consultants.

However, methodologically, the approaches to language description by 'insiders' and 'outsiders' are productively *complementary* – not mutually exclusive; in fact, for any given language we ideally need both – a methodological point which I hope will encourage people from different language backgrounds to make contributions not only to their mother tongues but also to other languages. The advantages of being an 'insider' are quite obvious; but there are also advantages in being an 'outsider,'[9] two central ones being the experience of reflecting on the language as a learner (if one gets to the point of learning the language in one's descriptive project) and the comparative point of view.[10]

In my own work, I have always been an 'outsider' – I have hardly done any work on my own mother tongue, Swedish, partly because I was always keen

---

[8] My first professor of linguistics – a committed European structuralist, Bertil Malmberg, once told me that he felt he'd been fortunate in that he'd started with the expression plane of language (in the 1930s) and had an opportunity to study general linguistic principles within that domain before he moved onto the content plane. There is definitely something to be said for this progression, even if one's target is the lexicogrammatical system of a particular language – as illustrated in this book. I was reminded of Malmberg's insight when I began to sketch a description of the phonology and lexicogrammar of Akan about a decade later.

[9] The history of English reference grammars in the twentieth century provides an interesting example. The first half of the century was dominated by 'outsiders' – Jespersen, Poutsma and other non-English Europeans; the second half by 'insiders' – notably Quirk and the team he established (though Jan Svartvik and later Stig Johansson came to represent the 'outsiders').

[10] This was clearly an advantage Halliday brought to his investigation of English: he came from his research into Chinese, and then expanded his studies to include English.

to transcend my own environment, partly because since Swedish is hardly a 'major' language (having approximately as many speakers as, say, Akan), I knew that international interest would be very limited. Even when I have worked on English, which has now become my primary language, this has always been against the background of the experience of studying and learning the language, moving in from the outside. So I am keenly aware of the value of being an outsider – also in the case of languages I have never been a learner of but have dabbled with, like Japanese, Kannada and Marathi.

When I worked on Akan as a linguist – initially over three decades ago but now again together with Isaac Mwinlaaru, I would have benefitted enormously from the present volume. Exploring the language in the mid-1980s with a wonderful language consultant, I tried my best to work systemic-functionally; but I had to develop the kind of trinocular reasoning modelled throughout this book on my own (just as Martin had to do when he worked on Tagalog). By taking another step – maybe in this case a knight's move, I am sure that we can draw on the trinocular reasoning in this book even when we work as 'outsiders' with language consultants – or, even better, as members of teams of insiders and outsiders.

**Descriptive Methodology**

As I recall my early work on Akan, I would like to return once more to descriptive methodology as a way of rounding off my afterword. In SFL, methodology is derived from the theory in the following sense: the systemic functional theory of language in context is a relational one rather than a modular one; the relations that are posited have as their domains the intersecting semiotic dimensions that constitute the 'architecture' of language in context according to SFL (see Matthiessen, forthcoming, including comments on problems with the term 'architecture'). The methodology is essentially one of shunting along these dimensions, exploring the relations trinocularly. This methodology has been foregrounded very effectively in this book; the authors show the power of reasoning 'from above', 'from below' and 'from roundabout' in terms of the hierarchy of stratification (but also in terms of rank, axis and – working sideways, as it were – metafunction) as they develop their descriptions.

The method of shunting applies equally to the cline of instantiation. Because of the importance of authentic natural text in context in empirical, evidence-based descriptive linguistics, the authors show how to move in 'from below' along the cline of instantiation, and how to generalise instantial patterns inductively by positing systems (while at the same time being informed by stratal considerations 'from above' – guidance coming from semantics and context). And it is possible to imagine how this process could be partly (but only partly!) automated by using the tools and techniques (including machine learning) of

NLP (Natural Language Processing), which tends to be (far) ahead of corpus linguistics in terms of computational power and sophistication (inside SFL in the identification of register profiles of different disciplines, Teich et al., (2016); outside SFL, see Lee (2018) on unsupervised machine learning in the development of descriptions, with reference to the Linguistica morphological analyser developed by Goldsmith and his team, e.g. Lee and Goldsmith (2016)).

Whether the process of moving in 'from below' in terms of the cline of instantiation is manual or partially automated, the selection of text types or registers is methodologically very important since different registers may put different lexicogrammatical sub-systems at risk, as illustrated in this book by the selections of texts from different registers (stories, interviews, procedures, service encounters, court trials and conferences: see Table 1.2) – as outlined in Chapter 1, Section 1.2.1: see Table 1.1 for the use of the registerially different texts in the exploration of the different areas of the grammars of the three languages.

But what about other methods widely used in language description? If we add typological generalisations based on many descriptions of particular languages to our theoretical resources, we can operate with certain expectations. For example, we might tentatively posit a specific system as we develop a description of a particular language, and then look for examples (what I called 'paradigm probing' above) – possibly using elicitation in working with a language consultant. This would appear to be a deductive method; but it should really be abductive since we will need to adjust the systemic description as we go along, testing the description as it is being developed against new samples of texts from different registers. This approach is of course a staple in traditional linguistic fieldwork, but we can enhance it by taking semantic and contextual considerations into account. Thus in developing a description of any given language, we actually need to keep shunting up and down the cline of instantiation. Michael Halliday has observed somewhere that people don't speak in paradigms, so we need to posit potential paradigms as we describe a particular language and then probe them.

As long as we shunt along the cline of instantiation, the hierarchy of stratification and the other semiotic dimensions presented in this book, we remain – as it were – within our own projection of the emergent description we are working on. But there may be other descriptions that can serve as secondary sources – as there will be in the case of languages such as English, Chinese and Spanish with a long descriptive history; and we should make good use of them while obviously assessing their quality at the same time (for example, are they based on naturally occurring texts in context or not?).

Making use of secondary sources is a form of meta-translation – reinterpreting the descriptions they present in systemic functional terms. This requires a great deal of training and practice, and the 'harvesting' of secondary sources would require another book (which would include guidance in the use of typological accounts).

The degree to which we have access to secondary sources will vary considerably as we move around the languages of the world. In the case of 'major languages', there will very likely be more sources than is humanly possible to consult (as in the case of Chinese, English and Spanish), and since they will be of variable relevance and quality, one has to develop methods of informed selection. In the case of 'non-major languages', the availability of secondary sources will vary considerably – say from descriptions with reasonable coverage via brief field notes to nothing at all. But it is vitally important to do a stock-take at the outset of any descriptive project, preferably using a tentative function-rank matrix to develop a sense of the nature and degree of previous descriptive coverage.

In my own descriptive projects, I have ranged from relying largely on primary sources to relying largely on the reinterpretation of secondary sources. Thus when I developed my systemic functional descriptive sketch of the lexicogrammar and phonology of Akan a bit over three decades ago, I had to rely mainly on primary sources – texts and elicited examples provided by a great language consultant. The most comprehensive secondary sources at the time were the grammar and dictionary by Christaller from the 1870s[11] (though some relevant work had been done in generative phonology).

At the opposite end of this scale from primary to secondary sources, I was given the task in the last couple of years by my friend and colleague Professor Bhimrao Bhosale to sketch a systemic functional description of Marathi as input to a series of lectures we gave in May 2018 at Dr Babasaheb Ambedkar Marathwada University in Aurangabad. As I was preparing material for the lecture series, all I had were secondary sources, so I set out to interpret them (including the examples provided) in systemic functional terms, drawing on similar 'exercises' I have undertaken since the late 1970s (originally with MSA).

This is a perfectly reasonable way of preparing for the development of the description of a particular language – as long as one recognises it for what it is: a preliminary guide – perhaps akin to a transfer description (as discussed by Halliday and by Elke Teich). It is a stepping stone – but like other forms of scaffolding and tacking, it needs to be set aside once the description gets airborne (actually, I'm just testing the tolerance for mixing figures of speech in close clausal proximity).

---

[11] Here a kind of meta-shunting becomes relevant and important: Christaller was naturally aware of what has come to be known as 'serial verb constructions', but they were not captured descriptively until Westermann (e.g. 1907, 1930). As I pondered various accounts at the time, which tended to be based on constituency, I could interpret them as verbal group complexing based on the primary sources.

## The Need for Descriptive Guidance

On one of our many hikes in the Santa Monica Mountains, Halliday and I discussed the need to produce a paper on how to develop systemic functional descriptions of lexicogrammatical systems. I was well enough into the development of the systemic functional computational grammar known as the 'Nigel grammar' and may have started my work on the systemic functional description of Akan, so I was experienced in developing systemic functional descriptions. We thought we might use as an example the development of a systemic description of bound clauses in English since this was one area that still needed some basic work, and we added the task to our agenda.

That was over thirty years ago, and the task still remains on the agenda – except now we have this book, the third step in the series of steps in the development of systemic functional theory and systemic functional descriptions. So many thanks to Martin, Quiroz, and Wang – and congratulations on your achievement!

# Appendix 1  Systemic Conventions[1]

## [i] System network

| | |
|---|---|
| a → [x, y] | **system:**<br>if 'a', then 'x' o 'y' – abbreviated: as 'a: x/y' |
| a → {[x, y], [m, n]} | **simultaneity:**<br>if 'a', then simultaneously 'x/y' and 'm/n' |
| a → [x → [m, n], y] | **delicacy ordering:**<br>if 'a', then 'x/y'; if 'x', then 'm/n' |
| a, b → [x, y] | **conjunction in entry condition:**<br>if 'a' and 'b' (abbreviated 'a & b'), then 'x/y' |
| a/b → [x, y] | **disjunction in entry condition:**<br>if 'a/b', then 'x/y' |
| a → {[x ! ->, y], [m ᵀ ->, n]} | **conditional marking**<br>if 'x', then also 'm' |
| a → {[x, y], [∥, 'go on']} | **recursive system (logical):**<br>if 'a', then 'x/y' and simultaneously option of entering and selecting from the same system again |

---

[1] This Appendix is largely adapted from Matthiessen and Halliday (2009).

Appendices

In this book conditional marking has been formalised through if/then superscripts (formalised in networks as e.g. exclamative$^I$, positive$^T$).

## [ii] Realisation statements

A realisation statement consists of an operator, such as insert or conflate, and one or more operands, at least one of which is a grammatical function.

| major type | operator | operand 1 | operand 2 | example |
|---|---|---|---|---|
|  | insert (+) | Function |  | + Subject |
| (i) structuring | expand (()) | Function | Function | Mood (Subject) |
|  | order (^) | Function | Function | Subject ^ Finite |
| (ii) layering | conflate (/) | Function | Function | Subject / Agent |
| (iii) inter-rank realisation | preselect (:) | Function | feature(s) | Subject: nom. gp. |

The expand statement has not been introduced in this book.

One of the operands of 'order' may also be a boundary symbol, as in # ^ Theme and Moodtag ^ #.

The different types of realisation statement are outlined in more detail below:

(1) Presence of Functions in the structure: the presence of a Function in a Function structure is specified by inserting the Function into the structure; the operation of insertion is symbolised by '+'; e.g. +Subject, +Mood, etc.
(2) Functional constituency relations: two Functions may be related by constituency and to specify this constituency relationship in the Function structure one Function is expanded by the other; the expansion is symbolised by putting the expanding constituent Function within parenthesis, e.g. Mood (Subject), which means that Mood is expanded to have Subject as a constituent Function. A Function may be expanded by more than one other Function, e.g. Mood (Subject, Finite).
(3) Relative ordering of Functions and ordering relative to unit boundaries: two Functions may be ordered relative to one another in the Function structure and this relative ordering is symbolised by '^'; e.g. Subject ^ Finite, Mood ^ Residue. The ordering may also be relative to the left or right boundary of a grammatical unit (represented by #), e.g. # ^ Theme and Moodtag ^ #.
A distinction can be made between sequencing Functions directly after one another, e.g. Subject ^ Finite, and sequencing Functions with respect to one another, e.g. Subject → Finite (meaning that the Subject comes

before the Finite but that another function, for example a Mood Adjunct, might intervene).

(4) Conflation of one Function with another: one Function from one perspective is conflated with a Function from another perspective, i.e. the two Functions are specified as different layers of the same constituent – they are identified with one another. Conflation is symbolized by '/'; for example, Subject/Agent means that Subject (interpersonal) and Agent (ideational) apply to the same constituent.

(5) Realisation of a Function in terms of features from the rank below: the realization of a function in a Function structure is stated by preselecting one or more features from the unit realising it; preselection is symbolised by ':', e.g. Subject: nominal group, Finite & Predicator: verbal group, etc.

A distinction can be made between the realisation of a Function through a feature (formalised as Function:feature) and lexicalisation of a Function through a specific lexical item (e.g. formalised for Tagalog interrogatives as Q::*ba*). Embedding can be defined as the realisation of a Function through a feature from the same or a higher rank.

# Appendix 2.1

**Big waves and Bondi Beach have always gone together, writes Peter FitzSimons, but no one had ever seen the ocean rise up with a strength such as this ...**

**And so there they lie, happily sweltering in the** summer sun on Australia's most famous beach, just as they have for so many generations past. It is such a wonderfully peaceful scene – of people and nature as a happy whole – that it is simply unimaginable that nature could ever rear up and savage the lot of them.

Ah, but those 35,000 Sydneysiders who were lying in those very spots on the afternoon of February 6, 1938, surely felt equally at peace.

The day was, in the vernacular of the time, a "stinker", and some thought it was in fact a record turnout on the beach, with the numbers perhaps swelled by the fact that those bronzed boys of the Bondi Surf Bathers' Life Saving Club had turned up in force to have one of their popular surf competitions.

At three o'clock there was still not the slightest clue that this afternoon would forever be known as "Black Sunday" in the annals of Sydney. Then it happened. With a roar like a Bondi tram running amok, an enormous wave suddenly rolled over the thousands in the surf, including those many standing on the large sandbank just out from the shore – knocking them all over as it went. And then another wave hit, and then another.

The huge waves, just like that, piggy-backed their way further and further up the beach and grabbed everything they could along the way – from babies to toddlers to adolescents to beach umbrellas, to old blokes and young sheilas alike, and then made a mad dash for the open sea again, carrying all before it and sweeping everyone off the sandbank and into the deep channel next to it in the process.

In no more than 20 seconds, that peaceful scene had been tragically transformed into utter chaos. Now, the boiling surf, with yet more large waves continuing to roll over, was filled with distressed folk waving for help.

In their long and glorious history, this still stands as the finest hour of the Australian lifesaving movement. For, ignoring their own possible peril, the Bondi boys now charged into the surf, some attached to one of the seven reels available, some relying only on their own strength. As one, they began pulling the people out.

On the shore, many survivors were resuscitated, as the Bondi clubhouse was turned into a kind of emergency clearing house, and ambulances from all over Sydney town descended and carried the victims away.

Finally, just half an hour after the waves hit, the water was cleared of bobbing heads and waving arms, and it was time to take stock: 250 people had needed the lifesavers to pull them out, of whom 210 were OK once back on land.

Thirty-five needed mouth to mouth to be restored to consciousness, while five people perished.

Do you have a historical anecdote about a place in Sydney?
Write to Peter FitzSimons at pfitzsimons@smh,com.au

*Source*: P. FitzSimons (2005) Place in time, *The Sydney Magazine*, 23 February.

# Appendix 2.2

Hi everybody and I am going to do just a random chatty vlog for you guys. I had a video for today. I filmed it and I was going to edit it. It was a type one Tuesday. I was showing all the diabetes supplies like the extra supplies we brought on vacation but I had bent down like before I started filming and my shirt got caught in my bra so it was it was like sitting- it just- it's all I could see the whole time so I was like "I am not posting this video" because that's all people would be looking at. So this is what you get today. So many of you actually love these sit down chatty videos so I thought it would be kind of fun. It is two twenty and I just got out of the shower and I just put some makeup on because it is national night out and I put I fancy shirt on. I like never wear this. I think I have worn this one time since I got it. I'm usually in like a tank top with sports bra with these like yoga pants. So. But it is national night out like I said and our neighbourhood gathers together and we have like a pot luck and the police come and the fire truck come and there are neighbours that I see like once a year and I wanted to look- I wanted to look presentable. Different than they probably see me every single day walking with the kids. I wanted to look nice. So that's kind of exciting. I'm bringing two big macaroni and cheeses. Just like the Stouffer's brand I think. Andy went and got it yesterday at the store. I got two big ones. I thought that would be really good for the kids and myself since I'm a picky eater. Oh and you're probably seeing how dark my hair is well, one it's wet, but I could not find the hair dye that I bought previously when I dyed my hair which I loved- I loved the first time. So I ended up having to do like a different shade that I didn't use previously and it's so dark I hate it. I hate it. I hate the- the colour of it so I've tried washing it out. It's lighter than it was a few days ago but yeah it's such a bummer and then I went to Target like two days later and there was a whole stack of them so I three of them. So hopefully next time I will get my hair colour back but for now this will do. What else can we talk about? I hear children coming. They're going to ask for more food. I just gave them Chex Mix and applesauce squeezes. What's up? [break in filming] I'm back. [laughs] So my kids just came upstairs and of course asked me for more food which they had a big lunch. Then they had a snack. I gave them each a bowl- like a heaping bowl full of Chex Mix and an applesauce squeeze and they want more food but they cannot have more food. I was going to vlog the day. I went to the dermatologist because I have these like marks on my feet. I'll show you. Let's see if I can show you from here. [lifting up leg] ooh. I don't know if you can see that. I have that mark and then there's another one and then another one and then on my other feet and it was all like bumpy and stuff. And it was spreading and it tripled quadrupled in size in a year. It actually was there for two years. Anyway, it was some granuloma something I don't know- it's called- it's some sort of skin thing. And so the dermatologist took like this needle and under each like bump and injected this like steroid and it all bubbled up. It was really gross and it hurt so bad but I didn't film it because there's like feet people out there that like are obsessed with feet and I didn't want to- you know. I didn't want those people attracted to my videos so Andy said not to film it but it was really itchy. And the bumps are supposed to go away and it shouldn't spread anymore but the discoloration might stay there for a really really long time so. Yeah. But that was good to get checked out. Oh another thing that has been really annoying this summer is you know when you go to a parking lot and it's a busy place. You get in your car and you don't necessarily want to leave immediately. Like you might want to- I might want to have Henry test his blood sugar, give the kids snacks. Or if we were at the pool, like change or look at my phone or send a text message or whatever. It drives me crazy when a car is like sitting there following you and then they just wait for you to leave. I cannot stand that. And that has happened so many times. And I was just at the mall of America and I got back to my car and I went into-. And I met up with a Kimmy from the Dodge family and I went to- I wanted to like Instagram a picture of us and FaceBook whatever. And as I was doing that I- I had just got in my car, got my phone and as I was doing that some guy was sitting there and there was cars behind him and he was like [mimics man's gesture] like waving me out. And I was so upset. Like I immediately got up, put my phone down. I immediately drove away but- I wasn't even thinking. I shouldn't have done that. I should not have done that. But it was just like "what!" There's a guy sitting there waving and angry at me because I was sitting in my car. It's like I am sitting in my car. I shouldn't have to leave. Mad at myself that I did that but from now on I am not moving. I don't care if they follow me around the whole parking lot get to my car. I am not moving. I don't want this video to like ramble on. I want it to be kind of short. But I do want to start going live either on Instagram, FaceBook, YouTube, I don't know. I don't know what exactly. I started doing like Instagram stories for like three days but then I lost a huge chunk of people that were following me so I don't if people like hated it or I was really annoying. So I stopped doing that and I did- I'd posted like four little clips of videos so I don't know if people just realised and didn't know who I was or didn't like me in their feed or what not. So that like tur- totally turned me off from Instagram. Then I thought "well maybe I'll do it on my Facebook page" but only about two hundred of you follow me there and I feel like so many of you would miss out. And then on YouTube, if I go live on YouTube, the only thing I don't like, you know, you have all the comments and stuff but when you play it back people watching can't see the comments so I just think it's kind of weird, I don't know. Because I would be talking to the people in the comments and the replay viewers would be like "what?", you know. Like I don't know. I don't know but I really think it would be fun to go live and answer questions and things. I have not done a Q and A, years. It's been years and all the one's that I've done prior, like many, many years ago, Andy and I used to do them all the time. I for some reason deleted them all. Every single one. Every Q and A I have deleted. So when I hit twenty thousand subscribers. That is my goal. That's always been my goal. I just hit nineteen although I just lost like thirty eight subscribers yesterday. So I was like at nineteen thousand and one. So I don't if I'm there- if I'm at nineteen thousand anymore. [talking to child] Just a second honey. [break] I totally forgot what I was just saying. Charlie just came up here and was talking to me [laughs]. [break] I remember what I was talking about. So when I hit twenty thousand subscribers I am going to do a big Q and A with the family, with Andy or whoever has questions and I'm going to do that for you guys. Clock is dinging, Charlie needs me, kids are hungry so I better go. Thank you for watching guys. [break] I will see you Thursday at for a day in the life video. It will be live at two PM eastern standard time. So don't miss it. Thanks for watching guys. Bye. [child walks in] You need a drink. OK. [reaches to turn off camera]

*Source*: Let's talk: Random Chatty vlog. *Youtube*. Retrieved on 13 March 2021 from https://youtu.be/YRx-zDoPbVw

# Appendix 3.1    La Ola Maldita

## La ola maldita

**Se ha dicho casi todo sobre el terremoto y posterior tsunami que asoló las costas de las regiones del Maule y Biobío. En este reportaje, el periodista Juan Andrés Guzmán reconstruye el pavor que experimentaron quienes acampaban en la isla Orrego, en la desembocadura del Maule, mientras sentían el agua subiendo despacio hasta inundarlo todo. Aquí, los sobrevivientes cuentan qué vieron exactamente.**
Por Juan Andrés Guzmán    7 Abr 2010 10:20 am

El bote pesquero Pinita estaba a 5 millas al oeste de Constitución cuando comenzó el terremoto. Su capitán José Ibarra y sus seis tripulantes habían pasado la noche preparando todo para la pesca del bacalao al día siguiente. Se acostaron tarde y se durmieron rápido, mecidos por un mar tranquilos e iluminados por la luna llena.

Entonces, el Pinita, de 50 toneladas, empezó a brincar como si fuera un bote a remos, o mejor, como si una ballena se estuviera rascando el espinazo con la quilla, según describió otro capitán que también pasó el terremoto en el mar. Los tripulantes del Pinita saltaron de sus camarotes y se asomaron por la borda. El agua borbotaba y hacía crujir el barco. Todos estuvieron de acuerdo en que eso tenía que ser un terremoto.

El capitán Ibarra llamó a su mujer por celular. Vivían en el cerro O'Higgins de Constitución y ella estaba sola y lloraba. En el barrio un edificio de tres pisos había colapsado matando a una pareja y a su guagua. Más tarde se sabría que las 16 manzanas del casco histórico de Constitución, construido enteramente de adobe, se había transformado en una trampa mortal para decenas de personas.

Mientras hablaba con su mujer, Ibarra recibió un llamado por radio de la Capitanía de Puerto de Constitución. Los marinos querían saber si veía olas yendo hacia la costa.

– Negativo – respondió.

Tras hacerlo brincar, el mar había vuelto a tener la quietud de un estanque. Y eso fue lo que informó.

Los tripulantes del Pinita se quedaron especulando sobre cómo estaría su ciudad. Pero entonces, a 10 minutos del terremoto, ocurrió algo que nunca habían visto. El mar empezó a succionarlos, a llevarlos aguas adentro con tal fuerza que cortó de un tirón la soga de 10 centímetros de diámetro que los ataba al ancla.

Lo que los absorbía era una ola de 15 metros de alto que cerraba el horizonte. Estaba a 200 metros y se acercaba a toda velocidad por el costado de la nave.

– ¡Tsunami, tsunami! ¡Apróate!, ¡apróate! – le gritaron los tripulantes al capitán.

Ibarra intentó ir hacia la ola de frente, remontarla con la proa hacia adelante, pero ella los chupó velozmente y no pudo maniobrar. La ola tapó la luna y la nave comenzó a escalar de lado esa pared oscura que rugía como si estuviera a punto de desmoronarse sobre ellos.

– Era terrorífica, negra. Era fea la hueá de ola, fea – recuerda el capitán. Ibarra tiene 30 años navegando en todo Chile y ésa es la peor ola que ha visto. En el Golfo de Penas le ha tocado cabalgar sobre masas de agua de más de 20 metros. Pero ésas son lentas y gordas e incluso con el mar embravecido los barcos las remontan con calma.

Esta ola era distinta.

–Venía arqueada y chispeando. Todo el tiempo parecía que nos iba a reventar encima.

El Pinita la escaló a una velocidad vertiginosa mientras su capitán la miraba por el ventanuco de la cabina y rezaba un Ave María agarrado al timón. Los marinos gritaban. El agua empezó a caer sobre la embarcación. Todos estaban seguros de que se volcarían.

Tras una eternidad el Pinita llegó a la cima y pasó al otro lado, bajando a gran velocidad.

Allá adelante una nueva montaña de agua se les acercaba.

–¡Viene otra!– gritaron todos.

Esta vez Ibarra alcanzó a "aproar" la nave y la pasaron con menos terror. Esta segunda ola tenía cerca de 8 metros de altura.

Luego, el mar volvió a quedarse tan inmóvil como antes.

En esa quietud fantasmagórica, reponiéndose del susto de sus vidas, tomaron conciencia de que ahora esas montañas iban hacia su ciudad.

Durante los siguientes minutos, sólo se oyeron los gritos del capitán que trataba de comunicarse con los marinos de Constitución.

Nadie le contestó.

El capitán siguió intentándolo hasta que todos entendieron que las olas ya habían llegado a la ciudad. Que ya no había nada que hacer.

**Sin permiso**

Al igual que miles de chilenos, apenas se detuvo el terremoto Nora Jara llamó a su hijo Jonathan Romero para saber cómo estaba. El joven de 18 años le contestó que no se preocupara, que él y sus tres amigos –René Godoy, Fabián León y Gabriel Jaque– estaban bien. No le dijo que estaban en una isla, Orrego, en la desembocadura del río Maule. Tampoco le dijo que en ese momento el agua empezaba a subir, que la gente a su alrededor pedía ayuda y que nadie venía a rescatarlos. Le ocultó todo eso para no preocuparla y porque sus amigos no habían dicho a sus padres que irían a la playa. Oficialmente estaban acampando cerca de casa, en San Javier, a casi 90 kilómetros, y aún tenían la esperanza de que nadie supiera la verdad.

Después de la llamada, el agua siguió subiendo con velocidad, aunque sin demasiada fuerza. Las familias con niños se aferraban lo mejor que podían a los eucaliptos para evitar que la corriente los llevara. La crecida les llegó arriba de la cintura y luego empezó a bajar. Jonathan recuerda que un hombre gritaba que se le había soltado su hija de dos años.

–Decía que la niña lo mordió porque el agua estaba helada y ahí se le cayó– relata el joven.

Los cuatro amigos estaban en la isla Orrego por pura mala suerte. Ellos querían pasar ese último fin de semana de verano en Iloca, la playa que estaba de moda. Pero llegaron tarde a Constitución y no alcanzaron a tomar el bus. Buscando dónde dormir, terminaron en la ribera del río Maule y vieron esa isla boscosa, de 600 metros de largo y 200 de ancho, salpicada de carpas y fogatas. Parecía el lugar ideal. Cruzaron en el bote de Emilio Gutiérrez, a quienes todos en la zona conocen como el Gringo. El hombre iba con su nieto de 4 años, Emilito, que entregaba los salvavidas a los pasajeros para la breve travesía de 150 metros.

Eran las 21:30 hrs de la noche del viernes. Los cuatro amigos fueron los últimos en llegar a la isla. Seis horas después el botero y su nieto habían muerto. Al cierre de esta edición sólo el cuerpo del abuelo había sido encontrado varios kilómetros por el río hacia la cordillera.

**El canto de los niños**

Nadie sabe aún cuánta gente había esa noche en la isla Orrego. Los sobrevivientes hablan de entre 50 y 100 personas, de las cuales al menos doce eran niños. Jonathan y sus amigos, por ejemplo, repararon en ocho chicos que jugaban en la playa cuando ellos llegaron. Y durante esa noche terrible vieron a otros cuatro más. De ellos no se sabe nada, salvo de uno: Timmy, de 4 años. Él y su madre, Mariela Rojas, fueron arrastrados por el torrente y tocaron tierra varios kilómetros río arriba. Mariela no sabe cómo lograron salvarse. Timmy estaba desmayado de frío cuando salieron del agua y no reaccionó durante un buen rato. "En nuestro grupo éramos nueve. Quedamos tres vivos y hay dos cuerpos que no encontramos", resume la mujer.

Tras el terremoto y antes que el mar empezara a subir, los atrapados en la isla Orrego se juntaron en torno a un kiosko que tenía generador eléctrico.

–Para que sus hijos no se asustaran una madre los hizo cantar "Está linda la mar, muy linda"–, recuerda Hugo Barrera, un sobreviviente.

Los adultos empezaron a pedir ayuda a gritos. Constitución estaba a oscuras y ellos, en medio del río, eran el único punto de luz. Era imposible que nadie los viera. ¿Por qué nadie los socorría?

Lo cierto es que sí los veían y sus llamados se sentían hasta en los cerros, donde se había refugiado casi toda la ciudad. Miles de personas observaron desde allí la isla iluminada, luego la llegada de las olas y, finalmente, no oyeron nada. La agonía y muerte en medio del río es un recuerdo que comparten hoy los habitantes de Constitución. Difícilmente lograrán borrarlo.

Hasta donde se sabe, sólo el pescador Mario Quiroz Leal se lanzó al río desde la isla Orrego. Estaba de vacaciones con su pareja Mariela –embarazada de 4 meses– y sus dos hijos de 4 y 9 años. Quiroz sabía que tenían que escapar.

–Le dije a mi mujer: "Agarra a los cabros chicos, no los soltís, yo voy a buscar un bote y vuelvo"– recuerda.

Apenas llegó a la orilla corrió a la Capitanía de Puerto a pedir ayuda. Dice que los marinos no le hicieron caso, que le dijeron que no había posibilidad de un tsunami. Quiroz los mandó a la cresta y volvió a la costa a buscar botes. Entonces empezó a subir el agua y él retrocedió por la calles esperando que la marea descendiera. Cuando lo hizo y pudo volver a la ribera, ya no habían embarcaciones.

El agua volvió a subir. Esta vez la corriente fue más fuerte y Quiroz corrió a los cerros para evitar ser arrastrado.

–Todavía me acuerdo de cómo la gente gritaba en la isla. Ahí estaba mi familia. Todos murieron– dice–. Nadie nos avisó, nadie nos ayudó.

Testigos afirman que los marinos evacuaron la Capitanía durante esa segunda subida. Cuentan que iban en su camioneta, con el agua llegándoles hasta la ventanilla y que la misma corriente los empujaba por la ciudad.

En la isla las familias flotaban con sus hijos y se aferraban a lo que fuera. Algunos se habían encaramado en los árboles, pero a los que tenían niños les fue imposible hacer eso.

El agua duró unos minutos arriba y bajó por segunda vez. En Orrego todos estaban mojados y entumidos.

Jonathan y dos amigos treparon a los árboles. Abajo quedó Gabriel Jaque, que no logró subir. Jonathan decidió que tenía que avisarle a su madre y decirle la verdad. Nora no lo podía creer. Su hijo, que minutos antes estaba sano y salvo, ahora figuraba atrapado en una isla inundada.

Ella estaba en San Javier. Ni siquiera se atrevió a retarlo. Muerta de miedo se contactó con los padres de los otros jóvenes y también llamó a un familiar en Constitución para lograr que Carabineros fuera a la isla.

Para entonces ya había pasado media hora del sismo. En todo Chile los servicios de emergencia intentaban restablecer las comunicaciones. El fantasma del maremoto rondaba la mente de muchos chilenos. A las 4:07 hrs, el Servicio Hidrográfico y Oceanográfico de la Armada (SHOA) trajo calma. Por fax informaron que, aunque el terremoto podía producir un tsunami, éste no había ocurrido aún. Ellos avisarían oportunamente si esto pasaba. Minutos más tarde, a las 4:20 hrs, el contralmirante Roberto Macchiavello aseguró al intendente de Concepción, Jaime Tohá, que el tsunami estaba descartado. Tohá repitió ese anuncio por la radio Biobío, la única emisora que tenía señal en la zona. El intendente de la región más afectada por el maremoto dijo que las personas podían volver a sus hogares. Es probable que 20 minutos antes de esa declaración la gran ola haya entrado en Constitución.

**La ola**

Hugo Barrera la vio venir, encaramado en un eucalipto a unos siete metros de altura. Dice que era una masa café, furiosa, veloz, que arrastraba todo a su paso. Una masa que se extendía por todo el horizonte, que avanzaba en silencio y que cuando tocó la isla empezó a hacer un ruido ensordecedor, un "pac, pac, pac" siniestro e imparable que era provocado por cientos de árboles partidos como fósforos o arrancados de raíz.

La ola azotó el árbol en el que Hugo estaba, lo zarandeó un rato, como si el destino aún no decidiera qué hacer con él y finalmente lo lanzó al agua. Hugo cayó a ese furioso torrente sabiendo que moriría.

Él estaba en Orrego por trabajo. Era el encargado de instalar y operar los fuegos artificiales con los que la municipalidad de Constitución planeaba cerrar el verano 2010. En la tarde, mientras montaba el equipo, vio a muchos niños que correteaban por la isla y se bañaban en el Maule. Quedó tan impresionado por la belleza del lugar que hizo varias fotos. Hoy, esas imágenes, captadas pocas horas antes de la destrucción, producen escalofríos. Se ven los cerros que encajonan el Maule cubiertos de pinos; cientos de pelícanos y aves descansan junto a la isla; el río y el mar se funden con tanta calma que sólo evocan sentimientos de armonía. ¿Cómo es posible que toda esa belleza guardara algo tan feroz, tan demencial? Esa noche Hugo la pasó con una familia de Talca.Ellos eran una docena de personas y ocupaban 5 carpas. Veraneaban y trabajaban. En la mañana los hombres salían a estacionar autos a Constitución y las mujeres vendían dulces. El grupo andaba con cuatro niños. "Una chica de unos 12 años, crespa; una guagua y dos niños de unos 5 y 7 años", recuerda

Hugo. Cree que todos murieron. "Esperaron la ola abrazados a los árboles y vi que la ola se los llevó", dice.

La ola no pudo con los árboles donde estaban Jonathan y sus dos amigos. Pero a Gabriel Jaque, que esperaba abajo, se lo tragó. Los jóvenes oyeron su grito desesperado llamando a Jonathan por su apellido: "Romerooooo". Y luego el rugido de la montaña de agua que arrastraba casas enteras, árboles y cuerpos. Ellos gritaban "Gabrieeeeel", y siguieron gritando y sollozando mientras el agua destruía la ciudad. Pero debajo de ellos ya no se oyó otro ruido humano fuera de sus lamentos y los de otras cuatro personas también aferradas a las copas de los árboles. Después de esa ola, en la isla no se escucharon más cantos de niños ni gritos de padres. Hasta el amanecer, cuando los siete sobrevivientes se animaron a bajar, en esa isla no se oyó nada.

**No hay lugar para los débiles**

Cerca de las 5:30 hrs la Presidenta Bachelet dijo a los medios que no había habido ni habría un tsunami en nuestras costas. Se basó en la información entregada por la Armada, institución que aún a esa hora continuaba afirmando que en el litoral chileno sólo se registraban aumentos de caudal de 10 ó 20 centímetros. A partir de esas declaraciones, que se repitieron hasta bien entrada la mañana, el 18 de marzo pasado se presentó una querella por la muerte de dos hermanas en la playa de Dichato, al norte de Concepción. Ambas huyeron a los cerros tras el terremoto y bajaron cuando las autoridades insistieron a través de la radio en que no había peligro. Las mujeres volvieron a Dichato justo cuando entraba la ola.

Hugo Barrera salió del río más o menos cuando la Presidenta negaba el maremoto. Notó desesperado que la resaca lo llevaba hacia el mar y nadó con todas sus fuerzas para no terminar en el océano. Alcanzó la orilla con su último aliento y temblando de frío y de miedo, caminó por lo que quedaba de la costanera de Constitución buscando una edificación alta, pues estaba convencido de que la tragedia no había terminado. Descubrió una casa de dos pisos donde protegerse. Se metió en ella gritando "¡Aló!" y subió al segundo piso. Encontró ahí a una señora que con toda calma esperaba lo que el destino le ofreciera. Se llamaba Blanca. Tenía unos 70 años y necesitaba muletas para moverse. No intentó huir. Estoicamente resistió el sismo y luego sintió el mar entrando en su casa y escarbando en el piso de abajo.

Blanca vivía sola y había aceptado morir sola. Otros ancianos, en cambio, vieron cómo sus familias escapaban y los dejaban botados. El sargento de la Armada, Cristián Valladares, se encontró con uno de ellos cuando intentaba llegar a la Capitanía de Puerto para ayudar. Eran las seis de la mañana, ya estaba clareando. Mientras se acercaba a la costa oyó los gritos de la isla

Orrego y se preguntó si habría un bote con qué ir a buscar a la gente. Entonces vio cómo el río se recogía y se formaba otra ola gigantesca. Mientras huía vio que esa ola tapaba los árboles, por lo que calcula que tendría unos 10 metros. Debe haber sido la tercera o cuarta gran ola que azotó Constitución.

En su retirada, el sargento Valladares vio que una mujer pedía ayuda. Al entrar en la casa medio derrumbada, encontró a un anciano en silla de ruedas que los miraba con angustia. Sus familiares estaban en los cerros. La señora que pedía auxilio era la mujer que lo cuidaba. Ella vivía en otro lugar y corrió a ver al anciano y lo encontró solo. Estaba mojado y gemía de miedo. El sargento lo sacó de ahí y lo llevó a la casa de la mujer.

**El saqueo**

No es difícil imaginar la angustia de ese anciano abandonado. Tampoco es incomprensible el miedo que deben haber sentido sus parientes. El terremoto y el tsunami sometieron a los chilenos a pruebas difíciles y radicales: rescatar a otros o salvarse; acompañar o huir; resistir la marejada o rendirse. Pero esas disyuntivas no acabaron cuando se detuvieron las olas. Cuando la naturaleza nos dejó en paz, las ciudades devastadas y abandonadas ofrecieron otra bifurcación: ayudar o robar. Y, mientras los sobrevivientes de la isla Orrego aún pedían auxilio y los arrastrados por el río emergían como espectros, desnudos y golpeados, y cruzaban la ciudad sin entender qué les había ocurrido, personas que no habían sufrido daño se transformaban en una nueva ola, en un terremoto humano, como lo llamó el alcalde de Lota, dedicado a robar y destruir lo que quedaba en pie.

El dueño de un supermercado que prefiere mantenerse anónimo cuenta que a él lo saquearon personas con dinero que venían en grandes camionetas. "Les pagaban a los pelusas para que les cargaran el vehículo. Para abrirse paso, aceleraban y se iban gritando '¡Tsunami!, ¡tsunami!', y tocando la bocina. Así se llevaron todo".

Es probable que ése sea el motivo por el cual mucha gente en Constitución recuerde que hubo decenas de olas ese día.

Nora llegó a Constitución a las diez de la mañana, cuando los saqueos estaban en su apogeo. Venía acompañada de la madre de Gabriel. Durante la noche Jonathan, llorando, le había dicho que a Gabriel se lo había llevado la ola y Nora se lo transmitió a la madre. Pero ella no perdía la esperanza.

Fueron a la comisaría en busca de ayuda. Carabineros estaban superados. Les dijeron que no podían hacer nada. Y les insistían que en la isla Orrego no había quedado nadie, que se fueran para el cerro porque podía venir otra ola.

Nora lloraba y rogaba. Tenían que sacar a su hijo de ahí, sobre todo si es que creían que venía otro tsunami.

Ricardo Fuentes oyó los ruegos de Nora y se ofreció a ayudarla. En realidad era el único que podía hacerlo. Ricardo es radioaficionado local. Durante la madrugada, con sus equipos, captó el mensaje desesperado que el capitán Ibarra enviaba a la Capitanía. Según Fuentes, los marinos se quedaron sin comunicación y evacuaron hacia los cerros. Por ello le tocó a él dar aviso a los bomberos de que dos olas gigantes se acercaban a la costa. Según afirma gente de la zona, con esta advertencia se salvaron decenas de personas que viven en la zona costera de la ciudad.

Con sus equipos, Fuentes contactó a Celulosa Arauco y avisó de posibles sobrevivientes en la isla. A los pocos minutos se escuchó el helicóptero de la empresa volar rumbo a la isla.

Las madres llegaron a la orilla del Maule justo para ver cómo el helicóptero se llevaba los siete sobrevivientes. Eran las 11 de la mañana del 27 de febrero y el piloto Víctor González los transportó al único lugar donde se podía aterrizar: el estadio de Constitución. Al lado, en el gimnasio, se había montado la morgue.

En ese lugar la madre de Gabriel asumió que estaba desaparecido.

−Ése fue el momento más terrible− sintetiza Jonathan.

Los jóvenes decidieron ver si, por alguna casualidad, su amigo había llegado al hospital. La mujer, derrumbada, los esperó en la morgue, donde a mediodía se habían juntado unos 60 cuerpos.

Los jóvenes entraron al hospital sin esperanza. Era un caos de heridos y muertos. No creían que nadie pudiera sobrevivir a la ola que habían visto, pero en la lista de ingresados, el nombre de Gabriel les saltó en la cara.

Jonathan entró a la carrera a la zona de los pacientes y recorrió las camillas hasta que lo encontró. Le pegó tres garabatos y lo abrazó. Gabriel sólo tenía heridas en los pies. Tuvo la fortuna de que la ola lo llevara directo a la orilla.

Cuando los jóvenes y sus madres abandonaron Constitución, la ciudad estaba siendo saqueada sin piedad.

Hoy, varias semanas después de la tragedia, los cuatro jóvenes pueden reírse de la aventura secreta que terminó con rescate en helicóptero. Dicen que sus padres todavía los están retando.

**El capitán regresa**

Recién el domingo a mediodía el capitán Ibarra pudo traer al Pinita de regreso a Constitución. Mientras navegaba por el Maule no podía creer lo que veía. La destrucción era tan completa y enloquecida que los únicos referentes para describirla eran de películas de guerra. Había dejado una ciudad alegre, que disfrutaba los últimos momentos del verano. Ahora volvía a un lugar donde la muerte se había revolcado.

–Me va a creer que yo me vine a Constitución el año 85, porque el terremoto de ese año nos pilló en San Antonio y mi familia quedó espantada … –cuenta Ibarra–. Bueno, así es Chile.

A medida que avanzaban por la costa, se le caían las lágrimas mirando la ciudad. Un tripulante gritó que había un cuerpo en el río. Era una mujer.

Todos entendieron que el río estaba sembrado de muertos.

Ah, Dios mío.

Los hombres del Pinita subieron a la mujer y descubrieron que estaba embarazada. Era la pareja de Mario Quiroz, el pescador que cruzó a nado el Maule intentando conseguir un bote para rescatar a su familia. Quiroz e Ibarra son vecinos y amigos, pero no se habían visto desde antes de la tragedia. Quiroz lo abrazó y le agradeció haber encontrado a su mujer.

–¿Ah, era tu mujer?– le preguntó. Al capitán ya nada lo sorprendía.

Hasta el cierre de esta edición los dos hijos de Mario Quiroz seguían sin ser encontrados.

*Source*: J. A. Guzmán (2010) La ola maldita. *Paula*. Retrieved on 5 August 2021 from www.latercera.com/paula/la-ola-maldita/

# Appendix 3.2    El campamento de verano

Eeh el susto más grande fue ahora en campamento de verano. Lo que pasa es que soy dirigente de scout y de repente una niña tuvo un ataque respiratorio y claro me tocó correr cuatro cinco kilómetros buscando una ambulancia y en el momento estaba súper agotado había caminado todo el día, pero por el puro golpe de adrenalina al final corrí los cinco kilómetros y cuando ya iba a llegar al teléfono como que me avisaron ya se había mejorado que había sido algo momentáneo que en el momento no vimos bien la situación y llegamos y actuamos no más.

*Source*: PRESEEA (2014–21) *Corpus del proyecto para el estudio sociolingüístico del español de España y de América.* Alcalá de Henares: Universidad de Alcalá. Our special thanks to Dr Abelardo San Martín and Dr Silvana Guerrero, from the Universidad de Chile, who gave us full access to the sociolinguistic PRESEEA corpus from Santiago, Chile. The corpus is also available for consultation at http://preseea.linguas.net/Corpus.aspx

# Appendix 3.3 El cambio de plan (call n°5)

A:  *call center agent*
C:  *customer calling*
A:  [company name], buenas tardes
    atiende xxx xxx
    ¿con quién tengo el gusto de hablar?
Z:  deme un segundo, don xxx,
    buenos días
C:  ¿aló?
A:  buenas tardes,
    ¿con quién tengo el gusto de hablar?
C:  ehh, con xxx xxx
A:  don xxx, ¿en qué le puedo ayudar?
C:  ehh,
    sabe que quiero bajarme de plan a diecisiete mil trescientos, con dos decodificadores
A:  disculpe,
    nosotros no tenemos ningún plan de diecisiete mil trescientos
C:  eh … sí sale del …
    aquí sale en los folletos
A:  no hay ningún plan de diecisiete mil trescientos
    ¿qué folleto está viendo usted?
C:  eh, o sea, es del [company name]
A:  ¿pero el cable o televisión satelital?
C:  ehh … satelital
A:  hay dos planes uno de veinte mil quinientos y otro de quince mil,
    no tenemos ninguno de diecisiete y fracción
C:  es que yo tengo dos- dos cajas
A:  ya,
    los quince, más el arriendo de los deco podrían dar diecisiete y fracción

| | |
|---|---|
| C: | claro |
| A: | ya, necesito el rut del titular, por favor |
| | [...] |
| A: | un momento por favor |
| | ¿aló? |
| C: | aló |
| A: | está rechazada la solicitud |
| C: | ehh, sí la eh- |
| | me cortaron el- el- el (([company name] a mí)) el trece de enero |
| A: | tiene que cancelar la deuda |
| | no puedo cambiarlo de plan |
| | si no está cancelado |
| C: | pero ... si yo pagué el- el trece de di –de diciembre al trece de enero |
| A: | estamos en febrero, señor |
| C: | sí po, tamos en febrero |
| | y yo ten- tendría que pagar |
| | porque yo no estoy viendo el xxx |
| | porque bien claro me dijeron a mí, la señorita |
| | que cuando a usted se le corta el servicio |
| | a usted no se le cobra nada |
| | porque no está viendo televisión |
| A: | eh, sí, pero si se quiere cambiar |
| | tiene que estar todo pagado |
| C: | pero ... |
| | ¿cuánto es lo que tengo que pagar? |
| | eh, porque yo quiero de diecisiete mil trescientos |
| A: | vamos a verificar un momento, |
| | veintisiete mil trescientos ochenta y tres pesos |
| C: | ¿veintisiete? |
| A: | exactamente |
| C: | ¿y por qué tanto? |
| A: | vamos a verificar |
| C: | son veintidós quinientos lo que estoy pagando yo no más, po |
| A: | le está cobrando el plan de veinte mil quinientos pesos, más el arriendo del decodificador adicional, más el proporcional por cambio de plan |
| | tiene un cambio de plan acá |
| C: | ya |
| A: | de diciembre |

| | |
|---|---|
| C: | si ese pa' ver lo que tenía que ver el partido yo de fútbol, los nacionales |
| A: | claro, que cobra un proporcional por el cambio de plan porque usted se cambió del plan básico al plan de veinte mil quinientos eso es lo que se le está cobrando en enero y esa es la deuda que tiene |
| C: | ¿son veintisiete? |
| A: | exactamente |
| C: | o sea si yo no pago de aquí al trece de diciembre ¿qué pasaría? |
| A: | nada, po, entraría en Dicom, porque ya tiene el servicio cortado ya |
| C: | sí po, si tengo el servicio cortado y me están cobrando que- una cosa que no estoy viendo |
| A: | se cortó por no pago, no por un problema con la señal |
| C: | obvio, oh- oh eso porque no tuve plata como pa' pagarlo |
| A: | entonces, si usted me está diciendo que no lo está viendo, no lo está viendo porque no lo pagó |
| C: | no po, porque me cortaron la … |
| A: | si le cortaron por no pago |
| C: | sí po, por eso que me le [*sic*] cumplió la fecha … de pago |
| A: | entonces si usted me indica que no lo está viendo es porque no está pagado por eso no lo está viendo no porque tenga algún problema con la señal |
| C: | no no no yo no le estoy diciendo por señal es que resulta que cuando a mí me dieron el papel el folleto las niñas que andaban en la calle si yo no veía tele en [company name] |

|      | a mí no me iban a cobrar nada |
|      | porque no estoy viendo tele |
| A:   | claro, pero no habla de que le cortan el servicio, |
|      | y a usted le cortaron el servicio por no pago |
| C:   | ya |
| A:   | ¿ya? |
|      | si usted no está viendo por algún problema de señal, |
|      | obviamente no se le va a cobrar |
|      | pero usted no está viendo |
|      | porque no ha pagado, |
|      | y a usted se le cortó por no pago |
|      | no (porque tuvo un problema con la empresa) |
| C:   | (porque … porque) me le [*sic*] pilló la fecha |
| A:   | bueno, eso no es responsabilidad de la empresa |
| C:   | ¿hasta cuándo tengo que pagar eso? |
| A:   | usted lo puede pagar cuando quiera |
|      | si ya está cortado el servicio |
| C:   | ya |
| A:   | no hay una fecha para el pago |
| C:   | ya ¿pero ahí no me siguen cobrando más? |
| A:   | mientras esté cortado |
|      | no se le está cobrando |
|      | porque está cortado |
| C:   | ya, ya, |
|      | eeeeh … ¿y pa' cambiarme de plan, |
|      | o sea, tengo que pagarle esa deuda primero? |
| A:   | claro, exactamente, |
|      | claro po, |
|      | y si no tiene para pagar la deuda |
|      | menos va a tener para pagar un cambio de plan |
| C:   | ya, ¿o sea que cobran también por cambio de plan? |
| A:   | exactamente |
| C:   | ¿y cuánto cobran por bajar a diecisiete trescientos? |
| A:   | es el proporcional |
| C:   | ¿pero cuánto es más menos? |
| A:   | no puedo darle ninguna información acá en sistema |
|      | porque el sistema no me lo permite |
|      | porque está bloqueado por no pago |
| C:   | ya, ya, ya, |
|      | eso no más quería saber |

A: bien, muchas gracias por llamar a [company name], hasta luego

*Source*: S. Castro (2010) Las disfluencias en el habla espontánea de Santiago de Chile. Unpublished master's thesis in linguistics, Pontificia Universidad Católica de Chile, Santiago. Our special thanks to Sonia Castro for giving us full access to the recordings from this research.

# Appendix 3.4   El decodificador (call n°7)

A:  *call center agent*
C:  *customer calling*

A:  bienvenido a [company name],
    usted habla con xxx xxx,
    ¿con quién tengo el gusto de hablar?
C:  hola buenas,
    no sé
    si hablé contigo recién,
    habla xxx
A:  buenas tardes, don xxx
C:  buenas,
    eh … tengo un problema con la información de la programación
A:  indíqueme el rut del titular, por favor
    […]
A:  ya
    ¿y usted está en su domicilio, don xxx?
C:  sí
A:  ¿y cuántos decodificadores tiene?
C:  tengo tres
A:  ¿y en cuántos tiene el problema de la programación?
C:  en el principal, en el principal
A:  ¿qué problema tiene?
    ¿no se ve la programación que corresponde?
C:  no, si si si se ve claro,
    no, no se ve la corresponde
    está la de hace unos tres días o cuatro días atrás
A:  ok, presione 'menú'
C:  ya
A:  'información del sistema'
C:  ya
A:  'restaurar predex'

| | |
|---|---|
| C: | ya |
| A: | 'inicio' |
| C: | ya, |
| | espere un momento |
| | me dice |
| | primero salen los idiomas |
| | segundo, audio |
| A: | presione 'exit' tres veces, |
| | verifique la programación ahora |
| C: | a ver, |
| | no, no tiene información en ninguno de los canales |
| A: | ¿no tiene información? |
| C: | claro, en ninguno de los canales |
| | sale la hora solamente |
| A: | espere un momento |
| | presione 'exit' |
| C: | ¿'exit' o 'menú'? |
| A: | no deje la pantalla así en ... solamente en la imagen |
| C: | ahí estoy- ahí estoy viendo tele ya |
| A: | ya, y si presiona ahora para ver el 'epg' |
| C: | ya |
| A: | ¿usted ve información ahora? |
| C: | NO |
| A: | ¿no? |
| C: | está en blanco |
| A: | saque la tarjeta del decodificador |
| C: | ah, nunca he hecho eso |
| A: | mire donde hay una tapita al lado izquierdo que dice [nombre de la empresa] |
| C: | ya |
| A: | ya |
| | ahí usted la abre |
| | y ahí va una tarjeta |
| | esa usted la tira para afuera |
| C: | ah, ya, ya, ya, perfecto |
| | la voy a sacar |
| | ¿apago esto o no? |
| | ¿lo dejo así no más? |
| A: | no, encendido |
| C: | ya la saqué |
| A: | desenchufe el deco cinco segundos |
| | y lo vuelve a enchufar |

| | |
|---|---|
| C: | ah, no el enchufe de la tele |
| | ¿lo enchufo sin la tarjeta? |
| A: | sí, por favor, y lo enciende sin la tarjeta también |
| C: | ehm, ya |
| A: | ya |
| | ¿qué aparece en la pantalla ahora? |
| C: | sale la información pero no la imagen |
| A: | ¿dice 'canales codificados'? |
| C: | (()) acaba de aparecer 'canales codificados' y el signo ((p)) allá arriba |
| A: | ya |
| | abra la tapita |
| | ingrese la tarjeta con el chip hacia abajo y hacia el fondo |
| C: | ya |
| | 'leyendo la tarjeta' |
| | ahí t- aparece bien |
| | voy a cambiar el (()) |
| | ahí sí |
| A: | ¿ahí se ve la programación? |
| C: | ahí se ve la programación como corresponde |
| A: | ok ¿tiene alguna otra consulta don Pablo? |
| C: | sí, eh … yo no sé |
| | si contigo … |
| | pero el- ahm el- ahora que llamé recién me dijeron |
| | que- que mi cuenta estaba … estaba pendiente |
| | o sea, que tenía que pagar la factura |
| | no sé |
| | y no corresponde todavía |
| A: | ya, la fecha de vencimiento es el día trece |
| C: | claro |
| A: | sí, es que las grabaciones son así |
| C: | ¿es para todos? |
| A: | sí |
| C: | ¿pero y por qué me dice el valor? |
| A: | ¿diecinueve mil seiscientos? |
| C: | claro |
| A: | ese es el valor de su plan |
| C: | claro, |
| | pero resulta que el 13 está ven- |
| | ¿el 13 vence mi mi mi factura? |
| A: | sí |
| C: | pero resulta que a mí me dijeron |

|  |  |
|---|---|
|  | que me iban a cobrar a fines de febrero |
|  | porque enero y la mitad de diciembre era gratis |
|  | entonces febrero lo iban a- me lo iban a facturar |
| A: | la boleta [está el] tres de febrero |
| C: | [o estoy pagan-] el tres |
| A: | (()) sí, para que usted vea febrero la boleta |
| C: | ahh, se paga por adelantado |
| A: | o sea, eh … se paga mes en curso, no adelantado |
|  | porque la boleta se emite el tres |
| C: | claro, o sea, el tres de febrero yo pago |
|  | para ver febrero, o sea, por adelantado |
| A: | exactamente |
| C: | ya, ahh |
|  | es eso lo que- lo que no sabía |
| A: | ok |
| C: | ya |
| A: | ¿tiene alguna otra consulta, don xxx? |
| C: | ehh … no, eso no más |
| A: | ok, cualquier duda o consulta vuelva a comunicarse al |
|  | ochocientos xxx xxx, |
|  | que tenga usted muy buenas tardes |
|  | hasta luego |
| C: | hasta luego |

*Source*: S. Castro (2010) Las disfluencias en el habla espontánea de Santiago de Chile. Unpublished master's thesis in linguistics, Pontificia Universidad Católica de Chile, Santiago. Our special thanks to Sonia Castro for giving us full access to the recordings from this research.

# Appendix 3.5  Sopaipillas

**Sopaipillas**

**Por Centro de Cocina Paula**

**En los días invernales y fríos, olvídate de las cremas y chocolates. Date un gusto con esta receta de antaño.**

**Personas**

    6 – 8 personas

**Ingredientes**

    1 taza de zapallo molido
    2 tazas de harina
    2 cucharadas de manteca o grasa
    Manteca para la fritura
    Sal

**Preparación**

1. Todos estos ingredientes se revuelven, pero no se amasan.
2. Si la masa no se despega, se le incorpora un poco más de harina.
3. Se uslerea y se corta en discos. Se pican para que no se inflen y se fríen en manteca o grasa muy caliente.
4. Se sirve con salsa de chancaca caliente.

*Source*: Centro de Cocina Paula (2012). Sopaipillas. *Paula*. Retrieved on 12 August 2021 from www.latercera.com/paula/sopaipillas/

# Appendix 4.1　海洋所抗击浒苔自然灾害纪实

2008年6月,是距离第29届北京奥运会开幕仅仅两个月的日子,如果你走进中国科学院海洋研究所,你将被眼前空地上晾晒的一片绿油油的海藻所吸引,这些海藻就是被称为"突如其来的海洋自然灾害"的主角——浒苔。

## 浒苔:突如其来的海洋自然灾害

2008年5月31日,大面积浒苔进入青岛近岸海域,使滨海名城青岛的蓝海呈现绿色。随着时间的推移,越来越多的浒苔随潮水涌上岸,它们到达了青岛著名的栈桥、第一海水浴场和前海风景游览区一带的沙滩,没几天便堆起了厚厚一层,并迅速扩散,在太阳晒后更是臭气熏天,成为污染带。

据6月28日的卫星遥感监测结果显示,青岛近海持续有大面积浒苔漂入,最大影响面积约为1.3万平方公里,实际浒苔覆盖面积约为400平方公里;密集区主要集中在青岛—崂山近海海域,面积约160平方公里。

此时,大量的浒苔已让浅海变成了一片翠绿,在山东省东南部近海海域呈规模聚集,青岛市表示:"这是一场突如其来的海洋自然灾害。"

值得关注的是,奥帆赛警戒水域面积共49.48平方公里,其中有浒苔面积达15.86平方公里,占总面积的32.04%。大面积的浒苔对青岛奥帆赛海域水体形成了威胁。而同一时间,已有30多个国家的运动员驻扎青岛并开始了奥帆赛的赛前训练,大面积的漂入浒苔已经影响到运动员的正常训练。

党中央、国务院和山东省委省政府、青岛市委市政府高度重视,要求全力以赴做好浒苔的清理处置工作。

中科院海洋所第一时间成立了青岛海域漂浮绿藻应急领导小组以及应急专家组,开展了关于浒苔的科学研究。

## 五所联合:抗浒苔保奥运

7月2日,根据全国人大常委会副委员长、中国科学院院长路甬祥的批示,中国科学院资环局紧急组织来自中国科学院海洋研究所、生态环境中心、水生生物研究所、南京地理与湖泊研究所、遥感应用研究所的14位专家组成中国科学院专家组,赴青岛协助山东省、青岛市开展青岛海域突发海洋自然灾害治理工作。

7月2日上午,专家组实地考察了浒苔灾害现场。当天下午,在青岛市副市长张惠的组织下,专家组与在青多家涉海单位的专家、领导进行了座谈,了解相关背景情况。

根据研究情况,中国科学院专家组迅速提出建议表示:第一,在当前阶段需要进一步加强监测与预警;第二,针对奥帆赛所在时间段,加强对奥帆赛及周边海域灾害性浒苔或其他藻类暴发事件的预警、预报工作,为预防和治理争取时间,确保奥帆赛顺利进行;第三,加强实用性技术手段的研究、示范、推广,提高打捞浒苔的效率,达到尽快清除比赛海域浒苔的目的。其中,实用、高效的打捞技术、装置研发应用尤其重要。专家组的建议得到了山东省青岛市的高度重视。

7月2日晚,科技部、中国科学院、国家海洋局、山东省、青岛市青岛海域浒苔处置应急专家委员会成立。该专家委员会的成立,为青岛奥帆赛场海域浒苔暴发事件应急指挥部提供了决策依据和科技支撑。

中国科学院的专家在委员会中发挥了重要作用。海洋所研究员、海洋环境学家周名江担任专家委员会副主任委员,海洋研究所党委书记、所长孙松担任生态组组长,海洋研究所所长助理王凡和研究员李鹏程分别担任监测预警组和处置组副组长。此外,中国科学院生态环境中心、水生生物研究所、南京地理与湖泊所、遥感应用研究所的专家都分别进入专家委员会。

7月3日晚,中国科学院副院长丁仲礼来到青岛,紧急协调中国科学院参与浒苔灾害治理的工作,并指示尽快为青岛市应急指挥部提供卫星遥感资料,确定浒苔分布面积、漂移路径等,为指挥部决策提供科技支撑。

7月4日,海洋研究所迅速行动起来,和遥感应用研究所密切合作,快速及时地为山东省、青岛市指挥部提供了浒苔分布的卫星图像和海区动力环境情况,使指挥部准确科学的决策得到了重要保障。之后,两所继续利用科考船和卫星遥感等先进的观测手段开展浒苔大面积海域监测工作,持续为山东省、青岛市提供关于浒苔的各种科学数据。

## 为奥运"保驾护航" 服务国家重大需求

据中国科学院海洋研究所党委书记、所长孙松介绍,从2007年青岛近海海域首次发生大规模浒苔以来,海洋研究所就主动部署了科研骨干力量,开展了浒苔的相关研究工作,充分发挥了服务于国家重大需求的作用,成为各级政府信赖的高技术辅助决策手段,得到了各级政府的广泛认可。

2008年6月24日,海洋所成立了青岛海域浒苔发生应对专家组,部署了多学科研究力量,重点研究浒苔可能的来源及其生长、消亡机制,为灾害治理提供理论依据。

6月25日,海洋研究所就前期研究工作和当前应急部署向中科院及青岛市政府作了书面报告。

与此同时,海洋所紧急指派正在南黄海执行任务的"科学三号"科考船,密切关注浒苔发展动向,尝试寻找浒苔的水下可能集中分布区域;并派出"创新号"科考船,锁定青岛关键海域,开展断面调查,力求系统掌握浒苔发生的动态变化及其与环境的互动关系;且"科学一号"科考船随时待命,计划联合其他科研单位一同开展科考工作。

为探究本次大规模浒苔灾害的发生机理,为科学治理浒苔,保障"绿色奥运"、"平安奥运"发挥科技支撑力量,7月18日上午,2008年中国近海海洋科学考察开放共享航次从青岛起航,航次由中科院海洋所与青岛市科学技术局联合组织实施。来自中国海洋大学、中国电波传播研究所、国家海洋局第一海洋研究所、青岛海洋地质研究所、中国科学院烟台海岸带可持续发展研究所、中国科学院海洋研究所6个科研单位的25名科研人员参加了此次航行。本次航行历时16天,共完成了黄东海典型海域的8个断面、67个站位的观测调查,取得了一大批基础数据和资料,为浒苔灾害的治理提供了重要的科学依据。

通过研究,海洋所率先确定了本次绿潮的原因种属于绿藻门石莼目浒苔属浒苔(Entermorpha prolifera),为广布种,无毒,不是海洋环境恶化的标志,消除了社会舆论的担忧,澄清了国际新闻中的相关错误报道,维护了国家形象。

此外,作为驻青科研单位,海洋所第一时间发动全所师生为清除浒苔献计献策。在所党委副书记、副所长王启尧的带领下,全所师生利用午休、周末休息时间多次到青岛第一海水浴场,展开了义务清除浒苔的志愿活动。师生们表示:"我为奥运添光彩,要体现在实际行动中。"

在采访中,记者还得知了许多关于海洋研究所与浒苔"不得不说的故事"。一连月余,孙松带领着众多海洋科研人员奋战在科学应对浒苔危机的一线,衣不解带、披星戴月、不顾风雨,进行着样品采集、种类鉴定、生长状态观察、生理指标测定、生态毒理效应分析等工作。一位工作人员向记者透露:"连续的工作与每晚持续到后半夜的会议,让孙松所长体力极大地透支。有一次,他一天连续工作20个小时,没有合眼,却依然紧张有效地投入指挥工作,看不出丝毫的倦怠。当看到他因过度熬夜、操劳而生病,虚弱却坚强,仍然坚持与我们一同工作的时候,我就在想,这场浒苔大战一定要坚持下去,我们一定会取得最后的胜利。"

据监测数据显示,截至7月9日,奥帆赛竞赛水域内警戒水域,浒苔面积由最初占总面积的32.04%降到了2.8%左右。7月6日,奥帆赛参赛队伍绝大多数帆船已下水训练,没有队伍因为浒苔干扰而中断训练。美丽的青岛奥帆中心最终迎来了成功的第29届奥帆赛。

如今,残奥会即将开幕,奥帆赛区保障任务依然艰巨,海洋研究所一如既往,将治"浒"进行到底,为奥帆保驾护航。

*Source*: Chinese Academy of Sciences. Retrieved on 12 May 2022 from www.cas.cn/xw/yxdt/200809/t20080905_986639.shtml

# Appendix 4.2　国际博物馆日专访单霁翔

今天是5.18国际博物馆日,这一天,故宫箭亭广场上,高科技艺术互动展演《清明上河图》惊艳亮相,人们可以"走入"画中,穿越到繁华的北宋都城,一睹宋代人文生活图景,感受宋代艺术之美。

像这样生动有趣的高品质展览,故宫每年大概要举办40个。从最初的"十重门"危机,到如今因观众冲刺看名画引发的"故宫跑",自2012年单霁翔执掌故宫博物院以来,成功实现观众限流,开放面积不断扩大,爆款文创深受追捧,精彩展览应接不暇,六年间故宫的变化有目共睹,而他却谦虚地只给自己打70分……在国际博物馆日,人民网记者走进故宫博物院,独家专访院长单霁翔。

记者：博物馆馆长应该是严肃的,但您给我们的印象却是风趣幽默的。很多人用"段子手"、"网红"来形容您,您喜欢这样的评价吗？

单霁翔：其实我不是段子手,我不讲段子,我是讲故事,讲文物背后的故事。博物馆的文化需要通过喜闻乐见的讲故事的形式讲出来。我有个特点,讲话不用稿,说的时候还带点口头语。善于使用"幽默",是一种很有效的沟通交流手段。一段演讲在吸引观众会心一笑的同时,也会给他们留下深刻的印象。幽默只是形式,丰富的文化内容,以及它传递的"正能量",才是最重要的。我不仅是一个看门人,还应该是一个讲解员,把历史和文物藏品背后的故事讲出来,可能人们会更爱听一点。

记者：在《朗读者》节目中,大家惊诧于您不仅能准确记得故宫文物的数量,还用了整整五个月的时间走遍了故宫的9371间房间,能否和我们聊一聊您的"故宫情结"？

单霁翔：我是在北京长大的,住了很多四合院,我开玩笑说,没想到最后一个岗位是在北京最大的四合院看门。

　　我到故宫博物院之前,曾在北京市文物局及国家文物局工作过,调研与学术研究相结合,让我的视野、关注的重点紧紧锁定在文化遗产保护事业。文物局工作期间,很多方面的工作与故宫博物院的文物保护、博物馆管理有着较密切的联系,所以我对故宫并不陌生。2012年年初,我来到故宫博物院工作,担任这个知名世界文化遗产地的"看门人"。我深刻地感受到,故宫的文化底蕴深不可测,文化资源博大精深。面对故宫这处有着

|       |       |
|-------|-------|
| | 600年历史的文化瑰宝,面对故宫博物院这座有着90年历史的文化圣地,必须心怀敬意地加以研究、小心翼翼地进行保护。 |
| 记者: | 2012年年初您临危受命,执掌故宫,从"故宫黑""故宫跑"到"故宫萌",这六年故宫发展成绩不俗,回想当时入宫,您压力大吗? |
| 单霁翔: | 2012年年初进入故宫博物院,到现在已经整整6年了。在这六年的时间里,我的每一天都是新鲜、紧迫和深刻的。必须承认,故宫博物院院长是一个风险很大的岗位,一定要把每一件事都预想好、安排好。

担任故宫博物院院长,对我的能力、学识、经验都是一个挑战。因此,我的工作从调查研究开始。分别向各位院领导讨教,到故宫博物院的30多个部处走访,利用节假日拜访在职和离退休的著名学者、文物专家和历任院领导,聆听大家的指导和建议。可以说,故宫博物院开展每一项工作,往往都深刻而多样地交织着"两难"的问题,都需要"左顾右盼",三思而后行,都需要掌握其中的辩证关系,才能正确加以判断与应对。 |
| 记者: | 如果让您给这六年打个分,您给自己打多少分? |
| 单霁翔: | 我觉得能打70分,比及格好一点。因为故宫还有很多事情要做,满分还远远达不到。世界上没有一座博物馆的藏品中,珍贵文物的比例占比如此高,93.2%是国家一级、二级、三级文物,我们现在努力扩大开放,希望到2020年能有8%左右的文物展出来,比现在翻四倍,这样的目标其实还是很低的目标。

到故宫北院区建成时,我们想提高到15%或16%,现在我们努力使故宫文物走出红墙,到全国各地、世界各地展览,这些取得了很好的反响,也让文物能够真正活起来,活在现实社会中,不只是把它们作为保管、陈列的对象。这些方面,我们确实差得还很远,我打70分绝对高了。 |
| 记者: | 5.18国际博物馆日,故宫推出了高科技互动艺术展演《清明上河图》,让观众在愉快的沉浸式体验中领略繁华多彩的宋代社会生活。能跟我们介绍一下吗? |
| 单霁翔: | 大家看到的高科技互动艺术展演《清明上河图》,目的只有一个,就是让观众真正"进入"《清明上河图》,把原本隐藏在作品中不易被了解的细节,变成观众能"看懂"的故事,画中人物真正"活"起来,观众还能"走进"画中,或在船上观湖,或在茶馆里闲聊。这种展览对我们而言,是第一次尝试。 |
| 记者: | 除了"活起来"的《清明上河图》,接下来还有哪些新改变值得我们期待? |
| 单霁翔: | 今年5月,故宫博物院筹备许久的明清家具馆和石鼓馆将对外开放。年内还将正式对公众预约开放文物医院;故宫城墙在基本修缮完成后将继续扩大开放;珍宝馆、钟表馆、陶瓷馆、书画馆将于今年全面改陈,武英殿与文华殿展示功能对调,武英殿变为陶瓷馆,文华殿成为书画馆,计划在今年相继开放;吴昌硕书画篆刻特展、"四王"书画展等书画专题展也将于年内相继 |

|       |                                                                                                                 |
|-------|-----------------------------------------------------------------------------------------------------------------|
|       | 举办……我们将按照每年40个临时展览的力度,把故宫博物院的展览更丰富多彩地呈现给社会观众。按计划,今年故宫开放面积将超过80%。 |
| 记者: | 今年国际博物馆日的主题为"超级连接的博物馆:新方法、新公众",如果让您传授故宫经验,您觉得可以归纳为几点? |
| 单霁翔: | 今年国际博物馆日的主题非常接地气,其涵义就是让博物馆成为连接公众与多元文化的纽带,用创新的方式方法,吸引更多公众来到博物馆,感受博物馆的文化氛围,获得深刻新鲜的文化体验,共享丰富的文化成果。 |
|       | 总结故宫经验,我觉得最重要的一点,就是一切工作要以观众方便为中心,设身处地地在博物馆当个观众,每天走上一趟,你就知道观众在哪些方面还不方便,这样你就会有所改正。 |
|       | 要想向普通观众,尤其是年轻人打开尘封的历史,解读经典的文化,就需要用一种生动的、喜闻乐见的形式来加以表达。新颖的形式、生动的语言、丰富的内涵、传递出的"正能量",恰是讲好中国故事的重要元素。我们的成功案例很多,而归于一点,就是把故宫博物院丰富多元的文化元素以及强大的文化资源,与当下人们的生活、审美和需求有效地对接,为大家提供取之不竭的精神食粮,也努力让故宫博物院所代表的中华传统文化既有辉煌的过去,有尊严的现在,也能健康地走向未来。 |
| 记者: | 近年来博物馆、美术馆等公共文化服务机构,渐渐从重管到重服务转变,我们也深切感受到博物馆更贴近人们的生活,对此,您怎么看? |
| 单霁翔: | 我曾经用"诚心""清心""安心""匠心""称心""开心""舒心""热心"八个词,来总结故宫博物院应如何服务观众这一问题,其本质是要求故宫博物院要采用人性化、以人为本的服务理念,目的是让故宫文化资源走进人们的现实生活。对于我们来说这是一场管理革命。 |
| 记者: | 2013年我们采访您的时候,您提到遗憾:就是很多观众进到故宫后一直往前走,而错过两旁的精彩展览,现在这个问题解决了吗? |
| 单霁翔: | 这已经不再是遗憾了,这个问题的解决成为了让我极为欣慰的一件事情。 |
|       | 近年来,故宫博物院有两个现象特别突出,一是过去80%的观众"到此一游",没有看到故宫博物院的展览就出去了,现在80%的观众都要看院内的各个展览,无论是午门城楼上的各类特展,还是珍宝馆、钟表馆等常设专馆,以及2015年开放的外西路区域,每天都迎接熙熙攘攘的观众前来参观,节假日期间很多展厅门口还排起长队,这在以往是极为少见的;再有,过去看展览的观众中极少能看到年轻人,估计连30%都不到,现在这个比例彻底逆转了,展厅里70%的观众是年轻人。对于我们来说,现在真真切切地感受到了从"故宫"到"故宫博物院"的彻底转变。 |

记者： 这源于故宫近年来策划了一系列高品质展览,但随之也出现了"故宫跑"的现象。一方面体现了人们对优秀文化的热忱,同时也反映出优质文化资源供应不足的问题。您怎样看待这一冷一热?

单霁翔： 2015年的"石渠宝笈特展"和去年的"千里江山——历代青绿山水画特展"举办期间,都发生过"故宫跑"现象,我们及时采取相应措施,如分发号牌、分时段参观等,保证了观众参观秩序和安全,同时也收获了很多启示。

故宫博物院究竟怎样做到既妥善保护文化遗产,又满足广大民众的文化需求?最现实的做法,就是努力扩大开放,举办更多观众喜闻乐见的展览,让更多深藏不露的文物藏品以更加富有创意的方式与公众见面。同时,也要不断创新观众服务方式,避免观众长时间排队等候,以精细化的管理措施,保证观众的参观质量。再有,努力举办"立体化"展览,通过数字影像辅助导览、展览宣传策划等,并且针对重点展览研发相应的随展文化创意产品,让一项展览的社会影响最大化、观众体验最优化。

记者： "火"的不仅仅是故宫展览,还有多款"萌萌哒"的文创产品。您觉得怎样把文创产品的时尚化、年轻化和故宫深厚的文化底蕴相融合呢?

单霁翔： 很多媒体热衷于宣传故宫"萌萌哒"的文创产品,实际上"萌萌哒"的文创产品并不占故宫文创的主流,不超过总量的5%。去年年底,故宫已经研发了10500种文创产品,大量体现故宫文化底蕴、实用性强、制作精良、创意十足的故宫文化创意和数字作品,正在以各种鲜活生动的方式走出紫禁城、来到社会民众身边。

故宫博物院一直在思考故宫文化如何与今天的人们生活顺畅对话的问题,希望能够用文化创意,将文化遗存与当代人的生活、审美、需求对接起来,让故宫博物院更加"接地气"。希望能够通过文化创意产品的载体,让传统文化与观众的文化需求完美"对接",研发出具有故宫文化内涵、鲜明时代特点,实用性强、绿色环保、价格合理,贴近观众需求的故宫元素文化创意产品。

记者： 您提到要把紫禁城完整地交给下一个600年。故宫博物院新馆选址和设计已基本完成,未来在科技与文化方面将得到最好的交融呈现。能具体谈谈有哪些规划吗?

单霁翔： 作为"平安故宫"工程的核心内容之一,故宫博物院北院区项目目前进展顺利。新馆选址在海淀上庄地区,南面是颐和园、圆明园,北面远处是八达岭和十三陵,占地十万多平米。北院区将进行多功能的分区使用,包括文物修复与展示中心、故宫文化传播中心、宫廷园艺中心、科技保护研究中心等。

新馆的主要功能是作为大型文物保护修护中心和博物馆展厅,同时建设数字博物馆,使故宫博物院数字技术能够得到展示。一是文物修复地,比如1500块大地毯、33000件武备仪仗,这些大家具在故宫文物院没有空间修复,所以要建一个大型的文物修复地,让观众在这里既能够领略到故宫文物藏品的丰富多样,也能感受到各类文物修复技艺的精湛与高超,以及"数字故宫"成果的精彩纷呈。二是跟故宫历史文化关系不大的藏品展览,如白沙宋墓100多箱出土文物等建国以后陆续进故宫的藏品,可以在新馆气势恢宏地布置出来。

记者: 今年是改革开放40年,您说过改革开放带来的巨大变化是使人们的能力在为社会做贡献时得到巨大的提升。改革开放四十年,对您个人而言,带来了哪些影响?

单霁翔: 对我个人而言,改革开放的四十年也是我人生中最为重要的四十年。改革开放后不久,我得到了去日本留学的机会,开始从事关于历史性城市与历史文化街区保护规划的研究工作,回国以后也在工作的同时继续深造,从理论和实践上对文化遗产保护事业有了更加深入的认识和提升。同时有幸担任第十届、第十一届、第十二届全国政协委员,十五年共提交政协提案226件,而且我保持着对文化遗产事业的"执着"和"专一",每一件提案都是关于文化遗产保护的。我竭尽全力,在我的每一个工作岗位上努力做到尽职尽责,为我国的文化遗产保护、传承与发展的伟大事业贡献自己的一份力量。所以,这四十年也是我不断奋斗和收获最多的四十年,回头看这匆匆逝去的时光,我深切地感受到:奋斗是幸福的,也是无怨无悔的。

记者: 这些年,故宫发展有目共睹,不仅研发了数字故宫社区、网络预约购票,通过"互联网+"技术传播故宫文化。您觉得改革开放对于故宫而言,有哪些深远影响?

单霁翔: 改革开放前,故宫开放了很多年,一直被人们看作是旅游景点,但是现在它是文化古建,是一座博物馆,人们进入故宫后,有看不完的展览,有要针对性参观的地方,这是故宫一个非常大的变化。

这些其实来自于方方面面的提升。比如我们的藏品清理,前任院长郑欣淼当年带领故宫人用七年时间清理文物,今天才有这么多藏品可利用;比如古建筑修缮,郑欣淼刚当院长时,就启动了修缮工程,现在才有可能扩大开放;再比如当时很多单位在故宫里办公,这些单位现在都搬出去了,故宫得以更安全,开放区域进一步扩大。再加上文物修复人员、藏品修复、古建筑修复,都离不开非物质文化遗产传承的工匠们,这些缺一不可。所以观众看到的是今天故宫正在走向世界一流博物馆。

记者: 到2020年,您说"要把紫禁城完整地交给下一个600年",这几年还有哪些大事要办?

单霁翔: 2020年,即紫禁城建成600年,将迈进世界一流博物馆行列。

2020年的故宫博物院,是平安的、壮美的。我们正在实施两项工程,一是从2002年开始为时18年的"故宫古建筑整体维修保护工程",二是2013年4月16日被国务院批准立项的"平安故宫"工程。这两项工程的完成节点都是2020年。到那时,故宫博物院开放面积将达到80%。

  2020年的故宫博物院,是学术的、创新的。2013年成立的故宫研究院和故宫学院,将开展的十余项科研与出版项目在学术界具有前沿性和开拓性的特点,对今后文物博物馆界从事大型科研工作的模式具有积极的探索意义。

  2020年的故宫博物院,是大众的、世界的。故宫博物院不断"让文物活起来",在保护好故宫世界文化遗产的基础上,深度挖掘文物资源,促成文物保护成果创造性转化,成为服务于大众的故宫、走向世界的故宫,只有这样才能把壮美的紫禁城完整地交给下一个600年。

(采访整理: 黄维 摄像:陈博文、赵晨 视频剪辑:陈博文、韦衍行)

*Source*: Retrieved on 12 May 2022 from http://culture.people.com.cn/n1/2018/0518/c1013-29998548.html

# References

Abercrombie, D. (1967). *Elements of General Phonetics*. Chicago: Edinburgh University Press.

Akerejola, E. (2005). A systemic functional grammar of Òkó. Unpublished PhD dissertation, Macquarie University, Sydney.

Arús, J. (2010). On theme in English and Spanish: a comparative study. In E. Swain (ed.), *Thresholds and Potentialities of Systemic Functional Linguistics: Multilingual, Multimodal and Other Specialised Discourses* (pp. 23–48). Trieste: EUT Edizioni Università di Trieste.

Arús-Hita, J., Teruya, K., Bardi, M. A., Kumar, A. & Mwinlaaru, I. (2018). Quoting and reporting across languages: a system-based and text-based typology. *Word*, *64*(2), 69–102. https://doi.org/10.1080/00437956.2018.1463001

Bache, C. (2008). *English Tense and aspect in Halliday's Systemic Functional Grammar: A Critical Appraisal and an Alternative*. London: Equinox.

Bartlett, T. & O'Grady, G. (eds.) (2017). *The Routledge Handbook of Systemic Functional Linguistics*. London: Routledge.

Bartoš, L. (1980). La atribución relacional y el adjetivo de relación en el español. *Études romanes de Brno*, *11*, 69–77.

Bateman, J., Matthiessen, C. M. I. M., Nanri, K. & Zeng, L. (1991). The rapid prototyping of natural language generation components: an application of functional typology. In *Proceedings of the 12th International Conference on Artificial Intelligence, Sydney, 24–30 August 1991* (pp. 966–71). San Mateo, CA: Morgan Kaufman.

Bateman, J., Matthiessen, C. M. I. M. & Zeng, L. (1999). Multilingual language generation for multilingual software: a functional linguistic approach. *Applied Artificial Intelligence: An International Journal*, *13*(6), 607–39.

Bello, A. (1847). *Gramática de la lengua castellana destinada al uso de los americanos*. Santiago de Chile: Imprenta del Progreso.

Belloro, V. (2007). Spanish clitic doubling: a study of the syntax–pragmatics interface. Unpublished PhD dissertation, State University of New York at Buffalo.

Belloro, V. (2009). Doblado de objeto y accesibilidad referencial. *Actas del XV Congreso de la Asociación de Lingüística y Filología de América Latina*. Montevideo: Universidad de la República.

Benveniste, É. (1966). *Problèmes de linguistique générale*. Paris: Gallimard.

Berry, M. (1981a). Systemic linguistics and discourse analysis: a multi-layered approach to exchange structure. In M. Coulthard & M. Montgomery (eds.), *Studies in Discourse Analysis* (pp. 120–45). London: Routledge & Kegan Paul.

Berry, M. (1981b). Towards layers of exchange structure for directive exchanges. *Network*, *2*, 23–32.

Berry, M. (2017). Stratum, delicacy, realisation and rank. In T. Bartlett & G. O'Grady (eds.), *The Routledge Handbook of Systemic Functional Linguistics* (pp. 42–55). London: Routledge.

Bloor, T. & Bloor, M. (2013). *The Functional Analysis of English: A Hallidayan Approach* (3rd edn). London: Routledge.

Bogard, S. (1999). Duplicación y clausura argumental: dos funciones del clítico reflexivo en español. *Español actual*, *71*, 41–48.

Bosque, I. (ed.) (1990). *Tiempo y aspecto en español*. Madrid: Cátedra.

Bosque, I. (1993). Sobre las diferencias entre los adjetivos relacionales y los calificativos. *Revista Argentina de Lingüística*, *9*, 9–48.

Bull, W. E. (1960). *Time, Tense and the Verb: A Study in Theoretical and Applied Linguistics, with Particular Attention to Spanish*. Berkeley: University of California Press.

Burton, D. (1980). *Dialogue and Discourse*. London: Routledge & Kegan Paul.

Burton, D. (1981). Analysing spoken discourse. In M. C. Coulthard & M. Montgomery (eds.), *Studies in Discourse Analysis* (pp. 146–57). London: Routledge & Kegan Paul.

Caffarel, A. (1992). Interacting between a generalized tense semantics and register-specific semantic tense systems: a bistratal exploration of the semantics of French tense. *Language Sciences*, *14*(4), 385–418. doi: 10.1016/0388-0001(92)90023-8

Caffarel, A. (2006). *A Systemic Functional Grammar of French: From Grammar to Discourse*. London: Continuum.

Caffarel, A., Martin, J. R. & Matthiessen, C. M. I. M. (eds.) (2004). *Language Typology: A Functional Perspective*. Amsterdam: John Benjamins.

Caldwell, D., Knox, J. & Martin, J. R. (eds.) (2022). *Appliable Linguistics and Social Semiotics: Developing Theory from Practice*. London: Bloomsbury.

Camus, B. (1992). Negación doble y negación simple en español moderno. *Revista de filología románica*, *9*, 63–111.

Carbonero, P. (1980). Afirmación, negación, duda. *Revista española de lingüística*, *10*, 161–76.

Castro, S. (2010). Las disfluencias en el habla espontánea de Santiago de Chile. Unpublished Master's thesis in linguistics, Pontificia Universidad Católica de Chile, Santiago.

Catford, J. C. (1977). *Fundamental Problems in Phonetics*. Indiana: Indiana University Press.

Chao, Y. R. (1948). *Mandarin Primer*. Cambridge, MA: Harvard University Press.

Chao, Y. R. (1968). *A Grammar of Spoken Chinese*. Berkeley/Los Angeles: University of California Press.

Christie, F. & Martin, J. R. (eds.) (1997). *Genre and Institutions: Social Processes in the Workplace and school*. London: Continuum.

Cummings, M. (2021). Interpreting the Old English nominal group from a parsed corpus. *Word*, *67*(4), 493–520. doi: 10.1080/00437956.2021.1993589

Daneš, F. (1974). Functional sentence perspective and the organization of the text. In F. Daneš (ed.), *Papers on Functional Sentence Perspective* (pp. 106–28). Berlin: De Gruyter.

Davidse, K. (1991/9). *Categories of Experiential Grammar* (vol. 11, Monographs in Systemic Linguistics). Nottingham: Department of English and Media Studies, Nottingham Trent University.

Davidse, K. (1998). Agnates, verb classes and the meaning of construals: the case of ditransitivity in English. *Leuvense Bijdragen, 87*(3–4), 281–313.

Davidse, K. (2018). A tribute to M. A. K. Halliday (1925–2018). *Functions of Language, 25*(2), 205–28. doi: 10.1075/fol.00008.dav

Di Paolo, M. (1989). Double modals as single lexical items. *American Speech, 64*(3), 195–224. https://doi.org/10.2307/455589

Di Tullio, Á. (1998). Complementos no flexivos de verbos de percepción física en español. *Verba: anuario galego de filoloxía, 25*, 197–221.

Ding, L. (1999). 从问句系统看"是不是"问句 [Cóng wènjù xìtǒng kàn 'shì bù shì' wènjù, A study of 'shì bù shì' questions from the perspective of question system]. 《中国语文》 [*Zhōngguó Yǔwén*, Studies of the Chinese Language], (6), 415–20.

Doran, Y. J. & Martin, J. R. (2021). Field relations: understanding scientific explanations. In K. Maton, J. R. Martin & Y. J. Doran (eds.), *Teaching Science: Language, Knowledge, Pedagogy* (pp. 105–33). London: Routledge.

Doran, Y. J., Martin, J. R. & Zhang, D. (eds.) (2021a). The grammar of nominal groups: systemic functional linguistic perspectives (Special Issue on the nominal group, Part 1). *Word, 67*(3).

Doran, Y. J., Martin, J. R. & Zhang, D. (eds.) (2021b). The grammar of nominal groups: systemic functional linguistic perspectives (Special Issue on the nominal group, Part 2a). *Word, 67*(4).

Doran, Y. J., Martin, J. R. & Zhang, D. (eds.) (2022a). The grammar of nominal groups: systemic functional linguistic perspectives (Special Issue on the nominal group, Part 2b). *Word, 68*(1).

Doran, Y. J., Martin, J. R. & Zhang, D. (eds.) (2022b). The grammar of nominal groups: systemic functional linguistic perspectives (Special Issues on the nominal group). *Word, 68*(2).

Dreyfus, S., Humphrey, S., Mahboob, A. & Martin, J. R. (2015). *Genre Pedagogy in Higher Education: The SLATE Project*. Basingstoke: Palgrave Macmillan.

Dumitrescu, D. (1973). Apuntes sobre el uso enfático de 'sí' (adv.) en el español contemporáneo. *Revue roumaine de linguistique, 18*(5), 407–13.

Dumistrescu, D. (1979). El sistema de las respuestas minimales en castellano. *Revue roumaine de linguistique, 24*(1), 45–54.

Ellegård, A. (1953). *The Auxiliary 'Do': The Establishment and Regulation of Its Use in English*. Stockholm: Almqvist och Wiksell.

Enrique-Arias, A. (2003). From clitics to inflections: diachronic and typological evidence for affixal object agreement marking in Spanish. In B. Fradin (ed.), *Les unités morphologiques: Forum de morphologie (3e rencontres)* (pp. 67–75). Lille: Université de Lille.

Evans, N. (2010). *Dying Words: Endangered Languages and What They Have to Tell Us*. Oxford: Wiley-Blackwell.

Fang, J. (2022). *A Systemic Functional Grammar of Chinese Nominal Groups: A Text-based Approach*. Singapore: Springer.

Fang, Y., McDonald, E. & Cheng, M. (1995). On Theme in Chinese: from clause to discourse. In R. Hasan & P. H. Fries (eds.), *On Subject and Theme: A Discourse Functional Perspective* (pp. 235–75). Amsterdam: John Benjamins.

Fawcett, R. (1988). What makes a 'good' system network good? Four pairs of concepts for such evaluations. In J. D. Benson & W. S. Greaves (eds.), *Systemic Functional Approaches to Discourse* (pp. 1–28). Norwood, NJ: Ablex.

Fawcett, R. (2000a). *A Theory of Syntax for Systemic Functional Linguistics (Current Issues in Linguistic Theory)*. Amsterdam: John Benjamins.

Fawcett, R. (2000b). In place of Halliday's 'verbal group', Part 1: evidence from the problems of Halliday's representations and the relative simplicity of the proposed alternative. *Word*, *51*(2), 157–203. doi: 10.1080/00437956.2000.11432500

Fawcett, R. (2000c). In place of Halliday's 'verbal group', Part 2: evidence from generation, semantics and interruptability. *Word*, *51*(3), 327–75. doi: 10.1080/00437956.2000.11432503

Fawcett, R. (2008). *Invitation to Systemic Functional Linguistics through the Cardiff Grammar* (3rd edn). London: Equinox.

Fernández-Soriano, O. (1999a). El pronombre personal: formas y distribuciones. Pronombres átonos y tónicos. In I. Bosque & V. Demonte (eds.), *Gramática descriptiva de la lengua española* (vol. I, *Sintaxis básica de las clases de palabras*, pp. 1209–73). Madrid: Espasa.

Fernández-Soriano, O. (1999b). Two types of impersonal sentences in Spanish: locative and dative subjects. *Syntax*, *2*(2), 101–40.

Figueredo, G. (2014). Uma metodologia de perfilação gramatical sistêmica baseada em corpus. *Letras & letras*, *30*(2), 17–45. doi: 10.14393/LL60-v30n2a2014-2

Figueredo, G. (2021) The nominal group in Brazilian Portuguese. *Word*, *67*(4), 461–92. doi: 10.1080/00437956.2021.1993588

Figueredo, G. & Figueredo, G. P. (2020). A systemic dynamics model of text production. *Journal of Quantitative Linguistics*, *27*(4), 291–320. doi: 10.1080/09296174.2019.1567301

Fillmore, C. (1968). The case for case. In E. Bach & T. Harms (eds.), *Universals in Linguistic Theory* (pp. 1–88). New York: Holt, Rinehart and Winston.

Firbas, J. (1966). Non-thematic subjects in contemporary English. *Travaux linguistiques de Prague*, *2*, 239–56.

FitzSimons, P. (2005). Place in time: Bondi Beach. *The Sydney Magazine*, 23 February.

Fontaine, L. (2017). The English nominal group: the centrality of the Thing element. In T. Bartlett & G. O'Grady (eds.), *The Routledge Handbook of Systemic Functional Linguistics* (pp. 267–83). London: Routledge.

Fontaine, L. & Schönthal, D. (2019). The rooms of the house: grammar at group rank. In G. Thompson, W. L. Bowcher, L. Fontaine & D. Schöntahl (eds.), *The Cambridge Handbook of Systemic Functional Linguistics* (pp. 118–41). Cambridge: Cambridge University Press.

Fontanella, M. B. (1992). Variación sincrónica y diacrónica de las construcciones con 'haber' en el español americano. *Boletín de filología de la Universidad de Chile*, *33*, 35–46.

Fries, P. (1981). On the status of theme in English: arguments from discourse. *Forum Linguisticum*, *6*(1), 1–38.

Fuentes-Rodríguez, C., Placencia, M. E. & Palma-Fahey, M. (2016). Regional pragmatic variation in the use of the discourse marker *pues* in informal talk among university students in Quito (Ecuador), Santiago (Chile) and Seville (Spain). *Journal of Pragmatics*, *97*, 74–92. doi: 10.1016/j.pragma.2016.03.006

Fung, K. C. A. (2018). Analysing Cantonese doctor–patient communication: A semantic network approach. Unpublished PhD dissertation, The Hong Kong Polytechnic University, Hong Kong, China.

Garachana, M. (ed.) (2017). *La gramática en la diacronía: La evolución de las perífrasis verbales modales en español*. Madrid: Iberoamericana/Veuvert.

García, L. & Camus, B. (eds.) (2004). *El pretérito imperfecto*. Madrid: Gredos.

Gili, S. (1958/2000). *Curso superior de sintaxis española* (15th edn). Barcelona: Biblograf.

Greenberg, J. H. (1966). Some universals of grammar with particular reference to the order of meaningful elements. In J. H. Greenberg (ed.), *Universals of Language* (2nd edn, pp. 73–113). Cambridge, MA.: The MIT Press.

Gu, Y. (2002). Towards an understanding of workplace discourse: a pilot study for compiling a spoken Chinese corpus of situated discourse. In Ch. Candlin (ed.), *Theory and Practice of Professional Discourse* (pp. 137–85). Hong Kong: CUHK Press.

Guo, R. (1993). 汉语动词的过程结构 [Hànyǔ dòngcí de guòchéng jiégòu, Process structures of Chinese verbs]. 《中国语文》 [*Zhōngguó Yǔwén*, Studies of the Chinese Language], (6), 410–20.

Guzmán, J. A. (2010). La ola maldita. *Paula*. Retrieved on 5 August 2021 from www.latercera.com/paula/la-ola-maldita/

Halliday, M. A. K. (1956). Grammatical categories in modern Chinese. *Transactions of the Philological Society*, 55(1), 178–224. https://doi.org/10.1111/j.1467-968X.1956.tb00567.x

Halliday, M. A. K. (1959–60/1966). Typology and the exotic. In M. A. K. Halliday & A. McIntosh (eds.), (1966), *Patterns of Language: Papers in General, Descriptive and Applied Linguistics* (pp. 165–82). London: Longman.

Halliday, M. A. K. (1961/2002). Categories of the theory of grammar. In J. Webster (ed.), *On Grammar* (vol. I, *The Collected Works of M. A. K. Halliday*, pp. 37–94). London: Continuum.

Halliday, M. A. K. (1964). Syntax and the consumer. In C. I. J. M. Stuart (ed.), *Report of the Fifteenth Annual (First International) Round Table Meeting on Linguistics and Language Study* (Monograph Series on Languages and Linguistics, 17, pp. 11–24). Washington, DC: Georgetown University Press.

Halliday, M. A. K. (1964/76). English system networks. In G. Kress (ed.), *Halliday: System and Function in Language* (pp. 101–35). Oxford: Oxford University Press.

Halliday, M. A. K. (1965/81). Types of structure. In M. A. K. Halliday & J. R. Martin (eds.), *Readings in Systemic Linguistics* (pp. 29–41). London: Batsford.

Halliday, M. A. K. (1966). Some notes on 'deep' grammar. *Journal of Linguistics*, 2(1), 57–67. https://doi.org/10.1017/S0022226700001328

Halliday, M. A. K. (1966/76). The English verbal group. In G. R. Kress (ed.), *Halliday: System and Function in Language* (pp. 136–58). London: Oxford University Press.

Halliday, M. A. K. (1967a). *Intonation and Grammar in British English*. The Hague/Paris: Mouton.

Halliday, M. A. K. (1967b). Notes on Transitivity and Theme in English: part I. Journal of Linguistics, 3(1), 37–82.

Halliday, M. A. K. (1967c). Notes on Transitivity and Theme in English: part II. Journal of Linguistics, 3(2), 199–244.

Halliday, M. A. K. (1968). Notes on Transitivity and Theme in English: part III. *Journal of Linguistics*, 4(2), 179–215.

Halliday, M. A. K. (1969/76). Types of process. In G. Kress (ed.), *Halliday: System and Function in Language* (pp. 159–73). Oxford: Oxford University Press.

Halliday, M. A. K. (1970). *A Course in Spoken English: Intonation*. Oxford: Oxford University Press.

Halliday, M. A. K. (1970/2005). Functional diversity in language as seen from a consideration of modality and mood in English. In J. Webster (ed.), *Studies in English Language* (vol. VII, *The Collected Works of M. A. K. Halliday*, pp. 164–204). London: Continuum.

Halliday, M.A.K. (1977/2003). Ideas about language. In J. Webster (ed.), *On Language and Linguistics* (vol. III, *The Collected Works of M. A. K. Halliday*, pp.92–115). London: Continuum.

Halliday, M. A. K. (1978). *Language as Social Semiotic: The Social Interpretation of Language and Meaning*. London: Edward Arnold.

Halliday, M. A. K. (1979/2002). Modes of meaning and modes of expression: types of grammatical structure and their determination by different semantic functions. In J. Webster (ed.), *On Grammar* (vol. I, *The Collected Works of M. A. K Halliday*, pp. 196–218). London: Continuum.

Halliday, M. A. K. (1981). Structure. In M. A. K. Halliday & J. R. Martin (eds.), *Readings in Systemic Linguistics* (pp. 122–31). London: Batsford.

Halliday, M. A. K. (1982/2002). The de-automatization of grammar: from Priestley's an inspector calls. In J. Webster (ed.), *Linguistic Studies of Text and Discourse (vol. II, The Collected Works of M. A. K. Halliday*, pp. 126–48). London: Continuum.

Halliday, M. A. K. (1984a). Language as code and language as behaviour: a systemic functional interpretation of the nature and ontogenesis of dialogue. In R. Fawcett, M. A. K. Halliday, S. Lamb & A. Makkai (eds.), *The Semiotics of Culture and Language* (vol. I, *Language as Social Semiotic*, pp. 3–35). London: Frances Pinter.

Halliday, M. A. K. (1984/2002). On the ineffability of grammatical categories. In J. Webster (ed.), *On Grammar* (vol. I, *The Collected Works of M. A. K. Halliday*, pp. 291–322).London/New York: Continuum.

Halliday, M. A. K. (1984b). Linguistics in the university: the question of social accountability. In J. E. Copeland (ed.), *New Directions in Linguistics and Semiotics* (pp. 51–67). Houston, TX: Rice University Studies.

Halliday, M. A. K. (1985). *An Introduction to Functional Grammar*. London: Edward Arnold.

Halliday, M. A. K. (1985/2005). It's a fixed word order language is English. In J. Webster (ed.), *Studies in English Language* (vol. VII, *The Collected Works of M. A. K. Halliday*, pp. 213–31). London: Continuum.

Halliday, M. A. K. (1991/2005). Language as system and language as instance: the corpus as a theoretical construct. In J. Webster (ed.), *Computational and Quantitative Studies* (vol. VI, *The Collected Works of M. A. K. Halliday*, pp. 76–92). London: Continuum.

Halliday, M. A. K. (1992/2002). How do you mean? In J. Webster (ed.), *On Grammar* (vol. I, *The Collected Works of M. A. K Halliday*, pp. 352–68). London: Continuum.

Halliday, M. A. K. (1992/2003). Systemic grammar and the concept of a 'science of language'. In J. Webster (ed.), *On Language and Linguistics* (pp. 199–212). London: Continuum.

Halliday, M. A. K. (1994). *An Introduction to Functional Grammar* (2nd edn). London: Edward Arnold.

Halliday, M. A. K. (2003). Written language, standard language, global language. *World Englishes*, *22*(4), 405–18.
Halliday, M. A. K. (2008). *Complementarities in Language*. Beijing: Commercial Press.
Halliday, M. A. K. (2010/13). Language evolving: some systemic functional reflections on the history of meaning. In J. Webster (ed.), *Halliday in the 21st Century* (vol. XI, *The Collected Works of M. A. K. Halliday*, pp. 237–53). London: Bloomsbury Academic.
Halliday, M. A. K. (2014). That 'certain cut': towards a characterology of Mandarin Chinese. *Functional Linguistics*, *1*, 4–23. doi: 10.1186/2196-419X-1-2
Halliday, M. A. K. & Greaves, W. S. (2008). *Intonation in the Grammar of English*. London: Equinox.
Halliday, M. A. K. & Hasan, R. (1976). *Cohesion in English* (English Language Series; No. 9). London: Longman.
Halliday, M. A. K. & James, Z. L. (1993). A quantitative study of polarity and primary tense in the English finite clause. In J. M. Sinclair, M. Hoey & G. Fox (eds.), *Techniques of Description: Spoken and Written Discourse (A Festschrift for Malcolm Coulthard)* (pp. 32–66). London: Routledge.
Halliday, M. A. K. & McDonald, E. (2004). Metafunctional profile of the grammar of Chinese. In A. Caffarel, J. R. Martin & C. M. I. M. Matthiessen (eds.), *Language Typology: A Functional Perspective* (pp. 305–96). Amsterdam: John Benjamins.
Halliday, M. A. K. & Martin, J. R. (eds.). (1993). *Writing Science: Literacy and Discursive Power*. London: Taylor & Francis.
Halliday, M. A. K. & Matthiessen, C. M. I. M. (1999). *Construing Experience through Meaning: A Language-Based Approach to Cognition*. London: Continuum.
Halliday, M. A. K. & Matthiessen, C. M. I. M. (2004). *An Introduction to Functional Grammar* (3rd edn). London: Hodder Arnold.
Halliday, M. A. K. & Matthiessen, C. M. I. M. (2014). *Halliday's Introduction to Functional Grammar* (4th edn). London: Routledge.
Hao, J. (2015). Construing biology: an ideational perspective. PhD dissertation, University of Sydney. www.isfla.org/Systemics/Print/Theses/HAO_2015_PhD_THESIS.pdf
Hao, J. (2018). Reconsidering 'cause inside the clause' in scientific discourse: from a discourse semantic perspective in systemic functional linguistics. *Text & Talk*, *38*(5). doi: 10.1515/text-2018-0013
Hao, J. (2020a). *Analysing Scientific Discourse: A Framework for Exploring Knowledge Building in Biology from a Systemic Functional Linguistic Perspective*. London: Routledge.
Hao, J. (2020b). Nominalisations in scientific English: a tristratal perspective. *Functions of Language*, *27*(2), 143–73. doi: 10.1075/fol.16055.hao
Harrison, K. D. 2007. *When Languages Die: The Extinction of the World's Languages and the Erosion of Human Knowledge*. Oxford: Oxford University Press.
Hernández, A. (2006). Posesión y existencia: la competencia de 'haber' y 'tener' y 'haber' existencial. In C. Company (ed.), *Sintaxis histórica de la lengua Española: Primera parte – la frase verbal* (vol. II, pp. 1053–160). México: Universidad Nacional Autónoma de México/Fondo de Cultura Económica.
Hernanz, M. L. & Brucart, J. M. (1987). *La sintaxis* (vol. I, *Principios teóricos: La oración simple*). Barcelona: Crítica.

Hoang, V. (2012). *An Experiential Grammar of the Vietnamese Clause*. Hanoi: Vietnam Education Publishing House.

Hopper, P. J. & Traugott, E. C. (2003). *Grammaticalization* (2nd edn). Cambridge: Cambridge University Press.

Hu, Y. (2011). 《现代汉语》 [*Xiàndài Hànyǔ*, Modern Chinese]. Shanghai: Shanghai Education Press.

Huang, B. (1984). 《陈述句,疑问句,祈使句,感叹句》 [*Chénshù Jù, Yíwèn Jù, Qíshǐ Jù, Gǎntàn Jù*, Declaratives, Interrogatives, Imperatives, Exclamatives]. Shanghai: Shanghai Education Publishing House.

Huang, B. & Liao, X. (2002). 《现代汉语》 [*Xiàndài Hànyǔ*, Modern Chinese] *II*. Beijing: Higher Education Press.

Huddleston, D. R. (1988). Constituency, multi-functionality and grammaticalization in Halliday's Functional Grammar. *Journal of Linguistics*, *24*, 137–74. https://doi.org/10.1017/S0022226700011592

Iwasaki, S. & Ingkaphirom, P. (2005). *A Reference Grammar of Thai*. Cambridge: Cambridge University Press.

Jakobson, R. (1949). On the identification of phonemic entities. *Travaux du Cercle Linguistique de Copenhague*, V (*Recherches Structurales*), 205–13.

Kashyap, A. K. (2019). Language typology. In G. Thompson, W. L. Bowcher, L. Fontaine & D. Schöntal (eds.), *The Cambridge Handbook of Systemic Functional Linguistics* (pp. 767–92). Cambridge: Cambridge University Press.

Kim, M., Martin, J. R., Shin, G. & Choi, G. (2023). *Korean Grammar: A Systemic-Functional Approach*. Cambridge: Cambridge University Press.

Kumar, A. (2009). A systemic functional description of the grammar of Bajjika. Unpublished PhD dissertation, Macquarie University, Sydney.

Laca, B. (2005). Tiempo, aspecto y la interpretación de los verbos modales en español. *Lingüística ALFAL*, *17*, 9–44.

Lamb, S. (1964). The sememic approach to structural semantics. *American Anthropologist*, *66*(3), 57–78.

LaPolla, R. J. (2009). Chinese as a Topic-Comment (not Topic-Prominent and not SVO) language. In J. Xing (ed.), *Studies of Chinese Linguistics: Functional Approaches* (pp. 9–22). Hong Kong: Hong Kong University Press

Lavid, J. (2000). Cross-cultural variation in multilingual instructions: a study of speech act realisation patterns. In E. Ventola (ed.), *Discourse and Community: Doing Functional Linguistics* (pp. 71–85). Tübingen: Günter Narr.

Lavid, J., Arús, J. & Zamorano-Mansilla, J. R. (2010). *Systemic Functional Description of Spanish: A Contrastive Study with English*. London: Continuum.

Lee, J. L. (2018). On the discovery procedure. In D. Brentari & J. L. Lee (eds.), *Shaping Phonology* (pp. 223–33). Chicago: University of Chicago Press.

Lee, J. L. & Goldsmith, J. A. (2016). Linguistica 5: unsupervised learning of linguistic structure. In *Proceedings of the 2016 Conference of the North American Chapter of the Association for Computational Linguistics: Demonstrations* (pp. 22–6). San Diego: Association for Computational Linguistics.

Lemke, J. L. (1995). *Textual Politics: Discourse and Social Dynamics*. London: Taylor & Francis.

Li, E. S. (2007). *Systemic Functional Grammar of Chinese: A Text-Based Analysis*. London: Continuum.

Li, E. S. (2017). The nominal group in Chinese. In T. Bartlett & G. O'Grady (eds.), *The Routledge Handbook of Systemic Functional Linguistics* (pp. 338–53). London: Routledge.

Li, C. N. & Thompson, S. A. (1981). *Mandarin Chinese: A Functional Reference Grammar*. Berkeley/Los Angeles/London: University of California Press.

Liu, X. (2002). 现代汉语句尾"了"的语法意义及其解说 [Xiàndài Hànyǔ jùwěi 'le' de yǔfǎ yìyì jíqí jiěshuō, The grammatical meaning of the modal particle *le* and its explanation]. 《世界汉语教学》[*Shìjiè Hànyǔ Jiàoxué*, Chinese Teaching in the World], (3), 70–79.

Long, R. & Peng, X. (2012). 《现代汉语及物性研究》[*Xiàndài Hànyǔ Jíwùxìng Yánjiū*, Studies in Modern Chinese Transitivity]. Beijing: Peking University Press.

Lü, S. (1979). 《现代语法分析问题》[*Xiàndài Yǔfǎ Fēnxī Wèntí, Issues in Modern Grammar Analysis*]. Beijing: Commercial Press.

Lü, S. (1999). 《现代汉语八百词》[*Xiàndài Hànyǔ Bābǎi Cí*, Eight Hundred Words in Modern Chinese]. Beijing: Commercial Press.

Lü, S. (2014). 《中国文法要略》[*Zhōngguó Wénfǎ Yàolüè*, An Outline of Chinese Grammar]. Beijing: Commercial Press.

Ma, Q. (2005). 《汉语动词和动词性结构》[*Hànyǔ Dòngcí hé Dòngcíxìng Jiégòu*, Chinese Verbs and Verbal Structures]. Beijing: Peking University Press.

Martin, J. R. (1992). *English Text: System and Structure*. Amsterdam: John Benjamins.

Martin, J. R. (1996). Types of structure: deconstructing notions of constituency in clause and text. In E. H. Hovy & D. R. Scott (eds.), *Computational and Conversational Discourse: Burning Issues – An interdisciplinary Account* (pp. 39–66). Heidelberg: Springer.

Martin, J. R. (2002). From little things big things grow: ecogenesis in school geography. In R. M. Coe, L. Lingard & T. Teslenko (eds.), *The Rhetoric and Ideology of Genre: Strategies for Stability and Change* (pp. 243–271). Cresskill, NJ: Hampton Press.

Martin, J. R. (2004). Prosodic 'structure': grammar for negotiation. *Ilha do Desterro: A Journal of English Language, Literatures in English and Cultural Studies*, *46*, 41–83. https://doi.org/10.5007/%25x

Martin, J. R. (2008a). Boomer dreaming: the texture of recolonisation in a lifestyle magazine. In G. Forey & G. Thompson (eds.), *Text-Type and Texture: In Honour of Flo Davies* (pp. 252–84). London: Equinox.

Martin, J. R. (2008b). What kind of structure: interpersonal meaning and prosodic realisation across strata. *Word*, *59*(2), 1–31. https://doi.org/10.1080/00437956.2008.11432583

Martin, J. R. (2015). Cohesion and texture. In D. Tannen, H. E. Hamilton & D. Schiffrin (eds.), *The Handbook of Discourse Analysis* (2nd edn, pp. 61–81). Chichester: John Wiley and Sons.

Martin, J. R. (ed.) (2018a). *Interpersonal meaning: Systemic Functional Linguistics Perspectives* (Special Issue of *Functions of Language*). *25*(1). https://doi.org/10.1075/fol.25.1

Martin, J. R. (2018b). Discourse semantics. In G. Thompson, W. L. Bowcher, L. Fontaine & D. Schönthal (eds.), *The Cambridge Handbook of Systemic Functional Linguistics* (pp. 358–81). Cambridge: Cambridge University Press.

Martin, J. R. (2018c). Meaning beyond the clause: co-textual relations. *Linguistics and the Human Sciences*, *11*(2–3), 203–35. https://doi.org/10.1558/lhs.34711

Martin, J. R. & Doran, Y. J. (eds.) (2015a). *Around Grammar: Phonology, Discourse Semantics, Multimodality* (vol. III, *Critical Concepts in Linguistics: Systemic Functional Linguistics*). London: Routledge.

Martin, J. R. & Doran, Y. J. (eds.) (2015b). *Grammatical Descriptions* (vol. II, *Critical Concepts in Linguistics: Systemic Functional Linguistics*). London: Routledge.

Martin, J. R. & Doran, Y. J. (eds.) (2015c). *Grammatics* (vol. I, *Critical Concepts in Linguistics: Systemic Functional Linguistics*). London: Routledge.

Martin, J. R., Doran, Y. J. & Figueredo, G. (eds.) (2020). *Systemic Functional Language Description: Making Meaning Matter*. London: Routledge.

Martin, J. R. & Dreyfus, S. (2015). Scaffolding semogenesis: designing teacher/student interactions for face-to-face and on-line learning. In S. Starc, A. Maiorani & C. Jones (eds.), *Meaning Making in Text: Multimodal and Multilingual Functional Perspectives* (pp. 265–98). London: Palgrave.

Martin, J. R. & Matthiessen, C. M. I. M. (1991). Systemic typology and topology. In F. Christie (ed.), *Literacy in Social Processes: Papers from the Inaugural Australian Systemic Linguistics Conference, Held at Deakin University, January 1990* (pp. 345–83). Darwin: Centre for Studies in Language in Education, Northern Territory University.

Martin, J. R., Matthiessen, C. M. I. M. & Painter, C. (2010). *Deploying Functional Grammar*. Beijing: The Commercial Press.

Martin, J. R., Quiroz, B. & Figueredo, G. (eds.) (2021). *Interpersonal Grammar: Systemic Functional Linguistic Theory and Description*. Cambridge: Cambridge University Press. https://doi.org/10.1017/9781108663120

Martin, J. R. & Rose, D. (2003/2007). *Working with Discourse: Meaning beyond the Clause*. London: Continuum.

Martin, J. R. & Rose, D. (2008). *Genre Relations: Mapping Culture*. London: Equinox.

Martin, J. R. & White, P. (2005). *The Language of Evaluation: Appraisal in English*. Basingstoke: Palgrave Macmillan.

Martin, J. R., Wang, P. & Zhu, Y. (2013). *Systemic Functional Grammar: A Next Step into the Theory – Axial Relations*. Beijing: Higher Education Press.

Martin, J. R. & Zappavigna, M. (2019). Embodied meaning: a systemic functional perspective on body language. *Functional Linguistics*, 6(1). doi: 10.1186/s40554-018-0065-9

Mathesius, V. (1933). Double negation and grammatical concord. In *Mélanges de linguistique et de philologie offerts à J. van Ginneken* (pp. 1–33). Paris: C. Klincksieck.

Matthiessen, C. M. I. M. (1995). *Lexicogrammatical Cartography: English Systems*. Tokyo: International Language Sciences Publishers.

Matthiessen, C. M. I. M. (1996). TENSE in English seen through systemic-functional theory. In M. Berry, C. Butler, R. Fawcett & G. Huang (eds.), *Meaning and Form: Systemic Functional Interpretations* (pp. 431–98). Norwood, NJ: Ablex Publishing Corporation.

Matthiessen, C. M. I. M. (1999). The system of TRANSITIVITY: an exploratory study of text-based profiles. *Functions of Language*, 6(1), 1–51. doi: 10.1075/fol.6.1.02mat

Matthiessen, C. M. I. M. (2004). Descriptive motifs and generalizations. In A. Caffarel, J. R. Martin & C. M. I. M. Matthiessen (eds.), *Language Typology: A Functional Perspective* (pp. 537–664). Amsterdam: John Benjamins.

Matthiessen, C. M. I. M. (2006). Frequency profiles of some basic grammatical systems: an interim report. In S. Hunston & G. Thompson (eds.), *System and Corpus: Exploring Connections* (pp. 103–42). London: Equinox.

Matthiessen, C. M. I. M. (2007). The 'architecture' of language according to systemic functional theory: developments since the 1970s. In R. Hasan, C. M. I. M. Matthiessen & J. Webster (eds.), *Continuing Discourse on Language* (vol. II, pp. 505–61). London: Equinox.

Matthiessen, C. M. I. M. (2014). Appliable discourse analysis. In F. Yan & J. Webster (eds.), *Developing Systemic Functional Linguistics: Theory and Application* (pp. 135–205). London: Equinox.

Matthiessen, C. M. I. M. (2015a). Halliday on language. In J. Webster (ed.), *The Bloomsbury companion to M. A. K. Halliday* (pp. 137–202). London: Bloomsbury.

Matthiessen, C. M. I. M. (2015b). Reflections on researching and teaching Chinese as a foreign language. *Researching and Teaching Chinese as a Foreign Language*, *1*(1), 1–27.

Matthiessen, C. M. I. M. (2015c). Systemic functional morphology: the lexicogrammar of the word. In E. Rosa Francisco de Souza (ed.), *Estudos de descripção funcionalista: Objetos e abordagens* (pp. 150–99). Munich: Lincom.

Matthiessen, C. M. I. M. (2018). The notion of a multilingual meaning potential: a systemic exploration. In A. Baklouti & L. Fontaine (eds.), *Perspectives from Systemic Functional Linguistics* (pp. 90–120). London: Routledge.

Matthiessen, C. M. I. M. (2021). The architecture of phonology according to Systemic Functional Linguistics. In K. Teruya, W. Canzhong & D. Slade (eds.), *Systemic Functional Linguistics, Part 1* (vol. I, *Collected Works of Christian M. I. M. Matthiessen*, pp. 288–338). Sheffield: Equinox.

Matthiessen, C. M. I. M. (forthcoming). The 'architecture' of language according to systemic functional theory. MS.

Matthiessen, C. M. I. M., Arús-Hita, J. & Teruya, K. (2021). Translations of representations of moving and saying from English into Spanish. *Word, 67*(2), 188–207. https://doi.org/10.1080/00437956.2021.1909843

Matthiessen, C. M. I. M. & Bateman, J. A. (1991). *Systemic Linguistics and Text Generation: Experiences from Japanese and English*. London: Frances Pinter.

Matthiessen, C. M. I. M. & Halliday, M. A. K. (1997/2009). *Systemic Functional Grammar: A First Step into the Theory*. Beijing: Higher Education Press.

Matthiessen, C. M. I. M. & Teruya, K. (forthcoming) *The Routledge Guide to Systemic Functional Linguistics: Terms, Resources and Applications*. London: Routledge.

Matthiessen, C. M. I. M., Teruya, K. & Lam, M. (2010). *Key Terms in Systemic Functional Linguistics*. London: Continuum.

Matthiessen, C. M. I. M., Wang, B., Ma, Y. & Mwinlaaru, I. N. (2022). *Systemic Functional Insights on Language and Linguistics*. Singapore: Springer.

McDonald, E. (1994). Completive verb compounds in Modern Chinese: a new look at an old problem. *Journal of Chinese Linguistics*, *22*(2), 317–62. www.jstor.org/stable/23753925

McDonald, E. (1996). The 'complement' in Chinese grammar: a functional reinterpretation. In R. Hasan, C. Cloran & D. Butt (eds.), *Functional Descriptions: Theory in Practice* (pp. 265–86). Amsterdam: John Benjamin.

McDonald, E. (1998). Clause and verbal group systems in Chinese: a text-based functional approach. Unpublished PhD dissertation, Macquarie University, Sydney.

McDonald, E. (2017). Form and function in groups. In T. Bartlett & G. O'Grady (eds.), *The Routledge Handbook of Systemic Functional Linguistics* (pp. 251–66). London: Routledge.

Meillet, A. (1903). *Introduction à l'étude comparative des langues indo-européennes.* Paris: Hachette.

Melis, C. & Flores, M. (2007). Los verbos pseudoimpersonales del español: una caracterización semántico-sintáctica. *Verba: Anuario galego de filoloxia, 34,* 7–57. http://hdl.handle.net/10347/3467

Montgomery, M. B. (2009). Historical and comparative perspectives on a-prefixing in the English of Appalachia. *American Speech, 84*(1), 5–26. https://doi.org/10.1215/00031283-2009-002

Moyano, E. (2010). El sistema de Tema en español: una mirada discursiva sobre una cuestión controvertida. In E. Ghio & M. D. Fernández (eds.), *El discurso en español y portugués: Estudios desde una perspectiva sistémico-funcional* (pp. 39–87). Santa Fe: Universidad Nacional del Litoral.

Moyano, E. (2016). Theme in English and Spanish: different means of realization for the same textual function. *English Text Construction, 9*(1), 190–220. https://doi.org/10.1075/etc.9.1.10moy

Moyano, E. (2021). La función de Tema en español: sus medios de realización desde la perspectiva trinocular de la Lingüística Sistémico-Funcional. *Revista signos,* 54(106), 487–517. doi: 10.4067/S0718-09342021000200487

Mwinlaaru, I. (2017). A systemic functional description of the grammar of Dagaare. Unpublished PhD dissertation, The Hong Kong Polytechnic University.

Mwinlaaru, I. & Xuan, W. (2016). A survey of studies in systemic functional language description and typology. *Functional Linguistics, 3*(8). https://functionallinguistics.springeropen.com/articles/10.1186/s40554-016-0030-4

Mwinlaaru, I., Matthiessen, C. M. I. M. & Akerejola, E. (2018). A system-based typology of MOOD in African languages. In A. Agwuele & A. Bodomo (eds.), *Handbook of African Languages* (pp. 93–117). London: Routledge.

Navarro, T. (1944). *Manual de entonación española.* Madrid: Guadarrama.

Neale, A. (2017). Transitivity in the Cardiff Grammar. In T. Bartlett & G. O'Grady (eds.), *The Routledge Handbook of Systemic Functional Linguistics* (pp. 178–93). London: Routledge.

Nesbitt, C. & Plum, G. (1988). Probabilities in a systemic grammar: the clause complex in English. In R. Fawcett & D. Young (eds.), *New Developments in Systemic Linguistics* (vol. II, *Theory and Application,* pp. 6–38). London: Pinter.

Nespor, M., Shukla, M. & Mehler, J. (2011). Stress-timed vs. syllable-timed languages. In M. Oostendorp, C. J. Ewen, E. Hume & K. Rice (eds.), *The Blackwell Companion to Phonology* (vol. II, pp. 1–13). Malden, MA: Wiley-Blackwell. doi:10.1002/9781444335262.wbctp0048

Norman, J. (1988). *Chinese.* Cambridge: Cambridge University Press.

Ostler, N. (2005). *Empires of the Word: A Language History of the World.* London: HarperCollins.

Pamies, A. (1999). Prosodic typology: on the dichotomy between stress-timed and syllable-timed languages. *Language Design, 2,* 103–30. http://elies.rediris.es/Language_Design/LD2/pamies.pdf

Patpong, P. (2005). A systemic functional interpretation of Thai grammar: an exploration of Thai narrative discourse. Unpublished PhD dissertation, Macquarie University, Sydney.

Penny, R. (2002). *A History of the Spanish Language* (2nd edn). Cambridge: Cambridge University Press.

Picallo, M. C. & Rigau, G. (1999). El posesivo y las relaciones posesivas. In I. Bosque & V. Demonte (eds.), *Gramática descriptiva de la lengua española* (vol. I, *Sintaxis básica de las clases de palabras*, pp. 973–1023). Madrid: Espasa-Calpe.

Pike, L. K. (1945/72). General characteristics of intonation. In D. Bolinger (ed.), *Intonation: Selected Readings* (pp. 53–82). Harmondsworth: Penguin.

PRESEEA. (2014-22). *Corpus del Proyecto para el estudio sociolingüístico del español de España y de América*. Alcalá de Henares: Universidad de Alcalá. https://preseea.linguas.net/Corpus.aspx

Quilis, A. (1988). *Fonética acústica de la lengua española*. Madrid: Gredos.

Quiroz, B. (2008). Towards a systemic profile of the Spanish MOOD. *Linguistics and the Human Sciences*, *4*(1), 31–65. https://doi.org/10.1558/lhs.v4i1.31

Quiroz, B. (2013). The interpersonal and experiential grammar of Chilean Spanish: towards a principled systemic-functional description based on axial argumentation. Unpublished PhD dissertation, University of Sydney. www.isfla.org/Systemics/Print/Theses/BQuiroz_2013.pdf

Quiroz, B. (2015). La cláusula como movimiento interactivo: una perspectiva semántico-discursiva de la gramática interpersonal del español. *DELTA: Documentação de Estudos em Linguística Teorica e Aplicada*, *31*(1), 261–301. http://dx.doi.org/10.1590/0102-445023762456121953

Quiroz, B. (2016). Convenciones de notación sistémica. *Onomázein*, *33*(2), 412–26. doi: 10.7764/onomazein.33.24

Quiroz, B. (2017a). Gramática interpersonal básica del español: una caracterización sistémico-funcional del sistema de MODO. *Lenguas modernas*, *49*, 157–82. https://revistas.uchile.cl/index.php/LM/article/view/49231

Quiroz, B. (2017b). The verbal group. In T. Bartlett & G. O'Grady (eds.), *The Routledge Handbook of Systemic Functional Linguistics* (pp. 301–18). London: Routledge.

Quiroz, B. (2018). Negotiating interpersonal meanings: reasoning about MOOD. *Functions of Language*, *25*(1), 135–63. doi:10.1075/fol.17013.qui

Quiroz, B. (2020). Experiential cryptotypes: reasoning about PROCESS TYPE. In J. R. Martin, Y. J. Doran & G. Figueredo (eds.), *Systemic Functional Language Description: Making Meaning Matter* (pp. 102–28). London: Routledge.

Quiroz, B. (2021). Interpersonal grammar in Spanish. In J. R. Martin, B. Quiroz & G. Figuedero (eds.), *Interpersonal Grammar: Systemic Functional Linguistic Theory and Description* (pp. 34–63). Cambridge: Cambridge University Press.

Quiroz, B. & Martin, J. R. (2021). Perfil sistémico-funcional del grupo nominal en español: estructura, funciones discursivas básicas y organización sistémica. *Estudios filológicos*, *68*, 123–51. doi: 10.4067/s0071-17132021000200123

Quiroz, B. (in press) Procesos, participantes y circunstancias: una aproximación sistémico-funcional a la estructura experiencial de la cláusula española. Boletín de Filología.

Rochester, S. & Martin, J. R. (1979). *Crazy Talk: A Study of the Discourse of Schizophrenic Speakers*. New York/London: Plenum Press.

Rodríguez Espiñeira, M. J. (2000). Percepción directa e indirecta en español: diferencias semánticas y formales. *Verba: Anuario galego de filoloxia*, *27*, 33–85. http://hdl.handle.net/10347/3331

Rojo, G. (1974). La temporalidad verbal en español. *Verba: Anuario galego de filoloxia*, *1*, 68–149. http://hdl.handle.net/10347/2724

Rojo, G. & Veiga, A. (1999). El tiempo verbal: los tiempos simples. In I. Bosque & V. Demonte (eds.), *Gramática descriptiva de la lengua española* (vol. II, pp. 2867–934). Madrid: Espasa.

Rose, D. (2001). *The Western Desert Code: An Australian Cryptogrammar*. Canberra: Pacific Linguistics.

Rose, D. (2005). Narrative and the origins of discourse: construing experience in stories around the world. *Australian Review of Applied Linguistics*, *19*, 151–73. https://doi.org/10.1075/aralss.19.09ros

Rose, D. & Martin, J. R. (2012). *Learning to Write, Reading to Learn: Genre, Knowledge and Pedagogy in the Sydney School*. London: Equinox.

Sapir, E. (1921). *Language: An Introduction to the Study of Speech*. New York: Harcourt, Brace, Jovanovich.

Silva-Corvalán, C. (1980–1). La función pragmática de la duplicación de pronombres clíticos. *Boletín de filología de la Universidad de Chile: Homenaje a Ambrosio Rabanales*, *31*, 561–70.

Silva-Corvalán, C. (1981). The diffusion of object-verb agreement in Spanish. *Papers in Romance*, *3*(2), 163–76.

Soto, G. (2009). Vigencia y significado del pretérito anterior: un estudio a partir del español escrito en Chile. *Estudios filológicos*, *44*, 227–41. http://dx.doi.org/10.4067/S0071-17132009000100014

Steiner, E. & Yallop, C. (eds.) (2001). *Exploring Translation and Multilingual Text Production: Beyond Content*. Berlin: De Gruyter.

Suñer, M. (1978). Perception verb complements in Spanish: same or different? *Canadian Journal of Linguistics*, *23*(1), 107–27.

Taboada, M. (1995). Theme markedness in English and Spanish: a systemic-functional approach. Universidad Complutense de Madrid. www.sfu.ca/~mtaboada/docs/taboada-theme-markedness.pdf

Tam, H. R. (2004). A systemic-functional interpretation of Cantonese clause grammar. Unpublished PhD dissertation, University of Sydney.

Tann, K. (2017). Context and meaning in the Sydney architecture of SFL. In T. Bartlett & G. O'Grady (eds.), *The Routledge Handbook of Systemic Functional Linguistics* (pp. 438–56). London: Routledge.

Tao, L. (1998). "是不是"问句说略 ['Shì bù shì' wènjù shuōlüè, A brief account of 'shì bù shì' questions]. 《中国语文》 [*Zhōngguó Yǔwén, Studies of the Chinese Language*], (2), 105–7.

Taverniers, M. (2018). Grammatical metaphor and grammaticalization: the case of metaphors of modality. *Functions of Language*, *25*(1), 159–200. https://doi.org/10.1075/fol.17014.tav

Teich, E. (1999). System-oriented and text-oriented comparative linguistic research: cross-linguistic variation in translation. *Languages in Contrast*, *2*(2), 187–210. https://doi.org/10.1075/lic.2.2.04tei

Teich, E., Degaetano-Ortlieb, S., Fankhauser, P., Kermes, H. & Lapshinova-Koltunski, E. (2016). The linguistic construal of disciplinarity: a data-mining approach using register features. *Journal of the Association for Information Science and Technology*, *67*(7), 1668–78.

Teruya, K. (1998). An exploration into the world of experience: a systemic-functional interpretation of the grammar of Japanese. Unpublished PhD dissertation, *Macquarie University*, Sydney.

Teruya, K. (2007). *A Systemic Functional Grammar of Japanese* (2 vols). London: Continuum.
Teruya, K., Akerejola, E., Andersen, T. H., Caffarel, A., Lavid, J., Matthiessen, C. M. I. M., Petersen, U. H., Patpong, P. & Smedegaard, F. (2007). Typology of MOOD: a text-based and system-based functional view. In R. Hasan, C. M. I. M. Matthiessen & J. Webster (eds.), *Continuing Discourse on Language: A Functional Perspective* (vol. II, pp. 859–920). London: Equinox.
Teruya, K. & Matthiessen, C. M. I. M. (2015). Halliday in relation to language comparison and typology. In J. Webster (ed.), *The Bloomsbury Companion to M. A. K. Halliday* (pp. 427–52). London: Bloomsbury Academic.
Thai, M. D. (2004). Metafunctional profile: Vietnamese. In A. Caffarel, J. R. Martin & C. M. I. M. Matthiessen (eds.), *Language Typology: A Functional Perspective* (pp. 397–431). Amsterdam: John Benjamins.
Thompson, G. (2013). *Introducing Functional Grammar* (3rd edn). London: Routledge.
Tornel, J. L. (2001–2). Perífrasis verbales y consideraciones metodológicas (I y II). *Contextos, 37–40*, 39–88. https://dialnet.unirioja.es/descarga/articulo/2161011.pdf
Trubetzkoy, N. S. (1939). *Grundzüge der Phonologie* (Travaux du Cercle Linguistique de Prague, vol. 7). Prague.
Tsao, F. (1980). *A Functional Study of Topic in Chinese: The First Step towards Discourse Analysis*. Taipei: Student Book Co.
Vázquez, V. & García, M. (2012). A discourse-based analysis of object clitic doubling in Spanish. In K. Davidse, T. Breban, L. Brems & T. Mortelmans (eds.), *Grammaticalization and Language Change: New Reflections* (pp. 271–97). Amsterdam: John Benjamins.
Veiga, A. (2004a). Cantaba y canté: sobre una hipótesis temporal y alguna de sus repercusiones. *ELUA, Anexo 2 (El verbo)*, 599–614. http://dx.doi.org/10.14198/ELUA2004.Anexo2.29
Veiga, A. (2004b). La forma verbal 'cantaba' y la estructura modo-temporal del sistema verbal español. In L. García Fernández & B. Camus Bergareche (eds.), *El pretérito imperfecto* (pp. 96–193). Madrid: Gredos.
Ventola, E. (1987). *The Structure of Social Interaction: A Systemic Approach to the Semiotics of Service Encounters*. London: Frances Pinter.
Wang, B. & Ma, Y. (2022) *Introducing M. A. K. Halliday*. London: Routledge.
Wang, L. (2011). 《中国现代语法》[*Zhōngguó Xiàndài Yǔfǎ*, Modern Grammar of Chinese]. Beijing: Commercial Press.
Wang, P. (2020a). Construing entities through nominal groups in Chinese. In M. Zappavigna & S. Dreyfus (eds.), *Discourses of Hope and Reconciliation: On J. R. Martin's Contribution to Systemic Functional Linguistics* (pp. 57–83). London: Bloomsbury Academic.
Wang, P. (2020b). Axial argumentation and cryptogrammar in interpersonal grammar: a case study of classical Tibetan. In J. R. Martin, Y. J. Doran & G. Figueredo (eds.), *Systemic Functional Language Description: Making Meaning Matter* (pp. 73–101). London: Routledge.
Wang, P. (2021). Interpersonal grammar in Chinese. In J. R. Martin, B. Quiroz & G. Figueredo (eds.), *Interpersonal Grammar: Systemic Functional Linguistic Theory and Description* (pp. 96–129). Cambridge: Cambridge University Press.
Webster, J. (ed.) (2004). *The Language of Early Childhood* (vol. IV, *The Collected Works of M. A. K. Halliday*). London: Continuum.

Webster, J. (ed.) (2005). *Computational and Quantitative Studies* (vol. VI, *The Collected Works of M. A. K. Halliday*). London: Continuum.

Westermann, D. (1907). *Grammatik der Ewe-Sprache*. Berlin: Dietrich Reimar (Ernst Vohsen).

Westermann, D. (1930). *A Ststudy of the Ewe Llaanguage*. London: Oxford University Press.

Whorf, B. L. (1945). Grammatical categories. *Language*, *21*(1), 1–11. doi: 10.2307/410199. [Repr. In J. B. Carrol, (ed.) (1956). *Language, Thought, and Reality: Selected Writings of Benjamin Lee Whorf* (pp. 87–101). Cambridge, MA: The MIT Press.]

Wiessner, P. W. (2014). Embers of society: firelight talk among the Ju/'hoansi Bushmen. *PNAS*, *111*(39), 14027–35. doi: 10.1073/pnas.140421211

Wilson, E. O. (2019). *Genesis: The Deep Origin of Societies*. New York/London: Liveright Publishing Corporation.

Zappavigna, M. & Martin, J. R. (2018). *Discourse and Diversionary Justice: An Analysis of Youth Justice Conferencing*. London: Palgrave Macmillan.

Zavala, V. (2001). Borrowing evidential functions from Quechua: the role of *pues* as a discourse marker in Andean Spanish. *Journal of Pragmatics*, *33*, 999–1023. doi: 10.1016/S0378-2166(00)00049-7

Zhou, X. (1997). Material and relational transitivity in Mandarin Chinese. Unpublished PhD dissertation, University of Melbourne.

Zhu, D. (1982). 《语法讲义》 [*Yǔfǎ Jiǎngyì, Lectures on Chinese Grammar*]. Beijing: Commercial Press.

Zuo, S. (1999). 现代汉语中"体"的研究——兼及体研究的类型学意义 ['Xiàndài Hànyǔ zhōng 'tǐ' de yánjiū – jiānjí tǐ yánjiū de lèixíngxué yìyì, A study of 'aspect' in Modern Chinese and typological significance of aspect studies]. 《语文研究》 [*Yǔwén Yánjiū, Linguistic Research*], (1), 9–20.

# Index

abduction, 399
Accompaniment (Spanish), 375
accusative, 34, 124, 125, 126, 127, 137
activity, 4, 35, 73, 95, 237, 343, 369
actor
  primary, 170, 171, 212, 213
  secondary, 170
Actor (Chinese), 287
Actor (English), 245, 249, 252
Actor (Spanish), 259, 276, 277
addressee deference, 97
adjectival group, 143, 213, 283, 294
adjective, 24, 37, 38, 39, 40, 41, 53, 54, 68, 72, 74, 75, 77, 80, 81, 88, 92, 143, 153, 157, 213
Agent, 303, 404
agentive, 303
agreeing Participant, 259, 264, 266
Akan, 398
ALSFAL-lista, 380
anaphoric ellipsis (Chinese), 351
appliable linguistics, 17, 24, 252, 254, 299, 370, 372, 373, 378, 379, 380
APPRAISAL, 14, 29, 97, 111, 158, 169, 184, 189, 211, 230, 251
  ENGAGEMENT, 29, 111, 130, 158, 185, 189, 201, 204, 211, 230, 231, 233, 235
argumentation, 3, 17, 33, 373, 379
  evidence, 33
  from above, 2, 3, 17, 31, 33, 38, 46, 50, 52, 87, 148, 180, 181, 191, 233, 349, 385, 387, 398
  from around, 3, 17, 38, 46, 87, 100, 181, 191, 230, 349, 385
  from below, 2, 3, 17, 38, 101, 143, 148, 151, 181, 191, 228, 230, 233, 349, 385, 387, 391, 398, 399
  paradigmatic reasoning, 385
  trinocular vision, 385
ASFLAnet, 380
aspect, 143
  completed, 147, 148, 160, 286

experienced, 147, 148, 160, 286
neutral, 145, 148, 159, 289, 291, 294
perfective, 145, 147, 148, 151
progressive, 149, 151, 160, 286
Aspect (Chinese), 144, 145, 146, 147, 149, 151, 153, 155, 156, 160, 214, 223, 289, 291, 294, 390
Assigner (Chinese), 294
Attribute (Chinese), 157, 296
Attribute (English), 250, 251
Attribute (Spanish), 260, 265
attributive clause (English), 249
Attributor (Chinese), 294
axis, 2, 3, 167, 375, 377, 385
  axial relations, 383
  paradigmatic, 3, 17, 18, 21, 23, 24, 33, 68, 70, 114, 142, 177, 179, 374, 375, 383, 384, 385, 387, 391, 392
  syntagmatic, 17, 24, 28, 114, 142, 171, 383, 387, 391, 392

bǎ-phrase, 291, 293
behavioural clause (Chinese), 301
behavioural clause (English), 256
behavioural clause (Spanish), 267, 269

Carrier (Chinese), 296
Carrier (English), 250
Carrier (Spanish), 259
characterology, 387
Circumstance, 303
class, 20, 38, 73, 144
Classifier (Chinese), 72, 73
Classifier (English), 37, 40
Classifier (Spanish), 53, 54
clause complex, 2, 12, 63, 227, 292, 328, 336, 372
clitic, 74, 83, 127, 131, 136, 146, 151, 153, 261, 265, 274, 286, 291
  pronominal, 55, 62, 63, 67, 96, 124, 125, 126, 137, 140, 195, 259, 260, 276, 376
clitic doubling, 260, 265, 376

455

456    Index

Comment Adjunct (English), 180, 189
Comment Adjunct (Spanish), 207, 210
common noun, 37, 38, 52, 54, 71, 72
communicative dynamism, 369
complex, 29
    adjective complex, 40, 41, 75
    hypotactic complex, 57
    name complex, 82
    noun complex, 41
    paratactic complex, 57
    word complex, 136
    word complex (Chinese), 74, 76
    word complex (English), 41
    word complex (Spanish), 57
computational model, 383
conditional marking, 403
conflation, 145, 260, 278, 313, 343, 403, 404
congruent. *See* grammatical metaphor
CONNEXION, 12, 14, 95, 96
consciousness, 126, 241, 247, 256, 261, 263,
    267, 285, 287, 289, 293, 301, 376, 377
constituency, 29, 377, 403
contact, 96, 169
context, 4–9, 169, 237, 304, 372, 373, 385,
    386, 387, 398
context dependency, 304, 322
corpus, 17, 33, 56, 97, 167, 168, 271, 371, 372,
    379, 386, 394
Corpus Tool, 374
count noun, 49, 58
coverb, 151
coverbal phrase, 85, 145
covert, 24, 212, 379, 384, 385
cryptogrammatical categories, 383
cryptotype, 24, 240, 245, 254, 283

data, 7, 17, 24, 33, 371, 372, 374, 378, 379
dative, 34, 125, 126, 127, 137
declarative (Chinese), 215, 216, 231, 232
declarative (English), 176, 177, 178, 179, 180, 190
declarative (Spanish), 199, 208
Deictic (Chinese), 82
Deictic (English), 44
Deictic (Spanish), 67
delicacy, 33, 251–4, 271, 303, 385
demonstrative (Chinese), 82, 88
demonstrative (English), 46
demonstrative (Spanish), 60, 67, 263, 266,
    376, 377
descriptive generalisations, 394
directionality, 285, 290
discourse semantics, 2, 3, 10–16, 17, 29, 31,
    33, 35, 36, 38, 43, 46, 50, 55, 59, 65, 66,
    73, 77, 81, 87, 95, 96, 97, 100, 112, 114,
    133, 135, 136, 158, 169, 173, 184, 185,
    211, 230, 234, 255, 296, 303, 304, 309,
    356, 366, 373, 377, 378

embedding, 404
    clause, 45, 85, 86, 264, 269, 270, 272, 274,
        276, 277, 278, 285, 293, 308
    coverbal phrase, 85
    nominal group, 46, 50, 83, 84, 88
    prepositional phrase, 44, 65
enclisis, 135
endangered languages, 378
engagement. *See* appraisal
Ensemble (Spanish), 281
entity tracking (Spanish), 127
Epithet (Chinese), 73, 75
Epithet (English), 38, 40
Epithet (Spanish), 56
ergative, 303
Event, 96, 166
Event (Chinese), 144, 146, 147, 149, 151, 153,
    159, 213, 224
Event (English), 98, 101, 249, 255
Event (Spanish), 131, 137, 138, 140, 195, 259,
    260
evidentiality, 97, 395
exchange
    action, 170, 171, 182, 192, 211
    knowledge, 170, 171, 179, 192, 197, 199,
        211, 217
exclamative (English), 181
exclamative (Spanish), 200, 206, 209
Existent (Chinese), 285
Existent (English), 255
Existent (Spanish), 266
existential clause (Chinese), 283, 285, 286, 289
existential clause (English), 255
existential clause (Spanish), 266, 333
expand, 403

fact, 248, 263, 264
fast speech processes, 31, 266
field, 4, 10, 35, 37, 38, 52, 71, 73, 95, 97, 237,
    305, 313, 314, 315, 316, 317, 318, 319,
    321, 323, 329, 331, 333, 335, 346, 349,
    354, 356, 357, 359, 363, 364, 369, 378
figure, 12, 35, 95, 96, 97, 101, 102, 104, 114,
    115, 118, 120, 124, 135, 142, 144, 145,
    148, 167, 237, 242, 249, 256, 273, 287,
    296, 300
    occurrence, 11, 12, 95, 97, 99, 237
    positioned, 11, 242, 247, 289
    state, 11, 95, 97, 237
Finite (English), 176, 178, 179, 180, 183, 186
Finite (Spanish), 193
finite clause (English), 178, 186, 242, 308
finite clause (Spanish), 327
fixed word order languages, 393
Focus (English), 50, 51
formal, 16
free word order languages, 393

# Index

function, 20, 38, 73
Function Marker (English), 50
functional, 16
functional language typology, 374–8, 388, 391, 396
function-rank matrix, 387
future tense (English), 98, 100, 101, 244
future tense (Spanish), 123

gender, 66
general verb, 241, 261, 264, 287, 298
generic structure, 305
genre, 2, 3, 6, 9, 322, 371, 372, 373, 378, 379
  macro-genre, 322
gerundive (Spanish), 274
global language, 389
glossing, 34
Goal (Chinese), 287
Goal (English), 245, 249, 252
Goal (Spanish), 260
*gonna*, 101
grading, 39, 72, 75, 144, 213
grammatical metaphor, 11, 12, 13, 14, 15, 30, 31, 183, 234, 236
  congruent, 12, 31, 110, 180, 211, 212, 215, 217, 218, 224, 228, 233, 234, 235
  metaphorical, 11, 12, 13, 31, 234, 235
  MODALITY, 235, 236
  MOOD, 234, 236
graphology, 3, 101, 131, 200, 322

heterogloss, 29, 112, 138, 187, 235
holistic model, 373, 386, 396, 397
Hyper-New (Chinese), 361, 363, 364
Hyper-New (English), 318
Hyper-Theme (Chinese), 361, 363
Hyper-Theme (English), 318
Hyper-Theme (Spanish), 323

IDEATION, 11, 12, 35, 95, 237
ideational, 10, 15, 35, 95, 96, 107, 109, 114, 138, 144, 152, 153, 164, 218, 219, 220, 237, 313, 315, 333, 352, 357
IDENTIFICATION, 14, 36, 43, 59, 81, 377
identifying clause (English). *See* relational clause (English)
imperative (Chinese), 211, 212, 213, 214, 215, 230
imperative (English), 182, 183, 184, 186, 190
imperative (Spanish), 195, 196, 199, 206, 208
imperfect (Spanish), 115, 116, 118, 120, 124, 167
imperfective (Chinese), 214
imperfective (English), 111
indicative (Chinese), 211, 214, 230, 231, 232, 291
indicative (English), 179, 183, 184, 186, 190

indicative (Spanish), 193, 194, 197, 199, 200, 201, 205, 206
infinitive (Spanish), 274
information, 365
information (Spanish), 340
information flow (Chinese), 350
information flow (English), 310, 315
informative (English), 181, 189, 190
informative (Spanish), 199, 201
Inquirer (Chinese), 212, 218, 219, 220, 228, 229, 232
instantiation, 167, 385, 398, 399
instigation, 303
INTERLOCUTION (Spanish), 193, 195, 196, 200, 206
International Systemic Functional Linguistics Association, 380
interpersonal, 10, 13, 57, 96, 112, 114, 135, 138, 140, 144, 158, 161, 164, 169, 187, 221, 233, 348, 374, 384, 395
interrogative (Chinese), 217, 218, 228, 229, 231
  addressee-oriented, 220, 223, 231
  elemental, 218, 219, 232
  proposition-oriented, 224, 225, 226, 227
interrogative (English), 176, 177, 178, 179, 180, 190
  polar, 179, 180
  wh, 179, 180
interrogative (Spanish), 199, 201
  elemental, 200, 208
  polar, 199
intonation (Chinese)
  marked TONALITY, 356
  salient syllable, 354
  tonality, 360
  tone group, 354, 355
  tonic, 354
  tonicity, 360
intonation (English), 313
  foot, 313
  marked tonality, 314
  salient syllable, 313
  silent beat, 313
  tonality, 321
  tone group, 313, 314, 321, 322
  tonic syllable, 313
  TONICITY, 186, 321
intonation (Spanish)
  salient syllable, 339
  tonality, 340
  tone group, 339
  tonic, 339, 340
  tonicity, 340
intransitive, 19, 20, 30, 240, 252, 253, 301
item, 4, 35, 38, 73, 95, 143, 237

Japanese, 383

458   Index

knower
  primary, 170, 171, 172
  secondary, 170

layers of structure (Spanish verbal group), 143
lexical tone, 354
lexicogrammar, 3, 16, 31, 32, 95, 135, 137, 234, 322, 365, 382, 383, 384, 385, 387, 390, 391, 401
light verb, 253
logical, 107, 137

macro-phenomenon, 242, 244, 247, 263, 273, 275, 276, 277, 278, 289, 293
maintenance, 379
marked theme (Chinese), 358
marked theme (English), 321
marked theme (Spanish), 346
mass noun, 49, 58
material clause (Chinese), 282, 283, 287, 289
material clause (English), 245, 252
material clause (Spanish), 261
measure (Chinese), 78
Measurer (Chinese), 77, 78–81, 85
  presenting, 82
  word complex, 78
mental clause (Chinese), 282, 283, 289, 290
  affection, 290
  cognition, 290, 291, 292
  desideration, 290, 292
  perception, 290, 291
mental clause (English), 245
mental clause (Spanish), 262
  perception, 270, 272, 278, 280, 281
  reaction, 263
metafunction, 2, 10, 16, 25, 26, 384, 385, 387, 393
meta-phenomenon, 242, 244, 247, 256, 263, 285, 289, 293, 300
metaphorical. *See* grammatical metaphor
metaredundancy, 31
meteorological clause (Spanish), 333
method of development, 314, 319
methodology, 24, 370, 378, 398
micro-phenomenon, 242, 244, 247, 263, 273, 276, 277, 285, 289, 293
Mod (Chinese), 161, 163, 164
Modal Adjunct (Chinese), 212, 214
Modal Adjunct (Spanish), 207, 209
modal adverb, 161, 162, 163, 165, 166, 168
modal responsibility, 34, 333
modal verb, 28, 112, 130, 132, 161, 162, 163, 165, 166, 168
modal verb (Spanish), 130
modality, 21, 26, 27, 28, 29, 97, 130–3, 154, 156, 174, 395

modalisation, 21, 164, 166, 185, 189, 391
modulation, 21, 22, 27, 166, 183
MODALITY (Chinese), 158, 161, 163, 168
MODALITY (English), 111, 185, 186, 187, 191
MODALITY (Spanish), 130–3, 138, 195, 201, 204, 205, 206, 209
mode, 4, 6, 10, 36, 304, 305, 322, 349, 378
Moderator (Chinese), 212, 215, 216, 220, 221, 228, 229, 230, 231
monogloss, 29, 185
monoglossic, 112
MOOD, 2, 26
MOOD (Chinese), 143, 211, 230
MOOD (English), 178, 179, 182, 190, 191
MOOD (Spanish), 192, 200, 206
MOOD DEIXIS (English), 178, 179, 183
morpheme, 28, 29
morphology, 2, 18, 38, 46, 63, 98, 103, 127, 167, 195, 196, 197, 199, 200, 240, 325, 331, 337, 366
  inflectional, 67, 98, 194, 197, 199, 376
move, 169
  arguability, 173, 174, 191
  challenging, 171, 172, 173
  follow-up, 170, 171, 199
  nub, 173, 174, 175, 176, 177, 179, 181, 182, 183, 191, 192, 193, 194, 195, 197, 199, 207
  obligatory, 170
  optional, 171
  terms, 173, 174, 175, 176, 178, 182, 191, 192, 207
  tracking, 171, 172, 173
multilingual meaning potential, 383
multivariate structure, 32, 108, 138, 139, 142, 166, 168, 245

narrative, 41, 42, 81, 305, 329, 349
Natural Language Processing, 399
Neg (Chinese), 158, 160, 164, 289, 294
Negation (Spanish), 210
negotiability, 31, 110, 157, 178, 230, 309
NEGOTIATION, 13, 97, 130, 169, 184, 211, 230, 233
New (Chinese), 354, 355, 363
  Marked New, 357
  maximal New, 355
  minimal New, 355
New (English), 313
  Marked New, 316
  maximal New, 314
  minimal New, 314, 316
New (Spanish), 340
  extended New, 343
  minimal New, 340
  unmarked New, 342

# Index

nominal group, 2
  nominal group systems, 49
  post-positional nominal group, 50
nominal group (Chinese), 70
  nominal group systems (delicate), 89
  nominal group systems (general), 87
  realisation statements (delicate), 89
  realisation statements (general), 87
nominal group (English)
  nominal group systems (delicate), 48
  nominal group systems (general), 47
  realisation statements (delicate), 48
  realisation statements (general), 47
nominal group (Spanish), 52
  co-referential, 325
  nominal group systems (delicate), 70
  nominal group systems (general), 68
  realisation statements (delicate), 70
  realisation statements (general), 68
nominative, 34
non-finite clause (English), 178, 308, 309
non-finite clause (Spanish), 264, 327
non-finite verbal group (English), 110, 183
non-finite verbal group (Spanish), 274
notation
  pronominal clitics, 125
  tense (English), 108
  tense (Spanish), 118
NUCLEARITY (Spanish), 129, 138
number, 63
NUMBER (Spanish), 193, 194, 200, 323
numeral (Chinese), 78, 82, 88
numeral (English), 42
numeral (Spanish), 58
Numerative (English), 42
Numerative (Spanish), 58

occurrence, 35, 115
orbital structure, 138, 143

parataxis, 40
  branching, 310
  extension, 40
parataxis (Spanish)
  branching, 328
Participant 1, 34, 137
  P1, 34, 125, 267, 302
Participant 2, 34, 138
  P2, 34, 125, 261, 265, 302
  P2cl, 140, 260
Participant 3, 34, 138
  P3, 34, 125, 261, 279
  P3cl, 140, 261, 279, 281
passive voice (English), 106
passive voice (Spanish), 123
past tense (English), 98

perfect (Spanish), 115, 120, 124, 167
perfective (Chinese), 214
perfective (English), 110, 111, 183
PERIODICITY, 15, 304, 366
person, 63
PERSON (Spanish), 193, 194, 195, 200, 207, 323
phase
  directional, 153, 154, 286, 291
  resultative, 153, 154, 155, 286, 291
Phase (Chinese), 152, 153, 155, 156, 157, 163, 286, 289, 291, 294, 395
Phenomenon (Chinese), 289, 291
Phenomenon (English), 245, 249
Phenomenon (Spanish), 263, 273, 276
  secondary, 277, 278
phenotype, 240, 241, 253, 254
phonology, 3, 101, 313, 340
  prosodic, 2, 31, 247, 339
    intonation, 31
    rhythm, 31
    tone group, 31
point, 314, 319
Polar Adjunct (Spanish), 202, 203, 207, 209
POLARITY, 97
polarity (Chinese), 143, 158, 211, 214
  negative, 154, 158, 159, 160, 163, 214, 222, 223, 224, 286, 289, 291, 294
  positive, 154, 156, 158, 160, 163, 224, 225
POLARITY (English), 111, 113, 185, 186, 191
  negative, 113, 185, 186, 188
  positive, 113, 186, 187
POLARITY (Spanish), 130, 133, 134, 138, 195, 201, 202, 204, 206, 209, 270
  negative, 133, 201, 203, 204, 207, 210
  positive, 133, 195, 199, 201, 202, 204, 206
Polarity Adjunct (Chinese), 221, 222, 223, 224, 226, 229
pose (Chinese), 230, 232
Position (Chinese), 296
Positioned (Chinese), 296
possessive determiner (English), 44, 46
possessive determiner (Spanish), 60, 62, 65, 66
  non-salient, 67
  salient, 67
Predicator (Chinese), 143, 157, 212, 213, 215, 217, 221, 223, 224, 225, 226, 227, 228, 229, 232
Predicator (English), 183, 186, 192
Predicator (Spanish), 199, 202, 203, 204, 206, 207, 208, 210, 325, 326, 331, 333, 336, 338, 343, 369
prepositional phrase (English), 44, 51
prepositional phrase (Spanish), 54
preselection, 404
present tense (English), 98

present tense (Spanish), 115
presenting, 43, 59, 64
presuming, 43, 59, 64, 81
primary tense (English), 97–9
  primary tense system, 99
primary tense (Spanish), 115, 167, 207
  future, 207
  imperfect, 207
  perfect, 207
  present, 207
  primary tense system, 117
probabilistic systems, 372
procedure, 366
Process, 237
proclisis, 135
projection (Chinese), 285, 292, 300
projection (English), 29, 256
projection (Spanish), 267, 268, 270, 271, 336
pronominal clitic. *See* clitic
pronoun, 36, 374, 375, 377, 392
pronoun (Chinese), 81, 83, 88
pronoun (English), 43, 241
pronoun (Spanish), 61, 62, 63, 67, 195, 263, 376
pronoun systems, 375–8
proper name, 36
  challenge, 91
proper name (Chinese), 82, 87, 93
proper name (English), 43, 47, 92
proper name (Spanish), 60, 61, 68, 92
property, 143
proposal, 170, 189, 230
proposition, 157, 164, 170, 189, 230, 231, 232
prosody, 140, 164, 203, 204, 207, 210, 385
pro-verb, 241

Qex (Spanish), 200, 206, 207
Qint (Spanish), 200, 206, 207
Qualifier (Chinese), 85
Qualifier (English), 44, 45
Qualifier (Spanish), 55, 64
quantifier (Chinese), 78
quantifier (English), 42
quantifier (Spanish), 58
quantitative studies, 372

rank, 2, 26–9, 167, 194, 385
reactance, 24, 244, 254, 283, 285, 302, 379, 383
  action vs sensing clauses (English), 244
  behavioural, verbal and existential clauses (English), 257
  behavioural, verbal and existential clauses (Spanish), 269
  major types of clause (Chinese), 295
  material vs existential clauses (Chinese), 289
  material, mental and existential clauses (Chinese), 292
  material, mental and relational clauses (English), 248
  material, mental and relational clauses (Spanish), 261
  modality vs attribution (Chinese), 157
  subtypes of mental clause (Spanish), 271
  subtypes of relational clause (Chinese), 299
realisation, 9, 11, 22, 27, 28, 31, 49, 125, 234
realisation statement, 18, 47, 87, 187, 374, 383, 403
Receiver (Chinese), 301
Receiver (Spanish), 268
recursive system, 27, 33, 47, 107, 135, 137, 142, 167
reference grammar, 386
register, 2, 3, 4, 9, 167, 254, 303, 371, 372, 373, 378, 379
relational clause (Chinese), 282, 283, 292, 296
  attributive, 294, 296
    classifying, 296
    describing, 296
  circumstantial, 296
  identifying, 297
  possessive, 299
relational clause (English), 246–8, 252
  identifying, 249
relational clause (Spanish), 264
Romance languages, 394

Sayer (Chinese), 301
Sayer (Spanish), 268
Scope (Chinese), 288
Scope (English), 253
*se*, 125, 349
SECONDARY TENSE (English), 97, 99–100, 103, 186
  additional selections, 104
  future, 99
  past, 101
  present, 99
SECONDARY TENSE (Spanish), 115, 117, 167
  future, 119
  in modalised verbal group, 132
  past, 118
  present, 119
  secondary tense system, 120
self-contextualising, 43
Senser (Chinese), 289
Senser (English), 245, 249
Senser (Spanish), 263
sequencing, 49, 70, 89, 178, 181, 403
serial structure, 114, 138, 143
serial verb construction, 395
SFL. *See* Systemic Functional Linguistics
shunting, 385, 386, 398, 399
*sí*, 133, 202

# Index

social semiotic, 3
speech function, 169, 234
standard language, 389, 390
status, 96, 169
stop rules
   English tense, 107
   Spanish tense, 123
stratification, 2, 10, 25, 29–32, 377, 399
stress-timed, 266
structure, 20, 246
   particulate, 369
   prosodic, 211
   wave, 369
Subject, 384
Subject (English), 176, 177, 178, 179, 180, 181, 183, 184, 308
SUBJECT PERSON (English), 177, 179, 183
subjunctive, 119, 135, 195, 196
syllable-timed, 266
syntagm, 18, 21, 23, 24, 239, 240, 244, 245, 246, 283
syntax, 18
SYSFLING, 380
system, 2, 391
system network, 2, 20, 24, 47
Systemic Functional Linguistics, 1
Systemic Language Modelling Network,

Tagalog, 398
tender (Chinese), 230, 232
tenor, 4, 6, 10, 96, 169, 234, 236, 305, 349, 378
TENSE, 390
TENSE (English), 97
TENSE (Spanish), 138, 193, 195
tense names (English), 104
tense systems (English), 107, 109
tense systems (Spanish), 122
textual, 10, 14, 36, 46, 304, 313, 352, 354, 369
Theme, 2, 365
   Predicator Theme, 366
   unmarked Theme, 34
Theme (Chinese), 354, 358
   Marked Theme, 357
Theme (English), 313, 316, 321
   elliptical, 316
   implicit, 316
   interpersonal Theme, 316
   Marked Theme, 315, 316, 318
   predicated Theme, 322
   textual Theme, 316
   thematic equatives, 322
   topical Theme, 316
Theme (Spanish), 335, 369
   and Circumstances, 346
   and TRANSITIVITY, 338, 348
   following Predicator, 336, 340
   in attributive clauses, 338
   Marked Theme, 346
   post-Predicator Theme, 343
   Shifting Theme, 346
   thematic equative, 347
   Theme predication, 347
   unmarked Theme, 331, 342, 369
theory, 382, 393
Thing (Chinese), 71
Thing (English), 36, 37
Thing (Spanish), 52
time, 390
Token (Chinese), 297, 298
Token (English), 250
tone group, 15
topology, 4, 256, 304
transitive, 19, 239, 240, 252
TRANSITIVITY, 2, 30, 237
TRANSITIVITY (Chinese), 350
TRANSITIVITY (Spanish), 257

univariate structure, 33, 107, 138, 142, 168
univariate structure (Spanish)
   limitations, 137

valeur, 374
Value (Chinese), 297, 298
Value (English), 250
Value (Spanish), 265
verb class (English), 103
verb class (Spanish), 116
verbal clause (Chinese), 300
verbal clause (English), 255
verbal clause (Spanish), 267
verbal group, 2
verbal group (Chinese), 143, 289, 291, 294
verbal group (English), 183, 187
verbal group (Spanish), 64, 193, 195, 198, 199, 202, 259, 274, 367
   present subjunctive, 135
   systems, 129, 135
Verbiage (Chinese), 301
Verbiage (Spanish), 268, 269
Vocative (Spanish), 207, 210
VOICE (English), 250, 312
VOICE (Spanish), 138

Wh (English), 178, 179, 180
Whex (English), 181
word, 29
word order typology, 392

For EU product safety concerns, contact us at Calle de José Abascal, 56–1°, 28003 Madrid, Spain or eugpsr@cambridge.org.